Encountering the Holocaust

IN MEMORY
OF
HYMAN WEIN
and
SUSAN WEIN

ENCOUNTERING THE HOLOCAUST: An Interdisciplinary Survey

EDITED BY
Byron L. Sherwin
and
Susan G. Ament

IMPACT PRESS
CHICAGO

ISBN 088482-936-7

The bulk of this book was written with the assistance of National Endowment for the Humanities grant EH-24770-76-636. The views expressed herein are not necessarily the views of the National Endowment for the Humanities.

Distributed for Impact Press, Inc. by Sanhedrin Press, a division of Hebrew Publishing Company, 80 Fifth Ave., New York, N.Y. 10011.

Library of Congress Cataloging in Publication Data

Main entry under title:

Encountering the holocaust.

    Includes bibliographies.
    1. Holocaust, Jewish (1939-1945)—Addresses, essays, lectures. 2. Holocaust, Jewish (1939-1945), in literature—Addresses, essays, lectures. I. Sherwin, Byron L. II. Ament, Susan G.
D810.J4E525 1979   940.53'1503'924   79-9126

ISBN 0-88482-936-7

PRINTED IN THE UNITED STATES OF AMERICA

Table of Contents

Publishers' Acknowledgments

The authors and publishers of this work gratefully acknowledge their indebtedness to the following authors and publishers for granting permission to excerpt previously published material in this work:

Arbor House Publishing Co., Inc. *Star Eternal* by Ka-Tzetnik 135633, English trans. copyright 1971 by Nina De Nur, pp. 121-2.

Commentary. "Like Groping Fingers" by Abraham Sutzkerer, trans. by Joseph Leftwich, in "Songs of the Death Camps," September 1951.

Farrar, Straus and Giroux, Inc. *O The Chimneys* by Nelly Sachs, p. 35.

Fortress Press. *Luther's Works: Volume Forty-Seven.*

Ghetto Fighter's House, Kibbutz Lochamei Hagetaot. *Vittel Diary* by Yitzhak Katzenelson.

Hoover Institution Press. *The Green Shirts and the Others: A History of Fascism in Hungary and Rumania* by Nicholas M. Nagy-Talavera.

Jerusalem Academic Press. "Psychoanalytic Contributions to the Problem of Children of Survivors from Nazi Persecution" by Judith S. Kestenberg, in *Israel Annals of Psychiatry and Related Disciplines* 10:4 (December 1972), pp. 311-12.

Walter Kaufmann. *Cain and Other Poems.* Doubleday and Company, Inc., 1962. New American Library, 1975.

Little, Brown and Co. "Introductory Notes on the Concept, Definition, and Range of Psychic Trauma" by William Niederland, in *Psychic Traumatization*, 1971.

Christopher Middleton, ed. and trans. "Death Fugue" by Paul Celan, in *Modern German Poetry, 1910-1960: An Anthology with Verse Translation,* Grove Press Inc.

Union of American Hebrew Congregations. *Heritage of Music: The Music of the Jewish People,* by Judith Kaplan Eisenstein, pp. 109-110.

Vanguard Press. *Night of the Mist* by Eugen Heimler, pp. 128-9.

Viking/Penguin, Inc. "Babi Yar," in *Selected Poems* by Yevgeni Yevtushenko. *Survival in Auschwitz* by Primo Levi, p. 84.

George Weidenfeld and Nicholson, Ltd. *Commandant of Auschwitz* by Rudolf Hoess, pp. 80-81.

Leon Wells. *The Janowska Road,* recently republished as *The Death Brigade.*

Wesleyan University Press. "The Inner Part" by Louis Simpson, in *Jewish-American Literature,* Abraham Chapman, ed.

West Publishing Co. *Law of Torts* by William Prosser, p. 340.

World Zionist Association Publications Service. *Children of the Shadows* by Ben-Zion Tomer, p. 74.

Yale University Press. *The Code of Maimonides—Book Eleven—The Book of Torts,* trans. Hyman Klein.

Acknowledgments

This volume represents the confluent efforts of a variety of individuals jointly committed to ameliorating the quality and increasing the quantity of Holocaust-related studies in the United States and abroad. It is only proper that some recognition—insufficient though it may be—appear as a preface to the book they helped create.

The initial plan for the composition of an interdisciplinary manual-text in Holocaust studies emerged as the result of a generous grant to Spertus College of Judaica from the Hyman and Susan Wein Foundation of Chicago. Besides sections of this volume subvented by the Wein grant, a number of articles and essays, already published and to be published in the future, were spawned by this grant. Furthermore, research for a separate volume on Holocaust theology has been subvented by the largesse of the Wein Foundation. To Irving Wein I am sincerely grateful for his generosity and for his patience over the years it has taken to transform an idea into a reality.

The basic format and the bulk of the contents of this volume were developed by a team of scholars brought together to comply with specifications of a significant grant by the National Endowment for the Humanities to Spertus College of Judaica. This grant was for the purpose of developing a model interdisciplinary curriculum in Holocaust studies for American colleges and universities. This "project team" included personnel from Spertus College and other academic institutions. As "project director," it is my happy duty to thank those who participated with me in this endeavor. To the "Senior Project Associate," Nathaniel Stampfer, who generously appropriated many hours from his duties as dean of Spertus College to offer guidance and support, I am particularly indebted. The staff of the Spertus College library and museum aided in many ways. My research assistant, Beverly Yusim, and my administrative assistant, Terry P. Dick, have been of inestimable help.

If "two heads are better than one," then certainly six heads are better than one. The contribution of the six members of the "project team" who worked with me have supplemented my own abilities and experience. To these individuals my heartfelt admiration and appreciation:

Professor M. Cherif Bassiouni of DePaul University who served as a consultant in international law

Professor Yaffa Eliach of Brooklyn College, New York, who served as a consultant in history and literature

Professor Elmer Luchterhand of Brooklyn College, New York, who served as a consultant in social-psychology

Professor Arnost Lustig of the American University, Washington, D. C., who served as a consultant in literature and film

Professor Alvin Rosenfeld of Indiana University who served as a consultant in literature

Professor David Weinberg of Bowling Green State University, Ohio, who served as a consultant in history and film.

It would be remiss of me not to express a note of appreciation to the authors of the following pages who were not part of the "project team": Helen Fein, my close friend Josephine Knopp, Joseph Lustig, Jack N. Porter, Ruth Kunzer and Marie Syrkin.

To my co-editor, Susan G. Ament, I am indebted beyond words. Her personal encouragement and editorial exactness helped improve my work, my moods, and the quality of the diction and flow of the pages which follow.

This volume represents the initial effort of Impact Press, Inc. Hopefully, it will set a high and successful standard for future endeavors.

Byron L. Sherwin
Chicago, Illinois
August 1978

Introduction

Byron L. Sherwin

ENCOUNTERING THE HOLOCAUST

"Once upon a time, there was a dragon whose breath was fire. He consumed millions of people. Yet, no knight could be found to slay the dragon." The dragon was real. The people were real. The absent knight was also real. But the story happened during the Second World War, and not "once upon a time." Why the dragon? Why the victims? Why the absent knight? Is the dragon dead, or only in hibernation? These are the questions one must ponder while surveying the charred remains. These are some of the questions addressed in the pages which follow.

A separate universe, with laws of its own, the Holocaust defies every "final solution" to the problems it engenders. In preparing road maps for those daring enough to explore the Holocaust Kingdom, historians and poets, psychologists and theologians, sociologists and novelists have all attempted to unravel its mysteries, its absurdities and its contradictions. But, like the legendary Atlantis swallowed up by water, this historical Atlantis consumed by fire has eluded all such attempts. The silhouette of its terrain remains obscure. The ghastly horror of its topography transcends description. The abysmal depths of its hellish valleys surpass rational comprehension.

Cartographers have carefully researched and plotted our turbulent flight across the Holocaust Kingdom. Lexicographers have provided us with a dictionary of terms which introduces us to its language. As we glide high above the clouds of smoke and fire which hover over the Kingdom's surface, distance provides us with a deceptive clarity of vision. However, once we descend onto its soil, the eerie chill of "night and fog" jolts our emotions and obscures our vision. Strangers in a strange land, we search our psychological survival kits for a device which might improve our chances of emotional survival in a domain populated by the ghosts of the slain and the ghouls of their slayers.

Re-entry visas back to the state of intellectual and emotional tranquility are

1

unavailable. Passports to the Holocaust Universe are one-way tickets. The person who enters its borders can never truly become free of its power. The person who leaves its borders is different from the person who dared enter its dominion.

We know our maps are faulty, but they are all we have. We know the setting, the characters, and the story line, but the plot remains obscure. New approaches, additional paths to perceiving what occurred, increase the perplexity of the maze. The bloodstained mosaic is enlarged, only to indicate how many pieces are still missing. Finding all of the pieces is inconceivable. The pattern of the mosaic remains obscure.

Studying the Holocaust is an impossibility. The best we can do is to study *about* the Holocaust. No work that we read can be "definitive." No scholar can be considered "*the* authority." No curriculum that we construct can be "complete." Yet, despite the impossibility of our task, we must persist in our task. In spite of our faulty maps, we must undertake our survey. Despite our anticipated failure, we must continue our quest for meaning and understanding. Despite the tendency for our emotions to paralyze our intellects, we must fully exploit all of our conceptual resources.

To offer explanations of *why* the Holocaust ought to be studied would be to demean its overwhelming significance. No defense for studying the Holocaust is required. Reasons, rationalizations, and defenses are irrelevant. One need not apologize for studying about the Holocaust. One need only apologize for *not* studying about the Holocaust. Suffice it to say that the Holocaust merits our attention because *it happened.* It happened in our century. It is part of our recent history. And, in a sense, part of our current history. The better its implications are understood and the more people who understand them, the less chance it has of becoming not only our history but our destiny.

Some have mistakenly depicted the Holocaust as a "reversion to medieval barbarism." However, the systematic extermination of millions of people is unknown in the annals of medieval history. The Holocaust was not a medieval event which occurred in modern times but a modern event, perhaps the first truly paradigmatic modern event. The all-powerful sovereign nation-state which adopted a policy of genocide, the systematic and intricate planning for the implementation of that policy, the massive bureaucracy constructed to carry out the policy, the use of mass media to "explain" and "justify" that policy, and the technology utilized to execute the policy—all are not "medieval" but are paradigmatic of *modern* society. The confluence of all these factors, for the first time, in Nazi Germany, gives credence to considering the Holocaust the first completely modern event.

Just as the Holocaust was not a medieval event, so it was not totally a "barbaric" event. Those who planned it and those who executed it were not primarily "barbarians" and masochists. They were largely people of high culture and advanced education. For example, of the four commanders of the "mobile killing units" (*Einsatzgruppen*) which murdered about five million people, including one and a half million Jews, one was a lawyer and one was a Protestant minister. The music of Wagner and Beethoven, and the writings of Goethe and Kant were as much a part of Nazi Germany as was the "Final Solution." Thus, as long as "cultured" people can be cruel or apathetic to cruelty, as long as governments devise policies which dehumanize their citizens, as long as technology persists in the "inhuman use of human beings," as long as bureaucracies grow and bureaucrats unquestioningly "follow orders," study of the Holocaust is an imperative to be implemented and not a proposal to be evaluated.

UTILIZING THIS VOLUME

The volume which unfolds in the following pages was composed under grants to Spertus College of Judaica from the National Endowment for the Humanities and from the Hyman and Susan Wein Foundation of Chicago, Illinois. The expressed purpose of these grants was the design of an interdisciplinary text-manual and model curriculum in Holocaust studies for American colleges and universities. Though the present volume does address itself to college instructors, it may be used profitably by high school instructors, instructors in theological seminaries, and by any educated reader interested in an overview of attempts, from a wide variety of academic disciplines, to come to grips with the Holocaust.

The basic format and approach adopted in the subsequent chapters were determined to a large degree by a "project team," formed to comply with specifications of the aforementioned National Endowment for the Humanities grant. (The names and academic affiliations of the members of the "project team" are found above on the *Acknowledgment* pages.) In devising this format and approach, the "project team" had to contend with a number of issues—theoretical and practical—attendant upon formulating a viable and accurate approach to studying about the Holocaust. Among the theoretical problems, three were paramount.

The first issue was whether the Holocaust should be approached as a unique and unprecedented event, or whether it should be described as an event readily comparable to other events. To consider the Holocaust as a totally unique event would accentuate its particular and its peculiar nature; however, it would prevent comparison of the Holocaust with any other event. The possibility of discussing the Holocaust within the framework and jargon of a variety of academic disciplines would thereby be severely impaired. Examining the way in which the Holocaust has been approached by these disciplines would become irrelevant. Integrating study of the Holocaust into already existing disciplines and courses would become impossible. On the other hand,

making the Holocaust too relative and relinquishing all claims to its uniqueness would divest it of its particular character and nature. Possibilities of
comparing the Holocaust with other events and experiences could lead to
outlandish extremes. It was, therefore, decided that a fair presentation must
embrace both approaches. The "unique" and the "comparative" approaches
must function as complementary opposites in Holocaust studies. Just as every
human being is unique and yet comparable to other human beings, so is the
Holocaust unique but comparable (to a limited degree) with other events and
experiences. The various chapters which follow embrace the tension which
obtains between these two polar approaches to Holocaust studies. To posit
only the unique nature or the comparable nature of the Holocaust would be to
distort the event by presenting a portrait with only half a face.

The second issue was the particularistic or universalistic nature and relevance of the Holocaust; i.e., Is the Holocaust a particularistically *Jewish*
experience with pertinence only for Jews, or is it a universalistic event with
universalistic humanistic implications? To recognize the Holocaust as an experience endured by Jews and directed primarily at Jews might limit its
interest to Jews. To adopt this approach would be to construe the Holocaust as
solely a chapter within the Jewish experience and would be to depict
Holocaust studies as a subject *only* within Jewish studies. On the other hand,
to remove the particularly Jewish component of the Holocaust experience by
stressing only the universalistic nature and implications of the Holocaust
would be an affront to the millions of Jews who were murdered by the Nazis
simply because they were Jews. It would disenfranchise the primary victims
of the Holocaust from claiming the experiences which were tragically, but
uniquely, their own. The project team decided that here too a careful balance
between the universalistic and particularistic dimensions of the Holocaust
should be attempted. The Holocaust should be depicted as an essentially, but
not totally, Jewish experience. The Holocaust should be approached as an
event in which Jews were the primary targets of victimization, but the
victimization of the Jews during the Holocaust nevertheless has universalistic
implications.

One cannot understand a play by ignoring all characters but the main one.
Similarly, one cannot survey the Holocaust or the literature written in response to the Holocaust by limiting attention to the Jewish plight. Attention
must also be given to the perpetrators, to those who collaborated with the
perpetrators, and to the neutrals. This means that attention must be paid not
only to Germany, but also to other countries: Axis, Allied and Neutral. In
addition, this means that targeted victims of Nazi extermination policies other
than Jews must be considered. *The Jewish Holocaust* refers to the systematic
murder of six million Jews. However, *The Holocaust* must also refer to the
systematic persecution of Gypsies, Jehovah's Witnesses, homosexuals and
Slavs. One must constantly refer to the approximately twelve million civil-

ians, including six million Jews, systematically murdered by the Nazis. Especially because Holocaust studies have been *primarily* concerned until now with the Jewish experience, it is imperative to stress the *other* six million or more marked victims who were designated as being "racially inferior," or as "useless mouths to feed," or as "enemies of the Third Reich." Nor should victims of other genocides such as the Armenian genocide during the First World War or the genocide against the American Indian or the more recent genocides in Africa and South America be forgotten or eclipsed by the genocide of the Jews during the Second World War. Therefore, the present curriculum attempts to achieve somewhat of a balance between the particularistic and the universalistic, between the Jewish and the non-Jewish dimensions and implications of the Holocaust.

The third theoretical issue faced by the "project team" was whether our approach should be "value-free" or "value-laden." Though a general problem in academic and pedagogical methodology, this issue becomes amplified when dealing with so volatile a topic as the Holocaust. Since much writing and many curricula on the Holocaust distort facts in order to offer an overly emotional and homiletical approach to the Holocaust, it was felt that every effort must be made to insure as much objectivity as possible. A careful attempt to eliminate "preachy" language and overly emotional discourse was advised. The "project team" handily rejected the "don't confuse me with the facts" approach. While we recognize the need for emotion, we also acknowledge the need for rational and critical objectivity. As Uriel Tal put it, "tears are important, but tears obscure our vision."

Despite a commitment to scholarly objectivity, this volume is not completely "value-free." First of all, the very possibility of "value-free" scholarship is itself dubious. Indeed, the decision to strive for "value-free" scholarship is itself a "value-laden" decision. Secondly, it is virtually impossible to discuss the Holocaust without some reference to moral values and to subjective predilections. Finally, it is dangerous, in a sense, to affirm a "value-free" judgment of the Holocaust. The corollary of "value-free" analysis is moral and cultural relativism. Such an approach would lead to the conclusion that the systematic murder of millions of people was not morally wrong in an objective sense but only morally wrong from a subjective point of view.

The studies which comprise this book have striven not to be overly impressionistic or excessively emotional. The authors of the following pages have attempted to preserve a balance between heart and mind, emotion and reason, humane concerns and humanistic scholarship.

Besides these three basic theoretical issues and other less basic theoretical issues, the "project team" confronted a host of practical problems in constructing a curriculum for use in American colleges and universities. As these problems would be of specific interest primarily to college instructors, rather than to other readers, these problems are discussed in an appendix to the present chapter.

Having made the preceding remarks about the genesis of this volume, some of the problems it attempts to address and some of the possibilities for its utilization, we turn now to a survey of its contents.

Each essay in this volume offers the following information:

1. General and specific themes one will inevitably encounter when studying the Holocaust from the perspective of a specific academic discipline.

2. Significant works in which these themes are treated. Pivotal problems addressed in these works.

3. A selected and (if necessary) an annotated bibliography, i.e., additional works, primary and secondary, which may be consulted for additional relevant information.

In addition, most chapters also include suggestions for class projects or additional research.

In an interdisciplinary work of this kind written by a team of authors, it is inevitable that duplication of information should occur. We have attempted, however, to keep this duplication to a minimum. Often, where duplication of reference does occur, the approach differs, depending upon the perspective of the discipline under discussion. Such "duplication," therefore, is not a re-dundancy, but rather a supplement.

Having committed itself to an interdisciplinary approach to Holocaust studies, the "project team" had to discern the pivotal academic disciplines to be consulted for studying about the Holocaust. The Table of Contents of this volume reflects the product of this discernment. To be sure, a number of disciplines are not represented herein. Hopefully, in a sequel to this volume, they will be included.

This work is divided into three parts. Part One deals with the Holocaust from the perspective of history, law and the social sciences. Part Two dis-cusses the treatment of the Holocaust in the arts. Part Three examines philosophical, moral and theological implications of the Holocaust.

Part One begins with an "historical overview" of the Holocaust. This chapter (Chapter Two) presents a skeletonlike historical survey of the Holo-caust. It serves as a prelude to issues which are discussed in greater detail in subsequent chapters. Among these issues is the problem of identifying "contributing causes" of the Holocaust. This problem is examined in the third chapter, "Ideological Antecedents of the Holocaust." An attempt is made to link the Holocaust with the history of Western culture, rather than to perceive the Holocaust as a *creatio ex nihilo*. Anti-Semitic themes in Christian theology, modern philosophy, volkist ideologies, and "racial anthropology" are explored and compared with Nazism's teachings regarding Jews and Judaism.

The fourth chapter, "The Holocaust in Historical Perspective," provides a framework for evaluating the massive and numerous studies in the history of the Holocaust. The author identifies three fundamental approaches which historians have taken to the Holocaust event. One approach concentrates upon the policies, ideology and activities of Nazi Germany with little or no reference to the Jewish plight under the Nazis. This approach focuses upon "general history" and neglects the "particular" experience of the Jews during the Second World War. The second approach concentrates largely upon the Jewish experience but neglects the general historical, social and political setting in which the Holocaust took place. This approach focuses upon the "particularistic" and neglects the "general." The third approach strives to embrace both "general" history and Jewish history. It examines the Holocaust as a Jewish experience within the context of a broader historical panorama; it embodies the unique and the comparative, the particularistic and the universalistic dimensions of the Holocaust.

While much attention has been paid to the activities of Nazi Germany vis-á-vis the Jews and other persecuted minorities, scant interest is often shown regarding the activities and policies of other governments toward the plight of Jews and other persecuted groups during the War. Without the active or passive complicity of states other than Nazi Germany, the devastating impact of the "Final Solution" might have been significantly lessened. Any complete study of the Holocaust, therefore, must consider the reactions of Allied, Axis and neutral governments to the genocidal policies of Nazi Germany. Chapter Five, "Socio-Political Responses during the Holocaust," offers an extensive review of these reactions. Because no other extensive qualitative survey of these matters exists, this chapter is more lengthy than other chapters in this book.

Discussion of the Holocaust cannot be limited to the War years. The impact of the event in the post-War years must also command attention. The fates of the perpetrators and of the victims are relevant to any study of the Holocaust. Chapter Six, "International Law and the Holocaust," deals in part with the fate of some of the perpetrators after the War. Chapter Seven, "Social-Psychological Aspects of the Holocaust," deals in part with the fate of the victims of the Holocaust.

Few studies of the Holocaust include an analysis of the implications of the Holocaust for international law. Chapter Six attempts to fill this hiatus in Holocaust studies by tracing the development and application of three legal concepts—"war crimes," "crimes against humanity," and "genocide"— and by analyzing the Nuremberg trials and the Eichmann trial. In addition, this chapter addresses itself to three questions particularly relevant to American students of the Holocaust: (1) Did the United States commit genocide against the American Indian? (2) Did the United States commit genocide in Viet Nam? (3) Why has the United States not ratified the United Nations' Genocide Treaty?

The Holocaust experience spawned research in many new areas of sociology and psychology. Among these is the study of the impact of traumatic experiences upon survivors of those experiences. Chapter Seven deals with "survivor syndrome," especially as it relates to the survivors of the Holocaust. In addition, this chapter discusses the newly emerging area of "children of survivor syndrome."

The question of Jewish armed resistance and the lack of it during the Holocaust must be encountered by any student of the Holocaust. This question is addressed below in the discussion of "Social-Psychological Aspects of the Holocaust."

Art is classically identified with the beautiful, with the sublime. However, the horrors of the twentieth century have compelled art to become mated to the horrible, the terrible. Rather than depicting beauty, art began to mirror atrocity. Certainly, the major expression of "atrocity art" has been Holocaust-related art. The second section of this volume discusses the products of artists' confrontations with the Holocaust.

The first responses to the Holocaust by literary artists were those of the diarists, writing in the midst of the crucible of their experiences. After the War, some of those who survived attempted to bear literary testimony to that which they had experienced; they wrote memoirs and autobiographies. Chapter Eight introduces and analyzes some of the more significant diaries and memoirs written during and after the Holocaust.

After the War, survivors and non-survivors produced a literary response to the Holocaust in a variety of genre—novels, short stories, poetry and drama. Chapter Nine reviews the most significant Holocaust novels and collections of short stories.

Despite T. Adorno's famous adage, "there can be no poetry after the Holocaust," poetry was nevertheless written in response to the Holocaust. Chapter Ten surveys Holocaust-related poetry written in English, Hebrew, Yiddish, German, and other languages. This chapter also discusses the sparse amount of drama written as a reaction to the Holocaust.

The most popularly consumed art-form is film. More people view films than read literary works. Film-makers, especially from Eastern Europe, have attempted to convey various aspects of the Holocaust experience. Chapter Eleven, "The Holocaust and the Film Arts," offers a history of the Holocaust through film. However, unlike historical accounts of the Holocaust, artistic films are able to depict not only external facts and events, but also internal emotions and responses.

Resistance to Nazi oppression was not limited to physical, armed resistance. In camps and ghettos, artists and musicians mounted a form of "spiritual resistance" to dehumanization and oppression. At the pain of death, in the face of depredation and decimation, they created art and music. In a realm of destruction, they created. In a world dominated by transient existence, they produced works of enduring value. Chapter Twelve, "Music and Art of the Holocaust," introduces the reader to works of art and music which testify to the endurance of the human spirit under the most inhumane conditions.

The third section of this book begins with a discussion of theological implications of the Holocaust. Both for Jews and Christians, the Holocaust strikes at the vitals of religious faith. For Jews, the Holocaust calls into question the endurance of the covenant between God and the people of Israel which is the cornerstone of the Jewish religion. Christians must confront the relationship of Christian anti-Semitism—theological and social—to the Nazi plan for the "Final Solution of the Jewish Problem." Such confrontation calls into question the moral and theological viability of basic Christian doctrines. Chapter Thirteen, "Jewish and Christian Theology Encounters the Holocaust," reviews the responses of Jewish and Christian theologians to the challenges posed by the Holocaust to Jewish and Christian life and faith after Auschwitz.

Reflections upon the Holocaust and its implications by professional philosophers have been very limited. Therefore, a review of the literature of contemporary philosophy and the Holocaust could not merit a separate chapter. Consequently, the single chapter (Chapter Fourteen) entitled "Philosophical Reactions to and Moral Implications of the Holocaust" provides a review of the scant philosophical material available, but offers a more extensive discussion of some of the moral implications of the Holocaust. This chapter attempts to construct two models for dealing with moral problems engendered by the Holocaust. Specific attention is given to the moral dilemmas faced by the Jewish Councils (*Judenrate*) and to the problem of apathy. This sub-chapter on "Moral Implications of the Holocaust" would be of specific interest to those involved with high-school curriculum design. To be sure, it is the most "value-laden" section of this volume.

Finally, the "Appendix" to this volume provides a listing of (1) archives and libraries with major holdings in Holocaust-related subjects, (2) institutions and organizations which specialize in Holocaust research and curriculum development, (3) repositories of major collections of Holocaust-related oral histories and some information regarding how to do an oral history, and (4) journals which specialize in Holocaust-related subject matter.

Having outlined the essential form and content of this volume, only the task of reading it and of utilizing it remains. It is the sincere hope of all the contributing authors that these efforts prove worthy of you, the reader.

APPENDIX

In designing the present volume, the "project team" discussed the following "practical" issues relating to the design of a curriculum in Holocaust studies for use on the college level.

Holocaust studies may be integrated into college curricula in two basic ways:

1. Holocaust studies may be offered as a course in itself in a variety of departmental or interdepartmental settings.
2. Some aspect of Holocaust studies may be integrated as a unit of study within already established courses in a wide variety of academic disciplines.

For example, a history department might not offer a course in "History of the Holocaust," but it might want to include some discussion of the Holocaust in a course on "The History of World War II" or "The History of Modern Germany" or the "History of Modern Europe," etc. A course in sociology might integrate some discussion of the Holocaust into a unit of study on genocide. A variety of literature courses might want to include some discussion of the more significant works of Holocaust literature. An almost limitless list of other possibilities in which some area of Holocaust studies might amplify and enrich a wide variety of already established or contemplated future course offerings could be composed. The problem, therefore, became to construct a curriculum design which could be utilized both by instructors offering courses in Holocaust studies per se as well as by those who seek to integrate one or more subareas of Holocaust studies into courses not specifically in Holocaust studies. Furthermore, even those offering courses in Holocaust Studies per se do so over a variety of time frames. Some offer year-long courses. Some offer semester-long courses (fifteen or sixteen weeks). Some offer quarter courses (ten weeks), while others offer summer session courses (three to eight weeks). In designing the present curriculum—the present volume—the "project team" had to consider these realities.

As this volume is composed for utilization in a wide variety of settings, so is it directed toward a diverse audience of potential readers. The current mushrooming of Holocaust studies has produced a huge influx of newcomers to a new field. Many instructors whose field of expertise lies elsewhere and whose academic training may have been free of any involvement with the Holocaust have suddenly found themselves confronted with the challenge of studying and teaching about the Holocaust either as a separate course or as a subarea of study within an established course. For those who have only recently entered the field of Holocaust study and teaching, hopefully this volume should prove immensely helpful.

Besides newcomers seeking direction, data and ideas, there are many already involved in Holocaust studies from the limited perspective of a given academic discipline, usually the one in which they were trained. Many of these instructors offer the only course in Holocaust studies at their respective college or university. Consequently, they may wish to offer a more extensive and more broadly based course by integrating material from other disciplines as they intersect with study of the Holocaust. The instructors may be knowledgeable in a single area of Holocaust studies but ignorant of where to obtain resources from another area. An instructor of Holocaust literature, for example, might require some guidance in seeking information which might help root a novel or a poem in a historical setting. Some direction in the history and historiography of the Holocaust would be useful to such an individual. This volume design hopefully would prove useful to such an instructor. For those in a single discipline wishing to teach Holocaust utilizing an interdisciplinary approach, this volume should prove invaluable. It is important to note at this point that the "project team" which composed this volume is committed to an interdisciplinary approach to Holocaust studies. An approach to study of the Holocaust from the perspective of a single discipline is presumed to be too limited in scope.

Because of the wide variety of settings in which Holocaust studies are presently taught and because the members of the "project team" who designed this volume did not want to presume to tell their colleagues how to teach about the Holocaust, this book is primarily concerned with *what* can be taught rather than with the problem of *how* it might be taught. We offer a series of units which together would offer adequate material for a year-long course in Holocaust studies. Each individual chapter may also serve as the basis for a course in the Holocaust from the perspective of a single individual discipline, e.g., "History of the Holocaust," "Holocaust Theology," "Holocaust Literature," "Holocaust and the Film Arts," etc. Furthermore, material provided within each chapter may be integrated into already existing courses within a given academic discipline. Thus, the material presented herein may be utilized as it is, or it may be restructured in a vast number of combinations for use in an almost limitless number of academic settings.

Each chapter has been written by an academician with an expertise in a specific academic discipline (e.g., history), but with a special expertise in the Holocaust from the perspective of that discipline (e.g., history, historiography of the Holocaust). Thus, each chapter is addressed to (1) colleagues within the specific discipline and (2) those who desire an overview on how that specific discipline intersects with Holocaust studies. To allow each essay to be comprehensible to the latter group, every attempt has been made to keep discussion as jargon-free as possible.

The Holocaust:

An Historical Overview

David Weinberg and Byron L. Sherwin

The National Socialist Workers Party (NSDAP) or Nazi Party had its origins in the violent political atmosphere of Bavaria in the immediate post-World War I period. At first, its appeal was restricted to a handful of eccentric nationalists, racists, and war veterans who found its platform of extreme nationalism and social reform a reflection of their own hostility toward Weimar politics and society. By 1921, however, the Nazis had a new leader, Adolf Hitler, committed to transforming the fringe party into a mass movement. Thriving on popular insecurity and hostility toward the Weimar regime, the Nazi party grew slowly but determinedly in the 1920's. After the unsuccessful Beer Hall *putsch* in Munich in 1923, the Nazis made their first entry into national politics in 1924, garnering three percent of the vote and sending fourteen representatives to the *Reichstag* or National Assembly. An upswing in economic conditions saw a Nazi reversal in the 1928 elections, the party gaining only 2.6 percent of the vote and twelve seats. The onset of the Depression, however, enabled the Nazis to make impressive gains in 1930, receiving 18.3 percent of the vote and electing 107 representatives. Though never able to secure an absolute majority in the *Reichstag,* (the party actually suffered a slight reversal in the 1932 elections), the Nazis played a pivotal role in obstructing parliamentary activity during the waning years of Weimar. The appointment of Adolf Hitler as Chancellor in January 1933 climaxed the Nazi drive for power and sounded the death knell for the Republic. The conservative and nationalist forces that brought Hitler to power were convinced that they would be able to manipulate him for their own ends. They were sadly mistaken. Far from a willing servant of others, Hitler and the Nazis soon showed their determination to carry out their program despite opposition at home and abroad.

Most observers in 1933 assumed that Hilter would judiciously "forget" his anti-Semitic tirades upon his accession to power. Instead, anti-Semitism became the central focus of the Nazi regime. What had previously been only propaganda now became, in the hands of a totalitarian State, a determined policy to eliminate the Jew, root and branch, from German and later European life. There were three major stages in the Third Reich's plan to solve the "Jewish problem"—expulsion, ghettoization, and the "Final Solution"—extermination. Though it is unclear whether all three policies were fully envisioned before the Nazis came to power, there is little doubt that once the Third Reich committed itself to a policy of racial anti-Semitism, the progression from expulsion to annihilation was inevitable.

Expulsion of the Jews was preceded by withdrawal of their legal and civil equality and by social and economic segregation. As early as April 1933, the Nazis had declared a general economic boycott against German Jews. Within the year, Jews were dismissed from the army, universities, the government, and the judiciary. The public burning of books by Jewish authors signalled the official exclusion of Jews from German cultural life. Legislation was passed in the first two years to prevent social and economic interchange between German and Jew, culminating in the Nuremberg Laws of September 1935 which denied German citizenship to Jews and prohibited marriage and sexual intercourse between Jews and Aryans. Legal restrictions were accompanied by a massive propaganda campaign depicting the Jew as an alien in the German midst and a corruptor of Aryan values and beliefs. Effectively excluded from all aspects of German society, Jews were declared non-citizens and could now be expelled from the Third Reich.

Tens of thousands of Jews left Germany in the first years of Nazi rule. After the passage of the Nuremberg Laws, emigration became official government policy with the result that many Jews were forced to leave property and personal belongings behind. The tragic plight of German Jewish refugees was highlighted by the desperate act of Hermann Grynspann, a young Jew who assassinated a German official in Paris in November 1938 after hearing of his parents' internment in a refugee camp on the German-Polish border. In retaliation, the German government initiated the so-called *Kristallnacht*—Night of the Broken Glass (November 9–10)—during which Germans set fire to synagogues and Jewish businesses in the major cities of Germany.

Of the close to 600,000 Jews in Germany upon Hitler's accession to power, more than half managed to escape before the implementation of the "Final Solution." After the *Anschluss* or annexation of Austria by Germany in 1938, 120,000 of the 185,000 Jews living in Austria also fled westward. Although efforts were made by international Jewish relief organizations to alleviate the refugees' plight, they were stymied by the refusal of most countries to accept Jewish immigrants. At an international conference called by President Franklin Roosevelt and held in Evian, Switzerland in 1938, representatives from nation after nation rose to explain why they could not and would not accept Jewish refugees. The tragic fate of the St. Louis, a German ship carrying Jewish refugees which in 1939 was denied entrance into Cuba and the United States and only at the last moment found temporary refuge for its passengers in France, Belgium, and England, highlighted the failure of the western nations to respond to Nazi anti-Semitism.

The advent of World War II in September 1939 marked a new stage in the Nazi plan to eliminate Jewry. In conquering the greater part of Poland, the Third Reich inherited a population of some three million Jews. Expulsion was no longer feasible. More importantly, Hitler and the Nazis viewed the War as a struggle to the death between Aryan and Jew. There could be no room for compromise with the racial enemy. Jews in conquered territories had to be "concentrated" in preparation for the "Final Solution."

The policy of forced concentration or ghettoization was initiated in September 1939 with instructions given to local Nazi officials in occupied Poland to transfer Jews living in scattered villages to the larger Jewish settlements, such as Lodz and Warsaw. By the winter of 1940, over a half a million Jews were living in the sealed-off ghetto of Warsaw, an area of no more than a few square city blocks. With ghettoization came restrictive measures isolating Jews from the outside world and further aggravating their miserable living conditions. After being forbidden to trade with Poles living outside the ghetto walls, Jews were forced to leave the ghetto and work in Nazi-controlled factories and plants. The *Judenrate* or Jewish Councils established under Nazi auspices could do little to counter the hunger and disease caused by inadequate food supplies and medical services. For example, it is estimated that over 100,000 Warsaw Ghetto residents died of hunger and disease before the mass deportations of July 1942.

The third and final stage of the Nazi solution to the "Jewish problem" began with the German invasion of the Soviet Union in June 1941. Hitler had envisioned the attack upon Russia as part of a master plan to destroy "Judaeo-Bolshevism," the last stage in his crusade against world Jewry. Not surprisingly, the Nazi invasion was accompanied by the wholesale slaughter of Jews. The massacres were carried out by the so-called *Einsatzgruppen* or Operational Brigades who first crossed over into Polish territory occupied by Russia in September 1939 and then carried their murderous campaign into the heartland of the Soviet Union. "Killing operations" followed a set pattern. Jews were marched to the outskirts of their village, forced to dig a mass grave, and then shot. All in all, the *Einsatzgruppen* murdered over two million Jews.

For Nazis committed to the total annihilation of Jewry, such operations were deemed insufficient. It would take too long to eliminate the Jewish population of Europe through mass shootings. There were also disturbing reports of "inefficiency" in the killing operations—wasted bullets, disobedient soldiers, escaping Jews. In January 1942, a meeting was held in the Berlin suburb of Wannsee (The Wannsee Conference) to coordinate plans for the "Final Solution" of the "Jewish problem" within Nazi-occupied Europe.

Mobile gas ovens had been used occasionally during *Einsatzgruppen* operations. They were now to become the major implement in the destruction of European Jewry.

Within months after the Wannsee Conference, death camps were established to carry out the Nazi plan. The major camps—Chelmno, Auschwitz, Belzec, Sobibor, Treblinka, and Maidanek—were set up in strategic areas of occupied Poland close to major concentrations of Jews. Thus Treblinka was the final destination of Warsaw Jewry after the *aktion* or roundup of July 1942 while Lublin and Lvov Jews arrived in Belzec in March 1942. Auschwitz, the most infamous of the death camps, served as the killing center for Jews transported from other countries conquered by the Nazis.

Besides these six major centers for mass murder, the Nazis also set up hundreds of labor camps in Poland and in Germany where Jewish and non-Jewish prisoners were forced to produce material necessary for the Nazi war effort. In addition to the extermination camps and labor camps, concentration camps had been established in the early 1930's for "enemies of the Reich." While Buchenwald was the best known of these camps, scores of concentration camps were sprinkled across Nazi-occupied Europe.

The Nazis also set up Theresienstadt, situated near Prague, as a "model" camp where representatives of international relief organizations and foreign governments were shown the "humane" conditions under which Jews were allegedly being interned. Though not actually killing centers, such camps took a heavy toll of Jewish internees. Tens of thousands died from disease and starvation while hundreds of thousands eventually met their deaths after being transported to Auschwitz and Treblinka, no longer needed as slave laborers or "model" prisoners.

In almost every case, Nazi conquest was quickly followed by the deportation of Jews. In western Europe, however, Nazi efforts to round up Jews sometimes met with resistance from the local non-Jewish population. Denmark, where only about 500 of the nearly 7000 Jewish residents were deported, is the most memorable example of non-Jewish efforts to save Jews. In other countries with larger Jewish populations, the picture was less clear.

There were few attempts to defend Jews in eastern and southeastern Europe. Indeed, in some cases, local residents outdid their Nazi occupiers in brutalities against Jewish citizens. In areas such as Slovakia, Hungary, Rumania, and Croatia, local and national government officials actively aided German administrators in the roundup and deportation of Jews until the desire to join the winning Allied cause in 1944 led them to back down. The active collaboration of government leaders in the "Final Solution" is revealed in the grim figures of murder and death: about 55,000 of the 75,000 Jews in Yugoslavia, over 70,000 of the 90,000 Jews of Slovakia, about 425,000 of the nearly 850,000 Jews of Rumania and 450,000 of the almost 650,000 Jews of Hungary. By far, the most decimated community was that of Poland. The center of world Jewish culture and learning before World War II, only about 400,000 of the approximately 3,300,000 Jews in Poland in 1939 survived the Holocaust. The murderous activities of the Nazi occupying forces were not limited to Ashkenazic Jewry. Once a center of Sephardic Jewish life, the Greek Jewish community lost over 60,000 of its 75,000 members in the Holocaust, including almost the entire population of Salonika, its most vibrant and populous settlement.

Given the brutal efficiency of the Nazi extermination machine and the active collaboration of many non-Jews, it was almost impossible for Jews to resist the Nazi onslaught. Powerless, cut off from the rest of the world, lacking arms, despised by both Nazi occupier and local resident, and steeped in a historical tradition that emphasized passive acceptance of one's fate, the Jewish communities of Europe were no match for the massive might of the Third Reich. And yet, despite incredible odds, Jews resisted. The example of the uprising in the Warsaw Ghetto in April 1943 is only one of the many recorded examples of armed defense in the face of the Nazi enemy. Hopelessly outmanned and lacking arms, the unseasoned troops of the Warsaw resistance held out for weeks as Nazi soldiers were forced to take each street and each house. Revolts even occurred in death camps such as Treblinka and Sobibor, desperate efforts in the closing days of war to counter the frantic attempts by Nazi officials to complete their program of annihilation. More common was the creation of underground movements among Jewish youth in cities such as Warsaw, Bialystok, and Vilna to ferret Jews out of and smuggle arms into various ghetto communities.

Yet, for all the recorded incidents of heroic defense, there were countless examples of resistance that went unrecorded and even unnoticed. The smuggling of food into the starving ghettos, the hiding of wanted Jews, the continuance of religious and cultural life, the maintenance of educational institutions—all represented an attempt to maintain Jewish identity and Jewish life itself in the face of the concerted effort by the Nazis to destroy Jewry and Judaism. Those Jews who marched to their deaths with dignity, despite efforts to dehumanize them, manifested a form of resistance which is too often ignored in discussions of the Holocaust.

The liberation of the death camps in 1945 did not mark the end of the Jewish tragedy. The European Jewish population had been reduced by two-thirds and world Jewry by one-third, yet murders continued as Jews attempting to return to their homes in Poland were viciously attacked by local residents. Equally tragic was the plight of the *heimlosen* - the nearly 250,000 stateless Jews who did not want to return to their former residences but were denied admittance to new homes. The successful struggle by nearly 100,000 Jews to emigrate to Palestine in the years 1940–1948 lies beyond our concerns but it is an important component of the history of the Holocaust. Other Jews would eventually find refuge in western countries but only after years of anxious waiting in displaced persons' camps.

Though Jews were the primary targets of the Nazis' plan for mass murder, members of other specific social, religious and ethnic groups, considered "enemies of the Reich," were also earmarked for persecution and extermination. The Allied armies represented the external enemies of the Reich which had to be conquered. However, others within Nazi-occupied Europe, were construed by the Nazi leadership to be "internal enemies of the Reich." For complete victory, these "internal enemies" also had to be subdued. While the Jew represented the primary "internal enemy," who must be destroyed to insure German survival and Nazi victory, others were also considered "a-social elements," "unproductive," "useless mouths to feed," and as having "lives unworthy of being lived."

In the very same month in which the war against the external enemies of the Reich began, Hitler signed an order aimed at destroying "unproductive" people, mostly non-Jewish Germans. This decree initiated the "Euthanasia Program," designated by the code T-4 (referring to 4 Tiergartenstrasse in Berlin where the operation originated).

Under the guise of a program for the health care of the physically and mentally disabled, T-4 was actually a program for the mass murder of the insane, mongoloids and retarded children. Eventually, political dissidents and random victims were also sent to their deaths.

The Euthanasia Program, in a sense, was a "dry run" for the extermination of Jews a few years later. Many of the personnel later used to staff the Nazi extermination centers received their "training" in the T-4 program. Franz Stangl, Commandant of Treblinka, is one notable example.

The killing process was carried out in secrecy. People were arrested by police with warrants issued by courts of law. Physicians "certified" the "illnesses" of candidates for destruction. Families, more often than not, trusted the "authorities."

Euphemisms helped to obscure the actual aim of the program. For example, the "Health Department" administered it. Transports to death were provided by the "Charitable Foundation for the Transport of the Ill." The operation itself was called "The General Foundation for Institutional Care."

Doctors and nurses greeted the "patients" at "hospitals" and "sanitoria." The "patients" were put at ease. Their temperatures were taken. Within a few hours, patients were informed that as part of the admissions process, they would have to take showers. These rooms which had the appearance of showers were actually gas chambers. Carbon monoxide asphyxiated the victims. Their remains were cremated so as to obscure evidence regarding the manner of their deaths. A form letter notified their family that death was from "natural causes." Often, the family of the deceased was given the option of buying the "ashes" of the victim.

Despite the guise of secrecy surrounding the actual activities of the Euthanasia Program, the German people eventually discerned its true intent. Public protests were made by Germans, including Nazi party members and

Church leaders. In the summer of 1941, Hitler's train was jeered as "patients" were being "loaded" onto a nearby train. On August 24, 1941, possibly as a result of these protests, Hitler ordered a halt to the T-4 program. It is not clear as to how many non-Jewish Germans and Austrians were murdered in this manner. At the Nuremberg trials, the number of victims was estimated at 275,000. Other, lower estimates, range between 50,000 and 80,000. What is significant is that at the height of Hitler's power, protest against a supposedly "secret" program appeared to have been efficacious. No such protest regarding mass murder of the Jews was forthcoming from the German people.

A second group marked for mass murder by Nazi eugenic policies was the Gypsies. The Nuremberg Laws of 1935 specifically defined the Gypsies as non-Aryans. In 1937, Laws against Crime labeled the Gypsies as "asocials." In 1939, the "resettlement" of the Gypsies was put under the jurisdiction of Adolf Eichmann.

Thousands of Gypsies were transported to concentration camps such as Buchenwald, to ghettos such as the Warsaw Ghetto and to extermination centers such as Auschwitz. Upon their arrival at extermination centers, Gypsies were often murdered at once, without any "selection" process. In addition, Gypsies were often used as subjects for medical experiments. Besides death from disease, starvation, medical experiments and gassing, thousands of Gypsies were murdered by the "mobile killing units" (*Einsatzgruppen*). The actual number of Gypsies murdered is impossible to ascertain. Figures vary from 100,000 to 400,000.

A third group marked for persecution by the Nazis was the Jehovah Witnesses. Considered "a-social" because they would not take an oath of allegiance to Hitler, say "Heil Hitler," or serve in the armed forces, massive arrests of Witnesses occurred in 1936. Many were taken to Buchenwald. Nazi propaganda identified the Witnesses as "defeatists," and as collaborators with Judaism and with the "Jewish World Conspiracy." In fact, the Witnesses were only being faithful to their religious convictions which forbade all but minimal recognition of temporal, political powers. These convictions did not permit them to take oaths recognizing any sovereignty, except the sovereignty of God's Kingdom.

In 1937, Witnesses came under the administration of the Gestapo. Rather than being perceived as a religious group, they were considered a dangerous, a-social and criminal enemy of the State. Religious, personal or moral opposition to the *Fuhrer* was considered a political crime.

In 1938 and 1939, Witnesses were given the option of taking the oath of loyalty to the State and of joining the armed forces, but they refused to comply. Of the 6,034 Witnesses in Germany, 5,911 were arrested. Many were brutally tortured. Approximately 2,000 were murdered. One may claim, with some justification, that the Witnesses were the only *religious* group persecuted by the Nazis for their religious convictions.

A fourth group persecuted by the Nazis was homosexuals. Categorized as "a-socials," homosexuals and those suspected of homosexuality were arrested and sent to penal colonies as slave laborers and to concentration camps, Buchenwald in particular, where many died. As the War progressed, many more were transported to extermination camps. Sparse data regarding the fate of homosexuals under the Nazis is presently available. One cannot even offer a viable estimate as to the number of homosexuals persecuted and murdered by the Nazis.

The fifth and largest group destined for slavery and extermination by the Nazis was the Slavs. Included within this group were Russians, Ukrainians, Byelorussians, Serbians, Bulgarians, Slovaks, Croats, Poles and all Slavic-language-speaking peoples.

Heinrich Himmler had told his SS generals that thirty million Slavs would have to be killed. The plan for the Slavs was to be one of "delayed genocide." Considered a "racially inferior" group, the Slavs were supposed to undergo massive sterilization and to be enslaved to support the Aryan race as a prelude to genocide. Though this plan was not completely implemented, its partial execution led to the enslavement and murder of millions of Slavs.

While some Slavic countries such as Bulgaria were allied with Germany, and while members of some Slavic groups such as Ukrainians were utilized by the Nazis as militia, helpful in the military war effort and in the mass murder of Jews, other Slavic groups—especially Poles and Russians—were enslaved and systematically murdered by the millions.

Himmler had declared that it was the mission of the German people to destroy the Polish people. He predicted the "disappearance of the Poles from the world." To a significant degree, Himmler's prediction came true. Besides the massive hardships endured by the Polish people under Nazi occupation, about 5,000,000 non-Jewish Poles were forced into slave labor by the Nazis. Furthermore, about 2,200,000 non-Jewish Poles were systematically murdered.

The number of Poles—Jews and non-Jews—in German-occupied Poland was about 22,000,000. Of these, about 3,000,000 Jewish Poles and 2,200,000 non-Jewish Poles were murdered. Adding the 5,200,000 enslaved Poles, it emerges that almost one of every two Poles in Nazi-occupied Poland was either enslaved or murdered by the Nazis.

In addition to being considered racially inferior, Russian Slavs were held guilty of the "sociological crime" of Bolshevism. Hitler perceived his war with Russia as a struggle to the death between two antithetical ideologies: Nazism and Communism. Therefore, Hitler maintained, no rules of law ought to apply in the battle against the Russians. The Russian "beasts" must be murdered. Russian prisoners of war, especially "Asiatic" Russians, were not to be sent to Prisoner of War Camps, but to extermination camps. It has been estimated that more than 4,000,000 Soviet prisoners perished in the execution of this policy. While many died of starvation and exposure, many were systematically murdered in extermination centers in a manner not unlike other Slavs, Jews and Gypsies, and by the *Einsatzgruppen*.

Thus, the Holocaust emerges as a particularly, but not exclusively, Jewish tragedy. In the narrow sense, the Holocaust was a specific disaster which befell Jews, Slavs and others. In the broadest sense, it was a horror which implicates all human beings. Each of us is a potential murderer, bystander, or victim. Consequently, study of the Holocaust is not only an attempt at historical understanding, but a frightening exercise in self-knowledge.

APPENDIX

APPENDIX I

DEATH CAMPS

CAMP	LOCATION	NUMBER OF JEWS KILLED
Chelmo	Wartheland	Over a hundred thousand
Belzec	Lublin district	Hundreds of thousands
Sobibor	Lublin district	Hundreds of thousands
Lublin	Lublin district	Tens of thousands
Treblinka	Warsaw district	Hundreds of thousands
Auschwitz	Upper Silesia	One million

Taken from Raul Hilberg, *The Destruction of the European Jews*, (Chicago, Quadrangle, 1961), p. 572.

APPENDIX II

ESTIMATED NUMBER OF JEWS KILLED DURING THE HOLOCAUST

COUNTRY	PRE-WAR POPULATION	NUMBER OF JEWS KILLED
Baltic countries	250,000	230,000
Belgium	90,000	40,000
Bulgaria	65,000	15,000
Denmark	8,000	—
Finland	2,000	—
France	300,000	90,000
Germany/Austria	785,000*	210,000
Greece	75,000	60,000
Hungary	650,000	450,000
Italy	40,000	8,000
Luxemburg	5,000	1,000
Netherlands	150,000	120,000
Norway	2,000	800
Poland	3,340,000	2,940,000
USSR:		
Russia	975,000	107,000
Ukraine	1,500,000	900,000
White Russia	375,000	245,000
Rumania	850,000	425,000

*On eve of Nazi accession to power in 1933

Continued

COUNTRY	PRE-WAR POPULATION	NUMBER OF JEWS KILLED
Slovakia	90,000	70,000
Yugoslavia	75,000	55,000
TOTAL	9,627,000	5,956,800

Figures extrapolated from: Lucy Dawidowicz, *The War Against the Jews* (New York, 1975), 403; "Holocaust," *Encyclopedia Judaica,* (Jerusalem, 1972), 890; and *The Holocaust and Resistance: An Outline of Jewish History in Nazi-Occupied Europe* (Jerusalem, 1972).

APPENDIX III

Estimated Numbers of Non-Jews Systematically Murdered

Jehovah Witnesses	—	about 2,000
Gypsies	—	100,000–400,000
Poles	—	about 2,200,000
Soviet POW's (mobile killing operations and extermination camps)	—	about 4,000,000*

TOTAL: Approximately 6,500,000

(Figures extrapolated from a variety of sources, including Hilberg, Levin, etc.)

THUS, THE TOTAL NUMBER OF DEAD FROM MAJOR GENOCIDAL OPERATIONS BY THE NAZIS IS ESTIMATED AS BEING BETWEEN TWELVE AND THIRTEEN MILLION.

*of this number, about 3,500,000 were in mobile killing operations (*Einsatzgruppen*)

Ideological Antecedents of the Holocaust

Byron L. Sherwin

Any forthright encounter with Holocaust studies must confront the compelling questions: Why did the Holocaust occur? What caused the Holocaust? More specifically, one must query: Why were the German people under Hitler the perpetrators of the Holocaust? Why were the Jews the primary targets of Nazi extermination policies?

Some historians of the Holocaust respond to these questions by attempting to identify the specific cause or causes which engendered the Holocaust. This approach implies that the Holocaust might have been predictable, that it was not an accident of history. Though historians maintain this position in the retrospective comfort of hindsight, one cannot assume that their view is merely an expression of intellectual curiosity. A personal motivation must also be present to justify their arduous, tedious and intricate research.

It would appear that these scholarly efforts are engendered by the existentially inspired quest for meaning, by the will to believe that history is not a game of dice in which chance supplants rational explanation. In searching out causes of the Holocaust, the historian is groping for a comprehensible rubric with which to understand an otherwise baffling event. His passion for rational explanation articulates a personal desire to uncover coherency and meaning within a seemingly incoherent and meaningless experience.

The historian's perspective may express not only his own existential crisis, but also his "egocentric predicament." His "explanation" may precede his collection of data. His ideological bent may presuppose the findings of his research. He may twist the material he collects to force it to correlate with his presuppositions. The Marxist historian, for example, might marshal his data to demonstrate an already assumed premise—that the Holocaust was a product of the class struggle, that its causes were economic in origin. A Zionist historian might interpret the data as confirmation of the claim endemic to certain varieties of Zionism that Jewish life in the Diaspora must inevitably lead to trauma and tragedy. The historian who presumes a cyclical view of history might interpret the Holocaust as an unavoidable predictable event which fits into the scheme of history in general, Jewish history in particular. The national determinist might contend that the intrinsic nature and destinies of individual peoples move history in a certain inevitable direction. He would assume that the Holocaust was the product of innate tendencies in the German nature toward tyranny, totalitarianism, and anti-Semitism. He would then summon data to justify the already assumed claim.

One might advise both the student and teacher of Holocaust studies to approach the works of such historians with skepticism and with caution. For a number of reasons, their studies are helpful but not conclusive.

First of all, the historian's reconstruction of the "causes" of the Holocaust represents a retrospective attempt to "predict" that which has already occurred. If the Holocaust was predictable, then why was it not predicted? One reason may be that its "causes" were not as clearly discernible in foresight as in hindsight. A second reason may be the unprecedented nature of the Holocaust. An event of the devastating dimensions of the Holocaust becomes believable only after it has occurred, not before. Prediction is based most effectively upon past experience. For example, we can predict that to touch hot metal will burn us because we know from experience that such a cause produced such an effect.

Unique events such as the Holocaust cannot be predicted as there is no basis in past experience for such predictions. The causes, even if they are correctly identified, had never before produced such an event. At best, the identity of such causes might predict future events. However, if the Holocaust was indeed a unique event, its causes must be incomparable and indeed irrelevant to explaining or predicting any other event.

Thirdly, the "causes" identified by a number of historians of the Holocaust were present in countries other than Germany. Totalitarian tendencies and anti-Semitic precedents, for example, were equally present in Russia and France. Why, then, did the explosion occur in Germany and not in these other lands? If such "causes" already existed in medieval Christian Europe, as some historians claim, then why was the systematic extermination of Jews first undertaken by twentieth century Germany? Thus, if the Holocaust is construed to be the effect of discernible causes, one must ask why the presence of these causes at other times and in other places did not inevitably produce the same effect. A cause-effect argument must assume that identical causes produce identical effects.

A further difficulty with the cause-effect argument is that it often attempts to identify a single cause for the Holocaust. To do so, however, distorts the problem by oversimplifying it. To do so commits the "reductionist fallacy." An event as complex as the Holocaust simply cannot be explained from a single perspective, whether it be economic, sociological, psychological or theological. The "causes" of the Holocaust, if they can be reconstructed, will emerge only from an interdisciplinary mosaic of investigation. A single cause, denoted by an individual discipline, cannot suffice.

To deny that the Holocaust may be explained as the effect of clearly discernible causes does not necessarily infer that the Holocaust was solely a product of chance; nor does it mean that "causes" should not be sought, that the event is beyond all comprehension or explanation. It only means that one should not be convinced too rapidly that the Holocaust was the effect of specific identifiable causes.

One may posit an intermediary approach that denies that the Holocaust happened by chance and that rejects any claim to have discovered *the* cause of the Holocaust. Such an approach would attempt to uncover the social, intellectual, and cultural preconditions without which the Holocaust might not have occurred. Such an approach would limit itself to identifying "contributing causes" of the Holocaust without affirming a definite cause-and-effect relationship between these "contributing causes" and the Holocaust. Such "contributing causes" would describe the ingredients which were *necessary* but *not sufficient* in themselves to engender the Holocaust. Thus, while it is possible to identify conditions that helped to precipitate the Holocaust, it is not completely possible to explain how the coexistence of these particular conditions at a given time in a given place necessarily produced the Holocaust. Nevertheless, the inconclusiveness of positing contributing causes of the Holocaust does not diminish the importance of efforts to describe them. The partial illumination they shed upon the event must be considered in any study of the Holocaust.

Rather than reviewing individual works that attempt to establish specific causes of the Holocaust, the following discussion will focus upon the development of various motifs, stereotypes, and concepts which helped to make the Holocaust possible.* The analysis below will be directed towards establishing the nature of intellectual and social preconditions without which the Holocaust might not have occurred. The bibliography at the end of this section will indicate relevant source material.

FIRST ATTEMPTS

Directly after World War II, a number of historians claimed that Hitler's Germany was an aberration in history, the product of tragic chance, the result of a state in which a group of madmen gained control. This approach, psychoanalytically oriented, attempted to demonstrate that the leaders of the Third Reich were clinically insane individuals who drew the German people

*For an analysis of some key works, see the following chapter.

and the world into a catastrophic war. The extermination of the Jews was interpreted as the insane policy of an insane German leadership.

This approach was widely accepted in the late 1940's and early 1950's when the United States and other western powers were pledged to normalizing political and economic relationships with West Germany in order to strengthen West Germany as a bulwark against the Soviet Union. Given the political realities existing at the height of the Cold War, the claim that the German people as a whole were not responsible for the War, but rather were victims of insane men at the helm of their government, was widely embraced.

This theory, which held the Holocaust to be a tragic and unprecedented historical fluke, stimulated a number of historians to maintain that the War in general and the Holocaust in particular were not events of chance and were not perpetrated solely by an insane German leadership. These historians contended that Nazi ideology and Nazi policies did not emerge out of a void, but were the result of intellectual and social conditioning. These historians were unwilling to so felicitously exempt the German people from responsibility. They wanted to demonstrate that Hitler's power and policies were supported by a wide variety of sectors within Germany—the intellectuals, the military, the industrialists, the people at large. They labored to prove that prewar conditions might have explained the events of the War. They refused to interpret the War in general and the Holocaust in particular as a total outburst of irrational behavior. Motivated either by the "aberration theory," by intellectual curiosity, or by existential crisis, they began to look for the seeds of the catastrophe in the periods preceding the ascent of the Third Reich.

TWO APPROACHES

Amongst those historians seeking to identify the significant (but not necessarily definitive) conditions leading to the Holocaust, two approaches may be identified. Some claim that the cultural, philosophical, or theological antecedents without which the Holocaust might not have occurred are to be found specifically in the generations immediately preceding the Holocaust. The Holocaust in this view was the product of a specifically modern anti-Semitism which somehow differed from earlier forms of anti-Semitism. These historians differ as to when this new, modern variety of anti-Semitism developed. Some examine the eighteenth and nineteenth centuries; some examine Enlightenment thought; some scrutinize Germany during the period of the Second Reich (1870–1914). A second group of historians looks to earlier periods and maintains that the seeds of Nazi anti-Semitism were sown throughout the history of Christian Europe.

An alternative to these two approaches maintains that there is a continuity of development from early European anti-Semitism to modern European anti-Semitism, culminating in the Nazi Holocaust. Certain motifs, such as the demonic nature of the Jew, were articulated first in the early periods and were nurtured and expanded in later times. These motifs appear in a variety of forms in ancient, medieval, and modern anti-Semitism. Thus, while modern anti-Semitism may have supplemented earlier notions, a continuum of ideas may still be discerned throughout European history. Modern anti-Semitism added to, but did not displace, former stereotypes. Rather than discarding the past, modern anti-Semitism in general and Nazism in particular built upon it.

Three areas are of specific relevance to the attempt to discern the preconditions that helped make the Holocaust possible. The first is the history of Christian anti-Semitism. Here one encounters the genesis and development of stereotypes and motifs that played a significant role in Nazi thought. The second is the response of Enlightenment thinkers to the "Jewish problem," which emerged as a result of the political and social emancipation of Western European Jewry in the eighteenth century. The third is the development of German *volkist* thought in the nineteenth century. The repetition of various ideas and motifs in each of these three areas will clearly link together various ancient, medieval and modern manifestations of European anti-Semitism. Nazi ideology will be portrayed as not having made neat distinctions, such as those presently being made by historians, between earlier and more recent notions. Hopefully, the material presented herein will demonstrate that Nazism was not a product of *creatio ex nihilo,* and that any serious discussion of the Holocaust must begin with a discussion of the genesis and development of the conditions which made it possible.

THE CHRISTIAN ROOTS OF NAZI ANTI-SEMITISM

On April 26, 1933, Wilhelm Berning, Bishop of Osnabruk, and Monsignor Paul Steinmann, Vicar General of Berlin, met with the German Chancellor, Adolf Hitler. The *Reichsfuhrer,* who had called the meeting, assured the prelates that National Socialism was committed to joining the Church in its struggle against Bolshevism and Judaism. In its anti-Semitic program, Hitler insisted, the Nazi regime was only continuing the 1500-year-old policies of the Church vis-à-vis the Jews. In dealing with the preconditions of the Holocaust, one must confront the question of whether Hitler's claim was accurate or libelous.

When Hitler harangued against the Jews, he struck a responsive cord amongst his listeners because he was speaking in a language already familiar to them. Much of the vocabulary of this language was drawn from the long history of Christian anti-Semitism. Hitler reiterated motifs and stereotypes nurtured by centuries of Church teachings. His denunciations of the Jews were not considered the maniacal ravings of a lunatic, but the restatement of notions upon which Christian theology had bestowed an aura of "respectability."

In the words of the prominent Church historian Alan Davies, "Without the Church, Hitler would not have been possible." Jules Isaac's writings on Christian anti-Semitism helped to persuade Pope John to alter the Church's official doctrine on the Jews. As Isaac so effectively put it: "Without centuries of Christian catechism, preaching and vituperation, the Hitlerian teachings, propaganda and vituperations would not have been possible." Thus, the Nazis did not discard the past, as some have suggested. Instead, they built upon it. They did not begin a development of ideas regarding the Jews. Rather, they completed it.

In the New Testament, in the writings of the Church Fathers (specifically, the Patristic "Adversos Judaeos" tradition) and in medieval Christian theology, art, law and literature, a portrait of the Jew emerged that was later utilized by Nazi theoreticians and propagandists in their "war against the Jews." We shall not attempt to trace historically the development of each of the individual motifs that constitute the mosaic of this portrait of the Jew. Rather, we shall strive to reconstruct the caricature of the Jew developed in Christian teachings, which provided material for Nazism's attack upon the Jewish people.

The "political theology" of Nazism perceived the world as a battleground where the forces of God, the forces of goodness and God's "chosen people"—the Aryans—wage a defensive war to the death against the forces of the Devil, the powers of evil, the Antichrist, symbolized by the Jew. The German people suffered degradation and defeat in the First World War and in the period immediately following it because they had been betrayed, "stabbed in the back" by the innately criminal and foreign element within Germany— the Jew. Adolf Hitler was then sent by God to redeem Germany as Christ was sent by God to redeem mankind. The *Fuhrer* is the Christ, the Messiah of Germany, whose mission is to fight the battle of God against the Antichrist, the Jew. As the *Fuhrer* is a messenger of God, his will expresses the Divine will; allegiance to him is faithfulness to God. For example, the German Christian Church (*Deutsche Christen*) proclaimed as follows: "In the person of the *Fuhrer* we behold the one sent from God. . . . we German Christians are the first trenchline of National Socialism. . . . to live, fight and die for Adolf Hitler means to say yes to the Path of Christ."

Nazism's portrait of the enemy—the Jew—embraced a contradiction. On the one hand, Jews were a powerless nuisance, like lice or vermin, which must be exterminated. On the other hand, the Jews were a worldwide power to be confronted and annihilated. The Jews were perceived simultaneously as superhuman powers posing an essential threat and as subhumans or animals to be exterminated for the "racial health" of mankind. The roots of these ideas, constituting the political theology of Nazism, derive largely from Christian traditions.

Already in the New Testament the Jews are described as being "not of

God'' but ''of the Devil.'' The Jews are depicted as an apostate people who had rejected God and who consequently had been rejected by God. The Jews' supposed rebellion against God was not only expressed by their rejection of His teachings, but by the murder of prophets whom He had sent to them. Specifically, the Jews had murdered Jesus, the messenger of God, the Son of God, God incarnate. As innately criminal apostates, the Jews are now despised and rejected by God. A new ''chosen people'' has replaced them—the Christian community.

In the literature of the Church Fathers, these themes were amplified and expanded. The Jews were now construed as the embodiment of the demonic, and Jewish history was portrayed as a sequence of sin and crime. The Jews were claimed to be criminal by nature. Hedonism, sensuality, and gluttony were claimed to be true to their essential dispositions. The Jews were understood to be the antithesis of the rest of humanity—anti-human, anti-God, anti-Christ. Eternally rejected by God for their sins and crimes, especially for the crime of deicide, the Jews must now be rejected by mankind. For many of the Church Fathers, to oppress, to persecute, to degrade the Jews was to fulfill the will of God and to demonstrate the truth of the Christian claim that the Church is now the chosen of God while the Jews have been abandoned by God.

By the fifth century, the Jew was no longer described as a human being. He was a demonic monster, a theological abstraction, a useless obsolescence, a subhuman creature. The scene for the future was already set before the Middle Ages. The ''moral'' and theological basis for persecuting and even for murdering Jews had been established. Jews might be killed because they killed Christ; Jews might be oppressed because it is the will of God; Jews must be subdued because otherwise their demonic power will contaminate or will destroy mankind. Thus, the struggle against the Jews was portrayed as a self-defensive battle for God against the Devil.

Many of these ideas developed by the Church Fathers attained legal status and became socially acceptable modes of behavior when Christianity became the official religion of Europe. In medieval Christian Europe, Jewish rights were legislated out of existence and Jewish degradation became the legally, socially, and theologically accepted norm.

The canonical measures taken in the Middle Ages began to clearly foreshadow legal measures taken against Jews in Nazi Germany. Earlier ideas were strengthened. For example, concrete legal and social measures helped to insure Jewish degradation and serfdom. Medieval legal codes depicted Jews as a species unto themselves. Compared to deer and other animals in the royal forest, they became the *property* of Kings. For example, the penalty in a number of kingdoms for killing a Jew was a fine for having destroyed the King's property. Like the Nazi Nuremberg Laws of 1935, canonical law forbade intermarriage between Jews and Christians. The ''Jewish badge,'' reinstituted by the Nazis, was anticipated by the decrees of the Fourth Lateran

Council in 1215. The burning of Jewish books by the Nazis was anticipated by the widespread confiscation and public burning of Jewish books, especially the Talmud, by medieval church authorities. Compulsory ghettoization, part of the Nazi plan of extermination, was instituted by the medieval German Church in 1267 (Synod of Breslau). Forced expulsion of Jews from various principalities and nations throughout the Middle Ages was the harbinger of the Nazis' attempt to make Europe *Judenrein* (free of Jews).

Throughout the history of early and medieval Christianity, the option of conversion to Christianity was open to Jews. Any Jew could remove his pariah status by embracing the Christian faith. However, by the early sixteenth century in Spain, this option became problematic, for the Jew was now identified by blood rather than by religion. Being a Jew was now considered a genetic trait which could not be erased by baptism. The Jew was believed to be of a different essence than the Christian. Baptism could not change the indelible Jewish nature.

Under threat of expulsion from Spain and Portugal in the late fifteenth century, many Jews had converted to Christianity. By the sixteenth century, the Inquisition sought to "purify" the Church hierarchy, the military, the universities, and the nobility of Jewish "corruption." Statutes concerning "purity of blood" (*limpieza de sangre*) were issued stating the degree of Jewish blood an individual might have. Being a Jew, having Jewish blood, was compared to an incurable disease. Once afflicted, there was no cure, not even baptism. Thus, in sixteenth century Spain, one may perceive the harbinger of the Nuremberg Laws for the "Protection of German Blood and Honor." One may discern the beginnings of *racial* anti-Semitism.

The underlying assumption of racial anti-Semitism, introduced by the Spanish Church, is that Jews are essentially and unalterably different from and inferior to other human beings. This notion was fundamental to the medieval Christian perception of the Jew.

The Jew was considered physiologically different from other humans because of his supposed relationship to the devil and to the demonic realm. Because of his alliance with the devil, the Jew was believed to have specific bodily characteristics in common with the devil. Like the devil, he was depicted in the form of a goat, with horns, a beard and a tail. This identity of the Jew with the demonic as well as with the animal world projected the contradictory, dual image, later utilized by Nazi ideology: the Jew as a powerful demonic force and the Jew as a subhuman animal.

When Shakespeare wrote, "Certainly, the Jew is the very devil incarnate," he was accurately summarizing Church teachings about the Jews which have their roots in the New Testament, and which were nurtured by the Church Fathers and developed by the medieval Church. When Julius Streicher, in 1941, recommended "the extermination of that people whose father is the Devil," he was reiterating a tradition long established by the Church.

Throughout the Middle Ages and until the present day, Jews have been charged not only with the murder of God (deicide), but with the premeditated murder of individual Christians, specifically children, for the purposes of drinking their blood. The "blood libel" is rooted in the aforementioned claim that the Jews are innately disposed toward murder. As late as the sixteenth century, the old German proverb that "Jews cannot exist or live without Christian blood" was current. The image of the blood-sucking Jew, prominent in Nazi propaganda, has its roots in this medieval imagery. On May 1, 1943, the entire issue of *Der Sturmer,* Julius Streicher's infamous organ of Nazi propaganda, was dedicated to the "blood libel." Hardly an issue of that journal omitted an illustration of a Jew sucking blood from an "Aryan" child.

Nazi researcher Helmut Schramm collected all the legends about Jewish ritual murder. His book was an immediate success, with Himmler personally ordering many copies for himself. Schlamm wrote:

> For our generation which currently is engaged in the severest struggle with this world pest in view of the Jewish ritual murders which ultimately sought to represent symbolically the annihilation of the non-Jewish world, there is only one possible conclusion: Spiritual and physical annihilation of the hereditary Jewish criminality.

The depiction of the Jews as a demonic alien, as hostile enemies within the boundaries of Christendom, inspired the notion that the Jews are the "enemy from within." They must therefore be eliminated in order to insure the safety of Christendom.

As a "fifth column," the Jews, it was insisted, should appreciate their "guest" status. As a "guest people," as an apostate people, and as a people destined to deprecation by the teachings of the Church, any economic success enjoyed by Jews made them subjects of attack. As financial success would deny the validity of the eternal "curse" upon the Jews, this success was to be suppressed. Furthermore, the accumulation of Jewish wealth—especially by means of money-lending—was interpreted as a gesture of the ingratitude of the Jews towards their "host people." Worse, it was considered to be an exploitative betrayal by the Jews of the benevolence of the people who had provided them with a home. The apostate Jew, who was innately a betrayer according to the aforementioned Church doctrine, was increasingly identified in medieval Christian thought with the paradigmatic betrayer, Judas. The medieval passion plays reinforced this identification of the Jew with Judas. Thus, to the medieval Christian mind, the Jew came to epitomize the exploitation, betrayal and "blood-sucking" of a host people by a demonic alien. This depiction of the Jew figures prominently in Nazi literature. The Jew, even the German Jew, was claimed to be an alien within Germany. He was at best an unwanted guest who had to be eliminated for the well-being of his host. Consequently, he had no rights, no status. His property could be expropriated because it was "stolen" from the German people. He had betrayed the German people by stabbing them in the back through economic exploitation during the First World War. He was sucking the blood, polluting the blood of Germany and of the Aryan race. The demonic Jew had to be eliminated for the Aryan people to survive. To destroy the Jews was to do the will of God.

In *Mein Kampf,* Hitler wrote:

> Hence today I believe that I am acting in accordance with the will of the Almighty Creator: by defending myself against the Jew, I am fighting for the work of the Lord.

For Hitler, this struggle had to be to the death. In a speech delivered in 1922, Hitler maintained:

> There can be no compromise—there are only two possibilities: either victory of the Aryan or annihilation of the Aryan and the victory of the Jew.

In 1943, when the extermination of the Jews was well under way, Heinrich Himmler addressed a group of SS soldiers and reiterated the claim that the war against the Jews was a moral duty, motivated by the need for self-defense:

> We had the moral right, we had the duty toward our people, to kill this people which wanted to kill us.

In February 1943, Goebbels' propaganda ministry issued the following instructions:

> Stress: If we lose this war, we do not fall into the hands of some other states but will be annihilated by world Jewry. Jewry firmly decided to exterminate all Germans.

In 1943, Himmler told his officers that,

> We had the moral right vis à vis *our* people to annihilate *this* people which wanted to annihilate us. . . . on the whole we can say that we have fulfilled this heavy task with love for our people, and we have not been damaged in the innermost of our being, our soul, our character.

In his last political testament (April 29, 1945), Hitler again portrayed the Jew as "the universal poisoner of all peoples" and charged all Germans with the task of "merciless opposition" to the Jew.

As Jews represented the Antichrist, Hitler represented the German Christ, sent by God to redeem Germany from its enemies. In schools in Nazi Germany, for example, students would recite the following grace after meals:

> *Fuhrer,* my *Fuhrer*
> Bequeathed to me by the Lord
> .... Thou has rescued Germany
> from deepest distress.

Some find the direct origin of Nazi anti-Semitism in the teachings of the Church as articulated by Martin Luther. For Luther was not only the founder of the Protestant Church; he was the founder of the specifically *German* Church. Furthermore, Luther was not only a theologian but one of the founders of German nationalism. It is, therefore, worthwhile to review Luther's teachings regarding the Jews.

In Luther's early writings, he urged kindness towards Jews on the hope that a cessation of persecution would precipitate widespread conversion to the Church he was then in the process of founding (e.g. in his tract, *That Christ was Born a Jew,* 1523). But, despite his early overtures to the Jews, Luther soon found that the Jews would not accept goodwill as an adequate incentive for conversion. Furthermore, when he tried to convert some rabbis, they in turn tried to convert him. Finally, in Luther's later days, when he heard that Moravian Christians were adopting many Jewish practices, Luther assumed that the cause was Jewish missionary effort. At this point, Luther could restrain himself no longer. In 1543, he wrote a tract highly favored by Nazi spokesmen, *On the Jews and Their Lies.* This treatise is so vitriolic that one biographer of Luther writes that "one could only wish that Luther had died before ever this tract was written." In this essay, Luther expounds what appears to be his true beliefs regarding the Jews. The attitudes he expresses here correlate with those found in his "table talk."

Luther not only reiterates many themes found in classical Christian anti-Semitic literature but goes beyond them. That his remarks were written in German, for Germans, about Germany, struck a responsive cord four hundred years later in Nazi Germany.

Luther reiterated such earlier themes as these: the dejected state of the Jews is proof of their rejection by God; the Jews are murderers of the prophets; the Jews are usurers in violation of their own law, the law of Moses; the Jews are demonic; their synagogues are homes for devils; Jews poison and exploit Christians; the Jews are criminal by nature; the Jews want to kill Christians and do indeed kill them; Jews are greedy and exploitative by nature; etc. Luther, however, not only went beyond these themes, but related them to the specific relationships of the Jews to the German People. His response to the "Jewish problem" of his day was as follows:

What shall we Christians do with this rejected and condemned people, the Jews?

First, to set fire to their synagogues or schools and to bury and cover with dirt whatever will not burn, so that no man will again see a stone or cinder of them. This is to be done in honor of our Lord and of Christendom.

Secondly, I advise that their houses also be razed and destroyed. . . .

Fifth, I advise that safe-conduct on the highways be abolished completely for the Jews. They have no business in the country.

Sixth, I advise that usury be prohibited to them and that all cash and treasure of silver and gold be taken from them and put aside for safekeeping. . . . they have stolen and robbed from us all they possess. . . . One should toss out these lazy rogues [from Germany] by the seat of their pants. . . . eject them forever from the country [i.e., from Germany]. . . . Thus the Jews, our guests, treat us; for we are their hosts. They rob and fleece us and hang about our necks, these lazy weaklings and indolent bellies; they swill and feast, enjoy good times in our homes, and by way of reward they curse our Lord Christ and all of us, threatening us and unceasingly wishing us death and every evil.

Thus the accursed Jews encumber us with their diabolical, blasphemous and horrible sins in our own country. . . . I am extremely surprised that the devil can be so powerful as to delude a person, to say nothing of an entire nation which boasts of being God's people. . . . Whenever you see a genuine Jew, you may with good conscience cross yourself and say: There goes the devil incarnate.

Luther's last sermon, delivered three days before his death, urged that the Jews be exiled from all of Germany.

Thus, in Luther's plan for the Jews, one may discern the prototype for much of the Nazi programme regarding the Jews. The destruction of German synagogues, as suggested by Luther, occurred on November 9-10, 1938, during the *Kristallnacht,* the "Night of Broken Glass." His description of the Jews as a criminal, betraying, exploitative, demonic force within Germany was clearly reiterated by Nazism. His plan to make Germany *Judenrein* after expropriating Jewish property "stolen" from the German people became a basic feature of the Nazi programme. It is no wonder, therefore, that Luther's German nationalism, coupled with his theologically inspired plans for the Jews, was popular in Nazi Germany. The Nazis showed their indebtedness to Luther's views on the Jews when they staged the first large-scale pogrom in November, 1938, in honor of the anniversary of Luther's birthday. Luther's tract, *On the Jews and Their Lies,* was republished by Nazi presses. It is no wonder that Julius Streicher asked that Luther be co-indicted as a defendant in the Nuremberg trials.

From the previous discussion it should be apparent that Christian anti-Semitism was a contributing factor to Nazi anti-Semitism, that Christian teachings were a necessary precondition for the Holocaust. As one prominent historian put it, "In our own day, and within our own civilization, more than six million deliberate murders are the consequence of the teachings about

Jews for which the Christian Church is ultimately responsible, and of an attitude to Judaism which is not only maintained by all the Christian churches, but has its ultimate resting place in the teaching of the New Testament itself.'' (James Parkes)

THE ENLIGHTENMENT: MODERN ANTI-SEMITISM

Though many ''Enlightenment'' thinkers rejected Christianity to some significant degree, they retained many of the anti-Semitic motifs characteristic of Christian teachings.

With the Enlightenment, Jews were afforded the opportunity of leaving their ghettoized, sequestered existence and of entering society at large. Enlightenment thinkers, generally speaking, developed two approaches to this new situation. ''Liberals'' were willing to admit Jews on the condition that they ceased being Jews. If Jews wanted the same rights as everyone else, they claimed, Jews had to become like everyone else. The liberals offered ''everything to Jews as individuals and nothing to them as Jews.'' ''Conservatives,'' on the other hand, maintained that since Jews are essentially different from other men, they could never be granted equality.

The ''liberal'' position emphasized the need for liberation from religion. It attacked Christianity by attacking Judaism. It maintained that Christianity was a form of Judaism imposed upon Europeans, an alien graft upon the European culture. It stressed the need to revert back to the authentic origins of European man—paganism.* It insisted that rationalism was the pathway to truth and that the Jew represented the antithesis of rationalism. The Jew epitomized superstition and mysticism. Like the early Luther, Enlightenment thinkers suggested that once oppression of Jews was assuaged, the Jews would dispense with their Judaism. The ''liberal'' approach to the ''Jewish problem'' was for the Jews to surrender their Judaism.

To some degree, Jews in Western Europe, especially in Germany, responded to the ''liberal'' position by offering a counterposition. They liberalized or reformed Judaism by emphasizing its rational nature and by expunging Judaism of its ''nationalistic'' tendencies. However, not only was this an unacceptable compromise for the liberals who wanted Jews to totally surrender Judaism, but it ironically became the basis for later claims, including eventually the Nazi assertion that since Judaism lacks irrationalism and emotion, it is not a real religion.

The ''conservative'' position held that even by religious conversion, the Jew could not be admitted into general society since he is essentially different from other men. The Jew is a ''resident alien'' within Europe. He is Oriental

---

*By ''paganism,'' this position meant the Greco-Roman culture of pre-Christian Europe.

and not Occidental. The climate of his Oriental origins has caused him to be of a nature different from that of Europeans. As a pariah people, as a "nation within a nation," the Jews could provide no basis for fraternity with Europeans. They must remain a "nation within a nation." As such, they are potentially subversives. They are the "enemy within." Consequently, conservatives queried as to whether economic or political power could be granted Jews. As Jews were not actual members of the peoples amongst whom they lived but rather part of an international element residing in a particular country, they posed an internal threat to the security of that country. The "Jewish problem"—what to do with the Jews—became a preoccupation during the eighteenth and nineteenth century. Finally, in the twentieth century, Hitler offered his "Final Solution" to this "problem."

French and German philosophers of the eighteenth and nineteenth century discussed the "Jewish problem." Some adopted the liberal stance while others took the conservative position.

French philosophers of a more liberal bent, such as Montesquieu, suggested equal rights for Jews if they would become like everyone else, if they would cease to be Jews. "If you do not want to be Christians," wrote Montesquieu, "at least be human."

Philosophers of a more conservative bent, such as Voltaire, held the Jews to be incorrigible aliens, of an essentially different nature from other men, a nation within a nation, an internal danger, a perennial evil. Even the most "enlightened" Jew, Voltaire claimed, could not escape his innate nature. The very existence of the Jews threatened European civilization. Conversion might change their religion, but it could not alter their nature.

Immanuel Kant, the leading German philosopher of the eighteenth century, also addressed himself to the Jewish question. In his discussion of moral theory, Kant claimed that since Judaism was concerned only with external laws and meaningless ceremonies, it was devoid of morality and religion, as he understood them. Consequently, Jews could never become part of the German people. Furthermore, Kant claimed that the Jewish notion of the "chosen people" implied hatred of non-Jews. Kant, therefore, suggested "the euthanasia of Judaism."

In the nineteenth century, G.W.F. Hegel, foreshadowing Arnold Toynbee, considered Judaism an anachronism. As such, it has no right to exist.

In the nineteenth century writings of Johann G. Fichte, the eminent German philosopher, one finds a foreshadowing of many of the nationalistic ideas later expressed by Nazism. Particularly in his *Address to the German Nation,* one finds the claim that the Jew is the implacable foe of all mankind. For Fichte, each Jew is part of an international force at war with every nation:

> A mighty state stretches across Europe, hostile in intent and engaged in constant strife with everyone else. . . . This is Jewry.

Thus, for the German people to fight the Jew is a totally justified measure of self-defense.

In the nineteenth century, while Karl Marx held the "liberal" view that Jews could enter western society by relinquishing Judaism, Bruno Bauer held the "conservative" position that the Jewish nature could not be altered, hence Jews could not and should not enjoy political and social emancipation.

Karl Marx followed the liberal position of extending rights to Jews once they surrender their Judaism. In his tract *On the Jewish Problem* Marx insists that the liberation of the state means the liberation of the state from religion — Judaism and Christianity. However, the liberation of Christianity, for Marx, entails its liberation from Judaism. Furthermore, "the social emancipation of Jewry is the emancipation of society from Jewry."

Marx stressed the need of Europe to free itself from the influence of Jewry because he identified Jewry and Judaism with the cause of European enslavement — money and egotism. For Marx, "What was the essential foundation of Judaism? Practical needs, egotism . . . The God of the Jews has become secularized and is now a worldly God. The bill of exchange is the Jew's real God." Marx furthers the notion of Jewish power by claiming that the Jew, with his money, "decides the fate of Europe." Thus, for Marx, "Jewish emancipation means, ultimately, the emancipation of humanity from Judaism."

Dealing with the "Jewish problem" was not restricted to philosophers. In the nineteenth century, literary, political, and popular writing and thought, especially in Germany, were profoundly concerned with the status of Jews and Judaism. Much of this concern is found in writings of what came to be called *volkist* thought.

VOLKIST THOUGHT

An essential component of Nazi ideology was the notion of the *volk,* specifically, the German *volk.* The roots of the Nazi plan for Jewish extermination may be clearly discerned in the writings of leading volkist thinkers.

When Hitler spoke to the German people about the German *volk,* he was reiterating ideas that mostly developed in the nineteenth century and which had become part of popular thought in Germany by the twentieth century. Allied with the supposed "scientific" findings of "racial anthropology," volkist ideology helped provide the philosophical, "moral," social and "scientific" justification for the elimination of those who were perceived as enemies of the German *volk;* i.e., Jews, Gypsies, Slavs, etc.

The volkist ideology crystallized with the establishment of nation-states in Western and Central Europe. It sought to define a nation as being more than a group of people living within common geographical boundaries, more than a community of citizens bound together by a "social contract," more than a people bound together by laws and traditions. Volkist ideology held that a nation was not *essentially* determined by geography or politics, but was the product of a unique national essence.

The formulation of volkist thought was largely a reaction to the rapid cultural, economic and social changes that accompanied the industrialization and urbanization of European life. It was part of a desperate search for roots amid radical change, a quest for orientation in a time of political and social revolution. It was the effort of conservatives seeking an anchor amidst turbulence. At a time when traditional sources of self-identity had begun to dissolve, volkist thought provided the alienated individual with a source of identity: individual identity may be found in the *volk*. The *volk* provided a link between the individual person and a "higher," immutable reality. The *volk* offered a common feeling of belonging, a shared destiny, a unified emotional expression.

Volkist thought claimed that the present may be an unfortunate abyss in the historical drama, but that the idyllic medieval past might be resurrected in the future. Present degradation of the *volk* is not a permanent condition, but a hiatus which may be overcome in the future as it had been in the past. A leader, a *fuhrer*, a political messiah who will unify the *volk*, is destined to arise. The spirit of the *volk*, the divine spirit, will act through him and will assure the resurgence of the *volk*.

While Enlightenment conservatives had often stressed the exotic nature of the Jewish foreigner, nineteenth century thinkers emphasized the threat posed by the corrupting influences of the resident alien Jew. While Enlightenment conservatives had often depicted the Jew as an Oriental sage, a master of wisdom, nineteenth century conservatives portrayed the Jew as a pernicious element that sought to subvert European culture, politics, economics and morality.

German volkist thought portrayed the Jew as a symbol of everything that was antithetical to the *volk*, as a corrupting force within the *volk* and as its natural enemy.

The *volk* was described as being rooted in the German soil, in rural Germany and in the ancient Teutonic heritage. The Jew was described as a rootless, wandering, urbanite, heir to a foreign cultural and religious heritage. The Jew was stereotyped as the epitome of modern influences which threatened to contaminate the purity of the *volk:* industrialization, liberal religion and morality, democracy, urbanization, rationalism, capitalism *and* communism.

As the antithesis of the German *volk*, the Jew could never become part of the *volk*. He must remain a foreign element, a potentially dangerous resident alien. For example, Julius Langbehn (b. 1851) who had called for the extermination of the Jews, "a passing pest and cholera," rejected the assumption that Jews could become Germans. "A Jew," he wrote, "can no more become a German than a plum can turn into an apple." A year after its founding, the Nazi Party drafted its platform. Plank four reads: "None but members of the nation may be citizens of the State. None but those of German blood, whatever their creed, may be members of the nation. No Jew, therefore, may be a member of the nation." Similarly, in 1941, Goebbels reiterated this doctrine, "The Jew has no voice in German questions. He is a foreigner, a stranger in our midst who enjoys rights only as a guest, but these he abuses without exception."

Because the very existence of the Jew in Germany was considered to be a threat to the German *volk,* a "Final Solution" to the "Jewish problem" was sought.

"FINAL SOLUTIONS"

One "final solution" was assimilation. By converting to Christianity and by intermarriage with non-Jews, Jews would disappear and the "Jewish problem" would be solved. This position was generally held by the political and church liberals in Germany. However, when Jews did not completely avail themselves of this option, the liberals found themselves disappointed and became hostile toward Jewish claims of the right to remain "Germans of the Mosaic persuasion." For the conservatives and for the volkist thinkers, conversion and intermarriage were never viable options. As the Jew was of an essentially different nature from others, conversion would be to no avail; he would remain a Jew. Furthermore, permitting the Jew to intermarry with Germans, allowing the Jew to enter the Christian fold, would only extend his "corrupting" influence upon the German *volk*.

For the volkist thinkers, every effort had to be made to remove Jewish influence and not to encourage it. For example, Wilhelm Marr, who is generally credited with coining the term "anti-Semitism," called for the de-Judaization of society. The Jew, he contended, is a formidable enemy who must be counterattacked lest the Teutonic people be forced into complete capitulation. Marr lamented the "Jewish Reich" of Bismarck and hoped for the emergence of a *German* Reich. Like other writers of the 1870's, Marr reiterated the stereotype of the materialistic, soulless Jew who weakened the German people by "predatory capital."

Richard Wagner, writing in 1881, expressed views similar to these of Wilhelm Marr. Wagner wrote:

> It is an established fact that I consider the Jewish race to be the born enemy of true mankind and of everything that is noble; it is quite clear that we Germans. . . . will perish through them, and I am probably the last German who knew how to maintain himself against an overbearing. . . . Judaism.

Paul Lagarde (b. 1827) already warned against the growing "Palestiniza-tion" of German cultural institutions and the German economy. He called for the immediate confiscation of all credit and banking facilities, thus depriving the Jews of all means for their sustenance.

In the 1880's and 1890's, anti-Semitism became a political as well as a social force in Germany and Austria. Conservative political parties began to infuse volkist ideas into their platforms, and began to win political power and influence. For example, the Conservative Party in Germany included the following plank in its platform of 1892: "We fight the multifarious and obtrusive Jewish influence that decomposes our people's life."

Around the turn of the century, the "Farmer's League" began to play a central role in the Conservative Party in Germany. Dedicated to outspoken anti-Semitism, the Farmer's League adopted the slogan, "War Against the Jews." The League preached that the essence of Germanism is the polar antithesis of Judaism.

Thus, for volkist thinkers, the Jew is an eternal enemy to be fought and not a potential "convert" to be embraced. The only "Final Solution" to the "Jewish problem" is to remove the Jewish influence. The best way to accom-plish this would be to remove the Jew from Europe in general and from Germany in particular. Two means of doing so are discussed in volkist writ-ings: expulsion and extermination.

The *volk* was compared to an organism which must be protected against its enemies: parasites strained the *volk's* vitality and germs infected its health. The Jew became the paradigm of the *volk's* natural enemy. Hence, in volkist thought, the Jew was already compared to an economic and political parasite that exploited the German *volk* and should be removed in order to insure its vitality and natural growth.

The *volk* required room for growth, *lebensraum*—living space—and pre-supposed the removal of inferior, parasitic elements, such as the Jews. Al-ready, in Lagarde's writings, the notion later termed *lebensraum* was stated. Lagarde linked his plan for the German colonization of Eastern Europe, especially of Poland, with the expulsion of Jews from that area.

Volkist ideology identified the Jews with bacilli and other germs, infecting the health of the *volk*. For example, the German philosopher Eugen Duhring maintained that the "Duty of Nordic peoples is to exterminate such parasitic races (as the Jews) as we exterminate snakes and beasts of prey." "Jewish-ness," wrote Duhring, "can only be ended by putting an end to the Jews themselves."

Langbehn, writing in the late nineteenth century, held that the Jewish *volk* and the German *volk* were both culturally and racially incompatible. While Lagarde had rejected a racial distinction between Jews and Germans and posited only a cultural and religious one, Langbehn went further. He directed his remarks especially toward the assimilated German Jews who had tres-passed their natural limitations and, by infiltrating the body of the German *volk,* had polluted its essence. The only way to deal with these Jews, he concluded, was to exterminate this "pest and cholera."

For Lagarde, compromise with "usurious vermin" was impossible; extermination was required: "With trichinae and bacilli one does not negotiate, nor are trichinae and bacilli subject to education; they are exterminated as quickly and as thoroughly as possible." In 1944, when the Nazi policy of extermination was at its height, an anthology of Lagarde's work, including his call for extermination of Jews, was printed and distributed to the German army.

Volkist thought described the struggle of the German *volk* against the Jew not only in biological terms, but in theological terms as well. The Jew was not only compared to vermin and bacteria, but to the demonic force in the world. Drawing upon notions deeply rooted in Christian theology, volkism portrayed the world as a battleground where the "chosen people"—the Aryans—are locked into a battle for survival with the demonic, epitomized by the Jew. Only removal of the Jewish threat, only a "Final Solution" to the "Jewish problem," could insure the survival of the German *volk.*

RACIAL ANTHROPOLOGY—ENTER SCIENCE

With the development of racial anthropology and Social Darwinism, an attempt was made to invoke the supreme source of authority in the nineteenth century—science — to justify the political, social and economic ends of volkist thought. Allied with "scientific" justification, volkist thought burst upon the twentieth century, a ready tool for utilization by Nazi ideologists.

Racial biology replaced humanitarian consideration or concern for individual human rights. The volkist notion that the German *volk* must be defended at all costs became a paramount concern. The rise of Hitler provided the means whereby "racial hygiene" could be converted from theory into action. Typical of this attitude is the profession of faith adopted by "racial hygienists" shortly after Hitler's rise to power in 1933:

> The significance of racial hygiene in Germany has for the first time been
> made evident to all enlightened Germans by the work of Adolf Hitler, and it
> is thanks to him that the dream we have cherished for more than thirty years
> of seeing racial hygiene converted into action has become a reality.

The German Society for Racial Hygiene counted many leading scientists amongst its members. In 1934, for example, Eugen Fischer, a respected anthropologist who became the first Nazi rector of the University of Berlin, restated the volkist notion that saving the *volk* transcends all individual and moral concerns. "Is any sacrifice too great," he wrote, "when a whole people is to be saved?"

Racial anti-Semites of the 1890's already stressed the notion of "blood pollution" and the need for racial purification. "Thou shalt keep thy blood pure" became the third commandment of the racist's "Ten Commandments of Lawful Self-Defense" adopted in 1893. It was considered a crime to have sexual relations with a Jew. The Nuremberg Laws translated these sentiments into legislation. Intermarriage with Jews, decreed as illegal in 1935, was not simply a social preference, but an attempt to "protect" the Aryans from racial "pollution." It should be remembered that the Nuremberg Laws were "for the Protection of German Blood and Honor."

In 1929, Goebbels' *Angriff,* speaking for the Nazi Party, reiterated this claim:

> Whoever spares the Jew, commits a sin against his own people. One can only be a servant of the Jews or their enemy. Enmity to Jews is a matter of personal hygiene.

Most influential upon Hitler and Rosenberg were the writings of Houston Stewart Chamberlain. A son-in-law of Richard Wagner, Chamberlain was an Englishman who lived much of his life in Germany. An Orientalist by training, Chamberlain had lived and taught in Japan before coming to Germany. His major work, *The Foundations of the Nineteenth Century,* became a classic of racist literature.

Chamberlain identified four major "races": Greeks, Romans, Jews and Teutons. The dispersal of Jews throughout Europe was a major calamity, according to Chamberlain. In order to save Europe from the continuing, pernicious Jewish influence, Chamberlain insisted that the Jews must be removed from Europe and that no humanitarian concerns should hamper the fight against the Jewish menace:

> The presence of an indefinite number of Jews is so pernicious to the welfare of a European state that we dare not be influenced by general humane principles.

Reiterating volkist motifs, Chamberlain identified the Jews with cold rationalism, calculated egotism, and crass materialism. He maintained that unless Aryan contact with Jews ceased, and unless a stop was put to intermarriages between Jews and Aryans, the Aryan race would be irretrievably polluted, and Europe would eventually become "a herd of pseudo-Hebraic mestizos, a people beyond all doubt degenerate physically, mentally and morally." Not only did Jews need to be eliminated, but all Jewish cultural and social influence had to be extirpated.

Hitler's plan to exterminate the Jews and other "inferior races" gained support in all sectors of the German people: the military, the Church, industry and academics. The German academic community provided the "scientific" and "philosophical" justifications for the plan. Industry provided the means and the military provided the manpower to execute the plan.

Agencies of the Nazi government employed scientists and academicians to translate theory into government policy and eventually into action. An expert for race study in the Reich Ministry of the Interior, for example, elucidated the principles he expected to follow in his work:

> First of all, we have the negative side of our work which translated into race technique means: extinction. . . . Let us not bother with old false humanitarian ideas. There is in truth only one humane idea, that is: furthering the good, eliminating the bad. The will of nature is the will of God.

Any questions as to the morality of extermination were assuaged by academic pronouncements and church support. The two most authoritative and respected institutions in Germany—the Church and the academic community—informed the average German that the racial policies of the Reich were justified. For the individual German to reject those policies was not only political treason, but a denial of Church teachings and a rejection of scientific "truth."

Leading German scientists and philosophers affirmed the correctness of Nazi racial doctrines. The study of "racial anthropology," "political biology" and "racial science" was established in most major German universities. "Jewish" physics, mathematics, biology, etc. were distinguished from "Aryan" physics, mathematics, biology, etc. Nazi physicists, for example, attacked Einstein on the grounds that his theory of relativity was a product of the Semitic mode of thinking, unworthy of acceptance by the German people. "To the abstract mathematical junk of the Jewish physicists," they opposed "the living conception of high and holy laws of nature, such as the Nordic investigator wins for himself." A book on *German Physics,* published by a distinguished scientist in Nazi Germany, begins as follows:

> German Physics? One asks. I might rather have said Aryan physics, for the physics of the Nordic species of man. . . . But I shall be answered—science is and remains international—It is false. Science, like every other human product, is racial and conditioned by blood.

This attempt to keep the Aryan race "pure" was linked to the notion that the purest race would rule the world. Purity of race was construed to be the only guarantee for the survival of the *volk* against its natural enemies. This idea, already expressed in the 1890's by Hermann Ahlwardt and others, was adopted by Hitler. In 1890, Ahlwardt wrote, "The people which first and most thoroughly rids itself of its Jews and thus opens the door to its innate cultural development is predestined to become the bearer of culture and consequently the ruler of the world.'' In *Mein Kampf,* Hitler paraphrased these words:

> A state which in the days of race poisoning endeavors to cultivate its best
> racial elements is bound to become some day the master of the world.

The leading Nazi ideologist, Alfred Rosenberg, maintained that the destiny of Nazism is to build a golden age by purifying the race-soul. To do so requires that alien elements be cut out as ruthlessly as a surgeon cuts out a cancer.

THE "PROTOCOLS"

A classic of anti-Semitic literature is the *Protocols of the Elders of Zion.* A favorite of Nazi authors, a compulsory text in Third Reich schools, the *Protocols* claims that world Jewry is involved in an international economic and political conspiracy to take over the world. Reputed to be a copy of the secret details of this plan, the *Protocols* began to appear in print in the 1860's. Over the years individual protocols or chapters were added until the final version consisted of twenty-four such protocols, purporting to be speeches of the Jewish elders at their secret meetings.

The *Protocols* reiterates the stereotype, rooted in Christian theology, which portrays the Jew as the devil incarnate, aimed at subverting the world from noble purposes. Widely used in Russia to provoke pogroms and other anti-Jewish action, the *Protocols* became popular in post-World War I Germany. In fact, a group of youths who assassinated the Jewish foreign minister of the Weimar Republic, Walther Rathenau, in 1922, did so on the conviction that he was either one of the elders of Zion or that he was acting on their orders. Allied with volkist thought, the *Protocols* became a powerful force in pre-Nazi and Nazi Germany. The *Protocols* had a direct effect upon the writings of Alfred Rosenberg, Adolf Hitler and Julius Streicher. The perpetual claim in Nazi literature that the war against the Jews was a self-defensive war against a powerful international force drew heavily upon the text of the *Protocols of the Elders of Zion.*

TOWARD NAZISM

Volkist thought provided an alternative to capitalism and Marxism, both identified with the Jew. It represented a "third way" which gained support during the Weimar republic. Democracy was never an option for volkist thinkers. They considered democracy a threat to the unity of the *volk,* as democracy supports the "racial mixture" of society. Wagner and others claimed democracy to be an unvolkist idea, part of the attempt of Jewish finance to rule Germany.

The Nazi Party offered volkism as a political alternative. The Third Reich attempted to express the ideology of the "third way" in concrete social and political programs. One of the programs was the "Final Solution" of the "Jewish problem." Thus, Hitler was not an innovator when he declared a war of extermination against Jewry. He was, rather, an adapter, a molder of prevailing Volkist theories. The German people had heard his message before. But it was Nazism which translated it into a ghastly reality. Hitler translated volkist themes into action. He called and the people responded.

In the wake of German degradation following World War I, a scapegoat was sought upon whom to transfer guilt and level responsibility for the German defeat. The Jew, the natural enemy of the *volk,* was an obvious candidate for this role. German thinkers and propagandists declared that for self-serving reasons, especially economic ones, the Jew had caused the German defeat, the Jew had "stabbed Germany in the back." The international Jewish conspiracy had brought Germany to its knees.

The portrayal of the Jew as a Trojan Horse, as a betrayer of the German people in times of crisis, had already been expressed by volkist thinkers, such as "Father Jahn" (b. 1778). Fredrick Ludwig Jahn and others considered Jewish support for Napoleon to be a betrayal of Germany. In addition, the music of Richard Wagner had nurtured the idea amongst the German people that the German hero cannot be defeated, save by a stab in the back. Hitler's claim that the Jews had betrayed Germany through a "stab in the back" translated Wagnerian opera into a political and social policy.

Throughout his life, Hitler was obsessed with Wagner's music and with his thinking. "At every stage of my life," Hitler once commented, "I came back to Richard Wagner." Hitler recognized "no predecessors except Wagner." According to Hitler, "Whoever wants to understand National Socialist Germany must know Wagner."

The volkist notion that a *fuhrer* would arise to redeem Germany from degradation was both utilized by Hitler and was applied to him. Already in 1814, Jahn called for a *fuhrer,* a "unity creator," an unparliamentary dictator, a savior. Wagner, too, stressed, the need for a *fuhrer* who would personify the German *volk.*

In 1923, before Hitler's abortive *putsch,* Wagner's son-in-law, Houston Stewart Chamberlain, acclaimed Hitler to be the fulfillment of Wagner's prophecies regarding the *Fuhrer* who would save Germany from democracy, capitalism, and the Jews. In a letter to Hitler, Chamberlain compared himself to John the Baptist, announcing the coming of the Savior. Now that the messiah of Germany had appeared, Chamberlain wrote, he could die in peace knowing the Germany destiny was secure.

CONCLUSIONS AND OBSERVATIONS

The ideas discussed above paved the way for Nazi policies and actions vis-à-vis the Jews. They provided the intellectual and social conditioning that made the Holocaust possible. Without them, the Holocaust might not have occurred.

As we have shown, Nazi ideologists and propagandists utilized motifs and stereotypes that were nurtured by Christian theology, developed by Enlightenment thought, expanded by volkist ideology and translated into action by Nazism. Consequently, no complete study of the "Final Solution" can overlook these "contributing causes" of the Holocaust. One cannot begin to comprehend the "success" of Hitler's programme for the Jews unless one is aware of the roots of the notions utilized to justify genocide morally, politically, socially and theologically.

Themes such as:

• the essential distinction between Jews and other people;
• the claimed demonic nature of the Jews;
• the perception of the Jews as a powerful enemy who must be defeated as a matter of self-defense;
• the portrayal of the Jews as powerless pariahs, subhuman nuisances, as parasites;

run throughout the history of Western culture. The "Jewish problem" confronted churchmen as well as men of the Enlightenment, volkist ideologists and racial anthropologists. Their responses to this "problem" paved the way for Nazi action. Their "solutions" were translated from theory into history by the "Final Solution."

SUBJECTS FOR FURTHER STUDY AND DISCUSSION

Inquiry into the possible causes of and preconditions for the Holocaust is just beginning. Much work remains to be done in this general area. Specifically, a number of topics warrant examination. A number of possibilities are as follows:

The development of German Christian anti-Semitism, specifically in the Reformation period, has received scant attention.

The influence of volkist thought upon modern Jewish philosophy and upon German Jewish Zionism requires additional analysis.

The influence of Christian motifs and volkist stereotypes upon the average German in Nazi Germany requires elucidation from untapped archival sources.

The persistence of the motifs discussed above in postwar Germany and elsewhere is an urgent *desideratum*.

Discussion of "political theology" in the United States—comparisons and contrasts with Nazi Germany—might yield both disturbing and comforting results.

A comparative study of the Armenian genocide by the Turks in 1915 and the decimation of the American Indian to the destruction of European Jewry might be helpful. A comparison of the theological, political, moral, social, and intellectual "justifications" for these tragedies, offered in light of "pre-conditions" and contributing causes, would prove fruitful.

A study of racial stereotypes and actions which they have engendered might provide an interesting contribution to the study of oppressed minorities.

BIBLIOGRAPHY

The books and articles noted below represent a limited selection of significant works on ideological precedents for the Holocaust. Paperback editions are so indicated. Where necessary, annotation is appended. Subtitles are often included in lieu of description.

1. Writing Holocaust History: Problems and Prospects

DAWIDOWICZ, LUCY S. *A Holocaust Reader* (New York: Behrman House, 1976). "Introduction: On Studying Holocaust Documents," pp. 1–25.

KATZ, JACOB, "Was the Holocaust Predictable?" *Commentary* 59:5 (May 1975) 41–48.

2. Writing History: The Problem of Cause and Effect

DRAY, WILLIAM. *Laws and Explanation in History* (Oxford: Oxford University Press, 1957).

―――. *Philosophy of History* (Englewood Cliffs, New Jersey: Prentice Hall, 1964).

DRAY, WM., ed. *Philosophical Analysis and History* (New York: Harper and Row, 1966).

GARDINER, PATRICK, ed. *Theories of History* (New York: Free Press, 1959).

WALSH, W. H. *Philosophy of History* (New York: Harper and Row, 1967).

3. Approaches to Anti-Semitism
(Sample Approaches)

PSYCHOLOGICAL AND PSYCHOANALYTIC
LOEWENBERG, PETER, "The Psychohistorical Origins of the Nazi Youth Cohort" *American Historical Review* (December 1971) 76:1457–1502.

POLIAKOV, LEON. *The Aryan Myth: A History of Racist and Nationalist Ideas in Europe* (New York: Basic, 1971).

SIMMEL, ERNST. *Anti-Semitism: A Social Disease* (New York, 1946).

ECONOMIC
ROSCHER, WILLIAM, "The Status of the Jew in the Middle Ages from the Standpoint of Commercial Policy" *Historia Judaica* (1944) 6:13–26.

4. Christian Anti-Semitism
(Some works relate Christian anti-Semitism to the Holocaust; others do not; some do in passing; others posit a strong relationship.)

BARON, SALO W. *A Social and Religious History of the Jews, Volume Eleven* (New York: Columbia University Press, 1967).

―――. *A Social and Religious History of the Jews, Volume Thirteen* (New York: Columbia University Press, 1969) pp. 206–299.

DAVIES, ALAN T. *Anti-Semitism and the Christian Mind* (New York: Herder and Herder, 1969).

FLANNERY, EDWARD H. *The Anguish of the Jews* (New York: Macmillan, 1965) (available in paperback).

HAY, MALCOLM. *Europe and the Jews* (Boston: Beacon, 1960) (available in paperback).

HILBERG, RAUL. *The Destruction of the European Jews* (Chicago: Quadrangle, 1961) (available in paperback). Especially, pp. 1–18.

ISAAC, JULES. *The Teaching of Contempt* (New York: Holt, Rinehart and Winston, 1964).

LESCHNITZER, ADOLF. *The Magical Background of Modern Anti-Semitism* (New York: International Universities Press, 1956).

LITTELL, FRANKLIN H. *The Crucifixion of the Jews* (New York: Harper and Row, 1974), pp. 52–53; also 24–44.

Luther's Works (Vol. 45) - The Christian in Society Volume II (Philadelphia: Muhlenberg Press, 1962); W. I. Brandt, ed.; "That Jesus Christ Was Born A Jew" pp. 195–231.

Luther's Works (Vol. 47) - The Christian in Society Volume Four (Philadelphia: Fortress Press, 1971), Franklin Sherman, ed.; "Against the Sabbatarians"; "The Jews and Their Lies."

PARKES, JAMES. *The Conflict of the Church and Synagogue* (New York: Atheneum, 1974) esp. pp. 151–307.

_____. *The Jew in the Medieval Community* (New York: Hermon, 1976 - 2nd ed.) (available in paperback).

POLIAKOV, LEON. *The History of Anti-Semitism* (New York: Schocken, 1965) (available in paperback).

RUETHER, ROSEMARY. *Faith and Fratricide: The Theological Roots of Anti-Semitism* (New York: Seabury, 1974).

ROTH, CECIL, "Marranos and Racial Anti-Semitism: A Study in Parallels" *Jewish Social Studies* (1940) 2:239–48.

RYAN, MICHAEL D., "Hitler's Challenge to the Churches: A Theological Political Analysis of *Mein Kampf*" in F. Littell and H. Locke, eds. *The Church Struggle and the Holocaust* (Detroit: Wayne State University Press, 1974) pp. 148–167.

SIIRALA, AARNE, "Luther and the Jews" *Lutheran World* (July 1964) 3:337–357.

TRACHTENBERG, JOSHUA. *The Devil and the Jews: The Medieval Conception of the Jew and Its Relation to Modern Antisemitism* (New Haven: Yale University Press, 1943) (available in paperback).

5. Modern Philosophy and the "Jewish Problem"

AVINERI, SHLOMO, "Hegel's Views on Jewish Emancipation" *Jewish Social Studies* (1963) 25:145–51.

_____. "Marx and Jewish Emancipation" *Journal of the History of Ideas* 25:3 (July 1964) pp. 445–50.

AYINN, SIDNEY, "Kant on Judaism" *Jewish Quarterly Review* (July 1968) 59:9–23.

BLOOM, SOLOMON, "Karl Marx and the Jews" *Jewish Social Studies* 4:1 (1942) pp. 3–16.

FACKENHEIM, EMIL. *Encounters Between Judaism and Modern Philosophy* (New York: Basic, 1973); especially chapters Two and Three on Kant and Hegel.

————. "Kant and Judaism" *Commentary* (December 1963) pp. 460–467.

HERTZBERG, ARTHUR. *The French Enlightenment and the Jews: The Origins of Modern Anti-Semitism* (New York: Schocken, 1970) (available in paperback).

McGOVERN, WILLIAM M. *From Luther to Hitler: The History of Fascist-Nazi Political Philosophy* (Boston: Houghton Mifflin Co., 1941).

ROTENSTREICH, NATHAN, "Hegel's Image of Judaism" *Jewish Social Studies* (1953) 15:33–52.

————. *The Recurring Pattern: Studies in Anti-Judaism in Modern Thought* (London: Weidenfeld and Nicholson, 1963). Kant, Hegel, Toynbee.

6. Volkist Thought

KOHN, HANS. *The Mind of Germany* (New York: Scribner's, 1960). Studies of Goethe, German Romanticism, Father Jahn, Wagner, Nietzsche, etc.

LOUGEE, R. W. *Paul de Lagarde* (Cambridge, Massachusetts, 1962).

MOSSE, GEORGE L. *The Crisis of German Ideology: Intellectual Origins of the Third Reich* (New York: Grosset, 1964) (available in paperback). The best available study on volkism.

————. *Germans and Jews* (New York: Grosset and Dunlap, 1970) (available in paperback).

STERN, FRITZ. *The Politics of Cultural Despair: A Study of the Rise of the German Ideology* (University of California Press, 1965) (available in paperback). Studies of Lagarde, Langbehn, van den Bruck, etc.

VIERECK, PETER. *Meta-Politics: The Roots of the Nazi Mind* (New York: Knopf, 1941) (available in paperback). Studies of Father Jahn, Wagner, Rosenberg, etc.

7. The Holocaust and Modern Anti-Semitism—General and Miscellaneous Studies

ARENDT, HANNAH. *Antisemitism* (New York: Harcourt, Brace and World, Inc., 1951) (available in paperback). A controversial analysis of the roots of totalitarianism in the nineteenth century. Discussion of the relationship between Jews' social, economic and political condition in the nineteenth century and the rise of anti-Semitic movements.

COHN, NORMAN R. *Warrant for Genocide: The Myth of the Jewish World-Conspiracy and the Protocols of the Elders of Zion* (New York: Harper and Row, 1966) (available in paperback).

EPSTEIN, KLAUS. *The Genesis of German Conservatism* (Princeton, 1966).

GOLDHAGEN, ERICH, "Pragmatism, Function and Belief in Nazi Anti-Semitism," *Midstream* 18 (December 1972) pp. 52–62. Author claims that while one part of the German mind pursued scientific reasoning, another sank into primitive magic.

MASSING, PAUL W. *Rehearsal for Destruction: A Study of Political Anti-Semitism in Imperial Germany* (New York: Harper, 1949).

PINSON, K. S. ed., *Essays on Anti-Semitism* (New York: 1946).

PULZER, PETER. *The Rise of Political Anti-Semitism in Germany and Austria* (New York: Wiley, 1964). Study of the politicization of anti-Semitism in central Europe at the end of the nineteenth century.

TAL, URIEL. *Christians and Jews in Germany: Religion, Politics and Ideology in the Second Reich, 1870–1914* (Ithaca, New York: Cornell University Press, 1974).

————. *Religious and Anti-Religious Roots of Modern Anti-Semitism* (New York: Leo Baeck Institute, 1971).

TALMON, J. L., "European History—Seedbed of the Holocaust," *Midstream* 19:5 (May 1973) pp. 3–25.

8. Nazi Racism

SCHLEUNES, KARL A. *The Twisted Road to Auschwitz* (Chicago: University of Illinois Press, 1970). Investigation of racial policies in the Third Reich in the period before the "Final Solution."

STEIN, LEON. *The Racial Thinking of Richard Wagner* (New York, 1950).

WEINREICH, MAX. *Hitler's Professors* (New York: Yivo Institute, 1946).

ZMARZLIK, HANS-GUNTER, "Social Darwinism in Germany," in Jaho Holborn, ed. *Republic to Reich: The Making of the Nazi Revolution* (New York: Random House, 1972) (available in paperback).

The Holocaust in Historical Perspective

David Weinberg

THREE HISTORICAL APPROACHES TO THE HOLOCAUST

Since the end of World War II, the historical study of the Holocaust has been dominated by two major approaches. One approach, whose proponents include European historians and students of totalitarianism, has concentrated on detailing the destruction process itself. Drawing upon captured documents of the Third Reich, it has emphasized the role of the Nazi bureaucracy in the execution of the "Final Solution" while relegating its Jewish victims to a minor or passive role. From this perspective, the Holocaust is seen as part of general history, the culmination of political and ideological currents already discernible in nineteenth-century Europe and in Germany in particular. Some historians of the "Final Solution" have gone so far as to argue that the murder of the Six Million, in challenging the basic tenets of Western Civilization, transcends both Nazi and Jew to imply a moral judgment concerning the nature of modern man.

The second approach, generally associated with survivors of the Holocaust and with Jewish historians, has sought to explain the "Final Solution" within the context of Jewish history. For proponents of this view, the Holocaust is a watershed in modern Jewish history, marking the destruction of an important center of Jewish culture and of one-third of the world Jewish population. Searching through the scattered documents of the vanished communities of Central and Eastern Europe, these historians have attempted to discover the nature of the Jewish response to the "Final Solution." Rejecting the passive role assigned to Holocaust victims by chroniclers of the "Final Solution," historians of the Jewish Response have emphasized the martyrdom of European Jewry, reflected not only in physical resistance but also in the daily struggle for survival against overwhelming odds. In contrast to those who would seek to transcend the Holocaust through philosophical and moralistic generalizations, these historians have argued that only a detailed analysis of the Jewish plight can bear witness to man's inhumanity to man.

In recent years, as the initial horror of the Jewish catastrophe has given way to intellectual soul-searching and as educated opinion has been replaced by cautious historical analysis, the two standard approaches have begun to be questioned. For many critical observers, the plethora of works by historians of the "Final Solution" and of the Jewish Response ironically seemed only to point up their inability to adequately describe and evaluate their awesome subject. In some cases, the growing concern over the inadequacies of Holocaust research has led to a questioning of the historical discipline and to a call for a moratorium on Holocaust study. Others have argued, more realistically, that the polemical debates between proponents of the two views point up the need for a separation of the dual concerns of historical investigation—the chronicling of the events of the "Final Solution" which may be possible and the evaluation of their significance which continues to elude our understanding.

From intensive discussion and criticism, a third historical approach has emerged. Though unwilling to cease Holocaust research and rejecting the division between chronology and interpretation as artificial, proponents of the new approach are troubled by the one-sided and often irresponsible nature of the two standard views. Attempting to integrate the two approaches, they call for an understanding of the Holocaust as a tragic conjuncture of general and Jewish history. Thus they argue for an investigation of both victimizer and victim, of the complex interrelationship between European and Jew from pre-Emancipation to the advent of Nazism that explains both the brutal efficiency with which the Third Reich attempted to make Europe *judenrein* (free of Jews) and the varied responses of the defenseless Jewish communities. If there are lessons to be learned from the Holocaust, these historians conclude, they must be drawn from an appreciation of its effect both upon modern society and upon contemporary Jewish consciousness.

An examination of the three approaches, the major works that typify them, and the questions and problems they raise can help clarify the complex nature of the historical study of the Holocaust and define its goals and concerns for the future.

THE "FINAL SOLUTION"

In order to fully understand how and why the "Final Solution" occurred, it would seem logical to first study the ideological roots of anti-Semitism in Europe in general and in Germany in particular.* With the exception of a few

*Also see preceding chapter.

highly emotional works written in the period directly after World War II,
however, historians have taken little interest in the origins of Nazi racism.
Most tend to dismiss Nazi tirades against the Jew as propaganda masking the
political machinations of Hitler and his underlings. Historians of the
Holocaust have proven no exception. Raul Hilberg, in his impressive study of
the "Final Solution," *The Destruction of the European Jews,* for example,
devotes only seventeen of his 771 pages to what he calls "precedents" for
Nazi anti-Semitism.

A notable exception and a pioneer in the study of the ideological roots of the
"Final Solution" is Léon Poliakov, a French scholar whose works are generally unknown in America. For Poliakov, anti-Semitism is no mere prop to a
cynical political administration but Nazism's very raison d'être. In his ency-
clopedic three-volume work, *Histoire de l'Antisémitisme* (the first volume of
which has been published in an English paperback edition), he explores the
development of anti-Jewish hatred from Golgotha to Auschwitz, emphasizing
the hostility manifested by the Christian world toward the living symbols of its
"rejected father." Racial anti-Semitism merely represented the imposition of
"scientific" categories upon the traditional notion of an unredeemable
people. The intervention of biological science with its presumption of human
infallibility, however, meant that punishment would be meted out by man and
not by God. Thus, the crematoria of Auschwitz and Treblinka replaced the
fires of Hell.

Poliakov's attempt to establish a historical continuum from Christ to Hitler
must be understood in the context of the immediate postwar period. The
desperate effort to comprehend the then recent revelations of the "Final Solution" led many historians to search the distant past for precursors of Nazism.
Poliakov's book, the culmination of work begun in the late 1940's, was only
one of many attempts to establish links between early and modern forms of
persecution in Germany. No less a scholar than A. J. P. Taylor in his book
The Course of Modern Germany, published in 1946, blamed Martin Luther
and the Protestant Reformation for modern Germany's penchant for au-
thoritarianism and mass murder. Other works delved even deeper into Germany's barbaric past to discover Nazi ideology and behavior in embryo.

Often attacked as simplistic and unscholarly, such sweeping theories of the
historical origins of the "Final Solution" have been revived in a number of
recently published books. Poliakov's most recent work, *The Aryan Myth,* is
by far his most ambitious study of the roots of modern anti-Semitism. By
means of "depth psychology," he examines the development of racial myths
in the European collective mind from their first expression in Ancient Greece
to their culmination in the Third Reich. Similarly, the "Luther to Hitler"
thesis has been reevaluated in a provocative book written by Uriel Tal of Tel
Aviv University. *Christians and Jews in Germany* traces the complex interrelationship between the two religious communities in the Second Reich with

particular emphasis placed upon Lutheran antecedents to Nazi anti-Semitism. Its attempt to prove a continuity between religious and racial anti-Semitism challenges those historians who deny the existence of pre-modern roots of the "Final Solution."

Of more limited scope are the growing number of studies of the nineteenth century origins of Nazi ideology and of Nazi racialism in particular. Typical of such works is George Mosse's *The Crisis of German Ideology,* which explores the psychological crisis that befell the German populace in the period after the French Revolution. Politically disunited and economically backward, Germans sought refuge in the ideal of a *volk,* a spiritual nation which, in the absence of political boundaries and industrialization, united Germans through a common language and folklore. Its symbolic representation was the Aryan, the blond-haired demigod who worked the land and shared in the German "soul." Its antitype was the Jew, the embodiment of the hated modernity that Germany could not hope to achieve and at the same time paradoxically the reason for its backward status among European nations. With the advent of pseudoscientific theories of race at the end of the nineteenth century, the Aryan assumed physical characteristics which made him innately superior. The Jew, in turn, became imbued with biological traits that stamped him as inferior and prevented him from successfully assimilating into the larger German community. It was a short step from theories of racial separateness to the preservation of Aryan purity through the physical extermination of the Jewish enemy.

Ideology provided the direction and purpose for the "Final Solution." The elaborate Nazi bureaucratic machine provided the means by which it was to be carried out. This was not the irrational anti-Jewish outburst of religiously motivated pogroms and demonstrations of the past, but the application of modern technology to a planned program of mass murder. Devoid of emotionalism and armed with a racial ideology that dehumanized the Jew by defining him as "subhuman," the German officials in charge of the "Final Solution" accomplished their task with an efficiency and grim determination that is unmatched in the annals of history. If the Nazis succeeded in murdering only a third of the Jewish people, it was not out of misguided humanitarianism but a result of the breakdown of the normally well-oiled bureaucratic machine.

The intricacies of the extermination process have been studied by Raul Hilberg in his work *The Destruction of the European Jews.* In over 700 pages, Hilberg paints a grisly tale of mass murder by an efficient and uncaring Nazi bureaucracy. The result of twelve years' research of German documents, the book traces the complicated interrelationships among ministries and Nazi officials who viewed the "Final Solution" as nothing more than one of many administrative tasks in the Nazi war effort. In thorough fashion, Hilberg examines the fate of Jewry from country to country, highlighting his account with detailed statistical charts on expropriations, deportations, and mass kill-ings. A concluding chapter discusses the fate in the postwar world of those responsible for the atrocities, making it clear that justice was rarely if ever meted out. The overall impression upon reading the book is one of horror and despair, made more powerful by the dispassionate writing style and meticu-lous devotion to detail. Though Hilberg steers clear of making value judgments about Nazi officialdom (with the notable exception of the last chapter), the compilation of statistics, documents, and charts provides a chilling insight into the depravity and inhumanity of the Third Reich which no emotional accounting could hope to convey.

Hilberg was not the first historian to examine the complex nature of the Nazi extermination process. Pioneering works by Gerald Reitlinger and Léon Poliakov in the early 1950's called attention to the need for a serious investi-gation of the "Final Solution." Hilberg's work, drawing upon documents un-available to previous historians, clearly surpassed its predecessors in scope and authority. In turn, *The Destruction of the European Jews* has spawned numerous studies of the execution of the "Final Solution" in specific countries. Within the past decade, books have been published on the murder of the Jews of Bulgaria, Slovakia, Hungary, Italy, and France. A cursory glance at *Dis-sertation Abstracts* during the same period reveals countless other studies of the "Final Solution" that owe their inspiration (and much of their documenta-tion) to Hilberg's work.

The attitude of Germans toward the "Final Solution" has occasioned serious historical debate. Most historians still tend to dismiss Nazism as the creation of raving madmen maintained through a sophisticated system of mass terror. Walter Langer's *The Mind of Adolf Hitler,* a psychological study of the *Fuhrer* originally commissioned by the Office of Strategic Studies (OSS) during World War II to gauge the policies of Nazi Germany, was the first of many studies that emphasized Hitler's personality as a major determinant of Nazi ideology. Despite the book's rigid Freudianism and general disregard for factual data, its view of the Third Reich as the creation of the psychological dementia of the Nazi leadership has been strongly supported in more serious biographical works, such as Alan Bullock's *Hitler: A Study in Tyranny* and Joachim Fest's *Hitler.* Best-selling sensationalistic books highlighting Nazi brutality and torture as well as the published revelations of Nazi officials who alleged that they were "only following orders" reinforced the commonly held view of an all-powerful State led by maniacal leaders and a well-meaning but terrorized populace.

But the unprecedented scope of the atrocities committed by the Nazis and the implication of thousands of seemingly "normal" Germans in the "Final Solution" have raised serious questions concerning the nature of totalitarianism and its effect upon individual conscience. Already in the immediate postwar period, it was clear to both Allied leaders and intellectuals that Nazi atrocities could not be simply explained away by glib allusions to "madmen" and "gestapo tactics." On a pragmatic level, the problem of ascertaining individual responsibility for the "Final Solution" stymied Allied legal experts seeking to "denazify" Germany and to prosecute Nazi war criminals after the War.* More disturbing was the realization that Nazi racial ideology and German complicity in its actualization challenged the fundamental moral canons of Western Civilization. As early as 1950, Hannah Arendt in her book, *The Origins of Totalitarianism,* questioned the "madmen and terror" thesis. A student of the philosopher Karl Jaspers, who had authored a probing work on *The Question of German Guilt* in 1947, Arendt contended that modern man is insecure, continually searching for direction in a world which is in a state of flux. At certain times in modern history, she argues, nations have opted for a totalitarian State which lifts the burden of responsibility and decision-making from the individual and invests it in an all-powerful personality or ideology. The totalitarian State, in turn, by virtue of its dictatorial control over all aspects of society, can reorient the values and attitudes of weak-willed individuals with little or no opposition. The result, Arendt concludes, is a society where traditional judgments concerning right and wrong, justice and injustice, morality and immorality, no longer apply.**

In her controversial book, *Eichmann in Jerusalem,* Arendt attempts to apply her ideas to the Third Reich and to the Nazi bureaucrat as personified by Adolf Eichmann. Based loosely upon the proceedings of the Eichmann Trial held in Jerusalem in 1961, the work argues for a reevaluation of the nature of the Nazi regime and of the German response to the "Final Solution." Though led by madmen, much of the day-to-day activity was carried out by individuals who were mediocrities in their daily lives and attitudes. Singling out Eichmann (whose position as official in charge of the deportation of Jews to concentration camps made him the subject of an intensive search by the Israeli Secret Service), Arendt argues that in reality he bore few of the signs of an evil genius. On the contrary, a study of his statements both before and during the trial reveals a petty administrator carrying out Hitler's orders and hardly ever reflecting about his role in the extermination of Jews. A perennial failure in life, Eichmann saw in his job a means toward achieving social acceptance and personal advancement. Eichmann thus becomes in Arendt's view a telling example of the "banality of evil" which typified the Nazi extermination process.

Brilliantly conceived but poorly written and researched, Arendt's book continues to be the subject of a raging controversy among historians of the

---

*See the discussion below on the Holocaust and International Law.
**On Jaspers, see below "Philosophical Reactions to and Moral Implications of the Holocaust."

Holocaust. The work suffers from an overall glibness; the book is actually a compilation of articles on the Eichmann Trial hastily written for *The New Yorker*. Aside from the questionable applicability of her "banality of evil" thesis to Eichmann, Arendt's work is marred by unfair criticisms of the trial itself and of the role of Jewish Councils in the success of the "Final Solution." Nor does she take into account the influence of racial ideology upon the Nazi bureaucrat charged with carrying out the extermination process. No wonder that Jacob Robinson was moved to title his point-by-point refutation: *And the Crooked Shall Be Made Straight!*

Despite the innumerable faults contained in Arendt's work, her general thesis cannot be easily dismissed. If Eichmann was not as banal as Arendt believes (and Robinson effectively proves the contrary), there nevertheless were millions of average-thinking Germans who were caught up in the Nazi movement. To place blame on a few sick individuals who gained power in 1933 is to ignore the national sickness that beset the German people in the period between the wars. To speak of a people cowed into submission by torture, brutality, and terror is to ignore the popularity of the Third Reich and the unwavering loyalty of Germans to its leadership. The "banality of evil" thesis, whatever its problems, helps to explain why most Germans willingly accepted a movement with a theory and a program that ran directly contrary to Judaeo-Christian values. By making evil banal and even "decent," the Nazis succeeded in creating a society of inhumanity. By making the banal evil, they implicated all of Germany in the murder of the Six Million.

Arendt's philosophical musings have taken us far afield of the history of the Holocaust. Indeed, there is a marked tendency in her works and in the works of other historians of the "Final Solution" to transcend their subject matter. Thus the Nazi bureaucracy becomes an example of modern political adminis- tration; the Nazi bureaucrat a prototype of modern man. Similarly, the "Final Solution" becomes only one example of technological mass murder. Indeed, terms borrowed from historians of the "Final Solution" have become com- monplace in general discussions of oppression and exploitation of minorities. Concepts such as the "ghetto," "Gestapo," and "racial genocide" are as much a part of Black consciousness in America today as they were of Jewish consciousness in Europe a generation ago.

The transcendence of Holocaust history is most noticeable in the treatment of the Jew. In almost all of the works discussed above, the Jew is relegated to a minor role in the "Final Solution." He is the victim—a passive and faceless figure who is the object rather than the subject of history. Thus, none of the investigations of the roots of anti-Semitism and its realization in Nazi racial policy discusses the complex relationship between European and Jew that explains the virulence of anti-Jewish hatred in modern history. Arendt, in *Origins of Totalitarianism,* does argue that the Jews' pariah status and special relationship to the State were major factors in the growth of anti-Semitic movements in Europe at the end of the nineteenth century. She concludes, however, that anti-Semitism was only a vehicle through which discontented elements voiced their hostility to the State; meanwhile the Jewish victim stood by a mere spectator, naive and unaware of the growing resentment against him. At best, as in the works of Poliakov, the Jew is defenseless and innocent but there is little concern with the relationship between anti-Semitism and the Jewish condition in European society. For this French writer, the Jew is merely a scapegoat for the psychological and spiritual frustrations of Christian Europe. Hilberg goes so far as to deny that his work has anything to do with Jews, much less with Jewish history. As he notes in the preface to *The Destruction of the European Jews:*

> Lest one be misled by the word 'Jews' in the title, let it be pointed out that this is not a book about the Jews. It is a book about the people who destroyed the Jews. Not much will be read here about the victims. The focus is placed on the perpetrators.

With *Eichmann in Jerusalem,* we are even further removed from the Holocaust and its victims. In Arendt's discussions of totalitarianism, both the Nazi official and the Jew in the concentration camp are merely case-studies of human beings succumbing to institutionalized evil. Her unacceptable thesis concerning the participation of Jewish Councils in carrying out the "Final Solution," for example, strongly implies that in extreme conditions the victim is often implicated in his own destruction. By reducing the Jew to a submissive victim, a number on a statistical chart, or the object of the extermination process, the historians of the "Final Solution" have eliminated the Jew from the Holocaust historian's concern.

THE JEWISH RESPONSE

The elimination of Jewry from Holocaust historiography (strangely paralleling its dehumanization in the "Final Solution" itself) has not gone unanswered. The work by Robinson has already been mentioned. It would be impossible to synopsize *And the Crooked Shall Be Made Straight.* Its sole purpose is to methodically destroy Arendt's book through a detailed refutation of her basic theses. The work with its page after page of facts and copious footnotes is a masterful accomplishment but it is clearly more relevant to specialists than to general readers. Other recently published books and articles have attempted to investigate the plight of Jews in Nazi-occupied Europe with emphasis placed upon their armed resistance to Nazism. Equally important have been the discovery and publication of memoirs and personal accounts by Jewish victims of the Holocaust.

The result of these works has been a new appreciation of the Jewish response to the Holocaust. Far from passive observers, Jews resisted openly and actively. Those who did not or could not resist by physical means saw in their continued Jewish identity and in the mere act of survival an act of defiance against those who sought to obliterate the Jew from history.

The so-called "Jewish Response" in Holocaust historiography has its origins during the War in attempts of Jewish relief organizations and refugee groups to make the world aware of the Jewish plight. The Institute for Jewish Affairs, created by the American Jewish Congress and World Jewish Congress in 1940 and headed by Jacob Robinson, published a number of important studies in the early 1940's chronicling the Jewish catastrophe. Similar work was carried on by the YIVO Institute for Jewish Research, founded in Vilna in 1925 but forced to flee to New York City in 1939. Refugee and relief organizations such as the American Federation for Polish Jews, which published *The Black Book of Polish Jewry* in 1943, were also instrumental in publicizing the fate of European Jewry. Mention must also be made of the early publications of research institutes such as Yad Vashem in Israel and the Centre de Documentation juive contemporaine in Paris which were established immediately after the War to serve as repositories for documents on the Jewish Response. The end of the War also saw the publication of numerous personal memoirs by survivors of concentration camps and ghettos which confirmed the existence of a Jewish underground in Eastern Europe.

The history of the Jewish Response gained new impetus in the 1950's and 1960's as a result of a number of factors. As we have seen, the revelations of the Eichmann Trial in 1961 and the publication of Arendt's and Hilberg's books triggered controversy concerning Jewish involvement in the "Final Solution." Israel's struggle for independence in 1948 had raised interesting questions concerning violence in Jewish history; the lightning victory of the Six-Day War in 1967, which averted Israel's physical annihilation, renewed interest in the roots of Jewish resistance. Of more scholarly interest were the works of Bruno Bettelheim on the social psychology of concentration camps. It was Bettelheim's contention, in books like *The Informed Heart* published in 1961, that Nazi officials had succeeded in breaking down the individuality and self-respect of concentration camp victims in preparation for their efficient liquidation in the gas ovens. The result was that Jews went like "sheep to the slaughter," passively accepting their fate after having lost the will to live. Not surprisingly, historians of the "Final Solution" such as Arendt and Hilberg were quick to seize upon Bettelheim's thesis to support their own minimization of the Jewish response to the Holocaust.

Bettelheim, released from Buchenwald and seeking asylum in the United

States in 1939, did not witness the "Final Solution." Neither he nor historians of the Holocaust who draw mainly upon German sources are aware of physical resistance in the ghettos before the final deportations and in the camps themselves. If they grudgingly acknowledge Jewish resistance, as in the case of the Warsaw Ghetto, they tend to accept the validity of their German sources' contention that it was insignificant and unique. More importantly, lacking a groundwork in Jewish history and tradition, Bettelheim and others mistake spiritual resistance—a defiance of the enemy based largely upon beliefs and attitudes rather than overt action—for meek acceptance and dehumanization.

Jewish historians and survivors of the Holocaust were not long in responding to the allegations of Jewish passivity. Works such as Marie Syrkin's *Blessed Is the Match,* published in 1947, and Bernard Goldstein's *The Stars Bear Witness,* published in 1949, recounted in highly emotional terms the heroic response of Jews to Nazi persecution. Other books chronicling Jewish resistance followed in the 1950's and 1960's. Many of these works were published in Israel under the auspices of the Yad Vashem Institute, whose journal, *Yad Vashem Studies,* continues to provide a forum for specialized research into the Jewish Response. Of particular interest have been the works on the Warsaw Ghetto uprising of April 1943. The discovery of the diaries of Emmanuel Ringelblum and Chaim Kaplan, two residents of the ghetto, has provided important information on the last months of what was once the largest Jewish community in Eastern Europe. The heroic resistance of the Warsaw Ghetto was paralleled in other Jewish communities during the Nazi occupation and has been documented in books such as Yuri Suhl's *They Fought Back.* Special mention should be made of the publications of Kibbutz Lochamei ha-Getaot (Ghetto Fighters' Kibbutz), which have been of inestimable value in shedding light on the activities of Jewish partisans during World War II. Other writers and historians have investigated the desperate revolts in concentration camps in the last days of the "Final Solution." Jean Francois Steiner's *Treblinka,* for example, though not a historical account *per se,* captures the attitudes and behavior of the participants in the revolt at the Treblinka extermination camp in August 1943.

But if Jewish historians have succeeded in arighting the balance between victim and victimizer in the Holocaust, they must still confront the awesome truth that the overwhelming majority of Jews did not actively resist their slaughter. In attempting to answer this question, historians of the Jewish Response have pointed to the many obstacles facing Jewish communities which prevented the mounting of an effective resistance campaign. Studies of life in concentration camps, such as Primo Levi's *Survival in Auschwitz,* as well as the growing body of memorial books of destroyed communities, clearly show that it was impossible for a powerless and unarmed people to mount an effective defense against the most powerful military and political force in Europe. The fact that there were nevertheless numerous examples of physical resistance thus becomes all the more remarkable.

More importantly, in investigating primary sources of the annihilated Jewish communities, historians have discovered that lack of physical resistance did not always mean passive acceptance. Indeed, a close examination of the day-to-day activity of individual residents of the ghettos and camps, often unrecorded in German documents, reveals a pattern of resistance that manifested itself in a commitment to Jewish identity and a will to survive as witness to Nazi brutality.

The commitment to Jewish survival during the Holocaust is chronicled in the contemporary works of Ringelblum and Kaplan. For both men, the keeping of diaries represented a commitment to Jewish history and to the Jewish future. Ringelblum actually organized a research group, the so-called *Oneg Shabbos* or "O.S.," to compile documents and personal accounts of the Nazi brutalization of the Warsaw Jewish community. In his diary, he describes the O.S.'s task as a "sacred duty" and voices the hope that it will make sure "that not a single fact about Jewish life at this time will be kept from the world." Similarly, Kaplan saw his diary as a "scroll of agony," noting in his prefatory remarks that he felt obligated to "record every event, every small detail which might shed light upon the darkness of foul, depraved souls." Ringelblum, Kaplan, and other contemporary chroniclers of the Jewish catastrophe clearly saw themselves as witnesses to inhumanity. By meticulously transposing evidence of this inhumanity to writing, they were resisting the attempt by Nazi officialdom to obliterate the Jew from history.*

In chronicling the daily existence of the Warsaw Ghetto, both Ringelblum and Kaplan revealed the unsung bravery of countless Jews whose resistance rarely took overt form. As both writers point out, the mere observance of Jewish religious practice took great courage. Daily rituals such as maintaining *kashrut* (dietary laws), putting on *tefilin* (phylacteries), and participating in communal prayer, which would normally go unnoticed in a traditional Jewish community, assumed heroic dimensions under Nazi occupation. The obsession with Jewish survival often took bizarre forms. Both Ringelblum and Kaplan write approvingly, for example, of the activity of Jewish smugglers and thieves who ferreted illegal food and clothing into the ghetto, thus enabling the Warsaw community to survive. Far more common were the hundreds of secretive acts that assured physical and cultural survival—the harboring of "wanted" Jews, the maintenance of charitable institutions, the continuance of Jewish education, and the vocational training of craftsmen and artisans. Rabbi Yitzchak Nissenbaum, himself a victim of the Holocaust, described this behavior as *kiddush ha-chaim*—the sanctification of life. In contrast to *kiddush*

---

*For further information, see the discussion below on Holocaust diaries and memoirs.

ha-shem which demands religious martyrdom for the sanctification of God's name, Nissenbaum noted that *kiddush ha-chaim* assumes that "the enemy demands the Jew's body and it is the Jew's duty to protect his body, to preserve his life."

Even those committed to physical resistance were not unaware of the importance of both *kiddush ha-chaim* and *kiddush ha-shem*. The personal accounts of revolts in ghettos and concentration camps continually allude to the participants' determination that there be survivors to tell the world about the extermination and the bravery of Jews. The close relationship between physical and spiritual resistance was also reflected in the adoption of the concept of *kiddush ha-shem* by secular members of the resistance. Once narrowly defined as religious martyrdom, it was broadened during the Holocaust to include anyone dying heroically for the sake of the Jews.

And what of the concentration camp victim who allegedly went passively to his death? The numerous works by concentration camp survivors attest to the stoic nature with which many Jews marched to the gas chambers. In *Survival in Auschwitz,* Primo Levi describes an incident as his group was preparing to enter the boxcars that would take many of them to their deaths at Auschwitz:

> When all was ready . . . they [women] unloosened their hair, took off their shoes, placed the *Yahrzeit* candles* on the ground and lit them according to the customs of their fathers, and sat on the bare soil in a circle for the lamentations, praying and weeping all the night. We collected in a group in front of their door, and we experienced a grief that was new for us, the ancient grief of the people that has no land, the grief without hope of the exodus which is renewed every century.

For Levi, an assimilated Italian Jew, such expressions of collective strength were strange and new. For Jews steeped in religious tradition, the singing of *Ani Maamin* expressing belief in the coming of the Messiah "no matter if he may tarry," the wearing of prayer shawls while marching to their deaths, the insistence upon remaining together in family groups, and the reciting of *kaddish* (prayer for the dead) were a continuation of a form of spiritual resistance with deep roots in the Jewish past. Far from dehumanized "sheep," many Jews continued to defy their Nazi oppressors by refusing to deny their Jewish identity and their humanity, even when all hope was lost.

The rather complicated history of spiritual resistance has only recently begun to be investigated. The practice of Jewish martyrdom is an ancient one but it has yet to be fully understood as it applied to Jews living under Nazism. Unlike previous forms of persecution, Nazism deprived Jews of the choice between saving themselves from death by renouncing their faith and avoiding

*AUTHOR'S NOTE: Candles lit annually to commemorate the death of a relative.

apostasy by giving up their lives for *kiddush ha-shem*. Though, as we have seen, there are numerous personal accounts of both *kiddush ha-shem* and *kiddush ha-chaim* during the Holocaust, we must await a more general study which would put them in a broader historical context. What were the traditional forms of protest and resistance within Jewish communities and how do they manifest themselves during the Nazi occupation? What, after all, are the alternatives for prisoners with no hope for escape?

A beginning effort to answer these questions can be found in the published proceedings of a colloquium on *Jewish Resistance in the Holocaust* sponsored by the Yad Vashem Institute in Jerusalem in 1971. In articles such as M. Dworzecki's "The Day-to-Day Stand of the Jews" and Y. Gottfarstein's "*Kiddush Hashem* in the Holocaust Period," participants in the colloquium attempted to examine the objective and subjective conditions that shaped the Jewish response to the Nazi threat. Though debate was heated, and few if any definitive answers were offered to the complex problem of defining Jewish resistance, it is clear from an examination of the proceedings of the colloquium that the Jewish response cannot be simply defined by the extremes of sheeplike passivity and doomed armed revolt.

In defining the Jew as victim, historians of the "Final Solution" have tended to ignore the response of Jewish communities not directly threatened by Nazism. Not surprisingly, therefore, historians of the Jewish Response have placed emphasis upon the rescue of European Jewry by international Jewish relief agencies and organizations. Such investigations have often been coupled with a condemnation of the apathy of the international community during World War II toward the plight of Holocaust victims.

By far, the most telling attack upon the apathy of the non-Jewish world was levelled not by a historian of the Holocaust but by an Austrian playwright troubled by his discovery that the Vatican remained silent during the War after having received information concerning the "Final Solution." Rolf Hochhuth's *The Deputy,* produced in 1963, created a scandal in both Europe and America with its revelations concerning the unwillingness of Pope Pius XI to speak out against Nazi atrocities after having been personally apprised of the existence of extermination camps by Kurt Gerstein, a Nazi official in charge of supplying lethal gas for the "Final Solution." Hochhuth's allegations were corroborated by Guenther Lewy in his book, *The Catholic Church and Nazi Germany,* which pointed to the Church's paranoiacal fear of Bolshevism and traditional anti-Semitism as factors that led the Vatican to silence criticism of and at times even endorse Nazi policy.*

Subsequent books and articles have shown that the Vatican's lack of concern with the murder of Jews was shared by other members of the interna-

---

*On apathy and the Holocaust, see below, "Philosophical Reactions to and Moral Implications of the Holocaust."

tional political community. Arthur Morse's book, *While Six Million Died,* shocked Americans with its accusation that American government officials (and elements in the American Jewish community) sloughed off the plight of Jews in Nazi-occupied Europe as insignificant and, at times, actively worked against their rescue and escape. More scholarly works such as Henry Feingold's *The Politics of Rescue* and Saul Friedman's *No Haven for the Oppressed* clearly show the unwillingness of the Allies to take action in defense of a stateless and powerless people. From the half-hearted attempts to solve the refugee problem at the Evian conference in 1938 to the refusal of American military leaders to bomb the concentration camps in 1943, international efforts to rescue Jewry proved far less successful than the Nazi practice of genocide.*

Yet rescue and escape from the Holocaust did occur, thanks largely to the efforts of the two Jewish communities that would assume leadership after the destruction of European Jewry—the United States and Israel. The activities of American-based relief organizations such as the Hebrew Immigrant Aid Society (HIAS) and its international affiliate, HICEM, the Joint Distribution Committee, and the Organization for Rehabilitation and Training (ORT) have yet to be fully researched. Much of their work was never documented and is known only by those who benefited from it. Many documents fell into the hands of the Nazis and were destroyed along with their bearers. It is only in the past few years that efforts have been made to collect the scattered and uncatalogued files of these international organizations. And until this work is completed, students of the Jewish Response must be satisfied with general works on emigration, such as Mark Wischnitzer's *To Dwell in Safety* or specific works on relief organizations such as Yehuda Bauer's *My Brother's Keeper* that deal only tangentially with the Holocaust.

Probably the most famous Palestinian participant in the struggle against Nazism was Hannah Senesh. Parachuted into the Balkans in 1944 by the British army along with forty-three other Palestinian Jews as part of a counterintelligence operation, she was immediately captured and tortured to death. Though never directly involved in the rescue of Jews, her commitment to the Jewish plight in Europe, as outlined in her published diary, had great symbolic importance in the mounting of an all-out rescue effort by Zionist groups immediately after the War. Zionist efforts were not restricted to the postwar period, however. The efforts to smuggle Jewish refugees into Palestine before and during the War is the subject of Jon and David Kimche's book, *The Secret Roads.* Yehuda Bauer, historian of the Holocaust at the Institute for the Study of Contemporary Jewry in Jerusalem, has devoted a great deal of attention to the role of Zionist movements in the rescue effort. In his book, *Flight and Rescue: Brichah,* he traces the successful rescue of 250,000 Jews from East-

---

*For further information, see the following chapter.

ern Europe after World War II by Palestinian and European based Zionist organizations. A companion volume, *From Diplomacy to Resistance,* examines the development of Jewish self-defense in Palestine in response to the Holocaust.

With serious research into the Jewish Response during the Holocaust has come a growing awareness of its roots before World War II and its effect upon postwar Jewish attitudes and behavior. The study of European Jewish communities on the eve of the Holocaust presents the historian with a rare opportunity to examine the Jewish Response in a period when the "Jewish question" existed but genocide was not its only "solution." Not surprisingly, the German Jewish community, the first community to be affected by Nazi racism and the most ill-prepared, has been singled out for specific study. The temptation to condemn with hindsight is noticeable in almost all the works dealing with German Jewry, but there is little agreement concerning its response to the rise of anti-Semitism. Thus while Jehuda Reinharz in his *Fatherland or Promised Land: The Dilemma of the German Jew, 1893–1914* and Sidney Bolkosky in *The Distorted Image: German Jewish Perceptions of Germans and Germany, 1918–1935* emphasize the naiveté of a largely assimilationist community, Ismar Schorsch in *Jewish Reactions to German Anti-Semitism, 1870–1914* sees an important reassessment of the assimilationist ideal in the growth of German Jewish defense organizations at the turn of the century. German Zionist leaders, whom one might assume to have been more aware of the dangers of anti-Semitism than their assimilated coreligionists, have fared little better. Reinharz, for example, concludes that on the whole, there was little difference between supporters of the German Fatherland and the Zionist "promised land" in the period 1893–1914, a conclusion echoed by Stephen Poppel in his work, *Zionism in Germany, 1897–1933: The Shaping of a Jewish Identity.* Similar studies of French Jewry by Michael Marrus and David Weinberg point up the silence and naiveté of native Jews during the Dreyfus Affair and the 1930's respectively.

Only scattered efforts have been made to examine the attitudes and behavior of Eastern European Jewry on the eve of the Holocaust. There are a number of important studies in Yiddish on specific aspects of Eastern European life in the interwar period in journals such as the *Yivo Bleter* but few have been translated into English. Weinberg's study includes an evaluation of Eastern European immigrants in Paris in the 1930's. His conclusions that immigrant Jews were more conscious of the threat posed by Nazism than Western European Jews are mirrored in Celia Heller's work, *On the Edge of Destruction: Jews of Poland Between the Two World Wars.* The fact that greater awareness of the dangers of racial anti-Semitism was not sufficient to save Eastern European Jewry from the "Final Solution," however, should guard against any glib comparisons between "committed" Eastern European Jews and "assimilated" Western European Jews. Whether consciously aware

or naively ignorant, there was little that a stateless people could do in the face
of a totalitarian movement pledged to its destruction and a world community
apathetic to its plight.

The study of survivors of the Holocaust is only in its infant stages. Most
historians of the Jewish Response have been reticent to pry into the lives of
concentration camp victims or have shied away from what they regard as
"current events." For the most part, the chronicling of the postwar fortunes
of survivors has been left to the survivors themselves. Works such as
Holocaust and Rebirth: Bergen-Belsen, 1945–1965, published by former inmates of the camp, reflect the survivors' dogged faith in the future and
commitment never to forget. The acclimatization of survivors to their new
homes in America and Israel has yet to be fully investigated. Dorothy
Rabinowitz's *New Lives* is a moving albeit impressionistic account of the
painful effort to live in both the past and the present which is the hallmark of
the concentration camp victim in America. While Rabinowitz and others have
begun to examine the question of "survival for what?," sociologists, psychologists, and philosophers have attempted to answer the equally telling
question of "why did I survive?" Terrence Des Pres' work, *The Survivor,*
presents a controversial thesis concerning the biological will to survive under
extreme conditions. Though hardly a historical study, the book is crucial for
an understanding of the attitudes and behavior of Jewish survivors in the
post-Holocaust world.*

THE HOLOCAUST AS A CONJUNCTURE OF GENERAL AND JEWISH HISTORY

Historians of the Jewish Response have clearly established the Holocaust as
a subject of serious study for Jewish historians. In examining the behavior and
attitudes of European Jewry faced with almost certain annihilation, they have
rescued the study of the Holocaust from anti-historical abstraction and transcendent theorizing. But in detailing the Jewish dimension of the Holocaust,
have historians of the Jewish Response fallen into the same parochialism as
the historians of the "Final Solution" whom they criticize? Can the Holocaust
be understood without both the victimizer and the victim? Is the student of the
Holocaust to be forced to choose between Hannah Arendt and Jacob Robinson?

The attempts by historians to avoid the polarities of the two standard approaches have led to the emergence of a new direction in Holocaust historiography. Its concerns and goals were originally outlined in a few prescient

---

*See below, "Social-Psychological Aspects of the Holocaust."

works published immediately after the War. As early as 1950, Philip Friedman, one of the first historians to devote himself exclusively to the study of the
Holocaust, argued against unrealistic compartmentalization of "Final Solution" and Jewish Response. In a speech delivered at the International Conference on World War II in the West held at Amsterdam in 1950 and again in an
article published in the July 1951 issue of *Jewish Social Studies,* he noted:

> (J)ust as the Jewish catastrophe in the Nazi era can be studied only in the
> broader context of the general events, so the general European history of the
> period cannot be adequately interpreted without full understanding of the
> German war against the Jewish people.

Friedman's attack, which was to be repeated many times until his death in
1960, has been taken up by a number of historians seeking to go beyond the narrowness of both the "Final Solution" and the Jewish Response. Gerd Korman, in two articles written in *Societas* and *Yad Vashem Studies* respectively,
devotes much needed attention to the development of historical analysis of the
"Final Solution" and its reflection in American textbooks. His major thesis—
that historians of the "Final Solution" and their textbook imitators have
tended to ignore the Jewish component in the Holocaust—argues for a synthesis of the two standard approaches. Surprising support for Korman's argument has come from one of the major historians of the "Final Solution,"
Raul Hilberg. In *Documents of Destruction,* a collection of German and
Jewish documents for popular audiences, Hilberg strongly implies personal
reevaluation of his attitudes toward the study of the Holocaust. No longer
denying the Holocaust as Jewish history, Hilberg speaks in his preface of
the need for a "balance, so that the destruction of the Jews might be seen
from beginning to finish, in various parts of Europe, and *as both German and
Jewish experiences.*" (Italics mine.)

   The attack upon the narrowness of European historians has been coupled
with a serious questioning of historians of the Jewish Response. No less
critical of his fellow Jewish historians, Friedman often denounced their efforts
as "khurbn" or catastrophe literature—lachrymose, highly emotional, and
oblivious to historical methodology. Friedman's criticism has been echoed by
historians in Israel and in America who have called for an end to polemics and
a return to serious historical research of the Jewish catastrophe. Though quick
to condemn the assumption of Jewish passivity by historians of the "Final
Solution," they have also criticized those historians of the Jewish Response
who exaggerate the incidences of armed resistance among European Jewry.
By concentrating exclusively on refuting the arguments of Jewish passivity,
these historians claim, the chroniclers of physical resistance ignore the more
significant issue of spiritual resistance. In failing to examine the subjective
and objective conditions shaping Jewish behavior during the Holocaust, they

unwittingly accept the definition of Jew as faceless victim made visible only through active intervention into history.

The new approach is reflected in two general works that attempt to view the Holocaust as a conjuncture of general and Jewish history. Nora Levin's *The Holocaust,* published in 1968, and Lucy Dawidowicz's *The War Against the Jews,* published in 1975, attempt to integrate the German and Jewish dimensions of the Holocaust into a logical and readable narrative. Their differing structures and only partial success reflect the difficulties involved in the synthesis.

In her foreword, Levin speaks of a "German-Jewish symbiosis" that culminated in the annihilation of one people by the other. Although she does not deal directly with the historical roots of this one-thousand-year relationship, she sees the Holocaust as a conflict between two peoples with diametrically opposed world views. As she notes:

> ... Germans have longed to transcend the shallow pockets of experience by plunging into great spiritual depths, by carrying ideas to their ultimate, by daring to plunge where man has not yet been. ... Traditionally, the Jew does not ask unanswerable questions, or, if he does, does not insist on answers to baffling paradoxes. ... Was it, one wonders, the ancient Jewish habit of submitting to the limitedness of all human knowledge and experience that the Nazis found most execrable in their enemy?

It is Levin's contention that the German's tendency to plunge into a "world without limit" explains the Nazis' dehumanization of the Jew and their attainment of a "new pitch of meaningless in history." Her goal is to trace the German's descent and the Jewish attempt to wrest meaning from it.

Levin's emphasis upon the conjuncture of German and Jewish history is reflected in her integration of material on the "Final Solution" and the Jewish Response. The book is divided into two parts. Part I, "The Preparation," is a chronology of events leading to the murder of the Six Million which borrows from both historical approaches. Included are chapters on Hitler, German Jewry in the 1930's, the beginning of World War II, and the fate of Eastern European Jewry in the wake of the German onslaught into Poland and Russia. The second part, "The Deportations," is a country-by-country account of the roundup of Jews which concludes with a discussion of rescue and "return" to Palestine. In attempting to bridge the abyss, in her words, "between those who have endured the unimaginable and those who did not," Levin has provided us with an important contribution to Holocaust historiography.

Dawidowicz's more recent book, *The War Against the Jews,* was immediately acclaimed as the standard work on the Holocaust. Like Levin's work, the book is divided into two parts, reflecting the dual concerns of the author. The first part, entitled "The 'Final Solution,'" seeks to answer the question of how a modern state could carry out the systematic murder of a whole people for no reason other than that they were Jews. The second part, entitled "The Holocaust," examines how and why a whole people allowed itself to be destroyed. An Appendix dealing with "The Fate of the Jews in Hitler's Europe" attempts in part to answer the question of why the rest of the civilized world stood by without opposing the Holocaust. In the first part, Dawidowicz traces the development of modern anti-Semitism in Germany, the institution of a bureaucracy for the "Final Solution," and the implementation of Nazi ideology in the concentration camps. In the second part, she examines Jewish life in Germany and Eastern Europe on the eve of the Holocaust, daily life in the ghetto, and the nature of both physical and psychological resistance. The Appendix examines the human cost of the Holocaust through a country-by-country analysis of the fate of Jewry.

Both books are impressive syntheses of the two standard approaches to the Holocaust. While Levin attempts to deal with the Holocaust chronologically, Dawidowicz chooses to divide it into its German and Jewish dimensions. Both works, freed from exclusive reliance upon either German or Jewish documentation, add new insight and understanding to the Holocaust. Neither book, however, chooses to view the Holocaust outside the context of the Third Reich. Though Levin alludes to events prior to the accession of Hitler to power, her book mirrors Dawidowicz's concern with the period between 1933 and 1945. Obviously, both authors are mainly interested in chronicling the complex details of the Nazi war against the Jews. But in failing to trace the roots of the Holocaust back in history, they gloss over its centrality in both general and Jewish history. If the reader gains greater insight into the relationship between the "Final Solution" and the Jewish Response through an integration of German and Jewish sources, he learns little of the "German-Jewish symbiosis" which Levin tempts us with in her preface, of those elements in general and Jewish history that shaped the actions of victimizer and victim.

It is perhaps utopian to hope for such a broad synthesis. For many historians, the Holocaust in its unprecedented destruction and evil defies comparison and evaluation. To generalize, to place the Holocaust in broad historical perspective, is to dehumanize and ultimately to trivialize the Jewish catastrophe. It is indicative of the general uncertainty and cautiousness that pervade the new approach to the Holocaust that Dawidowicz ends her book with a paradox. After devoting over 150 pages to an examination of the Jewish Response, she concludes by quoting from a resident of the Vilna Ghetto who, in noting the imponderable dilemmas confronting the Jewish community, remarked: "All are guilty, or perhaps more truly, all are innocent and holy."

It is not surprising, therefore, that a more successful integration of general and Jewish history has been achieved in specialized studies of Holocaust history. The methodological outlines of such an approach as it relates to the study of Jewish resistance, for example, have been discussed in Leni Yahil's

"Forms of Jewish Survival" published in *Jewish Resistance During the Holocaust*. Recognizing the Holocaust as a conjuncture of general and Jewish history, Yahil argues for an understanding of both internal and external conditions in evaluating Jewish resistance. Under internal conditions, she lists those factors associated with the life of Eastern European Jewry—size of the Jewish community, demographic makeup, internal organization, composition according to countries of origin, legal status, economic and social stratification, and religious and political composition. These concerns, along with subjective factors such as consciousness of the Nazi threat and attitudes towards resistance, form the "Jewish" component of the study of Jewish resistance. In addition, Yahil notes, there is a need to understand conditions external to the Jewish community which fall under the rubric of general history. Among these conditions are: economic, social, and cultural structures of the occupied country, its "spiritual heritage," geographic and physical factors that affected chances for escape, foreign policy toward Nazi Germany, and traditional attitudes toward Jews. Yahil also argues for an evaluation of the particular interests and attitudes of the German occupiers in each locality—their strategic considerations, interest in industrial and agricultural products, and relationship to the local population. Finally, she suggests that the progress of the War itself, in affecting both the pace of German annihilation and the degree of Jewish resistance, must also be considered in any historical investigation of the Jewish Response. The net effect of Yahil's approach is to lift the study of Jewish resistance from its insularity in "Jewish-centered" history and its insignificance in general history to a rich and tragic human event with relevance to both European and Jew.

A brilliant example of the value of such an approach is Isaiah Trunk's *Judenrat*. Winner of the National Book Award in History in 1972, the book attempts to deal with the perplexing problem of the role of Jewish Councils during the Nazi occupation of Eastern Europe. Trunk is aware of the central importance of this issue for historians of both the "Final Solution" and the Jewish Response. For historians of the "Final Solution," proof of the complicity of Jews in their own death could only reinforce their argument that Nazi extermination of Jews was a bureaucratic process that dehumanized its victims into passive submission. Similarly, historians of the Jewish Response have sought to restore the individuality and humanity of the Jewish victim by emphasizing either courageous resistance among Jewish leaders (the suicide of Adam Czerniakow, head of the Warsaw Council, after refusing to participate in the deportations of July 1942, is of particular interest here) or the hostility manifested towards the *Judenrate* by the Jewish populace.

It is not accidental, therefore, that Trunk begins his work with a criticism of the lack of serious and competent historical research on the activity of Jewish Councils. After over five years of painstaking research, Trunk concludes that it is impossible to make any sweeping generalizations about the response of

Judenrate under Nazi occupation. The reasons for his cautious conclusion provide an insight into what he undoubtedly hopes will be a new approach to Holocaust history. Agreeing with Yahil, he argues that internal and external conditions varied among Jewish communities. The participants in Jewish Councils were of diverse social, economic, and cultural backgrounds and thus reacted quite differently in similar circumstances. Although the ghettos were similar in their formal organization and in the role they were destined to play in the "Final Solution," they were far from homogeneous in their internal, demographic, and economic structure. The varied history and traditions of the communities as well as the geographic and physical conditions of the local area also left their mark on the Councils. What Trunk is demanding is an understanding of the Jewish Response as a complicated weave of subjective and objective conditions, of internal and external variables that reflect the position of the Holocaust as a conjuncture of general and Jewish history.

The scope and direction of Trunk's book clearly show the dimensions of the synthesis. A beginning chapter examines the official Nazi decrees establishing the Jewish Councils. Subsequent chapters deal with the internal structure of the *Judenrate*—the degree of their representativeness, their political and social composition, and the changeover in Council personnel. Special chapters are devoted to the social, economic, and cultural services provided by the Jewish Councils, a subject which has been generally ignored by those who see the *Judenrat's* function solely in terms of selection and deportation. Trunk does not shy away from the question of the Council's complicity in the "Final Solution." Separate chapters deal with the Jewish police, the Councils' relations with and attitudes toward German authorities and Jewish resistance groups, and the opposition to the Councils within the Jewish community. A concluding chapter examines the fate of Council members and ghetto policemen after the War and reveals that even Jewish survivors had difficulty evaluating the role of the *Judenrate* and their officials. A skillful blending of German and Jewish documents, *Judenrat* achieves a richness of historical presentation and analysis that is rare in Holocaust historiography.*

SUBJECTS FOR FURTHER STUDY

Trunk's book points the way to what will undoubtedly be a major reexamination of all aspects of Holocaust history. In the absence of a broad synthesis (which may not be possible), historians of both the "Final Solution" and the Jewish Response will be devoting their attention to specific problems and questions raised by the integration of general and Jewish history.

*On the *Judenrat,* see below, "Moral Implications of the Holocaust," Model #1.

Fresh insights into the Holocaust may also be expected as a result of the discovery of new sources of information. Historians of the "Final Solution" eagerly await the release of Allied government documents after thirty years of being closed to the public. Their revelations concerning Nazi foreign policy as well as the Allied response to the "Final Solution" will be of particular value. A major source of untapped documents are the archives of the countries of Central and Eastern Europe. So far, the archives of East Germany, Poland, Hungary, and other Communist Bloc nations remain inaccessible to scholars in the West but they are known to contain highly useful material on the plight of Jews in the particular countries during World War II. New information can also be expected from the proceedings of trials of Nazi officials, though such trials will become increasingly rare as the statute of limitations on the prosecution of war criminals takes effect.

Historians of the Jewish Response face particular problems in ferreting out new sources of information. Many of the documents of Jewish institutions in the ghettos of Eastern Europe were destroyed along with the communities they served. What exists is localized, scattered over many countries, and written in dozens of languages. Nevertheless, as Trunk's book so brilliantly demonstrates, Jewish historians have managed to surmount the problems of documentation through highly original research techniques. In the absence of official documents, historians of the Jewish Response have found useful material in such unorthodox sources as religious Responsa and children's notebooks. The attempts by survivors to preserve the memory of destroyed communities through the publication of *yizkorbukher* (memorial volumes) have been of immense help in recreating Eastern European Jewish life. The statements of Holocaust survivors, though often subjective and incomplete, continue to yield important information. Research institutes such as Yad Vashem and YIVO have only begun to tap the vast resource of memoirs, personal written statements, and oral testimony. Of particular value has been the study of the popular culture of ghettos and concentration camps—jokes, poems, caricatures, songs, etc.—which often contains valuable insights into contemporary attitudes and ideas. By far the most significant research development in the history of the Jewish Response has been the publication by Yad Vashem of a seven-volume *Guide to Jewish History Under Nazi Impact.* In collating the scattered research on the Jewish Response, the *Guide* serves as a useful starting point for the beginning Holocaust historian.

The subjects for future research are defined by both the new approach as outlined by Yahil and Trunk and the new sources being uncovered. Thus the availability of documentation on Nazi domestic and foreign policy from Allied archives will most certainly clarify the issue of whether the "Final Solution" was part of an original Nazi plan for dealing with Jews or developed as a result of wartime "exigency." The revelations of war criminals and former

Nazi officials will shed further light on the roots of Nazi ideology and the role of racial anti-Semitism in making the "Final Solution" possible. Similarly, the archives of Communist countries will reveal new information on Nazi extermination policy as carried out in particular countries. Historians will be especially interested in researching the participation of natives of occupied countries in the annihilation of Jewry and the effect of internecine rivalry in the Nazi bureaucracy upon decisions and actions concerning the "Final Solution."

Historians of the Jewish Response will find similar challenges. It is hoped that new sources will shed additional light upon the complex problem of physical and spiritual resistance in the ghettos and concentration camps. In particular, historians will be looking at the relationship between the maintenance of religious practice and commitment to resistance. (The recent publication of religious Responsa from occupied ghettos is of inestimable importance in this connection.) With the uncovering of new sources on Jewish resistance, historians of the Jewish Response will be able to investigate the complicated and often conflicting roles of the various resistance groups. Particular attention should be paid to the relations between Zionists and Communists, by far the two most important groups in the Jewish underground. In a more general sense, it is hoped that future research will reflect an awareness of historical patterns of Jewish resistance over the centuries. In his conclusion, for example, Trunk emphasizes the importance of viewing the *Judenrate* as part of a continuous chain of institutions of self-defense in Jewish history. Such an approach might also yield useful information on the links between resistance in the Holocaust and the mounting of Israel's struggle for independence. Similar historical evaluations are necessary for a correct understanding of spiritual resistance.

In addition to new sources, historians of the Holocaust must begin to engage in interdisciplinary study. Like their colleagues in other fields of history, historians of the "Final Solution" and of the Jewish Response should partake of the insights and methodologies offered by disciplines such as psychology, sociology, demography, and quantitative analysis. An interdisciplinary approach would be of particular value for an in-depth analysis of the European Jewish communities during World War II. In order to understand both the "Final Solution" and the Jewish Response, it is imperative that historians learn more of the internal structure of each Jewish community—its demography, social and economic stratification, and cultural life. Similar studies are needed for the surrounding Gentile community which was often instrumental in both the execution of the extermination program and the development of Jewish resistance. The tools of psychology and sociology might also prove valuable in examining the Nazi bureaucracy and its attitude toward the "Final Solution" as well as the fate of the Jewish survivor in the postwar world. Finally, the social sciences may also aid in comparing the differing attitudes and behavior of Western and Eastern European Jewry in the face of the Nazi threat. In examining the plight of the assimilated and non-assimilated Jew during the Holocaust, such a study may also shed new light on the challenge of Emancipation in modern European and Jewish history.

It has been over thirty years since the gas ovens at Auschwitz ceased to operate; yet, the problems raised by the Holocaust continue to perplex historians. Despite the many books on the "Final Solution" and the Jewish Response, the unprecedented nature of the historical event still defies description and evaluation. As Nora Levin notes in her foreword to *The Holocaust:* "To remember what happened and to know more about what happened assuage somewhat the acknowledged failure to comprehend what happened." Such humility was not always to be found among historians of the Holocaust. As the works of Arendt and others show, there are chroniclers of the Jewish catastrophe who have been more than willing to make sweeping generalizations concerning the "Final Solution" and the Jewish Response. With the advent of an integrative historical approach (typified by the works of Levin, Dawidowicz, and Trunk), polemic has been replaced by serious study and investigation. Through painstaking research and cautious analysis, these historians have begun to comprehend the most awesome event in Jewish history. In so doing, they are also making a significant contribution to human self-awareness.

SUGGESTED CLASSROOM TOPICS

In order to familiarize students with Holocaust sources, teachers may wish to make use of the various books of readings in Holocaust history that have recently been published. Works such as Gerd Korman's *The Hunter and the Hunted,* Raul Hilberg's *Documents of Destruction,* and Lucy Dawidowicz's *The Holocaust Reader* are compilations of German and Jewish sources in English translation that highlight the cruelty of the Nazi victimizer and the personal anguish of the Jewish victim. Students might supplement these readings with more extensive selections from memoirs and diaries of Nazi officials and Jews. (For a detailed discussion of such writings, see Chapter Eight.) Selections from primary sources may also be used to test the often unsubstantiated generalizations of historians of both the "Final Solution" and the Jewish Response.

A more difficult and challenging project involving individualized research is the collection of oral histories of the Holocaust. Students might be asked to interview survivors of concentration camps (including, if applicable, members of their own families), soldiers who participated in the liberation of camps, and local community leaders, both Jewish and non-Jewish, who were involved in efforts to publicize the plight of victims during the Holocaust. The teacher must make students especially aware of the difficulties involved in interviewing survivors and caution them against both the distortions of traumatic memory and the painfulness of recalling a past which many wish to forget. It is suggested that only the most mature and articulate students, well read in Holocaust history and sensitive to the psychology of Holocaust survivors, participate in the project. If successful, an oral history compilation can shed light on the historical events of the Holocaust and their repercussions in the present.*

A closely related project which requires substantial language skills is the reconstruction of destroyed Jewish communities in Eastern and Central Europe on the eve of the Holocaust. Students capable of reading Yiddish and having access to primary sources (memorial books, private journals of relatives and friends, recollections of survivors, etc.) should be encouraged to collect source material on *shtetlakh* (Eastern European Jewish communities) in the prewar period. Other students may wish to examine the response of local communities in America to the Holocaust. Through both oral interviews and investigation of newspapers and journals, students can attempt to evaluate the attitudes of their community during World War II or at present. Useful differentiations might be made between Jewish and non-Jewish, young and old, politically active and apathetic, and native and foreign-born members of the community. If students find little or no response to the events of the "Final Solution," the teacher may wish to examine the reasons for American apathy and ignorance both during and after the Holocaust.

Yet another project that gives students insight into American attitudes toward the Holocaust is an examination of popular films dealing with Nazism. Emphasis should be placed on evaluating the image of the Nazi and the depiction of his relationship to the German populace as a whole. Students should consider why American film-makers rarely if ever depicted the Third Reich as a popular regime. They should also question why there is little emphasis upon the Jew and practically no discussion of the "Final Solution" in such films. A close critical investigation of a number of war films should enable students to evaluate American perceptions (and misperceptions) of Nazism and the limitations of American support for its victims.

Films may also be used fruitfully in examining German attitudes toward Nazism and the nature of its appeal. German expressionist films of the 1920's such as *The Last Laugh* and *The Cabinet of Doctor Caligari* have often been used by cultural historians to examine the psychological preconditions for German acceptance of Nazism. (By far the most famous and controversial of these studies is Siegfried Kracauer's *From Caligari to Hitler.*) The teacher may also choose to screen documentary and propaganda films produced by the Nazis that reveal the ideological aims of the Third Reich and the reasons for its immense popularity. Leni Riefenstahl's *Triumph of the Will,* for example,

---

*For information on oral histories, see below, "Resources for the Study of the Holocaust."

is a masterful propaganda film documenting the Nazi Party's Nuremberg Conference held in 1934 that can be successfully used to emphasize the underlying irrationalism of the movement and its appeal among broad segments of the populace. Students may also wish to examine other aspects of Nazi popular culture for insights into the day-to-day functioning of the Third Reich. (George Mosse's *Nazi Culture,* an anthology of Nazi popular culture in English translation, is a particularly valuable source.)*

Nazi popular culture may also be studied to investigate the nature of Nazi anti-Semitism. Films such as *Jud Süss,* carefully presented and explained, are of inestimable value in understanding the roots of racism and the "logical necessity" of the "Final Solution." The teacher may wish to expand the study to include a general investigation of anti-Semitic stereotypes as revealed in German popular culture. Discussion should center on similarities and differences between Nazi anti-Semitism and previous forms of Jew hatred. Students might also attempt to compare and contrast Nazi racism with other forms of racism in modern history.

*See below, "The Holocaust and the Film Arts."

BIBLIOGRAPHY

The books below represent a limited selection of significant works in Holocaust history. They have been chosen for their scholarship and/or their influence upon the development of Holocaust historiography. Where possible, I have listed paperback editions.

The "Final Solution": Its Implementation

American Federation for Polish Jews. *The Black Book of Polish Jewry* (Roy Publishers, 1943). One of the first accounts of the Holocaust, compiled during the War from scattered reports of the implementation of the "Final Solution."

ARENDT, HANNAH. *Eichmann in Jerusalem: A Report on the Banality of Evil* (Viking Compass, 1965) (Available in paperback). A sloppy and often irresponsible account of the Eichmann Trial which nevertheless offers a fascinating insight into the appeal of Nazism.

BETTELHEIM, BRUNO. *The Informed Heart: Autonomy in a Mass Age* (Avon paperback, 1971). The classic description of concentration camp victims as dehumanized and depersonalized automatons and a central target of those arguing for the existence of an active Jewish response during the Holocaust.

BRAHAM, RANDOLPH. *Eichmann and the Destruction of European Jewry* (Twayne Publishers, nd) (Twayne paperback, 1961). Less heralded than Arendt's contemporaneous work, this is a thorough description of the "Final Solution."

BULLOCK, ALAN. *Hitler: A Study in Tyranny* (Harper, 1971) (Available in paperback). The standard biography of Hitler which, though discussing his obsession with Jews, says little about Hitler's implementation of the "Final Solution."

CHARY, FREDERICK. *The Bulgarian Jews and the Final Solution* (University of Pittsburgh Press, 1972). One of many specialized studies of the "Final Solution"; of particular importance because of the generally successful efforts by Bulgarian leaders to prevent the deportation of their country's Jewish population.

FEST, JOACHIM. *Hitler* (Random, 1975) (Available in paperback). A fascinating excursion into Hitler's mind by a German historian; extremely insightful in its discussion of the roots of Hitler's anti-Semitic beliefs but almost silent on the Holocaust itself.

HILBERG, RAUL. *The Destruction of the European Jews* (New Viewpoints, 1973) (Quadrangle, 1961) (Harper paperback, 1979). An indispensable work on the administration of the "Final Solution"; its massive compilation of factual data continues to provide important source material for students of the Holocaust.

INSTITUTE FOR JEWISH AFFAIRS. *Hitler's Ten-Year War on the Jews* (Institute for Jewish Affairs, 1943).

_____. *The Jewish Catastrophe* (Institute for Jewish Affairs, 1944).

_____. *Starvation Over Europe* (Institute for Jewish Affairs, 1943).

Three works hastily compiled during the Holocaust to alert the American community to the horrifying reality of the "Final Solution."

JASPERS, KARL. *The Question of German Guilt* (Capricorn paperback, 1961) (Peter H. Smith, nd). A short discussion of German guilt written in the immediate postwar period by an eminent German philosopher; surprising for its implicit recognition of the popularity of the Nazi regime.

KATZ, ROBERT. *Black Sabbath: A Journey Through a Crime Against Humanity* (Macmillan, 1969). A journalistic account of the events leading up to the roundup of Jews in Rome in 1943; the work is marred by a pseudo-Marxist attack upon ''rich'' Jews for allegedly saving their own lives at the expense of the Jewish masses.

LANGER, WALTER. *The Mind of Adolf Hitler: The Secret War-Time Report* (Signet paperback, 1973). A study commissioned by the OSS during World War II which seeks to explain Nazi policy in terms of Hitler's psychological delusions; the work suffers from a rigid Freudianism and a general sloppiness reflecting the haste with which it was written.

LÉVY, CLAUDE AND TILLARD, PAUL. *Betrayal at Vel d'Hiv* (Hill and Wang, 1969). A graphic description of the infamous roundup of foreign Jews in Paris in July 1942.

POLIAKOV, LEON. *Harvest of Hate: The Nazi Program for the Destruction of the Jews of Europe* (Syracuse University Press, 1954). A useful short account of the process of the ''Final Solution.''

PRESSER, JACOB. *The Destruction of the Dutch Jews* (E. P. Dutton, 1969). An examination of the fate of Dutch Jewry during the Holocaust which has particular significance because of the debate over the complicity of the Dutch *Judenrat* in the ''Final Solution.''

REITLINGER, GERALD. *The Final Solution: The Attempt to Exterminate the Jews of Europe, 1939-1945* (Perpetua, 1961). One of the first attempts to compile a history of the Holocaust.

ROBINSON, JACOB. *And the Crooked Shall be Made Straight: The Eichmann Trial, the Jewish Catastrophe, and Hannah Arendt's Narrative* (Jewish Publication Society, 1965). A devastating attack upon Arendt's *Eichmann in Jerusalem* which, in its point by point refutation, effectively proves the irresponsible nature of many of her arguments.

SCHLEUNES, KARL. *The Twisted Road to Auschwitz: Nazi Policy Toward German Jews, 1933-1939* (University of Illinois Press, 1970). A solid historical investigation of the racial policies of the Third Reich in the period before the implementation of the ''Final Solution.''

The Jewish Response: Before the Holocaust

BOLKOSKY, SIDNEY. *The Distorted Image: German Jewish Perceptions of Germans and Germany, 1918-1935* (Elsevier, 1973). An impressionistic analysis of German Jewish attitudes on the eve of Hitler's accession to power which argues forcefully that the German Jews' confidence in the efficacy of assimilation blinded them to the growing strength of anti-Semitism.

HELLER, CELIA. *On the Edge of Destruction: Jews of Poland Between the Two World Wars* (Columbia University Press, 1976). The only study of its kind available in English, the book is a sociological analysis of the largest Jewish community in Europe in the interwar period.

MARRUS, MICHAEL, ''European Jewry and the Politics of Assimilation: Assessment and Reassessment,'' *Journal of Modern History,* Volume 49:1 (March 1977), pp. 89-109. An insightful discussion of current literature on European Jewry in the interwar period; it argues, among other things, for a dispassionate analysis which eschews the extremes of assimilationist and Zionist viewpoints.

————. *The Politics of Assimilation: A Study of the French Jewish Community at the Time of the Dreyfus Affair* (Oxford University Press, 1971). An important study that asserts that the French Jewish community refused to recognize the significance of the Dreyfus Affair for its own cherished beliefs in emancipation and assimilation.

POPPEL, STEPHEN M. *Zionism in Germany, 1897–1933: The Shaping of a Jewish Identity* (Jewish Publication Society, 1977). A competent research effort which argues that German Zionists, much like their assimilationist antagonists within the Jewish community, were strongly tied to German values and beliefs.

REINHARZ, JEHUDA. *Fatherland or Promised Land: The Dilemma of the German Jew, 1893–1914* (University of Michigan Press, 1975). An interesting analysis of the confused self-definitions of German Jewry directly before World War I which occasionally falls into glib condemnations based upon historical hindsight.

SCHORSCH, ISMAR. *Jewish Reactions to German Anti-Semitism, 1870–1914* (Columbia University Press, 1972). A surprising thesis which argues that German Jewish leaders grew to recognize the danger of anti-Semitism in Germany before World War I and took effective action to counter it; an important counterargument to Bolkosky, Reinharz, and Poppel.

WEINBERG, DAVID H. *A Community on Trial: Jews of Paris in the 1930's* (University of Chicago Press, 1977). An analysis of Paris Jewry as a case study of the attitudes and behavior of European Jewry on the eve of the Holocaust.

The Jewish Response: During the Holocaust

BARKAI, MEYER, ed. *The Fighting Ghettos* (Tower, 1971) (Available in paperback). A compilation of personal accounts of armed resistance in Jewish ghettos during the Holocaust.

BAUER, YEHUDA. *Flight and Rescue: Brichah* (Random House, 1970). An investigation of the rescue operation conducted by Zionist and Palestinian-based organizations during and immediately after World War II.

————. *From Diplomacy to Resistance: A History of Jewish Palestine, 1939–1945* (Atheneum, 1973). A standard chronology of the development of Jewish resistance in Palestine which emphasizes the impact of the Holocaust.

————. *My Brother's Keeper: A History of the American Joint Distribution Committee, 1929–1939* (Jewish Publication Society, 1974). A general description of the activities of one of the major American Jewish rescue organizations; unfortunately, the work deals only with rescue and relief activity in the pre-Holocaust period.

DES PRES, TERRENCE. *The Survivor* (Pocketbooks paperback, 1977). A totally absorbing discussion of the psychology of survival in German and Russian concentration camps. Although the book says little about Jews and Jewish survival, the reader gains greater understanding of the awesomeness of the "Final Solution" and of the fierce determination of its survivors that the world never forgot.

GOLDSTEIN, BERNARD. *The Stars Bear Witness* (Viking, 1949) (Available in paperback). An early account of the Warsaw Ghetto uprising.

Holocaust and Rebirth: Bergen-Belsen, 1945–1965 (Bergen Belsen Memorial Press, 1965). A memorial book issued on the twentieth anniversary of the liberation of

Bergen-Belsen by survivors of the camp; valuable information on camp life and on the fate of Holocaust survivors.

KATSH, ABRAHAM, ed. *The Warsaw Diary of Chaim Kaplan* (Collier paperback, 1973). An absorbing personal account of daily life in the Warsaw Ghetto.

KIMCHES, JON AND DAVID. *The "Secret Roads": The Illegal Migration of a People, 1938-1948* (Secker and Warburg, 1954). A general description of Zionist efforts to rescue Jews from Europe and transport them to Palestine.

LEVI, PRIMO. *Survival in Auschwitz: The Nazi Assault on Humanity* (Collier paperback, 1973). By far the most compelling account of life in a Nazi concentration camp; unfortunately, the work deals only tangentially with Jews.

MARK, BER. *Uprising in the Warsaw Ghetto* (Schocken paperback, 1975). An emotionally charged description of the events of April 1943.

RABINOWITZ, DOROTHY. *New Lives: Survivors of the Holocaust in America* (Knopf, 1976) (Available in Avon paperback). An impressionistic account of the fate of a group of Holocaust survivors living in America; a sympathetic view which successfully avoids romanticization.

RINGELBLUM, EMMANUEL. *Notes from the Warsaw Ghetto* (Schocken paperback, 1974). An indispensable resource for material on daily life in the Warsaw Ghetto; its meticulous attention to detail reflects the author's commitment to chronicling the events of the Holocaust for future generations.

ROSENBAUM, IRVING. *The Holocaust and Halachah* (Ktav, 1976) (available in paperback). A discussion of religious Responsa during the Holocaust which attempts to understand the role of religious belief and practice in enabling traditional Jews to cope with the nightmare of the Holocaust.

SENESH, HANNAH. *Hannah Senesh: Her Life and Diary* (Schocken, 1973) (Available in paperback). The personal musings of a young woman whose commitment to rescuing her fellow coreligionists during the Holocaust and eventual death at the hands of the Nazis have served as a symbol of Jewish courage and fortitude during the dark days of World War II.

STEINER, JEAN FRANCOIS. *Treblinka* (Signet paperback, 1968) (Simon & Schuster, 1967). A fictionalized account of the revolt of prisoners in Treblinka in August 1943.

SUHL, YURI, ed. *They Fought Back: The Story of the Jewish Resistance in Nazi Europe* (Schocken paperback, 1975). By far the best compilation of accounts of Jewish resistance efforts during World War II.

SYRKIN, MARIE. *Blessed is the Match* (Knopf, 1947) (Available in paperback). The first significant work in English on Jewish armed resistance during the Holocaust.

WISCHNITZER, MARK. *To Dwell in Safety: The Story of Jewish Migration Since 1800* (Jewish Publication Society, 1949). A general study on Jewish migration which includes a description of Jewish emigration from Europe after the Holocaust.

YAD VASHEM INSTITUTE. *Guide to Jewish History Under Nazi Impact* (Yad Vashem Institute, 1960-1966). The most important bibliographical source on Holocaust historiography; works are arranged according to country.

YAHIL, LENI. *The Rescue of Danish Jewry* (Jewish Publication Society, 1969). A solid analysis of the largely successful effort by the Danish population to save its Jewish population from deportation.

ZIMMELS, DR. H. J. *The Echo of the Nazi Holocaust in Rabbinic Literature* (Printed in the Republic of Ireland, nd) (Reprint: Ktav, 1976). An exhaustive compilation of religious Responsa which reflects upon the nature of psychological resistance among Orthodox Jews.

The Holocaust as General and Jewish History

DAWIDOWICZ, LUCY. *The War Against the Jews, 1933–1945* (Bantam paperback, 1976). By far the most comprehensive study of the Holocaust, notable for its discussion of both the implementation of the "Final Solution" and the nature of the Jewish Response; an indispensable source for students of the Holocaust.

Jewish Resistance During the Holocaust (Yad Vashem Institute, 1971). Proceedings of a conference held in Israel which highlight the complexity of research into the Jewish Response; of particular significance is the paper by Leni Yahil which discusses the need to evaluate both internal and external conditions affecting the nature of Jewish resistance.

KORMAN, GERD, "The Holocaust in American Historical Writing," *Societas,* 2:3, (Summer 1972), pp. 251–270.

––––––. "Silence in American Textbooks," *Yad Vashem Studies,* (1970), 8:183–202.

Two valuable studies which attack American historians and American textbooks for ignoring Jewish victims in their discussions of Nazism.

LEVIN, NORA. *The Holocaust: The Destruction of European Jewry, 1933–1945* (Schocken paperback). Though not as comprehensive as Dawidowicz's work, this book nevertheless is an important contribution to the study of the Holocaust as both general and Jewish history; at times, Levin seems to imply a historical antagonism between German and Jew that preceded the Nazis' accession to power but, unfortunately, does not elaborate.

TUSHNET, LEONARD. *The Pavement of Hell* (St. Martin's Press, 1972). A fascinating insight into the personalities and behavior of the three major leaders of Jewish councils during the Holocaust.

TRUNK, ISAIAH. *Judenrat: The Jewish Councils in Eastern Europe Under Nazi Occupation* (Macmillan, 1972) (Available in paperback). Winner of the National Book Award in History, this is by far the best of the specialized studies on the Holocaust; transcending the generalizations of proponents of Jewish complicity and of Jewish resistance, Trunk concludes that it is all but impossible to make any hard generalizations about the behavior of Jewish councils; a brilliant and thorough work that should serve as a model for all historians of the Holocaust.

General Holocaust Readers

DAWIDOWICZ, LUCY. *A Holocaust Reader* (Behrman House, 1972) (Available in paperback). A useful collection of readings reflecting in large part the author's approach in her work *The War Against the Jews.*

HILBERG, RAUL. *Documents of Destruction: Germany and Jewry, 1933–1945* (Watts, 1971) (Available in paperback). An undistinguished collection which is notable largely for its inclusion of Jewish sources, a significant departure from the author's attitude in his massive work *The Destruction of the European Jews.*

KORMAN, GERD, ed. *Hunter and Hunted: Human History of the Holocaust* (Delta, 1973) (Available in paperback). An uneven collection which, in emphasizing personal accounts by survivors, both clarifies and distorts the historical significance of the Holocaust.

Books Useful in Planning Classroom Projects

BARSAM, RICHARD M. *Filmguide to Triumph of the Will* (Indiana University Press, 1975) (Available in paperback). A detailed analysis and summary of the most famous Nazi propaganda film ever made.

HULL, DAVID ST. *Film in the Third Reich* (University of California Press, 1969). A chronological account of the German cinema during the Nazi period; of particular interest is Hull's discussion of the anti-Semitic film, *Jud Suss.*

KINSER, BILL AND KLEINMAN, NEIL, eds. *The Dream that was no more a dream* (Harper Colophon paperback, 1969). A remarkable collection of cartoons, paintings, photographs, film clips, etc. from the Nazi period that reflect the escapist nature of Nazi ideology; the prefatory essay, unfortunately, is poorly written and often confusing.

KRACAUER, SIEGFRIED. *From Caligari to Hitler: A Psychological History of the German Film* (Princeton University Press, nd) (Available in paperback). Methodologically weak yet always provocative, this is a pioneering work which attempts to examine German attitudes and beliefs through an analysis of German films; especially interesting for its discussion of German films in the 1920's.

MOSSE, GEORGE, ed. *Nazi Culture* (Universal Library, 1968) (Available in paperback). The only work of its kind available in English, the book is a selection of cultural artifacts—novels, poems, primers, speeches, plays, etc.—of the Nazi period; useful for examining Nazi ideology and the nature of its appeal.

Socio-Political Responses during the Holocaust:

Actions and Reactions of Allies, Axis Partners and Neutrals to the Destruction of European Jewry

Helen Fein

The Holocaust has often been interpreted in terms of an underlying model. This model assumes the omnipotence of Nazi Germany, the super-state—with no other nation-states in existence—poised to destroy a stateless people, the Jews. Those who have adopted this model have obscured the factual question of the responsibility and complicity of other states—Allies, neutrals, and Axis satellites—either as active collaborators or as passive witnesses to the destruction of European Jews.

We may view the sovereign state as an organization emanating from an internal social order—the array of parties and class hierarchy—and as a rational actor pursuing some concept of its own interests within an international order. Focusing on the Axis satellites, if we view the state as a rational actor, how do we explain the rationality of their decision on deporting Jews? To what extent was this action contingent upon each state's concept of its interests and the domestic interplay of parties, classes, and interest groups? How was this deportation decision altered by the action or inaction of the Allies? How was the state's orientation towards the Allies modified by the course of the War, and by its expectation of German victory or defeat? What opportunities for threat or intervention developed during the course of the War?

Focusing on the neutrals, how do we explain their policy towards the admission of Jews as refugees and the extension of sanctuary? What diplomatic actions were taken to inhibit deporting or discriminating against Jews? Neutrals, for the purpose of this discussion, are limited to Switzerland, Sweden, Spain and the Vatican, acting as a state.

Focusing on the Allies (the United States, Great Britain, and the Union of Soviet Socialist Republics), one must first ask what was done to impede the processes culminating in the mass murder of Jews, from the initial discrimination against German Jews to the incineration of the Jews of Europe? What means were available that were not used? Viewing the state as a rational actor, how do we explain why virtually nothing was done? How was relevant state information diffused to or concealed from the public? To what extent was the states' policy related to their treatment of their own Jews or the political strategy pursued by their Jewish community? What evidence is there of the primacy of the rescue of Jews or prevention of their murder as a policy goal? Looking at the role of organized groups in public decision-making, how do we explain the unity or disunity of the Jewish community when confronted by this challenge to its existence? What objectives, anxieties and ideologies conditioned its own responses? In the course of any study of the Holocaust, the aforementioned questions must be addressed. It is imperative to try to understand the reactions of governments, as well as of individuals, during the Holocaust. No complete study of the Holocaust can omit a consideration of political as well as social factors. To restrict discussion only to the activities of the German Nazi state is to present a pivotal, though incomplete portrait of the activities or inactivities of governments during the War years. The war was a World War. It is necessary therefore to review the reactions—malevolent, benign or indifferent—of Axis powers, Allies and neutrals, to the Nazi plan for the destruction of European Jewry. Because the Allies were the freest actors and the most powerful states, we shall assess their role first.

THE ALLIES: THE UNITED STATES, GREAT BRITAIN AND THE UNION OF SOVIET SOCIALIST REPUBLICS

The United States

The activities of the government of the United States and of the American people during the War years should be of specific relevance to American students of the Holocaust. The activities of the American Jewish community during this period should have particular pertinence for American Jewish students studying about the Holocaust.

Americans studying the reaction of their government to the Holocaust are not simply engaged in an objective historical inquiry but are involved with an exercise in political, social and moral self-understanding. The apparent disparity between moral values proclaimed by American credos and political activities during the Holocaust clearly emerges out of a consideration of the official reaction of the American government to the destruction of European Jewry during the War years. The implications of this disparity for understanding American political behavior both before and after the War are many. In addition, the reaction of the American Jewish community holds vast implications for understanding how the American Jewish community responded to the pressing crisis posed during the War and for understanding its reactions to crises in the post-War era.

In reviewing American responses during the War years, four notable works elicit attention. These books, all of which have appeared after 1968, have attempted to explain the inaction of the Roosevelt Administration between 1933 and 1945 towards the subordination, legal exclusion and later annihilation of European Jews. The first of these works which merits attention is Henry Feingold's *The Politics of Rescue, The Roosevelt Administration and the Holocaust, 1938-1945*.

Feingold's work is the most comprehensive and analytical examination of the sources of the Roosevelt administration's policy since 1933, its relation to intraparty politics, the New Deal coalition, and the divisions within the Jewish community. Unfortunately, Feingold primarily narrates the artifices rather than reflecting on the causes of American policy. This diminishes the reader's appreciation of the complexity of his analysis, as the very tediousness of the bureaucratic shuffle between agencies and between the United States and Britain becomes tedious to the reader after the description of the third conference convened to avoid a solution.

David Wyman's *Paper Walls: America and the Refugee Crisis 1938-1941* and Saul S. Friedman's *No Haven for the Oppressed: United States Policy Toward Jewish Refugees, 1938-1945* are more limited in scope, but both contribute insights from different perspectives. Wyman has fully utilized the archives of the American Friends Service Committee—an organization critical to refugee aid with representatives throughout Europe—and has interviewed many people active in such missions during the period. Friedman (1973) presents little new evidence on the course of American policy, but relates the evidence on the relationship of Stephen S. Wise, President of the American Jewish Congress, to the American President Franklin Delano Roosevelt, charging collusion in ''A Partnership of Silence''; his evidence (to be presented later) is convincing.

Arthur D. Morse's *While Six Million Died: A Chronicle of American Apathy* can be recommended, but with reservations, for readers with little historical background on the Holocaust. Because he relies only upon published sources, some of which are untrustworthy, Morse makes several notable errors. Unlike either the trained historian or the critical journalist, Morse does not compare his sources. Furthermore, he is rather disingenuous as to the role of American Jewish leaders. His book will be immediately comprehensible to those conditioned by the media to demand the integration of personal drama and bureaucratic performance: this is understandable, given Morse's own previous performance as a director for Edward R. Murrow's *See It Now,* a popular television dramatization of historical events.

Despite differences in focus and audience, all these books present a similar picture of American administrative refusal to incur any costs on behalf of European Jewry.

What could have been done? Two possibilities were open during the prewar period. The first was to assist the exodus of the maximal number of Jews between 1930 and 1940 by opening up American immigration and by exploiting American influence to secure refuges in other countries. Secondly, the United States could have imposed sanctions against Germany both to censure past discrimination and to deter further dehumanization.

In summary, the Roosevelt administration not only refused to aid Jewish and other religious, ethnic or political refugees by any attempts to amend the immigration laws of the United States (based on national origins quotas), but also further subverted those laws between 1933 and 1943. The State Department undermined fulfillment of the law by failing to approve enough visa applicants to fill the quota for Germany (despite the surplus of applicants), and repeatedly opposed allowing refugees into the United States or its territories by exploiting loopholes in the law. Proponents of rescue, such as Harold Ickes, Secretary of the Interior — who sought to admit any number who might escape to the Virgin Islands from which they could enter the United States without formal barrier—encountered unremitting opposition from the State Department. When confronted with such a conflict between these advocates and the State Department or the members of Congress, President Roosevelt unhesitatingly supported the opponents of rescue.

To divert attention from the American policy of noncommitment, the President convened multinational refugee conferences (Evian in 1938, Bermuda in 1943), instigated the establishment of the powerless Intergovernmental Committee on Refugees, and initiated diplomatic probes on the possibility of resettling Jews in undeveloped areas of Latin America, the Philippines and Africa. Palestine, advocated by the Zionists, was rejected because of British opposition. Feingold observes of the United States and Britain: "Both sides seemed to wax enthusiastic when the projected haven was in the sphere of the other nation." Both nations rejected the possibility of taking in substantial numbers of the Jews seeking to flee Germany for any possible destination. The American unwillingness either to amend or fully exploit its own immigration laws enabled other nations to justify fully the closing of their doors at Evian in 1938; interested and disinterested spectators alike saw the Evian Conference as an exercise in Anglo-American collaborative hypocrisy.

The Nazis exploited their perception of the West's indifference to justify their own Jewish policy; the *Danziger Vorposten* observed after the conference that, "We can see that one likes to pity the Jews as long as one can use this pity for a wicked agitation against Germany, but that no state is prepared to fight the cultural disgrace of central Europe by accepting a few thousand Jews. Thus the conference serves to justify Germany's policy against Jewry" (see Morse, p. 214).

Between 1938 and 1941, the Nazis calculated that expulsion was one way to rid the Third Reich of its Jews; coincidentally, expulsion provided a tactic to exploit prospective refugees by seizing their property and giving credits (on the value seized) to receiving nations of refugees to purchase German imports. Such an agreement had previously been made with the Jewish Agency, enabling German Jewish immigrants to draw on blocked accounts in Germany upon their arrival in Palestine. This arrangement—the *Haavara* [Transfer] agreement—aroused much controversy among Jewish Zionist and non-Zionist leadership, especially amongst those American Jewish leaders sponsoring a boycott of German goods since 1933. When, in 1939, the German government proposed an exchange plan of Jewish refugees with "international Jewry" — using the United States and Great Britain as intermediaries for this fictitious corporate organism—the same objections were reiterated both by Jewish leaders and the governments involved, each motivated by different sources of apprehension. Both correctly perceived it as ransom. Unlike exchanges in classic economic theory, the price did not go down because of lack of demand for the commodity marketed, but it escalated. Jewish leaders feared becoming commercial agents for a criminal regime (not realizing the immensity of the crime it intended) and the costs of rescue if Germany ploughed through eastern Europe and began auctioning off the Jews of Poland. American officials feared not only setting a precedent for the mass marketing of unwanted peoples, but also the effects on American world trade.

In 1939 the Inter-Governmental Committee on Refugees (IGC) played at responding to the proposal for refugee exchange that Hjalmar Schacht, President of the Reichsbank, made in 1939. But they neither explicitly rejected nor gave sufficient encouragement to the German "moderates" (such as Schacht) to prevent their defeat by the Nazi radicals who preferred to inter rather than to exploit Jews. The German Jews' immediate plight was not conspicuous to the administrators of this sham agency. The IGC officials perceived those pleading Jews in the way that bureaucratic professionals often view desperate clientele: they were surplus claimants, whose needs must not be permitted to reverse the agency's definition of the problem situation lest the agency be overwhelmed by an unlimited demand. In 1939 the Gestapo ordered the German Jewish community to list one hundred members daily to either leave Germany within two weeks or face incarceration in concentration camps; IGC officials refused even to pretend to respond to the Jews' dilemma.

The problem in the United States and Great Britain was not of inadequate resources for potential escapees but of a lack of commitment to saving lives.

Since 1933, Hitler's victims had been written off as casualties of the revolution which diplomatic observers recognized was occurring after his accession to power. They wishfully hoped that "excesses" against the Jews—street violence, Gestapo raids by night, sending home the ashes of those recently deported to camps—would disappear as the revolution rid the country of its internal enemies as well as the Jews.

The aim of American (and British) foreign policy before 1939 was to avoid war with Germany. The U.S. always maintained a correct, respectful, diplomatic posture, rejecting (1) negative economic sanctions (e.g., blocking currency or cutting off trade), (2) positive economic exchanges to save prospective refugees, and (3) any diplomatic sanctions. No protest was ever made against stripping the German Jews of jobs in 1933 or citizenship rights in 1935. Only after *Kristallnacht* in 1938 did the Roosevelt administration imply a rebuke against Germany by recalling the American Ambassador to Berlin home "for consultation." Again on this occasion, Roosevelt refused either to cut off trade with Germany or to propose new immigration laws. American protests were restricted to notes concerning American Jews in Germany.

Official denial, disbelief and dispassion were the prelude to later resignation. In order to maintain such detachment later, it was necessary to obscure the visibility of the genocide then being committed. Thus, the State Department in August 1942 refused to relay reports to Rabbi Stephen Wise (President of the American Jewish Congress) from the World Jewish Congress Representative in Switzerland regarding detection of the plan for the "Final Solution," claiming insufficient documentation. Furthermore, the State Department informed its Swiss representative not to accept any more messages of that type from the World Jewish Congress' Swiss representative, Gerhard Riegner.

The State Department's role in inhibiting public recognition of the Holocaust and preventing rescue was well known but not exposed until Henry D. Morgenthau, Jr., Secretary of the Treasury, became aware of this conspiracy of silence in December 1943, and supervised preparation of a personal report to the President (originally entitled by Morgenthau's staff the "Report to the Secretary on the Acquiescence of this government in the Murder of the Jews"), Feingold tells us. Only in January 1944, when Roosevelt was confronted with proof of the State Department's subversion, did he establish the War Refugee Board (January 1944), which agency was granted authority to forestall "Nazi plans to exterminate all the Jews."

For the first time, the United States authorized the use of the threat of sanctions—future punishment of war criminals—and notified foreign representatives of susceptible belligerents with still extant Jewish populations (Hungary, Rumania, and Bulgaria) that they would be considered responsible for their acts.

The most susceptible German target was the 825,000 Jews of Hungary;

threats of deportation to German extermination camps had been earlier checked in Rumania and Bulgaria by the indigenous opposition of Jews, church leaders, and politicians. The War Refugee Board attempted to deter deportations from Hungary by threats of postwar punishment from the President against collaborators and by shortwave radio appeals to hide Jews and to record collaborators; furthermore, the Board attempted to intensify threats and appeals by increasing the visibility of any action, and by pleading with the International Red Cross to increase its observers in Hungary and with the Pope to broadcast both his opposition and the further threat of ecclesiastical sanctions.

By June 1944, it was evident that the effort to deter extermination in Hungary by the threat of future sanctions was ineffective. The Regent's lack of a personal following and the always imminent potential for a coup by the eventually successful radical right (most of whose leaders were in the official party, not the Arrow Cross) made resumption of deportation a threat even after July. The question still arises: Why did all Allies reject the most direct means of preventing the extermination of the Jews of Hungary—bombing the rail lines leading to Auschwitz and the crematoria?

Eyewitness reports and drawings of the Auschwitz facilities (provided by two Slovakian Jews who escaped on April 21, 1944) had reached Roscoe McClelland, the War Refugee Board representative in Switzerland in June, and had been sent to Washington then. This data was first released by the War Refugee Board in a sixty-page report in October 1944. Erich Kulka, in "Auschwitz Condoned: The Abortive Struggle Against the Final Solution," relates the progress of the Auschwitz Protocol, taking issue with Morse's judgment that the War Refugee Board left "no stone unturned to save Jews"; Kulka concludes that ". . . by its half-hearted and protracted handling of the Protocols, they [the WRB] allowed the Nazis in Birkenau to send several hundred thousand more people to their death."

Feingold has also oversimplified the causes of this critical decision by accepting Leon Kubowitzki's account of the event in his *Unity in Dispersion: A History of the World Jewish Congress* (New York, World Jewish Congress, 1948), which is based on a recollection distorting his actual role. War Refugee Board records show that the proposal to bomb Auschwitz was rejected by the Assistant Secretary of War, John J. McCloy, *three times* and that the Director of the WRB, John Pehle, did not himself request its bombing until November 1944. Nor was there pressure from Jewish organizations and leaders, including Kubowitzki, who wrote on June 28, 1944, that he doubted the efficacy of bombing and suggested alternate tactics necessitating the cooperation of the Soviets and the Polish Government-in-Exile. Kulka observes that McCloy's stress on the technical unfeasibility of bombing Auschwitz was a blind, as buildings within seven kilometers of the crematoria (the rubber works, the town, and SS barracks) were bombed three times between April and December 1944.

The other Allies agreed to divert no resources to save the Jews in Auschwitz. Kulka relates that Vishinsky himself, speaking for the Russian Foreign Ministry, rejected the suggestion made to the WRB by Leon Kubowitzki to mount a special military operation to liberate Auschwitz.

The increased public awareness engendered by the War Refugee Board's publication of the Auschwitz Protocols incited demands by Jewish groups for a warning to Germans to abstain from exterminating prisoners still alive in Auschwitz and other camps. This led to a public warning to the Germans from the Supreme Allied Commander, General Eisenhower; significantly, references to Jews were deleted in the final version which directed the Germans to ignore "any order from whatever source" to injure prisoners in concentration camps and forced labor battalions "without regard to their nationality or religious faith." Other means used by the WRB to prevent further exterminations were appeals to the Soviet Union and indirect diplomatic approaches to Germany to deter the SS from killing their prisoners: these are not evaluated by Feingold, Morse or Friedman.

Strategies of Denial and Defense: Life-Voiding or Life-Saving Labels?

The special character of German policy towards Jews was denied by tagging the victims with the universalistic label of "political refugee." Being a political, or opponent of the regime is an achieved status; being a Jew, under the Nuremberg laws, is ascribed by ancestry. President Roosevelt helped create the impression of something voluntaristic in the Jews' plight. The President, in fact, refused to recognize a peculiar Jewish problem, never mentioning Jewish victims until 1944. This denial was facilitated by Jewish groups who publicly recognized only infractions of human rights; they rejected special pleas for Jews as Jews because they believed this recognition would validate Hitler's charges. Roosevelt's blurred perception is shown in Feingold's description (p. 59) of the President's 1939 encounter with an American official negotiating with Hjalmar Schacht for the emigration of 150,000 Jews from the Reich. "Among the first questions asked by Roosevelt, when Rublee visited the White House in early February [1939] to present his final report, concerned the reason for limiting the agreement to Jewish refugees. It took some doing to convince the President that Berlin only recognized a Jewish problem and refused to negotiate on anything else."

Wyman, who has shown how Jewish organizations concurred in labelling Jews as political refugees upon the advice of their Christian allies, does not consider how this tactic of de-emphasizing their Jewish identity had unanticipated negative consequences. When Jewish organizations failed to back the Wagner Bill in 1938, which would have admitted 20,000 German refugee children outside the quota, an argument deterring potential sympathizers was that this would encourage the breakdown of nuclear families. Only a frank acknowledgment that the crisis of German Jewish families (aggravated by the internment of 60,000 Jewish men in concentration camps after *Kristallnacht*) was first a problem of the survival of their now rightless and increasingly impoverished members could convince professional welfare advocates of the lack of realism in the rules serving the range of German Jewish family problems. Similarly, the failure to stress that Jews as Jews had been defined officially as the enemy of the new Germany produced the paradox that Jewish refugees from the expanded Third Reich could be denied entry after the start of the War through depiction by the State Department as potential spies, untrustworthy because of their German identity. Keeping potential German agents out of the United States was a persuasive argument to justify: (1) bureaucrats' keeping the victims out by withholding papers and (2) indefinitely stalling procedures on visa applications by security checks. Even after the Allies publicly acknowledged the extermination of the European Jews (in their declaration of December 17, 1942), they failed to recognize Jews among the victims in the Moscow Declaration of 1943 which promised postwar judgment "by the peoples whom they have outraged" for Germans participating in the shooting of "Italian officers . . . French, Dutch, Belgian or Norwegian hostages or of Cretan peasants, or who have shared in slaughters inflicted on the people of Poland or in the territories of the Soviet Union. . . ."

The refugees' Jewish identity, while not acknowledged publicly, was recognized by the American administration in its establishment of quotas. In 1940 the President recommended limiting Jews to ten percent of the projected number of refugees to be resettled in Alaska—a plan he quickly vetoed when opposition developed. Even as late as 1944, he wanted to avoid placing "undue proportions" of Jews in a temporary detention camp in Oswego (the first of its kind) for refugees without visas (see Feingold, p. 303).

Although rescue from German-occupied countries was not generally possible, the United States might have attempted to improve the status of the Jews interned in camps and ghettos by declaring them "prisoners of war," a strategy called for by the Emergency Committee to Save the Jewish People of Europe in 1943. Redefining their status would have made these Jews subjects of international law and might have impelled the International Red Cross to inspect the camps, deterring the internees' execution by increasing their visibility. The visibility of the victims' suffering did provoke the delegates of the International Red Cross (originally reluctant observers), who witnessed the forced marches of Hungarian Jews to the Austrian border, to grant 30,000 certificates of protection to Hungarian Jews. Some lives were also saved by the War Refugee Board not as a result of direct sanctions to prevent deportation, but through redefining the status of Jews and by conferring papers, certificates of immigrant status or foreign protection.

The most ingenious and dedicated exploiter of saving lives through documentation was Raoul Wallenberg, a Swedish emissary of the War Refugee Board who was stationed in Hungary. Wallenberg extended Swedish diplomatic protection to 20,000 Hungarian Jews and leased apartment houses for them in Budapest. Although he lacked arms and had no special diplomatic sanctions to inveigh against Germany to uphold the authority behind such recertification, he defended the status he had bestowed upon his clients to the point of physically interposing his own body when the German police came to the quarter to round up Jews for deportation, following (by auto) six of his "clients" on a train leading to Auschwitz, and intercepting the train before it reached the border.

One notes the negative contributions of the United States State Department to saving lives through assisting in deviant recertification measures for the victims. The Department even rejected the War Refugee Board's request to transmit a message to certain Latin American governments (through Switzerland as an intermediary) in 1944, imploring them to validate visas presumably fraudulent which were held by Jews then interned in a German camp in Vittel, France. After several internal skirmishes between WRB and the State Department, the message was transmitted, but too much time had been lost: sixty of the interned Jews had already been shipped to Auschwitz.

Explanations of Determinants of American Policy Towards Rescue

All authors agreee on the widespread American opposition to the refugees' influx before the War and the exclusionary function of the quota system which was approved by large majorities of the American public. Wyman stresses that Congress merely reflected public opposition. Xenophobia (often masking blatant anti-Semitism) was first justified by the Depression and decade-long high unemployment, while keeping refugees out later was legitimated during wartime as self-protection against Nazi agents. Although manifest anti-Semitism was usually muted in public halls, it was a widespread and growing phenomenon. Some evidence is presented of a sympathetic reaction among notables, church leaders, and major newspaper editors towards Jews after *Kristallnacht* that might have been successfully exploited but was not. There was a growing negative perception of Jews by the American public during the War. Public opinion polls taken before and during the War testify to the constant willingness of a significant portion of the public to blame the Jews for their troubles. One sign of the low status of Jews was the finding that in 1944 more of those sampled would have excluded Jews from entering the country than would have excluded any other group mentioned by the interviewer, excepting only the Germans and Japanese; these data are summarized by Charles Stember in *Jews in the Mind of America* (New York, Basic Books, 1966).

How did the American Jewish community reflect or attempt to alter this background? Feingold examines the divisions within the wartime American

Jewish community on tactics of appeal and methods of rescue—public boycott or private petition, mass demonstration versus elite representation, Zionism as a goal or as one of a number of means of rescue—which superficially account for that community's inability to present even a single demand with unified backing. Breckinridge Long, the Assistant Secretary of State who created the major procedural barriers for refugees seeking to enter the United States, saw that clearly; Feingold tells us: "Before he surrendered his strategic position in January 1944, he confided in his diary that 'the Jewish organizations are all divided amid controversies . . . there is no cohesion nor any sympathetic collaboration—rather rivalry, jealousy and antagonism . . .' " (quoted in Feingold, p. 15).

Feingold traces the splits in strategy, inititally represented by the division between the American Jewish Committee and the American Jewish Congress, to the cleavage between social classes and ethnic subgroups among Jews: "uptown" and "downtown" Jews who had arrived from different milieus and who had maintained distinctive life-styles and relations to the non-Jewish community which justified different forms of protest. The more assertive leaders, notably Stephen S. Wise, ignored messages received in the thirties from German Jewish spokesmen, testifying to their loyalty to the new regime and rejecting intervention by American Jews; by this means, the German Jewish representatives sought to appease the regime and to refute Nazi propaganda. The rise of anti-Semitism in the United States, as in Germany, caused some American Jews to inhibit the assertion of claims on their own behalf as they internalized hostile images of the stereotyped Jew and sought to disprove them by accomodative behavior.

While the American Jewish Congress sponsored rallies and public protests, the American Jewish Committee opposed these and any open condemnations of German policy, and sought no changes in the limited American quotas on Jewish refugees; nor did it press the Roosevelt administration to condemn discrimination and (by 1935) legal disestablishment of German Jews as citizens. Naomi Cohen, in *Not Free to Desist: The American Jewish Committee, 1906-1966,* attributes the Committee's inaction to its failure to understand the difference between the Nazis and previous persecutors, heeding the advice given by leaders of the German Jewish *Centralverein*—the leading Jewish defense organization of Germany. The American Jewish Committee itself was motivated by fear of provoking reprisals. Frederick Lazin, in a paper on "The Response of the American Jewish Committee to the Crisis of Jews in Germany: A study of Qualified Concern, and Possible Complicity," attributes their failure to respond first to calculation of their own interests: the fear that generating protests publicly would arouse anti-Semitism. They did not see Jews as a collectivity beyond national barriers.

Although most Christian colleagues associated with Committee members in such organizations as the National Conference on Christians and Jews advised against any distinctive protest as Jews for fear of arousing anti-Semitism, a significantly-placed observer, Secretary of the Interior Harold L. Ickes, saw their protective stance itself as arousing contempt. He recalls, in *The Secret Diary of Harold L. Ickes, Vol. II* (New York, Simon and Schuster, 1954), a prewar conversation with Justice Brandeis: "I spoke to him of the cowardice on the part of the rich Jews of America. I said that I would like to get two or three hundred of them together in a room and tell them that they couldn't hope to save their money by meekly accepting whatever humiliations others chose to impose upon them. . . . Justice Brandeis agreed with me completely. He said that there was a certain type of rich Jew who was a coward. According to him, these are German Jews, and he spoke of them with the same contempt that I feel for them."

But middle class and poor Jews did not behave differently; Ickes' and Brandeis' formulation was simplistic. Retrospectively, what alarms us most is not the division among American Jewry but the ineffectuality of its most celebrated militant leaders. Both Feingold's and Morse's stress on tactical differences distinguishing the American Jewish Committee from the American Jewish Congress leads them to overlook the fact that both groups relied primarily on normative appeal. They appealed in the name of (the real, the true) fatherland. Both saw Roosevelt as a patron, a benevolent master who was sometimes misled by underlings, as are all lords of great establishments. Emblematic of this relationship was the characteristic salutation of Rabbi Wise to the President: "Dear Boss" (see Morse, pp. 23–4).

Friedman shows how Wise had suppressed his earlier militant rhetoric, publicly counseling Jewish leaders in 1939 not to support the Wagner Bill; the Bill failed, due not only to the opponents of refugees but to the administration's failure to back it. Professional refugee advocates drawn from the White Anglo-Saxon Protestant community feared that any new proposal not only could not pass Congress but also might provoke Congress to cut down all present immigration quotas; however, this fear negated positive political support for their potential Jewish allies, thereby turning into a self-fulfilling prophecy.

Friedman charges that in 1942, ". . . Wise, . . . not only knew about the death camps in the summer of 1942, five months in advance of the aforementioned petition, but actively collaborated with the [State] department in keeping verified accounts of mass murder from the public" (pp. 139–140). Wise had received the same report through the World Jewish Congress representative in London, Sidney Silverman, M.P., and had contacted Undersecretary of State Sumner Welles about it on August 28, 1942, to confirm it. Wise then assented to Welles' request not to disclose it publicly. Yet, as Yehuda Bauer has noted in an essay, "When Did They Know?", the report essentially was

substantiated by the firsthand accounts of mass extermination in Poland—
collected by the Jewish Socialist Party of Poland (the Bund) and transmitted
by the Polish Government-in-Exile to London—that had been broadcast on
the BBC two months earlier. Friedman presents excerpts from the scathing
indictment of the American Jewish community's leadership during the extermination of European Jews delivered by Chayim Greenberg, editor of the
Jewish Frontier, in February 1943.

If their failure had been a personal failure attributable to character defects,
we might deplore it but fail to learn from it. However, their failure represented
a more general state of American Jewish consciousness. It reflected the status
of emancipated Jews in most western nations who were granted legal equality
as individuals by the French Revolution in exchange for the loss of any
specific identity or rights as a group. Therefore, any loyalty to a collectivity
other than the nation-state was held to be suspect; one must identify as an
American or Frenchman or Italian "of Jewish faith." Thus, American Jews
were motivated to deny particularistic concerns or obligations, especially
when others could interpret claims based on such interests as conflicts of
interest with the nation-state. The appropriate ideology to avoid such conflicts
was the reiterated expression of loyalty and the conformity of group interests
with the national interest. They were true believers (as characterized by Melvin Tumin in 1964) in the "cult of gratitude."

In 1943, a more militant leadership emerged from Palestinian and American Jews affiliated with the revisionist Zionists (*Irgun Zvai Leumi*), which
had achieved some success by public advertisement and secured, Friedman
tells us, endorsements of 33 senators, 109 representatives, 14 governors, and
assorted other notables. They were repudiated as "opportunists" by Wise's
American Jewish Conference. Later, he personally used his influence to
squash their campaign to raise money to ransom Jews in the Rumanian concentration camps of Transnistria by informing the public that the offer was
unconfirmed (untrue) and the cost too high. Wise did not need to grant the
request which cost six months and an additional million Jews' deaths to
confirm the plausibility of "the Final Solution." Bauer concludes that, "it is
somewhat difficult to put all the blame for complacency on British or American statesmen . . . when Jewish leaders made no visible attempt to put pressure on their governments for any active policy of rescue. The Jewish leadership could hardly plead lack of knowledge." Wise was also well aware of the
role he was playing. Friedman notes (p. 146): "He wrote to Felix Frankfurter
on September 16, 1942, 'I don't know whether I am getting to be a *Hofjude*,
[Court Jew], but I find that a good part of my work is to explain to my fellow
Jews why our Government cannot do all the things asked or expected of it.' "
Instead of serving as Jewish representatives to the President, Jewish leaders
had become the President's representatives to the Jews. Wise resolved a

potential role conflict by deflecting Jewish claims to lower pressure on the Administration.

Despite the Jewish voters' solid support of Roosevelt, it was never used as a resource for bargaining. Relevant to this point is data presented by Lawrence Fuchs in his study, *The Political Behavior of American Jews* (Glencoe, The Free Press, 1956). Fuchs cites estimates of the percentage of Jews voting for Roosevelt, showing a continuous increase from 1932 to 1944, when Roosevelt received an estimated 92.8 percent of the Jews' vote. This contrasted with other ethnic groups, in which Democratic majorities declined after peaking in 1936. The lack of correlation between voting Democratic and social class among Jews contradicts the inverse correlation usually found among American voters during this period, lower income strata being more likely to vote Democratic. Furthermore, there is no evidence that Jewish members of Congress, a few of whom held influential committee chairmanships because of their seniority, ever worked together or understood the opposition to rescue. An example of this failure to understand is demonstrated in the autobiography of Representative Emmanuel Celler, *You Never Leave Brooklyn* (New York, John Day, 1953, pp. 89–93), in which Celler recalls how painful it was to explain to a rabbi petitioning him that the Administration had done all it could diplomatically (in October 1942) and was still unable to save the Jews. Celler wrote:

> I believed this. But the rabbi kept interrupting striking his cane on the floor of the office, "If six million cattle had been slaughtered," he cried, "there would have been greater interest. A way would have been found." ... I dreamed about him that night. The old rabbi stood on a rock in the ocean, and hordes of people fought through the water to get to that rock. And the people turned into cattle and back again to the people. I was on shore, held by a rope which somebody was pulling back.

The Jewish community's commitment to Roosevelt had eliminated the possibility of an autonomous leadership electing alternate strategies, either bargaining within or threatening to withdraw from the New Deal coalition. Nor were the possibilities of symbolic or mass civil disobedience even considered, although A. Philip Randolph's threat of a march by Blacks on Washington in 1941 had caused the President to issue a decree against discrimination in employment. Friedman's casual evaluation of the consequences of civil disobedience—had Wise led American Jewry down that road — betrays real ignorance of the uses and limits of nonviolence in general and specific ignorance of the Indian nationalist movement and of A. Philip Randolph's threatened march on Washington. The threat of the latter by a group more subjugated, less integrated, and largely disenfranchised, brought immediate economic benefits to Blacks and served as a precedent for future legislation and for executive orders against discrimination in the armed forces, in employment, and in housing and education.

The American Jewish community was taken in by its own reified image of Roosevelt as a humanitarian; this reification obstructed it from pressing him to act humanely. The community was solidary not in its ability to mobilize members in its own behalf, but only in its dependence on Roosevelt, renewing the client-patron relationship. This pattern may have been the only political option for Jews within a feudal society, but it had now become dysfunctional in coalition politics.

One need not attribute the Jewish response to Roosevelt simply to the unwitting perseverance of an historical pattern of dependency upon patrons. The Jews' image of Roosevelt was intensely positive because he was seen as the enemy of their enemies, who berated him for supposedly identifying with the Jews. This reflects a psychic need (on a group level) to symmetrically "balance" positive and negative sentiments in relations, leading to the truism that 'My enemy's enemies must be my friend.' (see Fritz Heider, "Attitudes and Cognitive Organization," *Journal of Psychology* 21 (1946), pp. 107–112). Anti-Semites, representing both the elite and the masses, castigated Roosevelt publicly and privately and labelled his regime a "Jew Deal." The pejorative epithets thrust on Eleanor and Franklin for their alleged fondness of Jews and Blacks were avidly circulated among the White Anglo-Saxon Protestant (WASP) social elite from which Roosevelt originated (see E. Digby Baltzell, *The Protestant Establishment,* New York, Vintage Books, 1966, pp. 246–249). The State Department was largely staffed by members of this elite and believed to be restricted to them, a belief reinforced no doubt when the American Minister to Lithuania made a public anti-Semitic address in Minneapolis in 1940 (see Feingold, p. 158). Jewish attacks on the State Department provoked increased resistance within the Department to admitting Jewish refugees, rationalized as measures to keep out potential enemy agents. Roosevelt's sensitivity to rejection by the WASP elite may have reinforced his political calculation that it was imprudent to agree to Jewish appeals which aroused Congressional and Departmental opposition.

The President was confronted with a readily resolvable role conflict: on one side was a miniscule but strategically situated ally who escalated rhetoric but never would employ any sanctions, while on the other was a consensus of elite, ideological and interest groups, political managers speaking in the name of the masses — all of whom wanted to check any measures which might open the gates to more refugees. Roosevelt yielded without demurral to the party which threatened sanctions for nonperformance without incurring any costs from failing to satisfy the Jews.

Only when confronted with evidence of the State Department's subversion through suppression of information—as distinguished from its legalistic eva-sion of rescue—by Henry Morgenthau, Jr. in December 1943, did the President withdraw support from the State Department. The Morgenthau memorandum was presented at a time when Jewish protest against Nazi extermination was rising in public arenas, demanding immediate intervention. Given the fact that immigration to the United States was practically closed by 1943, the risks of commitment were much less than they had been in 1938. On the other hand, the risks attached to publicly repudiating rescue by supporting the State Department were higher. Though the calculus of political costs and payoffs had altered by 1943, Roosevelt consistently behaved as a rational political actor, maximizing payoffs and minimizing costs. Given the fundamental dissension between constituencies on ends which the law ought to serve, the least costly mode of resolution is to substitute symbolic reassurance for commitment. (See Murray Edelman, *The Symbolic Uses of Politics,* Urbana, University of Illinois Press, 1967.) Roosevelt achieved this admirably, having discerned how easily the Jews could be satisfied.

Great Britain

A. J. Sherman's *Island Refuge* is the most comprehensive study of the reactions of the British government to the Jewish plight during the War. Sherman utilizes recently opened Foreign Office files which reveal British motives similar to those of the American administration traced by Feingold. But, besides the fear of being held liable for costs, domestic apprehension of job competition with unemployed Britishers and fear that facilitating the exodus of German Jews would encourage Hitler to strip them of capital more rapaciously, there was also the legitimate fear of British diplomats that providing a precedent by accepting expelled German Jews would encourage Poland and Rumania to solve their "Jewish Problem" by expelling their Jews. Nevertheless, the British government, unencumbered by any quota system for immigrants, pursued a more open policy than the United States and accepted the assurances of the Council for German Jewry (representing the organized Jewish community), guaranteeing support for the Jewish refugees they certified. Britain admitted more Jewish refugees from Germany and Austria (proportionate to its population) than did the United States, and reacted to the expanded need for sanctuary after Germany incorporated Austria by admitting Jewish children swiftly. But not until 1938 did the Council for German Jewry ask for a public loan and did the British government assume any costs.

Several ironies emerge from Sherman's documentation:

1. Cabinet members' sensitivity to American criticisms of British unwillingness to open up areas for Jewish emigration in other parts of the commonwealth (the Colonial Office could not overcome the real resistance there);

2. the perception of the governing class that Jewish leaders themselves opposed enlarging Jewish emigration to avoid increased anti-Semitic agitation;

3. the Jewish representatives' unwillingness to move from tactics of appeal relying on their influence among the elite to political threat and alliance, mobilizing the support of the left.

Portents of the destiny of the Jews in Germany and German-occupied Europe increased after the *Anschluss*. An influential delegation of the Council for German Jewry in December 1938 bluntly informed Lord Winterton that ''it was convinced by recent information it had received that Jews remaining in Germany were in immediate peril of physical destruction'' (p. 196). This warning was paralleled by a memorandum from a British Consul in Germany who had informally conversed with a senior member of Hitler's chancellory in 1938 and related that the German official ''had 'made it clear that Germany intended to get rid of her Jews, either by emigration or if necessary by starving or killing them, since she would not risk having such a hostile minority in the country in the event of war.' The official had added that Germany 'intended to expel or kill off the Jews in Poland, Hungary and the Ukraine when she took control of these countries' '' (p. 183).

While Britain eased barriers for Jews fleeing to the United Kingdom, it raised them against Jews fleeing to Palestine. And Palestine was the nation which had absorbed more Jewish refugees between 1933 and 1939 than any other single nation regardless of size. Britain curtailed the legal and tried to suppress the illegal emigration there in order to implement its 1939 White Paper which promised to preserve the existing Arab-Jewish ethnic ratio there and pledged to give self-government to its inhabitants in ten years, maintaining the Arab majority. Britain was also confronted with an accelerated, covert Zionist drive after 1938 to bring in Jewish immigrants illegally. Pressure was put on Balkan governments, especially Rumania, where Jews fleeing from German-occupied territory used to disembark illegally for Palestine, to avert such departures. Leni Yahil informs us of new documents showing the consistency of British attempts to repress such flights. Ruth Kluger, a leading recruiter for the illegal emigration sponsored illicitly by the Haganah known as ''*Aliyah Bet,*'' relates in her memoir (with Peggy Mann), *The Last Escape* (Garden City, Doubleday & Co., Inc., 1973), how this policy affected thousands and led indirectly to the deaths of immigrants forced to depart on unseaworthy ships which Turkey would not let anchor in its harbor, due to British pressures.

Much attention has been devoted to the extent of British recognition of German brutality. Andrew Scharf, in *The British Press and Jews Under Nazi Rule* shows the explicitness and consistency of British coverage of German anti-Jewish measures and their isolation of commitment from acknowledgment, enabling the British press to constantly express censure of anti-Jewish persecution while not relating this to British policy towards taking in refugees and Palestine immigration. However, during the prewar years, Franklin Reid Gannon notes, in *The British Press and Germany 1933-1939* (Oxford, Clarendon Press, 1971, p. 227), it was taken 'for granted that anti-Semitism was intrinsic to Nazism ''and must be accepted as such. As long as the majority of the German people supported Nazism and as long as Nazi anti-Semitism was legislative and non-violent, then Britain had no right or obligation to interfere.'' The goal of European peace through appeasement was widely shared from right to left.

No public protest against German anti-Jewish policies was issued until after the outbreak of the War, when Britain issued a White Paper ''. . . concerning the Treatment of German Nationals in Germany'' (Cmd. 6120). Britishers promptly received news of extermination through their press, the BBC and Polish Government-in-Exile's exposes, beginning in June 1942. By July 14, 1942, they were informed in the press that the Germans had invented a new type of poison gas, Zyklon B.

One might argue that the British policy was a rational one, explicable in terms of the imperial class' interest (well represented in Churchill's Cabinet) in maintaining the Empire: hence, the need to pacify the Arabs to prevent their desertion to the Axis cause and preserve the loyalty of Indian Muslims to prevent their coalition with the Hindu-majority Indian National Congress, in order to maintain a hold over India. However, Reuben Ainsztein, in his article ''The Failure of the West,'' argues that the British policy was explicable in terms of their prewar perception of ''the Jewish problem,'' aggravated by the growth of proto-fascist movements in Britain led by lords and the prewar belief that adopting the demands (made by Poland in 1938 as well as Germany) to expel the Jews was the price of peace. He cites evidence from conversations between Ben-Gurion (head of the Jewish Agency) and Lord Moyne of the British Foreign Office in 1941 that Lord Moyne anticipated there would be at least six million Jews displaced after the War and believed ''that Jews could be resettled in a state in central Europe—maybe East Prussia which the victorious allies could compel Germany to vacate''; however, the British ruling class gradually accepted the fact ''that Germans were solving the Jewish problem for them,'' with the stoicism with which that class accepted the Irish famine of 1848 and Indian famines. This is a provocative hypothesis, but demands proof not yet brought forth.

How was the Government's policy related to British public opinion, party divisions and the role of the British Jewish community? Ernest Hearst examines ''The British and the Slaughter of the Jews.'' Hearst shows there was consistently more positive identification with the Jews among the Labour Party and Liberals, but they were easily deflected by the bureaucratic shuffles of Cabinet and Foreign Office representatives who consistently responded to their inquiries in Parliament by showing why they could not do what they never had any intention of doing. Little public empathy was shown in Britain before the disclosure in 1942 of the extermination of the Jews. Protests and calls for action were mobilized, as dramatic performances, as they were in the United States. Calls for action were usually spearheaded by religious leaders, notably the Archbishops of Canterbury and York and the Roman Catholic Archbishop. Little public leadership was exhibited by the British Jewish community, whose leaders were like those of the American Jewish community, evidently adherents of the "cult of gratitude." When the House of Commons responded by standing up in silence to Anthony Eden's condemnation of the extermination of two million Jews in 1942, Mr. de Rothschild thanked them. When *The Jewish Chronicle* noted with disappointment Eden's failure to offer Jews any sanctuary, it did so "without wishing to appear ungracious."

Unlike the American Administration's response which could be interpreted as an accurate reflection of public opinion, there was no evidence that British response reflected the British public. Hearst found, "There is no evidence to suggest that the abandonment of the doomed was, on the conscious level, motivated by any detectable anti-Semitic bias. On the contrary, contemporary researches record a strong preference for opening the country to the persecuted. A British Institute of Public Opinion Poll [of March 1943] revealed that a vast majority would have supported action to assist refugees. Asked whether 'the British Government should or should not help any refugees who can get away?' no less than 78 percent opted for such help." This is a significant finding, raising additional questions regarding the impact of majorities and minorities on public policy in the democracies.

The Soviet Union

The role of the Soviet Union's activities before its invasion in 1941 and between 1941 and 1945 has seldom been assessed without bias. It is known that the Soviet Union contributed to the rescue of Jews from German domination in three ways, despite the intentions behind these acts which were designed toward other ends.

First, the Soviet Union allowed the entry of some Jews from the portion of Poland and the Baltic states ceded to the Soviet Union by the Molotov-Ribbentrop Pact of 1939, and deported many others without their consent for political reasons before the German invasion. P. Glikson notes that estimates of Jewish deportees and refugees range between 150,000 and 500,000; of these he believes 200,000 to 250,000 were of Polish nationality before the War. Since we have no way of verifying the numbers who died in Stalin's prison and labor camps and those who did not return, a more exact estimate cannot be corroborated. He estimates that the maximum number of Jews returning to Poland after the War, who were repatriated from the Soviet

Union, "did not exceed 175,000." This estimate, of course, does not include Jews returning to that part of Poland incorporated by the Soviet Union or to the Baltic States which were also incorporated.

Secondly, a large number—possibly a majority—of Jewish citizens of the Soviet Union living before the War in territories later occupied by the German invaders were evacuated to the interior due to their occupational and urban distribution. Solomon Schwarz, who tendentiously denies this while citing the evidence for it, concludes in *The Jews in the Soviet Union* that "As a result, the percentage of the evacuated who were Jews seems to be more than proportionate to the number of Jews in the Ukraine's urban, let alone total, population" (p. 227). Reviewing sources on the prewar and postwar population for particular cities and the number German records confirm were killed, also shows that large numbers had escaped. Schwarz and others have held the Soviet Union responsible for the naiveté of the Jewish population in Soviet areas regarding German intentions toward Jews, citing the suppression of news of German treatment of Jews between 1939 and 1941. However, the signs of widespread flight by Jews before the German advance indicate that the selection of those who stayed behind may be partially attributable to such persons' denial of threat but do not indicate that such denial was the universal or majority reaction among Jews.

Thirdly, the Soviet Union's policy towards encouraging partisan activity and its use of Jewish partisans directly affected the survival of able young Jews in the Soviet territory. Zwi Bar-On discussed "The Jews in the Soviet Partisan Movement," analyzing the objective goals of the partisan movement, the functional prerequisites for assuming the partisan's role, and the goals, abilities, and other commitments of Jews apt to volunteer for such units, enabling us to realize there were imminent real conflicts. The partisan had to be mobile in the forest: potential Jewish partisan cadres were torn between their wish to defend their people in the ghetto and desire to fight the Germans which could only be done effectively by leaving the ghetto. The Jewish partisans could not blend into the countryside as could Christians; nor could they leave wives and children behind in good conscience, and some attempted to resolve this by establishing family camps, limiting their flexibility as partisans. To evaluate partisans' policies and behavior towards Jews, Bar-On's discrimination between "anti-Semitism from above" (legitimated or authorized by leadership) and "anti-Semitism from below" is helpful. Although he does not reach a definitive conclusion on the former because of the lack of sufficient evidence at that time, he indicates cause for concluding that *de facto* discrimination was exhibited in the systematic replacement of Jewish commanders — Soviet sources indicate there were ninety-two originally—by non-Jews when the Jewish detachments were integrated into mixed units in 1943; in the demand for exceptional feats of courage to test Jewish recruits before accepting them as partisans; and, in the judgment of conflicts between

Jews and the local population when Jews punished collaborators among them who had helped to kill the Jews. The wide latitude necessarily allowed partisan commanders could mask many instances of hostility despite the absence of anti-Semitism in Soviet ideology of the period, while the close dependence on other partisans (who often did not mask anti-Semitic sentiments) produced many occasions for betrayal. Bar-On concludes that there was general (but not universal) anti-Semitism from below: "It is a proved fact that dozens and perhaps hundreds of Jewish partisans and their families were murdered by non-Jewish partisans, generally by a treacherous bullet in the back, in circumstances that enabled the murderers to deny without difficulty either the deed itself or its deliberate intention. In many cases murder was accompanied by robbery, rape and savage mishandling." Nevertheless, organized killing of Jewish partisans and other Jews in the forest was not authorized by the Soviet movement as it was authorized by the Commander of the Home Army and the right-wing underground defense forces in Poland.

Recently, much more information on Jewish partisans and revolts in ghettos and death camps has become known to the English reader through the publication of Reuben Ainsztein's massive work *Jewish Resistance in Nazi-Occupied Eastern Europe*. Because Ainsztein's primary purpose was to disprove the myth of Jewish nonresistance to their extermination and to Nazi power in general, much space is devoted to documenting that Jews were prominent in the early leadership of the partisan movement and participated disproportionately to their percentage of the population (which can be confirmed for Lithuania only). This is a plausible finding, but Ainsztein's preoccupation deters him from seriously evaluating the questions which preoccupied potential Jewish partisans: Resistance for what? Survival for whom, at what expense? What costs were intrinsic to the partisans' role, and which were incurred because of the disinterest of other partisans in the Jews' survival? There is little systematic evaluation of how the other partisan units helped or hindered the Jews' defense of their family camps in the forest created by the evacuation of women and children from several villages. Nor is there any objective assessment of the magnitude and legitimation of discrimination and exploitation of Jews qua Jews. Ainsztein's qualification of his own observations lamely denies without refuting evidence others have interpreted as indications of popular anti-Semitism. Ainsztein seems determined to "balance" evidence of discrimination and betrayal with evidence of how non-Jewish partisans perceived some Jews' behavior as corroborating accusations and stereotypes against them, without evaluating to what extent the latter was actually a cause of the former or a justification for preexistent attitudes. Perhaps his perverse balancing of claims can be attributed to a need to commemorate the cause for which so many Jewish partisans died. His purpose prevents him from evaluating the ambiguities of Soviet policy and relating these both to the immediate political context of partisan action and to the long term ideological goal of dissolving the Nazi-alleged nexus of "judeo-Bolshevism" in the minds of the subject population of Eastern Europe which was incorporated in the zone of Russian domination. If we asked, "To what extent did the Jews, as compared with other Soviet nationalities, actively participate in defense of the Soviet Union?" and "How did Soviet strategy exploit the extreme situation of Jewish encirclement to recruit candidates for high-risk services when the native population, in many regions, was unwilling to enlist for them?", we would learn more.

Another question not yet addressed is the interest or disinterest of Soviet military strategists in liberating Jews remaining in ghettos in 1944 as a factor in determining their military tactics. This question pertains particularly to Lodz, whose last 60,000 Jews were transported in August 1944, and Budapest, in which tens of thousands of Jews were estimated to have been massacred between the Arrow Cross coup of October 1944 and liberation in January 1945. War Refugee Board records reveal an attempt to deter extermination of Jews in camps and ghettos by direct and indirect warning of the Germans in late 1944 and direct American diplomatic intervention with the Soviet Union to request them to do the same, but do not show that there was a Soviet response.

While there is yet no evidence on the causes of the lack of Soviet interest in rescuing the Jews, the Soviet Union was more willing to identify verbally with the Jews collectively than were Britain and the United States at the beginning of the War. To enlist western sympathies, the Jewish Anti-Fascist Committee was created in Moscow in 1942. That this was simply a rhetorical and opportunistic use of Jews rather than a commitment to recognize their collective identity was shown by the Soviet Union's murder of the first two nominees for leadership of that Committee in December 1941—Victor Ehrlich and Henryk Alter, leaders of the Polish Jewish Socialist Bund, who had proposed sponsorship of the committee by Jews of all the Allied nations and broad representation which would have prevented effective Soviet control. Both S. Redlich and L. Schapiro believe that the Committee had positive functions for Soviet Jewry, increasing their self-consciousness and self-esteem, moving noted Soviet Jews to become concerned with the others, and enabling them to establish contacts with worldwide Jewish organizations. Redlich, in "The Jewish Anti-Fascist Committee in the Soviet Union," shows how the Soviet Union's willingness to identify publicly with Jews was limited to international audiences. The Soviets did not publicly identify the special character of Nazi extermination of the Jews in internal media during the War, and overlooked both the increasing popular manifestations of anti-Semitism during this period and the contributions of Soviet Jews to the war efforts (derogated popularly) in order to reinforce unity based on its ideology of a battle of all Slavs against the Germans. The recruitment patterns of committee members and the reason for their murder and for the imprisonment and liquidation of the committee in

1948 are described by Leonard Schapiro in "The Jewish Anti-Fascist Committee and Phases of Soviet Anti-Semitic Policy during and After World War
II," in *Jews and Non-Jews in Eastern Europe 1918-1945.*

Soviet rejection of particularistic Jewish claims—both as victims and as
citizens—in the name of a universalistic credo functioned as did nationalism
and the "cult of gratitude" in the West to diminish the possibility of Jews
maintaining their collective identity. A more comprehensive analysis of the
Jews' place and identity in the USSR is Y. A. Gilboa's *The Black Years of
Soviet Jewry.* The Soviet strategy was similar to that of the United States and
Britain in its indifference to Jewish survival. Saving the Jewish population
was not a war goal, but saving valuable categories of Soviet citizens was. No
concern was shown for the Jews at any time (to our present knowledge) in war
strategy and tactics. The extent of the verbal commitment of concern for the
Jews depended both upon the cost of the rhetoric and resources committed,
and the symbolic value of identification with the audience addressed. Where
positive identification cost little for the U.S., Britain, or the USSR and was of
potential benefit, it was employed; when it threatened the imperial or domestic order of domination (for Britain or the Soviet Union), it was not employed.

THE NEUTRALS: SPAIN, SWEDEN AND
SWITZERLAND

The neutrality of Spain, Sweden and Switzerland during the Second World
War was a tactical stance. Germany's plans in the event of victory were to
incorporate Sweden and Switzerland into the Third Reich and to overthrow
Franco so that a more pro-German clique could seize power in Spain. No
German pressure was exerted on them to institute anti-Jewish discrimination.
Neutrality was an expedient cover for both sides to protect present needs,
regardless of ideology and sympathies, giving the neutrals wide latitude in the
actions they could take toward Jewish refugees and could initiate diplomatically in capitals where they were represented.

The neutral which most exploited its position to help Jews of other
nationalities was Sweden. Once German intentions to exterminate the Jews
became clear, Swedish officials generally used all diplomatic means available
to help the victims. The Swedish Ambassador to Berlin, acting as a protective
power representing the Netherlands, inquired into the deaths of Dutch Jews at
Mauthausen in 1941, on the same date, requesting to visit the camp. Ironically, this only led the Germans to stop sending out death certificates to the
murdered Jews' relatives. When the Jews of neighboring Norway and Denmark were threatened with deportation in 1942 and 1943 respectively, Sweden guaranteed sanctuary to all Jews who crossed their border and supported

them in Sweden. Hugo Valentin relates these efforts in "Rescue and Relief Activities in Behalf of Jewish Victims of Nazism in Scandinavia." When deportations began in Hungary in 1944, the King of Sweden protested to the Regent of Hungary and employed the prestige of the Swedish government (also a protective power for Hungary abroad) to mask the mission of the Swede, Rauol Wallenberg, acting as an emissary of the War Refugee Board. This is not to say that any Swedish protest employed other than diplomatic means. Although a Swedish diplomat, Baron von Otter, had conversed with SS Lieut. Kurt Gerstein—an anti-Nazi German who had infiltrated the SS and been delegated to deliver the prussic acid used to kill Jews at Auschwitz-Birkenau—in the summer of 1942 and reported his tale to Stockholm, the Swedish government did not release the news. We know, however, that by then the Allies had received similar reports.

Sweden's activity and its motivation has seldom been assessed. Leni Yahil, in "Scandinavian Rescue of Prisoners," suggests that their initiative to protect other Scandinavians later in the War arose "from the desire to lay proper foundations for renewed cooperation after the war." One of the most confused instances of their help is the story of how the Swedish Minister of Foreign Affairs arranged the transfer of 2,700 non-Scandinavian Jews and about 5,000 other prisoners from concentration camps (released after Scandinavian prisoners were transported to Sweden) through the aegis of Dr. Felix Kersten, Himmler's masseur, who acted as an agent of the Swedish Government. Kersten also acted together with Hillel Storch, World Jewish Congress representative, to instigate Himmler to issue an order safeguarding Jews in concentration camps and allowing food and medicine to be imported there. Kersten's role was not represented in the memoir first describing the operation by Count Folke Bernadotte, the Swedish diplomat and Crown Prince, who accompanied the first buses of Scandinavian prisoners as a representative of the Swedish Red Cross. H. R. Trevor-Roper rebuts Bernadotte's account in his memoir *The Curtain Falls,* in Trevor-Roper's introduction to *The Kersten Memoirs 1940–1945,* and in an essay in *Commentary* of April 1975. Yahil relates the 1945 rescue operation to earlier behind-the-scene initiatives of Norwegian and Swedish officials and believes "this controversy has no historical value." Readers enticed by the drama of memoirs should be aware of their perils.

In contrast to Sweden, which accepted Jewish refugees openly and intervened diplomatically with some initiative, Spain tolerated Jewish refugees escaping over the Pyrenees, but intervened only belatedly to save Spanish nationals in Greece and protest deportations in Hungary in 1944 after other nations had done so. Although Jews were interned by the police, as were other foreign nationals who entered illegally without papers, no instances were recorded of their being repatriated to nations under German occupation.

Nehemiah Robinson provides a journalistic account of this period in a pamphlet published in 1953 by the World Jewish Congress, *Spain of Franco and its Policies Towards the Jews.* Spain's record in protecting Jews of Spanish nationality residing in German-occupied states is less straightforward. Haim Avni, summing up the tale of "Spanish Nationals in Greece and Their Fate During the Holocaust," shows how Spain was unwilling to immediately repatriate Greek Jews of Spanish nationality in Salonica in 1943. This led the Germans to intern all of them claiming such protection who were caught in Salonica (and in 1944 in Athens) in the Bergen-Belsen concentration camp. Spain sought guarantees that they could reemigrate from Spain, assurances of their financial support from the American Jewish Joint Distribution Committee, and maintained a numerical ceiling on their influx, forbidding entry until earlier entrants had emigrated. Estimates of the number of Spanish nationals among the Jews of Greece vary from 600 to 750; of these, 38 perished in German camps, according to Avni.

The neutral nation in Europe most hostile to Jewish refugees was the state in a geographic position of the utmost potential usefulness to those fleeing. Alfred Hassler, in *The Lifeboat is Full: Switzerland and the Refugees,* has documented with great clarity the mobilization of the Swiss Government to exclude Jews from 1938 to 1944. This began in 1938 when the Swiss Government categorically insisted that German Jews' passports be distinctively marked, leading to the "J" stamp stigmatizing German Jews at every port of entry. Illegal refugees were ordered expelled without opportunity to appeal after the War began; later they would be refused any opportunity to communicate with anyone on Swiss soil before being literally kicked back over the border. Yet legal refugees still mounted. On August 13, 1942, a month after the beginning of deportation to extermination camps from the Netherlands, Belgium, and France, the Chief of Police "issues orders that all civilian refugees be turned back at the border. These orders are enforced to the letter." Debate in the Swiss Federal Council fortified the Government's position. New interpretations by the police denied Jews admission as political refugees: "'French Jews are to be turned back without exception, since they are in no danger in their own country.'" Barbed wire was erected across the border while government censorship protected Swiss from reports of extermination in the East. This policy was only altered legally in 1944 after German defeat became certain. By November 1944, the same Dr. Rothmund that ordered Jews to be turned back was ordering protests of deportation to German authorities in Berlin. By February 6, 1945, "The Federal Council intercedes with the German government against the mass slaughter of the Jews."

Hassler thoroughly documents the extent of indigenous anti-Semitic sentiment in Switzerland (veiled in the self-justifying metaphor of the lifeboat), political and religious divisions bearing on the question, and how sources of information on extermination were suppressed. The absence of any recorded organized attempt to infiltrate Jewish refugees illegally is notable.

THE AXIS SATELLITES AND PARTNERS—AN INTRODUCTION

Before exploring the determinants of the policy pursued by these states, one must first identify the outcome of their policy on their Jews. This study of national differences in Jewish victimization during the Holocaust sought, as a first step, to refute that one could explain Jewish victimization adequately by the extension of German power alone (accepting their will to exterminate the Jews as a given end). States were differentiated by their degree of German control. The least controlled or most free were those in the colonial zone, whose governments had concluded agreements with Germany or were co-belligerents. These states were governed by the prewar Head of State and retained control of their police and army; although German troops might be stationed there, they were not occupational troops. Jewish victims in the colonial zone ranged from none to 90 percent; the range reflects deportation as an option, commencing only after the states' agreement to deport. Several states never agreed to deport any Jews when they were in this relationship to Germany—neither Finland, Italy nor Denmark—and Bulgaria and Rumania failed to execute commitments they had made to deport their Jews. Similarly, the Vichy regime of France retracted its commitment to extend the deportations. No reprisal was taken against any of these states for its refusal to deport its Jews or failure to fulfill its commitment.

Among German satellites, their allies and Denmark (a virtually self-governing colony of Germany between 1941 and 1943), Jews were a commodity for exchange with the Reich. Satellites' collaboration to deport was positively related to satellite obligations to Germany; the states which had received the most—Croatia and Slovakia, endowed by Hitler with sovereignty—collaborated completely, even agreeing to pay for transport of their Jews. States which received expanded territory—Rumania, Bulgaria and finally Hungary—agreed implicitly to deport all Jews; but Rumania and Bulgaria failed to implement their agreement, Rumania never deporting its established Jewish population (having virtually exterminated its "foreign" Jews itself) and Bulgaria halting after the deportation of Jews from the newly acquired territories. No previously sovereign states in the colonial zone, which had not acquired territory from Germany, agreed to the deportation of their Jews except France. Collaboration was most highly correlated with the development of anti-Semitic movements before 1936 in these states. Almost two million Jews lived in these states in June 1941 or about one out of every three Jews in Axis-dominated Europe outside the Soviet Union. These states created close to 1.17 million Jewish victims: almost one out of three of them was killed in his native land by his own countrymen.

Protests by the leaders of the dominant church preceded each instance in which nations in the colonial zone ceased collaborating and refused to enforce commitments they had already made to deport their Jewish citizens. Cases in this zone, where deportations were not halted before two out of three Jews were deported, are cases in which the dominant church leaders of the state had never made any categorical protest for Jews as Jews within the period in which the majority of Jews were deported. Where there was never an agreement to deport Jews, one usually finds that the dominant church had denounced "racialism" and/or anti-Semitism publicly before the War.

THE ROLE OF THE VATICAN

The demonstrable role of clerical authority in inhibiting Jewish victimizations prompts us to reopen the inquiry into the most significant neutral state in Europe, the Vatican. Was a difference in Jewish victimization in Roman Catholic—as compared to non-Roman Catholic—states attributable to the inaction of the dominant Roman Catholic Churches? Does this difference indicate that if the Pope had employed the sanctions at his command it could have made a substantive difference in lives saved?

The record clearly shows a substantive difference in victimization only among German allies and colonies. The majority of Jews were saved in all non-Roman Catholic states in this zone—Bulgaria, Rumania, Finland and Denmark—but in only two out of five predominantly Roman Catholic states—Italy and France—were the majority saved and these were the two states in which the local church hierarchy, either before or during the War, had condemned the government's anti-Jewish policies. The majority of Jews from Slovakia, Croatia and Hungary were exterminated without any protest from the highest cleric of the Roman Catholic Church in their native land or without sanctions threatened by the Papacy.

No difference was observed in terms of protest (public or private) against deportations between Catholic and non-Catholic churches in the occupied countries of western Europe and Greece—the command zone—and the SS zone of the Reich itself and occupied eastern territories, including what had been Poland, Serbia and the Baltic states. Among the former class of states, all churches protested; in the latter class, no church protested.

The controversy over Pope Pius XII's failure to protest Jewish extermination during World War II or to use any clerical sanctions to deter it, is now chiefly a controversy over motives and strategic (not moral) justifications of his policy. How far his policy was congruent with past Catholic theology or

the Church's history demands a much broader context for evaluation than can
be summarized here. The recent publication of the Vatican's own papers
should advance such research. The major interest here is in showing how the
Catholic Church's policy toward Jewish discrimination, civil disestablishment
and extermination developed between 1933 and 1945.

Guenter Lewy's *The Catholic Church and Nazi Germany* focuses chiefly
on the German Catholic Church's leadership and policy. He shows how the
Concordat of 1933 (so promptly negotiated) helped to legitimate Hitler's
extirpation of the constitutional structure of the Weimar Republic which was
made possible by the Catholic Center Party's members' votes for the Enabling
Act of 1932. Although lay Catholics had previously been warned against
joining the Nazi Party, now the censure was annulled and Bishops and laity
could wholeheartedly identify with the Third Reich. Bishops sang the Horst
Wessel song, eulogizing the flow of Jewish blood. The Church abandoned
attempts to enforce the terms of its agreement and, adapted by successive
retreats, compressed Catholic demands to preserve property and ritual. The
Bishops actively endorsed the German annexation of the Saar, Austria, and
Czechoslovakia. During the War they censured resistance to the state in the
name of religion; similarly, the church never challenged Nazi policy on "the
Jewish Question."

The one occasion when any Bishop publicly criticized the state was in a
public sermon delivered in 1941 by Bishop Galen against the gassing of
German children and older people who had been institutionalized for diverse
causes: Lewy unfortunately calls this "euthanasia," a tasteless misnomer for
the Hitler-authorized executions of "incurables" or "useless eaters." This
"experiment" provided specialists with an opportunity to develop the
technology for the "Final Solution." The Bishop's protest led to an order
curtailing gassing. Instead, the victims were poisoned; however, the program
was not abandoned in response to the public reaction, as Lewy alleges. Hitler's decision to take no action against Bishop Galen because of his popularity is significant, indicating that the potentiality for protest in Germany was
related to the identification with the protester and the object of the protest.
Since Jews were decreed public enemies, one identifying with them risked not
only incarceration in a concentration camp, but lack of public support in
contrast to the public's positive support for Bishop Galen. Though shocked by
the murder of their own relatives—anyone, after all, might have a retarded
child, a tubercular aunt, a schizophrenic cousin, or a mother with
arteriosclerosis—they were indifferent to the disappearance of the Jews.

Saul Friedlander's *Pius XII and the Third Reich: A Documentation* is of
broader scope than Lewy's work, but pertains only to 1939–1945. Friedlander
describes the unfolding of the extermination program and the Pope's response
as an aspect of the Pope's total response to the unfolding of the War and his
perception of Germany as the only defense against the spread of Bolshevism,

his greatest fear. The Pontiff's neutrality was always oriented towards Germany (for which his personal attachment was known), and he could justify to Harold Tittman, the American representative to the Vatican, his failure to condemn German extermination policies by stating that he would have to condemn Soviet policies simultaneously (which, he inferred, the Allies would not care for), thus equating the past massacre of thousands with present genocide of millions. Friedlander concludes with an observation and an anguished question of his own: ''. . . the German documents show . . . Pius XII feared a Bolshevization of Europe more than anything else and hoped, it seems, that Hitler Germany, if it were eventually reconciled with the Western Allies, would become the essential rampart against any advance by the Soviet Union toward the West. . . . How is it conceivable that at the end of 1943 the Pope and the highest dignitaries of the Church were still wishing for victorious resistance by the Nazis in the East and therefore seemingly accepted by implication the maintenance, however temporary, of the entire Nazi extermination machine?'' A letter from Cardinal Tisserant, Dean of the Sacred College of Cardinals in 1965, who in June 1940 had written that ''I have persistently requested the Holy See to issue an encyclical on the duty of the individual to obey the dictates of conscience,'' is printed in the prefatory pages of the book; the letter acknowledges the validity of Friedlander's documentation and implicitly disassociates the Cardinal from the Pope's policy.

Carlo Falconi's *The Silence of Pius XII* is a unique book, integrating evidence of the Pope's knowledge and failure to condemn the extermination of the Jews with his failure to condemn the persecution of Polish clergy and lay Catholics in the Polish territory incorporated in the Reich and his failure to condemn the ''extermination of at least half a million human beings''— Orthodox Serbs—by the professedly Catholic government of Croatia.

Falconi attributes Pius XII's failure to speak out to his fear of Communism, his knowledge of the ''psychological unreadiness of Catholics, especially German Catholics,'' his preoccupation with diplomatic means, his Germanophilia, and ''Most important of all. . . . his preoccupation with guaranteeing the Church's survival all over Europe. . . .'' He stresses that Pius XII's policy was not a break with his predecessor, Pius XI, who said nothing when the first anti-Semitic laws were passed in Germany in 1933, when the Nuremberg racial laws were promulgated in 1935, nor after *Kristallnacht* in 1938. He points out that ''The famous speech about Catholics being the 'spiritual heirs of the Jews,' for instance, was made behind closed doors and went unrecorded by the *Osservatore Romano*.'' The encyclical *Mit Brennender Sorge,* he observes, ''is famous without reason, for far from being an anti-Nazi document (as it is reputed to be) it did not even dare lay at Nazism's door the errors in dogma and morality then spreading throughout Germany . . . The one reproach made . . . was that the Concordat had been violated.'' Falconi, then, implicitly concurs with Friedlander's evaluation that the Pope's response to Nazi Germany was conditioned by his conception of the Church's political interests as a worldwide organization concerned first with perpetuating itself, more possible in totalitarian states of the right than of the left.

THE "NEW" STATES

Croatia

Croatia's independence derived from Hitler's offer of sovereignty (reserving the right to station troops there) in April 1941 to Anton Pavelic, the head of an exclusivist Catholic-Croat terrorist movement established in 1919 and banned in Yugoslavia. Since 1929, this Ustasi movement had been financed in exile by Italy. It was held responsible for the assassination of King Alexander of Yugoslavia in Marseilles in 1934. The offer to Pavelic followed the refusal of Vladko Macek, head of the dominant Croatian Peasant Party, to accept office and autonomy as Hitler's client. Hitler had assented to Croatia's falling within the Italian zone of influence: an Italian Army occupied its coast and enthroned the willing Duke of Spoleto, a member of the Italian royal house, to symbolize the relationship. Pavelic sought greater identification with Germany, even announcing in June 1941 that the Croats were not Slavs but descendents of the Goths, a Germanic people. Croatia, however, was not simply a puppet state, despite the avid relish with which it furthered German goals by slaughtering Jews and Gypsies. Croatia's policy of forced conversion and genocide of the Orthodox Serb minority was not instigated by Germany, and Rich tells us (p. 280) that the German officials there "concerned with the preservation of security and order were dismayed by the effects of these policies. Glaise protested regularly against the ruthless persecution of the Serbs and other minority groups. . . . Hitler, however, not only condoned but actively encouraged the Croatian government's racial policies." Hitler demanded that they respect the treaty of May 1941, guaranteeing non-intervention in Croat internal affairs, despite the urgent military situation threatening the Germans by the growth of guerilla insurgency in Yugoslavia, aggravated by the Ustasi policies.

To understand the genesis of such collective violence, one must understand: (1) how religious, ethnic and regional cleavages fell along the same lines in prewar Yugoslavia (only in existence since 1919) and (2) the prehistory of these peoples. Some basic works include Robert Lee Wolff's *The Balkans in Our Time* (Cambridge, The Cambridge University Press, 1956) and Wayne S. Vucinich's *Contemporary Yugoslavia* (Berkeley, University of California Press, 1969).

The literature of Croatia as an independent state (1941–1945) is sparse as most nationalist Croatian scholars would prefer to forget or deprecate the bloody record of that state, and in postwar Yugoslavia such ethnic nationalisms are officially repressed. Postwar responses to the Tito government's trial of Archbishop Stepinac—the highest Roman Catholic prelate— for his support of the Ustasi state, enabled his sympathizers to exploit the anticommunist antipathy to the regime prevalent in the West and to disregard the substansive evidence against him. Without denying the political functions of the postwar trials, we find that official Yugoslav, Catholic and anti-Catholic historians as well as neutral academics who have used the primary sources, concur on the evidence of state-planned and executed genocide against the Serbian minority which was related to state-initiated and enforced conversions and the role of the Catholic clergy in approving, leading, or tolerating these.

Edmond Paris' *Genocide in Satellite Croatia 1941–1945* most thoroughly describes the process of extermination of Serbs, Jews and Gypsies from boycott and civil discrimination to murder. By June 1941, signs on public establishments read, "No Serbs, Jews, nomads, and dogs allowed." Unlike the Jews, the Serbs were sometimes offered the chance to become acceptable citizens, although the means of salvation offered were sometimes a pretext. They would be locked in Roman Catholic Churches awaiting the priest and the churches set afire, as Jews had been set afire in synagogues in Poland.

The Croats' collective hatred of the Orthodox Serbs was explicit in folk sayings, such as "Serbs to the willows," while their anti-Semitism was less articulated, as Jews had not presented any political challenge to them in prewar Croatia. An excellent analysis of the status and self-identifications of those Jews is Harriet A. P. Friedenrich's "Belgrade, Zagreb, Sarajevo: A Study of Jewish Communities in Yugoslavia Before World War II" (unpublished doctoral dissertation, Columbia University, 1973).

Virtually all Jews who had not fled to the adjacent Italian zone or to the partisans in the mountains were exterminated, leaving few records behind. Some extant records of the Croat Jewish commissars and Jewish communities showing their decimation are reproduced in Charles W. Steckel's *Destruction and Survival* (Los Angeles, Delmar Publ. Co., 1973); these are not properly introduced nor explained, but are themselves fascinating.

The Ustasi regime was legitimated by Archbishop Stepinac's public celebration of Pavelic's return and his continued presence at public ceremonies, acclamation of its spirit by Catholic publications, and the participation of priests in extermination squads, especially of Franciscans. Paris tells us that nearly half of the twenty-two concentration-extermination camps were headed by priests. Carlo Falconi in *The Silence of Pius XII* substantially confirms Paris' indictment, showing the Vatican's indifference; its knowledge of the means taken to propagate the faith did not diminish the price expressed in the new, self-righteously Catholic state. This was exhibited by the honors accorded visiting Ustasi delegations in Rome and towards the state's official representative there. Although the Church within Croatia did attempt to deny the right claimed by the state to determine who might be converted (initially the government proscribed conversion for the Serbian intelligencia in order to liquidate them), never did it protest the terror utilized to induce Serbs to be converted. Falconi does try to convey the Catholic Croat's collective sense of grievance against the Serbs, as a minority upholding the true faith against inducements to assimilate, but himself sometimes confuses charges against the Serbs to justify the Croats' hatred with the causes of that hatred. Both Paris and Falconi cite estimates of 500,000 to 700,000 Serbs murdered.

Further confirmation of the Vatican's knowledge is provided by Branko Bokun's diary *Spy in the Vatican: 1941-1945* (New York, Praeger Publishers, 1973). Bokun was a young official in the Yugoslavian foreign office, delegated by it to go to Rome in August 1941 to appeal to the Vatican to stop the slaughter in Croatia, bringing a portfolio of evidence with him, including a copy of the speech of Mike Budak (the Minister of Religion in Croatia) on July 22, 1941, promising three million bullets for non-Catholics. Bokun was admitted to the office of Mgr. Montini, then a deputy to the Secretariat of State (Pope Paul VI), where he left his portfolio. Shortly thereafter he was told by Montini's secretary that the Croatian Ambassador had "'explained that the atrocities described in your file are the work of the Communists, but maliciously attributed to the Catholics.'" The secretary explained that nothing more could (meaning, would) be done.

Slovakia

To understand how the Slovak Parliament approved the proposed declaration of independence of Slovakia in March 1939, one must understand the century-long history of the Slovak People's Party, the intimate relation between clericalism and Slovak nationalism, and the tensions within that party before Nazi incentives were offered to the party's radical wing to complete the dismemberment of Czechoslovakia. Jozef Lettrich, in his *History of Modern Slovakia*, describes Slovakia's evolution from an unrepresented nationality within the Austro-Hungarian monarchy to a competitive nationality within Czechoslovakia, whose members lacked the education to derive proportional posts in the developing nation and perceived independence as subordination to the Czechs. Their sense of separate identity as a subjected minority was fortified by the religious division and clerical leaders of the Slovak Peoples Party. Nevertheless, the party never obtained more than one out of three Slovak votes before the War and was split factionally between the autonomists (who wished to remain within Czechoslovakia) and separatists, and it is likely that if the German nationalists of the Sudetenland had not split the Czech state in 1938 (confirmed at Munich), the radicals (secretly funded by the Nazis) would have been unable to create the bandwagon effect they did in 1939.

The Jews' status in prewar Slovakia and in the other central European Nazi satellites is concisely summed up in *Jews in the Soviet Satellites,* ed. by Peter Meyer et al. (Syracuse, Syracuse U. Press, 1953). The relationship between anti-Semitism and the nascent ethnic nationalisms in the area is well analyzed in S. Ettinger's essay on "Jews in Eastern and Central Europe between the Wars: An Outline," in *Jews and Non-Jews in Eastern Europe.* Since its origin, Jews in Slovakia had been conceived of as outsiders by the Slovak People's Party; anti-Semitic manifestos and street demonstrations were stirred up by the party in the 1930's. Livia Rotkirchen documents this period in an essay on "Slovakia, 1918–1938."

Deportations began on March 26, 1942, after definition, registration, systematic expropriation, segregating Jews thoroughly and separating families by interning the men in labor camps, stigmatizing them by affixing the yellow star, and establishing a government bureau to superintend a *Judenrat,* which, after the arrest of its first director in April 1941, faithfully executed government orders. By October 1942, two out of every three Slovakian Jews had already been deported. Livia Rotkirchen, in "Vatican Policy and the 'Jewish Problem' in 'Independent Slovakia (1939–1945)," relates the diplomatic efforts by the Vatican in Rome and Bratislava to protect Catholics liable to become victims and to appeal (never to forbid) to the government not to deport Jews, unmasking the meaning of "resettlement." The category of victims was then redefined in May 1942 to exclude individuals born as Jews who had converted to Christianity before 1939. Vatican diplomatic appeals in February and March 1942 were unavailing, as was the appeal by all the rabbis of Slovakia to President Tiso. Neither the Slovak nor the Roman hierarchy which could forbid it had done so. Rotkirchen reports how the Prime Minister (Tuka) replied to the Apostolic Delegate's protest when "'he appealed to the Catholic-Christian conscience' of Tuka . . . that for him there existed a higher authority in this matter, to wit, his confessor. The latter had asked him if he could take upon his conscience the responsibility for the deportation of the Jews as a thing done for the good of his people. When Tuka replied in the affirmative, the confessor, he said, had not opposed the actions involved." Nevertheless, continued diplomatic protests impelled Tuka to seek German reassurances on the fate of the deported Jews in 1942 to exculpate himself. This led the RHSA deputy in Bratislava, Wisliceny, to telegraph his superior in Berlin, Eichmann, relaying President Tiso's request to send a delegation to inspect the Slovakian Jews who had been resettled. Eichmann naturally refused. Repetition of such inquiry led the German Foreign Minister to instruct his minister in Slovakia to put no "official" pressure on the government to begin further deportations in July 1943. Deportations were not resumed until after the repression of the Slovak uprising in September 1944, in which Jews had heavily participated.

The most complete description of the demise of Slovakian Jewry is Livia Rotkirchen's *The Destruction of Slovak Jewry*. While the text is in Hebrew, there is a lengthy English summary and listing of documents reproduced (in Hebrew translation), indicating the range of sources explored. Her analysis may be faulted for not distinguishing between the actors' perceptions of causes and the causes of events themselves, including the causes of their perceptions. Rotkirchen uncritically accepts the belief of the Jewish leaders working together behind the scenes of the Jewish Council in late 1942—''The Working Group''—that their payments to SS Captain Wisliceny induced him to halve the extermination, not clarifying the pressures on the Slovakian government itself which caused them to demand German reassurances. Neither does Wisliceny's testimony at Nuremberg corroborate this. This appears to be another example of the SS' confidence game, also prevalent in Poland; it reassured the Jews because a bribe implies one can control the payee's behavior, assuming a state of mutual trust. Since the Working Group's leaders were used by Wisliceny to spread the illusion that the Jews of Europe could be saved by a greater ransom—the Europa Plan—this message was conveyed to Hungarian Jewish leaders—both conventional congregational spokesmen and Zionist—and must be taken into account (see the discussion on Hungary) in understanding their response.

EUROPEAN STATES EXISTENT BEFORE 1939 ALLIED WITH GERMANY

Bulgaria

Bulgaria had become progressively more dependent upon Germany during the 1930's and benefitted from Germany's adjudication of Balkan borders by acquiring territory from Rumania, Greece and Yugoslavia, fulfilling old claims to Macedonia. The prewar Bulgarian state was authoritarian, with a frequently disrupted tradition of party competition. By 1940, the Head of State, King Boris, led the governing faction, relying on manipulated elections to the *Sobranje* (Parliament) for a pretense of consent. However, excepting a significant Community Party, driven underground during the War, the state was stable; there were no popular radical right fascist movements waiting in the wings as in Rumania and Hungary or popular fascist contenders for power.

The government acceded on March 1941 to the stationing of 600,000 German troops in Bulgaria, but these had no occupational duties nor did they claim such rights. Although Bulgaria did make the gesture of declaring war against Britain and the U.S., no pressure was put upon her to join the war against the Soviet Union nor to sever diplomatic relationships.

Despite its commitment to Germany and its intended collaboration, Bulgaria deported no Jews from its prewar state. The causes of Bulgaria's policy have aroused much postwar discussion, but no analysis of why collaboration was stopped is possible without examining how it was stopped. The only scholarly exposition of the Bulgarian story is Frederick B. Chary's *The Bulgarian Jews and the Final Solution 1940–1944*, which we will draw upon to examine the critical interplay of collaboration and resistance. The government showed its respect for Germany by pushing through the *Sobranje* anti-Semitic legislation in January 1941, known as "the Law for the Defense of the Nation." This law defined Jews on racial grounds, registered them, stripped them of positions and rights, expropriated their property and allowed for suspension of free travel, residential control, and their future segregation. Members of the prewar anti-Semitic movements were appointed to key administrative posts; the Minister of the Interior (Gabrovski) and, later, the Commissar of Jewish Affairs (Belev) were members of the proto-Nazi Ratnitsi. Opposition to the law was widespread, including that of the Bulgarian Orthodox Church and professional associations of lawyers, writers, and doctors. Execution was lax. In August 1942, the law was amended to compel unemployed Jews in the capitol (Sofia) to leave on September 1, to seize Jews' private property, and to distribute identity cards to them. Simultaneously, wearing the Jewish star (earlier compulsory only for Jews drafted into labor brigades) became required of all Jews. But the decree could not be enforced. Metropolitan Stefan of Sofia protested against it publicly; to be sure, his concern was also directed to freeing Christians of Jewish birth from such a stigma. German diplomats complained that Jews would not wear the stars and the population supported them. Finally, by October 1942, the Bulgarian Government stopped producing stars, claiming that they had run out of electricity. German intelligence officials anticipated that the Bulgarians would not go any further.

To conclude an agenda to deport the Jews, the agreement was made but not publicized (to diminish visibility) and first directed against Jews to whom the Bulgarian leaders had no ties (the Jews from the newly-acquired territories) in order to deter opposition. This was done by asking the *Sobranje* (generally a Government rubber-stamp) to delegate the execution of the Law for the Defense of the Nation to the Cabinet (June 1942) which directly supervised the existing Jewish consistories in each community by its representatives. The Commissariat staff rose rapidly from thirteen in October 1942 to 160 in January 1943. The Commissariat arranged the agreement with the Reich Security Main Office representatives in February 1943, and it was approved by the Cabinet in March 1943, legally authorizing the deportation of up to

20,000 Jews "inhabiting the recently liberated territories." The Commissar knew well from his own census that there were under 12,000 Jews in these territories, meaning that 8,000 would have to be selected from Old Bulgaria, almost one out of six Bulgarian Jews. The decree was never published in the official gazette, testifying to high-level complicity in diminishing the deportations' visibility. The Commissariat contacted the civil and military rulers of the new territories (all from old Bulgaria) to notify them and make arrangements for the Jews' impending arrest by army and local police troops who cordonned off the towns' Jewish quarters on the dawn of the specified days.

While the arrests in Thrace and Macedonia were carried out without any prior awareness by the Jews, Bulgarians employed in the Commissariat and local officials who had been notified of the Commissariat's plans informed Jews in Sofia and Kiustendil as to the impending arrests of Jews in Old Bulgaria. Several Jews in Kiustendil got to Sofia despite travel restrictions and petitioned the Vice-President of the *Sobranje, D.* Peshev, as well as other notables to avert the deportations. Peshev demanded that the Minister of the Interior call off the deportations; after assessing the opposition, he called the Prime Minister who agreed to their postponement five hours before arrests were scheduled. Peshev raised a motion of protest and was joined by forty-two other members among the 160 delegates to the *Sobranje.* Metropolitan Stefan and the Bishop of Plovdiv protested most categorically, threatening to withdraw their loyalty from the King. Some diplomatic representatives also protested. Bulgarian leaders of democratic parties in exile and the underground Communist Party, broadcast protests against the anti-Jewish measures, urging noncooperation. Threats of later deportation in Sofia aroused a Jewish street demonstration, led by a rather unorthodox rabbi, Daniel Tsion, with many Bulgarian friends. The King staved off other German requests by telling the German Foreign Minister, Ribbentrop, that the Jews were needed for road construction, and he expelled the Jews from Sofia in May 1943 to rural towns. The German Foreign Office acknowledged its defeat as it had no means to force Bulgaria to deport its Jews in 1943.

What accounts for Boris' decision? His reputation has been enhanced by his subsequent sudden death, attributed by the western press to the Germans, although there is no evidence to support this. Chary reviews the role of King Boris, arguing against the popular legend that he saved the Jews. He concludes that the King's response at all times was a function of pressures put upon him. His reversal, Chary insists, was not attributable to popular attitudes alone, but "The relative lack of anti-Semitism among the Bulgarian peasants and the active objections from large segments of Bulgarian ruling society contributed to the prevention of deportations. The tolerant atmosphere was not unique to Bulgaria, nor by itself was it decisive. *Only through the channeling of popular discontent into political pressure could the political change required to eliminate deportations* occur." [my italics] Chary later reiterates how it was not opposition against the government which sought to undermine it (such as the Communist-dominated Fatherland Front) but opposition within the government that was most influential. The consistent opposition of church, elites and leaders of the democratic parties indicated that the government had no grounds on which to legitimate deporting the Jews and, thus had sought to diminish the visibility of deportations to impede the mobilization of resistance. Nissan Oren, an authority on the Bulgarian Communist Party of this period, reviews the question of "The Bulgarian Exception: A Reassessment of the Salvation of the Jewish Community," and reaches a similar conclusion. Despite some factual errors, this is a thoughtful essay. The *Annual* of the Social, Cultural and Educational Association of the Jews in the People's Republic of Bulgaria has published many documents in recent years aiming to demonstrate the Communist Party's leadership in defending the Jews and to show how widespread popular opposition was. These translated documents are fascinating in themselves. The authors sometimes show that they do not take their avowed theses as the explanation. The present Bulgarian Government's pride in its role seems consistent with the prewar repudiation by the Bulgarian intelligentsia of anti-Semitism and the past history of its Communist Party.

Finland

It is scarcely remembered that Finland was a Germany ally which never agreed to the deportation of her Jews, showing how nonoccurrences of the greatest significance tend to be overlooked. Scarcely any Finnish sources exist on this question, and there is no evidence of it being in controversy between Finnish parties, despite the presence of anti-Semitism among the prewar tenets of the extreme right—embodied in the Lapua movement, which staged an aborted uprising in 1931.

Finland became an ally of Germany against the Soviet Union in June 1941 to regain the land it had lost in the 1939–40 war against Russia precipitated by Soviet demands. No pressure was put upon Finland to deport its 2,000 Jews until Himmler's visit there in July 1942. Our knowledge of what occurred then is based on the *Memoirs of Dr. Felix Kersten,* Himmler's masseur, who acted to undermine his client's mission by offering his services as a translator. The Finnish Minister of Foreign Affairs, Witting, secretly informed by Kersten of Himmler's request, dissimulated with Himmler, pretending to agree to the request, but delayed action by stressing the need for Parliament to authorize such deportation at its meeting in November 1942. After November, Dr. Kersten told Himmler that because of the war situation such a subject was too delicate to raise.

We do know that some fifty Jewish refugees, purportedly accused of crimes, were being prepared for deportation by a Finnish police official, Arno

Anthoni, apparently acting in complicity with the Gestapo. Leonard Lundin reviews accounts of this incident in his *Finland During the Second World War* (Bloomington, U. of Indiana Press, 1957). We know from Finnish documentary sources, reviewed by Jaako Lintinen in the Finnish journal *Uvsi Maailma* on April 10 and October 23, 1964, that their resistance limited the victims to eight persons—five deportees and three relatives who accompanied them.

Italy

Italian policy toward Jews during the era of fascism (1922–1943) refutes the facile generalization that anti-Semitism is inextricably intertwined with fascism. Yet, the causes of Mussolini's turning from a pre-1939 philo-Semitic public policy to an anti-Semitic policy in 1938 with codified racial legislation and racist ideology, have been disputed. However, all reports of historians of Italy and observers during this period describe popular antagonism towards the racial laws, from the underground on the left to ardent pro-fascist prelates on the right.

Between 1938 and 1943, the Jews were disestablished and ejected from their well-integrated positions in Italian life: from public offices, the Army, the universities, managerial positions, and the Fascist Party. Jews were stripped of real estate and large firms. Segregation laws banned intermarriage with and domestic employment of non-Jews. Jewish refugees, welcomed into Italy from the Reich before the War, were interned in camps in the countryside; and some Jews were drafted into labor brigades in Rome, Bologna, Milan and Tripoli. However, the great majority of Jews were still free. No attempt was made to stigmatize them by the star nor to concentrate them into ghettos. Many could escape discrimination by securing exemption as a member of categories favored by the law—early fascists, war veterans and their families — these composed nine percent of all those defined as full Jews in 1938. An additional fifteen percent converted. Thus, the number of Jews estimated to be in Italy on September 8, 1943, was eighty percent of the number in 1938: the number (exceeding those removed from the rolls) is explained by the excess of refugees over emigres. German records show that Italian occupying forces generally prevented enforcement of racial legislation in the territories they occupied in France, Greece and Croatia (the record is more mixed in Croatia), physically interposing themselves against Vichy police in France and turning their territory into a haven for Jews. Arrangements for the exodus of those Jews to a safe haven in allied North Africa (initiated with the post-Mussolini Italian Government by Father Benoit and Angelo Donati) were impossible to execute because of (1) delay in securing approval from the U.S. and Britain and (2) General Eisenhower's premature announcement of Italy's joining the Allies. This news precipitated an immediate German invasion of Italian-occupied France and northern Italy.

The German invasion of Italy was followed by no immediate change in the Jews' status, leading many to deny their fears and to take no precaution to hide. Nor did the official community leaders lead or warn them, denying rumors of impending deportations. Many were reassured by SS Lieutenant Kappler's demand in Rome from the leaders of the Jewish community of fifty kilograms of gold, believing that the Germans would leave them alone once this ransom was paid. Commanded by General Stahel who did not trust Italian police, German police began rounding up Roman Jews at dawn on October 16, 1943. One out of every ten Jews was seized. The German Bishop signed a note to Stahel, warning that if the raids continued, the Pope might feel compelled to protest. But the raid was over—the Jews disappeared, and the Pope did not protest. The citizenship of Jews in occupied Italy was formally annulled by the puppet Republic of Salo—headed by Mussolini who had been captured by the Germans. Several other German military raids were staged in Italian cities. The German seizure of Jews was facilitated by the Italian records of their racial registration maintained by the Office of Race and Demography. The occupied Italian government's radio announced on November 30, 1944, that all Jews would subsequently be interned in Italy in concentration camps (allowing many exemptions). The record of Italian police cooperation in raids in other northern cities is mixed; records of the trial of F. Bosshamer, the Reich Security Main Office representative dispatched to Italy in 1944, show some belated cooperation and much unorganized noncooperation. Bosshamer arranged for surprise camp take-overs by German police, sending those Jews to Auschwitz. The Jewish refugees' relief agency of Belasem in Rome was taken over by Father Benoit, a French priest who had helped Jews evade deportation in southern France, had fled to Italy after the Gestapo sought him, and he provided false papers for foreign Jews. Informal networks to help Jews in hiding developed in other cities, some based on Protestant clergy and others on Catholic cadres. Much unorganized noncooperation was evidently shown. Many Jews were active in the partisans, involved in liberating or holding territory, and we have memoirs of how some of them warned other Jews of impending raids when they could. By liberation, one out of five Italian Jews had been either deported or massacred in reprisals for partisan activity in Italy or simply murdered there.

The most comprehensive source on the evolving status of Italian Jews under fascism is Renzo de Felice's *Storia degli ebrei italiani sotto il fascismo* (Torino, G. Einaudo, 1972). De Felice's findings are succinctly summarized in English by Michael A. Ledeen in "Italian Jews and Fascism." Meier Michaelis, in "The Attitude of the Fascist Regime to the Jew in Italy," explains Mussolini's shift to racialism as not inconsistent with his earlier pro-Zionist declarations, showing how the usual stereotypes of Jewish power and the belief in an international Jewish conspiracy had conditioned his perception of Jews' strategic importance. While such perceptions first motivated him to adapt policies favorable toward Jews—initially denouncing Germany's racial policy—he adapted a discriminatory policy later after the alliance with Germany was concluded not because of German pressure (as is often alleged without evidence) but because he was convinced that "international Jewry" was, of necessity, opposed to Germany and, therefore, could not be an ally of Germany's partner. Michael A. Ledeen expanded a similar explanation in "The Evolution of Italian Fascist Antisemitism," also stressing Mussolini's aspiration to transform the Italians into a new breed. Although racism was first introduced in 1936 into Italian legislation to prevent intermarriage with Black Africans (an unlikely possibility before Italy's invasion of Ethiopia), Jews were not discriminated against until 1938; and all evidence shows Mussolini never believed Jews (or Italians) were a distinct race—he always propagated racist ideology cynically. What really instigated Mussolini's ire against the Jews was the failure of Italian Zionists whom he had dispatched to London and Paris to get the sanctions against Italy (for the Ethiopian aggression) lifted. Ledeen observes that ". . . instead of drawing the reasonable conclusion that Zionists had little power over the decisions of the nations of the world, Mussolini felt that he had been betrayed by his allies, and that the international Jewish organization had turned on him." However, his suspicion of Zionism and "international Jewry" had been expressed earlier; the Jews were suspect as were all independent and international associations not enclosed by the fascist state. Periodic waves of accusation by the press appeared, such as the stress on the Jewish origin of the accused in the famed 1934 trial of anti-fascists. Discrimination against one category of Italians is seen by Michaelis and Ledeen as a warning to all Italians of what could happen to those who did not fit in: Ledeen remarks that "it was quite clear that Jews, or at least a high proportion of Jews, did not belong to the new breed."

Daniel Carpi relates, in "The Catholic Church and Italian Jewry Under the Fascists," how the Catholic Church in the latter half of the nineteenth century, adapted a tradition of religious anti-Semitism to the modern political struggle against the liberal democratic state. Under Mussolini's reign, the Church waged an aggressive struggle against Zionism, and emphasized "The Jewish Danger" in an official organ. The Church drew back only from the implications of Nazism (after the Concordat was concluded), as "With great reluctance, with hesitation and innumerable reservations, the Church was thus forced to see Nazism as a hostile and atheistic movement, even though the Nazis ranked only second in the scale of enemies of the Church, after the 'Communists-Jews-Freemasons' and their ilk."

For these reasons, Pope Pius XI denounced "'the myth of blood and race,'" and turned against the Church's alliance with fascism before his death, according to Carpi who is convinced that "after the death of Pius XI and with the accession of Cardinal Paccelli to the Holy Throne, Catholic anti-Semitism became stronger once again and increased steadily both in Italy and outside it." Clerical anti-Semitism was used as a justification for a fascist ideology in the newspaper *Il Regime Fasciste*. However, Carpi tells us ". . . it was soon known that their author, who appeared as a Fascist defending the Government's anti-Semitic policy, was a member of the clergy!"

Daniel A. Binchy, in *Church and State in Fascist Italy* (London, Oxford University Press, 1970), observes in his introduction to the republication of his 1939 manuscript how the opposition to the racial laws was more typical of the lower than of the higher clergy, thus running counter to the hierarchical pattern of church authority and control.

Documentation of the role of Italian troops and the Foreign Office in thwarting deportation in France, Greece, and Croatia is compiled in Leon Poliakov's and Jacques Sabille's *Jews Under the Italian Occupation* (Paris, Editions du Centre, 1955). Readers should also see contrary evidence of limited collaboration in and general toleration of Ustasi concentration camps in Croatia in Charles Stekel's *Destruction and Survival* (pp. 21–22) and the report by the Federation of Jewish Communities of Yugoslavia, *The Crimes of the Fascist Occupants and their Collaborators Against Jews in Yugoslavia* (Belgrade, 1957) [in Serbo-Croat, with an English summary].

The German occupation of Rome by strategically drawing a dragnet around the Jewish community in 1943 is contrasted with the lack of agreement and strategy among Jewish leaders in Rome by Robert Katz in *Black Sabbath*. This led to the Jews' failure to disseminate warnings of impending raids generated by German diplomats; Albrecht von Kessel, in "The Pope and the Jews," in *The Storm Over the Deputy* ed. by Eric Bentley (New York, Grove Press, 1964), confirms that such warnings were planted. Recriminations still fester over the responsibility of either the head of the Jewish community, Ugo Foa, or the ex-Rabbi of Rome, Eugenio Zolli. Zolli presents his effort to warn Jews in *Before the Dawn* (New York, Sheed and Ward, 1954), a confessional autobiography—significantly published only in English — intended to justify his conversion to Catholicism. Clarifying the dispute has probably been impeded by the acrimony over Zolli's apostasy after he was asked to resign as Chief Rabbi of Rome.

Katz holds the community leaders responsible for the vulnerability of the poorer Jews of Rome (living in the old Jewish quarter) for seizure because the leaders did not warn them, and the poorer Jews lacked contact with the more affluent Jews more likely to have fled the city. However, he presents no evidence on the number of Jews seized from such a residential district. He also indicts the Jewish leadership for espousing fascism and for failing to distinguish the moral responsibility for legitimating oppression from the guilt of initiating oppression.

Sam Waagenaar's *The Pope's Jews* (La Salle, Ill., A Library Press Book, 1974) presents some new evidence (in Chapters 38–41) on the extent of the Church's postwar posture of exaggerating its role in helping Jews evade capture. Otherwise, Waagenaar generally recapitulates what was known before, based primarily upon Italian sources and without systematically using German sources.

Considering the widespread public participation in strikes and anti-Fascist actions in Italy during late 1943 to 1945, it does not seem implausible that had the Pope publicly declared that trains carrying Jews were carrying them to their death and publicly urged noncooperation in their delivery, he could have instigated a railroad strike. The existence of sufficient evidence of internal German resistance within the Army and the SS to seizing Jews, leads us to suspect that a strike would have been welcomed by some, enabling them to carry out their orders without carrying out the objective. But if the Pope was intensely preoccupied during this period with the potentiality for Italian Bolshevism (perceived by him in popular demonstrations, strikes, and organized mass opposition to authority), as Friedlander has shown he was, how could he encourage mass disobedience? Would not workers who paralyzed the country one day to save the Jews paralyze it another day to bring down the order of domination?

Hungary

Hungary, as an Axis ally, was a completely autonomous, self-governing country until its invasion by Germany in March 1944. The government's commitment to Germany was based on a calculation of benefits received or expected from Germany, costs extracted for these benefits, and threats anticipated from Rumania, Germany, the United States and Britain and the Soviet Union. Hungary had received portions of Rumania, Czechoslovakia and Yugoslavia, much of which had been previously taken away from Hungary by the Trianon Treaty ending World War I which the party in power had never accepted. Between 1941 and 1944, policy zigzagged between what Hilberg refers to as ministries of "pro-German" politicians and "reluctant collaborators" (p. 511). The last of the latter before the German invasion was Nicholas Kallay (March 1942–March 1944), who describes in his memoirs, *Hungarian Premier* (New York, Columbia University Press, 1954), how he effectively masked his goal of protecting the Jews both from deportation and domestic discrimination by anti-Semitic rhetoric.

The government's allegiance to Germany was strained by the fatal Russian campaign of the winter of 1942–43 which decimated the Hungarian Second Army (cavalierly exploited by the Germans to cover their own retreat) and by the fear of Anglo-American arbiters determining the lines of central Europe between Hungary, Rumania and Yugoslavia in the postwar world: most feared was the Soviet Union's potential influence. Tentative advances made in the negotiations with the Western Allies in 1942 and 1943 were rapidly relayed to the Germans through their Hungarian allies in Parliament and the Army. The

Soviet advances and the Hungarian threat to "jump out," cutting off supply lines to Rumania, instigated Hitler to order the occupation of Hungary on March 19, 1944.

Before one can understand the responsibility for the subsequent annihilation of Hungarian Jewry, one has to understand: (1) the existent Hungarian political divisions, (2) commitments of both the elite and the Army leadership, and (3) how anti-Semitism symbolized the latent polarization of loyalties.

Prior to March 1944, the Regent had rejected requests emanating from the German Foreign Office to deport the Jews, despite the ruling party's official commitment to anti-Semitism and the rapid steady disintegration of the Jews' status in Hungarian life since 1938. The Regent—Admiral Horthy—represented the Magyar gentry or landed classes (known as "The Magyar Nation") which had, until then, coexisted in a tolerant symbiosis with the Jews who had originally filled the role of the absent bourgeoisie in Hungary. The Communist regime of Bela Kun in 1919 posed a direct threat to the Magyar gentry of losing control. Opponents of the revolution were divided into two camps: the Vienna group, headed by Count Stephen Bethlen, of traditional, authoritarian beliefs, and the Szeged group, identified with Gyula Gombos (Premier from 1932 to 1936), a radical rightist movement espousing national socialism. The latter exploited the visibility of a disproportionate number of Jews (or converts of Jewish origin) in the revolutionary regime's leadership to raise the rallying cry of a new counterrevolutionary ideology, the Szeged Idea, despite their awareness of how unrepresentative those Jews were of the political interests and identification of the majority of Hungary's Jews. Both groups were responsible for the White Terror, implemented throughout the country by the officer corps and secret nationalist societies, such as the Association of Awakening Hungarians and the Association of Hungarian National Defense (M.O.V.E.), headed by Gombos.

The government began stripping Jews of civil equality twenty-four years before the German invasion with the passage of the first *numerus clausus* act in 1920, limiting the entry of Jewish university students. Jews were further excluded from posts attained in the official bureaucracies, police, and schools between 1920 and 1938, but the first comprehensive racial code defining Jews by racial ancestry was passed in 1938. Further discriminatory legislation expropriating Jews was passed in 1942, but it affected only Jewish landowners.

Although Hungarian Jews in 1944 were still unsegregated, in 1941 the police agency expelled about 15,000 to 20,000 non-Hungarian born Jews from Transylvania (Hungary's easternmost part, yielded to Rumania in 1919 and reannexed in 1940). These people were driven across the border to Poland where they were massacred. News of general extermination came with the return of some escapees of this group and from Polish Jews fleeing into Hungary. The intentions of the generals were clear: General Heszlenyi had requested German aid on July 21, 1942, to deport "about 100,000" Jews who had entered Hungary illegally (a significantly larger estimate than others). Eichmann then refused, anticipating that he would be able to catch all the Jews of Hungary in his net if he waited.

Jews, except for men up to the age of forty-eight who served in labor brigades as a compulsory alternative to military service in Hungary, were nominally free until 1944. Because of the imposed punitive conditions and occasional torture of their commanders, they incurred a high risk of death. Testimonies tell of commanders sending men out in wintertime clad in summer clothing, employing Jews as human minesweepers, and shooting and torture parties against Jews. The Army was responsible for the 24,456 Jews officially reported as killed, wounded, or missing of the 37,200 sent to Russia in 1941, and for the massacre of about 3,300 Serbs and Jews in the Ujvidek area (formerly Yugoslavia) in 1941.

The swing towards the radical right was a popular movement: Nagy-Talavera, evaluating the popular vote in 1939, estimates that acknowledged native fascist parties won forty-five percent of the total votes cast and in the industrial zone of Budapest, formerly called the "Red Belt," they took 41.7 percent, emerging as the strongest single party; they consistently gained as the Social Democrats' vote diminished. The Army, whose officer class was often active in radical right movements and frequently of Swabian (ethnic German) origin, was an unreliable instrument of the Regent, and of dubious loyalty. The Social Democrats, Workers Party (Communist), Smallholders and the Peasants Party alone defended the civil equality of the Jews, but their constituency was dwindling. Both the dominant Roman-Catholic Church and the Lutheran Church had approved the 1938 Jew Law, seeking only to exempt converted Jews from its coverage (see Nagy-Talavera, pp. 152–153).

Only against this background, may one understand the consequences of the German invasion of March 19, 1944, authorized by Hitler to ward off Hungary's defection from the Axis alliance. Under pressure to appoint a pro-German cabinet, the Regent agreed not to resist the entry of German soldiers and to supply 100,000 Jews for labor in German aircraft factories. The Hungarian Under-Secretaries for Jewish Affairs, Laszlo Endre and Laszlo Baky, *requested* the deportation of the Jews, and the Council of Ministers approved the request to Germany on April 20, 1944. Eichmann recalls this period in a 1960 interview given to a journalist in Argentina before his capture: "It was clear to me that I, as a German, could not demand the Jews from the Hungarians. We had had too much trouble with that in Denmark. So I left the entire matter to the Hungarian authorities. Dr. Endre, who became one of the best friends I have had in my life, put out the necessary regulations, and Baky and his Hungarian gendarmerie carried them out. Once these two secretaries gave their orders, the Ministry of the Interior had to sign them." (see interview article with Eichmann in *Life*, November 28, 1960, p. 110.) Without the Hungarian gendarmerie of 20,000 men, German Ambassador Veesenmeyer testified after the War, the deportations would not have been possible. Eichmann's force in Hungary consisted of only eight SS officers and forty enlisted men. In Veesenmeyer's words (cited in Nagy-Talavera, p. 243, from testimony at Nuremberg):

> If the Hungarians had refused the German demands regarding the Jews with an iron consistence, there was nothing the Germans could have done about it on their own. There would have been pressure, but 1944 was already a 'crisis year' — there would have been no way to mark, concentrate and deport a million people. Such a task is a police task of tremendous nature, the accomplishment of which in three months was made possible only through the enthusiastic help of the Hungarian police and authorities. There was no way to bring help for this task from the outside—such a task could be carried out only by those who knew the land and the people. Eichmann had only a small staff. Such speed and smooth work was only possible with the full help of the Hungarian government.

Between May 15 and July 9, 1944, 437,402 Jews were deported from Hungary. In no other nation were so many so quickly consumed by the death machine. The Budapest Jewish Council was devoted to assuaging Eichmann's incessant demands for goods and to implementing German orders to segregate Jews. The energies of the leaders of the Budapest refugee-aid committee—Rudolph Kastner and Joel Brand — were channeled into negotiations proposed by the SS, who initially demanded 10,000 trucks from the allies for the German war effort (which, they were assured, would only be used on the eastern front) in exchange for 1,000,000 Jews. Joel Brand was sent to Istanbul on May 17, 1944 (accompanied by a Gestapo double-agent), to make contact with the Jewish Agency and the Allies. These negotiations masked Himmler's bid for a separate peace with the West, and the Jews selected were voluntary and/or involuntary agents of the SS Reichsfuhrer. Adolf Eichmann, Chief of the Reich Security Main Office team in Hungary, pledged these leaders to secrecy during Brand's mission, while deportation trains were rolling daily to Auschwitz. The Allies responded negatively to the Gestapo agents' request for war material to be used against their ally. Brand, instead of returning to Hungary as he had promised Eichmann, went on to Syria—despite advice that he would be arrested there, and was. Kastner, however, reestablished SS ties and was allowed to select about 1,700 Jews from the ranks of deportees. This choice of beneficiaries (some of whom bought their place on the train) and the undisputed failure of the committee's leadership either to arouse Jewish and other domestic resistance to the isolation of the Jews or to incite protest among the foreign emissaries and observers in Budapest, were part of the grounds for postwar charges of collaboration against him. Kastner, by then an Israeli government official, was pressed by higher officials to exonerate himself. The government, on his behalf, brought a suit for libel in the Jerusalem District

Court against Malkiel Gruenwald, who (in a political newsletter) had accused Kastner of collaboration and "preparation of the ground for murder" of the Jews of Hungary. The trial in 1954 initially resulted in the exoneration of Gruenwald and the judge's conclusion that Kastner had "sold his soul to the devil" in allowing himself to be used thusly, but Israel's Supreme Court exonerated Kastner on the grounds that his intent was not to destroy Jews. Nevertheless, Kastner could no longer benefit by being cleared; he was assassinated on the streets of Tel Aviv in 1957.

During June 1944, foreign observers' reports, instigated within Hungary by Kiklos (Moshe) Krauss, executive of the Jewish Agency's emigration office for Palestine, aroused international protest. Private protests from the Vatican (called for by the American WRB), the United States, the King of Sweden and other neutrals impelled the Regent to cancel deportations on July 5, 1944, thus sparing the Jews of Budapest. Despite appeals by the Jewish Council, some Bishops, and the plea of the Nuncio (the Vatican's Foreign Office representative) to the Prince Primate of the Hungarian Roman Catholic Church, he refused to protest either publicly or privately while almost three of every five of Hungary's Jews were being deported. Not until July 16, after the deportations were stopped, did the Primate authorize a statement about the deportation which specified Jews as past victimizers, but not as the victims, and refrained from urging Christians not to cooperate in further deportation; nor did it threaten sanctions against collaborators—it simply renounced all responsibility for what had been done.

Initially, the Budapest Jewish Council leadership's apprehension of a threat to them was allayed by a rumour (which Eichmann has said that he planted). According to this rumour, only the unassimilated non-Magyar Jewry of the "east" would be deported. By June some of its members unofficially issued a pamphlet called "An Appeal to the Christians of Hungary"; others surreptitiously appealed to the Regent's son, Miklos Horthy, to save the Jews and prevent a threatened right-wing coup against the Regent. Between July and October, M. Krauss and others, working with the Swedish emissary of the American War Refugee Board, Raoul Wallenberg, and with friendly foreign diplomats, sought to protect tens of thousands of Jews in Budapest by issuing certificates of foreign citizenship or protection; for each legitimate certificate, Zionist youth printed three times the number. Wallenberg and others even housed their protected Jews in special buildings: ironically, the most populous of these, nominally under Swiss protection, was known as "the glass house." The Budapest Jews' precarious security was again threatened in October 1944, when an Arrow Cross coup, backed by the Germans, succeeded. The Germans, who had preferred the more politically astute politicians of the right, backed the coup because the Regent was planning to surrender to the Allies and physically resist German control. The Regent's intention to arm workers and Jews to defend themselves against the native fascists had not yet been implemented. Scarcely any Jews had weapons excepting a small Zionist youth group, who exploited their few arms and captured German uniforms to liberate their members from captivity. After the coup, gendarmes and Arrow Cross members invaded the Jewish hospitals and the starred houses, massacring Jews routinely. There was virtually no opposition to the coup, just as there was no Hungarian resistance to the German invasion. The Protestant Bishops did urge the Prince-Primate on November 26, 1944, to intervene against the Arrow Cross slaughter of Jews with the Head of State (Ferenc Szalazi, Arrow Cross leader), as did the Jewish Council of Budapest on January 14, 1945: on both occasions, he refused.

After liberation (in February 1945), only seventeen percent of Hungary's Jews recorded in 1941 were listed as still alive on Hungarian soil: this number was later swelled by victims returning from the extermination camps or labor camps and Jews who had fled to neutral countries or Rumania so that those "of Jewish faith" recorded on December 31, 1945, constituted thirty-six percent of those listed in 1941.

There is no one altogether adequate study of the Holocaust in Hungary and its foundation in Hungarian politics. The first account by Jeno Levai, a Hungarian journalist, in *Black Book on the Martyrdom of Hungarian Jewry,* ed. by Lawrence P. Davis, is a chatty, daily reconstruction of events marred by the lack of identification of the witnesses used to reconstruct them and an uncritical presentation. G. A. McCartney's *A History of Hungary Part II. 1929–1945* (New York, Frederich A. Praeger, 1957) covers Hungarian politics like a chess tournament in which a player's strategy is not comprehensible without having followed each of his fifteen previous moves (and those of all other players). One's general confidence in McCartney's interpretations is jarred by his naive assertion that the Hungarian players authorizing the deportation of the Jews had no idea they were sending them to their death—only Randolph Kastner knew.

Nicholas M. Nagy-Talavera's *The Green Shirts and the Others: A History of Fascism in Hungary and Rumania* is a provocative work, showing how the rise of radical right anti-Semitic movements was a populist response caused by the failure of the respective ruling classes of these nations to integrate unrepresented classes to modernize their countries, and to provide means of social mobility for the educated. He consistently relates political ideologies to class constituencies and alliances, subtly exposing the underlying conditions and differing motives of classes leading and following these movements. The work on Rumania is less developed, but contains some powerful observations on the self-identification and strategies of Rumanian and Hungarian Jews: "The Jews had, nevertheless, one effective means of checking the Szeged Idea. The Trianon Treaty guaranteed equal rights to all Hungarians, regardless of their creed, race or nationality. The Rumanian Jews, through their connections abroad, forced the victorious Rumanian state into granting full citizenship to their unassimilated masses—many of them barely able to speak Rumanian—in 1923. The powerful Alliance Israelite now offered its services to the Hungarian Jews. They refused in categorical terms. . . . 'We are not Hungarian Jews but Jewish Hungarians.' Ultimately the 'bad' Rumanian Jews got better treatment as punishment than the 'good' Hungarian Jews got as a reward.'' He is consistently critical of the lack of foresight and of the absence of a political consciousness of the bourgeois Hungarian Jewish leadership's own self-interest. Braham points out in a review in the *American Political Science Review* (March 1972, 261–2) that the book is marred by inconsistent orthographic usage and some factual errors; he also contests some of Nagy-Talavera's interpretations. Nagy-Talavera brings passion, intelligence, and personal experience (as a Hungarian emigre) to this significant social analysis of fascism and problems of order in underdeveloped nations.

The most comprehensive and reliable work on Hungarian Jewry is that of Randolph L. Braham, who has rendered an enduring service to non-Hungarian readers by his bibliographic reference work *The Hungarian Jewish Catastrophe: A Selected and Annotated Bibliography* and through his compiling of original sources of lasting significance in *Hungarian-Jewish Studies*. For an effective, succinct account of the political responsibility for the extermination of Hungarian Jewry, one should see his essay ''The Holocaust in Hungary: An Historical Interpretation of the Role of the Hungarian Radical Right.'' Original documentation of the German and Hungarian role is compiled in Braham's two volumes on *The Destruction of Hungarian Jewry: A Documentary Account*. Braham is currently writing a four-volume history of Hungarian Jewry which readers concerned with the Holocaust and/or Eastern European political development can await with expectation.

No adequate account has been written of the lethargy of the Roman Catholic Church. However, Jeno Levai's *Hungarian Jewry and the Papacy: Pope Pius XII Did Not Remain Silent* provides some background, especially on the Hungarian Church, headed by the Primate, Cardinal Serenedi. His evidence belies his own defense in the title—all that was said came too late, too low, too evasively and with too many contradictions to instigate noncooperation. War Refugee Board records referred to earlier contain significant proof of the Pope's time lapses in responses and failure to respond after July 1944. The War Refugee Board began urging the Apostolic Delegate to appeal to the Holy See to protect the Jews of Hungary and Rumania in vague, general terms on March 24, 1944. Once isolation began, the Board initiated a request of the Pope (through the State Department's Vatican representative, Harold Tittman) to appeal to the people and the authorities of Hungary, on May 26, 1944, threatening ''ecclesiastic sanctions.'' The Pope continued his policy of restricting himself to diplomatic means, only appealing personally to the Regent in a telegram on June 25th. The Regent ordered deportation stopped on July 9, 1944, citing the Pope's intervention and appeals of other neutrals and the Allies. War Refugee Board records reveal the promptness of the response of the Apostolic Delegate in Washington (Msgr. Cicognani) and in Ankara (Msgr. Angelo Roncalli, later to become Pope John), showing how time lapses could not be attributed to poor communication. Between April 26 and June 25, 1944, 371,427 Hungarian Jews were deported, not including those dying or committing suicide in camps and ghettos in Hungary. Subsequent appeals by the Director of the War Refugee Board, John Pehle, to the Vatican to publicly broadcast appeals to clergy and laity to conceal Jews (after the Arrow Cross coup of October 16, 1944) on October 20, 1944, failed to elicit a response.

Similarly, no adequate account has yet been rendered as to the genesis and failure of Joel Brand's mission and, more significantly, whether the attempt was justified or itself helped to incapacitate the Jews of Hungary, by the Nazi design of the terms of the mission itself or by the failure of the mission. This question logically precedes the question of whom to charge with its failure—Joel Brand, the Jewish Agency, and/or the Allies? Alex Weissberg's re-creation of Joel Brand's story, *Desperate Mission: Joel Brand's Story as told by Alex Weissberg,* is an irresponsible mélange of firsthand testimony retrospectively reflected by guilt and second and thirdhand accounts of events of which Joel Brand was not a witness, with no sign that the author tested any assertions by the ordinary canons of evidence. Brand's account of the failure of his mission, casting blame on the Jewish Agency, is filled with clues as to his own ambivalent role—one day Brand is at a British cocktail party, the next day on a prison hunger strike. Bela Vago assesses "The Intelligence Aspect of the Joel Brand Mission" and how it prejudiced its avowed object, showing the manifold relations Brand and Grosz had had earlier with the Abwehr and Gestapo which negated their credibility as Jewish agents.

Andreas Biss, in his memoir, *A Million Jews to Save,* recalls his activities with Kastner while continuing negotiations with the SS after Brand failed to return from Istanbul, knowingly walking into a snare in Syria. Biss derogates Brand's character and his representation of his trip, attempting to persuade the reader that he and Kastner pursued an authentic and effective strategy of resistance, resulting later in Himmler's issuing orders to cease extermination in the camp. He attributes the failure of negotiations to Brand, who acted to oust Kastner from the spotlight, according to Biss. But Biss's account, written twenty-two years after these events, is filled with internal inconsistencies in reporting sequences of events and their causes and some dubious, controversial historical judgments. Only one who did not have to justify his own past could reconstruct the scenario and weigh his claims versus those of Brand, Kastner, and the trial witnesses, and also those of Kersten, Bernadotte and other purported negotiators with Himmler later involved in negotiations to liberate particular groups of Jews.

There is no account of the Kastner trial in English adequately assessing the substantive evidence and ethical issues involved in Kastner's and Brand's strategy. Walter Laqueur wrote a perceptive article on its political implications in the fifties in Israel for *Commentary* (December 1955). The English reader can best follow the trial itself through the reports on the trial and judgments reported in the English language *Jerusalem Post* between 1954 and 1958.

Randolph L. Braham, in an unpublished paper, "What Did They Know and When?" (International Scholars Conference on the Holocaust in New York, March 1975), shows the abundance of evidence available to Brand and Kastner and (to a lesser extent) to Jewish Council leaders before March 19, 1944, on German plans and facilities to exterminate the Jews. Braham considers numerous questions—why they did not inform provincial Jewish leaders and alert the Jewish population generally on German strategy, why they did not begin before mid-June to appeal directly to the Regent and to foreign observers using the Auschwitz protocol, and why they had not planned any anticipatory strategy before the invasion? He reviews the explanations—offered by Eichmann and Revisionist and Marxist critics—that Kastner simply collaborated in assuring the Jewish masses' ignorance in order to select the few he favored out of personal or political consanguinity. He relates Kastner's policy to the policy of the *Judenrat* heads in central and eastern Europe who took responsibility, first, for not informing the community to avert futile despair, and then, of selecting the victims in order to save those they considered to be the most valuable members of the community. This policy contradicted the normative Talmudic doctrine, enunciated by Maimonides: ". . . if pagans should tell them [the Jews] 'Give us one of yours and we·shall kill him, otherwise we shall kill all of you,' they all should be killed and not a single Jewish soul should be delivered." Isaiah Trunk in *Judenrat* (New York, The Macmillan Company, 1972) relates incidents in which rabbis employed this as a standard of reference in Vilna, Kovno, and Bedzin. The policy of leaders who made selections from potential victims was justified by Jacob Robinson in his introduction to Trunk's *Judenrat* as consonant with Jewish tradition, taking the selection of Jewish youth for the Russian Army during the reign of Czar Nicholas I (1825–1856) as the precedent. (The likeness of the assumptions that some members are more valuable than others and that the weaker ought to be sacrificed for the stronger for prevailing fascist ideology was not noted by Robinson or the original spokesmen for this strategy.) Braham does not choose between these explanations but does assess the contribution of such leadership to the Hungarian Jews' vulnerability: "Uninformed, unprepared, and disunited, the Jews became an easy prey in the hands of the SS and their Hungarian hirelings. They were isolated, atomized, dispirited and demoralized at a lightening speed. . . . Trapped and abandoned by their own Government, the traditional official as well as the Zionist leaders tried desperately to save what could still be saved under the given conditions . . . The Zionists, while agreeing with the objectives, if not the tactics, of these leaders basically believed that only by direct dealing with the SS, the real holders of power in Hungary, could the maximum be achieved for Hungarian Jewry.''

Braham also assesses "The Role of the Jewish Council in Hungary," in *Yad Vashem Studies X* (1974). His essay incorporates new reconstruction based on important testimonies from Budapest Jewish Council and Zionist leaders—Samu Stern, Erno Peto, Fulop Freudiger, and Otto Komoly—which are published in *Hungarian-Jewish Studies, III* (1973).

"Eichmann's Own Story," as dictated by Eichmann before he was apprehended in Argentina, was published in *Life* magazine of November 28 and December 5, 1960. Evidence developed at the trial is summed up by the Israeli prosecutor in Gideon Hausner's *Justice in Jerusalem* (New York, Harper and Row, 1966) and by Levai in *Yad Vashem Studies VI* (1963).

The great difference between the fate of the Jews of Hungary and of Rumania, where extermination began in 1941, renews our need to understand how the extermination process was checked in Rumania.

Rumania

Rumania has been one of the most puzzling of chapters in the Holocaust, indicating the inadequacy of interpreting political outcomes as a simple function of prewar attitudes toward the Jews. For Rumania began extermination of its own Jews before Germany did, and later concluded an agreement to deport Jews but failed to implement it. Later in 1943 it permitted Jewish emigration but released only Jews incarcerated in Rumanian concentration camps in Transnistria in the last moments before Soviet liberation in August.

In 1938 Rumania was ruled by a royal dictatorship which had replaced earlier parliamentary competition among its political parties, most of whose leaders, Nagy-Talavera tells us, took anti-Semitic ideology for granted (p. 248). Its stability was threatened by a growing radical-right mass movement, the Iron Guard, founded in 1927. To counter its popularity, competing fascist leaders incorporated elements of its program, especially the anti-Semitic elements. The government had begun attempting to disenfranchise Jews in 1936 but was thwarted by the courts and foreign pressure until 1938, when it annulled the citizenship of thirty-four percent of all Jews it had challenged. To suppress the Guard, the Government murdered its leaders in prison, leading to more assassinations, terror and counter-terror, and reinforcing their determination for vengeance. After the fall of France (Rumania's traditional ally), the state's policy became oriented toward Germany and the King attempted to pacify the New Guard leaders. The regime's popularity declined due to its loss of Rumanian territory. The government presided over the incorporation of substantial segments of Rumania in the west (Transylvania) by Hungary and in the east (Bessarabia and Bukovina) by the Soviet Union in 1940 after Hitler backed these states' demands. The King appointed General Ion Antonescu as Head of State in September 1940 to thwart an Iron Guard coup. King Carol, previously detested because of his prominent Jewish mistress and his own corruption, was induced by Antonescu to resign and flee. The new regime attempted to incorporate the Guard; the Vice-Premier, Horia Sima, was its commander. However, constant violence against Jews and political opponents plus spontaneous attacks on foreign diplomats were unchecked by the Government as Sima refused to accept Antonescu's demands to discipline the Guard. In January 1941, the Iron Guard revolted against Antonescu's regime and was put down: Antonescu earlier had requested Hitler's support to sustain him, but Hitler had feared the disorder and disorganization of production which could result from Iron Guard rule. Both during the retreat from lost territories and during the attempted coup, pogroms were staged: the Jewish victims of the attempted January coup were hung in the kosher butcher market in Bucharest.

During June 1941, Rumania joined Germany in attacking the Soviet Union, expecting to recapture her lost territories. Between June and December 1941, an estimated 130 to 160,000 Jews in the recaptured provinces were slaughtered and 140,154 deported to Transnistria; many died on the way. Julius S. Fisher shows that General Antonescu authorized the killing in Bucharest, being unready to wait for the Germans, and assesses the toll of victims in his *Transnistria, the Forgotten Cemetery*.

The Jewish leadership in Bucharest, drawn from the leadership of the Zionists and of assimilated Jewry, began to petition to General Antonescu directly. They also threatened the withdrawal of capital and held out the inducement of obtaining foreign exchange in order to stop deportations and to liberate the Jews of Transnistria. Despite the appointment of an unrepresentative Jewish Council in February 1942, responsible to the government, they persisted. They also appealed to the Rumanian Patriarch, the Queen, and diplomatic representatives, who, in turn, appealed to General Antonescu. Theodor Lavi describes these links in his *Rumanian Jewry in World War II*. The protests of W. Filderman, head of the prewar Jewish community organization, to General Antonescu, his childhood classmate, are reproduced in Lavi's "Documents on the struggle of Rumanian Jewry for its rights during the Second World War." These are fascinating but there is little analysis of Antonescu's constraint in response to Filderman. Excepting a two month internment in 1943 in Transnistria (where he continued his activities and his status was evidently protected), Filderman remained free. Lavi's analysis is contained in an essay, "The Background to the Rescue of Rumanian Jewry during the Period of the Holocaust" in *Jews and Non-Jews in Eastern Europe*. Antonescu's initial readiness to listen to Filderman is attributed to his previous awareness of (1) the effect that the Jews' challenge of former Rumanian governments had had earlier at Berlin in 1878 and at Paris in 1919 and (2) how their challenge led to the dissolution of the rabidly anti-Jewish Goga-Cuza regime in 1937. Once he was committed to listening to Filderman, he could not deny awareness of the violence his soldiers perpetrated. Antonescu was moved to reverse his policy by the internal growth of opposition, "evinced by even such traditional anti-Semites as former political leaders, the Church and the Court" and his desire to extricate Rumania from the German alliance, accelerated by the German defeat at Stalingrad.

Stephen Fischer-Galati presents a novel view in his essay "Fascism, Communism, and the Jewish Question in Rumania," in *Jews and Non-Jews in Eastern Europe,* maintaining that, "The preservation of the Jews should be ascribed primarily to Antonescu's integrity and to the absence of rooted political anti-Semitism or anti-Semitic brutality among the country's population." He maintains that the violence against Jews of Bukovina and Bessarabia was attributed to hostility aroused by their identification with the new Soviet regime which they welcomed in 1940; and that Rumanians distinguished these Jews, as well as those of Transylvania who often identified with the Hungarian nationality, from the assimilated Jews of Rumania proper identified with the Rumanian nationality. While Nagy-Talavera reiterates that the perception of the Jews of the outer provinces as hostile reinforced Rumanians' anti-Semitism, he shows that the ideology of the Guard which depicted the Jew qua Jew as diabolical maintained no distinctions.

In an informative essay on "The Attitude Towards the Jews as a Criterion of the Left-Right Concept," in *Jews and Non-Jews in Eastern Europe,* Bela Vago tells us that despite pervasive identification of the Jew as the alien, the Jews' influence on Rumanian parties exceeded their influence in Hungary and Slovakia. Vago shows how the Rumanian Jews' political commitment was conditioned by their class interests and negotiated by political bargaining between leaders, giving Jews more input in prewar Rumanian politics than would be evident from party platforms. Elsewhere, Vago has described the tactics of "Jewish Leadership Groups in Hungary and Rumania During the Holocaust," showing how the former were unused to relating politically to the Hungarian gentry on behalf of Jews as a collectivity, despite their personal assimilation, while the latter all used their roles politically and were accustomed to bargaining for political rights for Jews irrespective of their party or ideology. Despite disunity based on ideology and personalities among Rumanian Jewish leaders, the latter could adapt to employing their roles strategically during the Holocaust while most Hungarian Jewish leaders could not.

We can best explain Antonescu's response as a reaction consistent with both the pressures upon him and his own goal of preserving Rumanian sovereignty. In 1942, Antonescu, anticipating a German defeat, entertained the possibility of exploring a separate peace with the West. While he concluded an agreement with the Germans to deport the Jews from old Rumania in July

1942, it was never implemented. Simultaneously, disengagement was being investigated by J. Maniu, leader of the National Peasant Party, who maintained contact with the British Near East command. Antonescu dragged out the investigation of such illegal activities to prevent Maniu's exposure. In his memoir, *Lost Opportunity* (London, Jonathan Cape, 1957), Alexandre Cretzianu relates how he acted as Maniu's representative and was sent to Ankara in 1943 by Antonescu as Rumanian Ambassador, fully cognizant of his objectives. Maniu was one of the leaders with whom Jewish leaders maintained contact. Vago shows how they exploited the illusion of international Jewry's influence over the Western Allies with Maniu and other Allies in order to obtain their support.

In 1943 the Rumanian regime switched course, attempting to exploit the Jews via confiscatory taxes and expropriation, and offered to allow 70,000 to 80,000 to emigrate in exchange for foreign currency. This plan was never consummated, Friedman relates in *No Room for the Oppressed,* because of American delays attributable both to the State Department and suspicion among American Jewish leaders of the Emergency Committee to Save the Jewish People, which led Stephen Wise to deprecate the reality of the offer. The Jews had become a utility to be bought and sold, indicating the interplay of values among Rumanian men-in-power. When German victory seemed certain, they could be treated as objects and one might exterminate them as an end in itself. When German victory was uncertain and potential consequences could be anticipated, the use-value of existing Jews outweighed the intrinsic value of dead Jews. The greater willingness of Rumanian than Hungarian leaders to resist the German instigation and react rationally in defense of their national interests is attributed by Nagy-Talavera to the singular national identity of the Rumanians, which is contrasted to the non-Hungarian or frequent German origin of the Hungarian leaders.

A year later, the American War Refugee Board representative in Ankara, Ira Hirschmann, arranged a meeting there with Alexandre Cretzianu and asked him in March 1944 to (1) immediately disband the camps at Transnistria, (2) expedite passage and exit visas for 5,000 children through the port of Constanca to Palestine, and (3) end all persecution and repression against minorities in Rumania. Hirschmann specifies in his memoir *Caution to the Winds* that nothing was promised in exchange but the good will of the United States and personal visas for the Cretzianus. One week after this request was made, the camp was disbanded and the children were sent to Constanca. Hirschmann recalls how "Before he left, Cretzianu had said something which, while it caused a twinge of conscience, strongly reinforced my belief in unhesitant, affirmative action. He said, 'If this means so much to you in the United States, why didn't you come sooner. You could have saved more lives.' "

Based on Rumanian census statistics of 1930, 1941, 1942 and survivors' lists in 1946, several investigators have concluded that about fifty-two percent of all Jews within the October 1941 Rumanian boundaries were slaughtered or deported to concentration camps in Transnistria, excluding Soviet Jews slaughtered by the Rumanians and prewar Rumanian Jews under Hungarian and Bulgarian rule. One may see, for example, Nicholas Sylvain's article on Rumania in *Jews in the Soviet Satellites,* Julius Fisher's summary, "How Many Jews Died in Transnistria?" in *Jewish Social Studies* (April 1958), Dr. Sabin Manuila and Dr. W. Filderman's article, "Regional development of the Jewish population in Rumania," in *Genus* XIII (1957) and T. Lavi's article on Rumania in the *Encyclopedia Judaica* (14). Lavi concludes that 264,900 Jews or forty-three percent were murdered directly or died in camps and in transit.

CONCLUSION

German allies' and satellites' response to German pressure to deport their Jews was first a function of how consonant the Germans' end goal of eliminating the Jews was with the ideology of the state's ruling class or elite. This could best be predicted by the degree to which anti-Semitic movements had been legitimated by the mid-thirties. In states where anti-Semitic programs had been incorporated by the state (signified by adoption of the *numerus clausus,* other discriminatory legislation, or divesting Jews of civil equality) and such movements had attained a mass audience, there was no resistance. The Church proved to be the critical legitimating institution in all states. All instances where states refused to collaborate, or did not implement agreements to deport, were instances in which the head of the dominant church in that state had protested categorically and very early against deportation and/or previous discrimination against Jews. Roman Catholic Church heads in states allied to Germany were less likely to protest categorically than were non-Roman Catholic Church heads (ranking only states where each church was dominant); predominantly Roman Catholic states produced substantially more victims than did non-Roman Catholic states among German allies. Adding up the Jewish population in Roman Catholic and non-Roman Catholic Axis states separately, we find that three-quarters of the almost 1,000,000 Jews in Croatia, Slovakia, Hungary and Italy became victims as compared to less than half (48.5 percent) of the Jews in Finland, Bulgaria and Rumania in 1941.

In all states where deportations occurred, Jewish leadership petitioned church leaders to use their moral authority to halt them. Independent Jewish leadership, with contacts with native elites in Rumania and Bulgaria, did play a role in instigating domestic resistance. The emergence of such leadership seems to be related to the prewar political experience and to the degree of the collective consciousness of each nation's Jewry, rather than to the extent of assimilation of the Jews themselves or to the viability of anti-Semitic movements.

Germany never utilized either threats of sanctions or actual sanctions against its allies for failing to collaborate with deportations. This meant that any allied pressures against deportations would not have instigated German sanctions, given Germany's dependence upon her allies for raw materials, military bases and the resultant drain of her battle capacity caused by her occupation of these states. However, competing elites and movements in these states sought German intervention to gain access to power, using their anti-Semitism as a demonstration of pro-German loyalty. Germany did not support the more radical fascist anti-Semitic movements as a matter of course; it simply preferred governments that could guarantee order and economic productivity.

Domestic resistance against deportation reinforced state leaders' sensitivity to Allied (i.e., United States, Britain, etc.) disapproval of German extermination policy expressed in December 1942 and their later threats of postwar sanctions.

Where internal pressures were contradictory to Allied expectations and threats of future sanctions—as in Hungary—threats had to be reiterated before the head of state ceased collaboration. Orientation towards the West among these states intensified during the winter of 1942 and thereafter as they rationally calculated their future dependence on the United States and Britain and recognized the increasing likelihood of German defeat. The satellites [Croatia and Slovakia], which had never been sovereign before 1939, did not calculate their postwar interests because their leaders had always known of their states' demise if Germany were defeated. They fled or were tried as criminals after the War by the nations which they had severed by their collaboration.

At no point did the Allies threaten immediate sanctions against any state for deporting their Jews. However, the reported fear of Allied bombing and sensitivity to imputations of threat indicate that such a threat would have been effective and could have prevented consummation of the Hungarian Holocaust. Allied indifference to the rescue of Jews led to instances where the Allies' failure to respond promptly to the offers of German-allied states to save Jews caused many who could have been moved to sanctuaries outside occupied Europe to be deported or interned in concentration camps. These include the failure to arrange for the emigration of 80,000 Jews from Rumania to Palestine, offered by Rumania in 1943, and the failure of the American State Department and British Foreign Office to authorize the entry of Jews from the Italian zone of France to Allied-occupied North Africa in ships provided by the Italian government before Italy's defection was announced in 1943; the Italian government's preparations for this had led to a concentration of about 30,000 Jews there who were immediate prey for German police seizure after the precipitative Italian flight from France. Thus, Allied failure to use the means at their command, after they had publicly recognized the German policy of exterminating the Jews, led to the probable extermination of over half a million Jews in the colonial zone alone.

The structure of the alliance between the United States, Great Britain, and the Soviet Union, including the unconditional surrender demanded from all Axis powers, served to deter defections of Axis allies in eastern Europe (particularly Rumania and Hungary). These states feared postwar incursions of their independence by the Soviet Union and groped unsuccessfully to obtain assurances from the West before switching sides. The SS offer in 1944 to exchange Jews for trucks to be used against the Russians was a not-too-veiled bid to split the alliance. This caused reiteration of the Allied reluctance to "divert" war material or to do anything to save the Jews.

Why was rescue of the Jews believed by high Allied officials to be contrary to other war goals—diversionary—even when it was within their capacity and little cost was involved, e.g., in the request to bomb the lines to Auschwitz? No satisfactory answer has yet been given, but several plausible hypotheses can be proposed. The evidence shows that Germany was successful in persuading the western world that "the Jewish problem" was constituted by the Jews' existence itself: hence, the more Jews there were, the greater the problem. Denying any claims to aid Jews by labelling their requests as discriminatory or diversionary demands insured that one would not increase the number of Jews in one's sphere of influence. Systematic denials also made it less likely that the Jewish community of the Allies' homelands would press claims either unacceptable to those nations' constituencies or adversely influencing the loyalty of subject populations which the Allies were seeking to woo. The British sought to retain their imperial hold by preserving Muslim loyalties in the mid-East and the Soviets had to consolidate their postwar empire in eastern Europe; both might therefore hesitate to identify with the Jews, a people traditionally held in contempt or hated by dominant groups in these areas.

A cynic might argue that it was more economical to promise postwar punishment for a few war criminals than to commit any expenditures to preserve the lives of more Jews. Or perhaps, given the Jews' loyalty to the West and their lack of effective political strategy or collective consciousness, there was no incentive to incur any costs on behalf of them. Or perhaps, all of these explanations are correct.

BIBLIOGRAPHY

This bibliography is limited to a listing of works cited in the preceding discussion which relate to reactions of governments and of social groups within countries discussed above. Bibliographical material for other works discussed above has been incorporated into the text. This bibliography follows the order of countries discussed above.

I. General Works

AINSZTEIN, REUBEN. *Jewish Resistance in Nazi Occupied Eastern Europe* (New York: Barnes and Noble, 1974).

HILBERG, RAUL. *The Destruction of the European Jews* (Chicago: Quadrangle, 1961) (Available in Harper paperback).

MEYER, PETER et al. *Jews in the Soviet Satellites* (Syracuse: Syracuse University Press, 1953). See articles on Rumania and Bulgaria.

REITLINGER, GERALD. *The Final Solution* (New York: A. S. Barnes, 1961). (Also in paperback).

RICH, NORMAN. *Hitler's War Aims: The Establishment of the New Order*, 2 vols. (New York: Norton, 1974).

SNOEK, JOHAN M. *The Greybook: A Collection of Protests Against Anti-Semitism and Persecution of Jews Issued by Non-Roman Churches and Church Leaders During Hitler's Rule* (Assen: Van Gorcum, 1969). See discussions on Bulgaria, Hungary, Switzerland, Denmark, etc.

VAGO, B. AND MOSSE, G. *Jews and Non-Jews in Eastern Europe 1918-1945* (New York: John Wiley, 1974).

II. Allies

A. UNITED STATES

BAUER, YEHUDA, "When did They Know?," *Midstream* 14:4 (April 1968), pp. 51-59.

COHEN, NAOMI. *Not Free to Desist: The American Jewish Committee, 1906-1966* (Philadelphia: Jewish Publication Society, 1972).

FEINGOLD, HENRY. *The Politics of Rescue: The Roosevelt Administration and the Holocaust, 1938-1945* (Rutgers: Rutgers University Press, 1970).

FRIEDMAN, SAUL S. *No Haven for the Oppressed: United States Policy Toward Jewish Refugees, 1938-1945* (Detroit: Wayne State Press, 1973).

GOTTLIEB, MOSHE, "The Anti-Nazi Boycott Movement in the United States: An Ideological and Sociological Appreciation," *Jewish Social Studies* 35:3-4 (July 1973), pp. 198-227.

———, "The First of April Boycott and the Reaction of the American Jewish Community," *American Jewish Historical Quarterly* 57:4 (June 1968), pp. 516-556.

KULKA, ERICH, "Auschwitz Condoned: The Abortive Struggle Against the Final Solution," *Wiener Library Bulletin* (Winter 1968/1969).

LAZIN, FREDRICK, "The Response of the American Jewish Committee to the Crisis of Jews in Germany: A Study of Qualified Concern, and Possible Complicity," Unpublished paper presented at International Scholars' Conference on the Holocaust, New York; March 1975.

MORSE, ARTHUR D. *While Six Million Died: A Chronicle of American Apathy* (New York: Random House, 1968) (Available in paperback).

WYMAN, DAVID. *Paper Walls: America and the Refugee Crisis 1938–1941* (Amherst, Mass.: University of Massachusetts Press, 1968).

———, "Why Auschwitz Was Never Bombed," *Commentary* 56:5 (May 1978), pp. 37–47.

B. GREAT BRITAIN

HEARST, ERNEST, "The British and the Slaughter of the Jews," *Wiener Library Bulletin,* (Winter 1966/1967 and Spring 1967).

SCHARF, ANDREW. *The British Press and the Jews Under Nazi Rule* (Oxford: Oxford University Press, 1964).

SHERMAN, ALAN J. *Island Refuge: Britain and Refugees From the Third Reich 1933–1939* (Berkeley: University of California Press, 1973).

YAHIL, LENI, "Select British Documents on the Illegal Immigration to Palestine 1939–1940," *Yad Va Shem Studies* (1974) 10:241–276.

C. UNION OF SOVIET SOCIALIST REPUBLICS

BAR-ON, ZWI, "The Jews in the Soviet Partisan Movement," *Yad Va Shem Studies* (1960) 6:167–190.

GILBOA, Y. A. *The Black Years of Soviet Jewry* (Boston: Little Brown, 1971).

GLIKSON, P., "Jewish Population in the Polish People's Republic 1944–1972," Unpublished paper presented at the Sixth World Congress of Jewish Studies, Jerusalem, August 1973.

REDLICH, S., "The Jewish Anti-Fascist Committee in the Soviet Union," *Jewish Social Studies* 31:1 (January 1969) pp. 25–37.

RINGELBLUM, EMMANUEL. Kermish, J. and Krakowski, S., eds. *Polish-Jewish Relations during the Second World War* (Jerusalem: Yad Va Shem, 1974). On the diversion between Russian and Polish policies regarding treatment of Jewish partisans, see pp. 218–220.

SCHWARTZ, SOLOMON. *The Jews in the Soviet Union* (Syracuse: Syracuse University Press, 1951).

SHAPIRO, LEONARD, "The Jewish Anti-Fascist Committee and Phases of Soviet Anti-Semitic Policy During and After World War II," in *Jews and Non-Jews in Eastern Europe 1918–1945,* Vago and Mosse, eds. (New York: John Wiley, 1974).

III. Neutrals

A. SWEDEN

KERSTEN, FELIX. *The Kersten Memoirs 1940–1945* (New York: MacMillan, 1957).

VALENTIN, HUGO, "Rescue and Relief Activities in Behalf of Jewish Victims of Nazism in Scandinavia," *YIVO Annual of Jewish Social Science* (1953) 8:224–51.

YAHIL, LENI, "Scandinavian Rescue of Prisoners," *Yad Va Shem Studies* (1967) 6:181–220

B. SPAIN

AVNI, HAIM, "Spanish Nationals in Greece and Their Fate during the Holocaust," *Yad Va Shem Studies* (1970) 8:31–69.

ROBINSON, NEHEMIAH. *Spain of Franco and its Policies Towards the Jews* (New York: World Jewish Congress, 1953).

C. THE VATICAN

FALCONI, CARLO. *The Silence of Pius XII,* Trans. B. Wall. (Boston: Little Brown, 1965).

FRIEDLANDER, SAUL. *Pius XII and the Third Reich: A Documentation* (New York: Knopf, 1966).

LEWY, GUENTER. *The Catholic Church and Nazi Germany* (New York: McGraw-Hill, 1964).

D. SWITZERLAND

HASSLER, ALFRED. *The Lifeboat is Full: Switzerland and the Refugees, 1933–1945* (New York: Funk and Wagnalls, 1969).

IV. Axis Satellites

A. CROATIA

ETEROVICH, F. AND SPALATIN, C., eds. *Croatia: Land, People, Culture* (Toronto: University of Toronto Press, 1964). One of the few studies of Croatia as an independent state. The genocidal activities of Croatia are glossed over and ignored.

FALCONI, CARLO. *The Silence of Pius XII* (see listing under *Vatican*). Note Falconi's discussion of the mass murder of Orthodox Serbs in Croatia.

PARIS, EDMOND. *Genocide in Satellite Croatia 1941–1945* (American Institute for Balkan Affairs, no date).

B. SLOVAKIA

LETTRICH, JOZEF. *History of Modern Slovakia* (New York: Praeger, 1955).

ROTKIRCHEN, LIVIA. *The Destruction of Slovak Jewry* (Jerusalem: Yad Va Shem, 1961). (Hebrew text with English summary and document index).

⸻, "Slovakia, 1918–1938," in *The Jews of Czechoslovakia, Vol. I* (Philadelphia: Jewish Publication Society, 1968), pp. 85–125.

⸻, "Vatican Policy and the 'Jewish Problem' in 'Independent' Slovakia," *Yad Va Shem Studies* (1967) 6:27–53.

V. Axis Allies

A. BULGARIA

BENVENISTY, "Some Problems on the Reasons for Salvation of the Bulgarian Jews from the Camps of Death," *Annual of the Social, Cultural and Educational Association of the Jews in the People's Republic of Bulgaria* (1969) 4:63–103.

CHARY, FREDRICK. *The Bulgarian Jews and the Final Solution* (Pittsburgh: University of Pittsburgh Press, 1972).

COHEN, DAVID, "The Expropriation of Jewish Property During the Period of Hitlerite Occupation," *Annual . . .* (1967) 2:65–111.

CRISPIN, DONNA, "Protests Demonstration of the Jews of Sofia on May 24, 1943," *Annual . . .* (1970) 5:31–55.

IZRAEL, SALVADOR, "Historical Roots of the Fraternal Friendship between Bulgarians and Jews," *Annual . . .* (1971), 6:113–139.

NAIMOVITCH, ISAK, "The Struggle of the Bulgarian Communist Party Against Anti-Semitism," *Annual . . .* (1972) 7:275–307.

————, "Who Saved the Bulgarian Jews from the Death Camps?," *Annual . . .* (1966).

NATHAN, JACQUES, "From the History of the Jewish Fatherland Front," *Annual . . .* (1969) 4:21–41.

OREN, NISSAN. *Bulgarian Communism: The Road to Power, 1934–1944* (New York: Columbia University Press, 1971).

————, "The Bulgarian Exception," *Yad Va Shem Studies* (1968) 7:83–107.

VILI, MAYER, "The Bulgarian Writers in Defense of the Jews during the Years of World War II," *Annual . . .* (1970) 5:55–75.

B. ITALY

CARPI, DANIEL, "The Catholic Church and Italian Jewry Under the Fascists (to the Death of Pius XI)," *Yad Va Shem Studies* (1960) 10:43–56.

KATZ, ROBERT. *Black Sabbath* (New York: MacMillan, 1969).

LEDEEN, MICHAEL, "The Evolution of Italian Fascist Antisemitism," *Jewish Social Studies* (1975) 37:3–17.

————, "Italian Jews and Fascism," *Judaism* (1969) 18:272–288.

MICHAELIS, MEIER, "The Attitude of the Fascist Regime to the Jew in Italy," *Yad Va Shem Studies* (1960) 10:7–42.

C. HUNGARY

BISS, ANDREAS. *A Million Jews to Save* (New York: A. S. Barnes, 1975).

BRAHAM, RANDOLPH. *The Destruction of Hungarian Jewry: A Documentary Account, 2 vols.* (New York: World Federation of Hungarian Jews, 1963).

————, "The Holocaust in Hungary: A Historical Interpretation of the Role of the Hungarian Radical Right," *Societas* (Summer 1972) 2:195–219.

————. *The Hungarian Jewish Catastrophe: A Selected and Annotated Bibliography* (Jerusalem: Yad Va Shem and YIVO, 1962).

————. *Hungarian-Jewish Studies* (New York: World Federation of Hungarian Jews, 1966–1973).

DAVIS, LAWRENCE, ed. *Black Book on the Martyrdom of Hungarian Jewry* (Zurich, 1948).

LEVAI, JENO, ed. *Eichmann in Hungary, Documents* (Pannonia Press, 1961).

_____. *Hungarian Jewry and the Papacy: Pope Pius XII Did Not Remain Silent* (Sands, 1967)

NAGY-TALAVERA, NICHOLAS. *The Green Shirts and the Others: A History of Fascism in Hungary and Rumania* (Stanford: Stanford University Press, 1970).

VAGO, BELA, "The Intelligence Aspect of the Joel Brand Mission," *Yad Va Shem Studies* (1974) 10:111–128.

WEISSBERG, ALEX. *Desperate Mission: Joel Brand's Story as Told by Alex Weissberg* (Criterion, 1958).

D. RUMANIA

FISHER, JULIUS. *Transnistria, the Forgotten Cemetery* (New York: Yoseloff, 1968).

FISCHER-GALATI, STEPHEN, "Fascism, Communism and the Jewish Question in Rumania," in *Jews and Non-Jews in Eastern Europe*, Vago and Mosse, eds.

HIRSCHMANN, IRA. *Caution to the Winds* (New York: David McKay, 1962).

LAVI, THEODORE, "The Background to the Rescue of Rumanian Jewry during the Period of the Holocaust," in *Jews and Non-Jews in Eastern Europe*, Vago and Mosse, eds.

_____, "Documents on the Struggle of Rumanian Jewry for its Rights During the Second World War," *Yad Va Shem Studies* (1960) 10:261–316.

_____. *Rumanian Jewry in World War II* (Jerusalem: Yad Va Shem, 1965). Hebrew text with English summary.

NAGY-TALAVERA, NICHOLAS. *The Green Shirts and Others: A History of Fascism in Hungary and Rumania* (see listing under *Hungary*).

STARR, JOSHUA, "Jewish Citizenship in Rumania," *Jewish Social Studies* (1941) 3:57–80.

International Law
and the Holocaust

M. Cherif Bassiouni

No study or discussion of the Holocaust can avoid terms such as: "genocide," "crimes against humanity," and "war crimes." No thorough examination of the Holocaust event and its contemporary implications may ignore Nazi war crimes trials such as the Nuremberg trials and the Eichmann trial. Yet, these terms are primarily *legal* terms, and these trials were *legal* proceedings. It becomes necessary, therefore, for any study of the Holocaust to include some discussion of the Holocaust and international law. At present, most courses in Holocaust studies fail to consider the legal significance and legal implications of the crimes committed by Nazis and Nazi collaborators. Few texts and fewer courses in international law, international relations, political science and history deign to study the Holocaust and the pertinence it has for these academic disciplines. Utilization of this survey of the implications of the Holocaust for international law can only serve to enrich such courses and to supplement such texts.

The Holocaust was perhaps the most heinous international crime in world history. In order to comprehend the juridical attempts at prosecuting those responsible for having committed this crime and in order to appreciate attempts by jurists to prevent future occurrences of war crimes and genocide, it is necessary to discuss "International Law and the Holocaust."

The following pages will focus attention upon the emergence and development of three legal concepts and their relation to the Holocaust. These concepts are "war crimes," "crimes against humanity," and "genocide." Discussion of these three concepts will be interwoven within a discussion of the Nuremberg trials, the adoption by the United Nations of the "Nuremberg Principles" and of the "Genocide Convention," and the Eichmann trial. Finally, some suggestions regarding further topics for classroom discussion will be offered.

"WAR CRIMES"—FROM ANTIQUITY TO NUREMBERG

Laws aimed at "humanizing" armed conflicts have been a feature of virtually every civilization from ancient times until the present. A review of the development of such laws reveals that states always have been more willing to codify rules which should have been applied to the preceding war than they have been jointly to enforce violations of such laws both during and after an armed conflict. Thus, laws restricting actions taken by belligerents during times of war abound; however, until the Nuremberg trials, the occasions have been few in which individuals responsible for breaching those laws have faced criminal prosecution.

As we shall see in the following pages, the concept of "war crimes" was a relatively well-established notion by the beginning of the Nuremberg trials in 1945; however, the concept of "crimes against humanity" only emerged as a legal concept with the London Charter of 1945 and with the subsequent Nuremberg proceedings. Similarly, the legal notion of "genocide" emerged only in the years subsequent to the Second World War.

The first prosecution for initiating an unjust war is reported to have been in Naples in 1268 when Conradin Von Hohenstafen was put to death for that reason. The first reported international prosecution for war crimes was against one Peter von Hagenbach in Breisach, Germany, in 1474.

Peter von Hagenbach was tried before a tribunal of twenty-eight judges from the allied states of the Holy Roman Empire. While he was not tried for crimes committed during the war, this trial is significant in that von Hagenbach was stripped of his knighthood by an international tribunal which found him guilty of murder, rape, perjury, and other crimes "against the law of God and man" in the execution of a military occupation.

American military history contains a number of landmark cases in the history of war crimes trials. During the American Revolution, for example, George Washington appointed a board of officers to try Major John Andre. Virtually simultaneous with the Andre trial was the trial of Captain Nathan Hale by a British Military Court. Over a century later, the United States convened war crime military tribunals in the aftermath of the Spanish-American War and after the occupation of the Philippines. However, the most significant war crimes trial in American military history was undoubtedly the post-Civil War trial of Confederate Major Henry Wirtz for his role in the deaths of several thousand Union prisoners in Andersonville prison during the Civil War.

The most pertinent forerunner of the Nuremberg trials was the prosecution of war criminals by an international tribunal after the end of World War I. In 1919, the Treaty of Versailles established the punishability of war criminals, and ordered: the prosecution of Kaiser Wilhelm II by an International Tribunal

(Article 227); that Germany hand over to the Allies all Germans accused of war crimes to be tried by military tribunals (Article 228); and that the Allies may establish national war crimes tribunals (Article 229). In 1920, the Allies submitted to Germany 896 names of alleged war criminals. However, for political reasons, that list shrank to 45, and, of these, Germany tried only 12 before the Supreme Court of the Reich convened at Leipzig (six of whom were acquitted). The Kaiser, who found refuge in Holland, was never tried. Efforts of Germany to extradite him from Holland for trial were unsuccessful because Holland claimed that the Kaiser's alleged "crime" was a "political offense," exempting him from extradition.

By the outbreak of the Second World War, the legal precedents for the prosecution of war criminals had become well established. On November 1, 1943, the Allies stated their intention jointly to prosecute Nazi war criminals "whose offenses have no particular geographical location." In addition, the Allies declared that those responsible for atrocities in a specific country would be tried and punished in that country. The decision of the Allies regarding the method of trying the major criminals was embodied in the London Agreement of August 8, 1945, and its accompanying Charter which are the Constitutive authorities for the International Military Tribunal at Nuremberg. The prosecution of individuals to be charged with certain international crimes was to be divided between an international military tribunal which would try major accused criminals, and the Allies, who in their respective zones of occupation, would try other accused criminals. The Charter (Article 61) provided that:

> The Tribunal . . . shall have the power to try and punish persons who, acting in the interests of the European Axis countries, whether as individuals or as members of organizations, committed any of the following crimes: a) crimes against peace; b) war crimes; c) crimes against humanity.

"Crimes against peace," a relatively new concept which grew out of World War I, were viewed as the ultimate international crime. "Crimes against humanity" were a novelty, and what this meant in 1946, as well as how it was applied in the Nuremberg Trials, must be well understood if the impact of Nuremberg is to be correctly evaluated in international criminal law. "Crimes against humanity" related to a body of doctrine concerning the protection of human rights applicable at war and at peace. The problems it posed were many.

DEVELOPMENT OF THE CONCEPT OF "CRIMES AGAINST HUMANITY"

The initial legal basis for the concept of "crimes against humanity" was derived from the Fourth Hague Convention of 1907 concerning the Laws and

Customs of War on Land (Preamble, par. 8) in which it is stated that:

> the inhabitants and the belligerents shall remain under the protection of and
> subject to the principles of the law of nations, as established by the usages
> prevailing among civilized nations, by the *laws of humanity,* and by the
> demands of public conscience. (emphasis added)

Thus, the 1907 statement concerning the *"laws* of humanity" was deemed
one of the authoritative legal sources of international law which supported the
1945 claim to prosecute and punish those who committed *"crimes* against the
humanity." But those "laws of humanity" were neither defined by the Hague
Convention nor did the accompanying regulations concerning land warfare
refer to any specific violations as *"crimes* against humanity." A precedent
was needed, therefore, to give a more substantive definitional content to the
contemplated "crimes." Such a precedent was found in the massacre, during
the First World War, by the Turkish government of its own nationals (Armenians of Turkish citizenship). At that time, the governments of France, Great
Britain, and Russia declared that the massacres constituted "crimes against
humanity and civilization," and the three governments indicated that all the
members of the Turkish government would be held responsible. This was the
first time that "crimes against humanity" were given a substantive definitional content which placed criminal responsibility on individuals as well as
states, whether in time of war or peace.

Since these crimes were not within the prohibitions of the Hague Regulations on the law of armed conflicts, additional support was sought in connection with the post-World War I efforts to prosecute the German Empire and its
allies as well as individuals from these countries. To that end, in January of
1919, the Preliminary Peace Conference of Paris decided to convene a commission which, among other things, would find facts relating to violations of
the laws and customs of war committed by the German Empire and its Allies.
The commission found that breaches of the laws and customs of war had been
committed. Thus, the warning issued to the Turkish government four years
earlier by the Triple Entente that those responsible for the Armenian massacre
would be held accountable, was acted upon by the commission. Similar
offenses committed by the Germans were also made prosecutable. These
crimes, however, did not fall within the traditional definition of "war crimes"
(thus in 1945 they gave rise to the need to create a special category of offenses
which the London Charter distinguished from war crimes [Art. 6c]). The
1919 distinction between "war crimes" and crimes against the "laws of
humanity," however, was not formally embodied in any of the peace treaties
concluded after World War I. The reason was that American members of the
commission objected to the inclusion of reference to violations of the laws of
humanity in the Versailles Peace Treaty. Their view was that war by its very
nature is inhumane, and, therefore, acts consistent with the laws of war,

although inhumane, were not punishable. Considering the difficulty in determining a universal standard for humanity, the United States delegates concluded that judicial tribunals only deal with existing law. Therefore, infractions of the moral law and actions contrary to the laws and principles of humanity must be administered by a forum other than the judicial one.

The United States' position prevailed, and no provision regarding the commission of crimes against the "laws of humanity" was contained in the 1919 Versailles Peace Treaty. The Versailles Treaty (Art. 228) made provision only for the prosecution of those "accused of having committed acts in violation of the laws and customs of war." It should be noted, however, that the Treaty of Sevres between the Allies and Turkey did contain an article (no. 230) which stated as an offense "the massacres committed during the continuance of the state of war on territory which formed part of the Turkish Empire on 1st August 1914." The Treaty of Sevres was never ratified, but was replaced, in 1923, by the Treaty of Lausanne, which deleted a similar provision and granted amnesty to all persons who committed such offenses during the period 1914-1922. Thus, the commission of offenses by a government against its own nationals, one of the offenses covered by the 1945 London Charter (Art. 6c), had not in 1923 become part of conventional or customary international law. Indeed, the "laws of humanity" mentioned as a source of international law in the Fourth Hague Convention of 1907 did not ripen into substantive international crimes until 1945.

Until the London Charter (1945), the concept of "laws of humanity," and its successor "crimes against humanity," was unusually vague and could hardly satisfy the requirements of specificity of a criminal statute. Nevertheless, the acts committed against civilians during World War II did unequivocably violate the provisions of the 1899 and 1907 Hague Conventions on the laws and customs of land war. The Fourth Hague Convention of 1907 did contain specific provisions (Arts. 42–56) prohibiting the conduct in question. Furthermore, the 1864 and 1923 Red Cross Conventions covered some of the acts later included in the 1945 understanding of "crimes against humanity." (It must be emphasized that all of these earlier prohibitions of certain acts against civilians were related to war and its conduct but did not apply to peacetime.)

Those who framed the London Charter had to extrapolate the notion of "crimes against humanity" from a larger concept, "war crimes," which was well established. Thus, the definitions of "war crimes" in Art. 6b and of "crimes against humanity" in Art. 6c overlapped in several areas. They were defined as follows:

> 6b) War crimes: namely, violations of the laws or customs of war. Such violations shall include, but not be limited to, murder, ill-treatment or deportation to slave labour or for any other purpose of civilian populations of or in

> occupied territory . . . 6c) Crimes against humanity, namely, murder, exter-
> mination, enslavement, deportation, and other inhumane acts committed
> against any civilian population, before or during the war, or persecutions on
> political, racial or religious grounds *in execution of or in connection with
> any crime within the jurisdiction of the Tribunal,* whether or not in violation
> of the domestic law of the country where perpetrated. (emphasis added)

Thus, for example, crimes committed against civilian populations in occupied
territories would be "war crimes." At the same time, these offenses would
also fall within the definition of a "crime against humanity" if the "civilian
population of or in occupied territory" is included within the meaning of the
phrase "any civilian population." Similarly, "deportation to slave labour" is
a war crime and is included within the term "enslavement" which is also
considered a "crime against humanity." As a practical matter, however, most
offenses committed during the War could fit either category of "crimes against
humanity" or "war crimes."

The significant legal difference between the two is that "war crimes" could
be committed, logically enough, only during a war, while "crimes against
humanity" could be committed "before or during the war." Therefore, the
words "before or during the war" implied that international law contained
penal sanctions against individuals, applicable not only in time of war, but
also in time of peace. This, however, presupposes the existence of a system of
international law under which individuals are responsible to the community of
nations for violations of rules of international criminal law.

At the time of the Nuremberg trials, the new but imprecise concept of
"crimes against humanity" was generally understood to mean "an offense
against certain general principles of law which, in certain circumstances,
become the concern of the international community, namely, if it has repercussions reaching across international frontiers, or if it passes in magnitude or
savagery any limits of what is tolerable by modern civilizations" (Quoted in
Schwelb, "Crimes Against Humanity," p. 182, no. 18).

THE INTERNATIONAL MILITARY TRIBUNAL AT NUREMBERG

Besides the need to formulate and to define new legal concepts, the framers
of the London Charter were faced with the problems attendant upon the
creation of an international tribunal which was to operate on the basis of rules
yet to be agreed upon by its creators. Among these problems were the procedures to be employed in the proceedings, such as: how to proffer charges and
what rules of evidence to use. The conflict between the various legal systems
represented was ultimately resolved in favor of the Anglo-American adversary

system, which was used most prevalently. Thus, each defendant was presented with an indictment or statement of the charges against him, was entitled to counsel, could present evidence, testify in his own behalf, and particularly cross-examine prosecution witnesses. European lawyers and judges who were unaccustomed to cross-examination techniques found difficulties with it, but cross-examination did not play a critical role in the trial itself because the prosecution called only thirty-three witnesses. This was due to the fact that the United States' prosecutors (whose influence was significant) took the position that the case against the defendants should be based primarily upon documentary evidence which was abundantly available. Justice Robert Jackson's view was that "the disinterestedness and unquestioned authenticity of documents settle doubts which always would linger if the same story were told by witnesses, the best of whom always are open to suspicion of bias, bad memory, and influence." The tribunal consisted of four judges, one from each of the four major Allies (U.S.; U.K.; U.S.S.R.; France), and the prosecution consisted of four teams from the same four countries.

Twenty-four individuals were named in the indictment as defendants. They were charged with ten categories of "war crimes" in Count Three and with three categories of "crimes against humanity" in Court Four. The ten categories of "war crimes" listed in the indictment were: 1) murder and ill-treatment of belligerents' civilian populations, 2) deportation of belligerents' civilian populations for slave labor and for other purposes, 3) murder and ill-treatment of prisoners of war, 4) killing of hostages, 5) plunder of public and private property, 6) extraction of collective penalties, 7) wanton destruction of cities, towns and villages not justified by military necessity, 8) conscription of civilian labor, 9) forcing civilians to swear allegiance to a hostile power, 10) Germanization of occupied territories.

The facts alleged by the prosecution as constituting "war crimes" were also relied on as constituting "crimes against humanity" under Count Four. *Thus, "crimes against humanity" became the more inclusive category of crime.* "War crimes" committed against civilians were incorporated under the more general rubric of "crimes against humanity."

"Crimes against humanity" were understood to include not only "war crimes" committed during the War, but also acts committed against civilian populations before the War. Such acts were: murder, extermination, enslavement, deportation, and other inhumane acts. Furthermore, "persecution on political, racial, and religious grounds," both before and during the War, constituted two additional categories of "crimes against humanity" under Count Four of the indictment. In this regard, and with specific reference to Jews, the indictment charged that "Jews were systematically persecuted since 1933, they were deprived of liberty, thrown into concentration camps where they were murdered and ill-treated. Their property was confiscated."

The charges brought against the defendants were stated in the indictment in general language. For example, Goering, according to the indictment had "authorized, directed and participated in War Crimes . . . and . . . Crimes against Humanity . . . including a wide variety of crimes against persons and property." Such crimes could fall within any of the ten categories of "war crimes" or the three categories of "crimes against humanity" (such as crimes against civilian populations committed before the War, and persecution on political, racial, or religious grounds during the War). That was clear in Goering's case who, for example, had issued a decree on July 31, 1941, directing Himmler and Heydrich to "bring about a complete solution of the Jewish question in the German sphere of influence in Europe." Such a direction clearly constituted "ill treatment . . . of civilian population of or in occupied territory," a "war crime" under Art. 6b., and at the same time "extermination or persecution on religious grounds," clearly constituted a "crime against humanity" under Art. 6c. The confusion between "war crimes" and "crimes against humanity" could also be seen in the Tribunal's judgment which did not distinguish between "war crimes" and "crimes against humanity." The assumption is that they saw no need to do so because "crimes against humanity" included "war crimes" committed against civilian populations. This was reflected in the case of the sixteen defendants who were charged with and tried for both the commission of "war crimes" and "crimes against humanity". They all were found guilty of both charges or innocent of both charges.

Since the facts supporting the charges were unquestionable, the issues raised at the trial by the defendants were essentially questions of law. The defense questioned the tribunal's legitimacy to try the defendants and objected that the defendants were being tried under provisions not recognized by existing international law. Obviously, a nation like Germany that had unconditionally surrendered was in no position to resist whatever fate the victorious forces would deem appropriate. However, it was the view of the Tribunal that the Charter did not simply represent "an arbitrary exercise of power on the part of the victorious nations but was the expression of international law existing at the time of its creation" (I Judgment, 218). The United States was particularly eager to set the example of a valid precedent which could not be labelled "victor's vengeance." In that respect, the defendants and their lawyers helped in that they forced the Tribunal and the prosecutors to constantly seek justifications for their actions and thus to articulate the past, present and future of international law.

SOME LEGAL ISSUES CONCERNING THE NUREMBERG TRIBUNAL AND THE CHARGES

It is a principle generally recognized in criminal law that crimes must be clearly defined and that sanctions must be specified before one can be held responsible for committing a proscribed act. Some of the acts with which the defendants at Nuremberg were charged in Counts Three and Four were clearly in violation of the municipal law in effect where these acts were committed, but they were not violative of international law (without substantial extrapolation). Other acts held to be criminal were not criminal under municipal law or international law at that time. Furthermore, the defendants were charged with violating various treaties entered into by Germany which required, for example, the pacific settlement of disputes, non-aggression, respect of neutrality, et cetera. Chief among these was the Kellogg-Briand Pact (Pact of Paris) of 1928 which "condemn(ed) recourse to war for the solution of international controversies," and "renounc(ed) . . . war as an instrument of national policy . . ." (Indictment, App. C, 84–92). There is no question that the parties to the Kellogg-Briand Pact *declared and agreed* not to resort to war, but did this contract create *criminal liability* for those who broke the Pact? In other words, did the perpetrators of aggressive war commit merely an unlawful act or a *criminal* act as well? Since the Pact contained no sanctions and designated no tribunal to try its violators, according to general principles of criminal law it did not establish aggression as an international crime.

Because of the general legal principle that crimes must be clearly defined and sanctions must be specified before one can be held responsible for committing a proscribed act; because perpetration of an aggressive war was not deemed to be criminal by the treaties entered into by Germany before World War II; and, because of the general legal principle that individuals may not be held liable *ex post facto*—i.e., for acts committed before they had been deemed illegal—the basis for the criminal prosecution for the defendants at Nuremberg had to be established by the Tribunal.

The absence of clear definitions of "crimes against peace" and "crimes against humanity," and the absence of specified sanctions for those crimes and for "war crimes" was not deemed fatal by the Tribunal to the recognition of certain acts as being deemed "criminal." For the Tribunal, general principles of law recognized by civilized nations, which are a source of international law, may be binding upon states even in the absence of explicit agreement or specific definitional content. Furthermore, the Tribunal explicitly rejected the notion that only states, but not individuals, may be held liable for having committed such crimes. The Tribunal stated (I Judgment 223):

> That international law imposes duties and liabilities upon individuals as well as upon States has long been recognized . . . Crimes against international law are committed by men, not by abstract entities, and only by punishing individuals who commit such crimes can the provisions of international law be enforced.

The argument that the prosecutors were engaging in retroactive application of the law when prosecuting the defendants for planning and waging an aggressive war, was not persuasive when applied to the charge of "war crimes." The crimes defined in Art. 6c, in the view of the Tribunal, were "covered by Articles 46, 50, 52 and 56 of the Hague Convention of 1907 . . . [and] that violations of these provisions constituted crimes for which the guilty individuals were punishable, is too well settled to admit of argument" (I Judgment 253). Furthermore, the practice of the victorious nation punishing, let alone trying the vanquished for the commission of "war crimes," has precedent. Thus, establishing a special tribunal to administer punishment in accordance with a legal process, in the opinion of the Allies' judges, did what any one of them might have done singly. The absence of specific sanctions in the Hague Regulations was explained by the absence of an international legislature or a permanent international tribunal with jurisdiction to try international crimes. However, this weakness should not stifle the opportunity to advance international law and give it a more specific definitional and enforcement context.

The major innovation of the international Military Tribunal at Nuremberg, insofar as the trial of "war crimes" is concerned, was not the creation of offenses which had previously not existed or lacked definitional or enforcement context, but the fact that the trial was conducted *internationally* rather than by *individual states.* Also innovative was the inclusion of the London Charter's provisions for "crimes against humanity" as a recognized international crime. However, the difficulty in sorting out "war crimes" and "crimes against humanity" persisted throughout the trial, and the Nuremberg Judgment added more confusion than clarity to this new concept. The Court's approach was that insofar as most acts alleged to be "crimes against humanity" were also "war crimes," they were clearly violative of the generally accepted laws and customs of war. There was, however, substantial legal significance to the fact that "crimes against humanity" were defined as separate, technical offenses. Nevertheless, the crimes did cover the situations such as the killing of Germans by Germans in German territory. Such acts were not "war crimes"; they were not related to the War (i.e., World War II) and were wholly within the jurisdiction of Germany. The indictment's definition of "crimes against humanity" is: [those acts] "committed against any civilian population, before or during the war . . . whether or not in violation of the domestic law of the country where perpetrated." Therefore, the threshold issue posed by the prosecution of such offenses committed in Germany and against German nationals before the commencement of the War was whether international law can penetrate the domestic law of a nation. The language of the Charter clearly implies that international law is in some respect supreme to municipal law.

The question of the supremacy of international law presents serious questions affecting national sovereignty and intervention in the internal affairs of nations. Surely there is a certain interpenetration of international law and municipal law, but to assume that the jealously guarded concept of sovereignty has been bypassed is self-deluding. Nations are still very leery of supranational law and its effect upon their own municipal systems.

The framers of the Charter and the judges of the Tribunal were undoubtedly aware of the sensitive nature of inquiring into the domestic affairs of a nation and the precedent this would establish. This is why the Charter provided that "crimes against humanity" can only be committed "in execution of or in connection with any crime within the jurisdiction of the Tribunal," i.e., "crimes against peace" or "war crimes." This also explains why there was ambiguity about the separate nature of this crime. The tribunal always tried to link "crimes against humanity" to "war crimes" and to "crimes against peace," while at the same time underscoring the separateness of "crimes against humanity." One of the consequences of this approach, however, was that many crimes committed by the Nazi regime against German Jews prior to the commencement of war were deemed outside the purview of the Charter and the Tribunal's jurisdiction. This meant that such crimes went unpunished at Nuremberg. (Since then, however, the Federal Republic of Germany has vigorously prosecuted Nazis who had committed such crimes.)

While Art. 6c provided that "crimes against humanity" can be committed "before or during the war" (a step beyond the recommendation of the Commission after World War I), a connection still had to be established between those crimes and the plans for aggressive war. That necessary "connection" precluded the punishment of individuals who committed acts deemed "crimes against humanity" because they were unrelated to war or its initiation. The prosecutors attempted to establish the necessary connection, but the Tribunal was of the opinion that (I Judgment 254):

> revolting and horrible as many of these crimes were, it has not been satisfactorily proved that they were done in execution of, or in connection with (other crimes within the jurisdiction of the Tribunal).

Thus, the proposition implicit in the Charter, i.e., that international law is capable of penetrating municipal law outside the context of war, was once more limited by the Tribunal's opinion; which in that respect properly reflected the existing state of international law. The debate concerning the proper relationship between municipal and international law persisted after the War and continues today.

The final major legal question raised by the Charter centered around Articles 7 and 8 which stated:

> Article 7. The official position of defendants, whether as Heads of State or responsible officials in Government Departments, shall not be considered as freeing them from responsibility mitigating punishment.

> Article 8. The fact that the Defendant acted pursuant to order of his Government or of a Superior shall not free him from responsibility, but may be considered in mitigation of punishment if the Tribunal determine that justice so requires.

Aside from questions of: 1) whether the defendants were subject to international law, and 2) whether the law with which they were charged with violating was properly applied, a question also emerged concerning whether these defendants would benefit from certain defenses, namely: 1) were these acts immune from prosecution because they were acts of state, and 2) were these acts if committed pursuant to orders of superiors beyond punishment? The Charter answered these questions emphatically in the negative, as did the Tribunal in its judgment when it stated (I Judgment 223):

> [I]ndividuals have international duties which transcend the national obligations or obedience imposed by the individual state.

The Tribunal sealed the fate of the defense of "Act of State" by stating (I Judgment 223):

> He who violates the laws of war cannot obtain immunity while acting in pursuance of the authority of the state if the state in authorizing action moves outside its competence under international law.

This then left only one defense to the defendants, namely, that they acted in obedience to superior orders. Article 8 of the Charter, however, had rejected this defense. The defendants could then argue only that they were deprived of a valid legal defense by an *ex post facto* law.

The defense argued that an officer is in no position to determine the legality of or justification for war, especially when the definition of "aggression" is in dispute. However, that argument fails in respect to determining the criminal nature of orders constituting "war crimes" or such "crimes against humanity" as the intentional spreading of typhus disease, forced sterilization, and mass executions of civilian populations.

The Tribunal was of the opinion that Article 8 was not an *ex post facto* formulation of a novel principle of law and stated (I Judgment 224):

> The provisions of this Article are in conformity with the law of all nations. That a soldier was ordered to kill or torture in violation of the international law of war has never been recognized as a defense to such acts of brutality . . .

The Tribunal relied on the *Llandovery Castle Case,* a war crime trial held in Leipzig after World War I which considered the plea of "obedience to superior orders." The judgment of the German court trying the case was that:

subordinates... are under no obligation to question the order of their
superior officer, and they can count upon its legality. But no such confidence
can be held to exist, if such an order is universally known to everybody,
including also the accused, to be without any doubt whatever against the
law.

Although the Tribunal rejected defenses based upon obedience to orders of a
superior, it did hold that obedience to superior orders could be considered in
the mitigating of punishment.

As Article 8 precluded the possibility of pleading "obedience to superior
orders," the defense attempted to draw a distinction between *ordinary orders,* which would be covered by Art. 8, and *orders of the Fuhrer,* which
would not be included within the meaning of Art. 8. The argument, in essence, was that the Nazi regime was governed by the *Fuhrerprinzip* according
to which (I Judgment 176):

each *Fuhrer* (leader) has the right to govern, administer or decree, subject to
no control of any kind and at his complete discretion, subject only to the
orders he received from above.

The ordinary leaders, then, were subject to the directions of the highest
leader, Hitler, and there "was no contradicting the *Fuhrer*'s orders." Of
course, this inability to disobey according to the Nazi law was deemed irrelevant under international law which imposes duties (said the Tribunal) "transcending obligations imposed by the State." The *Fuhrerprinzip,* in the view
of the Tribunal, could not be accorded a position of recognition among the law
of nations (I Judgment 226):

They are not deemed innocent because Hitler made use of them, if they knew
what they were doing. That they were assigned to their tasks by a dictator
does not absolve them from responsibility for their acts. The relation of
leader and follower does not preclude responsibility here any more than it
does in the comparable tyranny of organized domestic crime.

Finally, it should be noted that the prosecution of war criminals and persons
accused of committing "crimes against humanity" was not confined to the
Nuremberg Trial. Many trials were held in the Allied occupation zones. Many
defendants in these trials were convicted and hanged. These trials were held
under the authority of Control Council Order No. 10, the purpose of which
was to "establish a uniform legal basis in Germany for the prosecution of war
criminals and other similar offenders, other than those dealt with by the
International Military Tribunal at Nuremberg" (UNWCC, 12).

Nuremberg was not set up as an international moot court to make decisions concerning theoretical problems. Rather, it was set up to accomplish a minimum of three things:

1. To express the moral outrage of the world community.
2. To resort to the rule of law to prosecute and punish those who had violated the law.
3. To set an example and a precedent, which might serve as a deterrent for such violative conduct.

THE FORMULATION OF THE "NUREMBERG PRINCIPLES"

The significance of the Nuremberg precedent is:

> The establishment of international human duties transcending both national obligations under municipal law and official orders of domestic authorities followed by the infliction of the highest penalty on the civil rulers and military leaders of a "criminal" state amounted to a revolution in the law. (Drost, *The Crime of State: Genocide,* p. 147)

After Nuremberg, the United Nations, during its formative years, dealt with the issues raised by the Nuremberg proceedings and sought to define the significance of this event. The United Nations Organization responded to the challenge provided by the Nuremberg Charter and its Judgment. The challenge was to develop a body of international criminal law that could be applied during wartime *as well as during peacetime* so that the Nuremberg difficulties could be averted. As a result, the first session of the General Assembly indicated its concern with that question in three resolutions which set forth the framework and the future direction of the international scheme for the protection of human rights.

The General Assembly also resolved that a committee be established to study the methods by which the General Assembly should encourage the progressive development of international law and its eventual codification. Taking note of the London Agreement and Charter, the Assembly affirmed the principles of international law recognized by the Charter of the Nuremberg Tribunal and the judgment of the Tribunal. The committee on codification of international law was directed to treat as a matter of primary importance plans for the formulation, in the context of a general codification of offenses against the peace and security of mankind, or of an International Criminal Code, of the principles recognized in the Charter of the Nuremberg Tribunal and in the judgment of the tribunal.

Some of the Principles of Nuremberg, formulated by the International Law Commission and adopted by the U.N. General Assembly in 1950, are:

Principle IV: The fact that a person acted pursuant to order of his Government or of a superior does not relieve him from responsibility under international law, provided a moral choice was in fact possible to him.

Principle VI: (b) War Crimes: Violations of the laws and customs of war which include, but are not limited to, murder, ill-treatment or deportation to slave-labor or for any other purpose of civilian population of or in occupied territory, murder or ill-treatment of prisoners of war of (sic) persons on the seas, killing of hostages, plunder of public or private property, wanton destruction of cities, towns or villages, or devastation not justified by military necessity.

(c) Crimes against humanity: Murder, extermination, enslavement, deportation and other inhuman acts done against any civilian population or persecutions on political, racial or religious grounds, when such acts are done or such persecutions are carried on in execution of or in connection with any crime against peace or any war crime.

With this formulation of the Nuremberg principles, the arguments concerning the existence of internationally enforceable proscriptions which were raised at the time would now be obviated in the future. Three questions, however, were not covered by this formulation; they are: 1) the creation of a permanent international criminal court, 2) the elaboration of a permanent international criminal code, 3) the applicability in time of the Nuremberg principles.

The third question, namely, the applicability *in time* of the Nuremberg principles, did not become apparent until the middle 1960's when the Federal Republic of Germany's statute of limitations on the crime of murder was to run out. The Federal Republic of Germany, like most countries, has a statute of limitations which bars prosecution of offenses after a certain period of time. The period of time for murder, the highest offense in its criminal code, is twenty-five years. This meant that by 1970 any person who had committed such a crime up to 1945 would not be subject to prosecution in Germany (the country with territorial jurisdiction over such offenses). Other countries could prosecute such offenders on the theory of universality of jurisdiction because such crimes are international crimes, but for practical reasons it would be difficult to prosecute outside Germany. Furthermore, many countries also have a similar statute of limitations. In response to that problem, prompted by concerned persons and groups (particularly, the International Association of Penal Law) the United Nations proposed an international convention the object of which would be to suspend any statute of limitations for "war crimes" and "crimes against humanity."

The more tangible result of the Nuremberg principles is the "Convention on the Nonapplicability of Statutes of Limitations to War Crimes against Humanity." If nothing else, it reveals the world community's persistence in not morally condoning these acts only because time has elapsed without its perpetrators being apprehended and brought to trial. Indeed, justice cannot hinge on the ability of those who evade it.

THE IMPACT OF WORLD WAR II "CRIMES AGAINST HUMANITY" ON THE REGULATION OF ARMED CONFLICTS AND THE PROTECTION OF CIVILIANS

When the extent of World War II's horrors became known, it was clear that the War had produced more harm to civilians than to combatants. The ratio of civilian to military casualties is estimated to be fifty to one. It consequently became incumbent upon the World Community to elaborate proscriptions capable of protecting civilians within the context of war. The Geneva Conventions of 1856 and 1921 were deficient in that regard; however, the efforts of the International Commission of the Red Cross culminated in the Four Geneva Conventions of August 12, 1949, which sought to ameliorate this situation. It was really the experience of World War II which brought about the required detailed regulation which was lacking in the 1899 and 1907 Hague Conventions. It was that insufficiency which made it difficult at Nuremberg to offer a substantive definitional content to "crimes against humanity." The Geneva Conventions have endeavored, therefore, to be specific in that respect. The Convention's proscriptions are clearly responsive to the type of acts committed during World War II. The Fourth Geneva Convention deals with the protection of civilians and prohibits those acts which were deemed "crimes against humanity" at Nuremberg. It deals, however, only with wartime situations.

The Civilians Convention contains 159 articles which state the fundamental and detailed rights of civilians in time of war. It attempts to extend to civilians those rights and protections that have been established for prisoners of war and the sick and wounded of the Armed Forces. Without enumerating each of these articles, some of its key provisions may be noted:

Article 13 specifies that the Convention applies to the whole population of countries in conflict, regardless of race, nationality, religion or political opinion.

Article 27 appears basic in that it carries on the theme of fundamental principles of Geneva, i.e., respect for the human person and the inalienable nature of his fundamental rights. Persons, honor, family rights, religious convictions and practices, and their manners and customs are protected against threats or acts of violence, insult or public curiosity. Women are protected against rape, enforced prostitution, and any force of indecent assault.

Article 30 provides that protected persons "shall have every facility for making application to the protecting powers, the ICRC, the national Red Cross (also Crescent, Lion and Sun, etc.), or any other organization that may assist them."

Articles 31–33 assert that physical and moral coercion to obtain information, murder, torture, mutilation, and medical or scientific experiments not
necessary for the health of the person are prohibited. Similarly, collective
punishments, terrorism, pillage, and reprisals against protected persons and
their property are prohibited.

Article 34 clearly and simply states, "The taking of hostages is prohibited."

Article 44 provides that refugees shall not be treated as enemy aliens solely
on the basis of *de jure* nationality of the enemy state if they, in fact, do not
enjoy the protection of any government.

One of the most important provisions expressed in Article 49 is that which
prohibits individual or mass transfers and deportation of protected persons
from occupied territory to that of the occupant or to that of any other power,
occupied or not, "regardless of their motives." It was this practice of deportation which added years to the Nazis' war effort when Germany's own resources were virtually exhausted. This same article allows the occupant to
evacuate protected persons in the interest of the safety of the population, for
imperative military reasons, or because such areas cannot be adequately
supplied. All transfers must be humanely conducted, and the protecting power
must be informed of them as soon as they have taken place. Conversely, this
article prohibits the detention of protected persons in danger areas and,
additionally, prevents the occupying power from moving parts of its own
population into the occupied territory.

As far as children are concerned (Art. 50), it is stipulated that the occupying
power will facilitate, with the cooperation of the national and local authorities, the proper working of all institutions which concern themselves with
the care, maintenance, and education of children. Identification and parental
registration are also to be facilitated.

The fact that a convention exists exclusively for the protection of civilians
is noteworthy in that it represents a substantial step in humanitarian progress.
The machinery available within the four corners of its provisions can provide
some humanization of war. Clearly, the Convention does not cover peacetime
situations which are presumably covered by the law of peace, more specifically through treaties on the international protection of human rights, and
other specialized Conventions.

THE GENOCIDE CONVENTION: PROVISIONS AND DEFINITIONS

Toward the end of World War II, when the mass murders committed by
the Nazis had become common knowledge, a new word entered our vocabulary—"genocide." Coined by Raphael Lemkin in 1944, "genocide"

joined "crimes against humanity" as a new term in the legal parlance. As a response to the Holocaust, and as a response to the challenge to international law posed by the Nuremberg trials, the United Nations attempted both to define "genocide" for international criminal law and to halt future occurrences of genocide, both in times of peace and war, by drafting the Genocide Convention of 1948.

In his work *Axis Rule in Occupied Europe* (1944, p. 79), Lemkin stated that "genocide" was intended:

> to signify a coordinated plan of different actions aiming at the destruction of essential foundations of life of national groups . . . The objectives of such a plan would be the disintegration of the political and social institutions of culture, language, national feelings, religions and the economical existence of national groups, and the destruction of personal security, liberty, health, dignity, and even lives of the individuals belonging to such groups.

Lemkin's definition was expanded, refined and concretized. On December 11, 1946, the "Convention on the Prevention and Suppression of Genocide" was adopted by the U.N. General Assembly. Unlike the Universal Declaration of Human Rights of December 1948, the genocide resolution was embodied in a treaty which was ratified by a sufficient number of states so that it might come into force.

The treaty defined "genocide" as follows:

> Art. 2: (W)ith intent to destroy, in whole or in part, a national, ethnical, racial or religious group as such:
> (a) Killing members of the group;
> (b) Causing serious bodily or mental harm to members of the group;
> (c) Deliberately inflicting on the group conditions of life calculated to bring about its physical destruction in whole or in part;
> (d) Imposing measures intended to prevent births within the group;
> (e) Forcibly transferring children of the group to another group.

The Genocide Convention also specifically states (Art. 1) that "genocide, whether committed in time of peace or in time of war, is a crime under international law . . ." Thus, the Convention, which it is hoped, must operate primarily, if not exclusively in times of "peace," took the logical stride beyond the London Charter and the Nuremberg Judgment. It included, however, within the definition of "genocide," serious bodily or mental harm to members of a group in terms as broad as what was encompassed in "crimes against humanity" as used in Nuremberg.

The original drafts of the Convention referred to "cultural genocide": "acts aimed at destruction of libraries, museums, schools, historical monuments, and religious edifices, or the suppression of language or printing media of a particular group." While such a notion is not included in the Convention, aspects of "cultural genocide" are within the coverage of other conventions.

The Convention provides that enforcement of its provisions is to be entrusted to the contracting parties. In accordance with their respective Constitutions the parties "undertake to enact the necessary legislation to give effect to the provisions of the (Genocide) Convention and, in particular, to provide effective penalties for persons guilty of genocide . . ." (Art. 5). As it seems unlikely that any individual is capable of committing genocide, the offense is only likely to be committed under governmental direction. A government that is intent upon genocide is certainly not going to allow its own municipal law to be applied against itself. Thus, although genocide may be considered an international crime, the government officials responsible are not subject to effective sanctions.

The main principles established by the Convention are the following:

1. The contracting states are bound to enact the laws needed to give effect to the provisions of the Convention; specifically, to provide effective penalties.

2. States undertake to try persons charged these offenses in their competent national court.

3. Parties to the Convention agree that the acts listed shall not be considered political crimes. Therefore, they pledge to grant extradition in accordance with their laws and treaties.

The Convention also envisages trial by an international criminal court should one be set up and should the contracting parties accept its jurisdiction.

If there is any dispute between one country and another on the interpretation, application or fulfillment of the Convention, the dispute must be submitted, at the request of any of the parties to the dispute, to the International Court of Justice.

Article 4 of the Convention declares that those guilty of genocide and the other acts listed shall be punished "whether they are constitutionally responsible rulers, public officials, or private individuals." This clause makes it impossible for a person to plead immunity because he was the head of a state or held some other public office.

Under Article 8 of the Convention, any contracting party may call upon the competent organs of the United Nations to take such action under the Charter of the United Nations as they consider appropriate for the prevention and suppression of acts of genocide or any of the related acts. The related acts are 1) conspiracy to commit genocide, 2) direct and public incitement to commit genocide, 3) an attempt to commit the crime, and 4) complicity in its commission.

During discussion by the Legal Committee in 1948, the question of an international penal jurisdiction was carefully considered. After studying the question, the International Law Commission concluded that an international criminal court was both possible and desirable but recommended that it be a separate institution rather than a Criminal Chamber of the International Court of Justice. Subsequently, in 1953 the Committee on International Criminal Jurisdiction submitted a draft statute for a separate court. The General Assembly agreed that the problems raised by this matter are closely related to the question of defining aggression and to the "Proposed 1954 Draft Code of Offenses Against the Peace and Security of Mankind" and, therefore, postponed consideration of an international criminal jurisdiction until it could consider all other reports on these related questions. It must be stated, however, that the repression of genocide can be effective only if in addition to municipal legislation an international criminal court can be established with effective means of exercising its jurisdiction and implementing its judgments. In addition, the convention must be supplemented with collective sanctions.

The collective aspect of genocide is to be seen in the protected groups under the Convention. According to the definition of the crime, the element of collectivity is to be found in the special intent to destroy a particular human group. It is argued that fundamentally genocide is but mass homicide with a special interest directed toward a special category of people but ultimately perpetrated on a particular person belonging to such group. The definition of "genocide" leads also to the conclusion that it amounts to an offense against the fundamental human rights of the individual.

THE GENOCIDE CONVENTION: PROBLEMS AND PROSPECTS

Despite the progress made by the adoption of the Genocide Treaty in 1948 and of the Principles of Nuremberg in 1950, a number of conceptual and practical problems remain.

As have been noted above, the Nuremberg trials did not adequately distinguish between "war crimes" and "crimes against humanity." No clear and distinct definition of "crimes against humanity" emerged from the Nuremberg proceedings. Nor did the Principles of Nuremberg, adopted by the U.N. in 1950, serve to clarify these distinctions further. While the adoption of the Genocide Treaty in 1948 introduced a new term and a new concept into the parlance of international criminal law, the treaty did not adequately distinguish "genocide" from "war crimes" or from "crimes against humanity." Though, in 1946, the U.N. General Assembly resolved that "genocide" is one category of "crimes against humanity," there was no clear conceptual or functional distinction made between the two notions. An attempt at clarification was made by the "Draft Code of Offenses Against the Peace and Security of Mankind." According to the Draft Code (1954; Art. 2,11), "genocide" may be committed by a private individual or a state, while "crimes against humanity" can be committed "by the authorities of a state or by private individuals acting at the instigation of or with the toleration of such authorities." This attempt at clarification, nevertheless, fails as there is no validity to the distinction between the two crimes since they both involve wholesale human depredation which could not occur without the state's instigation or acquiescence.

Thus, the introduction of new legal concepts—"crimes against humanity" and "genocide"—into the vocabulary of humankind in the post-World War II era may have conveyed the imperative need for repression and punishment of such crimes; however, those engaged in the progressive development of international law are still required to clarify and refine further the conceptual and functional meanings of these concepts and of the distinctions to be made between them (as well as their relationship to concepts such as "war crimes," "crimes against peace," etc.).

The aforementioned conventions and declarations aimed at protecting individuals from becoming victims of "war crimes," "crimes against humanity," "genocide," etc. However, a failure of these U.N.-sponsored enterprises was the absence of a provision for the prosecution (and extradition for prosecution) of those who had committed such crimes. No legal forum with jurisdiction to try such offenses was formed. In the absence of such a forum, nations continue to resort to political solutions rather than to legal ones in order to deal with aggression, "war crimes," "crimes against humanity" and serious violations of human rights. This means that retribution, if it is to occur, would be likely only in the case of an unconditional surrender—by a party to a conflict with the victorious party willing and able to carry out a scheme of prosecution and punishment. Since 1945, at least two conflicts have taken place (Biafra and Bangladesh) which should have given rise to international prosecution but did not do so.

As was noted above, the London Charter, the Nuremberg trials and the U.N. declarations and conventions firmly established the notion that not only states but individuals as well are culpable for crimes committed in violation of international law. Acts by individuals could no longer be defended on the grounds that such acts were committed under the umbrella of state-sanctioned legitimacy. In the absence of an internationally recognized legal forum to prosecute individuals for such crimes, the mere concept of individual responsibility cannot and has not served as an adequate deterrent. Individuals as well as states, have continued to commit these crimes and have continued to elude prosecution for having committed them. The present remedies for the repression of crimes such as genocide, are, therefore, severely limited. Unless provisions are made for the prosecution of such individuals, international declarations and conventions regarding such crimes are doomed to remain dead letters. Unless an international criminal court will be effectively able to exercise jurisdiction and to administer penal sanctions, it is likely that such crimes will continue to be committed and those responsible for committing them will elude prosecution.

THE EICHMANN TRIAL

Since the Nuremberg trials, many states have prosecuted Nazi war criminals in national tribunals or in specially constituted tribunals. No state, however, tried major war criminals, whether at large or dead. At the close of the Nuremberg trials, two major Nazi war criminals were still sought: Martin Bormann and Adolph Eichmann. Bormann was presumed dead; however, Eichmann was known to be alive. The relentless search for Eichmann resulted in his capture by Israeli agents in 1960, his "forced" extradition from Argentina, and his subsequent trial in Israel.

The legal questions raised by the Eichmann trial were many:

Did the Israeli courts have the jurisdiction and the competence for trying Eichmann for the charged offenses? This general question embraces a constellation of more specific questions.

While it was assumed that a state may prosecute an individual who harmed its nationals, all of those Jews who were affected by Eichmann's acts were not nationals of the State of Israel. Indeed, Israel was not yet in existence at the time of the crimes committed by Eichmann. How, then, could an Israeli court claim jurisdiction for prosecuting crimes against individuals who were not its nationals and for crimes committed before the State of Israel existed?

Eichmann was charged with having committed a variety of crimes, including "genocide" and "crimes against the Jewish people." As was discussed above, "genocide" was first codified as an international crime by the Genocide Convention of 1948. The concept of "crimes against the Jewish people" became law in 1950 by the Israeli parliament and was titled "The Nazi and Nazi Collaborators Law." As Eichmann's attorneys argued, these laws were being retroactively applied to acts committed during World War II. As has been noted above, it is a general principle of criminal law that one may not be held culpable for acts committed before a law deeming one culpable for such acts has come into existence; criminal laws cannot be applied *ex post facto*. If this principle of law were to be upheld, on what grounds did the Israeli courts have competence to try Eichmann?

Nazi war criminals, who committed crimes not limited to the geographical boundaries of a specific country, were to be tried by an international tribunal, according to the conditions of the London Charter and according to the precedents set by the Nuremberg trials and by a number of declarations and conventions adopted by the United Nations. Thus, the competence of a national court to try Eichmann for such crimes was at issue. Furthermore, the problem of whether a national law could prevail over international law was also involved.

Finally, the kidnapping of Eichmann from Argentina raised the additional question of whether the means of his apprehension voided the authority of the Israeli court to hear his case. The violation of Argentinian sovereignty and the kidnapping of one of its nationals, the absence of the legal extradition of an Argentinian national, raised additional complications from the perspective of international law.

Before discussing how the Israeli court responded to these questions, it is important to note the specific charges leveled against Eichmann. Besides being charged with "genocide" and with "crimes against the Jewish people," Eichmann was also charged with "crimes against humanity" as embodied in the Nuremberg Principles (discussed above). Specifically, he was charged: with having participated in the killing of Jews between 1939 and 1945 (Count 1 of the indictment); with having placed millions of Jews in living conditions which were calculated to bring about their physical destruction (Count 2); with having enslaved, starved, and deported Jews so as to deprive them of rights as human beings (Count 2); with having committed "crimes against humanity" (Counts 5, 6, 7).

The Israeli court rejected Eichmann's claim that it lacked proper jurisdiction and competence to try him for the aforementioned crimes. As to the question of whether Israel could claim jurisdiction for the prosecution of crimes against individuals who were not its nationals at the time when such crimes were committed, the Israeli court contended that it did indeed have such jurisdiction under three theories of extraterritorial application of laws. The first was the protected interest theory, which holds that acts committed outside the territory of a state may properly be brought before a court of that state if the acts in question affect significant interests of that state. The second was the nationality theory, where a state may prosecute a person who harmed its nationals. The use of these two theories can be questioned since at the time Eichmann's acts occurred, Israel did not exist as a state, and therefore could have no national interests in protecting people who were not its citizens. The State of Israel relied, however, on the theory that it embodies the "Jewish people" concept in its political existence and that this concept of Jewish peoplehood allowed it to extend its protective jurisdiction to all Jews wherever they are. This theory, however, has no basis in international law, particularly in respect to the jurisdictional applications given to it. Nevertheless, the State of Israel had another valid basis to try Eichmann. The District Court of Jerusalem appropriately held that (Verbatim Transcripts, Judgment, para. 12):

> the authority and jurisdiction to try crimes under international law are universal.

This is the doctrine of universality of jurisdiction in cases on international crimes.

By claiming the universality of jurisdiction in cases on international crime, the Israeli court responded to the question of whether a "national" court could prosecute a criminal for crimes violative of international law. Furthermore, the court noted that in the absence of an International Court to try criminals such as Eichmann, the judicial and legislative organs of each nation are not only permitted, but are obligated, to bring such criminals to trial.

According to the Genocide treaty, in the absence of a competent international court to prosecute individuals for the crime of "genocide," jurisdiction for prosecution vests in the territory in which the crime occurred. For this reason, the jurisdiction of the Israeli court to try Eichmann was problematic. One may claim, however, that the Israeli Court was justified in defending its jurisdiction to try Eichmann for two reasons. First, the universality theory of jurisdiction is relevant here. In the absence of an international court, Israel (as well as any state) could claim jurisdiction. Second, the "preferred theory of jurisdiction" (i.e., the crime is to be tried where it had been committed), is only meant to be an obligatory minimum which in no way bars individual states from punishing individuals found guilty of "genocide."

On the question of the retroactive application of the law of genocide, the court noted (excerpted from AJIL, 805,1962):

> ... It is indeed difficult to find a more convincing instance of a just retroactive law than the legislation providing for the punishment of war criminals and perpetrators of crimes against humanity and against the Jewish people, and all the reasons justifying the Nuremberg Judgments justify *eo ipse* the retroactive legislation of the Israel legislature ... The accused in this case is charged with the implementation of the plan for the "Final Solution of the problem of the Jews." Can anyone in his right mind doubt the absolute criminality of such acts ...?

Furthermore, the Court also realized that besides the Genocide Convention, Israeli law was also being retroactively applied. Nevertheless, the Court found that it "ha(d) to give effect to the law of the Knesset, and ... cannot entertain the contention that the law conflicts with the principles of international law." In other words, the Court was not empowered to review legislative acts. It should be noted that while most legal systems recognize the principle of *ex post facto*, it has been maintained that it is not a rule of international law.

The Court also addressed the question of the relationship between Israeli national law and international law as it pertained to the Eichmann trial. The Court found that national law would prevail over international law in an Israeli court.

The Court held that from the point of view of international law, the power of the State of Israel to enact the law in question or Israel's "right to punish" is based, with respect to the offenses in question, on a dual foundation: the universal character of the crimes in question and their specific character as intended to exterminate the Jewish people.

This dual foundation—the universal character of the crime, and the specific relationship of the crime vis-à-vis the Jewish people—led the Court to note that "all that has been said in the Nuremberg principles about 'crimes against humanity' applies *a fortiori* to 'crimes against the Jewish people.'" Thus, in effect, the court defined "crimes against the Jewish people" as a variety of "genocide" and defined "genocide" as "the gravest type of 'crime against humanity'" (i.e., "genocide" is a variety of the more embracive concept of "crimes against humanity").

Because Eichmann was specifically charged with "crimes against humanity," the claim that he was being prosecuted *ex post facto* is weakened. "Crimes against humanity," with which Eichmann was charged, were found to be in violation of the law of nations according to the Nuremberg Judgment. If the Nuremberg Judgment represents the application of general principles of international law, then the Israeli Court was correct in holding that Eichmann's acts were violative of the international law *when committed*.

After the Court had ruled upon the question of its rightful jurisdiction to try the Eichmann case, the defense raised many additional points of law regarding the culpability of the defendant. Primary amongst these legal issues was the question of whether the defendant was personally responsible for deeds committed as an "act of State." In simpler terms, the defense maintained that since Eichmann was only "following orders" of his government, he was free of any responsibility for acts performed in the course of his duties as a government official. Referring to the London Charter, the Nuremberg trials and the Nuremberg Principle, the Court affirmed the inadmissibility of the defense's position on this matter. The Court held that:

> The contention of learned counsel for the defense that it is not the accused but the State on whose behalf he had acted, who is responsible for his criminal acts is only true as to its second part. It is true that under international law Germany bears not only moral, but also legal, responsibility for all the crimes that were committed as its own "acts of State," including the crimes attributed to the accused. But that responsibility does not detract one iota from the personal responsibility of the accused for his acts. . . .

As to the question of its competence to hear the Eichmann case in view of Eichmann's improper apprehension from Argentina, the Court held that (excerpted from 56 AJIL, 1962):

> It is an established rule of law that a person being tried for an offense against the laws of a State may not oppose his trial by reason of the illegality of his arrest or of the means whereby he was brought within the jurisdiction of that

State. The courts in England, the United States, and Israel have constantly held that the circumstances of the arrest and the mode of bringing the accused into the territory of the State have no relevance to his trial. . . .

Indeed, there is no escaping the conclusion that the question of the violation of international law by the manner in which the accused was brought into the territory of a country arises at the international level, namely, the relations between the two countries concerned alone, and must find its solution at such level. . . .

According to the existing rule of law there is no immunity for a fugitive offender save in the one and only case where has been extradited by the asylum State to the requesting State for a specific offense, which is not the offense for which he was being tried. The accused was not surrendered to Israel by Argentina, and the State of Israel is not bound by any agreement with Argentina to try the accused for any other specific offense, or not to the offender, and the accused cannot compel a foreign sovereign State to give him protection against his will. The accused was a wanted war criminal when he escaped to Argentina by concealing his true identity. Only after he was kidnapped and brought to Israel was his identity revealed.

As to the question of the invasion of Argentinian sovereignty to apprehend the defendant, the Court held that this matter was a matter for negotiation between Israel and Argentina and irrelevant to the trial proceedings. Indeed, in such negotiations, Argentina waived its demand for Eichmann's return. In a joint communique issued on August 3, 1960, by the Argentine and Israeli governments, it was resolved by the two governments "to regard as closed the incident which arose out of the action taken by citizens of Israel, which infringed the fundamental rights of the State of Argentina." Thus, the Government of Argentina thereby refused conclusively to grant the accused any sort of protection. Therefore, the Court held that "the accused has been brought to trial before the Court of a State which charges him with grave offenses against its laws. The accused has no immunity against this trial and must stand trial in accordance with the indictment."

CONCLUSION

The Holocaust is all too often left only to Jews to remember and to commemorate. Yet, the Holocaust is not merely a Jewish tragedy; it is the tragedy of all humankind. Consequently, the Holocaust must not gradually become the exclusive concern of one people but must be considered part of the history of all people. "Never again" must become the motto of all humankind; otherwise, it would be all to easy to rationalize such events as simply being the result of intergroup conflict, as has been the case, for example, with regard to: Biafrans, the people of Bangladesh, black southern Africans and the Palestinians. It is all a matter of degree. Should human rights and their observance not become truly universalized, both in theory and in practice, acceptance of human depredation becomes all too inviting.

The conscience of the world must be constantly reminded of the Holocaust and other similar events so that genocide and other serious human depredations may be avoided in the future. What is at stake is the very preservation of humanity against the thin veneer of its civilization.

TOPICS FOR FURTHER STUDY AND FOR CLASS DISCUSSION

The preceeding pages have concentrated discussion upon three concepts— "war crimes," "crimes against humanity," and "genocide"—and upon two trials — the Nuremberg trials and the Eichmann trial. To be sure, other trials for war crimes committed during the Second World War have taken place. Therefore, one fruitful topic for class research and for class discussion would be a consideration of those trials. As has been noted above, the trials of Nazi war criminals in Germany continued after the close of the Nuremberg trials. Some of these trials were conducted by American judges (in the American Zone of occupation). The 1948 trials are of specific interest and may be studied in conjunction with viewing the film in which they are portrayed— *Judgment at Nuremberg.** In addition, trials of Nazi war criminals conducted by the West German government should be considered as they represent the judgment of Germans upon Germans for crimes committed during World War II. In the course of studying these West German trials, attention should be paid to the question of whether a "statute of limitations" ought to obtain regarding "war crimes." The question of whether to extend the "statute of limitations" on "war crimes" attained significant attention in Europe, Israel and the United States. As the result of this attention, the "statute of limitations" has been extended.

The trials of Nazi War criminals tended to eclipse the trials of Japanese war criminals held after World War II. A comparison of these trials would prove both interesting and instructive.

Study of the legal implications of the Holocaust raises a number of problems which are of particular interest to American students. For example, many comparisons have been made between Nazi atrocities and atrocities committed by Americans in the course of American military history. Nevertheless, it is our contention that the crimes committed by the Nazis are unique both in kind and in scope. The Holocaust is a unique event and should not be

---

*See chapter on "The Holocaust and the Film Arts."

readily compared to other acts of mass murder or genocide. The only possibly viable comparison to the Holocaust is the systematic slaughter of the Armenians by the Turks during World War I. In this regard, it should be remembered that when Hitler was asked how he expected to undertake the mass murder of the Jews without condemnation from the world community, he responded—''Who remembers the Armenians?''

Despite the inappropriateness of making close comparisons between Nazi atrocities and atrocities committed in the course of U.S. military history, such comparisons persist. Therefore, if and when such comparisons are made, it is best that they be done with proper care. In this regard, two specific problems present themselves:

• Has the United States committed genocide against the American Indian?
• Did the United States commit genocide in Vietnam?

The United States' involvement in Vietnam raised several controversial issues in the area of international law. Two such questions are 1) Whether the United States was guilty of genocide, and 2) Whether the United States committed ''war crimes'' in Southeast Asia.

''Genocide'' is defined in the Genocide Convention. The United States is not at present a signatory to this treaty. The Convention defines ''genocide'' as

> acts committed with intent to destroy, in whole or in part, a national, ethnical, racial or religious group by such means as killing members of the group, causing serious bodily or mental harm to members of the group, deliberately inflicting on the group conditions of life calculated to bring about its physical destruction imposing measures intended to prevent births within the group, or forcibly transferring children of the group to another group.

In the light of this definition, there are at least three essential elements to be considered in determining the material element and the mental element needed to prove a charge of ''genocide.''

1. The existence of a separate national, ethnical, racial or religious group sufficiently distinct and identifiable so as to be capable of being recognized as a victim of genocidal acts.

2. The commission of acts performed as part of a plan to destroy, in whole or in part, this national, ethnical, racial, or religious group.

3. A specific intent to destroy this group as whole or in part.

None of these elements are present in the facts surrounding the United States' activities in Southeast Asia for the following reasons:

1. The opposing parties in the Vietnam conflict did not include a separate national, ethnical, racial, or religious group. The nature of the Vietnam conflict was, at one time, a subject of strong political controversy. It has now, however, been internationally recognized as a civil war. The United States allied itself in this conflict with the South Vietnamese nationals and directed its activities against the Viet Cong, a term designating members of the insurgent military force. The Viet Cong did not qualify as, nor did they ever claim to be, a separate national, ethnical, racial, or religious group. In fact, the national, ethnical, racial and religious composition of the South Vietnamese nationals and the Viet Cong were essentially identical. The only groups so strongly concentrated on one side as to be conceivably in a position to suffer genocide were the Catholics, Cao Dais, and Montagnards, all on the *South Vietnamese - American* side. The absence of the one essential element of an identifiable group alone invalidates any legally defensible charge of "genocide" that might conceivably be made against the United States as a result of its activities in Vietnam.

2. American activities in Vietnam were not such as could be classified as part of a coordinated plan to destroy in whole or in part any particular national, ethnical, racial, or religious group. The only American actions which might even conceivably be argued as even approximating such acts were the establishment of free fire zones and massive bombing raids on North Vietnam. These two, however, clearly do not qualify but could constitute war crimes. However, there are the factors of military necessity and proportionality to be considered. Article 22 of the Hague Regulations establishes that the means by which one party may inflict injury upon another are not unlimited. Such means are subject to scrutiny in light of the military necessity of the particular tactical situation involved. Furthermore, Article 23 of the Hague Regulations establishes that there must be some proportionality between the amount and type of force used and the legitimate military objective that is being sought so that unnecessary injury and destruction are avoided. Additionally, military operations conducted as acts of political reprisal must not be out of all proportion to the provocation received. There is, however, a presumption of legitimacy given to any particular military operation. Proof of a violation of either the principle of necessity or of the principle of proportionality must be established before charges of war crimes may be confirmed.

As to any charges of genocide citing the establishment of free fire zones or American bombing raids on North Vietnam, it may be noted that the inhabitants of proposed free fire zones were warned prior to official designation of these zones to evacuate the area. Those who remained did so voluntarily and did not constitute a separate national, ethnical, racial, or religious group. Hence, any injuries suffered by them cannot be deemed genocidal. Moreover, in bombing North Vietnam, the United States utilized an internationally recognized military tactic against a legitimate military target. Specific individual casualties of noncombatants which resulted either during these raids or during other legitimate military operations were incidental to these operations. While special provision is made for such incidents in international law, they are not classified as genocidal acts.

3. American activities in Vietnam were not conducted with sufficient intent to support a charge of "genocide." It is firmly established that the crime of "genocide" is one of specific intent. There is no evidence sufficient to indicate that there was any specific intent, either expressed or implied, on the part of the United States to destroy in whole or in part, any national, ethnical, racial, or religious group. Because of the absence of such a specific intent, no charge of "genocide" can validly be made against the United States.

Finally, it may be noted that the absence of any *one* of the three essential elements of "genocide" sufficiently invalidates a charge of this offense made against the United States. That all *three* essential elements are absent in the facts of American involvement in Southeast Asia definitively defeats such an accusation and firmly establishes the innocence of the United States in this matter.

The question of American guilt has also been suggested in relation to the occasional war crimes that occurred in the more than decade of American involvement in Southeast Asia. None of these, however, was ever found to be part of a larger plan calling for the extermination, in whole or in part, of any given national, ethnical, racial, or religious group. The My Lai Massacre was the most widely publicized example of a war crime involving American personnel in Vietnam. The incident at Son My (My Lai) occurred on March 16, 1968. Lieutenant Calley, the principal offender involved, was charged with four counts of premeditated murder of 107 male and female Vietnamese civilians in the village of Son My (My Lai). Two additional counts were added alleging the premeditated murder of a Vietnamese adult and a Vietnamese child approximately two years of age. As no American civilian court had jurisdiction, the trial was conducted by military court-martial under the provisions of the Uniform Code of Military Justice. On November 24, 1969, MG Orwin Talbott, OG Fort Benning, Georgia, determined that there was sufficient evidence to warrant a trial and referred the charges against Lieutenant Calley for trial by the general court-martial. Evidence presented at trial indicated that Lieutenant Calley's platoon encountered no hostile fire in the village; the only casualty was a soldier who shot himself in the foot. The evidence indicated that the people whom Lieutenant Calley was charged with killing were unresisting, unarmed, and they had come completely within the control of Lieutenant Calley and his troops. Impanelling of the court began on November 12, 1970. The prosecution began to present its case on November

17, 1970. The court, on March 29, 1971, found Lieutenant Calley guilty of premeditated murder of not less than twenty-two noncombatant Vietnamese civilians and of assault with intent to murder one Vietnamese noncombatant civilian. On March 31, 1971, he was sentenced to confinement at hard labor for life, total forfeiture of all pay allowances, and dismissal from the service.

Action was also taken against two sergeants in Calley's company, who were court-martialed for intent to murder. These men, however, were acquitted. Several of Calley's superiors were administratively reprimanded for alleged attempts to cover up the My Lai incident. For example, Maj. Gen. Samuel Moster, Calley's division commander, was demoted and stripped of his Distinguished Service Medal by Army Sec. Stanley Resor, for failure to adequately investigate the My Lai incident. By May 1971, twenty-four men were charged by the Army with violations of the Uniform Code of Military Justice. Proceedings against twenty-three of these men resulted in the charges against them being dropped or acquittals.

The prosecution of these individuals, however, and the conviction of Lieutenant Calley clearly establishes that their conduct at My Lai was not an authorized part of planned American activities. Furthermore, all American armed forces personnel were instructed in the nature of and penalties for war crimes. They were required, as part of their standing orders, to immediately report the occurrence of any such crime if detected. These procedures clearly establish that any personnel who committed war crimes in Vietnam broke the bond of agency between themselves and the United States government prior to the commission of such acts. These war crimes, therefore, cannot be viewed as official acts of the U.S. government. The fact that at least twenty-one other U.S. personnel were convicted by the United States government for war crimes in Vietnam confirms that the commission of these offenses was neither the intent nor the desire of the United States. Thus, despite the contention of others— including the tribunal (a private initiative) convened by Bertrand Russell to try the United States for crimes committed in Vietnam—the present contention is that there are not sufficient legal grounds for considering the government of the United States guilty of "genocide" in Vietnam. Furthermore, any investigation of the question of whether war crimes were committed during the Vietnam War should include a discussion of whether such crimes were committed by the North Vietnamese against American prisoners of war.

The question of whether the United States has committed "genocide" against the American Indians, for the past two hundred years, is one which is not easily answered. The confusion lies in what is required to be convicted of "genocide" and in determining the past and present Indian policy of the United States government.

The most widely accepted international statement of what constitutes "genocide" can be found in "The Convention on the Prevention and Punishment of the Crime of Genocide" or, as it is usually called, "The Genocide

Convention.'' This convention was adapted by the General Assembly in 1948 and has been in effect since 1951 (see discussion on The Genocide Convention above).

In viewing this topic, two critical issues in charging the United States with ''genocide'' will be left out. First, the question of whether the United States can be convicted of a crime which it has never acknowledged; the United States has never ratified the Genocide Convention. Secondly, the issue of whether a *government* can be charged with ''genocide'' at all. The Genocide Convention in Art. 4 states that only *individuals* can be charged with ''genocide.'' If a government could be charged with ''genocide'' under the Convention, this would require a loose interpretation of the meaning of Art. 4.

Aside from the above problems in applying the Genocide Convention to the United States, the major issue in determining whether the U.S. has been guilty of ''genocide'' against the Indians is whether the U.S. has had the specific mental element to be charged with the crime. The Genocide Convention defines as ''genocide'' those acts if committed with intent to destroy, in whole or in part, a national ethnical, racial, or religious group—such as killing or causing serious bodily or mental harm to members of the group or deliberately inflicting on the group conditions of life calculated to bring about its total or partial physical destruction or imposing measures intended to prevent birth within the group or forcibly transferring children of the group to another.

In the Government's relations with the Indians, one can recall many horrible accounts of atrocities committed against the Red Man; the ''Trail of Tears'' and ''Wounded Knee,'' to name but two. However, it appears very difficult to attach any specific intent on the United States. It has been argued that one can imply the specific intent of ''genocide'' by means of circumstantial proof where a large number of victims have been affected. However, the contrary position seems to be the more prevailing view. For example, atrocities committed against American Blacks fail to qualify as acts of ''genocide'' since the requirement of an actual, specific intent cannot be proven with either a constructive or an implied malice model.

If we assume that there is a requirement for an actual, specific intent by the U.S., then it is difficult to prove any violation of the Genocide Convention, especially before 1887. For example, from 1790 to 1834 there were several statutes enacted to remove Indians from desirable eastern lands to the West, and, therefore, away from civilization. Even though there was a massive loss of life, there does not seem to be evidence that the statutes were intended to destroy the Indians. An example of this sort of act was the ''Trail of Tears,'' a forced migration of thousands of Indians from Georgia to Oklahoma. The Removal Act (June 1834), which authorized much of this senseless loss of life, had as its purpose to civilize and educate the Indian. In 1835 President Jackson said that he felt that the Indians would have a better chance of surviving if they were moved West. It would seem then that the specific intent for "genocide" is lacking up to this point. While isolated army and Government officials might have had the specific intent, it has not been conclusively established to determine that a nexus exists between their individual motives and official government policy.

The next era in American Indian - U.S. relations was heralded with the passage of the General Allotment Act of 1887, where tribal land was distributed to individual Indians. In the preamble to the act, the concept of assimilation, submerging one culture into another, does not appear. However, in debates and other reports it would appear that assimilation was the actual goal. It should be noted that this legislation did not terminate tribal existence if the Indians so elected; thus the Indians were able to preserve their tribal identity. In the New Deal this policy was temporarily halted with the Indian Reorganization Act, which attempted to reorganize the tribal units. In 1953 this policy seemed to be reversed again by House Concurrent Resolution 108 to end Federal regulation of Indians. The purpose of the Act was to end encroachments on the freedom of Indians, part of a major goal of the Eisenhower Administration to limit big government.

It can be seen through this period that the requisite specific intent would be difficult to prove, especially from the New Deal onwards. It might be argued that the aim of the General Allotment Act of 1887 was assimilation. This could be construed as containing the requisite specific intent to commit "genocide." By saying assimilation, one does not necessarily mean that the formulators of the policy wished to destroy the group, but rather, to change the group. As one government official noted at the time, "The American Indian is to become the Indian American." The Indian tribe was not prohibited from existing. Rather there seemed to be a desire on the part of officials for the individual Indian to become like other American racial and ethnic groups. While it is not denied that numerous atrocities were committed against American Indians, the requisite specific intent of the United States to commit "genocide" has not been established.

As has been noted, the United States consistently has refused to ratify the Genocide Convention, despite the fact that American presidents, including President Carter, have urged the Senate to do so. In view of all that has been said in this essay, it might be interesting for classes to discuss why the United States has failed to ratify the Genocide treaty until now, and to debate whether the United States should indeed ratify the treaty in the future. In any such discussion, the following information would prove helpful.

Since its submission to the Senate in 1949, the United States has consistently refused to ratify the Genocide Convention. That year the American Bar Association's special committee on the Convention opposed its ratification. The arguments at that time have since been reiterated.

The principal objections to the Convention are:

1. The Convention as drafted is imprecise in its language and vague in its specific prohibitions, particularly in respect to conduct which is anticipatory.

2. The mental element as described is believed to be sufficiently imprecise for enforcement in the United States' Courts.

3. The Convention prohibits 'incitement' to "genocide" which is believed to violate the First Amendment to the Constitution (freedom of speech).

4. All State criminal laws include what the Convention covers.

5. Concurrent jurisdiction over the same crimes creates confusion between the Federal and State Courts.

6. The Convention's creation of an international criminal court is unacceptable because citizens of the United States would not benefit in that type of a court from the constitutional safeguards otherwise available to them in American Courts.

Most of these arguments, however, have been discredited. In substance the American position is intended to prevent any form of foreign intervention in the domestic affairs of the United States. It is nonetheless valid to argue that the 1948 Convention suffers from imprecise drafting.

Finally, the question of German war reparations to individuals and to the Israeli government is relevant to a discussion of the implications of the Holocaust for international law.

Although the concept of war reparations had been employed many times throughout history, the circumstances after the Holocaust presented many new and different problems. According to customary international law, only states had the requisite standing with which to bring a claim against another state. An individual was virtually powerless in presenting claims against a foreign state within the international legal context. The only recourse available to such an individual was to petition his own government to present the claim on his behalf. Clearly, in light of the transnational character of the surviving victims of the Holocaust, this traditional espousal method was unrealistic.

Many writers, both during and after the War, suggested that the creation of a Jewish State would rectify this problem and possibly even promote the possibility of reparations. However, rather than solving the problem, the eventual creation of Israel complicated it. After all, how could a Mideast nation born in 1948 have the legal authority to represent the interests and claims of millions of people who were domiciled and murdered in Europe? Technically, Israel could not enter into a reparations agreement with Germany. Traditional international legal application of the reparation concept, as evidenced in the Versailles Treaty, was reserved solely to former belligerents and/or combatants.

In addition to the obvious legal problems, there were complicated logistical, political and emotional considerations. In Israel and Germany, the prospect of reparations was not unanimously accepted. The Germans worried that any such payments would ruin an already precarious economy. In Israel, many violently opposed any contact with Germany and viewed reparations as "blood-money." Nevertheless, after years of secret meetings, Germany and Israel negotiated a treaty which provided for German reparations to Israel.

The Luxemburg Treaty was signed on September 10, 1952. It consisted of four parts wherein Germany agreed to provide economic assistance to Israel and to Jewish survivors. Israel was to receive three billion Deutsch Marks (the equivalent of $715,000,000) in commodities and services. Along with this sum, two Protocols to the Treaty obligated Germany to initiate new legislation augmenting its then present laws compensating individual victims. An additional four hundred and fifty million Deutsch Marks were allocated to various Jewish organizations which represented individual survivors outside Israel.

Although many of the political, logistical and emotional problems lessened with the implementation of the treaty, there remained the problem of justifying the treaty within an accepted framework of international law. Many critics claimed that the treaty, being *sui generis,* a unique remedy to a unique problem, was therefore devoid of any legal significance.

The drafters of the Treaty tried to resolve this dilemma by claiming that reparations were not the basis of the agreement. Instead, they claimed that Germany was merely reimbursing Israel for its cost in absorbing thousands of postwar refugees. This was, to say the least, only a semantic victory, yet it did give the Treaty a much needed "basis." Another more plausible legal justification was voiced by those who claimed that international law was a dynamic entity which adapted itself to an ever-changing world.

Thus the reparations agreement reaffirmed the doctrine stated at the Treaty of Versailles which held states (and not only individuals) responsible for violations of international criminal law. A pertinent topic for discussion would be not only the legal ramifications of Germany giving reparations, but the moral implications of accepting reparations—i.e., do reparations represent (adequate or inadequate) compensation to Holocaust victims, to the State of Israel? Were reparations "blood money" as many have charged?

In addition to the aforementioned topics, a pertinent subject for discussion would be a review of trials in American courts of aliens or of naturalized American citizens alleged to have committed "war crimes" or "crimes against humanity" during World War II. The trial of Hermione Ryan in New York, which resulted in her deportation to Poland, is the most significant of these cases to date. The whole question of bringing such individuals to trial in the United States and the legal and bureaucratic obstacles involved is discussed by Howard Blum in *Wanted* (New York, New York Times Book Press, 1976). Relevant in this regard are works which discuss the process of finding Nazi war criminals both in the United States and elsewhere. The most important of these works are: Simon Wiesenthal's *The Murderers Among Us*

(New York, McGraw Hill, 1967) and Ladislas Farago's *Aftermath* (New York, Simon and Schuster, 1974). Furthermore, classes and instructors should continue to follow trials in the United States (most recently—1978—in Chicago and Albany) of alleged Nazi war criminals. The activities of legislators, such as Rep. Elizabeth Holtzman (D-NY), directed at making participation in Nazi war crimes grounds for deportation from the United States, should be followed with interest.

One may leave the introduction of additional topics relevant to "law and the Holocaust" to the discretion and to the imagination of instructors and students. Conceptual probing as well as "current events" may engender added topics for class consideration. For example, the recent resurgence of the American Nazi Party and the problems it poses politically, socially, and legally, would provide a stimulus for discussion of the implications of the Holocaust for contemporary American life. The questions of whether the Nazi Party should be outlawed in the United States and of whether free speech for Nazis is protected under the First Amendment to the U.S. Constitution, can be debated by students and instructors as well as by legislators and judges.

Another example of how "current events" may augment study of the topics outlined above would be a discussion of genocides being perpetrated today. Most recently, perhaps, has been the genocidal activities of the Paraguayan government with respect to its indigenous Indian populations (see, e.g., *Genocide in Paraguay,* ed. by R. Arens, Temple University Press, 1977, and the similarities drawn with the Holocaust in the epilogue by Elie Wiesel).

TABLE OF ABBREVIATIONS

A.B.A.J.	American Bar Association Journal
AJIL	American Journal of International Law
Am. Pol. Sci. Rev.	American Political Science Review
Ann. Dig.	Annotated Digest of International Law Cases
BYIL	British Yearbook of International Law
Col. L. Rev.	Columbia Law Review
Denver J. Int. L. & Pol.	Denver Journal of International Law and Policy
DePaul L. Rev.	DePaul Law Review
Duke L.J.	Duke Law Journal
Har. Int.'l L.J.	Harvard International Law Journal
Harv. L. Rev.	Harvard Law Review
Indictment, Proceedings, Judgment	Trials of the Major War Crimes before the Nuremberg International Military Tribunal (USGPO) 42 vols. (1947).
Int. & Comp. L.Q.	International and Comparative Law Quarterly
I.C.J.	International Court of Justice
I.C.J. Rep.	International Court of Justice Reports
Law Q. Rev.	Law Quarterly Review
Mich. L. Rev.	Michigan Law Review
Neth. Int. L. Rev.	Netherlands International Law Journal
R.I.D.P.	Revue Internationale de droit Penal
Santa Clara Lawy.	Santa Clara Lawyer
UNWCC	United Nations War Crimes Commission
U.S.C.	United States Code
Vand. L. Rev.	Vanderbilt Law Review
Yale L. Rev.	Yale Law Review

BIBLIOGRAPHY

I. General Works

BASSIOUNI, M. C., "An Appraisal of the Growth and Developing Trends of International Criminal Law," *Revue International de droit Penal,* 46:3 (1975).

————. *Substantive Criminal Law* (1978).

————. *International Terrorism and Political Crimes* (1975).

BASSIOUNI AND NANDA. *A Treatise on International Criminal Law* 2 vols. (1973).

OPPENHEIM, I. *International Law* (8 ed., ed. Lauterpacht, 1958).

SCHWARZENBERG, G. *International Law* (3rd. ed., 1957).

II. War Crimes - Before Nuremberg

8 American State Trials, 666 (1918), and *House Executive Documents* vol. 8, no. 23, serial 1381, 40 Cong. 2d S. M. (1868). For information on the Wirtz trial.

COLBY, "War Crimes," 23 *Mich. L. Rev.* (1925). Information regarding the trials of Nathan Hale and John Andre.

DAVIS, G. *A Treatise on the Military Law of the United States* (3rd rev. ed., 1918).

FENWICK, C. *Digest of International Law* 7 (1965).

FITZGERALD, C. *Peace and War in Antiquity* (1931).

Fourth Hague Convention Regarding the Laws and Customs of Land Warfare. Full text appears in 2 *AJIL* (1902 supp.), pp. 90–117.

GROSS, "The Punishment of War Criminals," 11 *Neth. Int'l. L. Rev.* (1955).

KADDURI, M. *War and Peace in the Law in Islam* (1955).

KEEN, M. *The Laws of War in the Middle Ages* (1965).

The Llandovery Castle (1923) *Ann. Dig.* No. 235.

Maine, H. *International Law* (2nd ed., 1894), pp. 138–40.

MULLINS. *The Leipzig Trials* (1921). For information about war crimes trials in Germany after WWI.

ROACH. *The Prisoners of War and How They Were Treated* (1865). For information on the Wirtz trial.

SCHWARZENBERG, "The Breisach War Crime Trial of 1474," *The Manchester Guardian* September 28, 1946.

SHERMAN. "The Civilianization of Military Law," 22 *Maine L. Rev.* (1970).

SWELB, "Crimes Against Humanity," 23 *BYBIL* (1946). Text of the Treaty of Sevres and other important documents.

WRIGHT, "The Legality of the Kaiser," 18 *Am. Pol Sci. Rev.* (1919).

————, "War Crimes Under International Law," 62 *Law Q. Rev.* (1946).

III. The Nuremberg Trials and Related Legal Issues

ARENS, "Nuremberg and Group Prosecution," *Washington University Quarterly* (1951).

BENTON, W. E. AND GRIMM, G. *Nuremberg: German Views of the War Trials* (1955).

BIAL. "The Nuremberg Judgment and International Law," 13 *Brooklyn Law Review* (1947).

BOSCH, W. J. *Judgment at Nuremberg* (1970).

BRAND, "Crimes Against Humanity and the Nuremberg Trials," 28 *Oregon Law Review* (1949).

CARTER, "The Nuremberg Trials: A Turning Point in the Enforcement of International Law," 28 *Nebraska Law Review* (1949).

DALY, "War Crimes Trials," 23 *Connecticut Bar Journal* (1949).

DAVIDSON, E. *The Trial of the Germans* (1966).

DINSTEIN, Y. *The Defense of Obedience to Superior Orders in International Law* (1965).

DOMAN, "Nuremberg Trials Revisited," 41 *ABAJ* (1961).

ERHARD, "The Nuremberg Trial Against the Major War Criminals and International Law," 43 *AJIL*(1949).

FERENCZY. "Nuremberg Trial Procedure and the Rights of the Accused," 39 *Journal of Criminal Law* (1948).

FINCH, "The Nuremberg Trial and International Law," 41 *AJIL* (1947).

GARNER, "Punishment of Offenders Against the Laws and Customs of War," 14 *AJIL* (1920).

GLUECK, "The Nuremberg Trial and Aggressive War," 59 *Harv. L. Rev.* (1946).

GOODHARD, "Questions and Answers Concerning the Nuremberg Trials," 1 *Int. Law Q.* (1947).

GREEN, "Trials of Some Minor War Criminals," 4 *Indiana L. R.* (1950).

HARRIS, W. R. *Tyranny on Trial: The Evidence at Nuremberg* (1970).

HILBERG, RAUL. *The Destruction of the European Jews* (Chicago: Quadrangle, 1961) (Available in Harper paperback). For a summary of the verdicts and punishments meted out to Nazi war criminals, see esp. pp. 704–715; on the trials at Nuremberg, see pp. 684–704.

International Military Tribunal. *The Trial of German Major War Criminals. Proceedings of the International Military Tribunal sitting at Nuremberg.* 21 vols. (London, H.M.S.O.; 1946–).

International Military Tribunal. *The Trial of German Major War Criminals by the International Military Tribunal sitting at Nuremberg. Opening Speeches of the Chief Prosecutors* (His Majesty's Stationery Office, London: 1946).

International Military Tribunal. *Trial of the Major War Criminals before the International Military Tribunal, Nuremberg, 14 November 1945–1 October 1946. Record of the Trial* (Published by the Secretariat of the Tribunal, 42 vols. Nuremberg: 1947–1949). Record of the trial.

International Military Tribunal. *The Trial of German Major War Criminals by the International Military Tribunal sitting at Nuremberg. Speeches of the Chief Prosecutors at the Close of the Case against the Individual Defendants* (His Majesty's Stationery Office, London: 1946).

International Military Tribunal. *The Trial of German Major War Criminals by the International Military Tribunal sitting at Nuremberg. Speeches of the Prosecutors at the Close of the Case against the Indicted Organizations* (His Majesty's Stationery Office, London: 1946).

JACKSON, R. *The Nuremberg Case* (1947). This work contains the full text of the London Charter.

LAUTERPACHT, "The Law of Nations and the Punishment of War Crimes," 21 *B.Y.B.I.L.* (1944).

MYERSON, M. H. *Germany's War Crimes and Punishment* (1965).

Nuremberg Military Tribunals. *Trials of War Criminals before the Nuremberg Military Tribunals under control Council no. 10, October 1946 to April 1949* (Washington: U. S. Government Printing Office, 1949–   ).

PARKS, "Command Responsibility for War Crimes," 61 *Mich. L. Rev.* (1973).

SWELB, "Crimes Against Humanity," 23 *B.Y.B.I.L.* (1946).

U. S. Chief of Counsel for Prosecution of Axis Criminality. *Nazi Conspiracy and Aggression* 8 vols., Supp. 2 vols. (Washington: United States Government Printing Office. Washington, 1946–48).

U. S. Chief of Counsel for Prosecution of Axis Criminality. *Nazi Conspiracy and Aggression. Opinion and Judgment Ed. by the Office of United States Chief of Counsel for Prosecution of Axis Criminality* (Washington: United States Government Printing Office, 1947).

U. S. Chief of Counsel for Prosecution of Axis Criminality. *Report to the President from Justice Robert H. Jackson, Chief of Counsel, for the United States in the Prosecution of Axis War Criminals, 7th June, 1945* 12 *Department of State Bulletin* (1945) 1071–1078.

U. S. Congress. *Committee of Foreign Affairs. Punishment of War Criminals. Hearings on H. J. Res 93 requesting the President to appoint a commission to cooperate with the United Nations War Crimes Commission* (Washington: U. S. Government Printing Office, 1945).

U. S. Department of State. *Trial of War Criminals. Documents: 1. Report of Robert H. Jackson to the President. 2. Agreement establishing an International Military Tribunal (Nuremberg). 3. Indictment. Department of State Publication 2420.* United States Government Printing Office (Washington, 1945).

U. N. International Law Commission. *The Charter and Judgment of the Nuremberg Tribunal: History and Analysis.* Memorandum submitted by the Secretary-General to the International Law Commission. Document A/CN.4/5. Lake Success, 1949.

United Nations War Crimes Commission. *Law Reports of Trials of War Criminals. Selected and Prepared by the United Nations War Crimes Commission.* 15 vols.

WOETZEL, R. *The Nuremberg Trials in International Law* (1960).

WRIGHT. *History of the United Nations War Crimes Commission* (1948).

———, "The Law of the Nuremberg Trial," 41 *AJIL* (1947).

———. "Legal Positivism and the Nuremberg Judgment," 42 *AJIL* (1948).

———, "War Crimes Under International Law," 62 *Law Q. Rev.* (1946).

IV. Other War-Crimes Trials After World War II

GUY, "Defense of Yamashita," 4 *Wyoming Law Journal* (1950).

KOESSLER, "American War Crimes Trials in Europe," 39 *Georgetown Law Journal* (1950).

International Military Tribunal. *Judgment of the International Military Tribunal for the Far East.* Parts A–C with Annexes, 1948.

U. S. Department of State. *Trial of Japanese War Criminals. Documents: 1. Opening Statement of Joseph B. Keenan, Chief of Counsel. 2. Charter of the International*

Military Tribunal for the Far East. 3. Indictment Department of State Publication 2613 (Washington: United States Government Printing Office, 1946). Contains indictment of Japanese War Criminals.

V. United Nations Declaration of Human Rights

BASSIOUNI, M. C., "The Human Rights Program: The Veneer of Civilization Thickens," 21 *De Paul L. Rev.* (1971).

BRIGGS, "Implementation of the Proposed International Covenant of Human Rights," 42 *AJIL* (1948).

BROWNLIE, I., ed. *Basic Documents on Human Rights*. This work contains the complete text of the U. N. Declaration on Human Rights.

LAUTERPACHT, "Universal Declaration of Human Rights," 25 *BYBIL* (1948).

SOHN AND BURGUENTHAL. *International Protection of Human Rights* (1973).

The United Nations and Human Rights (U. N. Publ. E.73.1.13, 1973).

VI. The U. N. Genocide Convention and Related Legal Issues

BROWNLIE, I., ed. *Basic Documents on Human Rights*. Contains the full text of the U. N. Genocide Treaty.

CARLSTON, "The Genocide Convention," 36 *ABAJ* (1950).

DROST, P. *The Crime of State: Genocide* (1959).

"Genocide: A Commentary on the Convention," 58 *Yale L. J.* (1949).

GOLDBERG AND GARDNER. *Time to Act on the Genocide Convention* 58 *ABAJ* (1972).

JOHNSON, "Draft Code of Offenses Against the Peace and Security of Mankind," 41 *Int. and Comp. L. Q.* (1955).

LEMKIN. *Axis Rule in Occupied Europe* (1944).

―――. "Genocide as a Crime Under International Law," 41 *AJIL* (1947).

MCDOUGAL AND ARENS, "The Genocide Convention and the Constitution," 3 *Vand. L. Rev.* (1950).

PELLA, "Towards an International Criminal Court," 45 *AJIL* (1950).

PHILLIPS, "The Genocide Convention: Its effects on our Legal System," 35 *ABAJ* (1949).

PHILLIPS AND DEUTSCH, "Pitfalls of the Genocide Convention," 56 *ABAJ* (1970).

REISMAN, "Responses to Crimes of Discrimination and Genocide: An Appraisal of the Convention on the Elimination of Racial Discrimination," 1 *Denver J. Int'l. L. and Policy* (1971). On the U. N.'s proposed draft of "Code of Offenses Against the Peace and Security of Mankind."

STONE, J. AND WOETZEL, R. *Toward a Feasible International Criminal Court* (1972).

SWELB, "The International Convention on the Elimination of All Forms of Racial Discrimination," 15 *Int'l. and Comp. L. Q.* (1966). On the U. N.'s proposed draft of "Code of Offenses Against the Peace and Security of Mankind."

"The United States and the 1948 Genocide Convention-Comment," 16 *Harv. Int'l. L. J.* (1975).

WHITEMAN. *Digest of International Law* (1963). See pp. 217-220 for background information on the U. N. Genocide Treaty.

VII. The Eichmann Trial and Related Legal Issues

ARENDT, HANNAH. *Eichmann in Jerusalem* (1964).

BAEDE, "The Eichmann Trial: Some Legal Aspects," 3 *Duke L. J.* (1961).

BASSIOUNI, M. C. *International Extradition and World Public Order* (1974). See esp., pp. 121–201, for a discussion of the problem posed by Eichmann's "forced" extradition for his trial in Israel.

CARDOZO, "When Extradition Fails, Is Abduction the Answer?," 55 *AJIL* (1961).

EICHMANN, A. 1906–1962, defendant. *The Attorney-General of the government of Israel v. Adolf, the son of Adolf Karl Eichmann.* Minutes of session no. 1 (n.p.) 1961–

EICHMANN, A. 1906–1962, defendant. 6,000,000 accusers; Israel's case against Eichmann. The opening speech and legal argument of Mr. Gideon Hausner, Attorney-General. Translated from the Hebrew and edited by Shabtai Rosenne, *Jerusalem Post* (1961). Documents of Eichmann's trial in the District Court of Jerusalem for Crime against the Jewish people. The opening speech and legal argument of Mr. Hausner from the Hebrew, and edited with some explanatory notes, by a well-known Israeli official and legal scholar.

EICHMANN, A. 1906–1962, defendant. *Transcript of the trial in the case of the Attorney-General of the Government of Israel v. Adolf, the son of Adolf Karl Eichmann, in the District Court of Jerusalem* (Microcard Ed. 1962). This is an unedited and unrevised transcript of the simultaneous translation and, as such, should not be regarded as stylistically perfect or devoid of linguistic errors. Based on the files of the New York Public Library, originally secured through the Jewish National and University Library.

GALES, "Genocide: Israeli Law," 42 *North Dakota Law Review* (1966).

Israel. Ministry of Justice. *Beit Ha-Mishpat Ha-Elyon* (High Court). Judgment: Criminal appeal in the case of A. Eichmann vs. Attorney General (Jerusalem, 1963).

FAWCETT, "The Eichmann Case," 38 *BYIL* (1964).

PAPADATOS, P. *The Eichmann Trial* (1964).

SILVING, "In Re Eichmann: A Dilemma of Law and Morality," 55 *AJIL* (1961).

ZEIGER, HENRY, ed. *The Case Against Adolf Eichmann* (N. Y.: Signet, 1960).

VIII. Genocide and the American Indian

BURNETTE AND KOSTER. *The Road to Wounded Knee* (1974).

COHEN, F. *Federal Indian Law* (1942).

JOSEPHY. *The Indian Heritage of America* (1969).

PRICE, M. *Law and the American Indian* (1974).

IX. Viet Nam

BEDAU, "Genocide in Viet Nam," 53 *Boston University Law Rev.* (1973).

Department of State, Officer of the Legal Adviser. "The Legality of the United States Participation in the Defense of Viet Nam," 75 *Yale L. J.* (1968).

FERENCZY, "War Crimes and the Viet Nam War," 17 *American University Law Review*.

HULL, R. M. AND NOROGROD, N. C. *Law and Viet Nam* (1968).

MOORE, "International Law and the United States' Role in Viet Nam: A Reply," 76 *Yale L. J.* (1967).

PAUST, "My Lai and Viet Nam: Norms, Myths and Leadership Responsibility," 57 *Mil. L. Rev.* (1972).

RUBIN, "Legal Aspects of the My Lai Incident," 49 *Oreg. L. Rev.* (1970).

SARTRE, JEAN PAUL. *On Genocide* (Boston: Beacon, 1968). A summary of the evidence and judgments of the International War Crimes Tribunal called into existence by Bertrand Russell to establish whether the U. S. committed war crimes during the Viet Nam War.

TAYLOR, T. *Nuremberg and Viet Nam: An American Tragedy* (1970).

X. Reparations

BALABKINS. *West German Reparations to Israel* (1971).

DAWIDOWICZ, L., "German Collective Indemnity to Israel and the Conference on Jewish Material Claims Against Germany," 54 *American Jewish Yearbook* (1953).

DEUTSCHKRON. *Bonn and Jerusalem* (1970).

HONIG, "The Reparations Agreement Between Israel and the Federal Republic of Germany," 48 *AJIL* (1954).

MARX. *The Case of the German Jews vs. Germany: A Legal Basis for Their Claims Against Germany* (1944).

MUNZ, "Restitution in Postwar Europe," *Contemporary Jewish Record* (1943).

PAGIS, DAN, "Draft of a Reparations Agreement" (poem), in *Selected Poems*.

ROBINSON, N. *Indemnification and Reparation: Jewish Aspects* (1944).

SCHWERIN, "German Compensation for Victims of Nazi Persecutions," 67 *Northwestern University Law Review* (1972).

VOGEL. *The German Path to Israel* (1969).

Social-Psychological Aspects of the Holocaust

Jack Nusan Porter

INTRODUCTION

The Holocaust presented social scientists with an extraordinary "case history." In the years following World War II, social scientists produced an overwhelming quantity of research in areas that either are directly related to the period or to issues which were raised by the War period.

World War II was massive in its scale of death and power, towering and complex in its elemental balance of good and evil, majestic and stirring in its multi-leveled meaning, overwhelming in its simplicity. Almost anything can be found within its confines—if only one wishes to look for it. At times, the questions become so profound that only poets, novelists, and mystics can provide "answers." Every scholar feels impotent, overwhelmed, and disillusioned by the enormity of the event. Social scientists have attempted to grapple with the questions raised by the Holocaust and they presently continue to do so. The various techniques they have used include: philosophical discourses, intensive interviews and case studies, laboratory simulation, historical analysis, psycho-history, participant observation and survey research.

The confines of the present chapter do not permit a discussion of all the socio-psychological "spin-offs" that the Holocaust has helped to engender. The present task is more modest: (1) briefly to introduce the subject, (2) to clarify two specific areas of research: (a) social and psychological obstacles to resistance and (b) the impact of the Holocaust on survivors and survivors' children, and (3) to outline directions for additional intensive research on these and other matters.

Almost any good introductory psychology textbook will include topics that seem to have gotten their impetus from the Holocaust. Examples include: the human struggle for freedom and the need to escape from freedom by embracing totalitarian systems, the susceptibility of individuals to mass movements, psychoanalytic and sociological studies of anti-Semitism and racism, and the structure and dynamics of prejudice. These, in turn, have led to innumerable studies in the following areas: race, racism, and race relations, most particularly black-white relations; the impact of group pressure on individual judgment (the "follow the crowd" syndrome); the question of conformity; attitude formation and attitude change; the sub-field of small-group research and, in particular, the influence of various types of leadership on group efficacy. The entire field of collective behavior was stimulated by the Holocaust and would include: the analysis of crowd behavior, rumors, and polical revolution; the art and science of propaganda and the impact of the mass media on popular opinion; and the new field of psycho-history which began with a psycho-sociological analysis of the mind of Adolf Hitler.

World War II ushered in an era of large-scale research that for the first time was funded by governmental agencies. Some of these funds went to university institutes and departments; others were funneled directly to the social scientists themselves. The Office of Strategic Services, the Department of Labor, as well as the specific research institutes of the Army, Navy and Air Force, were all responsible for the dramatic increase of research during and after the War. (One quick glance by the reader at the dates of the books referred to in the bibliography to this chapter will verify this fact.) Pioneering efforts were made to apply the latest techniques of modern psychology, sociology, and history, *not* to distant nor abstract issues, but to the most pressing issues of the day. The old adage is correct: "necessity breeds creativity," and there are few forces as compelling as a World War. Many of the studies made during and within a decade following World War II are today considered classics in the field.

SOCIAL AND PSYCHOLOGICAL OBSTACLES TO RESISTANCE

Until the Eichmann trial in 1961, most people assumed that the Jews "went like sheep to slaughter," without putting up the least bit of resistance. This passivity in the face of large-scale extermination raised a storm of controversy throughout the Jewish communities of the world, especially in Israel where the "tough" machismo *sabra* model was idealized. Subsequent research has shown that resistance did in fact take place on many "fronts": the Jewish ghettos, the concentration camps, and the forests. An entire literature exists describing this resistance.

Whether this resistance was effective from a strictly military point of view is debatable, but that is not the present concern. What is of interest are the obstacles to resistance in the face of genocide. One may agree with Elie Wiesel's observation that "the question is not why all Jews did not fight, but how so many of them did. Tormented, beaten, starved, where did they find the strength—spiritual and physical—to resist?'' (Quoted in ''Introduction'' to Suhl's *They Fought Back*).

Spiritual and moral forms of resistance will also be discussed in this chapter, but our concern is to define ''resistance'' in terms of military and physical resistance. Only a small percentage of Jews physically resisted. Our goal is to try to determine . . . why?

First of all, one must understand that these obstacles held true for many *non-Jews* as well, though the obstacles were more stringent for Jews. Furthermore, one could also say that some of these obstacles can account for the fact that in some cases, entire *nations* were paralyzed into inaction. By its very nature, resistance is engaged in by only a small minority of the total population. One is speaking here of armed resistance; yet, other forms of resistance are available to a larger segment of the population. Each person resisted according to his/her abilities. One cannot include the very young, the very old, the lame, the sick, and those who were executed so quickly that they had no time to resist. While spiritual/moral resistance was available to them, physical resistance was not.

The first and foremost barrier was simply the incomprehensibility of the Holocaust itself. It was unique in history. The audacity of this evil psychologically overwhelmed the entire world, let alone the Jews. One's first reaction was denial; i.e., to dismiss the entire idea as a cruel hoax, and most of the Allied nations and their leaders simply rejected early atrocity reports as wartime ''propaganda.''

Greuelpropaganda

Bruno Bettelheim describes three separate psychological mechanisms that were most frequently used in dealing with the horrors of genocide. They are based on the belief that a supposedly civilized nation could not stoop to such inhumane acts. The implication that modern man had such inadequate control over his cruelty was felt as a threat to the psyche.

The following defence mechanisms were used. First, its applicability to mankind in general was denied by asserting that such horrible acts (if in fact they did exist) were committed by a small group of insane or perverted persons. The Eichmann trial demonstrated just the opposite: that these acts were carried out with scientific and bureaucratic precision by thousands of ordinary people. Social psychologist Stanley Milgram has verified this phenomenon in his research: most people will harm their fellow human beings rather than disobey authority. Secondly, the truths of the report were further denied by ascribing them to deliberate propaganda; in fact, the Germans themselves, masters of the art, called it *greuelpropaganda* (horror propaganda), and were quite aware that the more outrageous the atrocity, the more difficult it was for the world to believe. The Germans also understood that the bigger the lie, the more it would be believed. Such lies had to exist in the realm of possibility and had to be based upon already manifested myths and prejudices. Thirdly, the reports were believed, but this knowledge was repressed as soon as possible. In addition to the individual's psychological mechanisms, the Germans were experts in unnerving their victims, in bewildering them, and in thwarting any plans for escape. The ploys used are well known. They had code words—"relocation," "Jewish problem," "Final Solution"—which camouflaged their real intent. They made people believe that the death camps were work camps. The victims were met by an orchestra at the train station; they were given bars of "soap" when they entered the gas chambers; moreover, the SS sent postcards back to the victim's friends and relatives describing how "wonderful" the situation was and how "well" they were being treated. It is not an exaggeration to say that it was a time in which morality was stood on its head: right was wrong, wrong was right, true was false, and false was true. This same thought was echoed by the French partisan leader Dominique Ponchardier in his book *Les Paves de L'Enfer* (quoted in Ehrlich, p. 272):

> ... It was by definition the era of the false; the false combatant, the false decent man, the false patriot, the false lover, the false brother, the false false. In a world of false noses, I was one of those whose nose was real and it seemed to me, as it did to all the "reals" that in reality we were all real cons.

This sense of existential unreality and dubious authenticity still plagues survivors to this day.

Collective Retaliation

The principle of collective responsibility baffled the Jews, prevented their escape from the ghettos, and helped suppress resistance. For example, in many ghettos when an escaped fighter was caught, not only he but his entire family, his neighbors, and even his work-unit were also killed. When a man or woman decided to resist, he/she knew that it would endanger not only his/her own life, but that of his/her parents, children, spouse, brother, sister, and acquaintances. Resistance could also be defined as escape, either from ghetto or concentration camp. Leon Wells, in his memoir *The Janowska Road* (p. 190) tells the following tale:

> Now the *Untersturmfuhrer* (SS officer) begins his speech, directing it at us: "One of you escaped. Because of him these people will be shot. From now on for anyone who tries to do the same, I will shoot twenty of you. If I find out that you are planning an escape, all of you will be shot." After his speech, he turns to the chosen six, and shoots one after another ... when finished, he calls for four of us to pick up the corpses and toss them into the fire.

The Jews in the ghetto faced a severe dilemma. If they left the ghetto to fight, they might save themselves but leave their families behind. If too many fighters left the ghetto, the remaining population would be vulnerable. But, if they did not resist in some way, they would be denied the privilege of avenging themselves. The late historian of the Holocaust, Philip Friedman, succinctly summarized this dilemma in the following quote (in ed. by Glatstein, p. 276):

> In the Jewish underground of Warsaw, Bialystok, and other ghettos, a passionate discussion was going on: What were they to do? Stay in the ghetto or leave it for the woods? It was primarily a moral issue: Were they entitled to leave the ghetto populace to face the enemy alone or did they have to stay on and to take the lead in the fight when the crucial moment of the extermination actions arrived? After heated debates, the opinion prevailed to stay in the ghetto as long as possible despite the disadvantages of the position, and to leave only at the last moment when there was no longer any chance to fight or to protect the ghetto populace.

The Germans understood the Jewish psyche quite well, and knew where the Jew was most vulnerable. Closely connected to the principle of collective retaliation were strong family ties among the Jews, and here the Jews were most vulnerable. Ironically, what had been a great strength to the Jewish people now became a pernicious trap. The close-knit family structure made it difficult for one or two members to leave the rest behind, and it became extremely difficult for an entire family to escape the ghetto together. To elect to leave the village or escape from the ghetto or camp in the hope of reaching the partisans, required a painful decision to leave a wife, mother, father, and child.

In an interview that the author had with his own survivor-father, this theme is constantly emphasized, and it is permeated with guilt, even when such leave-taking opened the opportunity to take *nekumah* (Yiddish for "revenge"):

> Am I no different from my parents or my daughters that I lived and they died? No, we are the same. Why, then, did I remain alive? I may not have been able to help them if I had stayed, but at least we would have been together to the end.

The Hope of Survival

As has been discussed, over and beyond all the concealed tricks, the half-truths and the devious ploys used by the Nazis to entrap the Jews (and the Allies), the most effective tool was the utter magnitude of the Nazis' own evil. This led, as was shown, to numerous ways of adapting to the incomprehensibility of the times. One of the most elemental drives of the human being is to try to survive. Many Jews felt they were not going to be killed; they were too valuable; the Germans "needed" their labor, their talents, or even their money.

Many believed that if they obeyed the law, they would be spared. In short: resistance to them meant suicide; not to resist meant the possibility of life, and why risk it? Hold onto life as long as possible. This was the attitude of many Jews. (This problem is examined by Arthur Miller, in his play *Incident at Vichy.*)

Orthodox Jews stubbornly refused to take part in military resistance. To them resistance was contrary to God's law; it was equivalent to a suicide mission, and suicide was considered a sin. Better to trust in God and His judgment. To the very end, they felt, one must do God's bidding, stay alive, and not risk death. One's goals should be *Kevod Hashem* (Hebrew term for "religious honor") and *Kiddush Hashem* ("sanctification of God's name," "religious self-sacrifice").

This form of nonviolent resistance (almost Gandhian in certain ways) has become a very controversial topic. Some readers will say that this form of passive resistance is not resistance at all but cowardice, and, furthermore, that it led to the deaths of many Jews who might have saved themselves (or died in active revolt) if they had not listened to the rabbis who forbade resistance. A Russian-Jewish partisan, Moishe Flash, whom the author has interviewed, echoed these same sentiments:

> Because of God and the religiously orthodox, many Jews died because it kept the people from fighting. The rabbis had a strong hold on the people. Because of that I had to leave my religion for a while and fight.

Nonviolent resistance took many forms. There were prayer groups and Hebrew classes that would congregate in ghettos and camps despite heavy penalties. There were attempts to rescue Torah scrolls from burning synagogues, although some people were killed in the act. There are stories of Hasidim who literally prayed and danced in religious ecstasy until the last minute of their lives!

Are these acts of bravery or cowardice? Is there an answer to such a value-laden, emotional question?

Lack of Arms, Lack of Trust

The most serious obstacles to resistance, once the psychological, theological, and family barriers were overcome, were: lack of arms, lack of communication between Jews and the outside world, and lack of trained leadership. Resistance comes down to basics: in any revolt, only a small minority are able to resist, and these few must have something to fight back with, and even here the Jews were not always successful.

As Philip Friedman states in his article "Jewish Resistance to the Nazis" (in ed. Glatstein, p. 277):

> A steady, uninterrupted supply of arms is a condition *sine qua non* for resistance operations. Most of the non-Jewish underground movements had received vast supplies of arms and other material from their governments-in-exile and from the Allied governments. But in no country was the Jewish underground treated on an equal footing with the recognized national underground organizations.

Whatever the Jewish underground was to receive had to pass through unfriendly national channels. Often the requests were refused outright (e.g., the Vilna and Bialystok ghettos), or came too late and in ridiculously small quantities (e.g., the Warsaw Ghetto). During the Warsaw Ghetto revolt (led by Mordecai Anilewicz) the Jewish partisans, after prolonged and maddening negotiations with the Polish underground, finally received only fifty revolvers, fifty hand grenades, and four kilograms of explosives. All this had to be used to fight off entire artillery regiments and air attacks—and some of the revolvers were defective and useless. One of the major reasons why the Jews received so little aid from the *Armia Krajowa* (the Polish Land Army), the largest underground movement in Poland, was that its leadership was permeated with anti-Semites.

Each gun, each grenade, and each rifle, were worth their weight in gold—because, quite often, each piece had to be literally purchased in gold on the black market from illegal arms dealers and army deserters, or had to be stolen from guards, soldiers, and peasants, or made in small clandestine factories and repair shops.

Aside from the lack of arms, there was often a lack of trust and communication between Jews and the surrounding communities. Some of this was due to anti-Semitism, but much of it was due to outright fear of the Germans who would retaliate for collaborating with the enemy (Jews, Communists, and partisans). In the words of Erich Goldhagen, Jews live not only like fish in a hostile sea, but like fish upon a hostile land. All this hampered the effective coordination between Jewish and non-Jewish fighting groups.

Conclusions

The above discussion has attempted to define the major social, familial, and psychological obstacles, including (briefly) the important military (non-psychological) stumbling blocks. These obstacles were effective in confounding the Jews and their sympathizers. The myth of total Jewish compliance and of total Jewish "cowardice" must not be replaced with a new myth, the myth of the Jewish "superman." There was heroism to be sure and in the most unlikely places, but the true picture of this tragedy lies beyond the myths that people have developed.

THE SOCIAL AND PSYCHOLOGICAL AFTEREFFECTS OF THE HOLOCAUST ON JEWISH SURVIVORS AND THEIR CHILDREN

The present purpose is to present a *survey* of the highlights of the socio-psychological literature concerning the aftereffects of the Holocaust upon the survivors. Literature in this area divides into two parts, each overlapping the other: (1) psychoanalytical case studies written by psychiatrists and psychoanalysts and (2) the personal memoirs and sympathetic interpretations done by the participants themselves or by journalists and sociologists. Though a significant body of literature exists in both cases, the field is not "over-researched." There is much more work to be done. The present discussion will concentrate on the psychiatric and sociological literature of the past two decades. Generally, studies of Holocaust victims fall under the category of disaster research. This general field will be immediately discussed.

Disaster Studies: An Overview

These studies go under various labels: "trauma," "stress," "siege," "catastrophe," and of course "disaster" research. There are three major approaches that social scientists can take:

1. *General Systems Theory* is concerned with the structure and process of concrete systems of social phenomena. The concepts of stress adaptation, equilibrium-maintenance in reaction to such stress, information-processing, inputs and outputs—all are used in this approach. General systems theory is useful in defining and manipulating social variables within the system, especially through the use of computers and statistical models. It is "scientific" and "objective" and it is an important tool. This writer finds it too "mechanistic." Consequently, it will not be used in the present discussion.

2. *Collective Behavior Theory* is the most popular approach to disaster studies. "Collective behavior" is actually a generic term which contains within it various social phenomena: crowds, propaganda, public opinion, riots, revolts, and disasters (natural and man-made). Such an approach emphasizes group morale, leadership, cohesiveness, collective defense, rumor control, and other manifestations of group behavior.

3. *Psychoanalytical Theory,* the approach which will be stressed in this section on survivors, puts its major emphasis on individual reaction to stressful situations. The vocabulary of this approach concentrates on such concepts as "trauma," "emotional reaction," "threat," "defense," "anxiety," "guilt," and "internal conflict." It is both a therapeutic and an analytical approach. Bruno Bettelheim and Viktor Frankl are the two most outstanding and widely-read figures in this area.

The weakness of a great deal of Holocaust research is that it is rarely comparative; that is, it rarely takes into account the literature of other stress phenomena. For example: concentration camp research is actually a subcategory of research on "total institutions" such as military prisons, Prisoner of War (POW) camps, and civilian prisons. If Jews in concentration camps were to be compared, for example, to soldiers in POW camps, a more balanced, less defensive, and more objective perspective could emerge. Furthermore, if the Jewish reaction to ghettoization and persecution were compared to reactions of civilians to such diverse phenomena as nuclear attack, natural disasters (floods, hurricanes, tornadoes), air raids and collective panic (for example, the fall-out shelter "scare" of 1962), then the picture that would emerge would show that the Jews reacted similarly to other groups. In short, the appearance of guilt and other psychological reactions are as normal for survivors of the Holocaust as they are for victims of nuclear attack, natural disasters, war combat, or intense life-depriving accidents.

What is a "Survivor"?

The definition of a "survivor" appears to be an easy one: a "survivor" is someone who sees himself/herself as a survivor after having confronted traumatic phenomena. Furthermore, a person is labeled a "survivor" by others when knowledge of this survivorship is made known. The question, that is more crucial, however, is: what is the *nature* of the "traumatic phenomena"? What is the magnitude, severity, and duration of the trauma? How does the trauma produce recognizable clinical effects? And, are these effects passed on to future generations? Many of these questions are extremely difficult to answer. It is, however, the dynamic process of the effects of the trauma on the individual and his family that will be discussed here.

Clinical Symptomology of Survivors

The question that psychiatrists have attempted to explain is whether or not there exists an entity called "the survivor syndrome" and, if so, what are the manifestations of such a syndrome. One of the world's foremost authorities on psychic trauma, William G. Niederland, had outlined some of the characteristics, both primary and secondary, of adults on whom repeated and brutal "traumata" have been inflicted (such as those inflicted on inmates of Nazi concentration camps and similar types of persecution). It must be added that these descriptions are of the most powerful effects. Not every survivor suffered from all of them: essentially these effects are those of the survivors of concentration camps. Other survivors, who have not suffered these extreme effects, will exhibit milder sequelae (Niederland, "Introductory Notes," pp. 1–9).

Personality changes in the survivor of such experiences are related to quantitative factors. Massive traumatic experiences of this kind have devastating effects on the total ego organization. Most survivors suffer from chronic or recurrent depressive reactions often accompanied by states of anxiety, phobic fears, nightmares, somatic equivalents, and brooding ruminations about the past and lost-love objects.

The sequelae of massive and repeated traumatization are:

1. Anxiety, usually associated with phobic or hypochondriacal fears, alone or in combination.

2. Disturbances of cognition and memory.

3. Chronic depressive reactions characterized by guilt, seclusion, and isolation.

4. Psychosomatic symptoms or disorders.

5. Psychosislike or psychotic manifestations.

6. Lifelong sense of heightened vulnerability to an increased awareness of dangerous situations.

7. Disturbances of sense identity, body-image, and self-image.

8. Permanent personality changes.

Let us examine in more detail what Niederland calls the sequelae or after-effects of traumatization. (See Niederland's "Clinical Observations....," p. 313).

1. Anxiety—the most common complaint, is associated with fear of renewed persecution, deep disturbances, multiple phobias, anxiety dreams, and "rerun" nightmares. Chronic insomnia occurs and is based on these recurrent nightmares and anxieties.

2. Disturbances of cognition and memory—such as amnesia or hyperamnesia, are manifested especially upon waking up from nightmares. "Lost and bewildered states" and a sense of disorientation from the present to the past are also found among survivors.

3. Chronic depressive reactions—cover the whole spectrum from masochistic character changes to psychotic depression. These reactions in their severity are correlated to the intensity of "survivor guilt" based on the loss of loved ones—children, spouses, parents, siblings, etc.

4. Tendency to isolation, withdrawal, and brooding—is marked by unstable relationships and problems with intimacy. These psychological states

manifest themselves in other social settings, such as withdrawal from political and community involvement.

5. Psychotic and psychoticlike states—occur in the most extreme cases of survivor traumata. Regressive and primitive methods of dealing with aggression can result in schizophreniclike symptoms, such as hallucinations, fantasy-building, states of depersonalization, hypochondriatic symptoms, or paranoid manifestations—all having a very specific history and determination.

6. Alterations of personal identity—include impairment of a sense of body image and self-image; frequent complaints of "I am a different person," "I am a weaker, more abhorrent person," and, in some extreme cases, "I am not a person" are heard. The image of the *musselman* or the "living corpse" appearance which some victims exhibit is an example of this. Robert Lifton makes similar comparisons with Hiroshima survivors who exhibit a type of "psychic numbing," a closing-off of feelings, manifested by a macabre, shadowy, shuffling, and ghostlike imprint, a type of all-encompassing psychological scar on the total personality often used as a defense against death anxiety and death guilt. In milder forms it can be seen as "sluggish despair" consisting of diminished vitality, easy fatigability, "weakness," "exhaustion" of the nervous system, and "inadequate functioning of an organ or organ system of the body." (On "psychic numbing " also see Lifton, *Death in Life*).

7. Psychosomatic conditions—which are quite common, and which form the basis for many German restitution claims, can exhibit themselves immediately after the traumata (after liberation) or many years later. These include: (a) diseases related to chronic states of tension; (b) gastrointestinal conditions, peptic ulcers and related symptoms; (c) cardiovascular disturbances such as angina pectoris, with or without states of hypertension; and (d) the typical "survivor triad" of symptoms: headaches, persistent nightmares, and chronic depression, accompanied by various psychosomatic complaints.

Coping Behavior of Concentration Camp Survivors: Psychological Adaptations

The various social and psychological ways in which survivors cope with their past and present have been systematically studied. The previous section has described the various psychiatric ailments that form what is called the "survivor syndrome." What will follow will be an extension of this work: a discussion of the coping behavior of Jewish inmates within the concentration camps. Following this section will come an analysis of the social and political forms of coping behavior. It is this latter area that, by and large, has been under-researched, while psychiatric and social-psychological studies have proliferated. It must be stressed that the coping behavior described here is of adaptation to the concentration camp. Those Jews who were not camp inmates exhibited similar coping behaviors in the ghettos and the forests, but perhaps not as intensely.

Dr. Joel Dimsdale, a Harvard Medical School psychiatrist at the time of the study, has outlined the following coping mechanisms from a sample of nineteen concentration camp survivors living in Jerusalem and the San Francisco Bay area of California:

1. Differential focus on the good

2. Survival for some purpose

3. Psychological removal, including: intellectualization, belief in immortality, time focus, and the "musselman" stage

4. Mastery—environmental and attitudinal

5. The will to live

6. Hope—active and passive

7. Group affiliation

8. Regressive behavior

9. Null-coping (fatalism) and anti-coping (surrender to stress).

"Coping" is difficult to define precisely. It would be said that any response to stress is coping behavior, but a more specific behavioral response to coping, according to Dr. Dimsdale, is: first, to lessen the immediate impact of stress, and, secondly, to maintain some sense of self-worth and unity with one's past and one's anticipated future.

Dimsdale, corroborating the findings of Viktor Frankl and Bruno Bettelheim, dismisses two false myths concerning survivors of the concentration camps: (1) that the individual was completely powerless to influence his fate and (2) that only the most barbaric inmates survived. Both of these popularly held opinions are false.

The first two means of coping, differential focus on the good and survival for some purposes, are also corroborated by Viktor Frankl. In the first case, the inmates concentrated on some minor gratification, e.g. getting through the food line without a beating or getting a slightly larger crust of bread. Those with a vision of life after the camps fared better. The love of a wife, a mother, a father, or a child was powerful motivation for surviving and bearing witness in order to tell the world what actually had happened. These were strong coping mechanisms.

The third means, psychological removal, led to an insulation from stress by developing ways of not feeling. By means of intellectualization, a person could withdraw into considerations of immortality, either personal immortality, the immortality of the Jewish people, or the immortality of a political movement such as Zionism or Communism. Strongly held religious beliefs were also good coping measures.

The fourth and most complete stage of withdrawal was the most dangerous of all. This was withdrawal into a *musselman* state, characterized by profound apathy and a total lack of response to stimuli.* If a person did not recover quickly from this stage, he died or was selected out and almost immediately killed by the guards. Null coping and anti-coping are similar to this stage of *musselman*, wherein fatalism and surrender to stress had completely overpowered the individual. He was now literally a "walking corpse."

Mastery, either environmental or attitudinal, meant autonomy. In fact, the will to live or any act that consciously reflected this will to live, was a form of autonomy. The camps and even the ghettos provided very little room for autonomy. The Nazis attempted to control every act of free will, but they could not control one's thoughts, one's dreams, and one's hopes. Within this realm, there remained some mastery over the environment.

The mobilization of hope and the will to live were also basic to survival. The possibility of hope was of two kinds: one was *active* hope, that the camps were so evil that they could not possibly continue for long; and the other was *passive* hope, conveying the message that where there was life, there was hope.

Group affiliation and regressive behavior were two methods of coping through interpersonal contact with another human being. Regressions such as crying occasionally helped, especially among the young. In this case, both parties were coping: the child received sympathy, attention, and even affection; and the adult who gave sympathy and affection reaffirmed his/her humanity and thereby strengthened his/her autonomy and mastery within an environment that "rewarded" hatred and evil rather than love and kindness. Group affiliation was also important in providing valuable information, advice, and protection. Within a group, one was no longer a number but an individual. A person could obtain a sense of self-worth and self-esteem by such affiliations as: being a member of a secret Communist Party cell or a religious group that attempted to pray or a group consisting of people from the same country speaking the same language or dialect, or a small family group. Size was unimportant: the dyad was common and extremely effective. If an inmate was unsuccessful in finding a group of *any* type in the first few days of internment, his chances for survival were severely limited.

These, then, were various means by which survivors of camps were able to cope. The camps were the most intense and most brutal form of oppression

---

*The term *musselman* was concentration camp slang. It was probably not a "sick" attempt at humor, i.e., "muscleman" to describe the weak and emaciated inmate, but more likely, from "muslim-man," the popular conception being that the Moslems were a robotlike people in their devotion to Allah and to their emirs.

and, therefore, the range of responses were likewise the most revealing. Those who were not camp inmates, but were still survivors of, let us say, the ghettos, the forests, or the partisans, used a similar but smaller repertoire of coping behaviors.

Coping Behavior of Survivors: Social and Political Adaptations

Research in this area is almost nonexistent. While there is some literature on the social and political acculturation patterns of most immigrant groups, studies that specifically analyze the social and political adaptation of Jewish survivors are in an early stage of development. Additional research in the future is inevitable; to date, most studies have concentrated on psychological adaptation. What follows is a brief series of hypotheses that require more scientific verification.

Jewish survivors of the Nazi Holocaust are also immigrants to a host country, whether that country be the United States, Canada, Israel, England, Argentina, etc. Their adjustment to this new situation depends on a host of variables: family situation (did they come alone, or with spouse, parents, children, or other relatives?); social and psychological maturity; age of entrance into the country; level of education; job opportunities; previous religious background; support of relatives and social agencies in the new country; and support within the ''community of survivors.'' These are some, but by no means all the factors that contribute to the positive or negative adjustment of immigrant survivors.

What confounds the analysis of survivors and their children is that it often is difficult to separate those variables that are distinctly related to the Holocaust experience and those variable adjustments made by any other immigrant group, Jewish or non-Jewish. The Holocaust and its wrenching impact upon the survivors were added burdens to all the other problems that any new immigrant faced.

Yet, despite the difficulties of acculturating to a new environment and despite the psychic and emotional burden of the Holocaust, one is impressed with the relatively good adjustment of the survivors. Financially, they are fairly secure with some having become quite wealthy. Doing ''fairly well'' does not mean that in terms of occupational status and prestige they have ''moved up,'' but survivors have done quite well, even better than expected, given generally low levels of education and training.* Many of the Russian

---

*One should make a distinction here between Eastern European (Polish, Russian, Hungarian) Jews and Central European (French, German, Austrian) Jews. The latter had left their European ghettos at a much earlier time in history and had entered the urban centers and acculturated more rapidly than the former. German Jews had higher levels of education and were more highly cultured urban people; Russian and Polish Jews were less urbanized and less educated. Therefore, these two groups adjusted differently in terms of occupations and other social and cultural forms of integration.

and Polish Jews became "marginal" tradespeople: tailors, caterers, scrap metal or used-auto parts dealers, "momma and papa" storekeepers and garment industry workers. A few became Hebrew teachers, cantors, sextons, and rabbis. Engineers, doctors, dentists, and professors are virtually nonexistent among Eastern European Jewish survivors. On the other hand, because of their education and training, German and Austrian Jews were more likely to be engaged in the "free" professions, arts, or journalism.

Because immigrant parents' lives and careers had been stunted by the Holocaust, the desire for their children to have the utmost in schooling was a *sine qua non,* whether pre-Holocaust or post-Holocaust. Within a single generation, their children very nearly "caught up," so to speak, with their host-country counterparts. A great many survivor-children "intermarried" with non-survivor children, and with as much education as they could muster, they entered into the free professions: e.g., teaching, social work, and other fields which their talents opened up for them. A few, however, joined their parents in the "family business" but this should be viewed as a "step-down" in mobility. The parents expected their children to surpass them in educational and occupational mobility, and though this may have caused some tension between generations, it was accepted. Many survivor-parents literally sacrificed their "lives" for the sake of their children's careers. This is not new; it occurred at the turn of the century during the great waves of immigration into this country, and Jewish parents have been sacrificing for their loved ones ever since.*

In most cases, survivor-parents tend to be members of Orthodox and Hasidic synagogues. While some may be nonobservant (or even antiobservant), most will live in religious communities and continue traditions out of respect for the memory of their parents or out of guilt. One impression that should be tested: survivors that were young adults or middle-aged during the Holocaust were more likely to remain "believers" and observant Jews than those survivors who were adolescents during the same period. The impact of the Holocaust on faith and observance deserves, of course, a fuller treatment.

Politically, survivors tend to be somewhat conservative. They keep a "low profile." They are rarely involved in local, state, or national politics. They try to avoid controversy, political or otherwise. Given their experiences, this is understandable. Another reason they are uninvolved is simply that, being "greenhorns," they are often ashamed of how they speak English or how they

---

*Two comments: first, my generalizations about mobility hold true for American and Canadian Jews outside of New York City. In New York (it may come as a surprise to some) Jewish income levels are lower than those of Jews in other parts of the country. New York Jews are more likely to be engaged in blue-collar occupations and, subsequently, their children are more likely to be engaged in these same occupations than their counterparts in other sections of the country. Mobility, in short, for New Yorkers, is somewhat more curtailed. Secondly, this ethos of parental sacrifice does not hold true for all immigrant families. In Italian and Polish families, there was much more resistance to the son or daughter gaining mobility as rapidly as Jewish children have done, and much more friction between the generations when this mobility occurred.

act or dress (they often "look" like new immigrants in style and decorum), and they feel that either they are too ignorant of the political process to become involved or that they will look foolish. Quite often, survivors are extremely embarrassed about their "Old World" habits and accents and many try to acculturate quickly. Some, however, give up and remain among their own kind. They feel that not only non-Jews but even other Jews do not really understand them or their world. They react to their "Americanized" children in the same way. At times, neither one understands the other and often each is ashamed of the other. Again, this is not historically different from any other immigrant conflict.*

In the areas of Israel and the plight of Soviet Jewry, however, survivors *are* politically involved, and their involvement comes with such force and devotion that it sometimes shocks non-survivor Jews. Survivors are very active in the various fund-raising activities, either within their synagogues or through survivor organizations. Their ties with Israel are close, not only spiritually, but also socially—many survivors have relatives there, and there is a great deal of inter-visitation. Furthermore, a disproportionate number of survivors support militant pro-Israel groups such as the Jewish Defense League or the Revisionist Organization of America. Many join the Pioneer Women, Farband, or other Labor Zionist Groups; if Orthodox, they support the Mizrachi (Religious) Zionist organizations in America. Many survivors were familiar with these organizations in Europe so they have no difficulty in joining them in other countries.

In conclusion, survivors are similar to other Jewish immigrants, except that they are a bit more "paranoid" about anti-Semitism and about Israel. They tend to live in tight-knit communities consisting of other survivors, speaking the languages and carrying on the customs of the "Old Country," of the *shtetle* and the European ghetto. They live a richly traditional but quiet life, apart even from other Jews in their communities, and they donate much of their energies to the lives of their children and grandchildren.

Coping Behavior of Survivor Children: Psychological Adaptations

First, the matter of definition must be delineated. Who is "a child of survivors"? Judith Kestenberg, an Israeli psychiatrist who has done extensive research in this area, defines "the child of survivors" as "one who was born after the Holocaust or has not been himself subjected to persecution or mal-

*Many of my generalizations also apply to survivors in Israel, including, I believe, this one, with, of course, the added depth of the Israeli situation, locked as it is in a life-death struggle for survival. The capture of Adolph Eichmann and the subsequent trial in 1961 made it possible for parents and children in Israel to "communicate." Yet, I must emphasize that some of my generalizations do not apply to survivors in Israel or their children. Comparison studies between Israeli and Diaspora survivors are necessary and fascinating.

treatment.'' A more complex definition is necessary because the impact of escape, migration, and childhood development in a family of survivors, regardless of direct persecution, can and does lead to emotional conflicts. Furthermore, a few months or even a few weeks in the European environment during the last days of the War and the subsequent postwar experience can also lead to psychological conflicts. Kestenberg's definition, however, proves adequate for this discussion.

There is little data on the subject, though there have been several symposia on the children of survivors, all of them emphasizing the psychological and psychoanalytical perspective. Interest among young Jews, and especially among the offspring of survivors, is growing. Much of the psychiatric literature is sketchy and all of the nonpsychiatric writings are impressionistic. However, the children themselves are now responding to their condition and that is good, but whether it will all add up to a definition of a ''survivors-children syndrome'' is difficult to say at present.

Kestenberg believes that there is no specific syndrome among children, but she is cautious about closing the book on the subject; she writes (pp. 311–312):

> Some years ago I analyzed a young adolescent who behaved in a bizarre way, starving himself, hiding in woods and treating me ... as a hostile persecutor. Soon after I connected his psychotic-like behavior with the real experiences of his parents' relatives in Europe, his symptoms abated but his analysis had to be prematurely terminated, chiefly because of his parental resistance. Haunted by the image of this patient, who came to me emaciated and hollow-eyed like a Musselman in a concentration camp, I looked at children of survivors in Israel and thought I could recognize in some faces a far away look, reminiscent of the stare of survivors of persecution.

Kestenberg does not tell us more about this patient. One conclusion made by Kestenberg, however, was that psychiatrists themselves (in the late 1960s) resisted unearthing the frightening impact of Nazi persecution on these children. This appears to have changed in the past few years, as more and more therapists are becoming aware of these children. My observations lead me to believe that a growing number of survivors' children are also seeking psychiatric treatment, and this should help in opening up the issue to more analysis.

Therapy can be of great help not only in relieving the stress of emotional conflicts, but, more importantly, in accelerating communication between parents and child. For example (Mostysser in *Martyrdom and Resistance*, pp. 4–5):

> My parents never told me anything about the war, ... It was like sex. You didn't talk about it in my house ... The house was like a tomb. Sometimes we went on picnics together. But underneath something was missing.

What was missing was emotional contact between the generations and a deeper sharing of the parents' fate and its effects upon the children. Too often, parents are too ashamed or too afraid of discussing the subject with their offspring. They do not wish to ''burden them'' with their suffering. Yet, the child can see the parents' suffering while not understanding its root cause. At times, children will blame themselves for the parents' suffering, and a complex web of guilt and helplessness will develop.

Despite what others say, I am beginning, more and more, to see that perhaps there is a ''syndrome'' at work, a ''secondary guilt syndrome'' that is passed on. Robert Lifton calls this the ''death imprint.'' Children themselves may feel ashamed of their parent's victimization. This, in turn, can often lead to a series of conflicts within the child, or between parent and child, or between the child and the outside world.

Often the parents are so preoccupied with the unending mourning process and the vicissitudes of making a new life in a strange country that they are unable to relate to the children's needs or respond with the necessary flexibility. The children's demands become overwhelming and are seen by the parents as straining them of already limited emotional resources. So the parents attack their children for not listening and for not understanding them. Often, it is difficult to tell who is the ''child'' and who is the ''adult'' in these cases. But these attacks are not ones that lead to disciplined behavior; they are cries of despair. Because they are unable to cope with the continuous anxious responses of their parents to their behavior, the children either go out of control themselves or respond by withdrawal, either into fantasy at best or into an affectless state at worst.

Another factor is the child's behavior toward authority figures, including parents, and the subsequent feelings of guilt provoked by aggression toward them. When the child has powerful and violent urges of aggression toward the parents, he is confronted with a paradox, a paradox fraught with conflict. It is as if he were saying: ''How can I attack someone who has already suffered so much?'' Parents and child then turn on each other, each escalating the other's feelings of guilt and guilt displacement, each blaming the other for their mutual sense of deprivation. A lack of communication and warmth, a blurred sense of identity, and a potential for depression can result from the dynamics of such guilt.

The Components of a Syndrome

Any syndrome that is developed among children of survivors will have to take into account the following variables:

1. Age: There is some evidence that the first child born after the parents' relatives (and even other children) were killed in Europe, may suffer more

intensely from the "secondary guilt syndrome" than the other siblings. This firstborn child carries a heavier burden than other siblings because he/she represents the "rebirth" of the family—he is often a "special" child, filled with promise and responsibility to the parents. While the firstborn child may carry additional burdens, he may also be far more successful and creative because he has been imbued with the hopes and ambitions of the parents. Subsequent children may suffer less than the firstborn, but also achieve less.

2. Time of Birth: Whether the offspring was born after the Holocaust either in the forest, the ghetto, the displaced persons (known as DP) camp after the War, or later in America, Canada, Israel, or other countries—may prove to be an essential variable.

3. Post-Holocaust Experience: The shock of liberation, subsequent recovery and the stages of acclimitization in the displaced persons camps and/or new countries in which new attachments were formed or families united—all are crucial components. This post-Holocaust phase is rarely mentioned in the literature and can be as traumatic to survivors and their children as the actual wartime experience.

4. Time of Departure: Did the survivors leave before or after the War? Many German and Austrian Jews were able to leave in the middle and late 1930s. Are their sequelae different from the Russian or Polish Jews who managed to survive the War? What were the different effects on their children?

5. Emotional Stability of the Parents: All persons suffered severe jolts to their personality during the War; however, their emotional maturity before and during the War are crucial in understanding to what extent the Holocaust effected them and their children. Furthermore, the intactness of the family is important. If there was a loss of a spouse, survivors tended to remarry soon after the War or before departing for other countries. These dyadic relationships were very strong, even if romance or deep love was missing. In a few cases, these were marriages of convenience, but they were still close-knit.

6. Participation in Wars of Liberation: Active participation in either the regular army, the resistance movements of World War II, or the Israeli wars seems to have a beneficial effect on both survivors and children. The channeling of feelings of powerlessness against a common enemy, whether Nazis or Arabs, is beneficial for mental health. The ability to take revenge was also satisfying, but never totally so, because no amount of revenge could replace the loss.

7. Reaction to New Stress: Adaptation after persecution is of course the key element. The uprooting and subsequent effects of beginning a new life in

a new country with all its inherent stresses have their impact on the children. Stress, especially success-stress, should be noted. Many survivor-immigrants work exceedingly hard; and work itself has become an anodyne, an opiate, a means to forget the past and to prove that one is still fully functioning. The tendency towards overachievement and social and political involvement among the children of survivors will be discussed in the next section.

8. Finally, the Impact of Therapy: Therapy itself can become problematic for the child and his/her parents. Studies have shown that survivors do not resist treatment of their children in most cases. Yet, very few children of survivors reach the offices of private psychiatrists, according to Kestenberg. I would tend to say that this is changing; more and more are seeking therapy. However, fewer parents are seeking such therapy, despite its availability and despite the fact that many survivors have achieved financial success. It is possible that survivors need special inducements and special settings and preparation for therapy before they will allow themselves or their children to be treated. For example, some psychiatrists feel that parents will accept a fellow-survivor as a therapist, especially one from a similar background or one who is acquainted with the Holocaust or who knows Yiddish. Others disagree and feel that a Gentile analyst might command more confidence by representing the "omnipotent *goy* (Gentile) who magnanimously hides survivor's children" (Kestenberg, pp. 318-19). Yet, no matter who the therapist is, the most beneficial form of therapy might be family therapy in which the entire "survivor unit" could benefit.

Coping Behavior of Survivor Children: Social and Political Adaptations

The social, political, and "countercultural" ways that survivor-children adapt are as fascinating as they are diverse. If there is a social-political syndrome in the making, distinct from a psychological syndrome, then it may have two major components, each with two parts:

1. Particularistic (in this case, Jewish involvement)
   a. Religious
   b. Political
2. Universalistic (that is, beyond the Jewish realm)
   a. Religious
   b. Political

Let us first examine some examples of the particularistically Jewish ways of adapting. I have found a large number of survivor-children involved in some form of Jewish commitment: many are Orthodox Jews (however, their parents were Orthodox so that the Holocaust does not seem to be the major independent variable there; the children would be involved in religion despite the Holocaust); a large number are active in Zionist youth movements; a large number are involved in "right-wing" revisionist Zionist groups, such as the Jewish Defense League and Betar; a large number are involved in Jewish student groups and in the editing of Jewish student newspapers and magazines; many are in religious communal groups; and many have intellectual pursuits of a Jewish nature. In short, whether because of the direct influence of their parent's home, their past education, the direct influence of Holocaust literature, or a visit to Israel and its Holocaust centers (Yad Vashem, Kibbutz Lochamei Hagettaot, Kibbutz Yad Mordechai, etc.), these Jewish youth and young adults are Jewishly active in one form or another. Some are religiously Orthodox or traditional.

These young people have made a religious response to the Holocaust, despite their expressed or unexpressed sentiments about the "absurdity" of the genocide. The creative tension is still present even though, outwardly, they are conformists.

A crucial political and historical "jolt" to the children of survivors (as well as to all Jews) came with the June 1967 Arab-Israeli "Six-Day" War and, later, the October 1973 Yom Kippur War. The 1967 war came exactly twenty-two years after the end of World War II and the liberation of the concentration camps. The children of survivors were now coming of age and had reached some level of maturity and sophistication. These wars intensified the latent emotions that were just below the surface.

Is There a Survivor Syndrome? A Conclusion of Sorts

What in summary can be said? First, regarding the presence of a psychological survivor syndrome among parents, the evidence is overwhelmingly "yes," a definite "yes." The works of Winnik, Krystal, Niederland, and others, plus the compendium of literature on the subject by Hoppe, confirm this conclusion. As for a socio-political "syndrome," again the evidence shows that there appears to be a constellation of adaptive mechanisms at work (conservatism, traditionalism, and political "paranoia"), but more research is needed to validate the parameters of this "syndrome."

As for the children of survivors, there exist some problems with generalizations. Some scholars feel that it is too early to report about the exact specificity of the formation of a syndrome or its lack (see, e.g., Kestenberg, pp. 322–3). More work needs to be done in the area in order to specify the content and dynamics of such a syndrome, but one can say that tentatively, "yes," there does exist the basis for such a syndrome. To be sure it is milder when compared with survivor-parents, but it may well exist. We need more data to confirm it. As for a socio-political or religious "syndrome," here too, my answer would be a tentative "yes." The various ways in which people respond to the Holocaust are difficult to predict. Much depends on such intervening variables as religious education, childhood traumas, political socialization, and situational factors, but a "syndrome" is in the making. Whether it is religious or political or both and whether it is particularly Jewish or not is difficult to forecast, but something is happening here. The offspring of survivors have to find some meaning and mold some form of response to the awesome "absurdity" of the Holocaust. What is certain is that the children of survivors have a fascination for radical and millenial movements, either political or religious, and this, in itself, is a significant finding.

FUTURE RESEARCH

Within another generation, many active participants of the Holocaust will no longer be alive. Death will rob us of the opportunity to more fully understand this traumatic event from people who had firsthand experience of it. Thus, it is with the utmost urgency that I recommend the following projects. My plea goes out not only to students and scholars, but to foundations and individual supporters of research:

1. Though there has already been a greal deal of analysis of survivors by psychiatrists and psychologists, there is now a need for synthesis. More has to be known about the social and psychological effects on the children of survivors. What effects are being passed on? Furthermore, as time goes on, we will have to deal with not only the children of the survivors but the grandchildren. What effect has there been on the present generation, and on those to follow?

2. After World War II there was a great deal of sociological research in areas concerning the Holocaust. Today, there is very little. We need more, and with the increasing interest in the field and with greater numbers of young Jewish scholars and students, there should be more. We need more interdisciplinary research. Too often, studies of genocide have been dominated by a few disciplines, i.e., psychiatry or history. With the aid of many approaches, such questions as the following beg for answers: What is the social and political impact of the Nazi genocide of the Jews on young people today—not only Jewish youth, but all youth, and especially German youth, and most importantly, the offspring of Nazi and SS "survivors"? What is the nature of the "community of survivors"? What is the structure of "survivor" organizations?

What is the imagery, mythology, and martyrology that has developed by the commemoration of the Holocaust? What is the relationship of survivors to the State of Israel? of Germans and ex-Nazis to the Jewish State? Compare the way that Israel has dealt with survivors and survivors' children with other countries to which survivors immigrated? Most writers maintain that Israel has been more successful in absorbing survivors than Diaspora nations for reasons outlined earlier. In general, we need a careful sample of children of survivors. Is there definitely a "transference" of the parents' survivor syndrome to the children; if so, what are its psychological, sociological, political, and religious ramifications? Do these children have a special bond? Do they have a special "contribution" to make to Jewish life? to society? Robert Jay Lifton had talked of the uniqueness of the *hibakusha,* the survivors of the A-bomb at Hiroshima. Is there such a "uniqueness" among Holocaust survivors?

3. There is a need for a more intense investigation of the behavior of the Jews in response to the traumatic disasters that have befallen them. We need to understand why some reacted with heroism, some with martyrdom, and many with submission. However, in order to present a complete picture, this research must be comparative; that is, it must analyze how non-Jews (for example, Russian POW's) reacted when faced with similar traumas; and it must compare how Jews reacted in various parts of Europe (French Jews as opposed to Polish Jews, for example).

4. Specifically, more research is needed on Jewish resistance or on the lack of such resistance. We know very little about the dynamics of resistance. Why do some resist and not others? Which forces in the Jewish community neutralize militancy and which do not? What is the impact of Jewish activism, Jewish militancy, and Israel's militarism on the Jewish community in America and in other parts of the world? If the "unthinkable" ever occurred "here" in America, what might be the response of the Jews? Would it be the same as that of Europe's Jews? These doomsday questions remind one of Herman Kahn's discussion of the aftereffects of nuclear war, but they are no less valid.

5. An extensive examination of the entire German *Wiedergutmachen* (restitution and indemnification) program must be made. As this program is presently constituted, children of survivors cannot receive compensation for psychiatric or social agency treatment (except for German Jews). Furthermore, lasting feuds have developed over this matter between psychiatrists appointed by German consulates, survivors, German restitution offices, and German courts. Even the Jewish community and local physicians in Israel have exhibited denial and avoidance attitudes regarding many claims by survivors and their children. Another legal question is the statute of limitations on war criminals and the fact that "death comes more quickly than justice"—the death of Nazis, their collaborators, and the death of Jewish witnesses who can testify against them.

6. There is also a need to clarify the concept of genocide from legal, political, socio-psychological, and administrative points of view. We need more comparative research on people effected by genocide—the Armenians during World War I, the Gypsies during World War II, American Indians in the 19th century, the Hottentots of Africa, and the Tasmanians in New Zealand. We need to understand why the United States has not yet signed the United Nations Genocide Convention. We need to understand how this Convention can prevent the destruction of groups and how it can punish those responsible for their destruction.*

7. There is a need to understand the impact of the Holocaust on young people, both Jewish and non-Jewish, and its impact on faith, identity, and religious commitment. We need to implement Holocaust studies in high schools, community centers and colleges in the world. We need to gain the support of political figures as well as educators on this matter. For example, New York Congressman Stephen Solarz has introduced legislation in the American Congress requiring the National Institute of Education to begin preparation of appropriate material on the Holocaust and to distribute it to every school in the nation.

8. Finally, we need to apply the insights of such people as Erich Fromm, Bruno Bettelheim, Viktor Frankl, and Robert Jay Lifton in order to examine the implications of unlimited technological violence and absurd death. To utilize the theories of humanistic social scientists and psychiatrists in order to build more healthy human beings is a crucial goal. In short, what can the survivors teach us about survival on this planet?

CONCLUSIONS

This chapter will conclude with a short synopsis of the major contributions of three psychotherapists regarding what the Holocaust can teach us about human behavior. These three psychologists are perhaps the three best known figures (aside from Erich Fromm) in this field: Viennese psychiatrist Viktor E. Frankl (author of *Man's Search for Meaning: An Introduction to Logotherapy*); University of Chicago psychiatrist Bruno Bettelheim (author of *The Informed Heart: Autonomy in a Mass Age*); and Yale psychiatrist Robert Jay Lifton (author of *Death in Life: Survivors of Hiroshima, History and Human Survival,* and with Eric Olsen, *Living and Dying*).

These three men have confronted the "unthinkable," and have forced their readers to confront the irrational and the evil in man. All three have not only

*For a discussion of the legal concept of "genocide," see the chapter, "International Law and the Holocaust."

confronted it but transcended it with a psychologically and politically healthier vision of the future.

Bettelheim and Frankl are both European Jews who not only survived World War II but who personally experienced the Nazi camps themselves. Their visions were fashioned while both served time in a concentration camp. Lifton, a younger man than the others and an American Jew, derives his lessons not from the Nazi Holocaust alone but from intense interviews with survivors of the first A-bomb blast in Hiroshima. Of the three, Frankl has developed the most comprehensive psychotherapeutic theory, called "existential therapy" or "logotherapy."

Logotherapy emerged in Frankl's mind as he was struggling to survive in a death camp where his father, mother, brother, and wife had died. With every possession gone, every value destroyed, everyone close to him dead, cold, hungry, and brutalized, how could he not merely survive but continue to find meaning in life?

He survived the camps with the same techniques that he later used in therapy with patients. He found meaning in life through several ways: by conjuring up happy images of his wife and family, by interviewing camp inmates and gathering material for his future book, and by controlling his thoughts in an institution that hoped to control not only bodies but minds. Bettelheim did the same though his camp conditions were much more comfortable than Frankl's. Both survived because they strove for "autonomy in a mass age." In a world that had gone beyond the wildest fantasies of Orwell's *1984* and Aldous Huxley's *Brave New World,* they and Lifton hope to teach others what integrity and hope mean, in a world that either pleasurably or painfully takes away freedoms and infiltrates minds with both trivia and perversions.

While Freud stressed frustration in our sexual life, Frankl stressed frustration in our will-to-meaning. To Frankl, our neuroses are existential in nature; they are caused by an estrangement from life and an inability to find a full and satisfying meaning in life. For Frankl, love and suffering are the solution. As he put it, "the crowning experience of all . . . is the wonderful feeling that, after all (man) has suffered, there is nothing he need fear anymore—except his God." For Frankl, the final destination of psychological health is a closeness to man and a reverence for God. More than either Lifton or Bettelheim, Frankl's ideas are a very religious psychiatric experience.

Bettelheim shares Frankl's ultimate vision of innerdirected autonomy in the face of overpowering technology and dehumanized bureaucracy, but his theory of survival lacks an inner coherence and is, in many ways, vaguer. His experiences at Dachau and Buchenwald led him to two conclusions (see his *Informed Heart*).

This first conclusion is that psychoanalysis was by no means the most effective way to change personality. Being placed in a particular type of environment could produce much more radical changes and in a much shorter time. The environment can be a negative or positive one. A concentration camp or prison can produce pathological behavior; a warm and happy setting can reduce psychopathology. In a sense, Bettelheim presaged Abraham Maslow, who also talked about growth-inducing environments. What Maslow called "self-actualization," joy and creativity, can be stimulated by such environments, while neuroses will develop within settings where the individual was not living up to his/her potential and where the surroundings were not conducive to growth. Later, Bettelheim, at the University of Chicago, would apply this insight to his school for emotionally disturbed children, the Sonia Shankman Orthogenic School. Bettelheim's second conclusion posited the inadequacy of psychoanalytical theory, that it was unable to explain fully what had happened to him and other prisoners. It gave little guidance for understanding what is meant by the "good" life or the "good" person. Psychoanalysis had its limitations: within the appropriate frame of reference, it clarified much, but applied to phenomena outside its province, it not only was inadequate but distorted meaning as well.

Rather than reject psychotherapy entirely, Bettelheim attempted to build an environment of love for his children, an environment where the "heart would be informed with reason" (hence the title of his book) while reason would be invaded by a daring heart. It is this symbiotic symmetry which should be the goal of humanity.

Bettelheim furthermore felt that the oppressive mass state of Hitler's Germany was a passing phenomenon. In fact, he saw it as a challenge and a temporary setback to people's ingenuity. He hoped that this challenge would force people to reach a "higher integration and a deeper consciousness of freedom." His final statement is one of hope but not false hope. The struggle for mastering the new conditions set by the atomic age will tax all our mental and moral powers if we do not want a "brave new world but an age of reason and humanity."

Robert Jay Lifton continues the work of Frankl and Bettelheim, lifting their vision to higher and higher planes. Unlike his elderly mentors, Lifton did not personally experience the Holocaust; in fact, his theoretical perspective is informed not by the destruction of the Jews in Europe but by two other phenomena: the Japanese survivors of the atomic bomb dropped on Hiroshima and Nagasaki, and the returning veterans of the Vietnam War. His writings almost beg inclusion of the Jewish survivors of genocide. While he is aware of the role they play in his theory and while he uses examples of their plight, one is surprised at the scarcity of references to Jewish concerns in his work. Regardless, this does not weaken his case. It only leaves it open to others (including the present writer) to apply his paradigm to the Jewish condition. Lifton has elevated the concept of survivor to include all of us. He has elevated the discussion of death and destruction to monumental psycho-historical heights, and in the process has made it possible for those who are not direct survivors or who have not directly experienced the Holocaust to gain access to the meaning of meaningless death. All of his books have led up to the one book, upon which I shall rely to present to the reader his most important contributions: *Living and Dying* (written in collaboration with Eric Olson).

Lifton wants us to understand the unscrutable face of death. He wants us not to turn away nor distort death, but to face it and to face the meaning of death in our lives. He feels that we have "buried death" the way the Victorians buried sex. In fact, though others have already used the term, Lifton speaks of the "pornography of death." But what makes death even more incomprehensible today is that while in the past, destruction had limits, today, mass destruction does not merely destroy: it destroys the very boundaries of destruction! We confront not only our own individual meaningless death but the meaningless death of our entire planet.

Lifton goes on to describe five modes or categories of immortality: biological, creative, theological, natural, and experiential. They are as follows:

Biological immortality is the most common mode. It means that a person lives on through his/her own children in an endless chain. This mode is never entirely biological, but is experienced emotionally and symbolically and transcends one's own biological family to include one's tribe, organization, people, nation, and even species. Furthermore, the sense of biological continuity becomes intermingled with cultural continuity as each generation passes its traditions on to the next. Lifton and Olson call this "biosocial immortality" and its implications for Jewish survivors are profound. Holocaust victims continually talk of the triumph not only of the family or individual but of the entire Jewish people as having outlived Hitler. The reverse is also shown: that Hitler and Nazism not only perished but that their names must be "blotted out" from memory and history. When referring to Hitler, Torquemada or Pharoah, Jews conclude with the Hebrew words, *Yismach Shimo* ("may his name be erased").

Creative immortality is a second mode, and this too has had a long Jewish tradition. One may feel a sense of immortality through teaching, writing, art-making, repairing, construction, composing, healing, inventing, or through some lasting influence on humanity. In some cases, writing a book or constructing a building may even serve as a substitute for having children. The hundreds of diaries and memoirs written during and after the Holocaust are testimony to this mode of immortality.

Theological immortality is the form of immortality that one might think of most readily. Historically, it has been through religion and religious institutions that people have most self-consciously expressed their aspiration for conquering death and living forever. All religions are faced with the concept of immortality and though each gives assurances of it in different ways, no religion is based on the premise that human life is eternally insignificant. Judaism however underplayed the image of ''afterlife'' in its theology by constantly stressing that the ''good works'' on earth will be their own best reward. The literature of the Holocaust rarely stresses ''afterlife.'' The struggle to survive and be witness here and now, rather than later, has been the key element in survivor accounts, except for a few ultra-Orthodox sects. Theological immortality raises the question of religious self-sacrifice. The implication that the Holocaust was part of God's will and that to struggle against the Nazis (who presumably were acting according to God's will) was useless has been rejected by most Jews.

Lifton's fourth mode of immortality is achieved through continuity with nature, again an ancient form of religious communion. Lifton quotes the Hebrew Bible: ''From dust you come and to dust you shall return,'' and comes away with a striking reflection that this represents a Biblical injunction against pride as well as an expression of confidence that the earth itself does not die. Mankind has always looked to nature for spiritual refreshment and revitalization of the spirit.

Lifton's final mode of immortality is what he calls experiential transcendence. This mode differs from the others in that it depends solely on a psychological state. This state is one of rapture, ecstasy, of being ''at one with oneself and with the universe.'' It can also be a state where one ''dies and is reborn.'' This mode can be found in the search for a theological rebirth, but there are other means: music, song, dance, battle, athletics, sexual love, childbirth, and intense comradeship. This experience can occur in relation to the four other modes (biological, creative, theological, natural) or in and by itself. Over the centuries, humans have used heightened states of consciousness to reach this form of immortality: fasting, drugs, liquor, or combinations of these plus other ways mentioned above.

In many societies and religions, including Judaism, experiential transcendence is encouraged through fiestas, carnivals, holidays, and celebrations which help people to break free from the restraint of routine and to sing, dance, drink, laugh, and love in a spirit of excess. The Hippie movement of the middle to late sixties was a movement of spiritual transcendence, and even though it was later overrun by hustlers, violent criminals, ''rip-off artists,'' and ''hard drugs,'' it nevertheless was a movement spawned by the threat of destruction and meaninglessness.

Lifton understands this generation well, and would easily understand the young children of Jewish survivors who took part in the ''anti-death'' movements of the 1960s and who continue to say a collective ''no,'' but in more quiet ways. In conclusion, Lifton's greatest contribution to these issues is his description of the impact of such "death imagery" on our society, and his hope in the ability to affirm life in the face of death. *L'chaim* ("to life") may seem to be just another cliche in Jewish life, but in the works of Frankl, Bettelheim, Lifton, and to all the survivors of all the holocausts from Hiroshima to Auschwitz to Vietnam, it is the single most important affirmation in the world today.*

*The author of this chapter offers his thanks to Harvard University's Frances Countway Library of Medicine and its staff for opening up their vast resources—to Dr. Robert Ravven, a special note of appreciation for his encouragement and support in this research.

BIBLIOGRAPHY

This bibliography is by no means exhaustive. The reader is advised to scan the bibliographies that are attached to the books and articles listed below. This "selected" bibliography contains only material in English or in English translation. The bibliography is divided into a number of sections which roughly correspond to the sections in the preceding discussion.

I. The Holocaust and the Social Sciences

ASCH, SOLOMON, "Opinions and Social Pressure," *Scientific American* (1955) 193:31–5. This, and others of Asch's experiments, examine the "follow the crowd" syndrome.

CANTRIL, HADLEY. *The Psychology of Social Movements* (New York: John Wiley, 1941). A study of the art and science of propaganda—an area of study stimulated by the War.

ELKINS, STANLEY. *Slavery* (New York: Universal Library, 1963). See especially the discussion of slavery in Nazi concentration camps and its relationship to other kinds of slavery, pp. 103–115.

FROMM, ERICH. *Escape from Freedom* (New York: Farrar, 1941) (Available in paperback). A discussion of the psychological implications of totalitarianism.

HOVLAND, ET AL. *Experiments on Mass Communications* (Princeton: Princeton University Press, 1949). A study of the art and science of propaganda.

_____. *The Order of Presentation in Persuasion* (New Haven: Yale University Press, 1957). Another study of the art and science of propaganda.

KRACAUER, SIEGFRIED. *From Caligari to Hitler: A Psychological History of the German Film* (Princeton: Princeton University Press, 1947). A study of Nazi use of film as a propaganda instrument. See also the chapter, "The Holocaust and the Film Arts."

KRECH, CRUTCHFIELD, AND BALLACHEY. *Individual in Society* (New York: McGraw Hill, 1962). A good example of an introductory text in psychology which includes topics which emerge from the Holocaust.

LANGER, WALTER. *The Mind of Adolf Hitler* (New York: Basic Books, 1972) (Available in Signet paperback). A psychosociological study of the mind of Adolf Hitler, written in 1943 for the office of Strategic Services. A pioneering effort.

MILGRAM, STANLEY. *Obedience to Authority* (New York: Harper and Row, 1973). (Available in paperback). A classic but controversial study which maintains that most people would harm others rather than disobey authority.

TURNER AND KILLIAN. *Collective Behavior* (2nd ed.: New York: Prentice Hall, 1972). The problem of crowd behavior, rumors and political revolution—an area of study stimulated by the War.

II. Socio-Psychological Aspects of Prejudice

ADORNO, FRENKEL-BRUNSWIK, LEVINSON, AND SANFORD. *The Authoritarian Personality* (New York: Harper, 1950).

ALLPORT, GORDON. *The Nature of Prejudice* (New York: Doubleday, 1958) (available in paperback).

BETTELHEIM AND JANOWITZ. *Dynamics of Prejudice* (New York: Harper, 1950).

III. Socio-Psychological Aspects of Anti-Semitism

ACKERMAN AND JAHODA. *Anti-Semitism and Emotional Disorder: A Psychoanalytic Interpretation* (New York: Harper, 1950).

BRUNBERGER, BELA, "The Anti-Semite and the Oedipal Conflict," *The International Journal of Psycho-Analysis* (April–July 1964), 45:380–85.

SARTRE, JEAN-PAUL. *Anti-Semite and Jew* (New York: Grove Press, 1960) (available in paperback). A study of anti-Semitism by one of the most influential philosophers of the postwar era.

SIMMEL, ERNEST. *Anti-Semitism: A Social Disease* (New York: International Universities Press, 1946).

VALENTIN, HUGO. *Anti-Semitism* (New York: Viking Press, 1936).

WANG, MARTIN, "National Socialism and the Genocide of the Jew," *The International Journal of Psycho-Analysis* (April–July 1964), 45:386–95.

IV. Social-Psychological Aspects of Resistance

AINSZTEIN, REUBEN. *Jewish Resistance in Nazi-Occupied Eastern Europe* (New York: Barnes and Noble, 1974). A massive work.

BAR KAI, MEYER, ed. *The Fighting Ghettos* (Philadelphia: Lippincott, 1962).

EHRLICH, BLAKE. *Resistance: France 1940–1945* (Boston: Little Brown, 1965).

FRIEDMAN, PHILIP, "Jewish Resistance to Nazism" *European Resistance Movements 1939–1945* (London: Oxford, 1960).

————, "Jewish Resistance to Nazism: Its Various Forms and Aspects," in J. Glatstein et al, eds., *Anthology of Holocaust Literature* (New York: Atheneum, 1973).

SUHL, YURI, ed. *They Fought Back* (New York: Crown, 1967) (available in Schocken paperback).

WELLS, LEON. *The Janowska Road* (New York: Macmillan, 1963) (Paperback Schocken 1978 edition, issued as: *The Death Brigade*). A memoir of a survivor.

V. Socio-Psychological Studies of the Concentration Camp

ADLER, H. G., "Ideas toward a Sociology of the Concentration Camp," *American Journal of Sociology* (1958) 63:513–22.

BETTELHEIM, BRUNO, "Individual and Mass Behavior in Extreme Situations," *Journal of Abnormal and Social Psychology,* 38:4 (October 1943). Probably the first study written in this area.

————. *The Informed Heart* (New York: Free Press, 1960). (Available in paperback).

BLOCH, HERBERT, "The Personality of Inmates of Concentration Camps," *American Journal of Sociology* (1946–7), 52:335–41.

COHEN, ELIE. *Human Behavior in the Concentration Camp* (New York: Grosset and Dunlop, 1953). See, especially, pp. 115–276.

FRANKL, VIKTOR. *From Death Camp to Existentialism* (Paperback: *Man's Search for Meaning*) (Boston: Beacon, 1959). The birth of "logotherapy" as a result of the author's experiences in Auschwitz.

KOGON, EUGEN. *The Theory and Practice of Hell* (Former title: *Der SS-Staat*) (New York: Berkeley Medallion, 1958). (Available in paperback).

VI. Socio-Psychological Studies of Survivors of Disaster: General Works

BAKER, GEORGE, AND CHAPMAN, DWIGHT. *Man and Society in Disaster* (New York: Basic Books, 1962). Psycho-analytic theories of survivors of disaster.

DES PRES, TERRENCE. *The Survivor* (New York: Oxford University Press, 1976) (Also available in paperback).

GROSSER, WELCHSLER, GREENBLATT, eds. *The Threat of Impending Disaster: Contributions to the Psychological of Distress* (Cambridge, Mass.: The MIT, 1964). See especially the articles by Lifton and Lang. This work represents "general systems theory," "collective behavior theory," "psycho-analytic theory."

"Human Behavior in Disaster: A New Field of Social Research," *The Journal of Social Issues* 10:3. Entire issue dedicated to disaster research.

LIFTON, ROBERT JAY. *Death in Life: Survivors of Hiroshima* (New York: Random House, 1967).

_____. *History and Human Survival* (New York: Random House, 1971). (Available in Vintage paperback).

LIFTON, ROBERT JAY, AND, OLSON, ERIC. *Living and Dying* (New York: Bantam paperback, 1975).

NIEDERLAND, WILLIAM, "Clinical Observations on the 'Survivor Syndrome'," *International Journal of Psycho-Analysis* (1968) 49:313-315.

_____, "Introductory Notes on the Concept, Definition, and Range of Psychic Trauma," in Niederland and Krystal, eds. *Psychic Traumatization* (Boston: Little Brown, 1971).

NIEDERLAND, WILLIAM, AND, KRYSTAL, HENRY, eds. *Psychic Traumatization* (Boston: Little Brown, 1971).

ROSENMAN, STANLEY, "The Paradox of Guilt in Disaster Victim Populations," *The Psychiatric Quarterly Supplement* 30:2 (1956), pp. 181-221).

VII. Socio-Psychological Studies of Survivors of the Holocaust (Refer also to references in works noted in preceding section on "General Works" on survivor research).

DIMSDALE, JOEL, "The Coping Behavior of Nazi Concentration Camp Survivors," *American Journal of Psychiatry* 131:7 (July 1974), pp. 792-797.

EITINGER, LEO. *Concentration Camp Survivors in Norway and Israel* (Oslo: Universitetforlaget; London: Allen and Unwin, 1964).

EITINGER, LEO, AND, STRØM, AXEL. *Mortality and Morbidity After Excessive Stress: A Follow-Up Investigation of Norwegian Concentration Camp Inmates* (New Jersey: Humanities Press, 1973).

KRYSTAL, HENRY, ed. *Massive Psychic Trauma* (New York: International Universities Press, 1968).

LUCHTERHAND, ELMER, "Early and Late Effects of Imprisonment in Nazi Concentration Camps: Conflicting Interpretations in Survivor Research," *Social Psychiatry* 5:2 (1970), pp. 102-110. Note the bibliography for this article for additional references of works on survivor-related research.

_____, "The Gondola-Car Transport," *International Journal of Social Psychiatry* (1966-67), 13:316-25.

———, "Prisoner Behavior and Social System in the Nazi Concentration Camps," in Rosenberg, Gerver, Hanton, eds. *Mass Society in Crisis* (2nd ed., New York: Macmillan, 1971).

NIEDERLAND, WILLIAM AND KRYSTAL, HENRY, eds. *Psychic Traumatization* (Boston: Little Brown, 1971). See especially the articles by Klein, Luchterhand and Hoppe. Hoppe's bibliography should be consulted.

WINNIK, H. Z., "Contribution to Symposium on Psychic Traumatization Through Social Catastrophe," *International Journal of Psycho-Analysis* (1968) 49:298–301.

——— "Psychiatric Disturbances of Holocaust Survivors," *The Israel Annals of Psychiatry and Related Disciplines* 5:1 (1971).

VIII. Children of Jewish Survivors of the Holocaust

ANTHONY, J. ed., "Symposium: Children of the Holocaust," *International Yearbook of Child Psychiatry and Allied Professions* 2 (1971).

EPSTEIN, HELEN, "Heirs of the Holocaust," *New York Times Magazine* (June 19, 1977), pp. 12–14, 74–77.

GOLDSTEIN, MEYER, et al, "Five Children of Survivors: A Conversation," *Response* 9:1 (Spring 1975), pp. 33–53.

KESTENBERG, JUDITH S., "Psychoanalytic Contributions to the Problem of Children of Survivors from Nazi Persecution," *Israel Annals of Psychiatry and Related Disciplines* 10:4 (December 1972), pp. 311–25. Pay attention to her references.

MOSTYSSER, TOBY, "Children of Survivors," *Martyrdom and Resistance* 1:6 (July–August 1975), pp. 4–5.

———. "The Weight of Past-Reminiscences of a Survivor child," *Response* 9:1 (Spring 1975), pp. 3–21.

SIGAL, JOHN. "Second Generation Effects of Massive Psychic Trauma," in Krystal and Niederland, *Psychic Traumatization,* pp. 55–65.

STEINITZ, LUCY, AND, SZONYI, DAVID, eds. *Living After the Holocaust* (New York: Bloch, 1975).

IX. Additional Listings on Survivors and their Children

ARLEN, MICHAEL. *Passage to Ararat* (New York: Farrar, Straus and Giroux, 1975). A fine personal account of the Armenian genocide on the child of survivors.

BARKUN, MICHAEL, "Survivors: Social Movements and the Sense of Victimization," Department of Political Science, Syracuse University, October 1975.

BARON, L., "Surviving the Holocaust," *Journal of Psychology and Judaism* 2:2 (Spring 1978).

CHADOFF, P., "Late Effects of the Concentration Camp Syndrome," *Archives of General Psychiatry* 8 (1963).

FOGELMAN, EVA AND SAVRAN, BELLA, "Therapeutic Groups for Children of Holocaust Survivors," *International Journal of Group Psychiatry* (1979).

GREENBLATT, STEVEN, "The Influence of Survival Guilt on Chronic Family Crises," *Journal of Psychology and Judaism* 2:2 (1978).

HOPPE, K. D., "The Aftermath of Nazi Persecution Reflected in Recent Psychiatric Literature," *International Psychiatry Clinic* 8:1 (1971).

KANTER, ISAAC, "Social Psychiatry and the Holocaust," *Journal of Psychology and Judaism* 1:1 (Fall 1976).

KENRICK, DONALD AND PUXON, G., *The Destiny of Europe's Gypsies* (New York: Basic Books, 1972). An account of the genocide of European Gypsies during World War II.

PHILIPS, R. E., "Impact of Nazi Literature on Children of Survivors," *American Journal of Psychiatry* 32:3 (1978).

RUSSEL, A., "Late Psychosocial Consequences in Concentration Camp Survivor Families," *American Journal of Orthopsychiatry* 44:4 (1974).

SIGAL, J. J. and RAKOFF, VIVIAN, "Concentration Camp Survivial: A Pilot Study of Effects on the Second Generation," *Canadian Psychiatric Journal* 16:5 (1971).

Introduction:

The Holocaust and the Arts

Byron L. Sherwin

From Plato to Hegel the concept of the beautiful has been the central concern of philosophies of art. While definitions of "the beautiful" have changed throughout the centuries, philosophers have concurred in the assumption that the artistic endeavor focuses upon the beautiful. The artist was perceived as one in quest of absolute beauty often equated with absolute truth. Some philosophers even identified the beautiful with the good and with the Divine. Only when the beautiful was divested of absoluteness by post-Hegelian philosophers did alternative theories of art begin to appear.

On the basis of this classical equation of art and beauty, some have denied the viability of Holocaust art. If art represents beauty, they claim, the Holocaust which represents the grotesque cannot be portrayed by art. If the product of an attempt to produce Holocaust art represents the Holocaust, then they insist, it is not art, and, if it is art, then it does not represent the Holocaust.

Others deny the viability of Holocaust art on the understanding that the function of art is to take "the sting out of suffering. . . . In the final analysis, therefore, art is pleasure even if the raw materials it works with are not." In this view, "any attempt to transform the Holocaust into art demeans the Holocaust and must result in poor art" (Michael Wyschograd). The philosophy of art underlying this stance seems to have been influenced by Schopenhauer's view that the function of art is to serve as a palliative against suffering.

Others assume the position of some of the French existentialists that art must impose meaning upon experience. Some of those who hold this position contend that Holocaust art is an impossibility because the Holocaust was an event bereft of meaning and purpose. To admit the possibility of Holocaust art would be to maintain that some meaning, some purpose could be discerned from massive atrocity. It would be to suggest that the Holocaust happened for a reason, for a purpose, and is therefore somehow justifiable.

Despite these refusals to admit the possibility of Holocaust art—some by Holocaust artists themselves—Holocaust art does exist in a wide variety of genres and forms. Perhaps Adorno's often quoted statement that there can be no poetry after Auschwitz should be juxtaposed to Aristotle's statement that poetry is more philosophical and more true than history.

Philosopher William Barrett has recast Aristotle's view in modern parlance to claim that "art presents us a deeper truth about human life than all the researches of the behavioral sciences." Thus, for Barrett, art is not primarily a quest for beauty, but an expression of the collective soul of a given generation aimed at understanding the depths of its own historical and personal predicament. For Barrett, echoing Aristotle, art provides us a deeper and more authentic record of an age, of an experience, of an event than any factual history. Nor, in this view, is art understood to be a palliative for suffering. To the contrary, art aims at immediacy, at confrontation and encounter with situations and experiences. Indeed, for John Dewey art is not merely a representation of experience, but experience itself, amplified to a heightened degree of intensity. More than a comfort, art is a challenge, an event, an experience. Art evokes rebellion, not complacency. Art jolts us with its questions, its insights, its challenges. For Albert Camus, the artist's credo is: I rebel; therefore, I am.

It may be a mistake to perceive art as a vehicle for imposing meaning and purpose upon dysteleological events, upon experiences devoid of purpose and meaning, upon the absurd. True, art is a quest for meaning and purpose, but it cannot guarantee nor can it create meaning and purpose where they are absent. Indeed, a major motif of contemporary art has been the affirmation of the absurd. Contemporary art has revealed the difficulty, if not the impossibility, of the attempt to find stability amidst the flux of appearance and experience. By attempting to express atrocity through art, contemporary artists are rejecting the validity of the equation of art and beauty. Nor do contemporary artists necessarily seek to apprehend absolute truth behind the veils of appearance and absurdity. Unlike classical artists and philosophers who equated the artistic endeavor with the quest for absolute truth, contemporary artists simply strive to understand the experiences of their age and to articulate the perplexities of their generation.

When art is equated with beauty, with truth or with being a palliative for human suffering, it becomes difficult if not impossible to defend the existence of Holocaust art. When art is perceived as the representation of reality or as the duplication of reality, the possibility for Holocaust art is largely stripped of viability. Plato's claim that art is an imitation of reality is inapplicable to attempts at Holocaust art. The Holocaust cannot be accurately reproduced, imitated or represented through art. However, when art is identified as an attempt to grapple with experience, to confront events, to express a response to those events, Holocaust art becomes both possible and necessary. The Holocaust artist is one who feels the centrality of the Holocaust to modern human experience and history. He or she attempts to encounter the Holocaust in all its terror and horror and to respond to it to the best of his or her artistic ability.

It would be a mistake to assume, as some do, that Holocaust artists or any artists describe actual events accurately and completely. What they do convey is their impressions of and reactions to events and experiences. As Jerzy Kosinski has observed, the literary artist does not describe what happened, but rather he depicts memories, impressions and reactions to what had occurred. Thus the claim that Holocaust art, or any art, can be assumed to be, or can justifiably claim to be an imitation, an exact replication of an event or an experience, is difficult to defend. When understood as a direct replication of the Holocaust experience, Holocaust art becomes impossible. However, when understood as an expression of impressions, as a response, as a reaction to events and experiences, Holocaust art and art in general become possible. To equate artistic expression engendered by an event with that event would be a mistake. The claim that Holocaust art is impossible because the Holocaust event cannot be represented in art is well taken. The consternation of those who fear that readers and viewers of Holocaust art will equate artistic responses to the event with the event is well founded. Nevertheless, once one understands that art can no longer be perceived in Platonic terms, as an imitation of reality, as a representation of reality, the cause of consternation dissolves, the viability of Holocaust art becomes manifest. Thus, Holocaust art is impossible only for those who define the artistic enterprise in a manner which eliminates the possibility of Holocaust art *a priori*. However, for those who perceive art in other terms, Holocaust art becomes viable, possible and necessary. One may therefore define ''Holocaust art'' as the expressive response of one's impressions to one's perceptions of the Holocaust event by means of media such as novels, poems, memoirs, diaries, short stories, drama, music, film, fine arts, plastic arts, etc. A survey of Holocaust art, expressed by means of these various artistic media, will be the concern of the chapters in this section.

Holocaust Literature I:

Diaries and Memoirs

Marie Syrkin and Ruth Kunzer

DIARIES*

There is no dearth of those who have tried to communicate the nature of what they experienced [during the Holocaust]. Leaving aside the reports of survivors and the testimony of witnesses, printed and unprinted (countless manuscripts still lie unpublished in such institutes as the Yad VaShem), a conscious, sustained effort to give form to what they endured was made by many Jews in Hitler's Europe. The manuscripts that have been found are evidence of probable larger numbers not recovered.

First of all there are the diaries. Anne Frank was not alone. In nearby Brussels another sensitive adolescent, Moshe Flinker, was keeping a Hebrew record which like Anne's would be found after his death in Auschwitz. In Warsaw another teenager, Mary Berg, was making notes in Polish while Emmanuel Ringelblum, the historian, and Chaim Kaplan, the Hebrew educator, were writing their respective scrolls of agony for the judgment of history. With the exception of Mary Berg, who reached the United States in 1944 in a prisoner-exchange because her mother was an American citizen, the writers were killed by the Germans; their diaries, dug up after the War, remain abrupt, incomplete, ending at the threshold of Treblinka or Bergen-Belsen.

Despite the differences in the persons and circumstances of the authors, the diaries have one quality in common which partially explains their effectiveness: they are written in innocence. Whatever the degree of foreboding—and the mature men in the Warsaw Ghetto have few illusions or hope—the impact of events is registered without benefit of hindsight; the reader knows what is hidden from the writer. This tragic irony makes the diaries peculiarly moving, and differentiates them from the many circumstantial accounts which will be written by survivors after a lapse of years.

*Originally published in *Midstream* May 1966; pp. 3–20.

The unfinished diaries affect us for still another reason. Not only Anne, the delightful little girl, but the baffled, suffering men are still without our grasp. Their questions, doubts and accusations are ours; we understand them as with the most desperate effort we do not understand what the survivors of the crematoria tell us. The experience of the diarists are still in the main human, and when in the Warsaw Ghetto they cease to be so, the immediate horror and amazement of the writer expresses what we feel. Our ability to sympathize with the diarist is due not merely to the fact that an individual moves us more readily than an anonymous multitude, but rather that his sufferings still wear a recognizable shape: they evoke fellow-feeling. This sense will paradoxically lessen when we enter the charnel house. The more direct the assault upon our sensibilities, the swifter the aversion, the turning away.

The three diaries of the Warsaw Ghetto are complementary, dealing with the same brief span of time—1940–1943—and with the same tight, confined existence. From November 1940, the creation of the ghetto, to July 22, 1942, the beginning of mass deportations from the ghetto, the chief events are recorded by each diarist writing in secret; each crucial date in the ghetto's history is marked by an entry. The facts are the same. Students of the period who scan the available data for confirmation of particular incidents will note that except for occasional differences of a day or two in the dating of an occurrence, there are no contradictions in the factual record. More surprising, in view of the different characters and ages of the writers, is the similarity of their reactions to what is happening. The social historian trained in political thought and action, the Orthodox Hebrew scholar, and the fifteen-year-old schoolgirl move from a confused hopefulness to hopelessness in the same baffled progression. Though they differ greatly in emotional intensity and intellectual resources, their basic responses are as tragically alike as the events they describe. Their unpreparedness, the comparatively long duration of their initial unawareness, indicate the state of mind of European Jewry, and help explain its inability to read the signs. Literacy came late to the wisest.

Emmanuel Ringelblum (born in Galicia in 1900), an active Labor Zionist deeply involved in party work and the organized communal life of Polish Jewry, is obsessed from the first with a sense of social responsibility. In his "Notes" he is meticulously writing history as well as an indictment; he trains a secret society of fellow-reporters whose records and interviews of refugees from other ghettos will in time form a priceless underground archive, composed and concealed at the peril of death. These records, some smuggled out in Ringelblum's lifetime, others found in milk cans after the War in the ruins of the Warsaw Ghetto, were to prove, as Ringelblum anticipated, major source material for the history of the catastrophe. His society of scribes, using the deceptive name of *Oneg Shabbat* (Sabbath celebrants) painstakingly keep the record of the Nazi Witches' Sabbath, the saturnalia of blood which engulfs European Jewry, till the "celebrants" themselves perish.

Chaim Kaplan (born 1880 in White Russia), a Hebrew teacher, has, like Ringleblum, spent his adult life in Warsaw. But unlike Ringelblum he is something of a recluse, more concerned with books and Hebrew manuscripts than with social action. He, too, is possessed with the need to "record," but his is a solitary voice, a personal cry to his God for a reckoning. He is less concerned with the drama of a dissolving society than with judgment for the malefactors, Jews as well as Germans. Ringelblum, aware of Kaplan's Diary, notes: "Several times I implored Kaplan to let me preserve his diary, assuring him that after the war he would get it back." But characteristically, Kaplan refused, offering merely to let it be copied rather than transferred to the archive. Ringelblum was convinced that the diary was lost. Fortunately, it was discovered years later by Professor Abraham I. Katsh and published in 1965.

Mary Berg, less introspective and anguished than her elders, has a keen eye for detail. Perhaps because she is young and healthy, biologically incapable of authentic despair, she has left extraordinarily vivid glimpses of the life rather than the death of the ghetto. When both the social historian and the stern moralist cry out, "The ghetto dances," the girl's account of how the young still seek ordinary pleasures appears as a corrective.

At the outbreak of the War Kaplan writes stubbornly (October 26, 1939): "Our existence as a people will not be destroyed. Individuals will be destroyed but the Jewish community will live on. Therefore every entry is more precious than gold, so long as it is written down as it happens, without exaggerations and distortions." At this stage Kaplan's optimism is hardly surprising. Seven months later (May 27, 1940) Ringelblum declares even more categorically: "If the war were to last as long as the Jews can hold out, that would be bad, because the Jews can hold out longer than the war can last." As defeats multiply, the ghetto continues to follow the fortunes of the war in the expectation of deliverance. On December 9, 1941, Mary Berg writes: "America's entry into the war has inspired the hundreds of thousands of dejected Jews in the ghetto with a new breath of hope. The Nazi guards at the gates have long faces."

Today we read these diaries no longer in the expectation of learning new facts, whose further compilation only adds to the known, but to share in the education of the authors. We are concerned with the education of Ringelblum and of Kaplan for theirs is still our education. The progressive discoveries they make about Germans, Poles, fellow-Jews, and about themselves confirm our darkest misgivings about the nature of man and offer new dimensions for the exploration of his condition. Throughout, both men, the secular liberal and the Orthodox Hebraist, suffer almost as much from the spiritual decline of all about them, as from their own physical extremity. One of Ringelblum's early entires (May 9, 1940) is of an eight-year-old child who goes mad, screaming: "I want to steal, I want to rob, I want to eat, I want to be a German." And he notes (September 9, 1940) that at the madhouse, Jewish lunatics praise Hitler and give the Nazi salute.

Kaplan is engaged in a more direct theodicy. As a religious man he interrogates God rather than society. His shift of mood can be gauged from two entries: During the first Hanukkah of the War (December 9, 1939) Kaplan writes: "A simple old woman asks me each day: 'Why is the world silent? Does Israel have no God?' I wished to comfort her in her agony, and so I lit four Hanukkah candles. And as I kindled the lights I felt they were as humiliated as I." Less than a year later (October 24, 1940) he will permit himself the Job-like outcry: "But He Who sits in Heaven laughs."

Ringleblum, using a different vocabulary, will reach the same despairing conclusion. Before this clarity is achieved, however, we get a graphic picture of the confusion in the ghetto as it is being established. Nobody understands the Nazi design because all insist on having the design make sense in terms they can rationally apprehend. Its cold logic is rejected for normal human explanations. That is why each new act of German savagery, each new decree continues to surprise the inhabitants. The Poles too are unclear about the fate of the Jews. The ghetto situation abounds in macabre ironies. There is a period just before the establishment of the ghetto when Poles masquerade as Jews so as not to be seized for forced labor for the Reich. And Polish parents hide their children in the homes of Jewish friends because the Aryan blood of Gentile children is useful for plasma for soldiers of the Reich. The gallows humor of these masquerades is lost on neither diarist, both of whom faithfully record grim ghetto jokes, among them that Jews who managed to escape return of their own free will to Warsaw. Kaplan writes of "tens of thousands of Jews who fled to Russia" who come back (1940) in the belief that the worst is over.

The agony accompanying the establishment of the ghetto is tempered by recurrent illusions. Perhaps with this sundering of the Jews from the rest of the world the Nazis have achieved their purpose and the Jews will be allowed to exist undisturbed in their wretchedness. Kaplan writes sardonically of the Jewish police (December 21, 1940): "The residents of the ghetto are beginning to think they are in Tel Aviv. Strong bonafide policemen from among our brothers to whom you can speak in Yiddish." Mary Berg is one of the simple souls whom Kaplan scorns. The Jewish policemen with their badges with a Star of David give her pleasure: "I experience a strange and utterly illogical feeling of satisfaction when I see a Jewish policeman at a crossing," (December 22, 1940) and she describes the "cordial" attitude of the ghetto dwellers to the Jewish police at this stage. Two months later (February 19, 1941) Ringelblum comments on the fact that in an altercation popular sympathy is with the Jewish police: "You would have minded a Polish policeman so why don't you mind a Jewish one?"

Within a year the Jewish police will be the most execrated element in the ghetto but in the beginning the policeman strutting with his badge is a symbol of Jewish authority. Kaplan's bitter observation ("they think they are in Tel Aviv") has its kernel of truth.

In a more sophisticated fashion, Ringelblum, too, nurses dreams of national revival within the enforced solidarity of the ghetto. Writing a few days before Mary Berg and Kaplan make their diverse comments on the Jewish police, he expresses another hope: "Today I was at a concert in the Judaic Library. Jewish artists appeared and sang in Yiddish for the first time. The program was entirely in Yiddish. Perhaps this is a beginning of a return to Yiddish." Ringelblum's optimism about the revival of Yiddish is premature. In May 1942 he will report that "Jews love to speak Polish." And he explains that very little Yiddish is heard in the streets because speaking Polish is a psychological protest against the ghetto.

In the grim parody of autonomy, the Jewish Council plays the grimmest role. At first Kaplan, enumerating all the tasks that have been delegated to the Council by the Germans, observes mildly enough (September 23, 1940), "The *Judenrat* has turned into a Jewish government, and by order of the conqueror it must now perform governmental functions it was never prepared for." Since the Jewish Council is responsible for food distribution, sanitation, schooling, work selection, tax collection, and housing, not only the Jewish Council but the ghetto inhabitants are under the illusion that the Council's activities are ways of prolonging the ghetto's life; the initial fury of the Council's critics is directed at the Council's failures in securing more food, more adequate medical help or more tolerable living quarters in the destitution of the ghetto. As late as April 20, 1941, Mary Berg expresses sympathy for Adam Czerniakow, President of the Council, who must deal with the "Germans every day and at the same time bear with the complaints and the reproaches of the starving, embittered and distrustful population."

Ringelblum makes short shrift of the composition of the Jewish Council from the outset (December 10, 1940): "Ruffians, nice boys all of them, wearing high shoes, have taken the reins at the Jewish Council. . . . Some of the leaders of the Council are honest people but without understanding of social problems." A year later (January 1942), when the ghetto is dying of typhus and starvation, he attacks "the inhumanity of the Jewish upper class" and the Jewish Council as its instrument. Those with money are faring better; bribes can secure not only bread but exemption from the dreaded labor camps. Up to a certain point the poorest of the poor will fill the quotas required by the Germans.

The charges that the members of the Council are weak, cowardly, and venal increase in vehemence as the agony of the ghetto approaches its climax. In this connection, Kaplan's evaluation of the composition of the *Judenrat* should be noted. He makes it abundantly clear that the members of the Jewish Council are not acknowledged Jewish leaders with moral authority in the community (October 27, 1940): "The *Judenrat* is not the same as our traditional Jewish Community Council which wrote such brilliant chapters in our history. Strangers in our midst, foreign to our spirit . . . the President of the *Judenrat* and his advisers are musclemen who were put on our backs by strangers. Most of them are nincompoops whom no one knew in normal times. They were never elected, and would not have dared dream of being elected as Jewish representatives; had they dared they would have been defeated. All their lives until now they were outside the Jewish fold."

Kaplan complains that for a while "even my Zionist friends" tried to get close to the seat of power to get jobs, but "generally our members ran from the *Judenrat*." He quotes an unnamed Zionist who declares: "We have a Zionist tradition to uphold and will never be a party to this criminal gang called the *Judenrat*."

It is apparent from the foregoing, as well as from Ringleblum's accusations, that while the administration of the ghetto by Nazi edict is delegated to the Jewish Council and the Jewish police, the leadership of the ghetto is in other hands. Imposed functionaries, at first the butt of Jewish demands they cannot fulfill, finally loathed as the executors of the Nazi deportation orders, unable to save themselves or their families, they are tragic, ambiguous figures. One thing is not ambiguous. With few exceptions the members of the Council neither were nor became Jewish leaders.

Yet when Adam Czerniakow, realizing at last that his fulfillment of the Nazi deportation orders meant not the partial salvation but the total annihilation of the ghetto, committed suicide on July 24, 1942, rather than sign the German decree, the three diarists exhibit varying degrees of sympathy. Predictably young Mary writes of his "great courage and energy till the last moment"; Ringelblum has only a brusque note: "too late, a sign of weakness—should have called for resistance—a weak man." Kaplan, who has been Czerniakow's and the *Judenrat's* most savage attacker, writes unexpectedly, "His end proves conclusively that he worked and strove for the good of his people; that he wanted its welfare and continuity even though not everything done in his name was praiseworthy."

This ambivalence of judgment is not merely the suspect charity of an obituary. It reflects the basic dilemma of the ghetto—that it had to live and die by quota if it were not to perish at once. At first the Council honestly believed that it was the buffer between the Nazis and the ghetto; its allocation of the little available, including work, would be kindlier than the dispensations of the Storm Troopers, each of whose intrusions filled the ghetto with terror and littered its streets with corpses. The ghetto shared this view. As long as they hoped for survival, the ghetto dwellers were each engaged in selection for life. Long before the deportation to the gas chambers, the choosing had started.

Among the most harrowing pages in Ringelblum's diary are his accounts of starving and freezing children. In November 1941, he writes: "Tonight, the

14th, I heard a tot of three or four yammering. The child will probably be found frozen to death tomorrow morning, a few hours off. Early October, when the first snows fell, some seventy children were found frozen to death on the steps of the ruined houses. Frozen children are becoming a general phenomenon." Death lies in every street: "In one courtyard the children played a game tickling a corpse." Kaplan and Mary report similar scenes of mass misery and the growing insensibility of the people to their own and others' suffering.

These are "natural" deaths—of hunger, cold and disease. Ringleblum listening to the cry of a dying child is no monster. He has nothing to share. Mary Berg, who has eaten that day, turns away weeping from a child "with big blue eyes" who cries, "I am hungry," and Kaplan records the hardening of the heart of all about him. From the start each lives at the expense of another. To give is to die oneself or to choose death for one's own child. Ringleblum puts it plainly (May 30, 1942): "What are we to do? Are we to dole out spoonfuls to everyone, the result being that no one will survive? Or are we to give full measure to a few—with only a handful having enough to survive?" And he proceeds to meditate on the categories that should perhaps be saved from death by starvation. This terrible choosing, demanded by every ramification of the Nazi scheme, will find its ultimate expression in the "selections" of the Jewish Councils but is implicit in every Nazi order from 1939 on. There will be degrees of guilt and horror but only degrees.

The ghetto's will to live expresses itself not only in the struggle for bare subsistence. Ringleblum has counted over sixty "night-spots." Kaplan mentions the "frivolity" in the ghetto despite sporadic slaughters and constant starvation, yet he adds, "It is almost a *mitzvah* to dance. The more one dances, the more it is a sign of his belief in the 'eternity of Israel.' Every dance is a protest against our oppressors." But secret dancing is the slightest of the protests; the ghetto's extraordinary intellectual and spiritual vitality glows till the end.

Young people take vocational courses given by the ORT. Mary Berg reports that "we" are urged "to study as hard as possible and to share among ourselves not only our bread but our knowledge." Ringelblum not only trains his underground research workers, the members of the Oneg Shabbat whose studies will result in the history of the ghetto, but participates in the organization of forbidden schools and lecture series. The question of language in the schools is debated: "There are to be three languages of instruction—Yiddish, Polish and Hebrew." A few months later, however, he reports the decision to concentrate on Yiddish. The Jewish Culture Organization organizes a whole courtyard in which only Yiddish will be used for lectures and instruction. "There is an intense cultural activity. More than ninety-nine courtyards have conducted Mendele academies—Yiddish schools." (February 27, 1941). And Kaplan records how cleverly Jewish children learn in secret: "In time of danger the children learn to hide their books. Jewish children are clever—when they set out to acquire forbidden learning they hide their books and notebooks between their trousers and their stomachs'' (February 15, 1941).

Mary Berg, many of whose friends are budding painters and musicians, describes the concerts and art exhibits of her fellow students. At an exhibition of the work of her school, ''still lifes'' are the most popular. ''The spectators feast their eyes on the apples, carrots and foodstuffs so realistically painted.'' Few people linger before the drawings of beggars. A particularly popular feature are the architectural designs for postwar houses surrounded by gardens: ''The visitors at the exhibition look with pride at these housing projects for Poland of the future . . . which of us will live to see it?'' (September 28, 1941).

While some dream of a free Poland, others are assiduously studying English in preparation for emigration after the War; at the same time Jewish scientists conduct scientific studies as best they are able, among them an investigation of the nature of hunger. As might be expected, the various political parties, Bundists, all shades of Zionists, and socialists are particularly active. The underground press publishes papers and leaflets which are openly distributed because for a while the ghetto believes that the Nazis are indifferent to its intellectual turmoil. ''Bloody Friday'' (April 18, 1942), when the publishers and distributors of the underground publications are executed, dispels this notion.

When the Jewish Council tries to suppress ideological debate on the grounds that continued political activity will invite further massacres and deportations, the timid agree, but according to Ringelblum, some believe that the ghetto has been morally ''rehabilitated'': ''This is the first time that Jewish blood has been spilled for reasons of political—not purely personal—activity.'' These are the beginnings of the debate on resistance which will soon shake the ghetto.

At which point do the diarists become aware of the ''Final Solution''? In April 1941, Ringelblum is still able to write that the ''news from the camps is not bad.'' Another year will pass before the knowledge of what is euphemistically called ''resettlement'' by the Nazis becomes inescapable. In July 1942 Warsaw has already received information as to the nature of Treblinka, but Ringelblum tells us that the Jews of Western Europe still think it is a work camp. They go to the death trains carrying ''brand new valises.'' And almost to the end the rumors which fly through the ghetto minimize rather than exaggerate reality. At a time when massacres in Vilna or Lodz run into the thousands during a single ''action,'' reports in Warsaw tell of fifty or sixty victims. Jews escaping from other ghettos in Poland flee to Warsaw because they have heard that it is an independent ''paradise.'' Not only the trickery of the Germans, with their blandishments of marmalade and bread for deportees who peaceably report to the transferpoint, is responsible for these delusions.

The Nazi propaganda campaign, calculated to lull the fears of the deportees so as to facilitate the process and prevent information from reaching the outside world, is only one element in the deception of the ghetto. The other is self-deception—the inability to believe what till then had been unbelievable. Ghetto rumors of atrocities lessen rather than exaggerate the truth, to reduce the event to psychologically manageable proportions. The new idiom of the twentieth century—extermination center—has not yet been learned.

When the truth is finally assimilated, the diarists lament the failure of the ghetto to resist. Kaplan, through the figure of a mythical Hirsch, appears in the guise of stricturing prophet (June 16, 1942): "My Hirsch is screaming: 'Cowards. . . . You delude yourselves out of hope that the evil will not reach you . . . Protest, alarm the world! Don't be afraid. In any case you will end by falling before the sword of the Nazis. Chicken-hearted ones, is there any meaning to your death?'"

Yet it is Kaplan who describes the results of two attempts at resistance: A mother refuses to surrender her baby. "They immediately grabbed the baby and hurled it out of the window." During a deportation two porters, "virile men," struggle with their captors. The next morning "the Nazis avenged the mutiny of two porters with a hundred and ten Jews." Not only foolish hope, but a sense of collective responsibility restrains the young and still vigorous. The others, the old, women, children, the sick—that is to say the bulk of the ghetto—are important, reduced by hunger and disease, and unarmed. On July 30, 1942, Kaplan adds another detail: "People come to the transferpoint voluntarily, saying 'Take me out of the quagmire of the ghetto. I will die anyhow.'"

As early as August 1941 Ringelblum comments on the passivity of the Jewish masses who die unprotestingly: "Why are they all so quiet? Why does the father die, and the mother, and each of the children without a single protest?" He gives two explanations; the fear of mass reprisals which will hasten the destruction of the ghetto; and, equally significant, physical weakness, a "direct result of hunger," which keeps the starving people inert and incapable of moral or physical reaction.

The diaries begin with "why" and end with "why" though the object of the query keeps changing. At the outset the writer tries to find rational explanations for the Nazi program which in the beginning is viewed not as a new mode, *sui generis*, but as an atavistic throwback to the familiar persecutions of the past. An ancient, much-enduring people can find comfort in historic parallels. When Ringelblum and Kaplan read the riddle of the Nazi "Final Solution," they abandon the quest for understandable motives, economic or political. The first stage in the education of the diarists—and they reflect presumably what is felt obscurely and less consciously throughout the ghetto—is the recognition of the existence of motiveless evil. Ringelblum poring over social causes, Kaplan, Job-like, mourning over the innocent in the hands of the unrighteous, at last stop asking why the murderer—German, Ukrainian, Lithuanian and Pole—murders. They are reduced to the simplest formulation: he murders because he is a murderer. This explanation, too primitive for a psychologist and too unsophisticated for a sociologist, is finally the only one the victim accepts.

The second "why" deals with the behavior of the world outside the Nazi realm of death and depravity. Why do Polish neighbors loot and betray the victims? Where are the "good" Germans? And, above all, what of the outraged conscience of the democracies when they learn about the fate of European Jewry? There is a jubilant moment in June 1942, when Ringelblum records that the "world knows." The British radio has been broadcasting information about Polish Jewry: "For long, long months we tormented ourselves in the midst of our sufferings with the questions: Does the world know about our suffering? And if it knows, why is it silent?" Now that the world has been alerted, measures to aid the tortured Jewries will be found. He rejoices particularly in the role of his O.S. reports smuggled out of the ghetto, in giving the alarm: "We have struck the enemy a hard blow. We have revealed his Satanic plan to annihilate Polish Jewry, a plan he wished to complete in silence." The realization that the world will accept the annihilation of European Jewry as one of the vicissitudes of the War and make no special intervention in its behalf dissipates his short-lived euphoria.

Kaplan, with fewer expectations of the social conscience of mankind, is at this time worrying about Rommel's successful drive in Africa; he permits himself a note on current Allied efforts unwonted in its bitterness even for so tart a commentator as Kaplan: "Perhaps here too Israel is at the heart of it. Our luck has caused it. You don't go into partnership with *idiots* and *failures.*"

After the world has been despaired of, the last "why" is addressed to the Jews. Ringelblum puts it directly (October 14, 1942): "Why did we let ourselves be led like sheep to the slaughter? Why did everything come so easy to the enemy?" In another entry he declares: "Now we are ashamed of ourselves, disgraced in our own eyes, and in the eyes of the world, where our docility earned us nothing." And he urges resistance.

It is apparent that the questions historians would pose two decades later were asked in bitterest soul-searching by the sufferers themselves. No cool retrospective critic, wise in hindsight, could write more indignantly than Ringelblum or Kaplan with his outraged cry of "Chicken-hearted ones!" However, the total effect of the diaries negates the self-castigation of the authors. Unlike the armchair commentators of the future, they are the agonized voices of the ghetto storming against itself. And, despite their self-contempt and anger, the image of helpless suffering they record provides the answer to what they ask.

For the last question can be asked only after the first two have been answered. As long as the Jews believe that Nazi barbarism is accidental, outside the norms of human behavior, they cannot credit a savagery beyond their imaginations to conceive. It is obvious from the ghetto's shock at each murderous action in the ghetto streets that they view these slaughters as episodes, to be explained by the viciousness of a particular German commander or a passing Nazi mood. The evil is piecemeal, as it has always been, and the killers, no matter how numerous, are individual. Hence the Jewish struggle to triumph over the accidental and to circumvent individual caprice. When the Jews reach the abyss of realization at the rim of the mass grave or the door of the gas chamber, they will be too worn down for any gesture of resistance. Similarly, as long as they believe that an outraged world will intervene in their behalf, every effort to defeat the will of the killer by remaining alive, whatever the conditions, seems meaningful.

"Why did we not resist?" the third question, is asked only when all hope has been abandoned, and hope in this context is more than the expectation of personal survival. When hope in man—German, Polish, American, English—is lost, the call to resistance is made. For at no moment do those who organize it nurture the illusion that resistance can achieve more than the death of most Jews and a few Germans. "To die with honor" becomes the slogan of the Jewish Fighting Organization. The notion that dismembered European Jewry had tangible means of resistance against the Nazi war machine is part of the mythology of hindsight.

Six months before the ghetto's last stand, Mary Berg describes the appeals of the Jewish underground (September 20, 1942): "The population is summoned to resist with weapons in their hands and warned against defeatist moods . . . 'Let us die like men and not like sheep' ends one proclamation in a paper called *To Arms.*"

We know from other accounts that the ghetto had no arms and that a few pistols and homemade grenades were smuggled into the ghetto with enormous difficulty through purchases from the Polish underground. The diaries of Kaplan and Ringelblum stop before the ghetto's uprising, and Mary Berg, already in France by April 1943, can offer only a hearsay report. Though Ringelblum puts special emphasis on recording the history of the underground movements for his archive, his diary devotes little space to their efforts. Yet knowledge of these heroic activities is as essential for a total view of the ghetto as Ringelblum's disenchanted picture of the brutalities of the Jewish police and the timidity of the Jewish Council.

However, at one point Ringelblum allows himself a paean to the heroines of the underground which obliquely casts a light on an aspect of the ghetto he does not generally dwell on. He writes: "The heroic girls, Chajke and Frumke—they are a theme that calls for the pen of a great writer. Boldly they travel back and forth through the cities and; towns of Poland. They carry Aryan papers identifying them as Poles or Ukranians. One of them even wears a cross, which she never parts with except when in the ghetto. They are in mortal danger every day. They rely entirely on their 'Aryan' faces and on the peasant kerchiefs that cover their heads. Without a murmur, without a second's hesitation, they accept and carry out the most dangerous missions." The girls travel from ghetto to ghetto bringing information, maintaining links between the severed Jewries and smuggling arms. Ringelblum concludes with unwonted enthusiasm: "The story of the Jewish woman will be a glorious page in the history of Jewry during the present war." Girls were more suitable for the role of emissaries between the ghettos than even blond young men since a physical examination would betray the latter.

To the end the remaining Jews of the ghetto worry about "the eternity of Israel." Ringelblum reports a debate about a proposal to rescue a few hundred children by hiding them in Polish monasteries which have agreed to accept them. The argument which ensues indicates the stress still laid on saving a few lives as a way of ensuring the people's survival. The fear that these children will be converted and that their numbers will be too small in any case to alter Jewish destiny is countered by the view that in a time of mass slaughter every Jew is precious as the possible preserver of Jewish peoplehood. Even the danger of conversion must be risked: "Sending a handful of Jewish children into monasteries will enable us to rescue those who will be the creators of a new generation of Jews."

The Ringleblum archives contain invaluable material on the history of the Jewish Fighters' Organization as well as on all aspects of Jewish self-help and resistance in Warsaw and other ghettos. This must be borne in mind as one reads the last despairing, fragmentary outcries of the "Notes." Ringelblum will take part in the ghetto's uprising and survive it only to be discovered and executed by the Germans in 1944. Before his death he will succeed in smuggling out an account of the underground intellectual life of the ghetto which will be its noblest memorial. In his valedictory he will write to his comrades proudly, "Know then that the last surviving educational workers remained true to the ideals of our culture. Until their death they held aloft the banner of culture in the struggle against barbarism." But in the diary written in staccato notes, half-completed sentences, during the death throes of the ghetto, there is no time to applaud the brave or recount their deeds. There remains only the throb of horror.

Kaplan's last entry (August 1942) expresses envy of the 5,000 Jews who went to the transferpoint of their own accord: "They had had their fill of ghetto life which is a life of hunger and fear and death . . . Would that I could allow myself to do as they did." These are his penultimate words. His last sentence is, "If my life ends what will become of my diary?" He managed to assure its preservation before his extermination in Treblinka.

Despite the fury of the writers and their unsparing criticism of their fellow-Jews no one can read these diaries—and this includes the less analytical account of young Mary Berg—without the conviction that the fortitude of ghetto Jewry sprang from a fierce will for national as well as personal survival. Anyone venturing to pass moral judgments on the conduct of European Jewry in the charnel house must marvel more at the good than at the base. Nothing more eloquently brings home Jewish helplessness in the Nazi vise than the self-accusations of its bravest spirits. No matter how vehemently or how often the diarists may stricture the "criminal Jewish police" or the "criminal Jewish Council," the very nature of their condemnation enables us to perceive the gulf that separates the ghetto's inner life and its acknowledged leaders from the so-called "authorities," appointees of the Nazis. And even the moral failures who fulfill the Nazi bidding in the vain hope of saving themselves and their families are not wholly excluded from the circle of compassion. Weak and corruptible though they be, indignant though the writer be, the fallen are presented as part of the Jewish tragedy and as fellow-victims.

In Western Europe Nazi persecution was more circumspect. Though the anti-Jewish laws were imposed on the Jews of the occupied countries, the drama of the "Final Solution" was in the main enacted in the East and in Central Europe where public opinion was more tractable and less squeamish, if not openly sympathetic to the Nazi program. Mass slaughters did not take place in the streets of Amsterdam nor were mass graves dug in the heart of Brussels. The chief exhibitions of violence were the roundups of Jews for deportation East. In the prison that was Nazi Europe, the West appeared to provide a larger cell with more opportunities for escape than the closed ghettos. Two remarkable diaries tell of attempts to hide in the West.

Both are the diaries of the very young. Unlike Mary Berg, whom the brutality of ghetto life forced out of the private world of adolescence, the diarists write to communicate what they feel rather than to record the history of time. No doubt many other young souls were keeping diaries to express their troubled emotions, their personal responses to the wonder of growing up and to the terror of being a Jew in Nazi Europe.

The most famous of these is, of course, that of Anne Frank whose diary, started in her Secret Annex in Amsterdam when she is thirteen years old, begins on June 14, 1942 and ends on August 4, 1944. Anne and her diary have been thoroughly publicized; the facts of her fate are familiar. That she has become the symbol of the Jewish tragedy for the non-Jewish world, to be viewed in motion pictures, is understandable. The bright little girl's humor, curiosity and unquenchable hopefulness beguile the reader. He is not obliged to face the meaning of her incarceration. Through her words he shares in an adventure in which the individual quirks of the participants are amusing, and Anne's adolescent longings poignant but not painful. When the diary concludes with Anne's expectation at the age of fifteen that "I may yet be able to go back to school in September or October" (June 6, 1944, D-Day), the reader is mercifully spared the need to follow her to Bergen-Belsen. He can, if he wishes, muse on her innocence and faith in man without being forced to consider what happened to that innocence and faith on the following day. Anne can be sentimentalized and gushed over by the unimaginative.

In her hiding place Anne is not unaware of what is happening. On October 9, 1942, she writes: "Our many Jewish friends are being taken away by the dozen. . . . We assume that most of them are murdered. The English radio speaks of their being gassed." But she is thirteen years old, with a quicksilver vitality and eagerness. She may be "terribly upset" but her moods shift and immediately after her reports of the doings "outside," she is able to write: "How fortunate we are here, so well-cared-for and undisturbed. We wouldn't have to worry about all this misery were it not that we are so anxious about all those dear to us whom we can no longer help."

The lucky Franks, aided by courageous Christian friends in Holland who risk their lives daily to keep them provided with food and minimal comforts, come to the same end as the Jews in the ghettos of Eastern Europe. Anne, caught in the turmoil of adolescent dreams, dwells occasionally on the possibility of capture, but her age and temperament enable her to create a world of make-believe in the attic with Peter. Her natural illusions require no explanation as do those of the ghetto dwellers.

At the same time, while involved primarily in the tremors of her own springtime and praying that "surely the time will come when we are people again and not just Jews," she cannot help meditating on Jewish fate in general: "Who knows, it might even be our religion from which the world and all peoples learn good, and for that reason and that reason only do we have to suffer now." And while declaring passionately, "I love the Dutch, I love this country," the young girl adds, "We can never become just Netherlanders, or just English, or representatives of any country for that matter, we will always remain Jews, but we want to, too."

Bruno Bettelheim in *The Informed Heart* blames the Franks' destruction on their desire to continue their private life "as usual." Had they tried to escape to the free world or tried to fight Germans instead of hiding passively, they might have survived. Anne should have gone to live with a Dutch family as their child. They should have had a gun to shoot down the police when they came for them. Bettelheim concludes that Anne died because her parents could not get themselves to face the facts of Auschwitz.

Judging from Anne's account, it is probably true that the family tried with incredible ingenuity to live "as usual" in their hiding place. They read, studied, and sought to remain human. Bettelheim's other strictures hardly bear examination. The Franks had fled from Germany to Holland in 1933, though they would have been wiser to have tried to get on the American immigration quota. They had no more foreknowledge than the rest of us. The notion that Anne could have been hidden with a Dutch family is dispelled by a glance at the photograph of the dark-eyed, dark-haired little girl. Aryan-looking small children were sometimes concealed in remote villages. Anne was too old and too marked a Jewish type for so public a solution. True, the family could perhaps have acquired a pistol, though it is not clear which member of the family would have been able to employ it. The only probable result of resistance would have been the death of the one survivor of the group, the father. In any case Anne, like other Annes in the Polish ghettos, would have perished.

The assimilated, well-educated, middle-class Franks living in Holland decided that their best chance to escape the Nazis was to hide in a secret apartment till the end of the War, however long that might be. Another well-to-do family in Holland decided on a contrary course. At about the same time that the Franks went into hiding, Polish-born Eliezer Flinker, an Orthodox businessman living in Holland, fled to Belgium with his seven children in 1942, to live openly in Brussels on an "Aryan" permit. During Passover 1944, the Flinkers, betrayed by an informer, were seized by the Gestapo. In their home was found the fatal evidence—matzoth, prayer books, ritual food. The family was sent to Auschwitz where the parents and the oldest son, eighteen-year-old Moshe, were killed; the six younger children survived. Like Anne, Moshe kept a diary which was discovered after the War in the basement of the Flinker apartment and published in Israel in 1958.

It is idle to speculate on why the Flinkers chose Belgium as their refuge, just as it is pointless to reargue the decision of the Franks. Both the Franks and Flinkers, by trying to escape the deportations to Eastern Europe, displayed exceptional enterprise if not perspicuity. Each family had a plan of action—the Franks relied on the goodness of a few trusted Gentile friends; the Flinkers speculated that survival might better be achieved in an environment where they were unknown and where their money would secure the neccessary residential permits. Each family managed to live for two years before capture and each family left an extraordinary testament in the diary of one of its children.

Young Moshe's Diary is written in Hebrew. Three years older than Anne, Moshe begins his diary when he is sixteen. As precocious and intense as Anne, he has none of her childish gaiety or effervescence. Brooding, scholarly, obviously an *Ilui* (a prodigy), he engages in a theodicy which rivals that of Kaplan in its probing. And yet he is a schoolboy with the good pupil's concern for marks. His first entry (November 24, 1942) deals with school. In 1940, when the Germans came to The Hague, he entered a special high school for Jews. Restrictions multiplied; he had to turn in his bicycle; then Jews were forbidden to ride on streetcars: "However, I continued going to school during those last days because I wanted to get my report card and find out whether I had been promoted to the next class."

In Brussels, unable to attend a Belgian school, Moshe spends his days reading Hebrew and Yiddish books which he borrows from a still existing

Jewish lending library. He starts resolutely to study Arabic because after the War he intends to be "a Jewish statesman in the Land of Israel." He studies diligently despite the difficulty of getting adequate textbooks; at one point he acquires an Arab-French grammar which necessitates the purchase of a French dictionary since his French is not as good as his German. But he perseveres for, "It is obvious that we shall have to live in peace with our brothers, the sons of Ishmael, who are also Abraham's descendants." While he mourns his inability to take special courses to qualify him for his future diplomatic career, he trusts with deep conviction that "the Lord will help me when my own intelligence is inadequate."

He reveals his plan to become a "Jewish statesman" in December 1942 when the fortunes of the War and of the Jews offer little reason for such extravagant anticipations. But the boy is not indulging in an idle fantasy; he is a believer waiting for Redemption. On the secular plane he is able to analyze the military situation, the political tensions among the Allies and the prospects for the Jews with an unblinking clarity rare among his elders. Comparing the present persecution of the Jews with those of the past, he understands that for the first time in history the whole Jewish people may face destruction. He early warns of "a coming war between England and America on one side and Russia on the other." He foresees the danger of "the final assimilation" of the surviving Jews after the War, and because of this menace he decides: "I am preparing from now on to emigrate to my homeland, and as soon as possible I shall try to do so, the Lord willing." This is five years before the establishment of Israel.

At no point does he lessen the horror of what is taking place. The boy receives its full impact, escaping only to the diminishing solace of his Hebrew studies. What sustains him in the midst of a sharply realistic appraisal of global catastrophe is his faith that these are the birth pangs of the Messiah. Amid such abominations salvation cannot come from the victory of one side or the other but only from God. The very intensity of his apocalyptic vision of the world's evil leads him to disdain human solutions. When the roster of sins is complete, the Lord will grant deliverance: "I think that this war will end with the downfall of most of the world because all have tortured our people. As I see it, the only thing that is delaying the approach of our salvation is that certain countries have not committed enough sins to blacken their names completely. The most important of these nations are England and America (the sins of Germany and Russia are now sufficiently enormous). Now, when England and America every day drop bombs on defenseless towns, on women, children and the aged, their list of sins must be getting longer. . . . But it is as yet impossible to be saved for the American has not amassed his quota of sin." (June 13, 1943)

Despite this passage, Moshe is no religious zealot complacently waiting for the Americans to fill their quota. While he never questions divine justice or divine wisdom, he pleads for divine help for his people. He is consumed by a sense of guilt because he is not sharing the sufferings of his fellow-Jews. Once while still in Holland, he was asked why he did not try to flee to Belgium or Switzerland: "Any girl or boy who can flee from the Germans is saved for our people and can be a hope for the future." In his Belgian refuge he writes: "Now I feel that I have not been saved for the future of my people; on the contrary, I see myself as a traitor who fled from his people at the time of their anguish."

On the day (June 22, 1942) that he learns of the extermination of Jews sent East he turns to his Bible but finds no consolation, "not in the Pentateuch with its lofty commandments" nor in the books of the Prophets. He chants the *Lamentations* and among his sorrows is that "I have done what I said I would do—study the Bible each day—but I have found nothing in it." Yet even as he ventures on this blasphemy, he blames himself rather than the Book.

At the same time, he is a lonely boy who wants friends, remembers a girl he knew in Holland, and watches the gaiety of the young Belgians from afar: "I see in the streets that the gentiles are happy and gay and that nothing touches them. It is like being in a great hall where many people are joyful and dancing and also where there are a few people who are not happy, and who are not dancing. And from time to time a few people of this latter kind are taken away, led to another room and strangled. The happy dancing people in the hall do not feel this at all. Rather, it seems as if it adds to their joy and doubles their happiness."

Moshe reports family quarrels; the mother wants to cross the border to Switzerland; the father refuses because a family of seven children is not mobile or likely to go undetected. The capture of a friend who made the risky move silences the mother.

The boy appears curiously indifferent to the question of escape to a neutral country. He is chiefly troubled by the premonition that the sufferings of the Jews will prove meaningless; the survivors will reject redemption: "I have often asked my Jewish acquaintances what they think the state of affairs will be after the war and I have always received the same answer—that everything will be as it was; we shall continue to stay where we now live and life will go on as before." (November 30, 1942) But this is not God's will, he declares firmly. The Jews were driven from their homes and cities to return to the Land of Israel. Such is the religious rationale of his hope, even while he soberly recognizes the human obstacle to its realization.

Was Moshe a victim of his family's passive acceptance of its doom? Bruno Bettelheim's suggestion that Jewish families could have saved their children by distributing them among friendly Christians presupposes the existence of numerous Christians ready to harbor a Jewish child. Nothing in the record warrants such an assumption. The Flinkers felt safer with their large brood in strange Brussels than in Amsterdam, their home-town. Courageous, self-sacrificing Christians who ventured to conceal Jews were rare individuals. The glimpses Anne and Moshe give us of seizures of Jews in the midst of a silent, cowed population show the Jews isolated in the West by the apprehension of the bystander as in the East by ghetto walls.

In Berlin, Ursula von Kardoff, a young German aristocrat, also kept a diary beginning in 1942. In *Diary of a Nightmare,* we see the reactions of a "good" German, an anti-Nazi, opposed to the persecution of the Jews. There is no doubting the writer's genuine distress at the deportation of the Jews. "No one knows what becomes of them all," but though many are depressed by the deportations, "the bulk of the population is quite indifferent to the whole business." The writer does not learn of Auschwitz till December 1944 and properly finds it hard to believe "such a ghastly story." She, however, forces herself to face the truth; but as late as June 1945, her fellow-Germans, when shown "ghastly photos of corpses piled up in the concentration camps," insist that these are really photographs of the bombing of Dresden.

The diaries of the Holocaust that I have discussed are not primarily emotional outbursts. A victim's lamentation, unless he is a great poet, can become tiresome even to the sympathetic reader. These hurried notes from Hell are precise in observation as well as eloquent, though apparently written without any self-conscious effort at restraint or "discipline," and differing in style and mood. The authors and their world emerge sharply etched. The quizzical little girl in her annex, the passionate historian and the sardonic scholar "recording" in the ghetto, and the possessed boy wandering on a Brussels street, come terribly alive; the unfulfilled futures of the wonderful boy and girl, reminders of what has been destroyed, tease the mind. Candid, acute, articulate, each writer bares more than his heart; he reveals, often unwittingly, how tightly shut was the trap in which the Jews of Europe perished and how few passersby even bothered to glance at the bars.

MEMOIRS

Holocaust diaries stop at the gates of the concentration camp. The diarist is cut off at a moment of hope or dread before his final seizure by the Germans. For an understanding of the ultimate horror experienced by survivors, one must go beyond diaries to autobiographies that were written after the liberation. The diaries, written in the early 1940's, reflect the immediate impact of events and the baffled search for some pattern or meaning in the happenings that befell the writer. The autobiographies, on the other hand, are composed in the fullness of knowledge, if not understanding. The individual writer looks back on everything; he does not have to speculate. When he seeks to reproduce the state of mind of the Jews of Europe from the beginning of the Nazi persecutions to the "Final Solution," he does so without the bewilderment of the diarist and without the fluctuations of mood—alternating between incredulous hope and tentative comprehension of the Nazi purpose—which characterize the writings of even such trained observers as Chaim Kaplan and Emmanuel Ringelblum. The diarist enters only the initial circles of Hell; he may have anticipated its depths, but the full story remains untold. Only the survivor who has completed every round emerges with the whole tale.

Autobiographies of survivors began appearing in the 1950's and more are being published as men and women, now middle-aged or elderly, seek to reconstruct what happened to them in the five or six years before the defeat of the Nazis. For the purpose of this study a limited number have been selected, one criterion being the availability of the work in English. Furthermore, an attempt is made to discuss works which differ sufficiently in style and emphasis: for no matter how inevitably similar the major outline of events appears to be, each writer adds his individual detail and perspective to the common experience.

Obviously, the element of repetition is unavoidable. However, this very element attests to the fidelity with which the concentration camp experience has been reported by those who endured and lived to tell their story. Just as the accounts of the ghetto written by the diarists contain redundancies, so do similar episodes reappear in the stories of the various survivors. Whether the death camp be Auschwitz or Maidanek, the same agonizing details of the Nazi technique of destruction are narrated—the terrible journey in the sealed trains; the selections for immediate or deferred death; the fatal showers; the divisions of the prisoners into categories ranging from the lucky German criminals, with their special privileges, down to the "subhuman" category of the Jews. Yet, each writer adds his special insight to the central question which torments mankind—how can people be so evil?

The first and most urgent problem of the concentration camp inmate is bare survival in conditions of such extremity that each day endured is a dreadful miracle—only a small minority survived. Yet concomitant with the story of physical and psychic outrage, each writer in his own fashion dwells upon the process of dehumanization and brutalization—a process deliberately engineered and structured by the Nazis as an essential means of carrying out the "Final Solution." Most of the narrators were in their teens or early twenties when they fell into the hands of the Germans (youth and vitality were essential for survival; children and the middle-aged or elderly were in the main foredoomed). Despite their youth, they wrestled with the immense questions of human evil and moral responsibility; they were pursued by a sense of guilt inherent in the very fact of their survival. For many, survival was a goal with a meaning transcending the purely personal. To survive meant to "bear witness," to let the world know what befell both the survivors and the millions who died, so that such horrors would never be allowed to happen again. They were so sure the world would care!

One of the most comprehensive and well-structured autobiographies, notable for its restraint, is Alexander Donat's *The Holocaust Kingdom*. Perhaps because the author was both a seasoned journalist and a mature man of thirty-four in 1939 when the German attack on Warsaw began, he was able to portray the years from the Nazi assault till his liberation and his family's arrival in the United States in 1946 with a completeness and literary competence to be found in few such narratives. He begins with a systematic analysis of the structure of the Warsaw Ghetto and the living conditions prescribed by German regulations. The diaries may be more moving because of the astonishment and disbelief of the individual when first exposed to the progressive barbarism of the Nazi regime, but for clarity Donat's exposition is equalled only by sociological or historical treatises. These treatises, however, lack the sense of personal dimension which Donat contributes. He provides the reader with a faithful description of the complex geography of the Warsaw Ghetto and of the various devices for maintaining life. Poignant vignettes illumine the familiar material. For instance, the famous scene of the deportation of two hundred children from an orphanage to the *Umschlagplatz* (assembly place) for transfer to the death camp (p. 70) accompanied by the head of the institution, the now famous Polish Jew Janus Corczak—a scene that has become a classic in accounts of the Warsaw Ghetto—is described with the added information that the *Judenrat*, the Jewish Council, tried to save Corczak but not the children whom they considered lost. Donat's descriptions of the Council, of the often vicious Jewish policemen trying to save only themselves, and, on the other side of the coin, of the heroism of various young women acting as couriers between the different ghettos, bear out what has been related by numerous witnesses. His description of the ghetto revolt is particularly moving. Donat's comment on "the entire cruel month of April," derisively beautiful because of the fine weather during which the German savagery was enacted, was surely written without knowledge of T. S. Eliot's "April is the cruelest month."

Donat's depiction of the burning ghetto is unforgettable:

> Then came Easter Sunday . . . Mass over, the holiday crowds poured out into the sun-drenched streets. Hearts filled with Christian love, people went to look at the new unprecedented attraction that lay halfway across the city to the north, on the other side of the Ghetto wall, where Christ's Jewish brethren suffered a new and terrible Calvary not by crucifixion but by fire. What a unique spectacle: bemused, the crowds stared at the hanging curtains of flame, listened to the roar of the conflagration, and whispered to one another, "But the Jews—they're being roasted alive!" There was awe and relief that not they but the others had attracted the fury and vengeance of the conqueror. There was also satisfaction. Batteries of artillery had been set up in Nowiniarska Street and were shelling objectives in the Ghetto from there. The explosions of grenades and dynamite could be heard as well, as Jews scrambled from their hiding places. Pain-crazed figures leaped from balconies and windows to smash on the streets below. From time to time a living torch would crouch on a window sill for one unbearably long moment before flashing like a comet through the air. When such figures caught on some obstruction and hung there suspended in agony, the spectators were quick to attract the attention of German riflemen. "Hey, look over there! No, over there!" Love of neatness and efficiency were appeased by a well-placed shot; the flaming comet was made to complete its trajectory; and the crowds cheered (pp. 152–3).

Here we have a devastating depiction of the role of the bystander during the Nazi Holocaust.

With Donat's arrival in Maidanek, we enter the world of the death camp:

> Maidanek was hell. Not the naive inferno of Dante, but a twentieth century hell where the art of cruelty was refined to perfection and every facility of modern technology and psychology was combined to destroy men physically and spiritually (pp. 167–8).

Having lived through the exaltation of the last days of the Warsaw Ghetto, Donat felt himself charged with the mission "of carrying the ghetto's history through the flames and barbed wire until such time as I could hurl it into the face of the world." He thought that this sense of mission would give him the strength to endure everything. But he had underestimated Maidanek. "Hell has no bottom" (p. 183).

The functioning of Maidanek, the formation of work-details known as *Kommandos,* and the role of the sadistic Kapos are explained and brought to life with horrifying exactness. The specialty of one Kapo was strangling prisoners with the heel of his boot "and he would stand erect in the pose of a Roman gladiator enjoying the approval of other Kapos for being a 'real master,' a strangler who did not need to dirty his hands." Another Kapo had a different method. He would lie on top of his victim "almost caressingly wrapping his fingers around his victim's throat." At such moments the Kapo had an orgasm while his companions snickered. Such sadistic amusements, encouraged by and participated in by the German guards, were variations on the program of extermination which led from killing labor to the chimneys. However, "most beat their victims because it was the custom of the place" (p. 179). Inside Maidanek one was either a victim or an executioner; there was no middle ground.

Similar anecdotes of horror fill all accounts of survivors, just as the reduction of the prisoner to the level of desiring only his ration of bread, and guarding his spoon and bowl from theft by another wretch, characterizes all the biographies. Yet, in the midst of the bestiality imposed by the Germans, some Jewish prisoners managed to discuss the "historical testament of Polish Jewry." A fellow-writer, also at Maidanek, enjoined Donat in words reminiscent of Ringelblum:

> Everything depends on who transmits our testament to future generations, on who writes the history of this period. History is usually written by the victor. What we know about murdered peoples is what their murderers vaingloriously cared to say about them . . . Their every word will be taken for gospel. Or they may wipe out our memory altogether as if we had never existed, as if there had never been a Polish Jewry, a Ghetto in Warsaw, a Maidanek. Not even a dog will howl for us. But if we write the history of this period of blood and tears—and I firmly believe we will—who will believe us? . . . Nobody will want to believe us because our disaster is the disaster of the entire civilized world (p. 211).

Similar scepticism about historical records is expressed by another Nazi victim, the German-Jewish social historian Walter Benjamin, who noted (in *Illuminations,* pp. 256–259) that historians inevitably sympathize with the victor, and who called on historians "to brush history against the grain" by empathizing with the victim.

Donat, his wife, and his child miraculously survived. (His wife tells her story in the second part of the book, and the events relating to the child are recorded by the Polish Gentile woman who saved him, at great risk to herself.) That a whole family emerged alive from the Holocaust gives *The Holocaust Kingdom* a kind of personal happy ending which only serves to underline the fate of the perished millions.

In *The Janowska Road* (also published as *The Death Brigade*), Leon Wells, sixteen years old when his travail begins and a member of a Chassidic family in the Ukraine, early learns that the whole world is the "enemy" of the Jewish

people. He describes the collaboration of the Ukrainian peasants with the
Germans, after the Russians withdrew. Following the German attack on Russia in 1941, the Ukrainians faithfully emulated the victorious Nazis in tortur-
ing their Jewish captives. In the Ukraine, as in Poland, enclosure in a ghetto,
murderous "actions" in which thousands were slaughtered, futile attempts to
escape to other towns in the hope that other localities may provide a refuge,
are recorded with the macabre detail which testifies to the ingenuity of Nazi
sadism.

Young Wells survives because of energy and resourcefulness and, paradoxically, because he has the "luck" to be chosen for the "death brigade," the
special work group consisting of Jewish prisoners who must burn the corpses
in mass graves and crush bones not completely burned; then others, the "ash
brigade," would search the ashes for gold teeth, jewelry, and other valuable
metallic items that may have been overlooked.

Wells' account of the functioning of the death brigade is one of the most
detailed in Holocaust literature (pp. 140–177). At the Janowska concentration
camp such later "improvements" as the gas chambers and the crematoria had
as yet not been introduced. Corpses had to be burned at a furious tempo to
escape the relentless beatings of the Nazi guards:

> One group worked with shovels—this meant digging out the bodies that had
> been buried or partly buried after former mass murders. Another group
> worked with the corpses directly. This was a terrible job. One had to grab the
> hands or feet of a corpse and pull it out from a veritable mountain of dead
> bodies. Very often the corpse slid out of their hands, or the skin of the body
> came right off and was left in their hands. Voices from the top of the hill
> constantly screamed, *Los, warum so langsam.* Quick, why so slowly . . .
> These were relatively fresh bodies—about two weeks old. That meant they
> were from the final liquidation of the ghetto. I think: Perhaps my two brothers
> were among them.

The Germans carefully tabulated the speed of the work and the number of
bodies disposed of. No amount of zeal prevented the periodic lashing of the
prisoners to keep them properly cowed. The stench of the putrifying corpses
clung to the workers. No amount of lysol freed them from their distinctive
smell. But they followed orders so as to defer the death they were certain
would come anyhow. When told to stop, he writes, "we sit on corpses" while
waiting for further instructions.

An advantage of working in the death brigade was a larger ration of food.
The soup was thicker; there was more bread. Wells relates that when he
escaped and went into hiding, though a teenage boy, he weighed 230 pounds
"owing to the plenitude of food we had in the last few months in the Death
Brigade" (p. 128).

It would be a mistake to assume that the dehumanization, which participation in this gruesome task involved, was total. The loss of sensibility, which

enabled a member of the death brigade to view this labor as merely another aspect of the Nazi scheme of torture and brutalization, was accompanied by a recurrent sense of guilt and shame. A father cries out: "... all, and my two daughters among them, were lying dead ... shot. What girls, beautiful, intelligent—what I wouldn't have done for them ... They told us to make a fire, and we threw all the bodies into it, my children, too" (p. 153). The author adds, "I didn't listen any more. How could I help him? The tragedy was universal, not particular any more." Incongruously, in this nihilistic setting, one member of the brigade was a religious man who fasted and kept the Sabbath insofar as he could.

Sometimes trucks came to the ravine with live victims who had to jump into the fire directly after undressing themselves and their children. When a child cried out, the German SD crushed its head against a tree and tossed it into the fire, but usually adults jumped into the fire without protest. They had been tortured too long. "Even the children in diapers feel this" (p. 207). The world is the enemy from whom escape is sought.

Death was omnipresent. Jews who escaped and went into hiding were in constant danger of betrayal by Poles, although a few Poles risked their lives to save some Jews. And even Jews who managed to survive were in many instances no longer capable of fellow-feelings, though they would assist a comrade if they could. "Help, yes—compassion, no," observes the writer.

Wells is nineteen when he is liberated by the Russian advance. What has his terrible adolescence taught him? Besides the knowledge that life, Jewish life, is cheap, and senseless savagery a daily companion, he has also learned "that logic is not always right." According to all the probabilities he should have perished like the rest of his family, but he had learned "not to give up," whatever the odds. In 1949, after getting a degree in engineering, Wells settled in the United States. The record he has left of man's capacity for inflicting and enduring brutality is one of unrelieved horror; however, he also shows that force of will and youthful resilience were important factors in survival.

One of the most profound and intellectually sophisticated accounts is *Survival in Auschwitz* (also published as *Auschwitz*), which first appeared in English as *If This is a Man*—a much better translation of the original Italian title. Primo Levi, the author, an Italian Jew, was a sensitive young intellectual when he was captured by the fascist militia in 1943 and deported to Auschwitz. A trained chemist, he was disposed to examine his experiences with scientific exactitude. He is as much interested in how human beings react to unspeakable torment, and in what animates the tormentor, as in relating his particular *via dolorosa*.

Levi describes himself at the outset:

> I was twenty-four, with little wisdom, no experience, and a decided tendency—encouraged by the life of segregation forced on me for the previ-

ous four years by the racial laws—to live in an unrealistic world of my own,
a world inhabited by civilized Cartesian phantoms, by sincere male and
bloodless female friendships.

He had fled into the mountains hoping to create the nucleus of a partisan band.
But nothing came of the attempt. An idealist, he was totally unprepared for
the lesson of the concentration camps: "that man is bound to pursue his own
ends by all possible means" (p. 9).

After his capture and arrest in the mountains in January 1944, Levi was sent
to the well known detention camp in Fossoli, near Modena. There were about
150 Italian Jews in the camp at the time, but within a few weeks their number
rose to over six hundred. On February 21 they learned that all Jews would be
leaving the following day and most of them knew that this meant the death
sentence. Yet life went on that last day, "even the teachers of the little school
gave lessons until the evening, as on other days. But that evening the children
were given no homework" (p. 11).

As he recounts the familiar atrocities to which each Jewish victim is
subjected—an account so familiar that the reader already anticipates the
sequence—he adds a fresh dimension to the already known. He has the
literary power and the intellectual awareness to highlight the offense, "the
demolition of a man." On the very first day, finding himself barefoot and
naked in the snow in Auschwitz, he realizes how much the affront to man goes
beyond physical suffering:

> It is not possible to sink lower than this . . . Nothing belongs to us any more;
> they have taken away our clothes, our shoes, our hair; if we speak, they will
> not listen to us . . . They will even take away our name; and if we want to
> keep it, we will have to find in ourselves the strength to do so, to manage
> somehow so that behind the name something of us, of us as we were, still
> remains (p. 22).

The first emotion is amazement at the fact that the savagery he encounters is
irrational, apparently causeless. Tormented by thirst he breaks off an icicle
near his window, but the guard outside snatches it from him. When he asks in
innocence, "*Warum?*" (why?) he receives the answer, "*Hier ist kein
warum*" (here there is no why) (p. 25). Even Jewish inmates tell the newcomers
contemptuously that queries are pointless; the only exit is by way of "the
chimney." Soon the meaning of that phrase is understood.

In time Levi learns the science of the tatooed numbers at Auschwitz which
epitomize various stages in the destruction of European Jewry. The low numbers,
30,000 to 80,000, of whom only a few hundred remain, represent the
survivors of the Polish ghettos. The select group of forty whose numbers run
between 116,000 to 117,000, represent the Jews of Salonika, a tough crew.
The higher numbers are the newcomers; Levi's tatoo is 174,517.

He also learns the arts of survival. One must wash even in dirty water, without soap, and dry oneself on whatever rag is being worn, because the purpose of the camp is to reduce men to beasts. Therefore, to survive so as "to bear witness," one must force oneself "to save at least the skeleton, the scaffolding of civilization." At the same time, like the rest, he learns how precious it is to get soup from the bottom of the pot—the privilege reserved for the Kapo who ladles it out—and how to value the gift of a tin spoon and bowl bequeathed to him by his friend Shmulek who is going to the gas chambers after a "selection." Levi describes Nazi bestiality and its effect on the sufferer as graphically as Wells or Donat, but his chief concern is the realization that "our personality is fragile, that it is much more in danger than our life" (p. 49).

In the midst of the inferno Levi sets himself the task of considering the camp as "preeminently a social and biological experiment." The pages devoted to this theme (pp. 79–90) are remarkably free of clichés and preconceptions. He denies the facile deduction of so many that man is fundamentally brutal and egoistic and that once all the restraints of civilized conduct have been removed, the prisoner is nothing but a bare forked animal without inhibitions. Instead, Levi concludes that in extreme situations of physiological necessity and physical suffering, "social habits and instincts are reduced to silence." A starving man thinks only of food, a tortured one only of the violation of his body. But he is nevertheless more than the creature to which persecution has reduced him.

At the same time Levi realizes that there are two categories of people in the concentration camp. He calls them the drowned, those who will inevitably perish, the *musselmen,* as the doomed are curiously called because they lack the ferocious ability to stay alive—and the saved. This survival of the fittest is not predicated on qualities which may avail in ordinary life, where the able succeed but the weak have a chance. In the savage world of the concentration camp, civilization offers no cushioning. Each man is fiercely alone and can only survive at the expense of another—in a selection, or by theft of food or a piece of clothing. Levi describes, without moralizing, those with the capacity to survive in this process of natural selection in unnatural circumstances. In one of the most frequently quoted passages of his book he writes:

One has to fight against the current, to battle every day and every hour against exhaustion, hunger, cold and the resulting inertia; to resist enemies and have no pity for rivals; to sharpen one's wits, build up one's patience, strengthen one's willpower. Or else, to throttle all dignity and kill all conscience, to climb down into the arena as a beast against other beasts, to let oneself be guided by those unsuspected subterranean forces which sustain families and individuals in cruel times. Many were the ways devised and put into effect by us in order not to die; as many as there are different human characters. All implied a weakening struggle of one against all, and a by no

means small sum of aberrations and compromises. Survival without renunciation of any part of one's own moral world—apart from powerful and
direct interventions by fortune—was conceded only to very few superior
individuals, made of the stuff of martyrs and saints (p. 84).

Levi himself survived because the Nazis needed a chemist with his training. In
1945 he was liberated by the Russians.

The above quoted passage, taken out of context, is often interpreted by
critics as Levi's credo of life and survival. Such a simplistic view does less
than justice to the complexities of Levi's book. Levi's memoirs are unlike
much of the writing on the Holocaust because he has the ability to transcend
fact while remaining factual. One of the most moving passages in this work is
the chapter, "The Canto of Ulysses." Primo, an Italian scholar, walks with a
young Alsatian and tries to translate, into bad French, the great passage from
the *Divine Comedy* in which Ulysses, in the Inferno, urges his men to remember what they are:

> Think of your breed; for brutish ignorance
> Your mettle was not made; you were made men,
> To follow after knowledge and excellence.

The Alsatian listens, trying to understand. And Levi, knowing that the next
day neither of the two may be alive, strives to convey the longing expressed
by Dante. It is a great scene in which the protagonists are given no quarter. As
they wait together for the turnip soup, the final line of the passage describing
how Ulysses founders with his men is recalled by Levi: "And over our heads
the hollow seas closed up" (p. 105). But, for a moment, Hell glowed with a
glimpse of what man could be.

In *The Forest My Friend*, Donia Rosen depicts inhuman brutalized peasants, treacherous and sadistic, cooperating with the Germans and outdoing
them, if possible, in mindless savagery. One meets a hunted child, cruel
bystanders, and Germans and their helpers among the local population. The
use of the Carpathian forests as a setting serves as a reminder of the role of
nature as helper—or obstructor—of efforts of escape and rescue. Written
simply, the book nevertheless conveys more than an individual exploit. Donia
Rosen's fate mirrors another dramatic part of modern Jewish history. After
recovering her health in a children's hospital in Czernowitz at the end of the
War, Donia, with other Jewish survivors, heads for the Land of Israel. She
succeeds in boarding an "illegal" immigrant ship, one immediately following
the notorious "Exodus," which also is apprehended by British naval vessels.
After describing her experiences in a British detention camp in Cyprus, Donia
ends her account with her arrival in Haifa as a Youth Aliyah immigrant.

Another child's story, this time of a non-Jewish witness, is Anatoli Kuznetsov's *Babi Yar*. The peculiar horror of the infamous ravine Babi Yar (Old Wives' Gully) on the outskirts of Kiev, where the Germans shot, buried, gassed, and burnt over a hundred thousand Jews, Ukrainians, and Russians between 1941 and 1943; had already been expressed in art in Yevtushenko's famous poem of the same title and in Shostakovich's Thirteenth Symphony. (For an analysis of this poem, see below, "Holocaust Literature III: Poetry and Drama.") Yet, when this documentary novel began to be serialized in the Moscow magazine *Yunost* (Youth) in the fall of 1966, it created a sensation. The publication coincided with the twenty-fifth anniversary of the Nazi massacre of the Kiev Jewish population, and the subject had become explosive in the Soviet Union. "Everything in the book is the truth," writes the author in his introduction to the story, and proceeds to give an autobiographical sketch of himself:

> I, Anatoli Vasilevich Kuznetsov, author of this book, was born on August 18th, 1929, in the city of Kiev. My mother was Ukrainian, my father Russian. On my identity card my nationality was given as Russian.
> I grew up on the outskirts of Kiev, in the Kurenyovka district, not far from a large ravine the name of which—Babi Yar—was known then only to the local people. Like the other parts of the Kurenyovka it was our playground, the place where I spent my childhood. Later it became famous, suddenly, in a single day. For more than two years it was a forbidden area, fenced off with high-tension wires which enclosed a concentration camp. There were notices saying that anyone who came near would be fired on (p. 2).

The writer was twelve years old when the Germans occupied Kiev in September 1941. His grandfather was an uneducated and bigoted Ukrainian worker of peasant background. He disliked Soviet rule and, like many other Ukrainians, first welcomed the Germans as liberators from an oppressive regime. But later he became a hater of fascism. His grandmother was an illiterate woman raised in a village, simple and kind. His father was a Communist who took an active part in the civil war. He divorced Anatoli's mother, a sensitive hard-working teacher who was rarely home. During the brutal Nazi rule of Kiev, the boy Anatoli matured at an early age, having to support himself as well as contribute to the upkeep of the family. With his own eyes he witnessed the extermination of Kiev Jewry and the tragic fate that befell many others of his fellow citizens. The longer he endured, the more convinced he became that it was his duty to tell the story of Babi Yar, especially in view of the increasing tendency in the Soviet Union to play down the Jewish aspect of the atrocities.

The issue was brought into the open by Yevgeni Yevtushenko's poem. In his autobiographical sketch, published in the French magazine *L'Express,* Yevtushenko relates that he had wanted to write a poem on anti-Semitism for a long time, but that it was only after he had visited Kiev and seen the place of the massacres that the words came to him. The literary journal *Literaturnaya Gazeta,* that published "No Monument Stands over Babi Yar," was sold out within minutes when it appeared on September 19, 1961. But the poet was sharply attacked by Soviet writers for his "Jewish Nationalism," and later he was castigated by Khrushchev at the Moscow Conference on Art and Literature for his lack of political maturity and his ignorance of historical facts.

Following in the footsteps of his illustrious fellow-Russian, Kuznetsov presents more than another atrocity story. He gives a candid picture of a child's discovery of the ravages of war and the depths of human brutality. His narrative more than hints at the complicity of many Ukrainians in the genocide. The author pieces the story together from his own memories, from notes he made at the time, and from what he was told by other survivors of the Nazi occupation and Babi Yar. While somewhat lacking in psychological depth, Kuznetsov has an eye for immediate physical detail, and many scenes, at times grotesque, come alive with horrifying vividness: the mobile gas-chamber that opened to show a hundred naked girls packed dead on each other's knees, with their head scarves on as if on their way to the baths; the German sense of precision in the final burning of the thousands of bodies neatly stacked crisscross in huge layered pyres with prisoners drawing "burning torches along the rows of projecting heads." It is this circumstantiality that makes the book memorable, rather than the author's more generalized comments, which add a layer of cynicism and angry pessimism to the work.

Within a few weeks of the Nazi occupation of Kiev, Anatoli had become a half-famished street urchin, selling matches or whatever he could get hold of, shining shoes, stealing potatoes from moving trucks, and prowling the city and countryside like "a young wolf." Living near Babi Yar, he could hear the machine guns firing almost every day as, according to Nazi custom, the Jews were succeeded as victims by mental patients, gypsies, political prisoners, victims of reprisal raids, thieves, and other "unreliable elements."

The book has an added interest in showing something of the workings of Soviet censorship. After coming to England as a refugee from Soviet Russia, Kuznetsov in 1969 published a second version of *Babi Yar,* indicating in heavier type the many deletions—from single words to whole pages—which the book suffered when published in 1966 in the Soviet Union. The anti-Semitism and anti-Sovietism of the grandfather were allowed but toned down in the original version. But the suggestion that the NKVD and not the Germans blew up Kiev's main street and a nearby monastery is removed. The frequent attacks on collectivization and the allusions to famine and even cannibalism are all deleted, as are the many emphatic parallels between Soviet and Nazi tactics of control. In addition to such ideological cuts, there are examples of Soviet prudery. There are no "sexual organs," "Russian prostitutes," "contraceptives," nor "circumcision." The comic description of German soldiers sitting in a row in an open latrine is left out, as well as the more significant detail of how some of the Jews who were shot in Babi Yar but not killed, crawled out from the pile "only to be knocked over the head and thrown back."

It is interesting that only now, so many years after the Babi Yar tragedy, and after several false starts, a monument has finally been erected at the site of the ravine on the outskirts of Kiev. But the character of the monument, as well as the inscription upon it, contain nothing that even remotely suggests the Jewish agony. In this respect the fifty-foot high monument, a bronze sculpture with eleven entwined figures, resembles the other Soviet memorials in Eastern Europe, including the memorial at Auschwitz. The stereotyped group includes a young girl bent over the slain figure of her boyfriend; a sailor shielding his mother with his body; a woman, her hands tied behind her back, but still suckling a child; another wounded young woman about to fall into the abyss; and, finally, a Red Army soldier and a partisan, the last two summing up the central theme of the monument. This description of the monument by the Novosti Press Agency highlights the typical "positive heroes" of this product of Soviet socialist realism. For Jews, the ultimate travesty upon truth is expressed in the monument's inscription: "Here in 1941–43, the German Fascist invaders executed over 100,000 citizens of Kiev and prisoners of war." The massacred Jews have been erased from the record.

In his autobiographical *Man's Search for Meaning,* psychiatrist Viktor Frankl develops the theory of logotherapy which brought him fame as the leader of the so-called Third Viennese School of Psychotherapy. Based on his experiences in Auschwitz and Dachau, Frankl approaches his subject with infinite compassion for his fellow-sufferers, a compassion that includes even the camp guards. His tolerant understanding is all-encompassing and extends to what he calls "the two races of men in this world: the 'race' of the decent man and the 'race' of the indecent man. Both are found everywhere; they penetrate into all groups of society. No group consists entirely of decent or indecent people. In this sense, no group is of 'pure race'—and therefore one occasionally found a decent fellow among the camp guards" (p. 137).

After discussing the "art of living," which is possible "even in a concentration camp," Frankl agrees with Nietzsche that "he who has a *why* to live for can bear almost any *how*" (p. 121). His own personal *why* was the love for his wife. During a painful forced march at night he relates how he managed somehow to get through: "my mind clung to my wife's image, imagining it with an uncanny acuteness. I heard her answering me, saw her smile, her frank and encouraging look. Real or not, her look was then more luminous than the sun which was beginning to rise" (p. 58).

While one may be critical of some of Frankl's psychological musings, one must admire his perceptiveness when he clearly recognizes the basic conditions for survival in a concentration camp: to get into a factory and work in a sheltered room was "a life-saving piece of luck" (p. 72). In spite of this theorizing, Frankl makes it clearer than most survivors that the ''luck'' of a prisoner was as decisive for survival as any attempt to give some meaning to life in a concentration camp. (For additional discussion of Frankl, see Chapter Seven.)

Compassion and helping others is also the survival message of Eugene Heimler's *Night of the Mist*. Like Viktor Frankl, Heimler is able, in retrospect, to regard his concentration camp experiences as a spiritual test revealing his inner strength. He notes that it was person-to-person relationships inside the camps which enabled him to survive the back-breaking labor, the savage beatings, and even torture. In their conversations, the prisoners always return to ''last things,'' such as questions of the destiny of man and the qualities of good and evil. A friend asks:

> What do you think determines the destiny of a person? What does it depend on, whether one is dragged down by suffering, or raised to a higher level by it? . . . The concentration camps have created a civilization within a civilization. And in this new civilization the truths and laws whose validity we believed in for centuries have been turned upside down. . . .

But then he finds the answer:

> many of the good have become bad, and many of the bad have become good. But it is the personalities that have changed not the values. The Good remains good even here; and Evil, evil . . . The impotent man is not the one who is incapable of having a sex life, but he who cannot receive God into his soul (pp. 128–129).

It is this final conclusion that Heimler takes with him out of Dachau into freedom.

Among other books that should be mentioned is Martin Gray's *For Those I Loved,* if only for the circumstance that here the triumphs of survival, material success and personal happiness are turned to dust and ashes by a pitiless fate reminiscent in cruelty of the envious gods of Greek tragedy.

Apart from the catastrophic ending, the book reads like a handbook for survival. Gray's father had taught him the basic rule: ''Never get caught. But if they catch you, think of only one thing, escape. Even if you're scared stiff. Escape . . . If you escape, there's always hope'' (p. 18). First, Gray survived the Nazi occupation of his native city of Warsaw. He even flourished as one of the blockade runners of the ghetto who brought food to the starving inhabitants. Next, and almost incredibly, he survived Treblinka; the tales of horror he relates of this perhaps most infamous of all the death camps bear out other accounts.

Gray's autobiography shows him as a kind of hero, but a flawed one. He had no intention of dying a hero's death on the barricades, so he escaped before they collapsed. On the other hand, he need not have returned to the ghetto to fight, nor did he have to join the partisans. It was his fierce drive to survive, his daring, and at times almost unbelievable luck which saw him through the War and then provided him with a new life of prosperity and family happiness. But in the end his luck ran out and fate turned against him. His wife and four children perished in a forest fire in the south of France in 1970. Ironically, Gray himself once more survived.

Nathan Shapell's autobiography, *Witness To The Truth,* holds special interest due to his treatment of the problems of the ''displaced persons.'' The exhausted survivors of the Holocaust at War's end found themselves once again behind barbed wire, this time in DP camps under Allied military administration. Shapell gives a vivid account of the lack of preparation on the part of the officers of the American military government in Bavaria when first confronted with the dishevelled concentration camp survivors. How much easier it was to deal with the clean, polite and obedient local Germans, rather than with such strange crude ruffians claiming to have suffered improbable experiences at the hands of those polite clean Germans. Nevertheless, though not at once able to absorb the meaning of the extermination camps and the horrendous happenings that had occurred in them, American military government personnel, with good will and fairness, soon learned what had to be done for the survivors. A native of Sosnowiec, Poland, and survivor of Auschwitz, Shapell served his fellow DP's by establishing good relations with the occupation forces and by helping to obtain proper quarters and facilities for the increasing number of survivors who found their way into the Bavarian countryside. Thus, Shapell treats an important part of the Holocaust, the immediate aftermath, that so far has been neglected and which deserves additional studies covering not only the American but also the British, French and Russian zones of occupation.

A totally different note is struck in the memoirs of a German Jew, Josef Katz, author of *One Who Came Back: The Diary of a Jewish Survivor.* Written with unpretentious candor and sober understatement, Katz's account is noteworthy because it describes the less known and rarely mentioned ghettos and concentration camps in Nazi-held Latvia, including the Riga ghetto and camp Stutthoff.

Born in Lübeck, the native city of Thomas Mann, which is so very differently described in Mann's classic novel *Buddenbrooks,* Katz provides insights into the early years of Nazi rule in Germany. He was seventeen years old when the Nazis came into power, but he and his family, like so many of their fellow German Jews, had no inkling of what was in store for them, and they were slow to learn. Yet there were many instances of Nazi brutality directed against Jews even in the early days. Katz's brother was the first to wake up. On April 1, 1933, ''Boycott Day,'' he writes, ''SA men are posted in front of our small leather goods store in the Braunstrasse to keep our customers from entering. One SA man punches my brother in the face when he tries to walk into his shop. He comes home very dejected and says to my mother, 'We Jews are finished now' '' (pp. 3–4). Then follows "race education" at school. Katz is told he no longer belonged on a German football field, and his former teammates ask him "if it's true that we always drink Christian blood for Easter" (p. 4).

After the night of November 9, 1938, the infamous *Kristallnacht*, Katz tries to get away. He has reached Hamburg when a telegram from his mother calls him back home since otherwise she will be arrested. On his return to Lübeck, Katz is jailed by the Gestapo. After his release, arrangements are made for his emigration to Shanghai. But, as he reports honestly and quite incredibly, "I decided not to go but to stay with my old mother, as the climate there would not be good for her" (p. 8). So Josef goes to Paderborn where he trains on a farm for life as an agricultural worker in Palestine. When sent to Berlin for a seminar on Palestine, he meets the famous Rabbi Leo Baeck, spiritual leader of German Reform Jewry, who was to survive the War in the Theresienstadt Ghetto. Katz listens to Dr. Baeck exhorting the young people "to observe the ancient Jewish tradition of study in order to understand the spiritual heritage of our ancestors" in these times "when the house we live in threatens to collapse" (p. 10). Shortly thereafter, Josef again is called back to his mother who has received her evacuation order. Katz dutifully returns to Lübeck where he voluntarily joins the transport deporting the Jews to points east.

The liberation of the concentration and labor camp Stutthof by the Red Army frees Katz, who, like hundreds of other survivors, suffers from typhus. After his health has been restored, Katz is ready to move on. But irresistibly he is drawn back to Lübeck. "The same old streets, the same old streetcars," he remembers the ghetto song. But he knows now that he no longer wants these streets. "People take little notice of the repatriates," he writes, himself one of a handful of survivors of the once flourishing Lübeck Jewish community. "Only the butcher with whom we used to do business for many years gives me an extra quarter-pound of sausage when he recognizes me." The final touch of irony is provided by the police clerk who returns the keys to Katz' home, "the same clerk who took my keys from me so long ago. 'But Mr. Katz,' he says, 'where have you been all this time? You never notified us of your departure' '' (pp. 268–269).

The triumph of the spirit of man over evil and degradation, recorded by survivors like Viktor Frankl and Eugene Heimler, among others, is the very theme and content of Josef Bor's unique eyewitness story *The Terezin Requiem.* A Czech writer and the sole survivor of a large Jewish family from Prague, Bor was imprisoned together with his entire family in the Theresienstadt (Terezin) Ghetto in Czechoslovakia in 1942.

At first, Theresienstadt was used by the Nazis as a "model ghetto" for propaganda purposes. Later it became the great assembly camp for Birkenau-Auschwitz and other death camps further east. However, many Jews died in Theresienstadt, among them a daughter of Theodor Herzl. But for a time Jews in Theresienstadt were allowed to conduct their own cultural activities, to organize concerts and other artistic events. Concerts and operatic performances were permitted to go on even when conditions deteriorated in the camp. They continued until hunger, disease and the death transports decimated the ranks of the performers and audience alike. Finally, in 1944, no musicians were left and music came to an end in Theresienstadt.

In this autobiographical fragment, Bor pays tribute to the tenacious spirit of an individual and a people. Narrating his story in a subdued voice and with great simplicity, Bor describes the struggle of a young and promising conductor, Rafael Schachter, and the nameless five hundred musicians making up the chorus, soloists and orchestra—all ghetto prisoners—who participated in the grim eighteen months of rehearsals for a performance of Verdi's *Requiem*. Only a few of the original group were among the "finalists" who performed the Requiem at what turned into a command performance for Eichmann, a visitor in Theresienstadt at the time, and the SS commandant of the camp.

There is no suspense in Bor's story. The end is obvious from the very beginning. Every day the conductor loses another performer to another death transport, despite a promise by the camp administration that the musicians would be allowed to stay together. Finally, this promise is grimly kept: after the performance, they are all shipped off together.

Why Verdi's *Requiem*? Busily adding the finishing touches to plans for the "Final Solution," the destruction of European Jewry, Eichmann was amused by the notion of Jews singing a Christian mass for their own imminent death. But the Jewish musicians rose above the warped Nazi sense of humor. In a state of exaltation the performers triumphed over hunger, exhaustion, provocation and terror, finding release and freedom in the transcendent power of music. Marshalling all the strength left in their starved bodies and tormented souls, they sang to their murderers in the audience: *"Libera me, Domine, de morte aeterna . . .* (Free me, O Lord, from eternal death)." The words are part of a Christian prayer set to music by a Christian composer; yet, they expressed the emotions of the Jews in Theresienstadt, most of them Jews from Western Europe who had made significant contributions to that culture. The performance of the Requiem in the very teeth of death was an act of spiritual resistance as moving and impressive as any act of overt resistance in the annals of the Holocaust. (On music in Theresienstadt, see Chapter Twelve.)

After a study of memoirs written by former inmates of concentration camps, the autobiography of Rudolf Hoess, *Commandant of Auschwitz*, makes extraordinary reading. Unblinkingly, Hoess admits that he "personally arranged on orders received from Himmler in May 1941 the gassing of two million persons between June–July 1941 and the end of 1943, during which time I was Commandant of Auschwitz'' (p. 17).

In March 1946 this murderer of millions was seized by the British near Flensburg, close to the Danish border. He was handed over to the Poles who tried and condemned him to death by hanging. While in prison in Cracow awaiting his execution, Hoess was asked to record his memoirs. He gladly complied, taking much care to give a full account and showing an amazing memory for detail.

Hoess was a good, obedient German, fulfilling as faithfully as he could the orders he had received from his superiors—orders he never presumed to question. He had been brought up in an affectionate religious family—his father was a devout Catholic—and Hoess had high praise for the moral values which his home life had inculcated in him. He loved his parents and was particularly fond of horses and dogs. At first he dreamt of becoming a missionary in Africa to redeem the heathens, but after World War I broke out, as a boy of fifteen, he managed to join the army in 1916. Curiously enough, he was wounded in Palestine and sent to a hospital in a German settlement near Jerusalem.

After the War, Hoess joined an extreme rightist group and was imprisoned for participation in a political murder in 1924. On the basis of his prison experience he viewed himself as a specialist in penal reform, believing that he had developed a deep insight into the psychology of condemned men. He was a model prisoner, obedient and neat. Released in 1928, his ambition was to become a farmer. The return to the soil seemed to him the essence of the moral life. This, however, did not prevent him from joining the Nazi party in 1932, a year before Hitler came into power. In view of his record and experiences, his progress was assured. Beginning modestly as a block leader at Dachau in 1934, he was posted to the Sachsenhausen camp in 1938, rising to the post of Commandant of Auschwitz in 1941. In the same year he was informed by Himmler of Hitler's order of the ''Final Solution of the Jewish Question.'' In his introduction to the Hoess autobiography, Lord Russell of Liverpool makes the interesting point that the Nazis, Hoess among them, were experts in the use of euphemisms. ''When it came to killing they never called a spade a spade. Special treatment, extermination, liquidation, elimination, resettlement, and final solution were all synonyms for murder and Hoess has added another gem to the collection, 'the removal of racial-biological foreign bodies' '' (p. 24).

In Hoess's autobiography one finds a complete authoritative account of the workings of the death camp as it appeared to the executioner. It is a remarkable record not only for what Hoess has described—his account has been carefully checked for accuracy—but also for the matter-of-fact manner in which Hoess has written it. Hoess describes the details of his job meticulously and with the pride of a good worker. His book consists not only of his autobiography but also of appendices containing documents with Hoess's extensive answers to interrogations conducted by examining judges. Consequently, we have here a work of incomparable historic importance for an understanding of the death camps and the psychology of Nazi executioners.

Hoess describes the management of the death camp as impersonally as though he were explaining the working of a clothing factory. There is the problem of inefficient help. Guards may be kind or malicious. The examples he gives of the cruelty of what he describes as "sadistic" guards fully duplicate the accounts given by the prisoners themselves, but there is no indication that a guard is ever dismissed or punished for the suffering he inflicted on the inmates. Hoess merely generalizes that the wisest and most kindly regulations may be circumvented by subordinates. In this discussion he manages to ignore the central monstrosity of the camp's purpose. But, like any student of penal institutions, he analyzes the result:

> To put it crudely, guards and prisoners constitute two hostile and opposing worlds. . . . If he (the prisoner) wants to fit into the scheme of things, then he has to look after number one . . . he becomes cunning, furtive and deceitful, and hoodwinks his opponent in order to obtain alleviations and privileges; or he goes over to the enemy and becomes a trusty, a Capo, a block senior, and so on, and manages to make his own life bearable at the expense of his fellow prisoners; or he stakes everything on one throw and breaks out; or he abandons hope, goes to pieces, and ends up by committing suicide (pp. 80–81).

Hoess is a great believer in the salutary effect of work as discipline and occupation for the prisoner. It is in this spirit that Hoess interprets the grim slogan *Arbeit macht frei* (Work Brings Freedom) which he had placed above the main gate of the Auschwitz camp. Wholly devoted to his task, the Commandant laments the difficulties of assembling an efficient staff and getting proper materials for building various structures.

At the same time, he is interested in the psychology of the prisoners, the brutality of the Capos, and the "crass egotism" evident in prison. "One would have thought that a common fate and miseries shared" would have led to comradeship, but such regrettably was not the case, Hoess moralizes. He also discusses how "the communal camp life" at Auschwitz affected various categories of prisoners.

The Germans, chiefly common criminals, had occupied almost all high camp positions, which enabled them to get decent portions of food, and fleece and torture the lesser breeds. The Poles, if they had the courage to try to escape—according to Hoess, the opportunities for escape were "innumerable"—could count on help from the local civilian population, once they got beyond the ring of sentry posts, but, of course, if they were caught, then there

would be reprisals and "the liquidation of ten or more fellow-sufferers."
Jehovah's Witnesses were a particularly valiant lot—Hoess obviously admires
them—ready to die fanatically and bravely for their ideals. The Russians were
"like animals who sought only food" and practiced cannibalism (pp. 135–
136). Gypsies, who were to be exterminated like the Jews, were unreliable
but a cheery lot and among Hoess's "best-loved prisoners." This did not prevent him from sending them to the gas chambers according to an order "which
until mid-1944 was known only to myself and the doctors at Auschwitz" (pp.
137–141).

Finally, Hoess discusses the effect of imprisonment on the Jews "who from
1942 on composed the greater part of the inmates of Auschwitz" (p. 142).
When the Reischsführer SS (Himmler) modified his original extermination
order of 1941, according to which all Jews were to be destroyed immediately,
and ordered instead that those capable of work were to be employed in the
armament industry established within the camp, "Auschwitz became a Jewish
camp" (p. 146). So Hoess had ample opportunity for his research into the
psychology of his chief victims.

He assures us that he never personally hated Jews, though he looked upon
them as "the enemies of our people" (p. 146). Probably quite accurately,
Hoess explains the high mortality among Jews as due not to the severities of
"camp life" but to their "hopelessness." They knew they were condemned
to death and consequently had no will to live. He adds that this was particularly true of Jewish women who deteriorated far more rapidly than the men,
"although from my observations they had in general far greater toughness and
powers of endurance than the men, both physically and mentally" (p. 147).

Hoess particularly comments on the brutality of female Capos, chiefly
non-Jewish criminals and prostitutes who exceeded the men in depravity.
"The Reichsführer SS regarded them as particularly well-suited to act as
Capos over the Jewish women, when he visited Auschwitz in 1942." Hoess
expresses outrage at their bestial behavior. He was shocked at how they
treated the French Jewesses, "tearing them to pieces, killing them with axes,
and throttling them—it was simply gruesome" (p. 149).

Hoess also had trouble with the *Hundestaffel*—the dog squad. Specially
trained dog handlers were to use the animals to keep prisoners from escaping,
but they often wasted their talents to have "some fun." When they were
bored, they set the dogs on the prisoners. This they could always explain by
maintaining that the dogs had been provoked by the suspicious behavior of the
victim. But sometimes the dog handlers were guilty of a grave offense: "they
had badly ill-treated or neglected their dogs" (pp. 156–157).

Hoess regarded his job as an important contribution to Germany's war
effort. When physical conditions in the camp worsened, he writes:

> I had to become harder, colder, and even more merciless in my attitude
> toward the needs of the prisoners. I saw it all very clearly, often far too

clearly, but I knew that I must not let it get me down. I dared not let my feelings get the better of me. Everything had to be sacrificed to one end, the winning of the war. This was how I looked on my work at that time. I could not be at the front, so I must do everything at home to support those who were fighting'' (p. 159).

In view of his passion for efficiency and order, Hoess naturally was relieved at the introduction of Cyclon B, the gas used in mass extermination. ''The order had been given, and I had to carry it out. I must even admit that this gassing set my mind at rest, for the mass extermination of the Jews was to start soon and at that time neither Eichmann nor I was certain how these mass killings were to be carried out'' (p. 163). Hoess had ''shuddered'' at the prospect of carrying out mass exterminations of thousands by shooting. Now the gas chamber provided a neat efficient procedure without ''blood baths.'' In fact, many members of the *Einsatzkommandos* who previously had to finish off the wounded, especially women and children, after mass shootings, had committed suicide or gone mad, according to Hoess. Now Auschwitz could fittingly play its part in becoming the ''greatest human extermination center of all time'' (p. 160).

Hoess never questioned the order for ''the Final Solution of the Jewish question.'' In fact, he states categorically that ''the reasons behind the extermination seemed to me right'' (p. 160). It was not up to him to doubt the wisdom of the *Fuhrer* who had so commanded. The notion that he might have disobeyed Hitler or Himmler seems to him outrageous. Many of the Germans involved in this ''service'' sometimes asked Hoess if the extermination of hundreds of thousands of women and children was necessary for the greater glory of Germany. Though he admits to an occasional inner queasiness on the subject, Hoess would reassure his wavering subordinates by telling them that this ''extermination of Jewry had to be, so that Germany and our posterity might be freed for ever from their relentless adversaries.'' At the same time, Hoess describes in detail scenes of such pathos that one is amazed to read them in his own account. He writes:

> I remember a woman who tried to throw her children out of the gas chamber, just as the door was closing. Weeping, she called out: ''At least let my precious children live.'' There were many such shattering scenes, which affected all who witnessed them. During the spring of 1942 hundreds of vigorous men and women walked all unsuspecting to their death in the gas chambers, under the blossom-laden fruit trees of the ''cottage'' orchard. This picture of death in the midst of life remains with me to this day (pp. 166–167).

In view of the controversy precipitated by Hannah Arendt's attempt to picture Eichmann as just a ''little man,'' a robot, it is interesting to note Hoess's comment on Eichmann's role. What were Eichmann's real convictions in regard to the "Final Solution"? Hoess leaves no room for misunder-standing the intensity of Eichmann's dedication: "He was completely obsessed with the idea of destroying every single Jew that he could lay his hands on. Without pity and in cold blood we must complete this extermination as rapidly as possible" (p. 172).

Hoess, like so many of his fellow Nazis, was a devoted family man. "When at night I stood out there beside the transports or by the gas chambers, or the fires," he writes, "I was often compelled to think of my wife and children, without, however, allowing myself to connect them closely with all that was happening" (p. 173).

Hoess's autobiography provides the fullest possible proof for every state-ment that the victims themselves have made. No list of atrocities described in anguish by the survivors deviates in ferocity from the factual account of the Commandant himself. Hoess was executed in April 1947.

After surveying the memoirs of survivors, the reader is impressed by the variety of explanations for the miracle of individual survival in the concentra-tion or death camps, and by the variety of judgments passed on the behavior of the inmates. Were the prisoners totally degraded by their efforts to scrounge a piece of bread or to devise a way of avoiding selection for extermination, even at the expense of another? Was luck the chief element which determined why one lived where so many perished? Was the determination to survive in order to bear witness the decisive factor? Or was there a social bond in misfortune which prompted individuals in extremity to help one another? The answers are conflicting. Is one to believe Hoess who saw only the worst in man, or Frankl who emphasized the best, or Primo Levi who attempted to balance the two extremes?

A serious attempt to prove "the capacity of men and women to live beneath the pressure of protracted crisis, to sustain terrible damage in mind and body and yet be there, sane, alive, still human," has been made by Terrence Des Pres, in *The Survivor: An Anatomy of Life in the Death Camps.* Like others who have studied the subject and have reached particular conclusions, Des Pres sees in survival an experience with a definite structure. However, he differs radically from many other commentators in his description of this structure as "neither random, nor regressive, nor amoral." Des Pres gives full weight to the bestiality and calculated degradation of the camp experience. He describes in horrifying detail the "excremental assault," motivated unmistak-ably not by random sadism but by a definite intent to reduce men and women to animal level. However, in the welter of abominations he describes, Des Pres discovers that despite all the factors that make for moral anarchy, despite the deliberate assault in the camps on man as a civilized being, nevertheless "order emerges, people turn to one another in 'neighborly help.'" While the testimony of survivors is full of instances of inmates savagely snatching a crust of bread from each other, there are as many examples of cooperation, of mutual aid, insofar as was possible, in the endurance of a common fate. Auschwitz Commandant Hoess saw only the first: the memoirs of survivors which Des Pres quotes (among them some discussed in this chapter) testify to the second. "Like the need to bear witness," which, he believes, might also be viewed as examples of rational thinking, "there was yet an instinctive depth to the emergence of social order through help and sharing" (p. 147).

Des Pres' thesis is the "depth and durability of man's social nature," which he illustrates by the fact that, though conditions in the concentration camps were designed to develop antagonism against each other among the prisoners, the inmates nevertheless persisted in "social acts." They sought to shield the sick so that these should not be immediately sent to the gas chamber; they tried to help those falling behind on a forced march, or on a labor detail, despite their own failing strength.

Des Pres makes still another point which is worth noting. He comments on the general bias on the part of society against "mere survival," as though to survive, to remain alive, had no moral value, and as though existence had to be justified by a higher purpose, or some ideological goal. Yet all human beings think primarily in terms of survival, though most are not obliged to endure conditions in which the will to survive is so nakedly tested. In this respect Des Pres takes issue with Bruno Bettelheim, who praises the readiness to die so as "to achieve autonomy."

Depending on one's character, empathy and experience, an argument can be made for the most negative as well as the most positive assessments of human behavior in extremity. Mass murderer Hoess piously moralized about the egoism of his victims. But the records of the martyrdom to which a whole people was subjected leave the reader with wonderment at the heroic endurance, at the social responsibility of the victims in their repeated desire to "bear witness," and at the persistence of the social bond which kept men human even in the death camp and the gas chamber.

BIBLIOGRAPHY

Diaries

BERG, MARY. *Warsaw Ghetto*. ed. S. L. Shneiderman (New York: Fischer, 1945).

FLINKER, MOSES. *Young Moshe's Diary*. transl. Shaul Esh (Israel: Yad Vashem, 1965).

FRANK, ANNE. *Anne Frank: The Diary of a Young Girl,* transl. B. M. Mooyaart (New York: Doubleday, 1952) (available in paperback).

KAPLAN, CHAIM. *Scroll of Agony.* transl. A. I. Katsh (New York: Macmillan, 1965) (paperback: Collier, 1973).

RINGELBLUM, EMMANUEL. *Notes From the Warsaw Ghetto,* transl. Jacob Sloan (New York: McGraw Hill, 1958) (paperback: Schocken, 1974).

VON KARDOFF, URSULA. *Diary of a Nightmare* (New York: John Day, 1966).

Memoirs

ARENDT, HANNAH. *Eichmann in Jerusalem: A Report on the Banality of Evil* (New York: Viking, 1965). (Available in Viking-Compass paperback).

BENJAMIN, WALTER. *Illuminations,* ed. H. Arendt, trans. Harry Zohn (New York: Harcourt, Brace and World, 1968).

BETTELHEIM, BRUNO. *The Informed Heart* (Glencoe, Ill.: Free Press, 1960). (Available in Avon Paperback).

BOR, JOSEF. *The Terezin Requiem,* trans. Edith Pargeter (New York: Alfred A. Knopf, 1963). (Available in paperback).

DES PRES, TERRENCE. *The Survivor: An Anatomy of Life in the Death Camps* (New York: Oxford University Press, 1976) (Available in paperback).

DONAT, ALEXANDER. *The Holocaust Kingdom* (New York: Holt, Rinehart and Winston, 1965). (Available in Schocken paperback).

FRANKL, VIKTOR E. *Man's Search for Meaning,* trans. Ilse Lasch (New York: Pocket Books paperback, 1963) (Available in other editions).

GOLDSTEIN, CHARLES. *The Bunker* (New York: Atheneum paperback, 1973).

GRAY, MARTIN. *For Those I Loved,* with Max Gallo, trans. Anthony White (Boston: Little, Brown, 1972).

HEIMLER, EUGENE. *Night of the Mist* (New York: Vanguard, 1960).

HOESS, RUDOLF. *Commandant of Auschwitz: The Autobiography of Rudolf Hoess,* trans. Constantine FitzGibbon (New York: The World Publishing Co., 1960).

KATZ, JOSEF. *One Who Came Back: The Diary of a Jewish Survivor,* trans. Hilda Reach (New York: Herzl Press and Bergen-Belsen Memorial Press, 1973).

KLEIN, GERDA. *All But My Life* (New York: Hill and Wang paperback, 1957).

KUZNETSOV, A. ANATOLI. *Babi Yar,* trans. David Floyd (New York: Pocket Books paperback, 1971).

ROSEN, DONIA. *The Forest My Friend,* trans. Mordecai S. Chertoff (New York: Bergen-Belsen Memorial Press, 1971).

ROUSSET, DAVID. *The Other Kingdom,* trans. Ramon Guthrie (New York: Reynal and Hitchcock, 1947).

SHAPELL, NATHAN. *Witness to the Truth* (New York: David McKay, 1974).

WELLS, LEON W. *The Janowska Road* (New York: Macmillan, 1963) (Available in Schocken paperback as *Death Brigade*).

Holocaust Literature II:

Novels and Short Stories

Josephine Knopp and Arnost Lustig

Somewhere in the Warsaw Ghetto a child wrote in a copybook: "I am hungry, I am cold; when I grow up I want to be a German; then, I shall no longer be hungry, and no longer be cold." As one who would discuss critically what has come to be called "Holocaust Literature," I find myself hard-pressed to deny to this outpouring of a young victim of the Holocaust the serious attention usually reserved for imaginative literature. Indeed, though these words fall outside the traditional limits of the literary preserve, they speak of nothing less than what man has become in our time and they allow us to glimpse what he is yet capable of becoming. In the aftermath of Auschwitz, therefore, literary criticism is called upon to broaden its purview in response to what has been called the "end of one era of consciousness and the beginning of another." The youthful diarist appears artless, ingenuous; clearly he intends his words to be understood in a literal sense—despite the inadequacy of the imagination to cope with the idea that they do, in fact, arise from a literal truth—yet within the context of their writing the words assume a meaning transcending that intention, taking on the metaphor for the very historical event which they describe. In this sense he is poet as well as chronicler, becoming—however unintentionally—spokesman for the victims through his act of bearing witness.

This brief example suggests one of the several difficult problems besetting the critic who turns his attention to Holocaust literature: the intermingling of genres, the frequent breakdown of the usual categories distinguishing diary from novel, literal account from imaginative fiction, and—more important— the impossibility of identifying those works which would best reward close scrutiny without applying a number of criteria extraneous to the traditional frame of reference of literary criticism. Furthermore, the unprecedented circumstances out of which this "literature of survival" has emerged add a special poignancy to the problem, as they do to all considerations related to the literature of the Holocaust.

Many victims of the Holocaust have published accounts of their experience. Impelled largely by the need to get the story to light, they feared that the tale might otherwise be lost with the slaughtered. Although all of these accounts are historically important, many are of only marginal literary interest (except insofar as they provide the underpinnings of the genre by offering a basis for comparison with Holocaust writings of real depth and power). Despite this, the story of victimization and occasional survival so deeply moves us that the absence of literary refinement seems irrelevant. That literary criticism does indeed play an important role becomes clear upon confrontation with those Holocaust works of surpassing literary merit. In fact, genuine literary skill, even when applied to the Holocaust, has a special power to convey these enormities.

The problem of distinguishing the writings of literary value among the many that have emerged from the Holocaust is beyond the scope of the present discussion. (The other side of this coin is the fact that a large number of works of undeniable literary merit must be omitted from the discussion, although many of these will be cited.) In any event, in the realm of Holocaust literature the issue of literary quality *per se,* usually regarded as the *sine qua non* of criticism, yields to the deeper questions implicit in T. W. Adorno's succinct proposition: "no poetry after Auschwitz... , " the questions whether the Holocaust is amenable to meaningful literary treatment at all and whether the attempt at such treatment should be made. The credibility of an affirmative response to the first of these questions, at least, continues to grow with the rapidly expanding canon of effective literary works dealing with the Holocaust and its aftermath, in a variety of languages, many of them now available in English. That Adorno probably did not intend his dictum to be taken too literally can be read from his own statement that the magnitude of the horror does indeed demand a voice, but a voice that will not betray it by a descent to cynicism. Requiring that the metaphor serve as a memorial to the event, at the same time he cannot avoid the feeling that "language itself had been damaged, possibly beyond creative repair, by the politics of terror and mass-murder." Adorno's position on this issue involves a dilemma reflected as well in the words of Elie Wiesel—perhaps the most important of the literary figures to emerge from the Holocaust—who has repeatedly acknowledged the dual and contradictory demands imposed by the Holocaust: response and silence.

Though Adorno and Wiesel describe essentially the same paradox, the basis for the contradiction differs markedly in the two men. As Lawrence Langer describes so well, Adorno sees "something disagreeable, almost dishonorable, in the conversion of the suffering of the victims into works of art, which are then ... thrown as fodder to the world ... that murdered them. ... Adorno appeals here not to latent sadistic impulses, but to the pleasures inherent in artistic response.'' Langer goes on to isolate a problem belonging uniquely to the art created in response to the Holocaust and one that surely counts among the deepest problems arising in the entire critical sphere: ''The prospect of art denying what it seeks to affirm (the hideous chaos of dehumanization during the Holocaust) raises a spectre of paradox for the critic, the reader, and the artist himself, that is not easily circumvented.'' Thus for Adorno, the tension between silence and literary response arises primarily from aesthetic considerations, grounded in questions concerning the very nature and purpose of art.

For Wiesel, by contrast, the contradiction has its roots in theological considerations, touching upon the nature of God and man, and especially upon the historical relationship between God and Israel. As one imbued from childhood with biblical and talmudic lore, the product of an Orthodox Jewish background, Wiesel views the Holocaust from within the framework of Jewish history and tradition, linking it with Sinai and Masada, his works at the same time illuminating its uniqueness within that framework. (Wiesel, indeed, would be the last to suggest anything that denies the historical uniqueness of the Holocaust.) For the theologically serious Jew, Sinai remains as clouded in mystery as God himself, a subject for study and discussion, but one destined ultimately to remain impervious to rational scrutiny. A serious Jew—and one with mystical leanings at that—Wiesel finds himself similarly overwhelmed by the impossibility of explaining the Holocaust and especially God's role in the event. ''Perhaps some day,'' he has said, ''someone will explain how, on the level of man, Auschwitz was possible; but on the level of God, it will forever remain the most disturbing of mysteries.'' If the problem of theodicy engendered by the Holocaust is insoluble, perhaps solutions should not be attempted at all; perhaps response is futile and the stance of the survivor (and with him the rest of us) should be a lapse into silence.

However, for one preoccupied with the power and necessity of silence in the face of the Holocaust, Wiesel has written remarkably often of the event, perhaps producing the largest canon on the subject by any single writer. And, of course, he is far from alone in his literary response. The nature of man mandates the continuing quest for an unattainable knowledge of the events of Sinai and the Holocaust, and none finds the mandate more imperative than does the creative artist, who must pursue the apprehension of ''truth,'' wherever that may lead. The act of writing is, furthermore, in itself a ''counterforce to nihilism,'' an attack upon barbarism, and an attempt to restore an articulate life, after Auschwitz. Hence the works of Holocaust literature which—in literary analogy to ''Russell's paradox''—themselves question the possibility of creating a meaningful Holocaust literature and the wisdom of making the attempt.

Even if one admits to the hopelessness of achieving real comprehension and one settles for the lesser goal of description, a serious problem remains inherent in the unprecedented nature of the events described. Langer has observed that "all serious art undoubtedly aspires toward the revelation of a new sense of reality," but Holocaust literature has "the curious advantage of having such a 'new' reality already available, pressing with equal force on the conscious and . . . preconscious life of the artist, and seeking only a way of being convincingly presented to an audience of contemporary readers." The problem then for the writer who adopts the Holocaust as a domain for literary scrutiny is in a sense the reverse of the usual problem confronting the would-be creator of imaginative literature, who strives to imbue his work—whether or not the subject is based upon actual events—with sufficient fantasy to warrant that appellation. Indeed, the Holocaust writer—virtually alone among writers—faces the difficulty of making a factual subject believable, of informing the actuality he describes with an aura of reality acceptable as such to his readers. He must somehow break through the barrier of nonacceptance engendered by an absence of that shared experience and sensibility upon which other writers may rely.

Among the group of writers who have successfully accomplished this, Wiesel, Andre Schwarz-Bart, Jerzy Kosinski, and Jakov Lind are generally acknowledged as outstanding examples. Schwarz-Bart, like Wiesel, reaches for the indispensable core of experience shared with his audience by placing the Holocaust within a (relatively familiar) super-structure of Jewish history and tradition. Kosinski and Lind, on the other hand, deal with the events of the Holocaust in isolation, presenting their lunacy directly and unsupported by a surrounding ambience of familiarity, logic or sanity. Drawing the reader into their unfamiliar world, they force him to accept its inverted logic and to perceive events from within a wholly altered framework of reality. These four writers are drawn together, however, by their common bond of survivorship, all of them having been victims of the Holocaust in their childhood years. Indeed, most who have written of the event are its survivors, a fact not surprising in view of the difficulties, already noted, in creating literature based upon it at all. The writer not directly touched must surely experience the same difficulty—greatly magnified and intensified—in moving across the threshold of ordinary reality into the special and distorted reality of the Holocaust Universe that besets the reader of Holocaust literature. In writing about the poet Sylvia Plath, George Steiner has in fact gone well beyond the observation of this difficulty to challenge the very right of the nonsurvivor to create a work of art based upon the Holocaust, to take on what he calls the "death-rig of Auschwitz." "What extraterritorial right," Steiner asks, in reference to Sylvia Plath's poetic "overdraft," does one have "to draw on the reserves of animate horror in the ash and the children's shoes? . . . Do any of us have the license to locate our personal disasters, raw as they may be, in Auschwitz?" Despite the objection raised by Steiner—and reiterated by other critics—some writers without direct experience of the Holocaust have indeed attempted to assimilate the event into the fabric of their imaginative works; these include Sylvia Plath, of course, and the poet Anthony Hecht, as well as the American novelists John Hersey, Leon Uris, Gerald Green, Bernard Malamud, and (in *Mr. Sammler's Planet*) Saul Bellow.

Green's *Holocaust,* in essence an historical novel conceived and executed upon a large scale, views the evolution of the Nazi ''Final Solution'' within the context of World War II. Tracing the varied fates of the members of the Jewish Weiss family of Berlin, as well as the career of the SS officer Dorf, the work provides a broad external perspective upon the Holocaust—even if it does not offer deep or original insights into those events. In a general way, the novel is historically accurate, enough so to serve as a factual introduction to a difficult subject for a large and possibly skeptical audience.

Bellow's work affords a good example of the uses to which Holocaust material may be applied by writers who are ''outsiders,'' not themselves survivors. Limitations upon the function of this material in the fiction of such writers is suggested by a comparison of Bellow's Sammler with the creation of an ''insider,'' the protagonist of Wiesel's novel *The Accident.* Both are Jewish survivors of Hitler's Europe living in New York after the War, yet the two men differ markedly in spirit. For Wiesel's character, survival has become the central experience; among the living he feels himself a ''messenger of the dead,'' life itself being too great a burden to bear. In the case of Sammler—though the Holocaust has left its mark, though he speaks of himself as a survivor, not the man he was before the War—there is the sense of a life shaped primarily by other, more normal and benevolent forces. Despite the setting of *The Accident*—New York after the War—its protagonist continues to be obsessed by the enormities inflicted upon him in an earlier time and a different place, and the novel, like all of Wiesel's, emerges as a response to the Holocaust and to the far-reaching consequences it has had for those touched by this perverted new reality. By contrast, Bellow's survivor-as-protagonist immerses himself in the new (and essentially normal) life he has established in the New World; *Mr. Sammler's Planet* does not treat the consequences of survivorship for the reestablishment of normalcy—as does *The Accident*—but deals rather with the reactions of a survivor to the new life he finds. Hence this work is, as Bellow intends it to be, an examination of contemporary Jewish-American life and morality through the eyes of one who knows it well, yet has the objectivity born of an earlier life first molded by a different culture and milieu and then destroyed, together with the world that nurtured it.

The American writers Norma Rosen and Susan Fromberg Schaeffer are two outsiders who—in the face of George Steiner's dictum and despite the difficulties we have already indicated—have produced novels with the specific and sole intention of responding to the Holocaust. Rosen's *Touching Evil* and Schaeffer's *Anya* are highly disparate works, differing radically in technique and substance, but firmly linked by this common intention. *Anya,* set for the most part in the Holocaust itself, attempts to re-create the unprecedented events and the bizarre atmosphere surrounding them, while Rosen's novel takes place in present-day New York and deals with the implications of the Holocaust for succeeding generations. In a *Midstream* article Rosen herself raises serious artistic questions about such an undertaking: "But how was the Holocaust to be written about? How could the virtues of fiction—indirection, irony, ambivalence—be used to make art out of this unspeakable occurrence?" Beyond raising these literary problems she expresses attendant doubts—which are far from trivial—of a philosophical/theological nature: "To make bad art would be unforgivable. Even to make good art would be in another way unforgivable. Because that would be transcendence. And it was not the right time for transcendence—it was far too soon, and maybe it would never be time." With Rosen's suggestion that "the best response to the Holocaust might be silence, or an endless scream—neither one makes art," we are back upon the familiar ground of the Adorno-Wiesel dilemma, especially in view of the prior existence of her own *Touching Evil.* Though she expresses the dilemma even more explicitly with the claim that "for the American Jewish writer, the Holocaust as subject was a double bind, as nearly impossible to write about as to avoid writing about," the fact remains that few American writers—Jewish or not—have approached the Holocaust in their fiction in as serious a way as have Schaeffer and Rosen.

Norma Rosen has expressed the view—one certainly worthy of serious discussion—that "the Holocaust is the central occurrence of the twentieth century, that it cannot therefore be more so for Jews and Jewish writers." Indeed, *Touching Evil* is constructed upon this concept, with the protagonists Jean and Hattie, non-Jewish Americans living in New York. The two women touch the evil of the Holocaust, become vicariously caught up in the death camp experience, through watching the Eichmann trial on television, which soon becomes a daily ritual, faithfully observed. Commenting upon her own work, Rosen reveals that to her "it seemed right . . . that the woman in my novel [Jean] should be determined that nothing in her life would, after she learned of the existence of the death camps, be as before." The other woman, Hattie, is pregnant and, once again in Rosen's words, "obsessed by the fear of what is passed on in the cycles of human generations." That these women are not Jewish plays a significant role in the author's design of the novel and her hopes for its impact upon the reader: "Clearly, a Jew might respond this way to the Eichmann trial. Non-Jews *ought* to respond in the same way and in my book at least, they would."

Rosen's reach for universality extends to the novel's New York setting, which, with the fearful residents locked into their apartments, serves as a metaphor for the fear-ridden ghettos of Eastern Europe. The metaphor is strengthened by the continuing demolition of Jean's neighborhood in the path of urban renewal, the white X's on the windows of those vacant buildings already marked for the inevitable destruction calling forth some of the horror of the Nazi destruction of the ghettos and their inhabitants. Toward the end of the novel Hattie, Jean's younger counterpart, gives birth to a child, complaining later of the careless treatment—she perceives it as brutal—which she and the other women in the maternity ward experienced. Hattie interprets her hospital experiences within the framework of her newly found awareness of the Nazi evil, becoming "in her hallucination, [symbolic of] the women who gave birth in the camps" and experiencing "the 'taking in' of the knowledge of the Holocaust."

For the author, some of the critical responses to *Touching Evil* were "painful because the novel was praised for what was not intended—for a depiction merely of the evil of everyday life." But to a large extent this disjunction between creative intention and critical interpretation results inevitably from the author's use of everyday evil as a metaphor for the greater evil of the Holocaust. With her newborn daughter in her arms, Hattie can barely remember the suffering of the labor room, and unlike the women who really did give birth in the camps, Hattie remains secure in the knowledge that she can keep the baby, that it will not be killed or its skin used for a lamp shade. Seeking to "take in" the knowledge of the Holocaust, both Jean and Hattie are overwhelmed—indeed Jean makes a conscious effort to be overwhelmed—by events which they have not themselves experienced (and here the fact that they are not Jewish seems to create even greater distance from the experience of survival); while many of the actual victims struggled every day for years to avoid being overwhelmed by what they did experience. Rosen's observation that "nothing about the Holocaust was metaphorical" yields some insight into the complexity of the task she has undertaken in her novel, as does the fact that no other writer has seriously followed her lead in this. If the success of her serious and important attempt to confront directly the implications of the Holocaust within the framework of the American experience is less than complete, it may well reflect a foreclosure of total success inherent in the very nature of the undertaking. And if the Holocaust indeed reveals "an evil so absolute that it overpowers all the old ideas of evil and good," the literary device for successfully representing it by some other (hence lesser) evil may simply not exist.

In contradistinction to Norma Rosen, who takes a literary gamble in serving the need for response to the Holocaust by building *Touching Evil* upon her concept of "witness-through-the-imagination," Susan Schaeffer reacts to this need by offering in *Anya* a written oral history, the true story of a real survivor based upon tape-recorded interviews between author and subject. Through this device and by presenting the story as a first person narration through Anya herself, Schaeffer overcomes the difficulties inherent in her lack of firsthand knowledge of the Nazi terror, thereby creating an effective novel of the

Holocaust. Schaeffer ultimately succeeds in identifying with the survivor virtually to the point of obliterating the distinction between author and narrator, of fusing outsider and survivor into a single consciousness.

The work begins as a *Bildungsroman,* chronicling the life and fortunes of Anya, a member of a wealthy and assimilated Jewish family in Vilna who enjoys a happy, comfortable childhood, later enrolling as a medical student at the University after overcoming the handicap of her Jewish background by virtue of outstanding academic achievement. Though the Holocaust sweeps up Anya, together with her entire family, in the German invasion of Poland, she senses from the outset her destiny to survive. Long after the War's end she reflects upon her fate, revealing an ambivalent obsession with survival that pervades much of Holocaust writing: "I believe there was something that wanted to keep me alive. . . . I was chosen to live or doomed to live, depending upon my mood for the day."

What strikes one most is the author's almost offhand manner: the fact, made clear by Anya's matter-of-fact description, that the participants—Jew and Gentile, victim and persecutor—do not find remarkable the Jew's role as the object of violence, that indeed violent anti-Judaism is accepted as normative behavior. Schaeffer never deviates from her understated style nor does she lapse into moral considerations upon the events as they occur. Perhaps for this reason Anya long avoids the guilt associated with survival in the midst of mass death, and only in the brief epilogue, describing her life in New York since the time of her arrival after the War, does that guilt become an important component of her personality. Instead of her earlier optimism and resourcefulness in the face of mortal danger, Anya reveals an inability to force the years of suffering from her consciousness. "I was a person who loved, who trusted, who never accepted defeat," she tells us. "And now I am not whole. There are chunks of flesh the war bit from me; my clothes cover them." Thus Anya's assumption that with liberation from the Germans there can be nothing further to fear proves no less a delusion that Hattie's hallucinatory terror. For she has failed to reckon with memory, to take into account the future effects of suffering so profound "that it teaches you you can never forget; you can only repeat and repeat." Jean and Hattie undeniably confront evil, but evil that can be put aside to allow room for normal life and thoughts of the future, while for Anya the future, preempted by the horrors of her past, has lost both hope and meaning.

The case of the novelists I. B. Singer and I. J. Singer does not fit neatly into a dichotomy between Holocaust "insiders" and "outsiders" since the two brothers were nurtured upon the rich Eastern European Yiddish culture destroyed by the Nazis, but they left it behind for the safety of America before the destruction began. Thus, while they cannot speak with firsthand authority about the events of the Holocaust itself, their work does offer a perspective informed by intimate knowledge, in its manifold complexity, of the world destroyed.

An instructive example is I. J. Singer's novel *The Family Carnovsky*, which traces the historic diaspora experience through several generations of a single family, illuminating the Jewish sensibility within the framework of the specific historicity provided by the Holocaust. In this work the Jew, as immigrant and as Holocaust survivor, is a victim of exile—ironically, both from a life-granting environment and from imminent death and destruction. With the history of the Carnovsky family as a vehicle, Singer exposes a good deal of the recent (and, indeed, not-so-recent) history of the Jewish people as a whole, presenting the eventual genocide as a consequence, in part, of historical Christian anti-Semitism and Jewish self-hate.

These two forces impinge prominently upon the life of David Carnovsky, a Polish *shtetl* Jew who settles in Germany, "the source of all goodness, knowledge, and light," where he seeks a life of enlightenment and movement in the larger society. Indeed, in Berlin David turns from the ways of the Polish Hasidim he disdains and establishes himself among the "distinguished descendants of long-settled German Jewry"—followers of Moses Mendelssohn—avoiding the "raggedy Eastern Jews" for which his wife Leah still yearns. In David, Singer suggests an essential link between the direction taken by the German-Jewish community in its efforts to merge into the surrounding German culture and the catastrophe that was to follow. This is not to suggest that the author is blind to the shortcomings of life in the *shtetl*: the superstition, the restraining customs and rituals, the inhibiting aversion to new ideas. Nevertheless, he condemns—at least by implication—the loss of Jewish traditions, the break with the Jewish past, as a factor in the Holocaust to come.

In Berlin David Carnovsky becomes a leading spokesman of "enlightened" Jewry, whose rejection of the Eastern European Jews results not only from the attractions of the larger society, but from a kind of anti-Semitic self-rejection as well. This denial of origins shapes David's daily existence, from his insistence that Leah give up the Yiddish language in favor of German to the ambivalence he exhibits in the naming of his son. The child, in fact, is given the two names Moses and Georg, the former the name "by which the boy would be called to the Torah when he grew older," and the latter—a German corruption of Gershon, the name of David's father—the "name with which he could go among people and use in business." David would teach his son to be a "Jew among Jews and a German among Germans," a Jew in the privacy of his own home, but a German in public. Singer exposes the bankruptcy of such a concept, observing—through the evolution of plot and character—that the effect is precisely the opposite, that in fact David and his fellow adherents of the Haskalah movement are looked upon as Jews among the Germans and as Germans among traditional Jews.

The second section of the novel introduces Solomon Burak, a Jewish storekeeper living in Berlin, a man who insists upon maintaining his ethnic identity with the Eastern European *shtetl* from which he emerged. In contrast to David Carnovsky and the Jews of his circle, Burak refuses to submerge his Jewishness or to conceal his origins. He does not change his name or drop his native Yiddish. To many of his fellow Jews in Berlin, Burak represents all that they seek to leave behind, an example of "typical Jewish impudence calculated to antagonize the gentiles. . . . They were uneasy because of people like him, who with their names, conduct and business tactics caused the gentiles to lump them, the long settled and German assimilated Jews, in the same category." It is interesting that this same denial of origins through rejection of Yiddish culture is described—in a post-Holocaust setting, however—by Philip Roth in "Eli, the Fanatic," a story in which a group of young Holocaust survivors cause embarrassment to the prosperous Jews of a suburban community in New York. In each instance members of the established Jewish community betray an unworthy cowardice, revealing themselves willing to abandon fellow Jews in need in order to preserve a fragile security built largely upon a separation from their own history.

This rejection of Jewish history explains the outrage of David Carnovsky's circle at Burak's success in buying his family out of the internment camps established by Germany to contain Polish immigrants during the First World War. Carnovsky—rich, respected, and a former Pole himself—feels that he "can't afford to get involved" to aid those Jews recently arrived from Poland, despite his wish to do so. But David's response to his own helplessness in this situation amounts to a profound reappraisal of his earlier involvement with the Jewish Enlightenment. He comes to believe that "the Melnitz Rabbi had been right after all. The ways of the philosopher led only to evil. It began with the enlightenment . . . it ended with apostasy. As it had happened with Moses Mendelssohn's descendents, it was happening with his. If Georg would not himself convert, his children surely would."

David's change of heart finds further justification in the altered social climate of Berlin following the World War—ably described by Singer—in the lawless hands of youths roaming the streets "screaming for Jewish blood," promising "dire revenge against the traitors of the *Vaterland*." The Jews are denounced—in traditional and familiar terms—as Christ killers, conspirators, devils in the disguise of ordinary people. But if the elder Carnovsky has grown sensitive to the dangers of assimilation, his son Georg—its victim— has not. Georg suffers the torments of growing up within conflicting Jewish and German traditions, rejecting the one and denied full access to the other, and his marriage to a Gentile woman serves only to alienate him further from both worlds. In him the notion of the enlightened "universal man" has become a mockery, a cruel and humorless joke, for, viewing himself as a free thinker, Georg remains a Jew to the world at large, subject to the sporadic anti-Semitic outbursts of a Gentile world. Nevertheless, like the earlier generation of German Jews during World War I, he maintains confidence in his credentials as a true German, naively believing himself immune to the Nazi onslaught when Hitler comes to power.

The final section of *The Family Carnovsky* depicts the life of Jegor Carnovsky, the son of Georg and grandson of David. Jegor is not merely an anti-Semite, despising his Jewish father, but one eager to further the Nazi war upon his father's people. David, now returned to the practice of traditional Judaism, understands the attitudes of his grandson as a sharp rebuke to the assimilationist practices of his own generation of Jews in Germany, as the inexorable consequence of Enlightenment thought. Jegor, indeed, expresses the ultimate form of Jewish self-hatred, going far beyond the simple wish to conceal his Jewish origins, to the point of willingness to participate in the destruction of the people and the culture of his father. Through the escalating self-rejection of successive Carnovsky generations, Singer suggests a possible role of the German Jews in their own destruction. Yet, in the end, with Jegor's return to the house of his father—despite the boy's flirtation with Nazism—the author seems to imply that Jewish history cannot easily be discarded, that—particularly under the cloud of anti-Semitism—Jews will seek out and identify with their origins. The implication remains as well that "enlightened Jew" is a contradiction in terms, that the path of Moses Mendelssohn inevitably leads to apostasy and eventual destruction for the Jew.

This raises a question with far-reaching implications, one that we can touch upon only briefly here. Namely, to what extent have Jewish identity and Jewish communal cohesiveness been shaped historically by the anti-Semitic threats—explicit or implied—of the surrounding culture? Related questions suggested by the contrasting viewpoints of the German Jews and the Jews of Eastern Europe in *The Family Carnovsky* are those of whether the Jew must remain isolated from the larger community in order to preserve his Jewish identity (and, in the long run, his existence), and whether it is possible at all for the Jewish community to retain its distinctive character, while at the same time it functions as a part of the dominant society. The attempt to support such a dual role within Germany, Singer makes it clear, led only to divided loyalty and an ambivalent self-image for the individual Jew, and to disaster for German Jewry as a whole. Perhaps it is too much to claim that Singer's work is a plea for a return to traditional Judaism as response to the Holocaust, but something of Emil Fackenheim's "614th Commandment"—the demand that Jews retain their Jewish identities in order to deny Hitler a posthumous victory—is surely here, at least by implication.

That David Carnovsky returns eventually to the traditional Judaism that he knew in Poland is perhaps less striking than Jegor's return at the novel's end, since, as Georg's son, he was taught nothing of the Judaism and the Jewish traditions that his grandfather knew. Still, the sense of diaspora that David has deep within him has somehow been transmitted to Jegor, through Georg. Franz Kafka observed this same phenomenon in his own life, commenting that "Jewry is not merely a question of faith, it is above all a question of the practice of a way of life in a community conditioned by faith"; "and by exile," he might well have added. For exile historically has been the Jewish experience par excellence, an experience deeply affecting Singer's characters, who live "on the fringes" of society, even when they are prosperous members of the middle class.

Like *Anya, The Family Carnovsky* does not end with the escape of the protagonists from the Nazis, but depicts their lives in America, where the sense of exile persists. Now safe, they have nonetheless become—in the phrase of Karl Shapiro's preface to his *Poems of a Jew*—"man left over, after everything that can happen has happened."

Enemies: A Love Story by I. B. Singer also focuses upon the lives of these survivor-exiles in New York after the War. The life stories here are of Jews trapped in the Diaspora, cut off from a *shtetl* culture that has been destroyed, people irretrievably damaged, alive but not whole after the Holocaust. Both Singer brothers suggest the impossibility of transporting intact—from one world to another—the multifaceted European Jewish culture, which necessarily undergoes a profound change with the migration.

With Jurek Becker's *Jacob the Liar,* we approach those Holocaust works produced by the Holocaust survivors themselves. Becker, now a resident of East Berlin, was born in Poland in 1937, later forced into a ghetto, and finally transported from there to a Nazi death camp. Despite these early experiences and despite the somber subject matter of *Jacob the Liar,* Becker evokes in this work humor of a kind almost never found in the literature of survivors. The work suggests nothing of the religious searchings of Wiesel and Schwarz-Bart, little of Kosinski and Lind's reconstruction of the horrors they have experienced, and none of the Christian-Jewish encounter that we find in Wiesel's later work, especially in *The Oath.*

Becker makes no attempt to salvage the remains, to seek reasons, to explain. Instead, *Jacob the Liar* presents a microcosm of Jewish life in the ghetto, not so much "under" Nazi authority as "with" Nazi authority. It is as if we had before us a world inhabited by "Lilliputian" Jews watched over by Nazi "big people," not malevolent or evil, but simply in a position of power and responsibility. Though they are unequal in stature, the lives of the Jewish prisoners of the ghetto and their German overseers are intertwined, the existence of each dependent upon that of the other, in a symbiosis of victim and executioner that has been remarked upon in a number of Holocaust writings. Here the Germans do not view the Jews as vermin to be exterminated, but rather as one might look upon dwarfs in a circus—as human freaks. As freaks, the Jews pose the problem of how the Germans ought to treat them; yet the reader is not allowed to forget that Auschwitz is the certain end which all of the inhabitants of the ghetto face. Until the final transport by freight train, however, the ghetto remains alive and—for the most part—intact, and it is the nature and quality of this life upon which Becker focuses the reader's attention.

Jacob's story is a simple one. A resident of the Nazi-controlled ghetto, purely by chance he overhears a few brief remarks indicating that Russian troops are close by and advancing. Jacob shares the good news with Mischa, who is on the verge of suicide and desperately in need of encouragement. To prevent Mischa from taking his own life, Jacob adds credibility to his rumor with an innocent lie: "I know—I have a radio." The virtual impossibility for a Jew to have a radio in the ghetto somehow does not dampen Mischa's belief, nor that of the other Jews of the ghetto, among whom the news spreads rapidly. They believe in Jacob's radio because, like Mischa, they must believe in order to preserve sanity and the will to go on living. Indeed, the radio brings about a profound change in the ghetto, whose residents go to Jacob for daily reports of the outside world, and especially news of the progress of the Russian troops. Unable to disappoint his friends, Jacob forces himself each day to an "act of creation," finding a new way to tell the same story so that hope would not die. Forced to defend this behavior toward his fellow Jews, Jacob justifies it on the grounds that "I try to use my very last means to keep them from simply lying down and croaking, with words, you understand. . . . Because I have nothing else, you see!"

Under the circumstances, Jacob's life becomes dominated by two fears— that the Germans might learn of the radio and that the Jews would stop believing in its existence. These fears eventually weary Jacob to the point that he can no longer hear the lie in solitude, and in his state of fatigue he reveals the secret to Kowalski, an old friend. Kowalski, having invested his last bit of hope in the advancing Russian troops, promptly throws himself onto the electrified barbed wire which surrounds the ghetto. In response, Jacob's despair deepens, as he realizes the untenable position into which he has maneuvered himself. Kowalski's suicide brings home clearly the dangerous double bind with which he must now live: while it is risky to continue to promulgate the lie, it is catastrophic to reveal the truth.

The charade continues, and the radio becomes the focal point of the novel, an inanimate "protagonist" about which Becker develops a series of vignettes concerning the ghetto residents, whose lives center more and more upon the outside "news" they receive from Jacob. One of these stories is of special interest since it reveals the sense of humor which lies at the heart of the novel. Jacob assumes the responsibility of caring for Lena, a young girl whose parents were transported one night to Auschwitz. Living with Jacob, Lena becomes curious about the radio, since she has never yet seen one in her young life. She looks through Jacob's things, finding a lantern which she decides must be the precious radio itself. As she has heard that a radio "talks," she speaks to the lantern, hoping for a response, and the ingenious Jacob devises a way to have the lantern answer her. Of course, contrast with the surrounding tragedy serves to emphasize the hilarity of this scene.

Humor is not the only characteristic of Becker's writing that sets him apart from the majority of writers on the Holocaust. He has, in addition, an intimate and disarmingly simple approach to his characters that allows the reader almost to forget from time to time that the world described is one of insanity, degradation, and horror. For the imminent, all-pervasive death receives muted treatment by Becker, without rage or outcry, without metaphysical speculation or vows of revenge. His perspective on the German enemy is equally understated and unusual. No need for the reader to recoil, Becker seems to imply, for they too are human. Jews die quietly, with a suggestion of heroism, of human dignity preserved, in their silence, as in the case of Herschl Stamm, a pious Jew who reveals a heroic side to his character. Yet the author suggests some disapproval at the absence of widespread, organized resistance in the ghetto against the prevailing evil social order imposed by the Nazis. But, finally, the passive resistance of ordinary people like Jacob, with their will to go on in the face of terrors unknown to earlier generations, amounts to resistance against the Nazis just as meaningful as armed uprising, and perhaps more profound as a statement of the power of the human will.

Like Becker's novel and like *Anya,* Ka-Tzetnik's *House of Dolls* chronicles the daily struggle of young Polish Jews to survive the degradations imposed upon them by the Nazis. Forced from her home into a ghetto, the schoolgirl Daniella eventually finds herself in a German labor camp. Because she is young and attractive, she does not share the manual labor done by the majority of the inmates, but serves rather in the "Doll House," established to fulfill the sexual desires of the German soldiers. The girls of the Doll House must serve their German masters with enthusiasm, the slightest indication of less than full attention to their work resulting in a much dreaded "report." In contrast to Anya, Daniella does not survive the experience, preferring finally to die in a heroic gesture of defiance, infuriated to the point of madness by the death of her beloved Harry, while her friend and fellow inmate Fella remains alive at the end.

Clever and resourceful, a tough survivor reminiscent of Anya, Fella—the reader is certain—will live to carry out the mission entrusted to her by Daniella: the delivery of a notebook and locket to Daniella's brother in Niederwalden. Indeed, the mission itself lends new purpose to a life drained of all significance beyond the instinct for survival. However, Anya's example serves to warn against the inference that Fella has found somehow the alchemist's secret for transmuting enormity into joy, death into meaning. Fella's mission can help her move more easily through the remaining days of torment perhaps, but it cannot erase the scars of survival. As Harry points out, in the Holocaust Universe "everything is mixed up. Life and death in one brew. A hereafter that's not here, not after. Fraud and hoax.'' Much as the thought violates our usual notions, we are forced to entertain the possibility, at least, that for the Holocaust victims, survival is not preferable to death, an idea which finds literary implications in Alvin Rosenfeld's observation that ''within the context of Holocaust Literature the living often carry a knowledge of death more terrible in its intimacy than that ever recorded in the writings of the [dead] victims.'' These remarks shed some light upon *House of Dolls,* written by the survivor Ka-Tzetnik whose very pen name contains the number branded into his flesh by the Nazis and translates roughly as ''Internee 135633.'' Rosenfeld pursues the idea further by raising a question which yields some insight into the fates of Daniella and Fella, one asked time and again in the writings of those who survived and implicit as well in the epilogue to *Anya*: ''Who, in fact, *are* the real victims here, the dead or those cursed back into life again, guilt-ridden and condemned by a fate that would not take them?''

The ambiguity of survival provides the central idea about which Arnost Lustig, himself a survivor of Theresienstadt (Terezin), has constructed his story ''The Return,'' from the collection *Night and Hope.* The story opens upon Hynek Tausig, a Jew who has escaped removal to the Theresienstadt Ghetto by hiding from the Germans during the roundup. Though his identification papers give him a new identity, Tausig walks the streets of Prague fearful of detection. Miserable, tired, and hungry, his fear impels him finally to rejoin his fellow Jews by slipping into the ghetto, where he finds a measure of contentment—despite the loss of freedom and cruel beatings—in the company of other Jews and in the knowledge that he will no longer need to hide. But Tausig eventually grows unhappy in the ghetto, reacting against its miserable conditions and the loss of dignity, despising his fellow Jews—and himself— for their fear and subservience, yet knowing that they cannot behave otherwise. Ultimately, he finds within himself that will to live which permeates *Anya* (and the autobiographical works of Kosinski and Lind), escaping from the certain death of the ghetto into the uncertain world outside to take up life once again under his false identity, and to struggle daily with that overwhelming fear of detection with which the story began.

''Rose Street'' is another story from *Night and Hope* which hints at the possible implication, through passivity, of the Jews in their own fate. In this tale the elderly Elizabeth Feiner, bringing to mind Hannah Arendt's famous denunciation of the *Judenrate,* suggests that by not cooperating so readily with the Nazis, perhaps by refusing or merely ''neglecting'' to conform to German regulations, the Jews might shorten the War and with it, their misery. But Elizabeth Feiner has her own method to resist ''the onslaught on human dignity that the present time brought with it''—silence, the refusal to speak or cry out in face of unspeakable horror, a response which runs as a thread throughout Wiesel's works and indeed forms the basis for the plot of *The Oath*. Mrs. Feiner remains silent during a brutal beating at the hands of First

Officer Herz and she finally dies in silence, refusing to yield to the pain and dehumanization which comprise the Nazi answer to "the Jewish question."

Within the domain of Holocaust Literature, this story is unusual in its partial shift of narrative viewpoint away from the victims to Herz and his driver Binde. Binde, in particular, arrests our attention for his silent disapproval of the way in which Herz mistreats the old woman, who somehow touches him, who reminds him, curiously, of his stepbrother. Binde's spark of decency finds expression in his feeling that Elizabeth Feiner is "a mediator between him and his future peace of mind." He brings her food, at great risk to himself, in an attempt to win her trust and salve his conscience, only to be met by a wary and suspicious silence. Later he assumes even greater risk, preventing the final humiliation to Mrs. Feiner by shooting a dog ordered to attack her. But Binde's actions, though heroic under the circumstances, serve more to highlight the brutal level to which the Nazis have sunk than they do to salvage the humanity of the German nation. Binde, representing a small minority among the Nazis, cannot save Mrs. Feiner—or the other Jews of the ghetto—from a horrible death inflicted by his compatriots, who have created the conditions which make impossible all but the weakest assertion of his humane instincts.

The role of the *Judenrate* in the fate of European Jewry is suggested in "Stephen and Anne," a story from the same collection, whose theme is that of awakening youthful love crushed by the circumstances of ghetto life. In "Blue Flames" Lustig focuses more intently upon this aspect of the tragedy, enlarging his treatment of the *Judenrate* to the status of theme. The story centers upon the relationship between Ignatz Marmulstaub, a member of the Jewish Council of Elders, and Herr von Holler, commandant of the ghetto. Holler confers favors upon Marmulstaub—in particular, keeping him alive— in order to turn to advantage his position as Council member. Although Marmulstaub is a coward, promoting his own interests even at the expense of his fellow Jews, the story cannot be read as a blanket condemnation of *Judenrate* members. Indeed, Lustig draws important distinctions, providing Lowenbach as counterfoil to Marmulstaub. Convinced that those in the forthcoming "labor transport" from the ghetto are never to return, Lowenbach, as head of the Council, withholds the signature that Holler—constrained by the rules of the Nazi bureaucracy—requires before the shipment can begin. Holler responds by summoning Marmulstaub to deputize for the imprisoned Lowenbach and to provide the needed signature. Too fearful to follow the heroic lead of his fellow Council member, Marmulstaub signs the paper and rationalizes his action on the grounds that "Holler had to call somebody." Lowenbach does not actually appear in the story, but his presence is powerful throughout, serving as background and silent rebuke to Marmulstaub's self-serving behavior. The same can be said of the young man, Woodpecker, who—calling to mind Elizabeth Feiner—emulates Lowenbach's refusal to cooperate, at first resisting with silence, and ultimately losing his life in a suicidal attempt to counter Nazi bullets with the axle of a carriage.

Woodpecker and Lowenbach, Mrs. Feiner and Tausig—all of these in their own ways rebel against the Nazi authority, choosing to maintain dignity and humanity, even at the expense of their lives. Their examples suggest a potential for Jewish resistance to the Nazis which, though perhaps not fully exploited, did occasionally make itself felt under virtually impossible circumstances. Indeed, the seven interconnected stories of *Night and Hope* demonstrate that in the face of the terror and misery of the Theresienstadt Ghetto a semblance of life did nevertheless carry on there, and it is Lustig's gift to recapture the spirit of this life for us. Focused closely upon the actions and fate of a few, the stories—however limited in intent—have sufficient cumulative impact to convey vividly the strengths and foibles of the victims and the complex interrelationships between them and their tormentors. Lustig's writings share with *Anya* and the works of Ka-Tzetnik—as they do with Wiesel's autobiographical *Night*—the force of actuality. The perceptive reader does not need to be told explicitly that the events described actually took place, that the characters depicted are real ones, however shattering one may find the acceptance of such truth.

Night and Hope, like many other works emerging from the Holocaust, batters the senses with the events of the present, describing the real actions of real people and leaving to the reader the inferences implicit in the situations described.

The same can be said of Lustig's novel *A Prayer for Katerina Horovitzova,* to my knowledge the only Holocaust work in which American Jews play a major role. The story, based upon an actual episode documented at Yad Vashem, concerns twenty American Jews taken prisoner by the Nazis after being trapped in Italy. These twenty men have been brought to Poland under the "protection" of a Nazi bureaucrat, Mr. Friedrich Brenske, to a concentration camp where they are held. Brenske has undertaken negotiations with the object—so the Americans are led to believe—of securing their release in exchange for a fortune in Swiss currency.

Katerina's life enters the negotiations when Herman Cohen, spokesman for the American group, overhears her plea to her father as she is being forced onto a death transport: "But I don't want to die.... " The figure of Katerina—like the American group—is based upon fact, modeled after an American-born Jewish ballerina of great beauty who was caught in Poland by the Nazis and sent to Auschwitz. Already on her way to the gas chambers, she so overwhelmed the guard with her beauty that he spared her life. Ultimately she was shot to death after wresting a gun from one of the guards and killing several. (See Borowski's "The Death of Schillinger," also based upon the story of this anonymous heroine.)

Although Lustig's novel contains little "action" in the conventional sense, the author brings to the work a manifold perspective successfully combining various levels of meaning. Katerina eagerly leaps at Mr. Cohen's offer of help, yet she cannot free herself of guilt rooted in her "reprieve." She acknowledges her cowardice under the threat of death, but, confronting death, in the end she emerges as a heroine. For their part, the Americans delude themselves with the belief that even warfare has rules to which both sides adhere. Gradually, painfully, Lustig exposes to light what the reader fears from the outset, that this belief is naive and unrealistic, that under Nazi rule the fate of Jews—regardless of their citizenship—is immutably sealed.

Especially significant in this connection is the failure of the American government to intercede on behalf of the group of twenty, who are "grossly rejected by their own authorities." Indeed, while Lustig does not formulate the notion explicitly, the suggestion nevertheless remains of a link between Hitler's successful campaign to destroy European Jewry and the silence of the world, of the Allied governments in particular.

As he does in *Night and Hope,* in *Katerina* Lustig has something significant to reveal concerning Jewish compliance and Jewish resistance. Finally understanding clearly and without self-deception that she is on the brink of death, Katerina seizes the gun of a Nazi officer and shoots several of the soldiers. Her behavior in death contrasts sharply with the passivity of the Americans, whose nudity—they have been forced to disrobe in preparation for the gas chamber—symbolizes an underlying moral nakedness, exposed in part by the diabolical, highly cultivated Nazi talent for dehumanization. Even more striking is the reaction of Brenske's commandos—Jewish inmates of long standing—who, though armed, fail to turn against their tormenters, instead aiming their "guns at the 19 men and one woman who stood huddled together," thus earning a brief respite from the fear of death and keeping alive a desperate and slim hope of survival.

But it is not Lustig's purpose to condemn these victims who remain passive or participate actively in their own extermination. Rather, he has undertaken the more difficult and subtle task of exposing to view the complexities inherent in the moral/psychological issues touching upon compliance and resistance among those exposed daily to physical torture and moral degradation. With regard to the Americans, Brenske understands that "a lot of people more vigilant and less credulous than they had been had also been lured from the path of judgement and reason. Mr. Brenske was an expert at the job." The Jewish tailor who acted as a commando upon Brenske's orders "understood a lot; there was a lot he didn't understand and there was a lot which had been inevitable," just as Brenske realized "that blood and blood relationships alone are never decisive.... It was strength that counted, rather, and the realization of which side has the superiority and power and who will be the one to present the bill when the rebellion is over." In view of the complete

Jewish powerlessness during the Holocaust, exacerbated by the silence of Hitler's enemies—Lustig may be suggesting—even the scattered, spontaneous resistance of individual victims such as Katerina and the people of *Night and Hope,* albeit restricted in scope, is a tribute to the human spirit.

The theme of resistance against impossible odds is taken up on a larger scale in Lustig's autobiographical novel *Darkness Casts No Shadow,* which tells the story of two teenaged boys who escape from a death transport and struggle for survival by hiding in the woods. The central episode of the work describes the boys' encounter with a German housewife, from whom they demand food. Though they understand well that the protection of their own lives dictates killing the woman, the boys cannot bring themselves to carry out the act, in part because she has a young child. They perceive that the will to live carries with it "the multiplied determination to kill . . . stronger than you are, but as long as you live, you can try to resist it." Indeed, they feel that there are "situations when . . . it would almost be better to be killed . . . than to kill." This resistance to killing has its inevitable consequence, as the woman reports the incident to the village authorities. Ultimately the boys are hunted down and executed by the old men of the village, men too old for the *Wehrmacht,* who want nonetheless to participate in the new dream—the work of the great German Reich.

Darkness Casts No Shadow is far from a self-conscious exploration of courage and morality in opposition to an all-pervasive and overwhelming evil; yet its sparse, elegantly executed narrative effectively carries the force and message of such an essay. Here, as elsewhere in his writings, Lustig has focused upon a narrowly circumscribed segment of Holocaust life, evidently believing—and with some justice—that assimilation of the larger picture is best left to the historians. Still, the behavior of two adolescent boys in this one small episode has universal implications, not about death, but about humane life, informed by the knowledge that "conscience is like your heart—you can't carve off a piece and expect the rest to function as before."

Jerzy Kosinski's *The Painted Bird,* similarly, emphasizes the immediate, but the narrative thread is overlaid with a quality of fantasy generated in part by the author's deliberate ambiguity concerning the protagonist's identity and the locale of his actions. (The fact that the events of *The Painted Bird* are even conceivable as actuality reveals the extent to which the Holocaust has altered our notions of reality by diminishing the scope of the impossible.) We are told only that "in the fall of 1939, a six-year-old boy from a large city in Eastern Europe was sent by his parents, like thousands of other children, to the shelter of a distant village" to the east, that in the War's disruption the parents lost contact with the boy, and that he "was considered a Gypsy or Jewish stray" by the villagers, who therefore could aid him only by risking severe penalties at the hands of the Germans. The work describes the boy's movement from village to village throughout the War, his exposure to bestiality and random, senseless violence, and his eventual liberation from the ordeal by Russian troops advancing westward during the War's concluding days.

The marked differences between Lustig's characters and this boy without family, past, name or language explain, in part, the off-center, disturbing atmosphere that Kosinski creates in this work. If we do not know in great detail the backgrounds of the people in *Night and Hope,* we nevertheless do have a grasp of the general outlines of their history. The contrast is even more striking when comparisons are made with Anya or Ka-Tzetnik's Daniella, whose history and family relationships receive detailed exposure, and who succeed in carrying with them—even into the ghetto and concentration camp—some of the artifacts and ambience of their past lives. Because of his youth, Kosinski's youngster remembers little of his past and dwells on it only at the beginning of the work, in anticipation of a reunion with his parents. But this expectation, crowded out by the immediate demands of bare survival, soon fades from his thoughts, leaving him to move from adventure to adventure, mute and in isolation. After the book's opening pages the boy remains sealed off from his past, establishing only short-lived human contacts, and these only from the necessity imposed by harsh circumstances.

The action of *The Painted Bird* is far removed from the ghettos and death camps described in much of Holocaust Literature; yet, the work succeeds in recreating the atmosphere of the Nazi universe of terror by depicting events which are equally devastating in their threat to destroy the boy's humanity. In this novel, indeed, Kosinski appears to mount an effective challenge—possibly the only one up to now—to what Alvin Rosenfeld understands as one of the "abiding laws" of Holocaust Literature: "there are no metaphors for Auschwitz." (Whether *The Painted Bird* will remain an isolated exception to prove Rosenfeld's rule remains, of course, to be seen.) Auschwitz, however, haunts the periphery of Kosinski's fictive world, a silent, though powerfully disturbing presence, a backdrop against which the primitive animalistic villagers act out their lives of violence and inarticulate superstition. Acutely aware of the contents and destination of the German death-camp trains which periodically move across their landscape, they believed that "the Lord was using the Germans as His instrument of justice," justly punishing the Jews "for the shameful crimes of their ancestors, for refuting the only True Faith, for mercilessly killing Christian babies and drinking their blood."

The boy, finding shelter where he can, moves from one peasant to another, mutely absorbing the scenes of death and bestiality which he confronts daily, his own life beset with constant pain and danger. One episode is particularly overpowering in its horror, as the boy witnesses the punishment a drunken miller inflicts upon a plowboy who lusts after his wife. The miller pushes the plowboy against a wall and gouges out his eye with an iron spoon. His terrible revenge as yet incomplete, the miller keeps the victim pinned against the wall and plunges the spoon into the other eye "which sprang out even faster." In an interview between Kosinski and Lawrence Langer (as quoted in Langer's *The Holocaust and the Literary Imagination*), the author attempts to explain the tendency of readers to reject this passage in his novel. Citing the instance of a woman who could not read through the episode, Kosinski wonders why she finds the eye-gouging too terrible to confront although she can contemplate the even worse realities of the gas chambers and concentration camps. His explanation of this phenomenon casts a good deal of light upon the literary and psychological considerations underlying the central design of *The Painted Bird*:

> The concentration camp as such is a symbol you can live with very well. We do. It doesn't really perform any specific function. It's not as close to us as the eyesight is. When you describe the atrocity of the concentration camp you are immediately reminding the reader that this is not his reality. . . . But when you describe the eyes being gouged out, you don't make it easier for the reader, he cannot help feeling his own eyes disappearing somehow, becoming blind.

The Painted Bird does indeed achieve its powerful effect through a succession of bizarre and violent incidents which evoke horror, a literary device that moves toward a re-creation of the atmosphere of Auschwitz without attempting to recreate Auschwitz itself. The life which the boy suffers has the expected result: having grown up with violence, he condones it and resorts to it. As Langer has observed, the boy's understanding of revenge as a mark of the true human being points to a reading of the novel as an intentional parody of the traditional *Bildungsroman*. Revealing in this connection is the contrast with *Anya*, which might be considered an incomplete *Bildungsroman*, describing a career interrupted precisely when it is about to mature into productivity. At the time of the German invasion Anya is an adult, with a firm grasp upon life, the values and goals instilled during her childhood already internalized, and indeed she retains her basic decency even in the ghetto and the concentration camp. Kosinski's boy, on the other hand, has nowhere to turn for humane guidance or example, the Holocaust itself acting as the societal framework—if one may use that term—within which he begins his growth to maturity. Not surprisingly, the values he has absorbed are a distortion, a parody of those that society normally attempts to inculcate. Only twelve years old at the War's end, as a result of his intimate knowledge of physical and moral degradation, he is violent and barely controllable, mute despite his need to communicate. Ultimately, the boy is reunited with his parents and he regains the power of speech as well, but optimism about his future is misplaced for, as the epilogue of *Anya* makes clear, liberation does not guarantee a return to prewar sensibilities, and the Holocaust survivor, indeed, may find impossible genuine liberation from the memory of his ordeal.

That the world has emerged from the Holocaust a radically altered place, its basic values and assumptions displaced beyond the point of return by the Nazi exploration in new regions of terror, is implicit in the final pages of *The Painted Bird,* suggested by the boy's great difficulty in readjusting to a measure of normalcy. The message becomes more explicit in Kosinski's later novel, *Steps,* a collection of loosely interrelated vignettes not describing a world going mad—as does *The Painted Bird*—but rather a world already in the throes of madness. In this sense *Steps* carries the central idea of *The Painted Bird* to its logical (or, rather, logically illogical) conclusion, surrounding the reader in an ambience bizarre enough to create a sense of disjunction from the familiar, yet too familiar to be dismissed as pure fantasy. As in the earlier work, the plot of *Steps* focuses largely upon bestiality, violence, and degraded, manipulative sexuality—but with an important difference. While the events in *The Painted Bird* shock the sense with their immediacy, often forcing one to turn away from the horror projected in its pages (the eye-gouging episode is a good example), those in *Steps* are presented in a detached fashion, calculated to make them appear unremarkable, almost acceptable as normal human behavior. The consequent tension established between surface appearance and underlying substance, between style of presentation and events presented, explains in large measure the power of *Steps* to disturb profoundly—if not immediately, then after reflection upon the implications for civilized society of Kosinski's fictive vision. In the sense that *Steps* is farther removed than is *The Painted Bird* from the actual events of the Holocaust out of which its world-view grows, it is a "second generation" work of Holocaust Literature, belonging among those artistic attempts to apprehend and assess a universe damaged, perhaps irremediably, by the knowledge of Auschwitz, rather than among those works grappling with Auschwitz itself.

The same may be said of much of the fiction—as opposed to the autobiographical works—of Jakov Lind, a Viennese Jew who survived the Nazi years in Germany itself, aided by false identity papers and an "Aryan" appearance. Lind's background of wartime life under an assumed identity, described in *Counting My Steps* and *Numbers,* explains the distance from the ghettos and concentration camps that his fiction shares with that of Kosinski. Even these autobiographies, like *The Painted Bird,* offer only the exterior view of the events of the Holocaust to which Lind, in his isolation from the great mass of Jewish victims, was himself exposed. This relatively distanced position, however, lies at the heart of Lind's uniqueness as a Holocaust writer and explains some of the intrinsic interest of his work. *Counting My Steps* and *Numbers,* as autobiography, do, indeed, depict reality, but reality of a kind quite different from that exposed in *Anya, Night and Hope, House of Dolls,* or Wiesel's

Night. In fact, Lind's life history brings to light the possibilities, however limited, for approximating normal existence in the midst of the Holocaust, for establishing a life outside of that death-in-life planned and executed by the Nazis as response to the "Jewish question."

These possibilities were realized for the teenaged Lind in the wake of his impulsive—and retroactively courageous—decision to ignore German orders to report for deportation with the Jews of Amsterdam. Instead, he separated himself from family and friends, going underground in search of freedom and sexual partners, to emerge later in the guise of ordinary Dutch citizen, Jan Overbeek, with papers entitling him to work to support himself. As Michael Berenbaum suggests, "Lind's life experience" contrasts with that of Anne Frank—who was about the same age—in illustrating the alternatives "available to one who faces his fear and admits to himself the magnitude of the problem." Indeed, Lind tends to be extremely critical of those Jews who, unable to face their situation directly and paralyzed by fear and disbelief, did little to save themselves from deportation and eventual death. Lind's frequently expressed ambivalence toward his Jewishness arises from revulsion against the kind of fear that reinforces powerlessness instead of combating it, the kind of fear that he associates with being Jewish: "My roots are in fear and fear is the marrow of my bones." Having himself survived by struggling in the face of fear and powerlessness, he reacts against what is—in his perception—the weakness of the vast majority of his fellow Jews, who could not—or simply did not—follow the same course of action. In Berenbaum's view Lind's career provides a small measure of evidence in support of the condemnation of the *Judenrat* and the Jewish willingness to cooperate with its leadership expressed in Hannah Arendt's claim that the total number of Jewish victims of the Nazis would have been reduced greatly "if the Jewish people had really been unorganized and leaderless."

As a Jew who finds fault with his own people while managing to "pass" among the Nazis, Lind is doubly an outsider, at home nowhere. This holds true even in Israel after his liberation, where he finds himself "turned back into Jan Overbeek on a visit to the Jews. Only more anti-Semitic than most Dutchmen." Lind's status as permanent (or, at least, long-term) outsider lends a special character to his fiction, adding an edge of objectivity to his description of chaos and abetting his violation—carried out repeatedly and with great effect—of the boundaries between sanity and madness, between historical truth and literary imagination. Lind presents his perception of the post-Holocaust era as a time in which such traditional distinctions no longer apply, having become largely irrelevant or meaningless. The first line of the title story in the collection *Soul of Wood,* rivaling in its searing effect the famous opening of Camus's *The Stranger,* illustrates the point: "Those who had no papers entitling them to live lined up to die." The reader who grasps at the hope that Lind's shattering conception is rooted only in the author's fantasy is very shortly disabused of that notion, alerted by the reference to freight cars packed with dying people, the alternative, more bearable interpretation swept away with a single reference to Auschwitz: "In the little town of Oswiecim they were taken off the train by men in uniform and cremated the same day."

As does most of Lind's fiction, *Soul of Wood* explores the state of mind that made Auschwitz possible and the resulting damage to the human spirit as revealed in both victim and executioner, rather than the events of the Holocaust itself. After his parents die on the way to Auschwitz, the crippled protagonist Anton Barth—even his eyelids were paralyzed—is removed by the faithful servant Wohlbrecht to a hut in the mountains, there presumably to starve or to be killed by forest animals, if the Nazis do not find him first. But Anton does not die in his isolation; miraculously, he survives a stag's attack, to develop the complete use of his body and voice. However, in order to survive in isolation, Anton is compelled to join a herd of deer, learning to live, eat, and run as the deer do, and, indeed, becoming the leader of the herd. Thus, upon his return to the hut at the War's end, an amazed Wohlbrecht finds Anton Barth whole in body but animal in spirit, deriving nourishment from hay but revolted by bread. Lind's transmutation of victim into beast is but one instance of a theme occurring frequently in the literature of the Holocaust— Schwarz-Bart's *The Last of the Just* and Kaniuk's *Adam Resurrected* come immediately to mind—an aspect of the new reality that the Nazi period has unleashed. The literary antecedent of this theme is to be sought in Kafka, for whom, however, the notion undoubtedly has significance more as symbolism for man's condition than as depiction of literal reality. The post-Holocaust writer, on the other hand, knows that Kafka's stunning conception has meaning beyond and outside of the symbolic, matching closely a reality that the Holocaust survivor has experienced firsthand.

Anton's transformation serves as a metaphor for Lind's own survival, made possible by the protective coloration of a new identity. Clearly, survival for Anton, as for Lind himself, depends upon an altered state of being, a descent from the usual self, which is doomed, to life upon a new level at which physical survival becomes possible. Thus, as we have noted in connection with *Anya,* survival, in itself, is far from an unalloyed good, tainted with the experience and memory of bestiality. Indeed bestiality pervades Lind's post-Holocaust fictive world, a place where modern-day cannibals ride Western European trains dressed in ordinary business attire and recruit potential victims, where nudists who drink fresh blood and eat their own children seem unexceptional. To our eternal horror, it is a place where the inverted logic of the Holocaust Universe has made mass murder of humans more acceptable than petty theft—a violation of "good breeding"—or the killing of squirrels and rabbits. After all, Bachmann tells us in *Landscape in Concrete,* "men can defend themselves, but what can animals do in this world without steel and dynamite? . . . Men are men, they have reason and weapons.''

The descent of the executioner to the bestial along with the victim is a commonplace of Holocaust Literature, but in the novel *Landscape in Concrete* Lind achieves an unusual and graphic treatment of this theme by employing the narrative viewpoint of the Nazis themselves in place of the more commonly adopted viewpoint of the victims. This literary strategy, available to Lind because of his unusual experience of survival in Germany, gives the author an internal view of the actions and motivations of the Nazis that has generally not emerged in the writings of those who were trapped in ghettos and concentration camps. The work, describing the chaotic state of the German mentality during the declining days of the War, emphasizes the human indifference to human suffering, the devolution of mass slaughter to the routine and tedious, the ''banality''—to use Hannah Arendt's term—of extermination through technology. It stresses as well a theme which is prominent in Lind's autobiographical works—the madness of defenseless passivity in a violent world.

In the end, however, it is not merely the victims of the Nazis who find themselves defenseless, as the executioners are themselves trapped in the Holocaust they have unleashed upon the world. The final pages of *Landscape in Concrete* describe an air raid and its aftermath, a sequence of events evolving into a metaphor for nothing less than the destruction of civilization as we know it. At the end, there remains only ''the gray ocean of an extinguished landscape, a colorless and bare'' stillness yielding no sign of the human or, indeed, of life in any form. The descent into nothingness is complete and irretrievable, it is ''too late for help . . . remedy is nothing but a word, stale medicine, nothing can revive dead cells.''

If the title of Lind's novel can serve as a clue to the mood of hopelessness in its final pages, the title of Yoram Kaniuk's *Adam Resurrected* is, similarly, an indication of the message its author intends to project. Like Lind, Kaniuk depicts a post-Holocaust world beset by madness, a reality distorted and misshapen by the enormity of events past but not forgotten. However, in contradistinction to Lind, for Kaniuk the madness is balanced by an ameliorating hope, the hope found in the ''resurrection'' of Adam, at the novel's end, from the inferno of insanity which he suffers throughout the work.

As with Lind's Anton Barth, the physical survival of Adam Stein has entailed a degradation of spirit from the human to the animal. Imprisoned in a Nazi extermination camp, Adam—a well-known clown before the War—was forced to provide humorous diversion for the benefit of the camp commandant while his fellow Jews, his own wife and daughter among them, marched to the gas chambers. This experience irreparably subverts Adam's humanity in his own eyes, and in the eyes of the Nazis, and in response he assumes the role of a dog, chewing on bones, eschewing human speech in favor of a remarkably doglike series of growls and barks, snapping and biting, and running on all fours, all to the great amusement of Commandant Klein. In keeping with the familiar pattern of survival, Adam's release from the camp at the War's end does not, in itself, provide an antidote to the spiritual poison methodically forced into his system by the Nazis. Indeed, the bulk of the novel's action centers upon an asylum for the insane near the Dead Sea, where, within his person, Adam as patient acts out the deep-rooted conflict between the world of normal human intercourse and the diabolical legacy of the Holocaust, struggling with the contradictory claims imposed by the need to reestablish sanity and the desire to preserve madness, the longing to forget and the impossibility of suppressing the past.

While Lind's writing has theological implications only in the sense of complete negation, Kaniuk's novel—beyond the obvious reference contained in its title—raises that bitter challenge to Judaism and the God of Israel which the works of Schwarz-Bart and Wiesel develop into a major and sustained theme. At the same time Kaniuk condemns the mainstream Western European civilization upon which the hopes of so many had been focused, but which in the end spawned the methodical slaughter of millions of innocents. With a searing irony, Kaniuk suggests that Adam found security in the Nazi camp because his classmates from the university designed and built it, that he understood where he was because "the culture which made Adam Stein also made the Camp." Kaniuk discredits the faith that Western civilization has traditionally invested in a scientific approach to the world, falling back instead upon the irrational power—bordering on the mystical—of Adam Stein as individual genius. Significantly, the persistent attempts by Dr. Gross to cure Adam's insanity prove futile, and in the end Adam—deliberately frustrating the psychiatrist's efforts—brings about his own "resurrection," not by application of scientific principles, but rather through the instinctual but difficult act of reaching out to another human being in distress. In helping David to throw off his doghood and become a whole child once again, Adam, in fact, succeeds in discarding the bestiality lying at the core of his own spiritual illness. In Kaniuk's world, then, science has proved itself—in Nazi hands—an effective weapon in promoting death, yet helpless in the face of the overpowering need to restore life.

Kaniuk's work shares with the writings of Wiesel a consideration of the efficacy of clinical madness as a response to the Holocaust, with *Anya* a depiction of the permanent emotional damage with which a survivor is burdened, and with both Kosinski and Lind a nightmare vision of the post-Holocaust world, a world in which sanity and madness are barely distinguishable. In several important respects it parallels Andre Schwarz-Bart's novel *The Last of the Just,* which also deals with the problem of human descent to the bestial within the context of the Holocaust. Indeed, the two works employ the identical image—metamorphosis of victim into dog—as the burden of humanity becomes unbearable. Though Schwarz-Bart's protagonist, Ernie Levy, does not survive the Nazi terror physically, as does Adam Stein, nevertheless his deeply sensitive humanity emerges intact, though profoundly altered by martyrdom. Adam, as victim, avoids martyrdom by exchanging his humanity for bare survival (ultimately regaining it only when the humanity of another is at stake), while Ernie Levy inverts the bargain to become a genuine martyr to man's spirituality. Ultimately, the lives of both emerge as testimony to the ambiguity inherent in man's nature, to the clash of self-destructive and self-fulfilling elements within the individual human being.

To find an appropriate context for his perception of the Jewish confrontation with the Holocaust, Schwarz-Bart turns to the legend of the *Lamed-Vov Zaddikim,* the thirty-six Just Men whose existence justifies the survival of Mankind within God's universe. In *The Last of the Just* he employs the legend as unifying theme and leitmotif, as a framework about which the intricate strands of plot are woven. Ernie Levy, the protagonist, is a twentieth century *Lamed-Vov,* descended from the Rabbi Yom Tov Levy, who was martyred by his own hand during the pogrom in York in 1185. Benjamin, Ernie's father, responds to a tragic Jewish past closely reflected in the history of his own family by opposing God, concluding that a Just Man is worth nothing either in this world or the next, that the suffering of the world and the *Lamed-Vov* "goes for nothing."

Travelling to Germany, Benjamin becomes intimately acquainted with the lacerating effects of Christian anti-Judaic teachings in his encounter with Yankel, the sole survivor of a pogrom who buried his entire village when it was over. No longer able to believe in God, Yankel turns his back on his people "to avoid spending his life on all fours." Benjamin later witnesses the return of an apostate seeking admission once again to the synagogue, confessing that—like Adam Stein's daughter—he had "wanted to live as the Christians do because he was ashamed to remain Jewish." As the congregation considers an appropriate penalty, Benjamin insists that the man has suffered enough already, quoting the words of the fifteenth century Rabbi Israel Isserlein: "he who returns to Judaism . . . imposes upon himself a continual penance." The extent to which persecution has influenced the Jews' view of themselves, with profound effects upon the Jewish community, is suggested in Benjamin's unanswered call for "one among us who never thought about" taking on "the advantages and felicities of Christianity." In the end Benjamin himself remains suspended between apostasy and tradition, neither turning away from Judaism completely nor able to accept the goodness of God or the efficacy of the *Lamed-Vov.*

Ernie Levy lives a life governed by the contradictory positions inherited from his grandfather Mordecai and his father. Mordecai teaches the young Ernie that the essential function of the Just Man is to sense "all the evil in the land, and take it to his heart,'' but the boy finds instruction in the streets as well: he is beaten senseless after Christian playmates force him to take the role of the accusing Jews in an impromptu play depicting the trial and Crucifixion of Jesus. Later—it is the mid-1930's in Germany—Ernie experiences the intense fear associated with the simple act of walking to the synagogue on the Sabbath. In one especially touching scene, Ernie and his younger brother Jacob consider the possibility of posing as Christians by removing the obligatory skullcap, but, fearing God as much as they do the hoodlums, they remain terrified, victimized by forces beyond their understanding. The boys' dilemma mirrors upon a personal level that of the Jewish community at large, who continue to pray in the synagogue, but with guards posted at the gate, unable to find peace either in worship or its avoidance.

With the advent of even greater danger the Levys contemplate escape from Germany, but remain unhappily aware that Jews—especially poor ones—are welcome nowhere, not even in the "democracies." Ultimately deciding it preferable to be "Germans in France than Jews in Germany," they cross the border. When Ernie later learns that the rest of his family has been removed from France to a Nazi extermination camp, he reacts with a renunciation of Judaism, damning God's name, wanting "to spit in his face." "To be a Jew is impossible," Benjamin had told him, and now, in the depth of crisis, Ernie goes farther, believing, like Yankel, that a Jew cannot even retain his humanity. In ultimate defiance of God, he adopts the identity of a Gentile and resolves to live henceforth as a dog, learning to bark and to consume raw meat. However, Ernie's disguise proves imperfect; he is recognized as a Jew by a French blacksmith who finds in his eyes the same qualities he has seen in those of Jewish children taken away by the Germans. The discovery of the blacksmith leads to a moment of recognition for Ernie, who realizes the baseness of his attempt to deny his humanity and his Jewishness by cultivating his lowest instincts. He undertakes a reintegration into life, rejoining his people not only in spirit but physically as well, going to occupied Paris and joining the Jewish community there.

Though Ernie's appearance in the old Jewish quarter of Paris marks his reentry into a familiar but terrible world of permanent fear, he manages somehow to find a measure of equanimity there, to summon up the resources necessary to accept his destined role of Just Man. Similarly, the doomed men of the Marais, everyday facing death at the hands of the Germans rather than simple brutality as was the case in earlier years, "never tired of God," defiantly refusing to miss religious services because "that's what they want." Once rejoined with his people, Ernie never again accepts separation from them, voluntarily entering the Drancy concentration camp, a staging point for shipment to Auschwitz and death. Here Ernie faces dehumanization once again, this time at the hands of the Germans, who try to reduce him—with the others—to a mere object, but bolstered by belief in Jewish peoplehood, if not in God ("wherever there are Jews, there is my kingdom"), Ernie refuses to succumb, maintaining his essential humanity to the end.

At Drancy Ernie encounters "a Catholic of vaguely Jewish ancestry," who wears a medal of the Virgin around his neck and a yellow star on his jacket. The man admits to shame at first learning of his Jewish ancestry, confessing that he was then still "on the other side," but at Drancy the focus of shame moves toward the part of him that is not Jewish. Uncertain whether he is Catholic any longer, he dwells "upon those two thousand years of catechism, those two thousand years of Christology," that prepared the ground for the Nazi terror, at the same time recognizing the mad innovations of the Nazis who no longer allow Jews to escape through baptism: "now it isn't your souls they're after, it's your blood." For Ernie the crisis of spirit has passed, but like the Jewish Catholic, he finds his faith in an omnipotent and just God challenged by daily encounter with incredible human suffering. Though Ernie dies in the gas chamber with the *Shema* on his lips, that ancient prayer professing the existence and uniqueness of the Hebrew God remains muffled, its meaning diminished and distorted by the sounds of innocent children and women dying anonymously around him. Yet, like his ancestor Yom Tov Levy, Ernie finds in loyalty to his people and their history a means to preserve his essential humanity, even in the face of cruel and senseless death.

Lawrence Langer has remarked that in locating the final action of his novel in the gas chamber itself—a step most Holocaust writers do not take— Schwarz-Bart in fact rejects Kosinski's artistic commitment to discovering "universal metaphorical equivalents for the grotesque horrors of our time." Nevertheless, even here, in "the deepest heart of Holocaust darkness," the author diverts his reader's attention from the horror—if only briefly—with the Talmudic legend of Rabbi Chanina ben Teradion, which comes to Ernie's mind as his death approaches. Wrapped in the scrolls of the Torah and thrown upon the pyre by the Romans for having taught the Torah, the Rabbi is asked by one of his disciples what he sees, and he replies that though the parchment is burning, "the letters are taking wing." Perhaps there is more than a touch of irony in Schwarz-Bart's juxtaposition of Ernie's situation with that of the ancient Rabbi martyred in the name of the sanctity of the Torah, since for Ernie, and the others who die with him, there is no question of choice, hence no question of martyrdom. If the Romans oppose the Rabbi's vocation, the Nazis find intolerable Ernie's mere existence. Nevertheless, while it may not mitigate the horrors of the gas chamber, the reference to Rabbi Chanina assumes significance in connecting Ernie and his fellow victims with the long and often tragic history of the Jewish people.

Another work which views the Holocaust in the light of Jewish history and tradition is Soma Morgenstern's *The Third Pillar,* which takes as its setting a "small half-burned bordertown" in Eastern Europe on the day of its liberation from Nazi occupation by the Russian army. The action of the novel centers upon the trial of a group of captured German Storm Troopers. Convened in the old synagogue of the town—erected, significantly, upon the ruins of a far older one destroyed by Chmelnitzsky—the trial functions as a literary framework for the narrative, which is biblical in tone and overlaid with religious mysticism. Within the context of the Holocaust, however, the trial emerges as more than a convenient—and particularly apt—narrative technique. It is, in fact, the civilized expression, consonant with principles both of secular and Jewish law, of the victim's overwhelming need to bring the defilers of humanity to justice and thus to seek a measure of redemption for mankind.

The trial is conducted by one called "The Messenger," a stranger of unknown origin and background ("in a certain sense I may be said to be Jewish"), who appears in the town on the day of its liberation. Although the few Jewish survivors of the town step forward to tell their stories indicting the Nazi prisoners—and with them the entire German nation—the most telling witness is an inanimate object, an innocent-looking but mysterious box that assumes mystical qualities as the plot unfolds. At the novel's opening "three Christian publicans" (one of whom later reveals himself as a Jew in disguise) find the box—apparently the property of the German army—and take it to the nearby synagogue after they find themselves unable to open it, despite their vigorous efforts. In the course of the trial that later unfolds, it is revealed that the box contains soap made by the Germans from the body of Jochanan, the pious thirteen-year-old son of the town's Torah scribe. With this revelation, it becomes clear that the dead themselves have returned to bear witness against their murderers, that any defense of the Nazis has become unthinkable.

The titular third pillar, the "pillar of blood" forged from Jewish sacrifice at Nazi hands, like the biblical pillars of fire and smoke, is to lead the Jewish people to their redemption, "through all the wildernesses into the Holy Land." Thus Morgenstern appears to suggest—as others have as well—that the founding of the State of Israel, the fulfillment of the biblical promise to establish the descendants of Abraham "in their land, that they be no more cast forth from their land," functions as a response to, perhaps a mitigation of, the annihilation of European Jewry. On the other hand, it can be, and has been, argued that the unprecedented destruction inflicted during the Holocaust was too high a price in blood for the Jewish people to pay, even to achieve the establishment of the Jewish national homeland. Elie Wiesel, whose entire career as a creative artist has been a response to the Holocaust, rejects the suggestion that Israel is an answer to the Holocaust and, in fact, as a survivor he refuses to acknowledge any lesson at all to be drawn from the event, despite its clear significance for Jewish history. Yet Wiesel shares with Morgenstern a preoccupation with religious mysticism and a perspective upon the Holocaust shaped by an acute awareness of the historical role played by the confrontation of the Jewish people with the effects of Christian dogma and the teachings of the church.

The two writers share as well in their use of the trial as a literary device to cry out against the demons raised by the Holocaust. However, while Morgenstern devotes virtually his entire novel to a trial in which the Nazis stand accused and condemned, Wiesel shifts the emphasis away from the executioners and puts God Himself on trial. An explicit instance occurs toward the end of *The Gates of the Forest,* in a Nazi concentration camp. One of the four rabbis summons the other three to convoke a special court to put God on trial, to accuse Him of murder, of "destroying his people and the Law he gave them from Mount Sinai. . . . The trial proceeded in due legal form with witnesses for both sides. . . . The unanimous verdict: 'guilty.' "

As witness to the Holocaust Wiesel remains firmly within the Judaic tradition—established by Abraham, Moses, Jeremiah, and Job—of condemnation of God for failure to intercede on behalf of His creatures. Indeed, Wiesel's first five works can be read as a sustained developing revolt against God from within a Jewish context. Jewish tradition provides not only adequate precedents for such revolt, but legal and moral sanction as well, in the covenant with God into which the Jewish people entered: "We are to protect His Torah, and He, in turn, assumes responsibility for Israel's presence in the world. . . . when our physical existence was threatened we simply reminded God of His duties and promises deriving from the covenant." Against this background the reality of Auschwitz confronts the Jew with a dilemma, an "absurdity" which cannot be easily dismissed and which stubbornly refuses to dissipate of its own accord. Since the Jewish God is "Lord of actual history," the Jew must conclude that God was somehow part of Auschwitz, thus calling into question the continued validity of the covenant itself. Clearly, any recognition that the covenant might no longer be operative would strike a devastating blow at the very foundations of Judaism and leave the theologically serious Jew isolated, to struggle in an unaccustomed loneliness with an indifferent, or worse, hostile universe. After Auschwitz, he is joined to the French existentialists in confronting the absurdity of the universe, an absurdity engendered and given substance by the Holocaust and signaling the breakdown of the covenant. The only possible response that remains within the framework of Judaism is rebellion against God, a denunciation of God that at the same time demands that He fulfill His contractual obligation. This is the religious/moral context within which Wiesel attempts to apprehend and assimilate the events of the Holocaust.

In his early works Wiesel's role as witness to the Holocaust predominates, perhaps in response to the survivor's fear that the tale would not be told or, if told, not believed. Hence, the autobiography *Night* exposes to view the inner life of the young Jewish inmate of a German concentration camp, while *Dawn* and *The Accident* are largely autobiographical works describing the torment that this survivor endures after liberation. As with other Holocaust writers, for Wiesel survival itself carries with it a stigma, engendering guilt and a sense that the survivor is no longer of the living, that he is—in Wiesel's phrase—"a messenger of death." If the enormities of the concentration camp experience lead Eliezer/Elisha, Wiesel's protagonist, to reject God in *Night,* the torment of survival brings him to question seriously and reject the Jewish moral commitment in *Dawn* and *The Accident,* not, however, without the sense that in violating the traditional Jewish code of morality he has violated his own being: "I've killed. I've killed Elisha." The rebellion against Jewish tradition, begun in the Nazi concentration camp of *Night* and continued in *Dawn* through Elisha's killing of a fellow human creature, reaches a climax in *The Accident* in the protagonist's act of attempted suicide. For the sacredness of life, God's gift to mankind, is basic to Judaism and, in fact, arguably the most basic tenet of the Jewish faith. Thus the Jew is not free to argue, as does Camus, that "there is but one truly serious philosophical problem, and that is suicide." It is not for the Jew to judge "whether"—in the words of Camus—"life is or is not worth living"; only the God of Israel, as Creator and Giver of Life, is to determine when life is to end. In Wiesel's Jewish context, therefore, the suicide attempt takes on significance as a kind of ultimate defiance of God, explainable only on the basis of a recognition, in reaction to Auschwitz, that God encompasses evil as well as good, that in violating His covenant with Man, God has not only withdrawn His protection, but has left man free of the restraints of His Laws and Commandments.

Wiesel's hero has thus come to share the attitude which characterizes Camus's protagonist, Meursault, at the beginning of *The Stranger*—a sense of the absurdity of the world and the pointlessness of human existence. In contrast to Meursault, however, Wiesel's character is obsessed by the relationship of man to God, never losing his belief in God's presence in the world, even while bitterly denouncing God's injustice toward man. While Meursault appears to have no past, living in a kind of timeless present devoid of history and human attachments, the narrator of *The Accident* cannot forget his past despite the horror of the memory, because "I am my past. If it is buried, I'm buried with it." He is at great pains to explain his desire to die, to make understood the tragedy of those "living-dead," who came back after merely lasting through the Holocaust, devoid of joy, hope, or delusions about the future.

The Town Beyond the Wall represents a new point of view in Wiesel's writing, emphasizing the culpability of man for the crimes of the Holocaust and indicting the indifferent observers equally with the executioners. Here the problem is couched primarily in terms of man's cruelty and indifference to his fellows, and the solution is sought within man as well. Indeed, in this work Wiesel clearly seeks response to the Holocaust in the secular existential philosophy of Camus. Following Albert Camus, Wiesel suggests that man's proper stance in the face of suffering entails a rejection of suicide and madness; it involves struggling against indifference, assuming responsibility for one's fellow man, retaining an essential core of humanity at all costs.

In contrast to the Jewish victims of his childhood, who were unable or unwilling either to surrender faith or to acknowledge the possibility of evil within God, the protagonist of *The Town Beyond the Wall*—now named Michael—frees himself to take positive action by refusing to shrink from these alternatives. Michael's ultimate victory over the tortures and loneliness of imprisonment comes about, not through prayer, which he rejects in spite of the danger of heading to perdition, but by extending his help to another human being, the demented young prisoner whose life he saves, whose mind he struggles with all his being to bring out of its catatonic state. The struggle to cure the boy saves Michael because it is a meaningful protest against the world's indifference, and thus, as for Adam Stein, an effective antidote to clinical madness. As Byron Sherwin has pointed out, Michael does in fact display a kind of madness in *Town Beyond the Wall,* the "moral madness" (in the sense of A. J. Heschel) of the ancient Hebrew prophets, which entails remaining human and retaining a concern for others in a world in which the social norm is hate and indifference. It is in this sense that Sherwin interprets the novel's epitaph from Dostoevsky: "I have a plan: to go mad." The moral madman is closely linked in spirit to the "absurd man," in the sense of Camus; both are able to face the world's absurdity unflinchingly, with aversion perhaps, but without denial. Where the absurd man may succeed in doing this on the basis of a rational decision, executed by force of will, the moral madman, like the Hebrew prophets, often acts upon inner compulsion, unable to do otherwise. The end result is the same in either case—that genuine confrontation with the absurd advocated in *The Myth of Sisyphus.*

Moral madness reappears as a theme of some importance in Wiesel's succeeding novel *The Gates of the Forest.* At the beginning of the work it is not the young protagonist Gregor, but Gabriel, his philosopher-teacher, who displays moral madness by reacting with laughter to the horrors of the War. Gabriel clings to this position even in the face of death; exposing himself to capture in order to save Gregor, he bursts into overwhelming laughter at the very moment he falls into the hands of the German soldiers. A similar response to enormity is urged upon Gabriel—in New York after the War—by the Hasidic Rebbe, who renews the emphasis, so prominent in *Night,* upon the implication of God in evil, but with a difference. Here there is a new awareness that the recognition of God's guilt is, in itself, not a viable solution to the problem of evil in the world, that there must be a constructive response from man as well. That response, Wiesel suggests, can be expressed in the Hasidic way of prayer and joy, through clinging to God until he is forced to recognize once again his covenantal responsibility for the preservation of the

Jewish people. Thus, Wiesel's protest against God is such that it allows him to remain a Jew, "within God"—in Wiesel's phrase. The object of this protest is not nihilism, not denial of God, but the very opposite—the reestablishment of God's order in a world which has witnessed the destruction of order. The boy of *Night*, who vows never to "forget those flames which consumed my faith forever," gives way to the man of *The Gates of the Forest*, who understands that "God's final victory . . . lies in man's inability to reject Him."

The Gates of the Forest provides the first instance within Wiesel's canon in which traditional Christian dogma concerning the historical role of the Jewish people assumes more than minor importance; this novel, indeed, marks only the beginning of an increasing preoccupation with that theme in the author's more recent writings. Wiesel's attention to the function of Christian attitudes in Jewish tragedy—especially in *The Oath*—where it serves as a framework supporting the entire plot—suggests that in the teachings of the Church, he has found (as have a number of Christian theologians in recent years) a clue toward understanding man's participation, whether active or passive, in Auschwitz. His recent work develops and builds upon the notion that men were freed to commit and accept the enormities of the Holocaust in part by the accumulation of centuries of Christian retribution against those among Jesus' people who did not accept him as Messiah.

Two episodes in *The Gates of the Forest* have particular interest in this connection. The first of these describes a school play performed in a Hungarian village upon the subject—"hatred of the Jews and its justification." During the performance the figure of Judas Iscariot—played, ironically, by Gregor, a Jew hiding from the Germans by posing as a mute Gentile—comes under verbal and physical attack as the other actors and the audience are carried away by hatred. As it happens, in his role of deaf-mute, Gregor has heard confessions of many guilty secrets by the villagers, who saw in him a completely safe confessor, one who could carry no tales. In danger of his life, Gregor briefly considers a public exposure of the villagers, who would then, he reasons, turn their hatred from him and toward each other. That Gregor rejects this plan in favor of a far more difficult and dangerous course of action indicates that this Jew-as-Judas, at least, is no betrayer. The impression seems unavoidable that Wiesel is attempting to reach a new understanding of the relationship between Judas and his master here, one that raises questions concerning the traditional Christian view of the betrayal, not only about the motivation of Judas, but about that of Jesus as well.

The second episode involves the village priest, who is harboring a Jewish fugitive. Having saved the Jew from capture by the Germans, he decides it is time to apply himself to the man's soul as well. The priest urges the Jew to accept Jesus, insisting that the trials of the Jewish people would end with their collective repentance. The Jew rejects the priest and his theology: "Stop thinking about our salvation and perhaps the cemeteries won't be so full of Jews.'' Unable to bear the Jew's dismissal of Jesus as Messiah, and indeed of the Hebraic God Himself, the priest loses control of his anger, ordering the man out of the house—and to certain death.

Consonant with Wiesel's reexamination of the figure of Judas is his reconsideration of the fundamental problem of the Crucifixion, from a Jewish perspective, in a brief episode in *A Beggar in Jerusalem.* The scene relates a conversation between the dying Jesus and one called Shlomo, who makes it clear to Jesus that he is not to be accepted as the Messiah by future generations of Jews: ''You think you are suffering for my sake and for my brothers, yet we are the ones who will be made to suffer for you, because of you.'' Through Shlomo, Wiesel expresses his sympathy for Jesus and a grasp of the moral dilemma posed for him by the ''actions his followers would undertake in his name to spread his word . . . the innumerable victims persecuted and crushed under the sign of his law.'' Wiesel perceives with Emil Fackenheim that ''the returning Christ would have gone to Auschwitz . . . involuntarily if not voluntarily.'' His artistic perception as expressed here foreshadows a significant theological insight: it is not in Jesus as man and prophet, but rather in the Church's conception of Jesus as Messiah that the genesis of Christian anti-Semitism is to be found.

In *The Oath,* Wiesel makes his most extensive attempt to date to gauge the role of Christian doctrine in the formulation of the ''Final Solution of the Jewish question,'' removing the major plot action to the Eastern European village of Kolvillàg in the 1920's—well before Hitler's rise to power—in order to add a new dimension to his understanding of the Holocaust by viewing the future from the perspective of the tragic Jewish past. The plot is set into motion by the confrontation in the present between two victims of past Jewish persecutions: Azriel, sole survivor of the pogrom in Kolvillàg some fifty years earlier, and a young man who shares in the agony of survival by virtue of his being the child of survivors of the Holocaust. The encounter between the two reveals that they are linked not only by the Jewish history of suffering but in their personal fates as well. It becomes apparent that only Azriel can prevent the young man's ''abdication'' from a life of despair, and only by revealing the secrets which he and the dead victims of the pogrom had sworn under oath not to reveal. After fifty years of silence Azriel, as the sole survivor and link between the victims of Kolvillàg and the living present, speaks out in order to avoid ''not suffering but . . . indifference to suffering.'' Azriel relates the circumstances leading to the final destruction of the Jewish community of Kolvillàg, and with his tale as vehicle, *The Oath* emerges as a quasi-theological inquest into the Christian roots of anti-Semitism. Through the novel's dramatic action, Wiesel examines the consequences of confrontation between the teachings of Judaism and traditional Christian dogma relating to the Jews, and in so doing he raises a number of serious and difficult problems that challenge both Jewish and Christian theology in the post-Holocaust era.

Azriel's story incorporates into the present the medieval accusation of ritual murder—the Jews of Kolvillàg are held responsible for the disappearance of a Christian youth—thus linking the circumstances leading to the destruction of Kolvillàg and, by implication, those surrounding the Holocaust itself with the pogroms of the Middle Ages. While the tale of "ritual murder" is central to the implication of Christianity in the Holocaust, the consequences for Judaic thought issue from the theological debate between the Rebbe and Moshe. Arguing within the framework of traditional *halacha* (Jewish law), the Rebbe opposes Moshe's offer of martyrdom, which can be justified only when the Torah itself is in danger. Moshe's counter-argument cuts deeper, reaching for another level of understanding of the covenant and describing the dilemma of the theologically serious Jew threatened with pogrom: "We must save the divine Law even if it places us in contradiction to the Law . . . Without Jews there would be no Torah. . . . They are inextricably bound." Moshe understands the paradox inherent in affirming God's presence during the Kolvillàg pogrom, that such affirmation would imply concomitant damnation of God for his complicity in the evil of the pogrom. Yet in characteristically mystical fashion, Moshe demands that the Jews of Kolvillàg remain Jews, continuing to praise God, but in "silence" rather than as witnesses. He concludes that despite the importance in Jewish history of the witness to disaster, of the "survivor-story-teller," they must now "adopt a new way: silence . . . we shall testify no more." Moshe's exhortation of his fellow Jews to remain with God does not in itself break new theological ground, reflecting rather the theological insight achieved in Wiesel's earlier work: man's need to define himself in relationship to God continues undiminished, even after Auschwitz. However—and we shall enlarge upon this presently—*The Oath* does offer fresh possibilities for assimilating the knowledge of God's implication in evil, despite Wiesel's assertion elsewhere of the impossibility of understanding Auschwitz on the level of God.

At the same time, the recognition with which *The Oath* is informed—clearer than elsewhere in Wiesel's writings—of the implication in Jewish suffering of Christian doctrine and Christian institutions, of the "love of God turned into hate of man," as Wiesel puts it, contributes to the possibility of comprehending Auschwitz on the level of man. This recognition is expressed in part through the concern with the history of Christian atrocity against the Jews displayed by Shmuel, who immerses himself in martyrology in an attempt to gain a better understanding of what is to come. In continuing to act as chronicler and witness, Shmuel rejects Moshe's oath, which has as its purpose the rupture of continuity in Jewish history, the abolition of suffering through an attack upon the history of suffering. This opposition of responses in Moshe and Shmuel serves as a focal point in the novel for the tension between the survivor's desire to remain silent and his need to record the event. This theme is a familiar one in the works of Wiesel, reflecting the author's personal dilemma as survivor, his feeling, often expressed, that the Holocaust demands response yet imposes silence. However, in *The Oath,* for the first time in Wiesel's fiction, this theme emerges as a central problem of the novel. Like Wiesel himself, Shmuel chooses to continue to serve as witness to history. Initiating Azriel into the tradition of the Book, he fulfills his chosen role, discharges his obligation to link Jewish past and future, denies the validity of Moshe's position.

With the killing already begun, the priest and the Bishop "decided this was the time to debate orthodoxy and heresy," giving credence to the Rebbe's position that "Help cannot come from the other side. A Jew must not expect anything from Christians, man must not expect anything from man. Consolation can and must come only from God." Consolation perhaps, but not rescue, and this is the heart of the difficulty Wiesel experiences in understanding the Holocaust on the level of God. Christian churchmen have not intervened on behalf of the Jews, but neither has the God of Israel, who, according to Jewish tradition, is bound to do so by virtue of the covenant. While Wiesel's earlier novels respond to this inherent paradox by declaring God guilty of complicity in evil, *The Oath* reaches toward a resolution within the Talmudic tradition of *Hester Panim,* the Hiding of the Divine Face, a point of view foreshadowed, however, in a legend appended to *The Town Beyond the Wall,* relating how God and man exchanged places, "so neither . . . was ever again what he seemed to be." Thus God may forfeit omnipotence and become, like man, not indifferent to history, but unable to control it, powerless to combat man's destructive impulse. The legend suggests that in observing helplessly the suffering of man, God suffers with him as well, since "the liberation of the one was bound to the liberation of the other."

In contrast to Wiesel, who has consistently admitted his inability to reconcile the Holocaust with the traditional Jewish view of the God of history and the covenant, Nelly Sachs in the verse drama *Eli* has employed the notion of *Hester Panim* in an attempt to achieve precisely such a reconciliation. *Eli* presents a plea for the survivors of the Holocaust to "re-establish their relationship to God and to regain his attention—in effect to bring him out of hiding" and an examination of the thesis that through prayer this can, in fact, be accomplished. While Wiesel does not go nearly this far in establishing upon *Hester Panim* a theological vantage point from which to view God's silence during the Holocaust, in *The Oath* he seems to weigh seriously the possibilities for understanding inherent in the concept. Illustrative are the Rebbe's questioning in the face of a pogrom, whether God "could be turning His Face away from His people," and Moshe's understanding—on his own terms, in terms of silence—of God's role in the affairs of men: "rather than speak, God listens; rather than intervene and decide, He waits and judges only later."

Though Wiesel implies, through Moshe, that God may have no choice in the Hiding of the Face, the suggestion remains as well that God is implicated in evil by virtue of his ambivalence: "Satan is more than evil," Moshe declares, "he is evil disguised as good, the link between the two . . . his place is at God's right. An awesome concept, leading to horror. How is one to distinguish God in evil, Satan in good?" Moshe's perception of the ambiguous and elusive nature of God's role in good and evil finds it counterpart in "the perplexing duality of the knowledge of God"—as theologian Eliezer Berkovits puts it—that confronts the Jew of faith after the Holocaust:

> He [the Jew of faith] knows of the numerous revelations of the divine presence as he knows of the overlong phases of God's absence. . . . But he also knows that God's absence, even at Auschwitz, is not absolute. . . . There were many who found him even in his hiding.

Between Berkovits and Wiesel there is an essential convergence of overall outlook, a unanimity in stressing the interconnectedness of all of Jewish history, the unbroken continuity of Jewish tradition. Shmuel's immersion in the study of the atrocities punctuating Jewish history, Moshe's teaching that "nothing in Jewish tradition was unconnected," find their counterpart in the observation of Berkovits that "a straight line leads from the first act of Christian oppression against the Jews and Judaism in the fourth century to the Holocaust in the twentieth."

Kolvillàg is a Jewish Everytown, whose destruction links past pogroms with future Holocaust. As he watched the town burn—destroying both Jew and Christian, both victim and executioner in a powerful evocation of the indivisibility of violence—Azriel, the sole survivor, the indispensable link needed to maintain the continuity of Jewish history, understood that he had just glimpsed the future. Kolvillàg provides a backdrop against which Azriel can view the Holocaust to come in terms of the accumulation of past events, but his view of the future is only one side of a dual truth. A description of the other is provided by Berkovits:

> The rabbis of the Talmud could speak of the silence of God at the time of the destruction of the Temple . . . and yet remain true to His word, because . . . Israel survived, remained historically viable, full of future expectation.

Azriel not only survives, but he survives to rescue the young Jew from self-destruction, to maintain Jewish continuity in *that* man's future by passing on to him, through the tale of Kolvillàg and its victims, the role of witness inherited from Shmuel. Like Azriel, who was saved from the flames of Kolvillàg in order to testify as witness, this young Jew no longer has the right to die. In spite of his initial reluctance, Azriel ultimately has rejected silence in favor of history, understanding the nature of man's encounter with God not as Moshe understood it, but as did his father Shmuel. As witness to future generations, Azriel becomes the fictive counterpart of his creator, carrying out the role that Wiesel, as writer and survivor, has taken upon himself.

APPENDIX

We conclude our discussion of Holocaust novels and short stories with an analysis of four powerful but often overlooked works. The first of these is Piotr Rawicz's *Blood From the Sky*.

It is possible to say that unless one has read *Blood From the Sky* one is not fully informed, not only about the literature of the Holocaust, but about the catastrophe itself; indeed, about the invisible dimensions of that catastrophe which can be discovered only by artists. And the time that has passed since 1961—when this book was published in Paris—has proven that the book is gaining in perspective—as do all good literary works—and that it can stand comparison with the best written parts of the Bible. It is, as a matter of fact, of the same breed as the Bible: it doesn't just repeat, as many others do, but it adds. It is really a beautiful, strong, and eloquent testimony, from which—almost from every line—can be written dozens of artistic and scholarly books.

Blood From the Sky is a poetic account of the catastrophe of the Jews in Eastern Europe. It takes place in one of the many small towns which were so simple to convert into ghettos, and then into slaughterhouses. The book is both intensive and extensive, covering the victim as well as the murderers. It is a story of a blond, well-educated Ukrainian Jew, Boris, who, in Paris after World War II, is telling his story, just as other people are telling their life stories, as casually as possible. The book has three parts, but any one part is as complete and as intense as the whole. The author, who tells the story seemingly without respect to time, unites the past, the present, and the future in one stream. He uses all possible means to let us know, feel and understand what happened. To do this, the author uses a literary strategy similar to Kosinski's in *The Painted Bird*—he has one foot inside and the other foot outside the world surrounding the Jews. He employs humor, cynicism, hallucinations, and a reality so brutal that it is hard to believe that what he described actually happened. The reader gets the impression that the author thought that he would be the only one able to give this testimony; Rawicz is obsessed with the task of giving testimony! The reader senses the flames which hover beneath the pages of this volume.

In this story, Boris and his girlfriend Naomi are among the few surviving people, and the story of their survival and the aftermath paints an historical, psychological and philosophical map of the landscape of the country known as the Holocaust. It is about ultimate degradation and ultimate human strength. The author compares Boris' situation in Paris after the War with life in the Ukrainian ghetto, and even with the distant past—which seems not so distant now—the pogroms in the previous century.

Rawicz is intelligent and pitiless. He describes the frantic activities of the doomed; he describes hopes, untempered with real possibilities. He discovers that irony is the most fitting tone for telling such a story. And he feels, as many others have, the responsibility to the dead, innocently killed.

Rawicz is proof for us that it is not enough to have only talent, just as it is not enough to have only the direct, firsthand experience. It is only when chance combines talent with experience that such a book can be born.

In spite of the fact that he writes in the end that his story is not an historical record, Rawicz still adds that "events here described could crop up in any place, at any time, in the mind of any man, planet, mineral . . . "

Like so many of the best literary works on the Holocaust, *Blood From the Sky* was written in French by an Eastern European Jew who adopted that language as his vehicle of expression. Because of this, American students of Holocaust literature often overlook important works written in Eastern European languages both by Jews and by non-Jews. Amongst the most significant works on the Holocaust written by a non-Jew in an Eastern European language is Tadeusz Borowski's collection of short stories, *This Way for the Gas, Ladies and Gentlemen.*

A Polish non-Jew who spent many years in Poland and Germany, and who finally married a Jewish woman with whom he had had an affair in Auschwitz, Borowski provides an added dimension to literary attempts to grapple with the Holocaust. His approach is possibly more objective than that of many Jewish writers on the Holocaust. His concrete mode of description engenders shock. With the possible exception of the Polish half-Jewish writer Jerzy Kosinski, Tadeusz Borowski offers the most enduring and most brutal portrayal of life and death during the Holocaust.

The importance of the book lies not only in the fact that the author was not Jewish and yet was a close witness to the Jewish Holocaust, having spent his apprentice years in Auschwitz and Dachau, but also in the fact that the author has been able to achieve a certain detachment. It is exactly this—his distance—that makes him important, that makes him different from others, and that makes his work seem to complete our picture of the Holocaust. Given the nature of the work and the talent of such magnitude, one must agree with Jan Kott in the introduction to *This Way to the Gas,* that this book will last as long as Polish literature itself. To this we might add, that it will endure as long as people think and read about the Holocaust.

Just as interesting as the lives of writers such as Joseph Conrad or Ernest Hemingway is the life of the writer Borowski. In his introduction to the American edition (one of the latest editions), Jan Kott compares the times which created and influenced Tadeusz Borowski's talent and writing to the era called, by another French Jewish writer, Romain Gary, "The European Education." It was indeed the European education of the years 1939–1945 which changed the lives of tens of millions and annihilated the lives of people in numbers never known before, as well as in brutality never experienced in such a manner and dimension before.

Borowski survived the camps only to gas himself to death in July 1951, when he was not yet thirty years of age. The disappointment of literary and political postwar Poland led to his suicide.

This Way to the Gas is a selection of Borowski's work limited to stories inspired by his concentration camp experiences. The core of this book are stories written and published in postwar Germany. After returning to Poland in 1948, Borowski added a number of stories to the original collection. Borowski's complete works, published posthumously, comprise five volumes. Amongst these is his first book, a collection of poetry, published by the Polish underground press in 1942, under penalty of death.

Borowski managed to survive the camps because he was made a *Kapo*. He was one of the privileged few in the machinery of death. However, unlike other Kapos, Borowski did not work in the gas chambers and ovens, but worked as a hospital orderly and a building laborer. Thanks to Jews coming into Auschwitz, who brought food and went directly from the trains to the gas, Borowski almost always had enough to eat. Every day and every night Borowski watched as thousands of Jews—men and women, the young and the old—were exterminated. In describing what he saw, Borowski uses the technique of letters, like short shots of a film camera, to pretend that his selection of facts has nothing to do with his tastes, desires, upbringing, or hopes for the future.

Nevertheless, in each of his twelve stories we can find more than one profound philosophical thought on the well-worn themes—what is man?—what is it that man is ready to do to his fellow man?—why did no one revolt?—why was it permitted to happen?—what can now be the future of man? After such degradation, the so-often-praised Jewish optimism takes on a different perspective:

> Never before in the history of mankind has hope been stronger than man, but never also has it done so much harm, as it has in the war, in this concentration camp. We were never taught how to give up hope, and this is why today we perish in gas chambers.

Borowski calls this world "the world of stone." And for him, for anyone who entered that world, there is no escape from it, whether he survives or not:

> The living are always right, the dead are always wrong—an optimistic statement. If the dead are wrong and the living are always right, everything is finally justified.

To this observation Kott adds, "But the story of Borowski's life and the stories that he wrote about Auschwitz show that the dead are right, not the living."

Borowski's stories are so unique and so simple that no one hesitates even for a second to accept everything that he writes as the truth. Chekhov once said of literature that if in love, church or the hospital, it is possible to lie and not to be caught, the very nature of literature excludes lying. In one of his stories Borowski takes another look at a brave girl, whose name was perhaps Katerina Horovitzova, who in the deepest Jewish tradition of revolt grabs, on her way to the gas, the pistol of First-Sergeant Schillinger in 1943, and shoots him, together with his adjutant. This girl actually existed, but no one knows any more than that of what happened, because everyone died. So, even in Auschwitz, in the midst of the War, a legend was born. Borowski takes a look at Katerina's fate from the viewpoint of First-Sergeant Schillinger. He completes the picture, which almost surely will be completed in the future by other writers.

Borowski proves that, as in the case of Piotr Rawicz, it is important to connect talent with firsthand experience, and his experience, though not Jewish, is, nevertheless, very Jewish.

To complete the picture are two more writers: the Polish Adolf Rudnicky, and Jiri Weil, one of the best Czech writers of this century, who did not board the transport, but spent the War in Prague. Rudnicky and Weil, in similar ways, escaped the destiny of the majority of the Jews in Europe and spent the War outside the ghettos, in hiding, in much the same way as do the heroes of Rawicz and Kosinski.

The Alive and the Dead Sea is a collection of Adolf Rudnicky's World War II stories. This volume completes the work of a significant Polish Jewish writer of the wartime. Many of his stories are autobiographical. The writer, who introduced himself into Polish literature with an impressive novel, *The Rats,* is, next to Borowski, the best Polish author preoccupied with the Holocaust. The fall of 1939 was for Rudnicky "the first initiation into history." He writes about the Jewish poor, about the fighters for a better future for mankind, about justice, which has never yet been achieved by man. His Jewish novels, short novels, and short stories were welcomed by Polish literary critics as works of great perfection from both an artistic and a moral point of view. "No writer," says a Polish critic, "has spoken so much truth about the time we have lived through." *The Alive and the Dead Sea* is filled with death, heroism, sadness, and survival. Sometimes its stories sound like prayers.

Some stories, like "The Golden Windows," explain something which still puzzles so many people: the total inhumanity of the enemy and the lack of preparation of the victims, the process they went through. This story of several people, facing the unbelievable destiny of many, is written in the spirit of Montaigne, who claimed that only people whose fate was kind could keep calm on their faces, but in the last role, alone with one's own death, there is no pretense and everyone speaks as he feels; everyone has to show what it is in him that is good and bad, pure and corrupt.

Jiri Weil is a necessary part of the picture, from another viewpoint, but for the same reasons as Rudnicky. He blends his great talent with his unique experience of hiding during the War. He was an authentic "submarine."

His novel *Life With a Star,* published in 1949, was attacked by leftist critics and silenced as an attempt to glorify cowardice, and as a decadent and existentialist work, improper in its concept of socialistic and realistic prose.

Unfortunately, works silenced in the East never crossed the borders of the West and so we are still waiting. The hero of the novel *Life With a Star* is a very small Jew, a bank clerk, Josef Roubicek. An antihero, he is ridiculous and always scared. He waits in his small room in a Prague suburb to get a call to a transport in the ghetto. Having parted from his girlfriend, he lives alone, by anti-Jewish orders, totally isolated from the neighboring world. After difficult interrogations, registrations and medical examinations, he goes to work in a Jewish cemetery. People of different professions are taking care of leaves and sand paths, and most important, they plant vegetables for their families and for the Jewish dining rooms of the community. By some mistake the hero never gets the order to enter the transport. He witnesses the whole line of tragedies of his fellow men who, in one way or another, are fulfilling the Nazi idea of the "Final Solution" of the Jewish question.

When alone, the hero carries on an imaginary dialogue with his girlfriend Rose and evokes the history of his love affair. One day he listens to the radio in Prague as people are being executed as blind punishment for the assassination of the *Reichsprotektor,* SS General Reinhard Heydrich, and he learns that Rose has been killed. The only non-Jew he can contact is a young worker, Materna, first a real stranger but later his bridge to the underground world, which Roubicek enters, thus becoming a "submarine." Here, in this strange world, he becomes the creator of his own life.

Life With a Star is the picture of an absurd world where the annihilation of the Jews is fulfilled step by step in a bureaucratic, pedantic, accurate action which seems to be not absurd but normal. The book is full of absurdity. That the wife and daughter of one Jewish friend of Roubicek would press the man to commit suicide and relieve them from trouble is absurd in itself, but it is even more absurd that the man understands and kills himself. It is a picture of an absurd world: the new Nazi world is a world without conscience, without dignity, an inhuman world. With the death of the Jews, the humanity of the whole world is murdered. Jiri Weil's second Jewish novel *Mendelssohn is On the Roof* describes the fate of the people caught in the monstrous world of the War.

Conclusion

No one writer but a collection of writers is needed to create a whole picture of what happened during the Holocaust. Several things can be learned from their work: Firstly, that art is able to go deeper than historical record. Secondly, that personal experience and firsthand account are not enough where there is a lack of talent; and talent is insufficient where there is no firsthand experience. Only when both—talent and firsthand knowledge—are connected, do we have results which are equal to the power of that historical occurrence, often compared either to Pompey or to Atlantis: the first buried for two thousand years under ashes and lava but preserved though dead, and the second, vanished forever, without the slightest trace; or comparable to events like the destruction of ancient Rome or the French Revolution. But the truth is that the Holocaust as an unprecedented historical event, is looking for appropriate means of expression. To date, this has come only through literature, the mother of the arts.

While the majority of writers seem to be shocked by the reality and enormity of the catastrophe, some authors are ahead of their time and are able to give literary testimony about the catastrophe in the way in which literature, from time immemorial, has grasped all that has happened in history and examined its literary dimensions: motive, action, and impact. Certainly, the works of these authors will be of more permanent value than others because they include a larger sum of reality, even though it is a shocking reality. These authors have captured the maximum truth, which is the ultimate gauge of literature.

There are some writers who claim, paradoxically, that silence is more powerful than words, and yet, they are not very thrifty with words, suggesting, at the end of many words, that silence is the goal to be achieved! These writers belong among the helpless who, as is often the case, are making virtue from their own necessity.

This chapter has concerned itself with authors who, thanks to their unique talents, have provided special scales and measures for the reality of the Holocaust, and, viewed objectively, belong among the best. They are connected by theme, not place of origin. For example, it is Weil from Prague and Rudnicky from Warsaw; earlier it was Ka-Tzetnik from Israel and Kosinski from New York. Of course, this is not to suggest that we need no testimony beyond that of these writers. On the contrary, we are waiting for it. But what we are waiting for is that which will earn the title "art" when measured against these books.

To write, for some, means to rid themselves of guilt and to state, with an almost absolute certainty, when, where and to whom the guilt belongs. Therefore, literature is one of the most important ways to share the picture of the Jewish Holocaust. Literature tells us what we know about the catastrophe now. Certainly literature is also important because while history, philosophy, psychology or sociology each stands alone, literature includes all of them and re-creates all elements into its own literary amalgam, out of which comes something that exists nowhere but in literature.

Just as every man is the same yet different, so it is that the Holocaust is one and the same experience, but different for everyone who survived it. Therefore, it is almost impossible for one person—though he be clever, experienced and sensitive—to grasp it all in a literary way, as a testimony or a documentation. It will require many people, perhaps in several generations, to compose the mosaic in which the single parts fit together to create the whole.

Ultimately, it will most probably be literature which will give us the most faithful picture of the Jewish catastrophe in Europe, thanks to the qualities and attributes which exist only in literature and which have secured for literature its place in human culture and civilization, where it can never be replaced. Aristotle was wise when he gave priority to poets over historians in the effort to find the truth.

BIBLIOGRAPHY

Annotation in this bibliography is generally limited to primary sources *not* discussed or analyzed in the preceding chapter.

I. Novels and Short Stories

AICHINGER, ILSE. *Herod's Children* (New York: Atheneum, 1963). Through fantasies and daydreams, children attempt to assuage the pain and horror of Nazi persecution.

ANDERSCH, ALFRED. *Efraim's Book* (New York: Doubleday, 1970). A philosophical novel.

BECKER, JUREK. *Jacob the Liar* (New York: Harcourt, Brace and Janovich, 1975).

BELLOW, SAUL. *Mr. Sammler's Planet* (New York: Viking Press, 1970) (Available in Fawcett paperback).

BOROWSKI, TADEUSZ. *This Way for the Gas, Ladies and Gentlemen* (New York: Viking, 1967) (Available in Penguin paperback).

DEL CASTILLO, MICHAEL. (New York: Dell, 1957). Autobiographical novel tracing childhood to adulthood. The child survives but the adult has little real commitment, except to those few who sustained him.

GARY, ROMAIN. *The Dance of Genghis Cohn* (New York: Viking, 1968). The narrator is the ghost of a Jewish victim who returns to haunt his Nazi murderer. This novel shows that the Holocaust is a problem for the perpetrator as well as the victim.

GREEN, GERALD. *Holocaust* (New York: Bantam paperback, 1978). Novel based upon the NBC Docu-drama *Holocaust*.

HERSEY, JOHN. *The Wall* (New York: Knopf, 1950) (Available in Bantam paperback). The story of the Warsaw Ghetto uprising, written in the form of a chronicle. Compare E. Ringleblum's *Notes from the Warsaw Ghetto*.

KANIUK, YORAM. *Adam Resurrected* (New York: Atheneum, 1971).

KA-TZETNIK (CETYNSKI, KAROL) *House of Dolls* (New York: Simon and Schuster, 1955) (Available in paperback).

KARMEL, ILONA. *An Estate of Memory* (New York: Houghton Mifflin, 1969). An intricately woven novel about four women in Auschwitz, committed to the survival of a child born to one of them.

KOSINSKI, JERZY. *The Painted Bird* (New York: Houghton Mifflin, 1965) (Available in Bantam paperback).

———. *Steps* (New York: Bantam paperback, 1969).

LANGFUS, ANNA. *The Whole Land Brimstone* (1962); *The Lost Shore* (1963). These two works trace the life of Anna from destruction to survival.

LIND, JAKOV. *Counting My Steps* (New York: Macmillan, 1969).

———. *Landscape in Concrete* (New York: Grove, 1966) (Available in Crest paperback).

———. *Numbers* (New York: Harper and Row, 1972).

———. *Soul of Wood* (New York: Grove, 1964) (Available in paperback).

LUSTIG, ARNOST. *Darkness Casts No Shadow* (Washington: Inscape, 1977) (Available in Avon paperback). The basis for the film *Diamonds of the Night*—see discussion of the film below in "Holocaust and the Film Arts."

_____. *Diamonds of the Night* (Washington: Inscape, 1978). A magesterial collection of short stories.

_____. *Dita Saxova* (New York: Harper and Row, 1979). The story of a beautiful teenaged girl who survives the camps and later commits suicide.

_____. *Night and Hope* (Washington: Inscape, 1977) (Available in Avon paperback). The basis for the film *Transport from Paradise*—see discussion below in ''Holocaust and the Film Arts.''

_____. *A Prayer for Katerina Horovitzova* (New York: Harper and Row, 1973) (Available in Avon paperback).

MORGENSTERN, SOMA. *The Third Pillar* (New York: Farrar Straus, 1955).

RAWICZ, PIOTR. *Blood From the Sky* (New York: Harcourt, Brace and World, 1964).

ROSEN, NORMA. *Touching Evil* (New York: Curtis, 1969) (Available in paperback).

RUDNICKY, ADOLF. *The Alive and the Dead Sea* (Warsaw: Polonia Publishing House, 1957).

SCHAEFFER, SUSAN FROMBERG. *Anya* (New York: Macmillan, 1974) (Available in paperback).

SCHWARZ-BART, ANDRE. *The Last of the Just* (New York: Atheneum, 1960) (Available in Bantam paperback).

SEMPRUN, JORGE. *The Long Voyage* (New York: Grove, 1964). The journey from the Warsaw Ghetto takes five days by boxcar. The lives and memories of the 120 political prisoners.

SINGER, I. B. *Enemies: A Love Story* (New York: Farrar, Straus and Giroux, 1972) (Available in Fawcett paperback).

SINGER, I. J. *The Family Carnovsky* (New York: Vanguard, 1969) (Available in paperback).

URIS, LEON. *Mila 18* (New York: Doubleday, 1961) (Available in Bantam paperback). The story of the Warsaw Ghetto uprising.

_____. *Q B VII* (New York: Doubleday, 1970) (Available in Bantam paperback). The basis for the ABC-TV movie QB VII.

WIESEL, ELIE. *Accident* (New York: Hill and Wang, 1962) (Available in Avon paperback).

_____. *A Beggar in Jerusalem* (New York: Random House, 1970) (Available in Avon paperback).

_____. *Dawn* (New York: Hill and Wang, 1961) (Available in Avon paperback).

_____. *Gates of the Forest* (New York: Holt, Rinehart and Winston, 1966) (Available in Avon paperback).

_____. *Night* (New York: Hill and Wang, 1960) (Available in Avon paperback).

_____. *The Oath* (New York: Random House, 1973) (Available in Avon paperback).

_____. *The Town Beyond the Wall* (New York: Holt, Rinehart and Winston, 1964) (Available in Avon paperback).

II. Literary Criticism

BERENBAUM, MICHAEL, ''An Examination of Jakov Lind.'' An unpublished paper delivered at the Modern Language Association, April 1975.

LANGER, LAWRENCE. *The Holocaust and the Literary Imagination* (New Haven: Yale University Press, 1975) (Available in paperback).

ROSEN, NORMA, "The Holocaust and the American Jewish Novelist," *Midstream* 20:10 (October 1974), pp. 54–62.

ROSENFELD, ALVIN, "The Problematics of Holocaust Literature," in, ed. by Rosenfeld and Greenberg. *Confronting the Holocaust* (Bloomington, Indiana: University of Indiana Press, 1978).

SCHOLEM, GERSHOM, "The Tradition of the Thirty-Six Hidden Just Men," *The Messianic Idea in Judaism* (New York: Schocken, 1971). Should be read for background material for Schwarz-Bart's *Last of the Just*.

SHERWIN, BYRON, "Elie Wiesel on Madness," *Central Conference of American Rabbis Journal* 19:3 (June 1972), pp. 24–33.

———. "Wiesel's Midrash: The Writings of Elie Wiesel and Their Relationship to Jewish Tradition," in, ed. by Rosenfeld and Greenberg. *Confronting the Holocaust* (Bloomington, Indiana: University of Indiana Press, 1978).

STEINER, GEORGE, "In Extremis" in *The Cambridge Mind,* ed. Homberger, Juneway and Schama (London, 1970).

Holocaust Literature III:

Poetry and Drama

Yaffa Eliach

POETRY

The Jewish poet does not permit his world to collapse because of catastrophe and calamity. Art becomes his vehicle to express the collective consciousness of his people. Time loses its chronological significance. Distinctions amongst historical events blend into a common historical-national experience. Individual experiences become confluent with the experiences of the entire people. One event comes to epitomize the history of all people. One person may represent all persons. In much of Holocaust poetry, this melting of individual events, individual places, and individual personalities occurs. One such poem is Abba Kovner's "Little Sister." The "Little Sister" is an allusion to Song of Songs (8:8–9):

> We have a little sister
> And she hath no breasts;
> What shall we do for our sister
> In the day when she shall be spoken for.
> If she be a wall,
> We will build upon her a torrent of silver
> And if she be a door,
> We will enclose her with boards of cedar.

The sister-bride of Song of Songs allegorically is the Jewish people, and God is her bridegroom. With this association in the background, Kovner transforms the "little sister" into the personification of the entire Jewish people.

She is alone in an alien world, a strange world of other "sisters" who are emotionally and literally betrothed to their god. It is a cold, barren world.

In the center of this poem stands the walls; the wall of the Dominican convent in which she seeks shelter during the War, and the city beyond the walls. Both worlds are imprisoned within their own walls: physical walls and spiritual walls of indifference. For the "Little Sister," there is no hope within and no hope without, no "scarlet thread" in sight. Again, the poet alludes to Biblical imagery—the scarlet thread that saved Rahab who dwelled in the walls of Jericho (Joshua, 2:18–21). For Abba Kovner's little sister there are no miracles; no walls will come tumbling down. Her world is one of walls, ghettos and camps, a world of death. Her bridegroom, her only hope of escape, is death.

Yet, despite the pessimistic mood of the poet, he cannot escape his tradition of hope in the face of despair. Hope comes with spring, with the whisper of chestnuts. This hope is for redemption; its symbol is the Messiah.

Like Kovner, Nelly Sachs (1891–1970) (the Nobel Laureate of 1966) resorts to the Bible, Jewish history and mysticism to provide a background for her poetry. Unlike Abba Kovner, she writes in German and discovers her heritage only after Hitler's rise to power. The Berlin-born poetess turned from the German romantic vein of Goethe and Schiller to the Bible and Kabbalah. Her allusions to the Bible and to Jewish mysticism are frequent ones but lack intense, intimate knowledge of the sources. Her allusions lack the deep, rich texture of classical Jewish sources. Her Biblical and Kabbalistic sources are simple. She refers mainly to personalities and events that are universally known and which, for the most part, are also within a Christian frame of reference. It is this familiarity with Nelly Sachs' cultural world that gives her poetry an aura of simplicity in which the Western reader can feel at ease. In the introduction to *O' the Chimneys* Hans Enzesberger wrote:

> Her poetry is neither a secret code nor a picture puzzle ... The work demands of the reader not cleverness so much as humility ... The work does not want to be made concrete or be transformed but experienced, patiently and with exactness.
>
> (Introduction to *O' the Chimneys,* p. vi)

Thus the Western European reader feels at home with Nelly Sachs' poetry both culturally and emotionally.

Throughout Sachs' poetry the Germans remain anonymous. There is no bitterness nor anger, neither biting humor nor the characteristic paralyzing fear of the artist-survivor. Sachs is a sad observer, consumed by melancholy, pain and loneliness.

But Nelly Sachs is also the traditional Jewish poet. Her private lamentations join the chorus of her people (*O' the Chimneys,* p. 13):

> When someone lifts us
> He lifts in his hand millions of memories
> Which do not dissolve in blood
> Like evening.
> For we are memorial stones
> Embracing all dying.

This poem, a rare outburst of force, does not have the visually gentle imagery of Nelly Sachs' butterflies and flowers.

In "But Who Emptied Your Shoes," Biblical imagery dominates. The burning sand of Sinai, the sand in the shoes of those that are going to die in the crematorium, and the sand in the shoes of those that will come, all merge into one: past, present and future.

Despite its occasional outbursts of national pain and anguish, Sachs' poetry is generally gentle. Her lamentations offer a note of solace. Because she wrote during the Holocaust in Sweden, and not under siege, the fear of living in a constant suspended terror between death and hope is not dominant in her poetry.

Gertrud Kolmar, who is virtually unknown to the English reader, shares many similarities with Nelly Sachs. She was born in Berlin in 1894 and grew up on its affluent West side. She wrote in German and only with Hitler's coming to power did she become aware of her unique Jewish heritage. Kolmar then began to study Hebrew and later even organized a Hebrew discussion group. Although some of her poetry was written in Hebrew, none of those poems survived. Not as fortunate as Sachs, Kolmar did not escape to freedom. She was murdered in Auschwitz at the age of forty-eight. Yet, it was not her fate, i.e., her death at Auschwitz, that justifies her inclusion among poets of the Holocaust, but rather the quality of some of her poetry.

One of Kolmar's major concerns is the woman. Her seventy-five poems of *Weibliches Bildens* ("Images of Woman" or "Feminine Portraits") deal with diverse varieties of women and her intense desire to identify with them. In September 1938, her book *Die Fraue and Die Tiere* (The Woman and the Animals) was published and received public notice. The pleasure of recognition was short-lived; *Kristallnacht* followed shortly. Kolmar's book shared the fate of all other works by Jewish authors; even the unsold copies of her book were destroyed. In her quest for identity with the many female characters, both mythical and historical, she is always a woman in love: lover of earth, people, men, children and her people. Kolmar turned to the Bible, to Deborah, for the archetype Jewish female figure of a prophetess-poet. She herself becomes part of the historical presence in the prophet-poet tradition. She is the Jewess who, along with her people, endures throughout the ages, despite unceasing persecution. With the increase of anti-Jewish measures in Germany, the anguish of Gertrud Kolmar increased. In the lines of her poem

"We Jews," the anquish of the individual poet merges with that of "we Jews." She shares their fate.

Unlike Nelly Sachs, Kolmar does not lament a destruction which already took place, but rather the impending doom. Years before the "Final Solution" actually took place, she painfully describes the lonely, helpless position of the Jew, the "darkened desert of the world." The world is deaf to the cry of justice. But the victim's "lips are sealed in glowing wax" and are unable to alert the world. The impending doom is inevitable. She feels her weeping head being dragged toward "the hill of ashes." Though her poetic imagery had not yet to cope with the realities of Auschwitz, her prophetic-poetic vision predicts it all in an almost frightening way. She herself became part of that monstrous "hill of ashes"—Auschwitz.

Unlike Kolmar's poetry, Yitzhak Katzenelson's (1886-1944) Holocaust poems survived. During the Holocaust, in Warsaw and Vittel, he wrote prolifically in both Hebrew and Yiddish. Katzenelson did not allow himself any distance from the events. He knew that death waited at every corner. Time was a luxury he could not afford. He did not indulge in self-deception, but grasped the enormity of the Jewish tragedy and its ramifications. His poetry is both the roar of a wounded lion and a chilling record of a trained historian. In this account, poetry, drama and prose blend to provide an account filled with dates, numbers, names of victims, places, and executioners. Unlike Nelly Sachs' poetry, the Germans and their collaborators do not remain anonymous in Katzenelson's writings. The Germans are identified individually and nationally. It is precisely the immediate response to the events, poetry forged under siege, that gives Yitzhak Katzenelson's poetry its singular monumental importance. In its own unique way, his writing transcends the boundaries of poetry and becomes an historical document.

Katzenelson's poem "The Song of the Slaughtered" is one of the greatest literary expressions of the Holocaust. He began to write it on October 3, 1943, and completed it in Vittel in 1944. The enormity of the tragedy would overpower him and he would be unable to express it in writing. Two and a half months before October 3, he felt some apprehension at his ability to handle the material. In his *Vittel Diary,* Katzenelson notes (p. 29):

> I could not draw up this bill of reckoning, the account for millions of murdered lives. I have not the strength for this task and I shall not do it . . . Whenever I begin to approach the subject, I feel that I shall lose my reason . . . So I stop.

Or, on another occasion, the entry in his diary reads (p. 35):

> I cannot write. It is impossible to describe the horrors that exceed anything in the history of mankind. There do not exist the words to describe them; they have not yet been created.

Nevertheless, he knew that his experiences must be recorded: "the whole world must know what happened. A whole nation has been murdered in broad daylight before its very eyes, yet no one has ventured to utter a word."

Katzenelson gives poetical expression to all his experiences during the Holocaust. His personal pain and national suffering are one. He expresses his boundless love for the Jewish people and deep hatred for the cruel enemy. Like the prophet Ezekiel, he faced a valley filled with bones, but a much larger one: the European continent. Facing this grim reality, Katzenelson asked Ezekiel's question, "Son of man, can these bones live?" He had to answer in the negative; European Jewry had come to an end. In "Song of the Slaughtered," he writes:

> The birds and fishes knew—all of us knew:
> The Gentiles all around us—they knew too.
> We would be murdered: each of us was doomed.
> No reason given; nothing to be done.
> The order had been issued, stark and plain:
> "Slaughter the Jewish people!"—child and man.

The great poet Aaron Zeitlin once said "to read Yitzhak Katzenelson is to suffer. More so, it is to be destroyed with millions of Jews, to be consumed by the flames and at the same time, to rise from the ashes and demand justice."

Abraham Sutzkerer (b. 1913) is another Yiddish poet who wrote in the ghetto. He lived through the Nazi occupation of the Vilna Ghetto, joined the Resistance and escaped to the partisans. He transformed his experiences into lyrics. His poetry metamorphoses suffering into beauty. Despite the morbidity of events, his poetry contains overtones of optimism, defiance and admiration for physical and spiritual resistance, expressed so well in the poem about the Rom Press (Ausubel, ed., p. 268):

> We dreamers must now become soldiers
> Melting words into bullets of lead.

This poem was written in the Vilna Ghetto in 1943, when the Jewish resistance fighters melted the lead plates of the famous Rom Press into bullets. In another poem, "The Schoolteacher Mira," also written in 1943, Mira becomes a symbol of courage in the Ghetto. Her class diminishes overnight from 130 children to only 40. She organizes a choir and teaches her children a hopeful song of spring. Mira Borenstein was a teacher in the Vilna Ghetto. She was deported and murdered in Treblinka.

In the "Secret Town," Sutzkerer combines his technical poetic skills with the main themes that dominate his poetry. It is a long poem which describes the survival of a group of ten Jews in sewers beneath the Vilna Ghetto.

Ten Jews, a symbolic number, cling to life in the filth and darkness of Vilna's subterranean canals. They defy darkness and dream about freedom, peace and the heroic resurrection of the Jewish people. Among the ten men was the poet. He survived in order to bear witness to suffering which must be transformed into beauty.

Sutzkerer's poem, "*A Vogn Shikh*" (A Freight Car of Shoes), was written in Vilna on January 7, 1943. It is a ballad with an initial strophe that is repeated in the last refrain. The poem is dominated by the rhythm and sound of the rolling train and the exclusive focus on inanimate objects—shoes. Piles of shoes are being taken to Berlin, shoes that belonged to brides, mothers, children: to people that are gone forever.

> There is no one I can ask,
> but it pains me in my heart:
> O shoes, tell me the truth,
> Where are they, the feet?

There is literally no one left to reply. The inanimate objects are all that are left. Yet, they have a strange life of their own, an echo of the "dance Macabre," the shoes click together in the rhythm of the moving train.

> The shoes—a full car load
> Like the people in a dance.

Inanimate objects that belonged to the victims very often assume a living dimension and the personalities of their dead owners. These things become their only extension, the only link between the dead and the living. With the absence even of a grave or a tombstone, any inanimate object becomes a cherished object. Shoes loom large in many poems, perhaps due to the fact that shoes, more than any other object, assume the personality of their owners. In a similar vein, Isaiah Spiegel (b. 1906) writes about his father's boots (Howe and Greenberg, eds., p. 349):

> Patched
> and cleated
> my father's boots
> are lying in the sand
> on the Auschwitz hill.
>
> From your holy patched boots,
> From your holy shining cleats,
> I hear you say in me:
> My son, with these patched boots

And these shining cleats
I can even go to meet the Messiah.

With everything destroyed and gone forever, his father's boots are the only
visual link with the dead, the past. (The identical motif is repeated in Ka-
Tzetnik's *Star Eternal*. However, the "inanimate" motif in Holocaust literature reaches its highest artistic expression and psychological insight in "The
Coat" by Chaim Grade.) The line between the living, lone surviving poet and
the inanimate object, is blurred. The poet and the object become interchange-
able aspects of one another, and both are extensions into the present of the
dead and the past. Even the cobblestones assume human dimensions. In the
empty streets of the ghetto there are only skulls, heads, faces. The closing
stanza also contains a common motif in Holocaust literature: at the edge of devastation there is a faint echo of redemption.

With the destruction of Eastern European Jewry, a community with its rich
life in *shtetl* and city, the Yiddish poet was forever uprooted from his source
of inspiration. After the War, all literary disputes that divided Jewish poets
disappeared as they now seemed trivial. The memory of the Holocaust became the decisive unifying force.

In their looking homeward, these poets seem to be returning to an old
direction—to God (Howe and Greenberg, ed., p. 289-90):

> In the desolation of memory, Yiddish poets find themselves turning back to
> the old Jewish God, not so much the God of Orthodoxy or event, the God
> their fathers had worshipped, but a God inseparable from Jewish fate, a God
> with whom one pleads and quarrels. It is as if, in a depopulated world, there
> must at least be someone to talk with: some figure or force, even if projected
> through images of denial and in accents of reproach, in whom the sheer
> possibility of meaning continues to reside.

As if God, whatever his projected image might be, is the only remaining link
with the past, a spiritual Wailing Wall, a remnant from a glorious past. Since
it is useless to talk to men, and the poet must speak, since silence is impossible, the poet turns to God.

Kadia Molodowsky speaks to God in anger (Howe and Greenberg, p. 331):

O God of Mercy
For time being
Choose another people.
We are tired of death, tired of corpses,
We have no more prayers.
For time being
Choose another people.

Jacob Glatstein conducts a dialogue with God:

> I love my sorrowful God,
> My wandering brother.
> I love to sit down with him on a stone
> And talk my heart out to him.

Wherever he may be, the Jewish poet is compelled to turn to God. Aaron Zeitlin in his poem *"Ani Maamin"* offers a most passionate expression of faith (in Howe and Greenberg, pp. 321–5). In one of his shorter poems, "Being a Jew," Zeitlin looks upon the turning to God, even for the non-believer, as the very essence of being Jewish.

> Being a Jew means running forever to God
> Even if you are his betrayer,
> Means expecting to hear any day,
> Even if you are a nay sayer,
> The blare of the Messiah's horn.

The motif, God and the Holocaust, is more pronounced in post-Holocaust Yiddish poetry; yet, it is not unique to it. This motif is found in the Holocaust poetry of Israelis, including Nathan Alterman (1902–1970) and Uri Zevi Greenberg (b. 1894). Greenberg, in bitter and sarcastic lines, explodes, "Sit, sit God in Your heavens." God, the Redeemer of Israel, has become "the keeper of the Jewish cemetery." More than others, Uri Zevi Greenberg is the prophet-poet of the Holocaust. Long before the event, Greenberg foresaw the European Holocaust and his poetry was obsessed with visions of horror. The Holocaust, in his view, was the culmination of two thousand years of Christian-Jewish hostile relations. Unlike Sutzkerer, he is less concerned with formal and aesthetic problems. For him, poetry is a medium to express his all-consuming ideologies. This does not preclude his employment of European poetic traditions. He draws mainly from Jewish sources, from Bible to Kabbalah, making the translation of his poetry a challenge even for the most skilled translator. Greenberg combines his national poetry with his personal history and turns it into a mythos, a unique combination of the European and Jewish traditions.

With little doubt, the two best known poems on the Holocaust, especially in Europe, are Celan's "Death Fugue" and Yevtushenko's poem "Babi Yar." One of the most outstanding European poets after the War, Paul Celan (1920–1970) was preoccupied with the search for a living language, a poetic voice echoing silence as well as speech. Though he was born in Czernowitz, Bokovina, Celan wrote in German. His Jewish parents were murdered in a concentration camp while he was sent to a forced labor camp. In his poem "Death Fugue" (*Todesfuge*) (1952), Celan attempted to reconcile language with silence. He writes:

> Black milk of daybreak we drink it at nightfall
> we drink at noon in the morning we drink it at night
> drink it and drink it
> we are digging a grave in the sky it is ample to lie there
> A man in the house plays with the serpents he writes
> he writes when the night falls to Germany your golden hair
>   Margarete
> he writes it and walks from the house the stars glitter
>   he whistles his dogs up
> he whistles his Jews out and orders a grave to be dug
>   in the earth
> he commands us now on with the dance

The first sign of the fragmentation of language is the lack of formal punctuation. In the poem's meter, in the poem's rhythm, one clearly hears the rhythm of trains. This sound of moving trains dominates many Holocaust poems; e.g., the poetry of Plath, Sutzkerer, Bochert. The metaphors used by Celan in 1952 have become common in Holocaust poetry. Celan continues:

> A master from Germany death comes with eyes that are blue
> Your golden hair Margarete
> Your ashen hair Shulamith

Blue eyes—the Germans as a master race—are motifs that reoccur in poetry identifying the Nazi-tormentor (e.g., "Daddy" by Sylvia Plath).

In a bitter ironic twist, another author, who writes under the name Ka-Tzetnik (prisoner), ridicules German "scientific" racist theory. Ka-Tzetnik describes his innocent Jewish sister murdered by the Nazis:

> My sister's hair was long and curly, the color
> of ripe gold
> My sister's eyes were blue like sky

Margarete's golden hair represents ideal German womanhood. One is immediately reminded of Goethe's heroine (*Faust*) of the same name. Shulamith's ashen hair suggests both death and color, ash being another constantly reoccurring metaphor. Celan's poem is a contradiction in color with gold and ash being dominant.

A generation after its composition, "the fugue of death" can be discussed within a much larger "tradition" of an emerging Holocaust literature. Yet, its initial impact still remains. One is still struck by a description of a reality where speech is lethal and silence is laden with terror. Words and silence are so orchestrated, simultaneously, that the reader encounters a paradox of silence and speech, silence and terror, a task which words alone cannot achieve.

Yevgeny Yevtushenko's (b. 1933) poetry continually shifts from the most intimate to the most public themes. One can sense both the European influence and that of the Russian poets of the 1920's and 1930's. With the possible exception of "Death Fugue," "Babi Yar" is the single best known poem on the Holocaust (September 19, 1961). Written in topical verse, it deals with historical and political events—the mass grave at Babi Yar, a ravine at the outskirts of Kiev and the refusal of the Khrushchev regime to erect a monument on the site. (In the summer of 1976, the newly built monument of Babi Yar was unveiled.) Probably the best known international poem, after Celan's "Death Fugue," partially because of Shostakovich's Thirteenth Symphony, Babi Yar is especially associated with the murder of over 33,771 Jews on September 29-30, 1941, and tens of thousands of others killed by the Germans and their collaborators during 778 days of the German occupation of Kiev.

In order to cope with the enormity of the crime, in order to grasp the incomprehensible, Yevtushenko, in the best European tradition, reduces the tragedy to a level of individuals. The mass anonymity of the victims assumes individual dimensions. The poet identifies himself with the victim, the Jewish people as a whole. He also identifies strongly with the individual victim.

> I was crucified. I perishing
> Even today the mark of the nails.
> I think also of Dreyfus. I am he.
> The Philistine my judge and my accuser.
> I am also a boy in Bialystok
> The dripping blood spreads across the floor,
> The public-bar heroes are rioting
> I an equal stench of garlic and of drink.

In the well constructed graphic narrative order, Yevtushenko selects an innocent victim to represent the suffering of the Jews. The victims have both universal and Jewish dimensions—Christ, Dreyfus, and the small boy from Bialystok. Both the poet and the reader may find it emotionally easier to identify with these heroes. Their Jewishness is marginal. The boy from Bialystok appeals to the humanitarian, a small suffering child in a bloody pogrom.

The faceless millions murdered during the Holocaust are reduced to recognizable human beings.

I seem to myself like Anna Frank
To be transparent as an April twig
And am in love, I have no need for words,
I need for us to look at one another.

Anne Frank, the best known victim of the Holocaust, becomes the personification for all who perished. The poet can cope with suffering only on an individual level. A young innocent girl in love is being brutally separated from her young lover. The description of the spring of their love, life and season has flashes of brilliance.

In the closing lines of his poem, Yevtushenko assumes his Russian nationality. These lines have more of a political ring than a poetical one.

No Jewish blood runs among my blood,
But I am as bitterly and hardly hated
By every anti-Semite
As if I were a Jew. By this
I am a Russian.

To end a poem like "Babi Yar" with blood as a yardstick for nationality is anti-climactic and ironic, even if the pen was subconsciously guided. Yevtushenko briefly returned to the subject of the Holocaust in "The Bratsk Station" (1966) in which a protagonist, Izi Kramer, a Jewish survivor of a Nazi camp and now an engineer in Siberia, continues to be haunted by his past.

The poems of Sylvia Plath (1932–1963) are more of a personal confessional nature. The majority of the poems in *Ariel* reflect an inner personal world. Three poems, which combine the private with the public, are: "Daddy," "Fever 103°," and "Lady Lazarus," all written in the autumn of 1962, close to her suicide. In all three poems, Sylvia Plath parallels her feelings about the concentration camps and the bombing of Hiroshima to her inner pain.

Plath was not a Holocaust survivor and her "concentration camp universe" was not based on personal experiences. The poetess' use of a set of images derived from the concentration camp experiences poses some questions. In this regard, G. Steiner asks ("In Extremis," p. 305): "Does any writer... other than an actual survivor, have the right to put on his death-rig?... What extraterritorial right had Sylvia Plath... to draw on the reserves of animate horror in the ash and the children's shoes?... Do any of us have license to locate our personal disasters, raw as these may be, in Auschwitz?"

Sylvia Plath's use of concentration camp imagery is indicative of a literary trend which was only at its very beginning in the 1960's, i.e., borrowing concentration camp imagery to describe situations of a victim and a victimizer. The atrocities of the Hitlerian era are at the center of modern thought. They have given rise to poetry, prose, and drama of cruelty and oppression. For the artist who is not a Holocaust survivor, it is a reference point which has now become part of his cultural heritage. It is mainly the ability to reconcile horror with aesthetic creativity that troubles many, including Theodore Adorno and George Steiner.

Sylvia Plath transferred her personal pain onto the greatest possible suffering in Western civilization. Concentration camp imagery was the "natural" choice. The transformation was not to gain a better comprehension of the Holocaust victim, but rather to employ the extreme in human suffering to describe one's own agonies. In "Daddy," Sylvia Plath "maneuvered" herself into the utmost extreme position of a concentration camp victim with all the racial and psychological "credentials."

Her father, Otto Plath, was born in 1885 of pure Prussian descent and came to America when he was fifteen. He died when his daughter was nine. Her mother, Aurelia Plath, is of Austrian descent and could have been Jewish. Given those circumstances, her father could have become a Nazi and her mother, a Jewess, could have been one of the Six Million. In terms of the poem, the mother figure is unimportant. The daughter appropriates the mother's attributes; she becomes the victim, the Jew, while the father becomes the Nazi. In "Lady Lazarus," the companion poem to "Daddy," Plath equates her suffering as a result of her unsuccessful suicide attempt to that of a Jew in a concentration camp.

Despite its artistic and intellectual merit, it is difficult to cope with the aesthetic and moral aspects of Plath's poetry. For example, the father image in Holocaust literature is that of strength, comfort and love. Plath's "Daddy" has nothing in common with literature of the Holocaust, except external descriptions of German-Jew camp relations based on deep-rooted male-female, hate-love relationships. According to A. Alvarez, it is rather an exploitation of Freudian psychology "spoken by a girl with an Electra complex." Steiner's question still haunts us. "Does any writer . . . other than an actual survivor, have the right to put on his death-rig?"

To a generation of Israeli poets, the Holocaust is more than a national, personal memory. As a result, there is a constant undercurrent in their creativity. The Israeli population with its large number of survivors and their children, the struggle for survival within hostile borders, the fears on the eve of the Six Day War and during the Yom Kippur War make the terror of the Holocaust a constant one. The struggle for survival makes the Holocaust an ever-present reality in Israeli literature, even when it is not directly mentioned. Nevertheless, the Holocaust is more central a theme in the works of Israeli authors of European birth than it is in the writings of the native Israelis.

Amir Gilboa (b. 1917) and Yehudah Amichai (b. 1924) were both born in Europe. Both served with the Jewish Brigade in World War II. Both came face to face with the German atrocities, the remnants of European Jewry, and the destruction of their European childhood world. Gilboa first began to publish while serving in the Brigade. In his poems, his childhood and the European landscape are darkened by the Holocaust and the death of his relatives. In his more recent poems, published after the Yom Kippur War, one can sense the fear and terror of an isolated lonely Israel during the war. It strongly echoes the loneliness of the Jew during the Holocaust.

Yehudah Amichai's poetry tends to focus upon individual problems and strivings. His poetry is more of a confessional, personal nature. Yet, his personal history overlaps and coincides with national themes and ideologies. His novel *Not of This Time and Not of This Place* (1967) focuses upon an Israeli seeking revenge upon the Germans who participated in the extermination of the author's native town.

The theme of "My Father Fought Their War for Years" is the tragedy of the twentieth century—war! During World War I the father fought for Germany, with the hope of ending all wars in order that his son might inherit a better world. Now, the son must fight his own wars; however, his share of wars is even greater than his father's. One of these wars is against Germany, his father's country. The bitter irony and the futility of war are common themes in Amichai's poetry.

For Dan Pagis (b. 1930), the Holocaust is a central theme. He was born in Bukavina and during World War II was in a concentration camp. Pagis lives with the memory of annihilation as something he has both experienced and survived. At times, his work is tinged by guilt for having been spared. In "Footprints," one of the major poems on the Holocaust, the theme of survivor-guilt is most pronounced. Pagis does not make any extraordinary attempt to join either the living or the dead; his existence is suspended between life and death.

M. L. Rosenthal refers to Pagis as a poet of survival and compares him to other Eastern European poets who write out of memories of the concentration camps and resistance. However, he is also an Israeli with unique traits:

> But he does not resort to anti-rhetoric, their almost deadpan restraint. Pagis and other Israeli poets have certainly been affected by the reaction against overt emotionalism in the wake of violence to the human spirit that no verbal violence could match . . . They have not, however, had the paralyzing political experience, leading to spiritual isolation, of moving from one kind of brutal repression directly into another. An ultimately humanistic and even romantic affirmation is implicit in Israeli thought and life. (In Carmi and Pagis, p. 100).

Dan Pagis, though also Eastern European, combines in his poetry the prophetic-poetic Jewish tradition, colloquial voices, and a detached intellectual observation of self. It is this unique combination that distinguishes Pagis from other Eastern European poets and gives his poetry a distinct place within Israeli poetry. These qualities are best demonstrated in a short poem called ''Written in Pencil in the Sealed Railway Car.'' This brilliantly written poem is a model of verbal economy. Explosive in content, it leaves the reader breathless, speechless, intellectually agile, and tuned to meaning and sound, as if all that had to be said about the death of six million was cramped into six brief lines. It is a combination of a sacred text, interpreted secularly against the background of the eternal journey to death, beginning with the first sense-less murder of Abel by his brother Cain and concluding with the brutal exter-mination during World War II. The poet and Eve are identical; they both ride the death train with dead Abel, unable to comprehend death, unable even to phrase their pain and bewilderment in words. The question of Eve remains unfinished and thus without an answer, just like our own.

Pagis' imagery is striking both in its poetic vividness of abstract and con-crete forms. It is in a constant state of flux, like colors fading and flowing one into another, never skipping stages, but moving from one state and level to another. In Pagis' poetry, death is up high, a cloud, a smoke; life is below. A ladder with many rungs extends between the various states and levels. There is no skipping of stages. The dominant place of order is evident in a bitter, sarcastic poem ''Draft of a Reparation Agreement.''

> Everything will be returned to its place,
> Paragraph after paragraph.
> The scream back to the throat,
> The gold teeth back to the gums,
> The smoke back to the tin chimney and farther on inside.

His vision of self in the concentration camp universe is an existence in abstracts and demonstrates the most fundamental difference between the skin-deep concentration camp imagery of Plath and soul-deep scars of Pagis. (Pagis' ''Testimony'' is a fine example of this.) Celan wrote ''Death Fugue''—music with words and silence. Pagis painted abstract pictures of the concentration camp landscape with words of mind and memory.

For the European poet and for the Israeli, there can be no escape from the historical memory of the Holocaust. The American poet is less dominated and haunted by the European historical experience. The pre-Holocaust Jewish Europe with its teeming life and bustling creativity, a Europe which is the major undercurrent of the Yiddish poet, is a vague reality for a whole genera-tion of American poets. As sons and daughters of immigrants, the Europe that was destroyed was the land of their grandfathers and grandmothers and not the land of their fathers. Their reaction to the Holocaust is more of a personal individual nature rather than a national one. The extent of their familiarity with Europe was limited to family stories and old photographs. Rhoda

Schwartz (b. 1923) in "Old Photographs" is traveling on a European train: "the train is a black holocaust going through the mountains." The passing sights merge with photographs and the family history.

Other American poets were in the army and encountered the European atrocities as victorious liberators. There was pride in being a liberator, a modern St. George slaying the European dragon. For example, Louis Simpson (b. 1923), a winner of the Pulitzer Prize for Poetry (1964), described that American exhilarated feeling in his poetry.

American self-esteem immediately following the War is expressed in his poem "The Inner Part" (in Chapman, ed., pp. 376–8):

> When they had won the war
> And for the first time in history
> Americans were the most important people . . .

Yet, it is not the victorious mood over Germany's defeat that prevails in American poetry, but rather the initial shock of the concentration camp reality, and coping with one's own emotions upon confronting the Germans.

Unlike Nelly Sachs, the American poet is not inhibited in naming the enemy. Simpson, for example, in his poem "A Story of Chicken Soup" (in Chapman, ed., pp. 374–5), strongly feels that the murdered Jews were his own relations, relatives he knew only from his grandmother's stories told over chicken soup. Despite the embarrassment, he singles out the accused by name. He refers to them as "Germans" rather than "Nazis" (the more common noun in European poetry). His dislike for the Germans is a controlled one. In Simpson's description of a German girl and her "mechanical brothers," there are elements of caricature and black humor. In a poem by C. K. Williams, "A Day for Anne Frank," (1936) the element of black humor, cynicism, and grotesque imagery reaches an extreme.

Irving Feldman, in his poem "Pripet Marshes," attempts to transplant his own non-Holocaust friends into the European reality. He transplants his friends to the marketplace to be deported. A moment before the Germans arrive, he rescues his friends. In this regard, Sidra Ezrahi comments, "The American poet as a creator can rescue his Jews only because they were not the real victims."

Nevertheless Feldman's fantasy cannot roam free. Like most post-Auschwitz poets, Feldman is reconstructing a Holocaust reality. The "novel" element is the American poet's quest to understand and explore the sufferings of the victims and his attempt to identify with them. The intense identification of the American poet with the European victims also occurs in the poetry of Anthony Hecht (1923), a Pulitzer Prize winner for poetry (1968).

Hecht was among the victorious American soldiers in Europe. The sights of the camp haunt him. In his poem, "In the Room," the poet strives to achieve an authentic identification with the victim. He shares with him a common God, a common enemy, a common destiny.

More than any other event, the Holocaust shocked the Jewish artists and intellectuals into realization of their Jewish origins. Irving Howe quotes a statement to that effect by an unidentified intellectual in the aftermath of the Holocaust. In *World of Our Fathers,* Howe writes (p. 607):

> But we knew that but for an accident of geography we might also now be bars of soap... Our Jewishness might have no clear religious or national context, it might be helpless before the criticism of believers; but Jews we were, like it or not, and liked or not.

It is this realization, in the aftermath of the Holocaust, that marks the distinction between the poetry of Sylvia Plath, European poets, and poets of Jewish origin. Their identity with the concentration camp universe, the realization of their fate during the Holocaust, "if not for an accident of geography," provides them with a special insight and identification with the victims' fate.

Charles Reznikoff's (b. 1894) *Kaddish* is based upon the traditional prayer *Kaddish d'Rabbanan.* This is not a *Kaddish* for the dead, but rather a prayer for the living, requesting abundant peace, grace, lovingkindness, mercy, long life, ample sustenance, and salvation. In *"Kaddish,"* Reznikoff enumerates the many sufferings of the Jews prior to, during and after World War II.

In this poem, the concluding words in consecutive stanzas are "peace, safety, a living and life." Unlike other poets who are unwilling to be consoled and to forget and whose imagery is dominated by death, Reznikoff, the Brooklyn-born poet, responds by affirming life. One of his finest poems, *In Memoriam: 1933,* is a fine example of Reznikoff's faith in the Jewish people, despite oppression. Though dominated by elegaic tones, his poems vibrate with affirmations of faith, placing his poetry in the tradition of the Jewish prophet-poet.

Ani Maamin by Elie Wiesel (b. 1928) is a cantata set to music by Darius Milhaud. It reflects the major sources of influences upon Wiesel's writings: Midrashic and Hasidic sources and postwar French literature. *Ani Maamin* is neither poetry nor drama. It does not achieve the poetic and dramatic quality characteristic of other major Holocaust poetry nor of his own literary style. It is basically a dialogue with a silent partner—God. The founders of the Jewish people—Abraham, Isaac and Jacob—confront God. They question His commitment and His promise to the Jewish people in view of the mass destruction of the Jews during the Holocaust.

Through the dialogues, most of the modes of destruction are described, from the open air killings to the gas chambers. It is a cry of despair and anguish with the characteristic themes, motifs and imagery that dominate suffering and loneliness of the individual victim, and the guilt of the survivor for having survived. Images that populate his other works—rabbis, beggars, students—reappear here. The period of the Holocaust is referred to as *Night,* which is a familiar motif from his autobiographical novel, *Night.* Throughout the cantata, Abraham, Jacob and Isaac's confrontations and arguments with God assume a national character, and thus the author deals with the entire people through the individual. The Holocaust experiences of the Jewish people are superimposed upon the Biblical experiences of the forefathers. The lines between past and present, individual and nation, are blurred. Biblical and modern imagery blend. It is here that *Ani Maamin* achieves, at times, glimpses of greatness.

Each of the three forefathers confronts God with an argument based upon his previous personal contacts with God, dealing with His promise that there *would be* a people of Israel. While all three patriarchs confront and argue with God and with the authority and strength of survivors, Isaac emerges as the classical model of a survivor, a theme that Wiesel develops in *The Messengers of God.* Thus, Isaac becomes the symbol of all Jews who went to the slaughter and survived. Despite the national symbolical dimensions of Isaac's sufferings, in *Ani Maamin* Isaac's thoughts during the *Akedah* have Christian overtones. While on the altar, his thoughts do not focus upon the survival of the Jewish people. If sacrificed, Isaac's death would have constituted the annihilation of the Jewish people; nevertheless, Isaac contemplates only his own suffering. Suffering for the sake of suffering was never a Jewish virtue. Isaac's emphasis on suffering, rather than survival, is intriguing. While the Jewish people is central to the arguments of Abraham, Isaac and Jacob, the Land of Israel and the newborn State are marginal. Despite the birth of the State, they are not willing to be consoled.

Wiesel is careful in not linking the Holocaust to the birth of the State of Israel, thus making one event dependent upon the other. Wiesel's heroes are more preoccupied with survival and suffering than they are with the Land and its rebirth. In *The Messengers of God,* where many of the ideas of *Ani Maamin* are fully developed, among the seven messengers of God, conspicuously absent is King David, one of the most central figures in Judaism, a symbol of Messianic redemption and of a physically strong Israel.

Yet, despite the resolution not to be consoled and despite the silence of God, Wiesel concludes *Ani Maamin* with a declaration of faith in the eternity of the Jewish people and in redemption.

The post-Holocaust trials attracted many artists including Peter Weiss, Robert Shaw and Walter Kaufmann. In "Portrait of A Lady," in his *Cain and Other Poems,* Kaufmann describes an interrogation center in Germany in 1945:

> In every cell they tell the same
> as children spell, scared without shame,
> and give no picture, dwelling on the frame.

Though the story was repeated in many cells, it is the same. Yet, the story provides a portrait of an individual: the one becomes the symbol of many.

Eichmann's trial in Jerusalem deals with both the witness and the accused. Kaufmann's poem "Witness" is based upon actual testimony, with the artist re-creating the conversation between child and mother prior to an open air killing. Facing the accused, Eichmann is not just the realization of "the banality of evil" (Arendt), but the bankruptcy of an entire system and a philosophy. For Kaufmann, the trial becomes a literary theme to be both historically and artistically recorded.

The Holocaust also changed the Jewish poets' attitude towards Europe and Germany. Its culture, historical sites, and landscapes which delighted and inspired artists for centuries, became sources for distress and pain.

"More Light More Light," a poem by Anthony Hecht, describes two episodes which deal with death. One is about a religious martyr during the earlier centuries; the other treats murder in a concentration camp. The title of the poem represents the words Goethe is reputed to have spoken on his death bed in Weimar. The Buchenwald concentration camp was built near the site. Goethe's favorite tree was actually in the camp compound. Can one ever seek Goethe's light while Buchenwald is nearby casting its long shadows? Can beautiful Bavaria ever again be to the Jewish artist just a lovely romantic country with excellent beer and smiling blondes?

The Jewish poet cannot find tranquility on German soil. Its forests, stars, birds and trees are ghosts in the land of the dead. For Michael Waters, who could not endure the emotional strain of a prolonged visit to Munich, the "Dachau Moon" was just too much.

The post-Holocaust poetry written in English in America is a poetry of despair. The elements of redemption and hope, common to Jewish poetry written under siege and since liberation, are absent from American poetry. Most often, Holocaust-related poetry is written from an individual confessional vantage point with rare outbursts of national visions in the poet-prophet tradition.

American post-Holocaust poetry completes a cycle in American Jewish literature. It is the *Kaddish* for the "land of the grandfathers." It is summed up by Kaufmann's poem "Religion."

> *Yisgadal v'yiskadash shmay rabo.*
> And the bones came together
> bone to his bone
> an exceeding great army.
> Distant voices from buried worlds
> grandfathers
> and their fathers beyond them
> straight backs

and stakes
and stiff necks
and soon
mountains of false teeth
an exceeding great army
May The Great Name Magnify and Sanctify Itself.

Kaufmann's "vision" is not that of Ezekiel. He does not ask for a new heart
but rather

and the gift of new eyes
not for dreams and visions and refuge
eyes that see dust as dust
without blinking
and the will to endure and defy and prevail.

The apocalyptic-messianic vision is not part of Kaufmann's poetry, nor is it a
dominant one. In other Jewish-American poetry, one of the undercurrents is
the realization of one's orgins and the affirmation of one's will to exist, to
survive and to defy the realities of the post-Auschwitz world—a conclusion
diametrically opposed to Sylvia Plath and Tadeusz Borowski. What Elie
Wiesel wrote about Kaufmann's poetry may be applied to post-Holocaust
poetry in general:

> Here, poetic vision and philosophical quest fuse movingly, eloquently: Wal-
> ter Kaufmann's song, in a world doomed by words, does not sin against
> silence. These poems full of vision and power prove that poetry, after Au-
> schwitz, is not only possible but also necessary.

DRAMA

The playwright, writing on the Holocaust, shares identical difficulties with
the Holocaust novelist and poet. He, too, must transform the unspeakable
atrocities of the Hitlerian era into words. He, too, must travel from documentation to art, from the horrors of the Holocaust to their imaginative realization
in literature. His creative task does not stop here, for he must carry the literary
imagination one step beyond the written word, back to its visual realization on
stage. There is no longer a word on a page between the artist and the audience,
but a controlled visual reality. Of those writing about the Holocaust, the
playwright's task may well be the most difficult and vulnerable one. The
playwright cannot hope to find guidance in either Western or Jewish tradition.
The mass anonymity of the victims and the overwhelming atrocities have

neither a precedent in Western drama nor in Jewish literature (where drama is a relative newcomer to millennia-old literary traditions). Can the medium of the stage convey the message of Auschwitz without minimizing or distorting the reality of that huge European wasteland?

In *The Theatre and its Double* Antonin Artaud (1896–1948) charts a new course for the theatre. His views have had a powerful impact upon the aesthetics of contemporary drama. His book was published in 1938 before Hitler's atrocities assumed monstrous proportions. Artaud argued for a return to drama as a primitive rite concerned with elemental human needs and emotions. Drama must protest artificial values imposed by a rationalistic culture. Such drama would repudiate established conventions and forms of the modern theatre with its reliance on texts, speech, plot, psychological analysis, and the proscenium arch in favor of purely irrational assemblage of sounds where gestures symbolize ideas and effigies and bizarre objects signify cosmic forces hostile to man. Audiences must be submitted to the maximum theatrical experience in order to undermine their assurance and revive latent external forces inside themselves and ranging outside of themselves. To make the theatre believable, providing ''the heart and the senses that kind of a concrete bite which true sensations requires,'' Artaud advocated the exteriorization of a depth of latent cruelty by means of which all the perverse possibilities of the mind, whether of an individual or a people, are localized. On the eve of the War, Artaud wrote as if, by means of his artistic intuition, he sensed the atrocities of World War II.

Artaud's avant-garde theories offer new vistas in the attempt to cope with the Holocaust on stage; nevertheless, the challenge to the artist remains monumental. Relatively few playwrights attempt to approach the subject and even fewer theatres dare to produce Holocaust plays. The European playwrights, especially in Western Europe, have taken the lead. The New York and London stage have also made significant contributions. The Israeli theatre, subsidized by the national and municipal government, has made only a token attempt to promote Holocaust-related drama.

Joze Szajna, the director of the Polish studio theatre, survived Buchenwald and Auschwitz. At the time of his liberation he promised that he would not allow the world to forget what happened during the War. His production, *Replika,* looks like a fulfillment of Artaud's theory. *Replika* is a wordless odyssey through the Holocaust; only a few single words are uttered throughout the duration of the entire play. The stage is filled with bizarre objects, effigies, piles of clothes and shoes. The actors convey their plight in grotesque, horrifying and graceful movements. *Replika* attempts to recreate Auschwitz, to reproduce man's indomitable spirit, tempered by the inhumanity directed against him by himself.

The Investigation by Peter Weiss is a condensed presentation of the trials of twenty-one individuals who participated in the destruction of millions of people at Auschwitz in the years 1941–1945. (These trials were held in

Frankfurt, Germany, in 1964 and 1965.) Weiss chose a new way to bring those events to the stage. The dialogue of *The Investigation* was not invented but consists of actual passages selected from the testimony of the accused and their accusers. It has been distilled to bring out what is essential to the author's vision. In the reproduction of the Auschwitz trials, in the form of an oratorio in eleven cantos, Weiss documents the negative achievements of a civilization: the use of concentrated power of a modern technology by a sophisticated leadership to draw a highly civilized people into an active or passive destruction of a segment of its own population.

Barbaric lawless acts unfold on an austere stage with no attempt to reconstruct a courtroom; nevertheless, the drama develops with the strict logic of court procedure. The judge and the attorney ask their questions; the named accused and nameless witnesses tell their story. There is no personal drama in the play, and all questions and answers are delivered in a monotone. There is no punctuation in the free-verse text, nor are there stage instructions. There is only a prefatory note which is partially cited here (p. ix):

> Personal experience and confrontations must be steeped in anonymity. Inasmuch as the witnesses in the play lose their names, they become mere speaking tubes. The nine witnesses sum up what hundreds expressed. . . .

Can an audience cope with the anonymity, bleakness and historical facts of the Auschwitz planet being recited in a monotone for the entire duration of the play? Distilled, shocking reality and the naked facts of atrocities are recited on stage. Can the audience transcend the notion of an observer?

Weiss is uncompromising in his refusal to allow the audience any form of classical catharsis. His drama is unyielding in its insistence on unmitigated evil. Yet, there seems to be a need for an aesthetic distance to modify realities. The artist's imagination must serve as a buffer between the historical event and the stage; otherwise, it may lapse into a repulsive experience. In *Marat/Sade,* Weiss brilliantly achieved such a transformation of an historical event into a theatrical experience.

Unlike *The Investigation,* Wolfgang Borchert's (1921–1947) *The Outsider* is written in an hysterical uncontrolled fury. Borchert was part of the Nazi system. Severely crippled on the Eastern front, he died at the age of twenty-six, on the day before the opening of his play. *The Outsider* concerns a crippled soldier, Beckman, who returns home to find his family gone and his house destroyed. Disillusioned, he jumps into the Elbe, cluttered with suicides. The play treats Beckman's futile attempt to find a place where he belongs after the Elbe spewed him out. He continues in his search but is unwanted everywhere. Only the well-fed undertaker is cheerful. The play ends when Beckman curses all who have rejected him, including the "Little Old Man Who Used To Be God."

Though the play does not deal with Germany's guilt towards other people, it is a perfect example of postwar German youth's disillusionment with the system which ruined their country and the best years of their lives. In its style, this play is a re-creation of Expressionism—where the human race and the entire cosmos are observed through the eyes of one character.

Like *The Investigation,* Rolf Hochhuth's play *The Deputy* was written in 1963, almost a generation after the events depicted. Like Weiss, Hochhuth bases his drama upon actual events. Hochhuth rejects extreme naturalism in art which, according to him, must fail when competing with the daily mass media for conveying a shocking effect. He also seems to reject the aesthetic approach which would transform the Holocaust into a detached metaphor, where victims and tormentors are turned into pure symbols. Throughout the play, Hochhuth relentlessly forces his audience into emotional involvement and moral judgment. For Hochhuth, the audience must confront reality and has no options of viewing it as a fantasy. Both the text and stage direction do not allow that lapse. Even the closing moments of the play during the shift from Auschwitz reality to the unemotional voice of an announcer on tape are a masterpiece of blending the literary creative imagination with the historical event.

Unlike Weiss, Hochhuth avoids anonymity. All major characters have names and are recognizably modeled after historical personalities. The only one unidentified by name is "the Doctor," who is modeled after the "Angel of Death," Dr. Mengele. Giving him a name would place this diabolic figure in the company of men. Since condensation of historical events has been necessary in the interest of drama, Hochhuth added an historical appendix to verify the historical reliability of both persons and events mentioned in the play.

In Borchert's *The Outsider,* the blame is placed on the German system. In *The Investigation,* guilt is diffused through the Nazi ranks and even taints the victims. The Western World is guilty: tormentor and victim alike. Hochhuth locates the guilt within individuals. He especially singles out Pope Pius XII, Christ's *deputy* on earth, for censure. Hochhuth stigmatizes the Pope for failing to protest and for remaining silent while six million Jews were murdered. The Pope is blamed as an individual who failed to use his powerful position. The blame falls upon a person rather than upon an institution. Father Riccardo Fontana and Kurt Gerstein, in their self-sacrificing acts of heroism, acted as individuals guided by deep personal convictions: that man must exercise his fundamental freedom and that, indeed, he is his brother's keeper. The play's theatrical power stems from the author's use of heightened verse dialogue mixing colloquialisms with ecclesiastical and Nazi Party jargon.

Arthur Miller's play *Incident at Vichy* does not have Hochhuth's historical scope. It is based upon a single incident told him by a friend. Fifteen years later, this episode materialized into a play. *Incident at Vichy* dramatizes approximately ninety minutes in the lives of a few men in a detention room in

Vichy, in the autumn of 1942. They sit on a long bench near the door of an inner office awaiting the mysterious interrogation that will decide their fate. They represent a cross section of European society including a waiter, an electrician, an actor, a nobleman, a psychiatrist, a gypsy, and a Jew. The gypsy sits alone at the edge of the bench, and the old Jew, his fate sealed, sits with his mysterious bundle and does not utter a word. The play touches upon the common themes of Holocaust literature, including disbelief in the German atrocities. When speaking about the camps and the furnaces, Monceau the actor says, "What good are dead Jews to them? They want free labor. It's senseless. You can say whatever you like, but the Germans are not illogical" (p. 37). But the preoccupation of the play is not with the villainy of Nazism; it is rather with the involvement of human beings with justice and injustice, guilt, self-preservation, and commitment to others.

The play lacks the dramatic fascination of Miller's earlier plays. The actions are compressed, linear, and void of any virtuosity and intricacy. Instead, Miller aims a blunt blow at his audience. The element of surprise comes at the very last moment, when Von Berg walks out from the interrogation office, a free man, and gives his pass to Leduc. In this last move, Von Berg shows Leduc that guilt can be particularized and transformed from masochistic despair into responsibility—guilt for being a survivor and responsibility to transform it into something more positive than self-pity.

The Man in the Glass Booth by Robert Shaw (b. 1927) is among the most dramatic plays dealing with the theme of Holocaust-related trials. Unlike the plays by Weiss and Miller, the strength of Shaw's play lies not in its original structure but in its dramatic and startling impact.

Arthur Goldman, a New York tycoon who has built his own real-estate empire since 1947, is the central character of the play. Throughout the play the author assumes that both the reader and the audience are thoroughly familiar with the Holocaust and its aftermath. To a degree, the dramatic impact of the play depends upon this assumption that the audience understands the inner, tormented world of Arthur Goldman.

Arthur Goldman goes to great lengths to "document" his own "guilt" as if he were a Nazi *Einsatzgruppen* commander. He achieves his aim. Goldman is abducted and brought to stand trial in Israel. The overtones from the Eichmann trial are quite apparent and dominant. This detracts from the artistic quality of the play, and prevents both reader and audience from penetrating the unique tragedy of Arthur Goldman—the need of the victim to assume the personality of his persecutor. In Goldman's case, the persecutor is his own cousin, the Nazi colonel Dorff. Robert Shaw knows the stage well. In the process of transformation from Goldman to Dorff, Shaw reaches the finest moments of the play. Shaw spares no one. All are guilty, both during the War and afterwards. Nothing was learned from the past.

The play is very compact. The transition from one abrupt situation to another is very smooth and creates a dramatically startling effect. At times, however, the compact form of the play is detrimental. The supporting characters are much more real and believable in Shaw's novel upon which the play is based. More apparent in the novel are the past of Mr. Goldman, the horror of the Nazi concentration camp and Goldman's fascination with it, and Nazi superiority. Also, Goldman's tragedy is more intensely felt in the novel. In the play, it is reduced at times to the level of shock treatment. For the American reader and audience, the play is of great importance, for it deals with the Holocaust in familiar surroundings and with genuinely American characters.

Erwin Sylvanns, like Weiss, Hochhuth, Miller and Robert Shaw, is also concerned with guilt: not the guilt of the protagonists on stage, but the guilt of the German public in the theatre. Upon returning to Germany, Sylvanns was horrified by the rapidity with which the Germans had succeeded in repressing all consciousness of their guilt or in transferring it to the dead. To shake them out of their forgetfulness, he wrote a play about the murder of Jewish children in the Warsaw Ghetto, *Dr. Korczak and the Children*. In order to enlist audience participation, Sylvanns hit upon a brilliant device. He selected a man who enjoys great sympathy in Germany—Dr. Korczak—but instead of telling Korczak's tragic story, he has the audience watch a group of people like themselves. Actors become affected by the story as they rehearse it. The actors have the same background as the audience, with the same likes and prejudices. From the first lines, Sylvanns establishes his rapport with the audience by allowing the actors to identify with the audience's prejudices. Sylvanns hoped that through these theatrical experiences and involvements the audience would realize that the ''characters'' are not characters but people like themselves

The Israeli playwright Gavriel Dagan, in a short play *The Reunion,* also aims at his immediate audience. He tries to prove to them that Jewish resistance within the Nazi system was almost impossible. To convey the message to the audience, he turns a friendly gathering between the playwright and his friends in a central European hotel suite in 1970 into a nightmarish experience. Within minutes, the guests comply with their oppressors and offer no resistance, in a play cleverly staged by the host. Like Sylvanns, Dagan's major concern is the audience, to show them that they, under similar conditions, would have behaved the same way.

Nelly Sachs' play *Eli: A Mystery Play of the Sufferings of Israel* also focuses on a central question: Why do the innocent suffer? It takes place in the market place of a small Polish town. Eli, an eight-year-old child, was murdered there during the War (p. 314):

> in his nightshirt and
> his pipe in his hand

> the pipe he had played in the fields
> to lamb and to calf

The play consists of seventeen brief scenes with Hasidic and mystical elements. It was written, Nelly Sachs tells us in the postscript, in a few nights, after her flight to Sweden. The play's poetic qualities surpass its dramatic strength.

Charlotte Delbo, in *Till Human Voices Wake Us,* is not concerned with guilt or with any other post-Holocaust obsession. As a playwright, she assumes the unmitigated position of an eyewitness, a survivor who was spared so that she may tell unbelievable stories of her survival which survivors themselves do not comprehend.

The play is about a women's death camp, a camp with thousands of women of various nationalities, including a newly arrived transport of two hundred French women. The play centers around twenty-three of these women between the ages of sixteen and thirty with the exception of Helen's mother, who is forty years old. It is an all female cast. The stage is a bleak place with an inclined plane to suggest the roll call square. The women are dressed in shapeless grey dresses (no stripes) with grey and other drab kerchiefs. Faces, including eyelids and lips, are powdered in grey. The story that unfolds on stage is of disease, hunger, suicide, torture, and all the other horrifying realities of a death camp and the will to cling to life, if only to bear witness. It is the agony of seven days in which each minute is a lifetime. On the eighth day in camp, Yvonne sums up her concentration camp experience (p. 12):

> I believed that nothing could divest a human being of his pride. Nothing
> except dysentery. You can no longer look at yourself when you gradually
> dissolve, turning into dirty water.

Charlotte Delbo does not spare the public the concentration camp universe with its sights, sounds and language. It is all enacted on stage as if she is constantly saying to the audience that the least you can do is to endure it and comprehend it on stage so that you may prevent it from becoming a reality again.

Not all playwrights who have tried to depict the atrocities of the Holocaust confront it as directly as Weiss, Borchert and Delbo. Friedrich Dürrenmatt (b. 1921) resorts to cynicism and tragicomedy. There are ways of bringing Auschwitz to the audience by not bringing the death camp to the stage but by inventing similar situations. *The Visit,* in which the grotesque revenge of a rich, old lady exposes her native town in a garish satirical light, is a fine example. He justifies his dramatic technique in his essay "Theatre Problems" (1955) as being the only one valid for this apocalyptically absurd age, an age when we are all collectively guilty, enmeshed in the sins of our fathers and of our fathers' fathers. We are simply the children of our fathers. This is not our guilt but, rather, our misfortune. Comedy alone is suitable for us.

Max Frisch (b. 1911), in *The Fire Raisers,* resorts to comedy and parables to attack the complacent irresponsibility of the average citizen who appeases and encourages the fire-raisers, the amoral. Every man's behavior in an incendiary world is criminal. One of Frisch's greatest plays is *Andora,* a tragedy about anti-Semitism and the destructiveness of complacency and prejudice. Unlike Dürrenmatt, who establishes a detachment from his characters, Frisch is involved with them.

In the Spring of 1973, the Uruguayan National Theatre produced a play on the Holocaust, *Yom Kippur,* by Louis Novas Terrara (Newlander). It is a play within a play, a farce dominated by black humor. It is an episode about three Jews in a death camp: an assimilated banker, a beggar, and a rabbi named Adolf. The Nazi executioners order the three inmates to put on an amusing play. If the inmates succeed in humoring the Nazis, they score points for each successful attempt. One hundred points will give them their lives. The audience is identified with the imaginary Nazi officers. It is to this silent audience that the three actors appeal for points and for life. The play takes place on Yom Kippur, the holiest of all Jewish holidays. For props and scenery, the three actors use objects taken from other murdered inmates. They fail to humor the Nazis and are short of points; hence, they are condemned to die. The play concludes with a shocking element of cannibalism. This play is at times an expression of some aspects of the Artaud and the Dürrenmatt theories, with a touch of Jakov Lind's characteristics; yet it is neither of them. It remains a replica of the authentic concentration camp universe. This macabre setting is neither a distortion of reality nor the creation of an illusory world. It retains the authentic reality of the ''other planet'' which made the events of *Yom Kippur* both probable and possible.

In *Mister Runaway,* Lilliane Atlan attempts to write a play on the Holocaust removed from any aspect of documentation. Interviewed in Tel-Aviv on the eve of the play's opening, she said ''what is taking place in my play is not from the realm of literature, it is not from the realm of the Holocaust, but from the realm of the imagination'' (ben Shaul, p. 21).

The play is about four Jewish children, two boys and two girls; a doll, representing their dead friend Tamar; and a German soldier. After the destruction of the ghetto they survive in sewers. On the eighth day they emerge, starved, delirious, and clothed in rags. They are caught by the waiting Germans. The children are placed on a truck that will take them to their final destination—the valley of the bones. A German soldier joins them. He is a strange, slightly mad fellow nicknamed ''Mr. Runaway.'' During the journey towards their death with Mr. Runaway, he tells them stories to forget death. It turns out to be a strange, horrifying adventure of life. Under the influence of Mr. Runaway, the children, starved and on the fringe of madness, tell their stories. They pretend and play games, such as "going to school," "being an adult," "getting married," "being prominent," and "getting old." They imagine the truck to be the land, the sea, and the forest. They act out their lives, which in reality they will never be permitted to live. Their tragic last journey ends when they reach the valley of the bones. When they are murdered, it is as if they die from old age and not from the German bullets. Their journey lasted a lifetime. The least that man's imagination could offer them was a dignified death.

The stage is dominated by the imaginary truck, the five passengers, the doll, and the guards dressed in green. It creates a peculiar blend of reality, illusion, and madness. Lilliane Atlan feels that documentation limits the creative imagination. For her, theatre is almost a religious experience, where there is a special bond between the audience and the actors; like a synagogue, each is an individual and suddenly all are united together (ben Shaul, p. 21). She is dominated by Artaud's reverence for the theatre as a universal place of prayer.

The few plays written in Israel after the Holocaust are not based upon extensive documentation like *The Deputy,* nor are they exclusively from the realm of imagination like *Mister Runaway,* but rather they develop from the survivor's experience and post-Holocaust reality. Where German guilt is only marginal, the Israeli playwright is concerned with the fate of the survivor, his ability or inability to cope with reality, and the central place in his life of Israel—the only positive force and solution for the Jewish survivor and for others seeking justice.

Yehuda Amichai's *Bells and Trains* is a powerful short radio play about the visit of Hans Wolf, now Yohanan, to an old-age home in his native town, Singburg. The old-age home was built by the German government "out of guilty feelings." It is a paradise of ghosts in the midst of a German town where many of its thriving businessmen were former SS and Gestapo men. In the background, the church bells toll and the trains run on their punctual schedules. The old live by those painful sounds and their ghastly memories. Each old person lives with his or her dead. Hans feels that he is like Orpheus who went down to hell to fetch his dead. He wants to bring his aunt to Jerusalem, but she belongs in Singburg among the living-dead. The old-age home assumes symbolic dimensions of the death of Jewish civilization in Europe, and the visitor from Jerusalem symbolizes the continuity of Jewish life.

Leah Goldberg's *Lady of the Manor* takes place in Europe in 1947. A librarian from the land of Israel, Michael Zand, and Dr. Dora Ringel, a social worker for Youth Aliyah, are in Europe on a mission; Zand is seeking rare Jewish manuscripts scattered by the Germans, and Dora seeks Jewish children in monasteries, convents, and other hiding places. They are forced by a raging storm to spend the night in the manor, where Zand was looking for manuscripts. The watchman reluctantly allows them to spend the night there. During the evening, a most ideological conversation develops among the three.

Each represents a different theological trend of the forties. During the course of the conversation, they learn that the watchman is the former owner of the manor, a Count, who after the Communist takeover, became the watchman. During World War II, the castle served as Gestapo headquarters and the Count was one of the most prominent members of the Resistance.

When Zand is left alone in the library, he touches an old cuckoo clock. The clock strikes ten. A secret door opens in the wall and a beautiful, bewildered young girl appears. Zand learns that her name is Lena. Saved by the Count during the War, she lives in constant fear in her hiding place, thinking that the War is still going on. The Count did not tell Lena that the War had ended over two years ago. She is the only thing left to the Count in his lonely, crumbling world, and he clings to her even if the price is deceiving the only person whom he loves. The girl, the lady of the manor, lives in an imaginary world of which she is a prisoner. Zand and Dora urge her to leave the manor and start a new life in Israel among her people and her peers.

It is a very simple plot, a mixture of ideological overtones and fairy tale touches. Neither the structure nor the language reflects the fine poetic style of Leah Goldberg. In Israel, the play is a favorite. The fairy tale element appeals to the younger generation since it lacks the usual morbidity associated with the Holocaust. The librarian and the social worker are true-to-life characters of the late forties and early fifties, and strike a chord of familiarity with a segment of the Israeli population. The theme, rescue of Jewish children after the War, is also a familiar subject. Thousands of similar episodes took place in real life. It is a pleasant play about the Holocaust where the horrors of the Holocaust are absent and the more profound questions are not asked. The play was staged in New York but was not a critical success.

Ben-Zion Tomer's play *Children of the Shadows* begins thematically where Goldberg's play ends, with the attempt of a young boy, a survivor, to rebuild his life. He came to the Land of Israel at the age of fourteen with the ''Teheran children,'' a group of children that managed to survive on their own in the Russian-Asiatic countryside. Unlike George Kaiser in his play *The Raft of the Medusa* (1943) and William Golding's novel *The Lord of the Flies,* Tomer is not interested in the children's savage struggle for survival, but, rather, their attempt to achieve normalcy in the post-Holocaust reality.

Yoram, the protagonist of the play, is twenty-eight years old. He was fourteen when he came to Israel. In his attempt to acculturate and assimilate into Kibbutz reality, he denies his past, changes his name from Yossele to Yoram, and severs all ties with friends and family. He succeeds and even marries a ''sabra,'' a native Israeli, named Nurit. In the fifties, the wave of new immigrants brings to Israel his family and friends and other Holocaust survivors. The past starts to haunt him day and night. His wife, Nurit, despite her attempts, finds it very difficult to cope with the unfamilar ''dark side'' of her husband.

Both Nurit and Yoram are followed by a mysterious stranger. He is a

homeless, lonely, half-crazed man, who sleeps on a bench at the Tel-Aviv boardwalk. The only man to whom he occasionally responds is a balloon seller who is also a survivor. The mysterious stranger refers to himself as ''Medusa—a kind of jellyfish who has no words.'' Yoram discovers that Medusa is Dr. Sigmund Rabinowitz, his brother-in-law, who, prior to the War, was a famous humanist and authority on Renaissance art. He lost his family during the War and paid a high price for his own survival—Sigmund cooperated with the Nazis.

In the final conversation between Yoram and Sigmund, Tomer delivers the finest dialogue of the play. When Yoram demands an explanation, Sigmund replies (p. 74):

> You want to understand, to understand . . . Here you will find the story of a certain commandment [commandant] of a concentration camp. . . . A boyhood friend of mine . . . A German . . . We studied together at Heidelberg . . . A humanist . . . He had a special way of torturing me: once a week he would invite me to discuss with him the future of humanity. Once he said to me: You Jews have given us Marx, Freud, Einstein, Heine. . . . But only Heine grasped the essential thing about the German temperament . . . that we've remained fire worshippers to this day. I want you to understand that I was a human being, and the most terrible thing of all was that they were human too. . . .

Unlike Yoram, Sigmund is unable to forget and unable to reconcile his pre-Holocaust humanism with his own behavior during the Holocaust and his post-Holocaust existence. Even madness is no escape. The guilt is overpowering. His only way out is suicide. The part of Sigmund with his tormented inner world was played by the late Aaron Maskin with superb inner strength and sensitivity.

Tomer is not interested in German guilt, a theme so common to German and other European plays. His main theme is the Jewish survivor's struggle with rehabilitation. For a country like Israel, where Holocaust survivors comprise a high percentage of the population, this has been one of the most difficult problems. In Children of the Shadows, young survivors like Yoram and Helenka are afraid of life; yet, youth is in their favor and they are able to overcome. Tomer seems to imply that ''normalcy'' for the adult survivor is a difficult task, beyond realization. In the waves of the ocean Sigmund finds the solution. Another survivor is selling balloons, a symbolic occupation of nothingness. Israeli society and its attempt to ''absorb'' the survivors is marginal to the play and is represented by Dubi and Nurit.

In The Last Jew by Uri Assaf and Yaffa Eliach, the lives of two generations are constantly marred by the trauma of the Holocaust. The children are Vladimir, a convert to Judaism, the son of a collaborator who murdered the Jews of Eisyski in 1941, and his wife Bluma, the daughter of the Last Jew. Both

Vladimir and Bluma immigrated to Israel from the Soviet Union and are psychiatrists in a mental institute in Israel. Yigal Sinai is an Israeli intelligence officer screening Russian immigrants. The fathers are Schneiderson, Bluma's father—he is the sole adult survivor of Eisyski who continued to live in the town for thirty years—and Levangorski, Schneiderson's business associate who is Vladimir's father and a former Nazi collaborator. Nachummadman and Maphtir-Yonah are two lunatic survivors from Eisyski living in a mental institution in Israel under Vladimir's care.

The protagonists, each from his own perspective, experience the guilt, pride, penance, revenge, and shame forced upon them by the daily events of the Holocaust. The play constantly alternates between the dead and the living, between Eisyski and Israel; flashbacks are dominant. The two madmen are not willing to accept reality. They choose the asylum out of sound calculations and convenience. There, within its walls, they recreate their *shtetl,* Eisyski, with its Eastern European lore and folklore. They are constantly busy constructing a strange surrealistic vehicle inspired by Ezekiel's divine chariot. Their "passengers" are nine life-sized effigies of their town's nine dead notables. They always await the arrival of the mysterious coachman, the tenth man. When Schneiderman, a former coachman, visits the hospital, the confrontation reaches its peak.

The younger generation have the misfortune of being their fathers' children. So eloquently stated by Dürrenmatt, they cannot escape their fathers' world which is now their own. Bluma fights for some share of normalcy, love, and justice. Vladimir is torn between guilt and penance, between Christian concepts and Jewish aspirations. He is forever marked with the sign of Cain as the murderer's son; Yigal Sinai, the Israeli officer, is committed to the idea that his generation will never allow it to happen in Israel.

Can one cope with the Holocaust 365 days every year—especially in a country with a large population of survivors, with a constant flow of new immigrants who reopen old wounds, and with hordes of hostile millions on the borders calling for annihilation? The fundamental issue is the price one had to pay "there" for one's survival. Was survival just a mere chance with fate on the crossroads directing "left and right"? Did only the Schneidermans survive? Are the characters of *The Last Jew* mere individuals involved in their daily personal affairs? As critic Gefen (p. 9) has written about *The Last Jew:*

> There is no doubt that each character in the play has not only its own personal existence but is intentionally symbolic. . . . Each is a defined archetype and as such the meaning of their activities and behavior is different from characters in a regular play.

In *The Last Jew* there is a continuity between the pre-Holocaust and the post-Holocaust eras. The world of the fathers, their ghosts and their guilt, still haunts and torments the lives of their sons and daughters. They attempt to build a better and safer world than the one they witnessed as young children in a Europe filled with dead bodies and decimated cities.

In 1977 a silent switch seems to have occurred in the presentation of the Holocaust in the public media. There was less focus upon the concentration camp universe, destroyed cities, war crimes and trials, but far greater focus upon the more flamboyant aspect of the Hitler-era: Nazi leadership and Hitler himself. Within months, four books on Hitler were published and two of them exceeded one thousand pages. One may attribute this to a new generation born after the Hitlerian era, physically and emotionally less scarred by the events of the World War than those of the previous generation. This new generation is fascinated with the Third Reich and tries to come to terms with the ghosts which clearly haunt the younger generation.

The screen, and, to a lesser extent, the theatre, also seem to follow the trend and the limelight, focusing upon Hitler and Germany's top leadership during the Second World War.

Three young Germans, among them two composers in their twenties (Walter Quintas and Lothar Siems), have written a new rock opera fittingly entitled *Der Fuhrer*. This rock opera, designed for stage production, traces Hitler's and Nazi Germany's bloody history: the burning of books, the murdering of Jews, the misery and destruction of war, and the War's ignominious end. The musical opens to the haunting, unholy sounds of an occult seance in which a Faust-like Hitler enters into a pact with Satan. Hitler promises Satan that he understands the pact and will do as commanded. In the end, when Hitler screams "there, there, over in the corner—it is he. It's he come for me!", the devil returns to take his prize. Joseph Goebbels, the Nazi propaganda minister, figures as an evil spirit and the devil's advocate. Eva Braun, Hitler's mistress and wife for the last few hours of his life, is the helpless victim of misled love. One of the recurrent leitmotifs is the yearning of bored alienated people for a leader. In one of the early numbers, called "*Fuhrer* Wanter," the crowd breaks into a chant of "How we want a man to lead us out of misery!" During the opera, the disaffected are shown to be mesmerized by Hitler's magical power and his pledge of "law and order," and work and bread. The musical ends on a pessimistic note, with a new cry "for another leading man to tell us how to live and what to do."

The entire musical takes place in a mystical occultlike pagan atmosphere and suggests that the entire Hitler period was the result of a spiritual seance that failed.

One rock opera with sixty participants and Hitler as its superstar does not clearly set a new trend. Yet, it introduces a new element in Holocaust drama—heroic Wagnerian-like characters as its protagonists may become a passing vogue. Despite this trendy rock opera, the current fascination with Hitler, both attraction and revulsion at the same time, hopefully is not a beginning of an overwhelming outpouring of Holocaust plays with flamboyant Nazis, but rather an indication that the time may be ripe for dramatists to make a more aggressive attempt to come to terms with the Holocaust.

The playwright, more than other artists, needs that historical latitude and the ample range of time and space. Unlike the poet, the novelist, and the diarist, the number of plays written under siege is minuscule. Even a generation after the Holocaust, the harvest of plays is rather unimpressive when compared with other areas of literature. When the artist confronts his empty page, he or she writes, consciously or subconsciously, for an individual at the other end of the printed page. An intimate relationship between two individuals is formed. The nature of this relationship, whether of contempt or admiration, is irrelevant. The literary artist creates a reality to be judged in public by a public, a reality upon which the author is losing some measure of control to the actors and the director. Due to the overpowering and paralyzing impact of the Holocaust, and to the sensitivity of the material and of the public, Holocaust drama remains a risky adventure for the playwright, the audience, and the theatre. "And let there be spotlights on the darkest episode in mankind's history" remains a lonely voice on the post-Holocaust stage.

BIBLIOGRAPHY

I. Poetry

AMICHAI, YEHUDA. *Selected Poems* (England: Penguin Books, Penguin paperbacks, 1971).

AUSUBEL, NATHAN AND MARYNN, eds. *A Treasury of Jewish Poetry* (New York: Crown, 1957). See especially, poetry of Sutzkerer.

BURNSHAW, STANLEY; CARMI, T.; AND SPICEHANDLER, E., eds. *The Modern Hebrew Poem Itself* (New York: Holt, Rinehart and Winston, 1965). See especially poetry of Gilboa.

CARMI, T., AND PAGIS, DAN. *Selected Poems,* trans. S. Mitchell (London: Penguin and Penguin paperbacks, 1976).

CHAPMAN, ABRAHAM, ed. *Jewish-American Literature* (New York: New American Library, 1974) (Available in Mentor paperback). See especially poetry of Simpson, Williams, Hecht.

FELDMAN, IRVING, "To the Six Millions," *Midstream* 10:3 (September 1964), pp. 63–67.

_____. *The Pripet Marshes and Other Poems* (New York: Viking, 1965).

GERSHON, KAREN. *Selected Poems* (New York: Harcourt, Brace and World, 1966).

HECHT, ANTHONY. *The Hard Hours* (New York: Atheneum, 1967).

HOWE, IRVING, AND GREENBERG, ELIEZER, eds. *A Treasury of Yiddish Poetry* (New York, Holt, Rinehart and Winston, 1972). See especially, poetry of Spiegel, Grade, Molodowsky, Glatstein, Zeitlin, etc.

HUGHES, TED. *Crow: From the Life and Song of the Crow* (London: Faber, 1970).

KA-TZETNIK 135633. *Star Eternal,* trans. by N. Denur (New York: Arbor House, 1971).

KATZENELSON, YITZHAK. *Vittel Diary* (Israel: Ghetto Fighter's House, 1972).

KAUFMANN, WALTER. *Cain and Other Poems* (New York: Random House, 1971).

KOLMAR, GERTRUD. *Dark Soliloquy,* trans. and introd. by H. A. Smith; forward by C. Ozick (New York: Continuum, 1975).

KOVNER, ABBA. *A Canopy in the Desert,* trans. S. Kaufman (Pittsburgh: University of Pittsburgh Press, 1973) (Available in paperback). Contains "My Little Sister," etc.

KOVNER, ABBA, AND, SACHS, NELLY. *Selected Poems* with an introd. by S. Spender (London: Penguin and Penguin paperbacks, 1971).

LEVERTOV, DENISE. *The Jacob's Ladder* (New York: New Directions Paperback, 1961). Note poems, "During the Eichmann Trial."

REZNIKOFF, CHARLES. *By the Waters of Manhattan* (New York: New Directions, 1962) (Available in paperback).

_____. *Holocaust* (Los Angeles: Black Sparrow Press, 1975) (Available in paperback).

PLATH, SYLVIA. *Ariel* (New York: Harper and Row, 1965).

SACHS, NELLY. *O' the Chimneys,* with an introd. by H. M. Enzensberger (New York: Farrar, Straus and Giroux, 1967).

STEINITZ, L., AND SZONYI, D. *Living After the Holocaust* (New York: Bloch, 1975). (Available in paperback). Note poetry sections, pp. 55–65, 83–93. This book is largely a reproduction of *Response* 1975.

WATERS, MICHAEL, "Dachau Moon," *Response* (Spring 1975) 25:58–61.

WIESEL, ELIE. *Ani Maamin* (New York: Random House, 1973).

YEVTUSHENKO, YEVGENI. *Selected Poems,* trans. R. Milner-Gullard and P. Levi (Baltimore: Penguin paperbacks, 1964).

YOLAVKOVA, H. ed. *I Never Saw Another Butterfly* (New York: McGraw-Hill, 1965).

II. Drama

AMICHAI, YEHUDA. *Bells and Trains, Midstream* 12:8 (October 1966) pp. 55–66.

ASSAF, YURI, AND ELIACH, YAFFA. *The Last Jew* (Israel: Alef Alef Multi Media, 1977).

BORCHERT, WOLFGANG. *The Outsider* in *Postwar German Theatre,* edited and trans. by M. Benedikt with G. Wellwarth (New York: Dutton, 1967), pp. 52–113.

DELBO, CHARLOTTE. *None of Us Will Return* (Boston: Beacon, 1968; Beacon Paperback, 1978).

GOLDBERG, LEAH. *The Lady of the Manor,* trans. T. Carmi as *Lady of the Castle* (Jerusalem: World Zionist Organization, 1974) (Available in paperback).

HELLMAN, LILLIAN. *Watch on the Rhine* (New York: Random House, 1941).

HOCHHUTH, ROLF. *The Deputy,* trans. R. and C. Winston (New York: Grove, 1964) (Available in paperback).

LAMPELL, MILLARD. *The Wall* (based on the novel by John Hersey) (New York: Knopf, 1961).

MILLER, ARTHUR. *Incident at Vichy* (New York: Viking, 1965) (Available in paperback).

SACHS, NELLY. *Eli: A Mystery Play of the Suffering of Israel* in *O' the Chimneys* (New York: Farrar, Straus and Giroux, 1967), pp. 309–385.

SHAW, ROBERT. *The Man in the Glass Booth* (New York: Harcourt Brace and World, 1967) (Available in Grove paperback).

SYLVANNS, ERWIN. *Dr. Korczak and the Children,* trans. G. Wellwarth, in *Postwar German Theatre* (New York: Dutton, 1967), pp. 118–157.

TOMER, BEN-ZION. *Children of the Shadows,* trans. H. Halkin (New York: World Zionist Organization, no date).

WEISS, PETER. *The Investigation,* Eng. version by J. Swan and U. Grosbard (New York: Atheneum, 1966) (Available in Pocket Book paperback).

WERFEL, FRANZ. *Jacobowsky and the Colonel* (New York: Random House, 1944).

III. Literary Criticism

AIRD, EILEEN. *Sylvia Plath: Her Life and Work* (New York: Harper and Row, 1975).

ALVAREZ, ALFRED. *Beyond All This Fiddle* (London: Penguin Press, 1968). See for poetry of Plath, especially "Lady Lazarus."

ARTAUD, ANTONIN. *The Theatre and Its Double,* trans. Mary E. Richards (New York: Grove, 1958).

BEN SHAUL, MOSHE, "Yim Lilliane Atlan Yozeret Mar Slik," (Hebrew) *Maariv*; January 4, 1972; p. 21.

EDER, RICHARD, "Drama: Polish Theatre," *New York Times*; May 26, 1976, p. 22.

EZRAHI, SIDRA, "Holocaust Literature in European Languages," *Encyclopedia Judaica Yearbook 1973* (Jerusalem: Keter, 1973), pp. 106–119.

GEFEN, "Ha-Yehudi Ha-Aharon," (Hebrew) *Al-Ha-Mishmar*; April 11, 1975; p. 9.

GOELL, YOHAI. *Bibliography of Modern Hebrew Literature* (Jerusalem: Israel University Press, 1968). On the poetry of N. Alterman, see pp. 2–5, on Uri Greenberg, pp. 22–28.

HAMBURGER, MICHAEL, AND, MIDDLETON, CHRISTOPHER, eds. *Modern German Poetry, 1910–1960: An Anthology with Verse Translation* (New York: Grove, 1962). Contains "Death Fugue" by Celan.

KABAKOFF, JACOB. *Modern Hebrew Literature in Translation* (New York: Selected Books, Jewish Book Council, 1976).

LANGER, LAWRENCE. *The Holocaust and the Literary Imagination* (New Haven: Yale University Press, 1975) (Available in paperback). Has analyses of Celan, Sachs, Steiner, etc.

MURDOCH, BRIAN, "Transformation of the Holocaust: Auschwitz in Modern Lyric Poetry," *Comparative Literature Studies* (June 1974) 11:123–150. Especially see discussion on Sylvia Plath.

ROBINSON, JACOB. *The Holocaust and After, Sources on Literature in English* (Jerusalem: Israel University Press, 1973). See section on drama, pp. 298–299.

ROSENTHAL, M. L. *The New Poets: American and British Poetry Since World War II* (New York: Oxford University Press, 1967).

ROUSSET, DAVID, "The Days of Our Death," *Politics* (July–August 1947), pp. 151–157.

SHENKER, ISRAEL. "A Conference Ponders: Who, and Why, is a Jew," *New York Times*; May 26, 1976, p. 18.

SPENDER, STEPHEN, "Catastrophe and Redemption: *O' The Chimneys* by Nelly Sachs," *New York Times, Sunday Book Review Section*; October 8, 1967, pp. 5, 34.

STEINER, GEORGE, "In Extremis," in *The Cambridge Mind,* E. Homberg, W. Janeway and S. Schama, eds. (London, 1970). See discussion on Sylvia Plath, esp. p. 305.

———. *Language and Silence* (New York: Atheneum, 1967). (Available in Atheneum paperback).

SYRKIN, MARIE, "Nelly Sachs: Poet of the Holocaust," *Midstream* 13:3 (March 1967), pp. 13–23.

ZOHN, HARRY, "Gertrud Kolmar: German Jewish Poet," *Jewish Spectator* 41:1 (Spring 1976), pp. 43–46.

The Holocaust and the Film Arts*

Arnost Lustig and Joseph Lustig

INTRODUCTION

At present, the film arts are the most popularly accepted mode of artistic
expression. Certainly, more people view films than read historical works. In
teaching about the Holocaust, one can successfully utilize the uniqueness of
film both to inform students about the Holocaust experience and to provide an
emotional impact upon them.

Films may be integrated either into a specific course on the Holocaust in
Film or into a course on the History of the Holocaust or the Literature of the
Holocaust. Since films related to the Holocaust are generally grounded either
in historical events or in literary works, the use of such films may help balance
the total picture of the Holocaust experience. In showing these films, one
should adequately introduce their historical framework. In addition, if a particular film also develops from a more richly textured literary work, one
should consider the study of the literary work itself as well as its relationship
to the film. In the following pages, a list of films will be provided to offer a
complete picture, a mosaic of the Holocaust experience.

The ensuing discussion is divided into three parts: films describing the
prewar experience, films describing the war experience itself, and films describing the aftermath of the Holocaust experience. In addition to plot outlines, themes, and a description of the unique qualities and contributions of
each of these films, one may find background bibliographical information

*Jewish Media Service has compiled a list of over 300 Holocaust-related films. The Center for
Holocaust Studies in Brooklyn, the National Institute on the Holocaust in Philadelphia, and Bnai
Brith Anti-Defamation League also have compiled lists of available films and where they may be
rented. Dissertations on Holocaust-related films are presently being completed by Judith Donen-
sen at Hebrew University and by Joseph Lustig at New York University.

provided, wherever pertinent, to explain these works. Film attempts to describe the human experience in all its complexity: literary, psychological, physical, historical and philosophical. For further enlightenment, supplementary Holocaust materials reflecting these various perspectives within other media should also be consulted.

Film, like literature, has been produced in a variety of genres and modes. Generally speaking, Holocaust films fall into two groups: documentary film and theatrical film. Documentary films are useful in completing the historian's portrayal of the Holocaust experience because these films provide a one-dimensional objective view of an event without penetrating into the subjective responses of individuals participating in an event. The theatrical film attempts to introduce the second dimension of subjectivity.

The film arts, like other disciplines and art forms, must attempt to ascertain whether the Holocaust is an event with universal implications or with only particular implications as a Jewish experience during the Second World War. Perhaps film can best embrace both the universal and particular implications of the Holocaust by describing personal conflicts developed within the framework of the Jewish experience but common to all human beings. Since the moral, intellectual, and existential conflicts inflicted upon human beings during the Holocaust years were present in the most extreme degrees possible, filmmakers felt that the most responsible manner in which to deal with such conflicts was through a strictly realistic film art form. Despite the international constituency of the film artists portraying the Holocaust and despite the specifically Jewish experience they are depicting, the universal human problems engendered by the Holocaust have united these filmmakers in attempting to artistically express an experience which, because of its horror, defies any possible expression. Consequently, the mosaic synthesized by many different filmmakers of various national and ethnic origins has produced a homogeneous presentation not only of the Holocaust experience but of the human conflict in the post-Holocaust world.

At present, an adequate number of films is readily available to provide a total, balanced view of the Holocaust. Only budgetary considerations in renting these films would preclude the portrayal of a full picture of the Holocaust through the medium of the film arts.

Despite the popularity of films in contemporary American society, one should not underestimate their impact not only in moving the viewer but also in providing factual information on an event. Since films may provide a perspective on the Holocaust experience which is unavailable through other media and art forms, a total study of the Holocaust would therefore be inadequate without the use of available film materials.

Here are twenty-four films, selected as the core of two twelve-film course units. The first film in each dyad is an ideal choice for the teaching of a historically grounded, human experience oriented course on the Holocaust and Film. The second film in each dyad is, then, a substitute should the first be temporarily unavailable. In addition, each twelve-film unit was designed to entirely and independently cover the Holocaust experience, thus constituting two separate courses on the Holocaust and Film.

THE PREWAR EXPERIENCE

Naiveté and Blindness

In an entertaining manner, the slightly melodramatic SHIP OF FOOLS explores the prewar attitudes of Germans, Jews, Americans and other nationalities soon to be involved in the horrors of the upcoming world conflict. Traveling on a German ship from Vera Cruz to Bremerhaven in 1933, tourists and season-workers reveal themselves to the viewer layer after layer as the voyage nears the German shores.

First, here are the diverse members of the German group. The kind ship doctor wishes that Germans did not think it the duty of an intelligent, civilized man to take orders no matter how foolish they might be. The captain refuses to take seriously the Nazi ideals of some of the passengers. The weak, divorced Aryan husband has left his Jewish wife for the fear of losing his job. The bourgeois couple's universe centers around their fat pet dog. Finally, the Nazi presence is a cheap, vulgar fanatical Austrian-turned-German, cruel and dangerous in his opinions. His cabin-mate is the German Jewish businessman Lowenthal, an optimist of suicidal proportions, who sees the world in 1933 as getting "better all the time." Ironically, after the Nazi succeeds in barring Lowenthal from the captain's table for meals, the relationship of the two cabin-mates begins to acquire a friendly dimension. Lying in bed, ill, the Austrian remarks that he is beginning to like Lowenthal who gave him some pills against a cold. The former asks why the latter is returning to a country where nobody wants him. "Why don't you go back to your own country?" he asks. "Germany is my country!" answers Lowenthal, adding that not only he himself but also his father and grandfather were born in Germany. Much like the majority of European Jews of the time, this Jewish businessman who sells religious articles exemplifies a terribly unrealistic attitude toward the sociohistorical situation of the day. This is seen most clearly when he shows his Iron Cross from World War I to an acquaintance of his, a midget traveling for pleasure. The latter remarks that Lowenthal is blind not to see the impending fate of the Jews in Germany, where every second person had voted for Hitler. Lowenthal replies that the majority of Germans are still anti-Hitler, for only 44% had voted for Hitler. In addition, what do the German Jews have to be afraid of, being "Germans first and Jews second? . . . There are almost a half million Jews in Germany, what will they do? Kill all of us? . . . "

Then there is the American group: a young couple consisting of a socialist painter and his middle-class fiancee, a frustrated baseball player, and a middle-aged, rich and spoiled divorcee. Their attitudes are childish, sometimes indifferent, sometimes just uninformed, yet always humane and honest. They characterize the distant America of isolation, concerned with freedom and material wealth.

Likewise, the Spanish—busy with their own narrow problems and existential interests—stay outside the arena where the German-Jewish relationship will soon reach its terrible proportions.

Cinematically, SHIP OF FOOLS is an accomplished film. Its structure, cutting, acting, cinematography and direction are functional—unified in the communication of central themes. It is an honest film and an interesting one to watch, an entertaining film as well as a useful educational instrument. Thanks to its quality direction (Stanley Kramer), performances (George Segal and Lee Marvin) and the overall value of Katherine Ann Porter's literary base, SHIP OF FOOLS offers a good first step toward intuitive as well as factual understanding of the period immediately preceding the Holocaust.

Not quite as cinematically accomplished as SHIP OF FOOLS but of an equal psychological and historical "eye-opening value" is the VOYAGE OF THE DAMNED. Situated in the late 1930's, the film tells the story of a group of several hundred German Jews who are permitted to leave Germany for Cuba (on special orders of the Nazi Propaganda Ministry which designed the entire operation). In Cuba, however, for a Nazi bribe, the group's visas are revoked. Therefore, the ship turns back toward Germany after it has been publicly demonstrated to the worldwide critics of Germany that Germans are not the only ones who do not want the Jews. A short time before reaching German ports, several countries (including Belgium and Luxembourg) offer to accept some of the Jewish passengers—ironically, just months before the Nazi invasion of their own territories.

There are three national groups depicted in the film: the Germans, the Jews, and the Cubans. While most of the German sailors are strongly anti-Semitic, a young crew member, quite untouched by the Nazi venom, falls in love with a Jewish girl passenger. The ship's captain also represents the better part of Germany: he bans the showing of German official newsreels which are offensive to the Jewish passengers and is ready to wreck the ship in British waters if no country will accept the ship's "cargo." Among the Jews, a great variety of social, economic and cultural backgrounds can be observed, ranging from the prominent aristocratic professor of medicine to the desperate individual jumping from the ship rather than having to face the return to Germany. The majority are despondent and indecisive middle-class Jews who obey orders and behave in an orderly "civilized" manner. Only a few are willing to join a revolt by a handful of their younger, more realistic, desperately anti-fascist brethren to commandeer the ship.

The Cubans, generally, are shown as indifferent self-absorbed individuals, most often involved in official or illegal money-making.

Like SHIP OF FOOLS, the VOYAGE OF THE DAMNED introduces the viewer to the themes central to the prelude of the Holocaust: clear vision, a realistic evaluation of the historical situation, values of property, national and religious identity, relationship with the land where one's forefathers and children were born, and cowardice and courage. Both historically and subjectively, the film succeeds in introducing the Jewish dilemma of the prewar years: the existential conflicts and physical experience, the Jewish naiveté and blindness, and faith in the future.

Inside the Trap

A taste of 1931 Germany is offered by the musical CABARET. Against the backdrop of a highly entertaining world of night clubs, the musical tells a story of an American journalist and a singer. More importantly, through their eyes one sees the inside of anti-Semitic Germany, where Jewish businesses are looted and Jews are terrorized in the streets and assaulted by Hitler-Youth under the eyes of ordinary Germans—all in an atmosphere of a vulgar, cruel Dionysian mentality. The German Jews' feelings surface, most notably, when a Jew hides his Jewishness all his life until the moment he confesses the fact to the Jewish girl he loves. Here the viewer can experience the insecurity of being a Jew in Germany. One sees the shame, confusion, fear and impossibility of claiming one's still legally sanctioned human rights. On the other hand, the Jewish self-deluding optimism is also palpably present in the film. When artistically juxtaposed with the growing pro-Nazi sentiment sweeping the country, this optimism becomes especially noticeable and physically painful. For example, one notes the sequences depicting school children and ordinary adults enjoying a day in a country inn, and then joining a Nazi group marching by in passionate patriotic singing.

CABARET, a rich aesthetic experience in itself, derives much of its entertainment value from its literary base in Christopher Isherwood's *The Berlin Stories*. For purposes of Holocaust study, this film is useful for many of the same reasons that the aforementioned films are. It, too, is concerned with the themes of cowardice and courage, and of one's relationship to his homeland; it, too, gives a viewer a sampling of the psychology of the victims-to-be.

A similar kind of a viewer's participatory experience is offered by the Italian THE GARDEN OF THE FINZI-CONTINIS. The film tells the story of an aristocratic Jewish professor's family in Ferrara. Quite distinguished and fully assimilated, these Jews become slowly aware that the unimaginable is becoming the new reality: their acquaintances and neighbors are going to accept and live by the fascist anti-Semitic laws passed in Italy. Continuing their social games, playing tennis and sending their children to the university as if nothing were changed, the Finzi-Continis refuse to confront the terrible reality awaiting them. Their blind deluding optimism leaves them sadly unprepared to avoid their ultimate deaths in the camps.

The film allows the audience to experience, almost physically, the frustration, shame, fear and hopeless optimism of the Jews. The Jewish fate contrasts sharply with the well-being, selfishness and lack of moral courage exemplified by the seemingly decent inhabitants of a previously friendly Ferrara. The inhabitants' conformity to the fascist rule and their seemingly unmotivated change in attitude toward the Jews, help explain the bewildered impotence and the late, ineffective defense of the majority of Jews not only in that ancient Italian town but in all of Europe.

The "Supermench": His Country and Times

It is as important to understand the world of the perpetrator as it is to understand the world of the victim. Therefore, one must penetrate the Germans' psychology, including their self-image and their fears and ambitions. One must see the world through their eyes and feel like them for a moment, at least vicariously. This end can be achieved through films, especially through Nazi films.

Although the German film establishment in the early 1930's contained only a few actors and directors who were "card-carrying" Nazis and early supporters of the Hitler regime, and although as a whole the "Filmwelt was a hotbed—however passive—of limited resistance to the government," there were some for whom "to choose between exile or stardom, a concentration camp or the veneration of sixty-six million Germans in 1933 was not hard . . . The fatal error, morally, was the supposition that governments come and go, but art marches on in a vacuum" (Hull, p. 7). One of such film artists was the ambitious, visually gifted Leni Riefenstahl. In 1933, she had been approached by Hitler to make a Nazi Party short, VICTORY OF FAITH [SIEG DES GLAUBENS], the completion of which resulted in Hitler's request the following year for another film, this time a feature-length coverage of the September 1934 Party Rally in Nuremburg.

The cast for the cinematic deification of the Party and its leaders (Hitler, Hess, Goering and others) utilized the 350,000 native Nurembergers and the 770,000 visitors to that city; the film showed thousands of them in Party uniforms, youth outfits and Labor Corps uniforms carrying standards, marching in formations, standing in crowds and pledging allegiance to the *Fuhrer* against the backdrop of heiling by German mothers and the shrieking of joy by German daughters. This visual information, interwoven with the mystical footage of the ancient Nuremberg veiled in mist, clouds and long shadows, makes up the core of the Nazi masterpiece TRIUMPH OF THE WILL [TRIUMPH DES WILLENS]. The track accompanying the picture consists of only live and authentic sounds: marching boots, folksongs, orations, soldiers' responses, and children's cries of joy.

Premiering in March 1935, this historical re-creation of an historical event stated in its opening credits: ''Produced by the Order of the *Fuhrer.*'' This film influenced many Germans to rally to Hitler's cause, mainly on the strength of the accurately re-created emotional level of its historical model. In this ''overwhelming propaganda success,'' many critics feel, ''the role of Leni Riefenstahl. . . . was unforgivable'' (Barnow, p. 105).

The key to the emotional functioning of TRIUMPH OF THE WILL is one of its first sequences. Hitler's trimotor junkers descends from the clouds like an eagle on an ancient city, lit by shafts of sunlight biting through a mystical mist. As the plane slowly lands and stops, the door opens and Hitler appears. A powerful ovation fills the soundtrack and a title fills the screen:

On September 5,
1934
20 years
after the outbreak
of the World War
16 years
after the start
of German suffering
19 months
after the beginning
of Germany's rebirth
Adolf Hitler
flew again to Nuremberg
to review the columns of his faithful followers.

Thus, the newly-found togetherness, comradery, the sense of belonging and discipline, the opportunity to follow a leader, patriotism, pride—a reaction to the paranoia and sense of inferiority instilled in Germans following the First World War--all of these dimensions are introduced, followed up, and climaxed in a mythical reconstruction of a mythical event. One can feel the dynamic of the Party style and its magical appeal for the masses; one can see and hear the leaders close up, passion filtering through the screen. For this emotionally re-created authentic depiction of the Party, the film is considered an accomplished product and as such is a useful tool for the study of the Holocaust.

Is TRIUMPH OF THE WILL a work of art or merely a weapon of propaganda? Is a piece of art with flawless form but defective content still art? Specifically, is Leni Riefenstahl (the directress of TRIUMPH OF THE WILL), in view of her pride and effort in the film as a work of artistic quality and in view of mankind's historical and moral judgment of its contents, a true "artist" or merely an evil genius? Aestheticians and social scientists have striven to answer these questions. However, film critic Sigfried Kracauer has noted that "films are never the product of an individual" (p. 5). Thus, one could argue that Riefenstahl was somewhat forced by circumstances to produce TRIUMPH OF THE WILL and, being a talented perfectionist, she produced it well. Possibly, Riefenstahl was not even anti-Semitic; for example, she attempted to employ on the film a non-Aryan cameraman, Heinz von Jaworsky (who in 1936 collaborated with her on OLYMPIA, and later emigrated to the United States). On the other hand, Riefenstahl's disclaimers of accusations that she was a sympathizing Nazi are doubtful in light of her often contradictory verbal defenses. For instance, according to the interviewer Robert Gardner, she claimed that Hitler persuaded her in 1934 to make the film, even though she told him that she knew nothing about the Party and its organization. But, how could she know nothing about the Party if the preceding year she had made a film about the Party, entitled VICTORY OF FAITH?! Thus, considering the contradictory nature of the available evidence, one must develop one's own conclusion. For the victims of the Nazi crimes, the verdict is unanimous.

Similar cinematic insight into the feelings of living in the legendary times of Nazi Germany, increasingly fanaticized and growing in might, is offered by German newsreels and military films. The New York Museum of Modern Art's Department of Film edited excerpts from such film into a feature length program entitled PROPAGANDA FILMS I. This document contains portions from TRIUMPH OF THE WILL, 1937 and 1940 "bugle-call" military films PILOTS, GUNNERS, RADIO OPERATORS and BAPTISM OF FIRE, respectively, and 1940 WOCHENSHAU Film Weekly. The military films glorify the German Air Force; the latter, for instance, centers around the role of the *Luftwaffe* against Poland and is effectively filmed in the style of Riefenstahl's TRIUMPH OF THE WILL. The formations of Nazis are substituted by formations of planes; the marching armies wear field uniforms rather than parade Nazi uniforms. In TRIUMPH the continuously screen-present Hitler, "a ranting, marching, saluting. . . . forbidding public figure" becomes "in image and content. . . . a more magnanimous leader" (Barsam, p. 166). These films, as well as the newsreels, continued to strive for two ends: "as to the faithful, to stir the blood, building determination to the highest pitch; as to the enemy, to chill the marrow, paralyzing the will to resist" (Barnow, p. 139). Three decades after the War, one can only approximately understand how these two-way weapons of propaganda relying on powerful music, natural sounds, authentic footage, mythical composition, the psychological use of camera angles, and dynamic editing, affected the victims and the murderers. Nevertheless, it is clear that these films affected the outcome of the Holocaust.

THE WAR EXPERIENCE

A City Given to the Jews

The Nazis sought to persuade the Western world, the inhabitants of occupied Europe and European Jewry, that the program for the Jews was not a program of murder but a radical transfer of population and normalization about which the Jews themselves had spoken for two thousand years. For this purpose, the Nazis created Jewish ghettos like Lodz, Vilna, and an exemplary ghetto intended to be used for propaganda purposes, the Theresienstadt Ghetto.

In this military garrison town and fortress, built 180 years earlier by the Austro-Hungarian empress Maria Theresa and designed originally for 6,000 people, the Nazis concentrated 60,000 Jews from twenty-one countries of occupied Europe. Under Nazi supervision, the Jewish self-administration was allowed to build a transit station midway between the countries from which the Jews came and various extermination camps to which these Jews were ultimately sent. In this ghetto, life was lived intensely. The residents sensed, but did not know, that they were condemned to death.

The film TRANSPORT FROM PARADISE shows a cycle of twenty-four hours during which a German General-Inspector prepares the "town" to become a showplace for a visit by the International Red Cross. The film introduces the cream of European Jewry: former generals, cabinet ministers, leading artists, scholars, wealthy bankers and industrialists, and, at the same time, underground fighters and young people for whom life existed everywhere—even in Theresienstadt.

The film begins with a dramatic irony of the Nazis filming a propaganda film about the ghetto where selected people from the Jewish crowd have to say smiling into the camera, accompanied by light music: "I am happy here in Theresienstadt; I don't miss anything." Various individuals state this line in twenty-one languages.

For the first time in the art of the Holocaust, the film accuses the traitors and collaborators among the Jewish self-administration, and draws a strict line between courage and cowardice, solidarity and carelessness, mercy and selfishness, between every man for himself and the fight of all possible groups against the Nazis. As a symbolic contradiction to the Nazi program of extinction of the Jews called "Operation Night and Fog," the film is based on the book *Night and Hope,* and expresses the theme of "never again like sleep" as its philosophical conclusion for the future of the Jews.

Among the cinematic qualities which enhance the historical and subjective value of TRANSPORT FROM PARADISE is Brynych's tender direction which helps accentuate the contrasts between courage and cowardice, and between decency and selfishness. For example, the boisterous style of the acquiescing present head of the *Judenrat,* Marmulstaub, contrasts with the somber decency of Lowenbach, the former head of the self-administration who refused to sign the transport lists and ended up in a transport himself. Furthermore, the film benefits from Curik's realistic yet poetic camera, which brings out the happiness of a few moments of love and friendship against the interplay of sinister lights and shadows. With his documentary-styled vertical and horizontal camera movement along the ghetto streets, the cameraman creates a gritlike pattern affecting the audience as if they too were in a prison. Also the film's sound track contributes significantly toward the viewer's emotional reaction. A mixture of German songs and jazz guitar over the presence of everyday military sounds, roll-call orders and the whisper of love and friendship, are all elements that mirror the life energies of the young people of the ghetto and the destructive forces in their environment.

A parallel to the message of TRANSPORT FROM PARADISE is offered in the documentary I NEVER SAW ANOTHER BUTTERFLY. The 15,000 children of Theresienstadt, of whom a bare 100 survived, are represented by this unique and poetic film composed of ghetto children's drawings from the years 1942-1944. The film shows another phase of life in many concentration, labor and transit camps in the territory of the Third Reich. The pictures tenderly portray life as an interesting privilege. The film is saturated by the indestructible creativity of man condemned to death. This creativity substitutes somewhat for the loss of all people close to one's heart, for the loss of one's possessions, leaving one alone with only secret hopes. The pictures show images of the old home, trees, flowers, sunny sky, sky with birds and clouds—all unconscious symbols of freedom.

Based on a book of the same title, published first in Czechoslovakia and later throughout the world, I NEVER SAW ANOTHER BUTTERFLY enables one to see the absurd world of concentration camps through the eyes of children, who knew nothing when first brought there. "They had come from places where they had already felt humiliation, they had been expelled from schools. They had sewn stars on their hearts, jackets and blouses, and were allowed to play only in the cemeteries. When they were herded with their parents into the Theresienstadt ghetto, they began to look around and tried to understand the strange world in which they had to live."

Cinematically, the film relies on its macro-lens to reveal the soul of the paintings. It records the details of faces, flowers and trees: it sweeps across the images of a countryside, a house, a group of school children and parents. Expressing the same joys, loneliness, hopes, and memories as the visuals, the sound contains these children's poems read by boys and girls barely out of first and second grades. Their tender voices communicate well the grim fates of the youngest victims of the Holocaust, in Theresienstadt, the city Adolf Hitler "gave to the Jews."

Internment

"The basis of the violence consists, for the most part, of harmless, kind people who are indifferent toward brutality. Sooner or later these people may overcome their indifference, but then it is usually too late" (Liehm, p. 407). This conviction of Jan Kadar is central to his THE SHOP ON MAIN STREET. It is a petty story about petty people in a small town. People know each other, visit one another, celebrate the births of their children and mourn their deceased elders. Time flows slowly. Everything new is observed by the citizens with suspicion, and thus also with distaste they accept the arrival of a thousand-year Reich in Slovakia. The players of the tragi-comedy include Rose Lautman, the owner and salesperson in a store with buttons, pins and laces. Others are the cabinetmaker Tono Brtko, his wife Evelyn, dog Essence, and his brother-in-law Marcus Kolkocky, a public official seeking the new possibilities offered by the new ideology. To please his brother-in-law, Kolkocky names Brtko the Aryan administrator of Mrs. Lautman's store. There Brtko soon discovers that she has nothing to offer him besides her ignorance and the approaching senility that spares her even the knowledge that there is a war. This petty plot develops into a deep drama which destroys human lives.

During the time allocated to build a wooden cone in the town square to symbolize the new times, the town must be cleansed of Jews—*Judenrein*. Kolkocky has received the order. Those who refuse to steal Jewish property and to treat their Jewish neighbors as third-rate citizens, like Mr. Kucharsky, are publicly denounced, publicly beaten and sent to a concentration camp as "White Jews."

Brtko, in exchange for the silent protection of Mrs. Lautman, receives financial support from the Jewish community to satisfy his wife who believes that every Jew owns a secret gold treasure. However, Brtko suddenly faces a new dilemma. While the Jewish population is being loaded from the town square onto trucks to be deported, Tono Brtko hesitates between the risk of keeping Rosalie Lautman in ignorance and the fear of what his brother-in-law would do to him if the next day, in a town which is purely Aryan, an old Jewish woman would be found. Without intending to hurt Mrs. Lautman, he wants to get rid of her by opening the door and showing her other Jews ready to be deported. The old woman, who until this moment knew nothing about Hitler, the new Europe, and the Nuremberg Laws, widens her eyes in terror and evaluates the situation in one word: *pogrom*. A brawl takes place in which Brtko tries to push her out of the store by force, and the fragile Mrs. Lautman falls dead on the ground. When Tono Brtko sees that he murdered an innocent Jewish woman, just like the rest of the Jewish population from town after town will continue to be murdered day after day, he sends his dog outside, takes a piece of rope and hangs himself at the moment when the first trucks with deported Jews leave the square.

It is one of those tales about which it is said that it is like the drop of dew in which the whole world is reflected. Immediately after its release, the film aroused an immense controversy, for it touched one of the sensitive spots of an era which is called Nazi but in which not all were Nazis and active collaborators. In the petty story, people were accused who did not support Nazism, but did not ever actively resist it, and without whose quiet acquiescence the "Final Solution of the Jewish Question" would not have been possible.

The film's quality is the result of the happy collaboration of the autobiographical elements provided by the Jewish writer Ladislav Grosman, the Jewish director Jan Kadar, and the Jewish actress Ida Kaminska. At the same time, the cooperation of the non-Jewish director Elmar Klos and the Slovak actor Jozef Kroner endow the film with inimitable realism. Visually, the film surrounds the spectator with the atmosphere of the clashing worlds; the film combines classically styled, poetic realist sequences with the dreamy flashbacks and dreams of Mrs. Lautman's past into a rich cinematic reality. Aurally, the Liska score functionally complements the images by surrounding them with a mixture of a delicious marching waltz and old Yiddish folk songs played on a turn-of-the-century phonograph. Thus, the sound, picture, and themes together create a film of absolute classical strength and beauty.

A suitable alternative for THE SHOP ON MAIN STREET is Brynych's AND FIFTH HORSEMAN IS FEAR. It is visually a rich film with Kafkaesque elements; a wealth of angle variations are used to convey the inner states of the characters. The film tells the story of a Jewish doctor during the Nazi occupation of Bohemia and Moravia; the physician is sought out by the underground in order to give medical assistance to an injured member of the resistance. Occurring primarily in an ordinary Prague apartment building and in the deserted streets, the action reveals the characters' strengths, weaknesses, and moral qualities, cutting across the human landscape within an occupied country. At the end, the underground, as well as the Jewish doctor, are betrayed to the Nazis by a pleasant, seemingly sympathetic informer, and these Jews are interned.

Thematically, the film is an odyssey in the nightmare and terror of fear and denunciation, lack of trust and indifference—turned—murderous lack of concern when human compassion is needed most. Cinematically, the theme is fortified by the formal structure and surrealistic style responsible for the communication to the audience of the atmosphere of fear, terror, cowardice and perfidy.

Struggle to Hide

Among the greatest of paradoxes in Holocaust art is the autobiographical story of the fifteen-year-old Anne Frank, written before she was deported to

Bergen-Belsen concentration camp where she died. Her one sentence, "I believe in the goodness of man" is engraved in the 10,000-year-old written history of mankind like the sentences written in the Bible. THE DIARY OF ANNE FRANK is the most understandable document of the Second World War available to the younger generation.

The George Stevens film, grounded in the spirit and the concrete context of Anne's images, is a key work in the art of the Holocaust. Through the eyes of a child one returns to the years 1942, 1943 and 1944—the worst years of the War. In accordance with children's abilities to perceive everything as original and fresh, one sees the last chapter of the age-old struggle for freedom taking place in an Amsterdam attic. The unbelievable strength of this story is based upon two things: first, on what we know today about Nazism, its roots, social background and results; and, secondly, but functioning simultaneously with the former, on that which Anne writes in her letters to a fictitious girl friend, Kitty.

The film's contribution lies in its ability to enable the audience to perceive these two poles. Furthermore, there is the mysterious question of a limited human existence versus the human dream of eternal life. And this is what the second unforgettable sentence from *The Diary of Anne Frank* means when Anne writes: "I want to go on living even after my death."

Director Stevens is indebted to the work of documentarians in creating this highly realistic film. It is classically constructed, with camera placements serving the location of a cramped attic and photographing action developing in front of its lenses as if the optical instrument were not present. The direction hides the clues of an a priori process, and in conjunction with the analytical editing, it unfolds the film's character as a work of art involving the process of growing awareness and analysis. The structure seems to have been constantly evaluated on location as the director's perception of the subject changed and his understanding of it increased. The film seems to serve the characters, employing a minimal stylization of its elements and striving to become a "creative treatment of actuality."

For similar motives that Stevens adapted into film *The Diary of Anne Frank,* that Shakespeare had written about his lovers of Verona, or that Romain Rolland his *Peter and Lucia,* Jiri Weiss adapted into film the story by Jan Otcenasek, *Romeo and Juliet and the Darkness.* Although the Jewish theme does not have a dominant position in the work of Jiri Weiss or his scriptwriter (Weiss spent the Second World War in England and Otcenasek is not a Jew), both men started from the feeling of limitation and tentativeness brought about by the War and, at the same time, by the years of maturation when one desires freedom and wishes to live a rich, exciting life.

In the middle of Hitler's war in Europe, Paul, the son of a Czech tailor, finds the Jewish girl Esther, a high school student before graduation. She is alone, sitting on a park bench, and he joins her. Her parents have been transported to Theresienstadt, but she did not obey the order of deportation. At the moment, she is without family or possessions, helpless. She confides in Paul and awakens his compassion. With a half-childish sincerity, Paul decides to hide the girl in a small room behind his father's tailor shop. It is, first, an unconscious love and, secondly, a kind of rebellion against the times which had changed everything into a huge prison. Paul sets himself free by his action and at the same time takes upon himself an impossible burden. He cannot confide in his parents who live in fear day and night—it is during the weeks of curfew after the assassination of the SS Reichsprotector Heydrich—and he is jeopardizing the safety of his entire family, the entire building. This is the time when the Nazis murder total families, buildings and villages. However, at this very time, friendship and compassion have already developed into first love between the two young people. It is a strong and desperate love.

The Nazis pay for armies of informers who willingly serve them for much less than the notorious thirty silver pieces. One of these informers begins to circle around the hiding place. When Esther realizes the consequences of her discovery, not only for Paul but for his family as well, she leaves her hiding place realizing she is going to death. She is killed at the moment that the German police are enclosing Prague's Ressl's Street church, the hideout for the London-based paratroopers who assassinated Heydrich.

Cinematically, the film is notable for its veneer of black and white light play. Scenes photographed during the night and in the hideout are poetic, tender and aesthetically pleasing, in addition to serving the overall narrative function exactly and succinctly. Indebted to its well-written literary base, ROMEO AND JULIET AND THE DARKNESS reveals not only the historical and psychological environment of the Holocaust in Bohemia, but offers a delicate depiction of an ill-fated love, much in the vein of the tragedy by Shakespeare.

The Nature of Nazism

The availability of historical archival footage in military war archives after the end of the War gave rise to a strong interest in using film materials as the raw material of history. Such footage was incorporated into feature-length and short compilation films, often producing new revelations about all aspects of the War. Freezing film frames, slowing down the projection speed, and magnifying details revealed an often overlooked detail; intelligent editing accentuated important developments and connections. One of the most thorough among the "historical chronicler films" is Erwin Leiser's MEIN KAMPF.

After a comprehensive historical background to World War I and the Weimar Republic, Leiser follows the rise of the Nazi Party and Adolf Hitler, constantly comparing their development with the social, economic and cultural situation in the country. The audience witnesses the lines of 3,000,000 unemployed in 1930—to whom Hitler promised jobs—the 1932 naturalization of the Austrian corporal, Hitler's speech as *Reichskanzler* ("we shall not lie and we shall not cheat!") against the background of Dimitrov's trial, and the bookburning orgies against the nineteenth century warning of Heinrich Heine that "where books are burned, people are burned."

The audience witnesses Nazi putsches in the German states and April 1933 anti-Jewish boycotts. The history continues: within eighteen months Hitler rises to absolute power; the first concentration camps are founded (Oranienburg, in February 1934); by 1935 compulsory military service is established; in 1938 Austria is occupied; in Germany itself hundreds of synagogues are burnt down; during the *Kristallnacht* 7,500 Jewish shops are plundered and 10,000 Jews are deported to Buchenwald. In 1939 Czechoslovakia and Poland are occupied, the war in Europe having started.

In October 1940 a 1.5 square mile Warsaw district is made into a ghetto for 240,000 Jews and 80,000 non-Jews, six persons per room (later rising to thirteen) and allotted 200 calories daily. Thanks to Goebbels' cameraman, one can witness footage of children that cannot walk because their legs are bare bone, children that search each other's heads for lice, and children that are starved to death and fill mass graves with their corpses. In the meantime, the War continues: Norway, Denmark, The Blitz, the invasion of Russia, El Alamein, Stalingrad.

In the Spring of 1943, a brave group of Jews rises against the Nazis in the Warsaw Ghetto Uprising, choosing to die a courageous death with dignity rather than to live and die in slavery. Their deed results in the total destruction of the Ghetto, but they show remarkable human qualities linking them to Jewish heroes like the Maccabees and Bar Kochba. (When the Germans count their booty, they find that against 100 tanks the Jews fought with nine rifles, 59 pistols and a few hundred hand-grenades.)

By 1944, when over 4,700,000 men and women are forced to work in Germany, a dense network of concentration camps built in Eastern Europe under Heinrich Himmler reaches new heights in efficient murder. In Auschwitz that summer, according to Hess, approximately 2,500,000 people are liquidated, 400,000 Jews dying under the command of Adolf Eichmann. Berlin is destroyed. Hitler commits suicide. Fifteen-year-old German soldiers surrender (although in 1939 Hitler had proclaimed: "One word I have never learned . . . surrender"), and the vanquished Germans fight among themselves for the meat of dead horses. When the Supreme Allied Commander, Eisenhower, looks at the dead bodies in liberated camps and turns around in shock, the audience too experiences a shock. One sees the survivors who lived through subanimal suffering and now face an uncertain life ahead, with decimated bodies, destroyed minds and no living relatives or friends. Such images juxtaposed with the overcrowded graves, yards of unburied corpses, skeletons, heaps of human hair, jaws stripped of golden teeth, thousands of spectacles, 500,000 articles of clothing, piles of suitcases, toys, and shoes create in the spectators a painful feeling of terror and pity.

What have the Nazis left behind? An estimated twenty-five million dead soldiers and twenty-four million dead civilians. Of the latter, nine million died in concentration camps, two-thirds of whom were the 72% of the entire prewar Jewry in Europe, approximately six million Jews.

Leiser's work relies on documentary authenticity and humane historical editing as its strongest points. The editing is serious, authoritative, strong, yet poetic (when such feeling is appropriate) and not bombastic. The commentary utilizes a degree of historical detachment but is still involved on a human level, carrying on the feelings of the filmmaker's heart and soul, which are definitely anti-fascist but not hysterical about it. The film relies upon a good use of rhythm and tempo in the intercutting of stills, frozen frames and live footage, always visually documenting the facts to make a point obvious in its historical and human context. Furthermore, the film is not redundant in image and sound, and moves ahead thematically and in time and place in order to offer wealth of detail and breadth of generality, both in the background and the present. MEIN KAMPF offers a slice-of-life picture on the everyday level as well as on the grander level of politics and history. It is a total document destined to testify, probe and provoke.

A film attaining the same heights of quality as MEIN KAMPF is Mikhail Romm's ORDINARY FASCISM. This part compilation—part real-life documentary, begins on a basic human emotional level; i.e., by showing pictures of children's drawings. These are today's children, and their pictures depict foxes, lions and bears. When a frame of a mother with a pretty child appears on the screen, Romm suddenly freezes it and the peace photo becomes a war photograph of a mother with a child, both undergoing intense suffering. One hears a shot, and the freeze-frame is followed by sequences of corpses in camps, heaps of hair, legs and shoes, empty furnaces and night-pots. Then the audience sees Hitler at a parade, and a number of stills and extensive footage documenting the rise of the Nazis to power. At the same time, one becomes acquainted with the environment surrounding Hitler, both inside and outside of Germany: huge parades of Nazis march at night with torches patterned into a swastika, and huge book-burning orgies light the sky; meanwhile the kings of other European countries play tennis and feed the ducks, thousands of spectators spend their time watching car races and listening to Cab Calloway, and the American girls attempt to find the one who fits the exact proportions of Venus styled after Marlene Dietrich.

The director follows the themes important to the viewer's understanding of Nazism: the racial theories (one sees the skulls which "look right"—Bormann's, Rohm's, Streicher's—and the skulls which "look wrong"—Einstein's, Tolstoy's, Chekhov's); the German unity—*Ein Volk, Ein Reich, Ein Fuhrer*—(the Krupps and Goering participate at a fest; and Hitler ceremonially inaugurates a new highway construction); the Third Reich art (Hitler attends a visual arts exhibit filled with Siegfried-like paintings and statues of the *Fuhrer* and German Infantrymen), and the German youth (goose-step marching go-go girls at a cabaret, Hitler Youth, massive induction into the *Wehrmacht,* and swearing-in ceremonies where masses of inductees rid themselves of the right to think and remain human beings).

On the Holocaust itself, Romm shows the prewar Warsaw Ghetto, examining its inhabitants' stills by stopping on faces and figures; he mentions Doctor Korczak and his children, and he points out the gate through which four million passed. He depicts the process of selection where "left" meant death and "right" meant labor, and stops his camera on the group of naked Jews awaiting their gassing—zooming in to the eyes of individuals awaiting their death.

At the same time, Nazi Germany is falling. Its citizens in destroyed cities swear faithfulness to Hitler only to give themselves up within a short time to the Soviet and Western forces.

At the conclusion of the film, decades after the War, the audience witnesses mass rallies of fascists and swastikas on Jewish tombstones—this time they are American and they demonstrate for the freedom of Rudolf Hess. The old Krupp, in the meantime (although his family made 100 marks for every dead), enjoys a peacetime chat. . . . Most significantly, the filmmaker finally asks what changes children, who all over the world are at first good and sweet, into soldiers. As the audience sees a little girl cleaning her nose and a little boy playing with a toy rifle, Romm answers: "We change them."

The strength of ORDINARY FASCISM lies in its instructional quality penetrated with historical richness, authenticity, art and serious wit. The images are chosen according to their historical and educational contents and are given life by the simple, colorful, Russian fablelike commentary which sometimes describes, sometimes contrasts with, the often Eisensteinian camera work. As opposed to the purely humanistic angle of the historian Leiser, Romm's approach to history is class-biased. Yet, even with this rather one-dimensional vision, ORDINARY FASCISM is a live and sensitive chronicler of the events of the Second World War.

Hostile Environment

DIAMONDS OF THE NIGHT is a film based on the autobiographical story *Darkness Casts No Shadow.* In the Spring of 1945, during the transport to death from Buchenwald to Dachau, two boys take advantage of the mistake of an American dive-bomber pilot, who confused their train for a German military transport; after a six-day starvation, the boys attempt a desperate escape. Alone in an unknown forest, they set out to travel east, exhausted and hungry, isolated from the entire world. The longer they are in the woods, the more they resemble animals. One day, they steal food from a German woman in an isolated cottage only to find out that they are unable to pass it through their bleeding mouths. The woman denounces them to the mayor of a nearby town. The last old men remaining in Germany, and not in the military close to the War's end, organize a hunt. The captured boys await the mayor's decision about their fates. Meanwhile three dimensions are visible in the mind of one of the boys. The distant past at home and the more recent past in the camps exist as one dimension; the present in which German old men celebrate the capture of the boys by dancing and eating is the second dimension; the future, where the hope for arriving home in Prague is mixed with fear that they will die close to their destination, is the third dimension. Later, without compassion, the old men hold a mock execution and send the boys into the forest to die.

One of the most notable aspects of Nemec's direction is that he accentuates the story's natural lack of reliance on the usually stressed horrors of war. The presence of armed German soldiers is minimal; there are no interrogations, camps or guards. The horror of the War is shown merely by following the exhausted boys throughout a seemingly hopeless situation during their torturous march. In the style of surrealism, the hand-held camera of Kucera becomes an intimate creative instrument as it intermittently takes on the character of one of the boys or serves the role of an independent observer. Together with the multi-dimensional editing, natural sound and sparse dialogue of six sentences within the film's seventy-one minutes, and the locations of the countryside which can be kind to the strong and cruel to the weak, the photographic elements create a cinematic experience filled with naked emotion and deep truth about the Holocaust and the human condition in general.

Different, yet complementary to DIAMONDS OF THE NIGHT, is the French THE SORROW AND THE PITY. In this four-hour part compilation, part live interview footage staged ingeniously by Marcel Ophuls, one witnesses what many call one of the most shameful periods of French history. Citizens of a small French town located near Vichy, members of the underground, a Jewish biologist, and the former prime ministers of France (Mendes-France) and Great Britain (Anthony Eden) give the viewer an impression that the Vichy period was one of collaboration, racism, cowardice and a lack of dignity. Much like DIAMONDS OF THE NIGHT, this documentary conveys the feeling of the hostile land, of the environment against which the Jews were pitted. For example, in July 1942, the French Police arrested nearly 13,000 Parisian Jews, including over 4,000 children. Although the Nazi orders for this action did not require the inclusion of children, according to Dr. Claude Levy, this was done from the French initiative, as the French racial laws were even stricter than the Nuremberg Laws.

In a gallery of faces and personalities one can observe a range of human reactions to the past: from self-respect to disdain, from apathy to disgrace.

From the mouth of Mendes-France, one hears what it was like to be a Jew in Petain's France and how he escaped from the French prison and became a pilot in de Gaulle's Army. One listens to the members of the resistance and to ordinary citizens (one man advertised in local papers that he was not Jewish) as well as to members of the nobility (a count explains that he fought with French fascist troops against the Soviets because he preferred Hitler to Leon Blum). These sequences are heightened in their effectiveness by being juxtaposed with newsreel footage of the political leadership of Germany, revealing that while the leaders performed state duties and committed crimes against humanity, French entertainers like Maurice Chevalier were entertaining German troops. Chevalier's or Brassens' songs in THE SORROW AND THE PITY ''all have the flavor of loud, buoyant cheerfulness superimposed on a great deal of mute suffering or guilt'' (*New York Times Magazine*, October 17, 1976, p. 4).

The End of a People

When World War II ended, everyone returned home: the French to France, the British to Britain, the Americans to America. Even the Germans went back to Germany; only the Jews did not return—their world was shattered. In Poland, for example, of the 3,500,000 Jews before the War, only 300,000 remained alive after the War. When they returned to towns and villages where they had lived for a thousand years, they found the ruins of their synagogues. In Kazimierz, for instance, only one Yiddish-speaking man returned to pray at the temple built six hundred years before by Kazimierz the Great. When a handful returned, like the ninety in Kelce, they continued to be slaughtered, this time by the anti-Semitic Poles. On July 4, 1946, in a pogrom precipitated by a rumor of the Jewish ritual murder of a Christian child, forty-six of the ninety Jewish survivors of the Nazi terrorism were killed. Thus ended the history of a people in one of Europe's countries; of the few remaining survivors most went to America where some passed the immigration health examination, and a few left for Palestine, landing clandestinely on the beaches near Haifa and Tel Aviv.

The history of the Jews of Poland is the subject of the film LAST CHAPTER. In a documentary form, it depicts the thousand-year flow of events culminating in the Nazi Holocaust: from the tenth century Jewish immigration of merchants from the Volga River, to the cobblers and sea captains of the Jagellonian times, to the seventeenth century nationwide Jewish Parliament, Chmielnicki's pogroms of 1648, to the *Shtetlakh*—Bund, Opatoshy and Ash.

In the 1930's, the Polish Jews did not want to leave their heritage of a millenium and emigrate. At that point Vilna, Bialystock and Cracow were heavily inhabited by the Jews who organized businesses, hospitals, Yeshivas and community centers. Warsaw, settled by Jews since 1430, developed into a center with eighty Jewish papers and magazines, Yiddish theatres and political and social organizations. At that point, every third Warsawian (of the one million total) was Jewish. Thus, after the fall of Poland, Hitler found it convenient that the Jewish population was already concentrated in the ghettos of the Polish cities, and merely walled them off, herding the remaining Jews inside.

The Warsaw Ghetto lived on, with its jester Shmuel Rubinstein and a symphony orchestra playing on homemade instruments, nourished by two hundred calories a day. In the summer of 1942, after one thousand died of starvation, the Jewish head of the *Judenrat* swallowed poison rather than sign a deportation order requiring ten thousand deportees per day.

While the Jews were loaded onto trains taking them to their death, and while Doctor Korczak went with his children to gas, London, America and Moscow remained silent, in spite of urgent cries for help from Jewish activists. In London, for instance, the Bundist member of the Polish Government in exile, Artur Sigelbojm, in desperation over the refusal to act upon the desperate Jewish pleas for action, committed suicide. In the ghetto, meanwhile (April 1943), under the leadership of Mordechai Anielewicz, the Jews rose to live a few days in freedom and die with dignity. No one even dropped medical supplies to the fighters.

The annihilation of most of Poland's Jewry ends the last chapter in the history of one people in a European country. This final chapter is covered in this film fully, powerfully, and sensitively. However, the other periods in Jewish Polish history are also well covered, which is one of the film's greatest strengths. It utilizes rare archival material not incorporated into other films: Yiddish theatre performances, Nazi footage of the Jews in Makov posing for German cameramen by showing noses from profile and heads from high angles through wide-angle, distorting lenses. The commentary, though excessive in a few places (for the pictures speak louder), is rich in the detail and texture added by the velvet voice of Theodore Bikel.

A similar ending to that of the LAST CHAPTER's scenes of the uprising in the Warsaw Ghetto in 1943 makes up a substantial part of the Polish film BORDER STREET. Showing the struggle of a few Jews fighting with homemade weapons and a few captured pistols against Nazi tanks and crack troops, the film does not rely on documentary footage as it attempts to reveal the subjective angle of the participants and other inhabitants of the Ghetto. The film's narrative follows little David, the protagonist, from the time when he plays in the streets with other children and experiences their anti-Semitism at the beginning of war in Poland to the time of the destruction of the Ghetto as he runs in the sewers of Warsaw, having lost his family. Watching little David, the audience experiences almost directly the terrible life and terrible death inflicted upon the Jews of the Warsaw Ghetto, offering them, at best, the sad existence of deserted animals.

Testimony and Comment

One of the most notable Holocaust films ever made is Alain Resnais' NIGHT AND FOG. In a pattern of alternation between the present (1955) in color and the past (World War II) in black and white, the documentary film shows "how simple it is to understand the camps and how impossible" (Hughes, p. 204). Tersely representing the terrible life in a death camp, NIGHT AND FOG moves at a walking pace, along the camp landscape, barbed wire, luscious grass, abandoned railroad tracks, wooden barracks— all in sun-illuminated color. As one senses the quiet atmosphere of an empty camp after the War, Resnais hits the audience with the horrors of the past: watching black and white documentary footage, one becomes aware that the green rich grass of today is nourished by fertilizer, the main components of which are the ashes of human heads and knotted limbs belonging to the shrivelled corpses of starved men and women, their skin tissue-thin. Once they had names: Burgher, German Communist; Stern, a Jewish student from Holland; Schmulski, a Polish merchant; Annette, a French schoolgirl. Then, their heads were shaven, their arms were tattooed and they were classified as Night and Fog [*Nacht und Nebel*]. They entered an Arbeitslager, having arrived in sealed trains, 80 per wagon, in filth, hunger and thirst. But in 1955, under the gates with inscriptions *Jedem das Seine* and *Arbeit Macht Frei*, these people were fertilizer in the earth.

One of the greatest strengths of the film is its poignant commentary by Jean Cayrol, himself a deportee. While selecting images with the richest detail, Cayrol comments, warns and explains. For instance, watching a still of the commandant posing on a camp wall, one hears the comment: "Highest of all: the commandant. From afar he presides over the rites. He pretends to know nothing of the camp" (Hughes, p. 240).

At the film's conclusion, the worried words of the once-hunted Cayrol resound through the theatre:

> The crematorium is no longer in use. The devices of the Nazis are out of date. . . . Who is on the lookout from this strange tower to warn us of the coming of new executioners? . . . . There are those . . . who sincerely look upon the ruins today, as if the old concentration camp monster were dead and buried beneath them. . . . Those who pretend to believe that all this happened only once. . . . who refuse to see, who do not hear the cry to the end of time (Hughes, p. 255).

A film of similar power is the Israeli THE 81ST BLOW. It tells the story of a survivor of Nazi concentration camps whose internment centers around an experience of special significance—he was dealt 80 blows by a stick at the hands of the Germans. When he comes to Palestine and testifies about his experience to his friends, his listeners voice their doubts about the veracity of his tale. Their disbelief is the 81st blow.

While THE 81ST BLOW depicts some of the same themes of Jewish war suffering and annihilation in Nazi camps as NIGHT AND FOG, it, like the French film, transcends the temporal borders of the Nazi rule. It concentrates on the early post-Catastrophe reality, and, in addition, it examines some of the Jewish reactions to the trauma, noticing that for some Jews facing reality is as difficult as it was before the Holocaust.

THE POSTWAR EXPERIENCE

Judgment

In contrast with the uncertain statements about the Nazis and their collaborators' guilt by Anthony Eden in THE SORROW AND THE PITY, in JUDGMENT AT NUREMBERG director Stanley Kramer is not afraid to take a stand. Based on the actual trials of Nazi judges in 1948, the film raises questions of innocence and guilt, cowardice and courage, moral maturity of a nation and an individual, and justice.

An American small-town judge, Dan Haywood from Maine, presides over the trial of four Nazi judges who "committed crimes within the law"— murder, brutality, injustice—by sharing responsibility for these crimes with the Nazi executioners. These judges are defended by a German attorney asking the tribunal to "judge the judges' characters" since they merely carried out the laws of their country. Therefore, this trial should be considered the trial of the German people.

In his free time, Haywood seeks to learn as much as possible about the private side of the German people. In court, he behaves like the epitome of the American spirit of fairness, giving the other side the benefit of the doubt. Nevertheless, the deeds of the defendants speak against them clearly enough. The prosecutor's chief witness, the former law school professor of one of the defendants (Ernst Janning, the Minister of Justice under Hitler), Dr. Wieck, testifies that the independent position of a judge in pre-Nazi Germany changed as the administration of justice was slowly turned over to the state and judges either adapted or resigned. He himself refused to wear a swastika on his gown and resigned as a judge.

In a series of long and absorbing courtroom scenes, the audience meets some of the Nazi judges' victims: a baker's helper, sterilized by Janning's orders since his father was a Communist; Irene Hoffman, sentenced by Janning as a young girl to two years in prison for the crime of "racial pollution" with her sixty-five-year-old Jewish benefactor who was sentenced to death. This notorious Feldenstein case was based on the testimony of a Nazi Party member who had seen Hoffman kissing the Jewish merchant and sitting on his lap; the prosecution headed by another 1948 defendant, Emil Hahn, made a mockery of all the accused said, and the audience laughed for two days, and the verdict was "guilty."

After a distasteful attempt by the defense attorney to imply that there must have been something between Hoffman and Feldenstein, Janning, admitting his guilt and choking with shame, talks about the case himself. At the same time, he gives the German key to the understanding of the rise of Nazism:

> It was like the story of the sacrificial lamb and for the love of Germany. There was fear: fear of the country's neighbors, of the present, past and future, of the Germans themselves. Hitler then was saying: there are devils among us (Jews, Communists, etc.)—destroy them, and there will be no reason to fear. Those Germans who knew better did it only for the love of Germany. What difference did it make that a few Jews or a few Communists would lose their rights or lives during the process? Germany, once again, would be a proud country. To this end, Hitler was to be the means; he was to have been discarded afterwards. But what was to be a passing phase became the way of life. And the world encouraged it. Hitler said Germany wanted the Rhineland; the world said: "Take it!" Hitler wanted Sudetenland; the world said: "Take it!"

Refuting German claims that they did not know what was happening, Janning asks: "Where were we? Were we blind? No, we did not want to know!" Furthermore, he adds, all the judges knew their verdicts before the trials, whatever the evidence.

The tribunal in 1948 found all defendants guilty and sentenced them to life imprisonment. Janning was remorseful, but the others remained convinced of no wrongdoing throughout the trials. Did Janning deserve the same punishment as they? The film attempts to answer by pointing out the parallel case of the German general Carl Berthold, executed for his involvement in the Malmedy case. Loathing Hitler throughout the War, Berthold was sentenced to death and hanged with other Nazis; however, his widow testified that, as a soldier only, he was entitled to a military death by a firing squad. Having been hanged with the other Nazis, he was indistinguishable from those he loathed.

The film also explores the question of collective guilt, fear and courage. Before Irene Hoffman agrees to go to Nuremberg as a witness, the American prosecutor works hard to persuade her. She must overcome the shame and fear of testifying against other Germans, her husband's unwillingness to permit her testimony, and the threat of a boycott of their photo shop. She finally agrees, however, for she feels that "she has responsibility to those who can't get up to the witness stand anymore."

Moreover, one senses this film's concern about the Nazis' disregard for the feelings of other human beings, even after the War, and the lack of desire to repent. These imprisoned criminals demonstrate with cool concern that it is simple to get rid of 10,000 people in half-an-hour, but ''it's not the killing, it's the disposing of the bodies that's a problem.''

Ironically, at the end of the film a caption announces that of the ninety-nine defendants sentenced at the 1948 trials, by the 1961 release of JUDGMENT AT NUREMBERG none are serving their sentences any more. As the caption fades out, clamorous Nazi marching songs fill the theatre. These joyous, vigorous songs create the feeling of respect and fear of the iron might with which Hitler's Germany inflicted pain upon millions. Shivering, the audience once again questions any compassion for and the humility of the sentenced judges (and, for that matter, all sentenced war criminals). The audience realizes, on an emotional level again, that the cruelty perpetrated by those in jail was committed by those in power upon those who could not defend themselves.

Cinematically, JUDGMENT AT NUREMBERG is an absorbing spectacle even though it relies, like most courtroom films, on the spoken word. However, its character portrayals are excellent, thanks to actors Spencer Tracy, Richard Widmark, Maximillian Schell, Marlene Dietrich and Judy Garland. Utilizing terse black and white, functional editing, realistic angles and actors' as well as camera movement, the film succeeds visually, aurally and thematically in presenting the viewer with a powerful and almost vicarious experience.

The pursuit of justice is the focal point of Marcel Ophuls' second four-hour film THE MEMORY OF JUSTICE. Produced along the same technical concept as THE SORROW AND THE PITY, this part compilation, part interview footage examines the trials at Nuremberg right after the War, and what followed.

The archival footage points out the Germany of triumph and defeat, including the beginnings of its new life, the concentration camps, and the Nuremberg trials. It also focuses on the war in Vietnam and Daniel Ellsberg's revelations. The interview footage covers varied spokesmen: the Nazis—Albert Speer, Admiral Doenita; Telford Taylor, the American prosecutor at the trials; and Hartley Shawcross and Edgar Paure, Taylor's British and French counterparts. Ophuls himself appears with his German non-Jewish wife, former German soldiers, Auschwitz inmates who survived, and American and German students.

Interweaving these sources, Ophuls asks questions: What are war crimes? Is there collective guilt? Is it possible to judge any atrocity and massacre with fairness? Are we all part of Auschwitz, Nuremberg and Vietnam?

Ophuls does not fully answer these questions. He attempts to help the viewer consider these questions, offering more than one point of view. Yet, Ophuls reacts on a personal level. When a student at one of his film seminars at Princeton University mentions the "alleged crimes of Goering," the filmmaker attacks the student for not being able to recognize evil because of his preoccupation with his own bad conscience (the war in Vietnam, in this case).

Although the documentary attempts to show a wide variety of viewpoints, in a demonstration of forced "fairness," the filmmaker's subconsciously-felt loyalties surface in the film. Thus, blurring together the differing terror of Nazi death camps, the liberation struggle of Algeria, and the war in Vietnam, the validity of the Nuremberg trials is affirmed in the film by Telford Taylor, the American prosecutor. Responding to the question of whether the Americans, the bombers of Dresden and Hiroshima, had the right to help judge Germany, the lawyer says (*N. Y. Times Magazine,* Oct. 17, 1976; p. 55):

> There are principles which persist . . . in spite of their frequent betrayal in the world. A judge should not think of himself as an exceptionally virtuous man, but as "merely the instrument through which the voice of principle speaks."

According to Ophuls then, "in unjust times . . . we have especial need of the 'memory of justice,' that ghostly reminiscence which makes us believe we know what justice might be, even if we don't see it practiced much around us" (ibid). That memory is the reason for the existence of this personal film composed of greatly diverse footage, commentary and music, a film which makes a full circle as far as Jewish attitudes are concerned. Like the Jews in the 1930's who hated Hitler but loved Germany, Ophuls finds himself in the same place only one level higher; he fully realizes the evil of Nazism, not considering Hitler a mere clown and his followers fanatical fools. Therefore, the filmmaker produces his painful documents.

The Survivor

Many claim that the survivor is a punished person. He is neurotic, troubled by guilt feelings, psychoses, nightmares and visions. He often demonstrates a strong personality, yet lives submerged in the past. A portrayal of this kind of person was attempted in a number of films, among which THE MAN IN THE GLASS BOOTH excels.

It is a story of Mr. Goldman, a wealthy New York Jewish builder who has visions of his dead father selling pretzels at a corner under his apartment's windows. Persecuted by hearing Hitler's speeches and the sounds accompanying a deportation, Goldman's greatest fear is that Nazi Colonel Adolf Dorf, responsible for his father's death, is free and conspiring to kidnap him. He spends time in his attic where he hides concentration camp memorabilia: striped shirts, yellow stars, menorahs, old wire-rimmed glasses, and *yarmul-*

kas. Among these items Goldman prays, and he burns his arm with a candle, crying over a trunk full of documentary photographs and newspaper clippings of camp inmates.

One day Goldman dresses in his best and, as if waiting for a visit, listens to Nazi marching songs. Suddenly, three Israeli agents armed with an Uzi submachine gun and revolvers burst into the apartment and arrest him. According to X-ray photographs of his teeth, a broken clavicle and vertebrae, they ascertain that the man is not the Jew Goldman who survived Nazi death camps, but Nazi Colonel Adolf Dorf, taking cover as the Jew, Mr. Goldman.

In the Israeli jail, Dorf is met by his prosecutor, the sabra lawyer Miriam, whom he treats with sexual vulgarity. However, for Dorf's admission that he had lied while entering the United States, she allows him to defend himself dressed in his Nazi uniform. He is also examined by an Israeli psychiatrist who pronounces him normal within a psychotic society of Nazi Germany, thus psychotic; a diagnosis which the Colonel scorns.

Put into a glass booth so as to be protected from the wrath of the courtroom audience, Dorf explains the working process of his camp. When it was cheaper to kill Jews than to keep them, they killed them. In Mauthausen, for instance, the Jews were killed in the "war effort"—stone carrying work during which whoever fell was shot. The system worked because of the total depersonalization of the inmates attained by taking away from them decisions and future, by creating a meaningless mass from what used to be individuals, and by constantly demeaning them.

The evidence against Dorf is overwhelming. A German cinematographer testifies that in the Talnia ghetto in Poland, Dorf ordered film coverage of an operation he commanded. Men gathered in a small room were closely fired onto by a cannon. Shattered into pieces by the shell, these people were piled up into a heap of body parts and then relatives were called to find their fathers' and brothers' pieces and reassemble them. Another witness had seen the Colonel shoot four camp inmates and make the others urinate on the corpses. When Dorf proudly admits all of his crimes, he asks why the Jews offered no resistance (at which point the glass booth is pounded into by angered Israelis).

Later Dorf is allowed to explain what enabled Hitler to rise to power and the Germans to carry out his internecine orders. The Germans feared the Jews; even Hitler feared them. And because they loved Hitler, they followed him. They felt "in fear . . . they . . . would kill and in killing . . . they would live," as the desire to kill is natural and a "murder keeps a man fit."

During the trial only one uncertainty arose. Was it certain that the man in the booth was Dorf? Mr. Goldman's assistant Charlie Cohen remained convinced that the man in the booth was Mr. Goldman who was ill. However, when an Argentinean surgeon admits that he forged Goldman's X-rays for $10,000, and when a West German dentist admits that he also forged Goldman's dental X-rays, it becomes obvious that the man in the booth is

Arthur Goldman, a psychotic Jew who in his schizophrenia wanted to taste what it was like to be a Nazi murderer who killed Goldman's father.

When asked by the judge why he wanted to take the guilt upon himself, Goldman becomes catatonic, locks himself in the booth and hears only German marching music, sounds of deportation and a transport train, crying of children and German orders, military noise and shots. He undresses, spreads his arms, (appearing like Jesus Christ) and dies of a broken heart.

One of the most remarkable aspects of the film is the ironic ambiguity between a camp survivor and a Nazi colonel. It is frightening how similar they can both be in their aesthetic, business, academic and living styles. The sympathy of the audience for Mr. Goldman changes into the hate for the same (in physical appearance, at least) man; moreover, while he looks like the Nazi, one has to admit he has many admirable traits: intelligence, wit, knowledge, courage, ingenuity. In this, the film helps one understand that the enemy was, indeed, a capable and forbidding one. The changing identification with the character helps one to understand his own soul a little better, for in everyone there is a little bit of both Mr. Goldman and Colonel Dorf.

THE MAN IN THE GLASS BOOTH is indebted to its literary base, Robert Shaw's play based on his novel *The Flag,* and the superlative acting by the Austrian Maximillian Schell in the role of Goldman-Dorf. He portrays both characters with chilling truthfulness, evoking in the viewer compassion for one and detestation for the other. Both states give rise to soul-searching on the part of the audience.

THE PAWNBROKER is another film which examines the difficult adaptation process of the concentration camp survivor. It is the story of the psychopathological adaptation by Sol Nazerman, a Jew who survived a concentration camp apart from his exterminated family. He cannot adjust to his new life as a pawnbroker in a shabby Harlem shop, a place also full of horror, cruelty and injustice. Painfully, Nazerman relives his old life via daily flashbacks which return him to his lost loved ones. Every outward similarity to a previous situation stimulates him to evoke traumatic memories. One example is a ride in a New York subway car which changes into a crowded transport train wagon where his son had been crushed to death; at another time, seeing a partially dressed woman, Nazerman cannot help remembering the scenes of the rape and death of his wife at the hands of German soldiers.

Although the survivor's adjustment is painful and difficult—he has been punished far too heavily for one human being to withstand—it can proceed toward a satisfactory state of the strained psyche. The selfless death of Nazerman's assistant during a robbery of the shop awakens in him the long dormant affective mechanisms which function in the present, and the survivor begins to look for a new meaning in life.

The film's notable structure, reminiscent of DIAMONDS OF THE NIGHT, also centers around the inter-cutting of sequences occurring in the present and the past to the point where the structure becomes an aesthetic and emotional experience in itself. By this means, the audience experiences the frustration and helplessness of the past and the flattened effect of the present. Heightened by the strict, realistic black and white rawness of the footage, the honesty of Steiger's Nazerman, and the visual weight of the grey shadows on the oppressive Harlem walls contrasting with the lighter tone of the happier memories, THE PAWNBROKER is a sad testimony of the continuing punishment of the victims of the Holocaust.

Because the postwar experience is represented considerably less than the war experience, a second alternative is presented here in addition to THE PAWNBROKER. This exception is dictated by an attempt to present a well-rounded course on the Holocaust.

Of the same breed as the last film is the Czech DITA SAXOVA, written according to events which actually occurred. It is the story of an 18-year-old Jewish woman who returned to Prague as a survivor of Nazi camps together with children after whom only memorabilia like those of the children of I NEVER SAW ANOTHER BUTTERFLY were left. On the outside, it seems this girl is happy only because she survived Hell. She is blond, blue-eyed, merry at every occasion, ready to make up for the three years spent in a concentration camp by living up the rest of her life. In reality, she is attempting to overcome isolation and disappointment in a world not completely ready to right the wrongs of the past.

The film expresses the thoughts of the novel *Dita Saxova,* on which it is based; namely, that the sickness of mistrust and loneliness is strongest in the handful of people who came back from the War and the camps too young to be left to their own devices, and yet too old to allow others to look after them.

The film emphasizes what a few realized after the War, that the tragedy of people who lived through concentration camps did not finish by exiting through a camp gate, that for many the second chapter of the tragedy occurred simultaneously with the moment which outwardly seemed the happiest of all—the moment of liberation. The concentration camps may have ended in the real world, but not within the souls of the victims. Besides, not even the real world is peaceful; contrary to all calls for peace, the world of peace is not quite normal.

Dita Saxova embodies the people who were returning from the Nazi camps. She is considerably more sensitive than other youths of her age toward the abnormalities of the normal world. Her effort at reconstructing the postwar world in her soul is wrecked; even weak tremors seem enormous, even merely unquiet dreams appear as nightmares, and Dita Saxova ends up in suicide.

The tender sensitivity of DITA SAXOVA is the result of the cooperation between Antonin Moskalyk (the director of, among other films, PRAYER FOR KATERINA HOROVITZOVA—the winner of the Monte Carlo Television Film Festival and eight other international awards*) and the cinematographer Jaroslav Kucera. The film's visual richness is enhanced by the poetic black and white, with a multitude of gray middle tones. Audially, one hears a concert of symphonic pieces and jazz songs textured by past dreams and an uncertain future, composed by Lubos Fiser. DITA SAXOVA is not as famous internationally as the other films of the Czech New Wave because it was the last film released before the Soviet invasion of Prague.*

CONCLUSION

The approach to the film selection for this course on Jewish Holocaust in Film has been a historical one. Of course, it is possible to use other criteria to organize the structure of such a course. For instance, one can emphasize form; one can select only documentary or only theatrical films, films produced by a certain studio, a certain country (with clear formal distinctions), or within a certain time limit (e.g., during the War years, or two decades after the Catastrophe). Using content or methodology as the criterion, one can select films concerned specifically with Eastern Europe's Jewish Holocaust, or films based on actual events, films re-creating imaginary Holocaust reality, other films utilizing the anthropological or the sociological approach to name a few.

The historical approach to the course in the Holocaust seems to contain elements of all the other possible approaches. First, considering the time period which has passed since the Catastrophe, it seems to be the most objective. Secondly, from the pedagogical point of view, the historical approach is the most understandable, covering the most extensive chronological stages of the Holocaust experience. Thirdly, this approach is the most universal vis-à-vis the Jewish experience and the audience, giving the student a feeling for the human elements of the experience, both academic and emotional. Thus, the historical criterion most naturally dictates the structure of this course on Jewish Holocaust in Film.**

---

*PRAYER FOR KATERINA HOROVITZOVA tells the story of a Jewish girl who, realizing that she and her fellow Jews are going to be gassed, takes a German officer's revolver from his holster and shoots him in a desperate affirmation of her human dignity. Banned in Czechoslovakia, this film is, at the moment, unavailable for distribution in the West as well.

**See discussion at the end of Chapter Four.

BIBLIOGRAPHY

General Works (quoted above):

BARNOW, ERIK. *Documentary* (Oxford: Oxford University Press, 1974).

BARSAM, RICHARD. *Non-Fiction Film* (New York: Dutton, 1973).

GRIERSON, JOHN. *Grierson on Documentary* (London: Faber and Faber, 1966).

HUGHES, ROBERT, ed. *Film: Book II* (New York: Grove Press, 1962).

HULL, DAVID. *Film in the Third Reich* (Los Angeles: University of California Press, 1969).

KRACAUER, SIEGFRIED. *From Caligari to Hitler* (Princeton: Princeton University Press, 1947).

LIEHM, ANTONIN. *Closely Watched Films* (New York: International Arts and Sciences Press, 1974).

New York Times Magazine, October 17, 1976.

FILMOGRAPHY

Films are listed according to the order in which they are discussed above. If a film is based upon a literary work, information regarding that work is provided.

SHIP OF FOOLS. Directed and produced by Stanley Kramer. United States, 1965. Distributed by Columbia Pictures. From the book: *Ship of Fools* by Katherine Anne Porter (Boston: Little Brown, 1962; paperback: Signet, 1963).

VOYAGE OF THE DAMNED. Produced by Stewart Rosenberg. Screenplay by S. Shagen and D. Butler. From the book: *Voyage of the Damned* by Gordon Thomas and Max Witts (New York: Fawcett Crest paperback, 1974).

CABARET. Directed by Robert Fosse. United States, 1972. Distributed by Allied Artists. From the book: *The Berlin Stories* by Christopher Isherwood (New York: New Direction, 1945).

THE GARDEN OF THE FINZI-CONTINIS. Directed by Vittorio De Sica. Italy, 1971. Distributed by Cinema V. From the book: *The Garden of the Finzi-Continis* by George Bassani (New York: Harvest paperbacks, 1977).

TRIUMPH OF THE WILL. Directed and produced by Leni Riefenstahl. Germany, 1934. Distributed by Images (Department of Film, Museum of Modern Arts).

PROPAGANDA FILMS I. Various producers and directors. Germany, 1934, 1937, 1940. Distributed by Images.

I NEVER SAW ANOTHER BUTTERFLY. Produced by the Studio for Popular Science Films. Czechoslovakia, 1961. Distributed by Contemporary Films.

TRANSPORT FROM PARADISE. Directed by Zbynek Brynych. Produced by Film Studio Barrandov, Prague. Czechoslovakia, 1962. Distributed by Impact Films. From the book: *Night and Hope* by Arnost Lustig (Washington: Inscape, 1977; Avon paperback, 1978).

THE SHOP ON MAIN STREET. Directed by Jan Kadar. Produced by Film Studio Barrandov. Prague, 1966. Distributed by Prominent Films and Jewish Welfare Board. From the book: *Shop on Main Street* by Ladislav Grosman (New York: Doubleday, 1970).

AND FIFTH HORSEMAN IS FEAR. Directed by Zbynek Brynych. Produced by Barrandov, Prague, 1964.

THE DIARY OF ANNE FRANK. Directed by George Stevens. United States, 1959. Distributed by Twentieth Century Fox, Incorporated Films and Jewish Welfare Board. From the book: *Anne Frank: The Diary of a Young Girl* (New York: Doubleday, 1952; Pocket Books paperback, 1953).

ROMEO AND JULIET AND THE DARKNESS. Directed by Jiri Weiss. Produced by Barrandov. Prague, 1966. Distributed by Promenade Films and Mac Millan Audio Brandon. From the book: *Romeo and Juliet and the Darkness* (*Sweet Light in a Dark Room*) by Jan Otcenasek (Prague: Artia, 1960).

MEIN KAMPF. Directed by Erwin Leiser. Produced by Tore Sjoberg. Sweden, 1961. Distributed by Columbia Pictures and Modern Sound Pictures.

ORDINARY FASCISM. Directed by Mikhail Romm. Produced by Mosofilm. Union of Soviet Socialist Republics, 1965. Distributed by Joseph Brenner Associates.

DIAMONDS OF THE NIGHT. Directed by Jan Nemec. Produced by Barrandov, Prague, 1964. Distributed by Impact Films. From the book: *Darkness Casts No Shadow* by Arnost Lustig (Washington: Inscape, 1977; Avon paperback, 1978).

THE SORROW AND THE PITY. Directed by Marcel Ophuls. France, 1972. Distributed by Cinema V.

BORDER STREET. Directed by Alexander Ford. Produced by Film Polski. Poland, 1948. Distributed by Globe Films and Jewish Welfare Board.

NIGHT AND FOG. Directed by Alain Resnais. France, 1955. Distributed by Argos Films and Contemporary Films.

THE 81ST BLOW. Produced by J. Aulich, D. Bergman and C. Guri under the auspices of the Kibbutz of Ghetto Fighters, Camp Inmates and Nazi Victims. Israel, 1975. Distributed by the American Federation of Jewish Fighters, Camp Inmates and Nazi Victims, New York.

JUDGEMENT AT NUREMBERG. Directed and produced by Stanley Kramer. United States, 1961. Distributed by United Artists and Jewish Welfare Board. From the book: *Judgment at Nuremberg* by Abby Mann (London: Cassel, 1961).

THE MEMORY OF JUSTICE. Directed by Marcel Ophuls. France, United Kingdom, Germany, 1976.

THE MAN IN THE GLASS BOOTH. United States, 1975. Distributed by American Film Theatre. From the book: *The Flag* and from the play *The Man in the Glass Booth,* both by Robert Shaw (New York: Harcourt, Brace and World, 1967; New York: Grove paperback, 1968). (See discussion of this play above in the sub-chapter on drama based upon the Holocaust).

THE PAWNBROKER. Directed by Stanley Lumet. United States, 1965. Distributed—Ely Landau-Herbert Steinman, and Jewish Welfare Board. From the book: *The Pawnbroker* by Edward Lewis Wallant (New York: Harcourt, Brace and World, 1961; paperback, 1962).

DITA SAXOVA. Directed by Antonin Moskalyk. Produced by Barrandov, Prague, 1968. From the book: *Dita Saxova* by Arnost Lustig (New York: Harper and Row, 1979).

Music and Art
of the Holocaust*

Susan G. Ament

INTRODUCTION

The paradox of the immortality of man's spirit despite his physical mortality, has long challenged those seeking to describe and interpret human civilization. The annihilation of European Jewry during the Holocaust dramatically illustrates this paradox. Much of Holocaust history, biography and literature reflects the power of the written word in portraying the indestructibility of the spirit of the Jew, even in the presence of acute suffering and apparent defeat. Less obvious, but just as powerful as written testimony, is the spiritual resistance engendered by the Jewish art and music of the Holocaust. Despite Nazi determination to obliterate Jewish artistic expression, there is abundant and varied evidence of Jewish art and music produced as part of the Holocaust experience in camps, ghettos, and forests.

This chapter will concentrate primarily on Jewish art and music *during* the Holocaust. In general, this chapter will focus only briefly on post-Holocaust responses in Jewish art and music. Occasionally, the Jewish art and music during the Holocaust will overlap with the post-Holocaust responses in Jewish art and music.

THERESIENSTADT

Most of the known art and music of the Holocaust came out of the Theresienstadt Ghetto (Czech: Terezin) because many of the best trained Jewish artists and musicians from Europe were sent there.

*The author of this chapter wishes to thank Janet Blatter, art archivist at YIVO Institute in New York, for her personal consultation and for making her excellent manuscript "The Holocaust in Art" available for this research.

Theresienstadt was created as a Jewish ghetto by Reinhard Heydrich. Originally a small military garrison town located thirty-five miles from Prague, Theresienstadt had been inhabited by 7,000–8,000 soldiers and peasants. The town was named after Maria Theresa, the Eighteenth Century Empress of Austria.

Under Heydrich's orders, Theresienstadt was first dissolved as a city and then the resident Czech population was evacuated. Next, multitudes of Jews began to inhabit the ghetto of Theresienstadt by the beginning of 1942. At first, this ghetto was intended for (1) the old and sickly, (2) prominent disabled Jewish World War I veterans, and (3) Jews too famous to merely disappear without inquiry from the world community. Later the ghetto was expanded to include many other residents. By the end of that first year (1942), this town that had housed 7,000–8,000 was inhabited by over 90,000 Jews.

Because the Nazis originally portrayed Theresienstadt as a "Paradise Ghetto," many German Jews sought to enter Theresienstadt in order to improve the quality of their lives from that which they were experiencing in Germany. In addition, more and more prominent European Jews were invited to share "special treatment" in Theresienstadt. Instead of finding a "Paradise Ghetto," Jews lost their material possessions and their freedom in Theresienstadt. Living conditions were crowded, uncomfortable, and unsanitary in this "model ghetto." Hard work, severe punishment, disease, and starvation were the norm. Between 1941 and 1945, nearly 140,000 Jews were deported to Theresienstadt. Of these deportees, approximately 87,000 were sent to the extermination camps, such as Auschwitz and Treblinka; over 33,000 died or were killed in Theresienstadt itself. Of the 15,000 children in Theresienstadt, only 100 survived.

In spite of the precarious living conditions in Theresienstadt, the people developed a full rich cultural program there. Eliminated from public life once again in their history, Jews once again found a sense of purpose and normalcy through cultural endeavors. Both professional and amateur artists and musicians viewed their cultural activities in Theresienstadt as continuing proof that the Jews were not subhuman, as Nazi ideology claimed, but were cultured human beings capable of making considerable contributions to European culture. Thus, artistic creativity served to instill feelings of self-worth and unity among the people of Theresienstadt.

At first, the Jewish cultural life of Theresienstadt developed secretly. Since so many of the best trained Jewish artists and musicians of Europe were in Theresienstadt, a fuller and richer secret cultural life developed in Theresienstadt than in the other ghettos or camps. Even after the Nazis became aware of this rich development, they seemingly did not fear that any of the Theresienstadt culture would escape that walled-in fortress. The Nazis presumably viewed the artists, composers, musicians, and audience of Theresienstadt as people with only doom in their future. Therefore, it seems that the

Nazis initially tolerated musical activity in Theresienstadt in order to pacify the Jews. Later, the Nazis permitted, and sometimes even encouraged, music and other Jewish cultural life to flourish in Theresienstadt in order to foster the "myth" of the idyllic life of the Jews of Theresienstadt. Decorating the ghetto with the "approved" art works of the contented prisoners served the Reich as further evidence for the world that Theresienstadt was a typical peaceful and comfortable Jewish ghetto. Art, music, literature, and lectures were all sanctioned and even encouraged if they were of an apolitical genre. However, when the artists of Theresienstadt dared to expose the sociopolitical realities about Theresienstadt through their "subversive" art, the Nazis eliminated these artists.

ART OF THE HOLOCAUST: THERESIENSTADT

Most of the known concentration camp art was created in Theresienstadt. The camp artists were allowed to perform a wide variety of "official" functions. At work in the "Drawing House," affiliated with the technical department of Theresienstadt, the artists created extensive graphic work, copied masterpieces, painted landscapes and portraits for the SS, and decorated the camp for propaganda purposes. As an elite camp group, these artists officially spent much of their time creating charts, blueprints, and posters for the Germans. Bedřich Fritta led the group, which included Felix Block, Leo Haas, Otto Ungar, and the architect Norman Troller.

In their free time, the camp artists were permitted to do other art work as long as it was neutral or nondidactic. Some of the Theresienstadt artists began to work secretly to depict actual conditions in the camp. Assuming a political role, they used their art to expose the reality behind the Nazis' model community of Theresienstadt.

The Nazis dealt harshly with those creating *greuelpropaganda* or "horror art," i.e., art which criticized the Reich. The interrogation and resultant imprisonment and death of some of the major Theresienstadt artists resulted from the fact that one of the Theresienstadt art collectors was found with some of the *greuelpropaganda* drawings. Ungar, Fritta, and Block died; only Haas survived. They were condemned for depicting "lies" about the Nazis in Theresienstadt. However, their work remains as examples of significant acts of defiance and resistance to Nazi oppression.

Art in a Concentration Camp: Drawings from Terezin was an exhibition organized in the 1960s that combined works of both the professional artists and the child artists of Theresienstadt. Consisting of paintings, drawings, and sketches, the exhibit was first shown at the New School for Social Research in New York. Afterwards, it traveled throughout the United States. Over 100 of these works of art were included in Gerald Green's *The Artists of Terezin.*

To better understand the backgrounds and achievements of the artists of Theresienstadt, Green provides a revealing picture of some of the artists and their art. Otto Ungar, Bedřich Fritta and Leo Haas were professionally trained illustrators. Tortured and crippled for his secret art, Ungar had utilized his art to sensitively and honestly portray ordinary camp people. Ungar's works have been preserved both in the Yad Vashem Museum in Jerusalem and the Prague Jewish Museum. Officially, Fritta was the head draftsman in charge of creating charts for the Germans. One of the two natural leaders of the Theresienstadt artists in their attempt to record the truth about Theresienstadt, Fritta was both political and anti-German for many years. His artworks are most somber and chilling. Bulging and blind, the eyes of Fritta's prisoners underline what remains of them as human beings. The darkness and boldness of his lines emphasize his recurring motifs of terror, gloom and impending death. In his sketches, one sees such images as buzzardlike ravens next to slumped figures, or gnarled dead trees. (This same artist also created a lovely children's primer for his young son Tomáš. The book survived and was used as a primer by Fritta's orphaned son.)

Haas, the other leader of the Theresienstadt artists, was already established as a satirical cartoonist and had already built up a sketchbook of prison conditions in a previous situation, utilizing merciless sketches of his jailers. Haas' powerful drawings document the incongruities of life in Theresienstadt. Recording the many daily events in Theresienstadt, his drawings effectively capture the people as they lose their human dignity and go through various stages of "psychological death." Although Karel Fleischmann was a dermatologist who was never part of the official Theresienstadt art group, he was another important artist who saw and depicted the truth in Theresienstadt. The camp inmates in his drawings struggle for human dignity and sanity in spite of constant horrors.

The "objectionable" secret works of the artists of Theresienstadt were clearly *greuelpropaganda*. Subjects covered include transports to extermination camps, overcrowded bunkers, long roll calls, working conditions in the ghetto, starvation, the hearse, and the nature of ghetto entertainment. The drawings capture such incongruities as that of the people, who had become zombies or *musselmen,* listening to a concert with blank eyes. Frequent themes in these drawings are: (1) slow deaths by uncertainty, (2) aging as a ghastly and premature process, (3) loss of dignity, and (4) arbitrary punishment and violence. A theme such as loss of dignity is illustrated vividly in the Theresienstadt drawings by portraying the people as numbers and by depicting many stooped figures. Working with the *greuelpropaganda* of the subjects and themes, the expressionistic techniques in these drawings tend to produce a disturbing repulsive effect. The emphasis on darkness and the harsh contrast between light and dark intensify the grimness and the impending doom that one finds in the drawings. Janet Blatter, art archivist, remarks that:

It seems almost as if expressionism, with its severe contrasts of light and dark, angularity and jagged lines, exaggerations and distortions in the style of caricature, had been developed through the years specifically for the visual realization of the Holocaust. . . . the effect is one of a curious mixture of repulsion at what one sees and attraction for the way it was accomplished.

Clearly, the Nazis objected to some of the Theresienstadt art not only as *greuelpropaganda* but also as examples of expressionism, a "degenerate modern art" style banned by the Reich for its political implications. Although many of these works exhibit some of the characteristics of expressionism, Blatter cautions against oversimplification in examining this Holocaust art:

In general, there is clarity in certain details (empty pots, signs to the entrances of the "shops," crutches carried by the blind) which take precedence over the more non-representational features of expressionism. After all, parts of the works were intended to serve a specific if not exclusive purpose of recording, informing and arousing to action those who were in a position to influence the policies of Terezin.

In contrast with some of the powerful expressionistic works of the major professional Theresienstadt artists portrayed by Green in *The Artists of Terezin,* simplicity and restraint characterize the works of young Alfred Kantor in *The Book of Alfred Kantor.* From the time of his arrival in Theresienstadt as a teenager, Alfred Kantor decided to keep a record of his imprisonment. During the three and a half years he spent in Nazi camps of Theresienstadt, Auschwitz and Schwarzheide, he sketched whenever possible. Kantor destroyed most of the sketches to avoid detection. Nevertheless, he notes (in *The Book of Alfred Kantor*) that "once drawn, these scenes could never be erased from mind . . . When I was free again, the rescued material—and the lost sketches I had committed to memory—made it possible to put together my diary."

Concerned with communicating his experiences effectively, Kantor first began to write the captions under his drawings in his native Czech. In his "Introduction" to *The Book of Alfred Kantor,* Kantor adds that he then wrote the captions in English because he planned to immigrate to America right after the War and wanted to be sure that people there would understand what he was saying. Kantor was so prolific that his art really comprises a visual diary of his life in Terezin, Auschwitz and Schwarzheide. Some of the watercolor sketches that he compiled in the displaced persons' camp at Deggendorf were based on the original pencil sketches he drew in earlier camps. Kantor, like the other artists of Theresienstadt, focuses on the loss of human dignity that accompanies both the loss of privacy and the crowded depersonalization of camp existence. When he depicts the daily activities of camp life, even Kantor's simple bold lines and lack of melodrama do not conceal the realities of Jewish life and death that he witnessed in Theresienstadt and beyond. His drawings from later camps feature crematoria, death lines, hearses, corpses and burning bodies.

Another Theresienstadt artist, whose drawings exhibit not only a detached style (like Kantor) but also detachment in subject matter, is Adolph Aussenberg. Confined in the Theresienstadt infirmary due to a heart condition, Aussenberg created ink sketches of daily life in Theresienstadt, both inside and outside of the infirmary. Although his drawings initially seem ambiguous in subject matter and location, closer scrutiny reveals that in some of the drawings he too has created *greuelpropaganda* depicting the horrors of life in Theresienstadt. However, Blatter emphasizes that, unlike the extreme visions of sickness and aging in the drawings of Haas or Fritta, the benign infirmary drawings of Aussenberg display "none of the bitterness or anger of these other artists. His works apparently belong to the type of art approved of by the Nazi officials, and it is possible that these works decorated the children's bunkers."

Each in his own way, the Theresienstadt artist utilized his work to record and to describe what he witnessed. The form that he chose for artistic expression was dictated not only by his training and preference but also by the availability of supplies and by the need for concealment. Due to their official camp assignments in the technical department, the official Theresienstadt artists had abundant supplies of paper, pens, ink, paints, and brushes for drawing. Flattering appropriate Nazi officers resulted in additional drawing supplies. When art supplies were difficult to obtain in Theresienstadt and other camps, some drawings employed such available materials as the back of official notices and posters, graph paper, paper bags, cardboard boxes, remnants of flour sacks, old cement bags, and old newspaper used as wrapping paper.

Because the artists never knew when the Nazis would search their premises or transport some of them, drawings were an especially appropriate form for their art of protest against the Nazis. Drawings were considerably easier to smuggle out or hide than paintings or sculptures. In fact, due to the danger involved, many of the artists did not even have ample time to develop sketches into drawings. What was done with some of the secret art that really recorded life in Theresienstadt? Artists such as Haas and Fritta, anticipating a possible Nazi search, had the foresight to hide many of their secret works either within wall paneling (Haas) or in a tin case in a farmyard (Fritta). All of these works of Fritta and Haas survived the War; most belong to the Jewish Museum of Prague. Whether they hoped to reclaim the works themselves after the War or merely leave them for another to discover, a number of the artists felt the importance of preserving their works for historical and/or psychological reasons. The spiritual resistance offered by their art of protest was destined to survive as a model for both old and new generations. Other means of preserving some of the secret Theresienstadt art included selling some works to ghetto art lovers in exchange for food and smuggling some works out of Theresienstadt to hopefully reach the appropriate foreign group.

Although sculptures were generally too difficult to either secretly create or to conceal in the camps, the sculptor Arnold Zadikow did plan sculptures during his internment in Theresienstadt. However, he did not survive to create them later; only a few of his sketches, camp drawings and sculpture plans are preserved at the Yad Vashem Museum.

A considerable collection that has been preserved is depicted in *I Never Saw Another Butterfly: Children's Drawings and Poems From Terezin Concentration Camp 1942–1944*. These Theresienstadt drawings, collected from the 4,000 drawings in the archives of the State Jewish Museum in Prague, represent the work of thirty-nine children (ages ten to fifteen). Some drawings were selected to illustrate poems written by the children in the ghetto; others were chosen for their artistic excellence. The girls' drawings show their interest in remembered and treasured features of nature that they had left behind them, such as butterflies, flowers, and cottages with flower gardens. The boys occupied themselves with more concrete details of nearby hills, vivid illustrations of battle scenes, and concrete pictures of the full range of daily camp experiences also depicted by many of the professional adult artists. Unlike the adult artists of Theresienstadt who primarily chose to depict the reality of life there in their personal artwork, the youthful artists of Theresienstadt drew both the real world that they saw and the dream world that they remembered and/or longed for. One cannot justly compare the children's drawings to those of the trained adult camp artists. Nevertheless, as individual expressions of the suffering and the hope of the children of Theresienstadt, the drawings preserve their voices and honor their memories. Of the 15,000 children (under age fifteen) who entered Theresienstadt, only 100 survived.

Focusing on the Holocaust art in Theresienstadt has disclosed a definite emphasis on creative art. In contrast, the examination of the musical culture of Theresienstadt will reveal more of a central stress on interpretative art rather than on creative art.

MUSIC OF THE HOLOCAUST—THERESIENSTADT

Musical performances in Theresienstadt during the Holocaust strongly reflected the living conditions there. Musicians used compositions that they had previously memorized plus whatever else became available. Standard works by masters were in much demand. Because scores were sparse, folk songs often had to be arranged for choral groups. Clearly this was primarily interpretative art rather than creative art. With freer expression permitted in Theresienstadt and more musical artists interned there, the musical life in Theresienstadt was much fuller than in other ghettos and camps. The thorough German documentation plus the souvenirs of survivors provide much information on musical expression in Theresienstadt. Musicians, like artists (e.g., Alfred Kantor), strove to preserve evidence of the music life in such a place as Theresienstadt. Evidence includes: (1) drawings depicting Theresienstadt musical activities, (2) a few concert bills, (3) a few musical manuscripts, (4) commemorative recordings of Theresienstadt musical performances, (5) a few sketches for the operas staged there, (6) other assorted documents, and (7) eyewitness accounts.

Milan Kuna points out that the central paradox of the rich musical activity in Theresienstadt was that amidst all the horror and darkness around it, the music functioned with immediate and immense ethical power. Somehow the strains of the music helped to blot out political, national, social, and intellectual differences. Both the audience and the performer welcomed musical performances with enthusiasm.

Operatic performances played a significant role in Theresienstadt. Most opera performed there was concert opera, often only excerpts. The majority of the operas had multiple performances. The psychological needs of the people are dramatically illustrated by Alfred Kantor's drawing of their enthusiastic attendance at a secret performance of Bizet's opera *Carmen* in a soundproofed attic and accompanied by a broken piano. Although several of the operas were fully staged and quite lavish, in general musical performances were set on simple stages, in lofts, or in quickly cleared rooms. The performances featured homemade costumes and undistinguished scenery. None of these factors destroyed the enthusiasm of the audience or the performers. For the many talented professional singer-soloists interned at Theresienstadt, the operatic performances there were their only artistic outlet. Eyewitness testimonies plus secret letters preserved from some of the singers substantiate the importance of the performances to the singers.

The greatest operatic success at Theresienstadt was the children's opera *Brundibar* by Hans Krása, which was performed fifty-five times with Rudolf Freudenfeld conducting. The public interpreted it as a declaration of victory and hope each time the children sang the song of victory over the mean organ-grinder. The tragedy of this opera was that part of the cast went to Auschwitz after each performance and had to be replaced each time. The Jews at Theresienstadt also found *The Bartered Bride* by Bedřich Smetana to be especially memorable, and the opera was performed about thirty-five times. Not only were the professional soloists of high caliber, but experiencing this opera infused the Jews with a feeling of human dignity.

Rafael Schächter, the main talent behind the operatic performances in Theresienstadt, handled diverse aspects ranging from choral and orchestral conducting to piano accompaniment and operatic staging. He worked with operas by composers such as Smetana and Mozart. Franz Eugen Klein, a former orchestra conductor, also helped to organize and conduct performances of famous operatic works in Theresienstadt, including Verdi's *Rigoletto,* Puccini's *Tosca,* and Bizet's *Carmen.* Klein also was the composer of one of the two operas written in Theresienstadt. His opera *The Glass Mountain (Der Gläserne Berg)* was screened once by a special camp committee which vetoed the work for public performances. The real explanation and the whereabouts of the score both remain unknown. Also never performed in Theresienstadt was the opera *The Emperor From Atlantis (Der Kaiser von Atlantis),* written by Viktor Ullmann to the libretto of Peter Kien, who was also a talented artist in Theresienstadt. This antiwar work about a cruel tyrant allegorically depicted Hitler's downfall in the mythical kingdom of Atlantis. The Germans withdrew their initial approval of the production and banned the work when they realized that the subject matter was really the Nazi regime. Furthermore, the Nazis deported Ullmann and Kien to Auschwitz, and the opera was never performed in Theresienstadt. The score was assumed lost after the death of the composer and most of the performers in Auschwitz; only in 1975 was it accidentally discovered in a London attic. Ullmann had hidden the script with another prisoner. The newsletter *Martyrdom and Resistance* points out that performances of the opera have included the premiere performance in London in 1975 and the first Israeli performance in Jerusalem in 1978, both by the National Opera of Holland. *The Emperor of Atlantis* has also been performed in San Francisco.

Not only operatic singing but also the whole range of choral activities led by the talented Rafael Schächter expanded as Theresienstadt expanded in size. Juvenile and adult choirs in Theresienstadt made many independent choices of compositions, including mostly composers such as Smetana, Dvořák, and Novák. Arrangements were made also of popular songs by the imprisoned composers. Singers frequently selected, with intent, songs embodying such concepts as native country, freedom, and the defeat of the mighty. Among the many excellent professional singers performing at Theresienstadt, a few of the world-renowned opera singers included David Grünfeld, Ada Hecht, and Karel Berman.

It was ironic that Jewish concentration camp audiences would be so enthusiastic about Verdi's *Requiem,* a Catholic mass for the dead. This performance was certainly an impressive act of spiritual resistance. Despite the victims' courage in performing the death melodies especially for their oppressors, Verdi's *Requiem* had to be studied three times because most of the choir was taken away with a transport after each first performance. At one point, almost the entire orchestra that Czech conductor Karel Ancĕrl had developed in the ghetto was transported to Auschwitz. Only Ancĕrl and three other musicians survived. In the ghetto Ancĕrl had conducted an international, predominantly professional, string orchestra of forty-five members. Of the musical artists surviving the Holocaust, Ancĕrl probably won the greatest postwar recognition. He was conductor of the Czech Philharmonic in Prague and then musical director of the Toronto Symphony. He was well known for guest appearances with the greatest orchestras in the world, and he made many recordings.

Certainly the development and perpetuation of orchestras was a significant achievement in the musical life of Theresienstadt. In addition, other small instrumental groups also flourished there. For example, several quartettes existed at different points in the life at Theresienstadt, even a piano quartette. Some prominent skilled musicians played in them. Repertoire ranged from Czech works to works by Beethoven, Haydn, Mozart, Dvŏrak, Schubert, Brahms, and others. In addition, the quartettes featured original works composed at Theresienstadt by Gideon Klein, Hans Krása, Egon Ledĕc, Pavel Haas, and others. The Theresienstadt piano trios also performed significant works. A jazz group, "The Fricek Weiss Jazz Quintette," was a talented, experienced group that the Nazis utilized successfully as a showpiece during visits to Theresienstadt by the International Red Cross. At approximately the same time, "Ghetto Swingers" was another successful jazz group. In his book, Alfred Kantor draws a jazz group in performance at the ghetto cafe. His accompanying note poignantly reveals that:

> They played daily, but one was allowed to visit the cafe for only two hours about once a year. . . . People sat quietly with tears in their eyes while they listened to the music. For each of us it was two hours of escape, of make-believe.

In addition to the instrumental groups at Theresienstadt, there were many talented solo performers. For example, many talented solo pianists played a range of composers from many eras. Some of the vocal soloists have already been mentioned.

The major Theresienstadt composers created musical works there that would serve much more than momentary needs. However, few of their works survived the Holocaust. In two years in Theresienstadt, Ullmann, for example, composed more than fifteen new works, including his previously-mentioned opera. His other compositions include a symphony, piano sonatas and songs. In addition, he renewed and rearranged some older works of his own and of others. Nevertheless, most of his works were lost. Very few of the Theresienstadt compositions of Krása remain either. Before Theresienstadt, Pavel Haas had begun to write both a symphony and a requiem. In Theresienstadt, Haas was a prolific musical composer of choral works, string orchestral works, and small musical forms appropriate for the group. His only surviving work is "Four Songs on the Words of Chinese Poetry," written for bass voice and piano. Little music remains either of another major Theresienstadt composer: Karel Reiner. More creative works composed by major Theresienstadt composer Gideon Klein do remain and attest to his perseverance during his short stay at Theresienstadt. From this professional pianist and self-taught composer, there still survives a string trio, a string quartette, a piano sonata and a cycle of madrigals. Only the few composers who returned after the War could rewrite their Theresienstadt compositions. František Domážlický had talents that were not fully developed during his days at the camps. After returning from the camps, he rewrote his male choir songs, the one-movement "Song Without Words," and the overture to another work.

In 1971, Joza Karas collaborated with CBS-TV to produce a special program of music from Theresienstadt. Entitled "There Shall Be Heard Again . . . '', the program featured works of Pavel Haas, Viktor Ullmann, Gideon Klein, Hans Krása, Egon Ledeč, Carlo S. Taube, Karel Berman and Ilse Weber, all performed for the first time in the United States. The program has been preserved both on video tape and on audio tape.

ART OF THE HOLOCAUST: OTHER CAMPS AND GHETTOS

Although so much of the Holocaust music and art was either created or interpreted in Theresienstadt, meaningful artistic expression certainly could be found outside of Theresienstadt. In looking at art outside of Theresienstadt, it is important to note that other camps and ghettos also created *greuel-propaganda* art: Auschwitz, Buchenwald, Bergen-Belsen, Dora, Warsaw, Vilna, Kovno, Gurs, Mauthausen, and Sachsenhausen. The art exhibit *Spiritual Resistance: Art From Concentration Camps, 1940–1945* consists of over one hundred works depicting life in four ghettos and twelve concentration camps. Although drawings and watercolors comprise the main part of the collection, it also includes several oil paintings and works in other media. Representing the work of forty-nine Jewish artists, the exhibit began touring the United States in May 1978. Despite the range of artists and locales included, this exhibit focuses on the more evocative Theresienstadt works of *greuelpropaganda* or "horror art,'' also emphasized in Green's *The Artists of Terezin.* One feature of the collection is Malvina Schalkova's works on Theresienstadt life; Green's book treats her works only briefly. The works in the exhibit were chosen from the Ghetto Fighters' Museum in Kibbutz Lohamei Haghetaot (Ghetto Fighters' House Kibbutz) in Northern Israel.

A focus on the art of the Kovno Ghetto reveals that the Yad Vashem Museum in Jerusalem has preserved some of Jacob Lifschitz's drawings of life in the Kovno Ghetto (e.g., children in class). Some of Esther Lurie's drawings from the Kovno Ghetto were rescued after the War and published in an album in Israel. The Yad Vashem Museum has preserved both the original drawings and her sketches from the Stutthof camp. Esther Lurie is one artist who carefully used her wiles both to save her own life and to obtain supplies for her secret artwork. She flattered the camp officers into having their portraits done.

Well-known camp artists with works preserved include Adolf Feder, Zaveli Schleifer, and Arnold Daghani. Feder was an established artist in prewar Paris. Several of the works he created in the French Drancy Camp have been preserved. Schleifer was a Russian artist living in Paris before the War. A few of his camp drawings from Compiègne were saved. Vivid paintings from the gifted artist survivor Arnold Daghani were saved from his camp experiences in Rumania-Transnistria.

Alfred Kantor's many Auschwitz drawings of winter-spring 1944 include such themes as (1) barefooted women with shaven heads doing difficult labor in subzero wet weather and (2) desperate women, oblivious of splinters, frantically scraping empty food barrels for any remaining scraps. Purposeless labor and the sadistic cruelty of the guards are features of these drawings of human degradation and dehumanization.

Leon Delarbre, a former museum "conservateur," was in Auschwitz, Buchenwald, Bergen, and Dora. He obtained materials for his gruesome drawings by offering to do portraits of the camp secretaries. A trained artist with an elegant, classical, subtle technique (unlike that of the Theresienstadt artists), he used it to sketch such gory Nazi atrocities as public hangings, corpses being transported to cremation, and victims of disease and dehydration. Using the subtle shading and fine lines of the Renaissance masters, Delarbre's works attract the viewer for their style in spite of their grotesque subject matter. Delarbre too hid some of his works, and they survived. Boris Taslitzky, another artist with a subtle classical technique, worked effectively in a controlled, objective manner in Buchenwald to sketch people who were near death.

Alexander Bogen's views on his own art help to define the historical, psychological, and spiritual purposes of much of the art of the Holocaust. Bogen, who served as a Partisan Commander near Vilna, was trained at Vilna's Academy of Art. His drawings of partisans show restlessness and tension. Interviewed by art archivist Janet Blatter after the War and reflecting on the work that he had created, Bogen emphasized that he was concerned with his art as (1) immortalizing him for posterity, (2) recording what had happened (a) to inform, (b) to leave permanent documentary reference for the future, and (3) allowing him (as the creator) to keep both his human dignity and his sanity. Likewise, when the mature Alfred Kantor looks back at the intensity with which he sought to record and expose the atrocities of such a place as Auschwitz, he now sees himself within a different context. He realizes that his self-imposed documentary role as observer at Auschwitz served his need for self-preservation. By momentarily detaching himself from the horrors of Auschwitz, he was better able to retain his sanity. For another example, Blatter suggests that Leon Delarbre's apparent detachment in his drawings aided his self-preservation in the camp.

Not all of those who lived and died as ghetto and camp artists were Jews. The non-Jewish Polish artist Mieczyslaw Kościelniak spent several years working in various slave labor gangs in Auschwitz, unable to use his hands to paint. Within a few days after his liberation from another camp in May 1945, he began to draw sketches of life at Auschwitz; he continued these drawings for several years. Kościelniak's works, like those of so many others, depict the daily suffering of the camp inmates. However, given the conditions of freedom and more time to draw, Kościelniak's sketches and drawings often contain considerably more detail than the quickly executed and hastily concealed works produced by many artists in the camps. Maria Hiszpanska-Neumann, another non-Jewish artist, was a Polish Catholic who created drawings of the difficulties of camp life and died in Auschwitz. Zinovii Tolkachev was a Russian soldier involved in liberating Auschwitz. His sketches of Auschwitz and Maidanek are compassionate but not sentimental.

In addition to the sketches and drawings already discussed, the range of camp and ghetto art "products" still available include: (1) technical work assigned by the Germans, (2) Theresienstadt stamps and currency with Moses' picture, (3) counterfeit money in Sachsenhausen, (4) German-commissioned forgeries of masterpieces in Bialystok, (5) portraits of the officers and (6) illustrated resistance posters.

MUSIC OF THE HOLOCAUST: OTHER CAMPS AND GHETTOS

Although the opportunities and the documentation from Theresienstadt were the fullest, evidence exists of beautiful musical performances in Gleiwitz, Auschwitz and Buchenwald, in spite of the terrors of those camps. A complete symphony orchestra played in the Warsaw Ghetto. However, most of the orchestra members plus Szymon Pullman, the conductor, were slaughtered in Treblinka. Erwin Palm, a young Düsseldorf conductor, also died in the camps. *Playing for Time,* Fania Fénelon's full-length eyewitness account of her life in the women's orchestra in Auschwitz-Birkenau, provides a vivid picture of how orchestra life enabled the prisoners to (1) stay alive and (2) retain some semblance of human dignity and sanity, in spite of the horrors and degradation around them.

At one point, Fénelon reflects on her initial awareness of the existence of an orchestra at Auschwitz-Birkenau. The psychological effect is most encouraging:

> I was in the quarantine block when a rumour came through that there was an orchestra. That day we were almost happy; if there was an orchestra at Birkenau, perhaps it wasn't as terrible as we feared.

Later, she expresses her conflict and disgust at finding such incongruities as

> The farcical nature of this orchestra conducted by this elegant woman, these comfortably dressed girls sitting on chairs playing to these virtual skeletons, shadows showing us faces which were faces no longer.

Fénelon felt extreme disgust at entertaining an SS woman after the woman had just finished participating in a selection. It was as if the orchestra served as the woman's dessert.

Fénelon's description of Alma, the orchestra conductor whose perfect concerts were her only goal, emphasizes how obsession with the orchestra served Alma's need for self-preservation. Alma's obsession with conducting a perfect concert helped her to forget the camp and the gas chambers.

Folk Songs

Permeating the lives of the Jews of Europe during the War, the folk songs of the ghettos and camps probably provide the most striking evidence of Holocaust music as an historical document of spiritual resistance. In the introduction to "The Song of the Ghetto," a collection she edited, Ruta Pups suggests that people wrote songs to express and report their painful ghetto experiences for future generations. The songs record both the events themselves and the feelings of the people. In the introduction of an earlier collection, Yiddish poet H. Leivick discusses ghetto and concentration camp songs, also from a historical perspective. Leivick feels that these songs facilitate the comprehension of the seemingly incomprehensible events of Jewish struggles and martyrdom in ghettos and camps.

In *Voices of a People,* Ruth Rubin classifies these Yiddish folk songs of World War II into six categories: ghetto songs, concentration camp songs, the plight of the children, resistance, partisan songs, and songs dealing with the German invasion of Russia. The themes of these songs range from suffering and shame to courage and heroism, from bitter hatred of the enemy to struggle and joy in victory. They include prayer songs, lullabies, satirical songs and work songs. Uneven in quality, the songs were created both by the common folk and the educated. One creator might be an eleven-year-old boy; another might be a youthful resistance fighter; yet another might be the old Rabbi Emanuel Hirshberg of the Lodz Ghetto. Many of the songs perished with their composers. Through all the songs runs a thread of a strong will to survive: a desire for both individual human dignity and the perpetuation of cherished traditions of the people. Unlike the slower development of most folk songs, these became folk songs almost overnight. Since texts were often hastily set to music, the songs frequently utilized traditional Jewish or secular European melodies, tunes from then current Soviet dances and songs, or old familiar Jewish or European folk songs.

In the songs of the ghettos and camps, rarely is there a song of normal life on such themes as love, marriage, family, or joy. In ghetto songs containing humor, such humor is bitter and satirical. If there had been laughter before, there was laughter no longer. For example, ''Dance of Death,'' a folk song of the Vilna Ghetto, transforms an older gay Yiddish wedding song into a bitter and macabre dance of death:

> Collars ripped, our throats are freezing, barely strength for groaning!
> Dance, dance, dance! It's one, two, three, you know.

The ghettos, concentration camps and death marches gave rise to many new folk songs of lamentation. Unlike the laments of the medieval Jews, their tone usually is not religious. Their language is not the Hebrew of the Bible or the prayer book. Yiddish, the language of the folk, is the language of Holocaust laments.

M. Gebirtig was Europe's most popular Yiddish folk bard between the First and Second World Wars. Popular in ghettos, his songs encouraged the suffering people to feel contempt for their cruel oppressors. However, the optimism in his earlier songs gave way to fear and despair as he watched the War progress. Gebirtig's *''Es brent''* (''It is Burning'') became popular throughout the ghettos and concentration camps. As a whole little town is burning, Gebirtig points accusingly:

> And you stand there looking on
> With folded arms,
> And you stand there looking on
> While our town goes up in flames. . . .

The poet Hirsh Glik, a youth fighting with the partisan groups, wrote the lyrics to a powerful partisan song of courage, defiance, and hope: *''Zog nit keynmol az du geyst dem letsten veg''* (''Never say that you are trodding the final path''). All the Partisan groups of Eastern Europe soon made it their official hymn; the song quickly became popular throughout the ghettos and concentration camps of Eastern Europe; it was subsequently translated from Glik's native Yiddish into many languages.

Of the few published collections of songs of this period, S. Katcherginsky, a Vilna poet-partisan, compiled the most valuable one. Containing 250 texts and 100 tunes, the collection was compiled from the ghettos, camps, and forests. Katcherginsky wrote many of the lyrics himself. The horrible conditions and problems of the period are vividly illustrated in this material.

Ruth Rubin perceptively evaluates the significance of all these songs:

> Taken as a whole, Yiddish folk song of World War II and the German occupation comprises a remarkable documentary chronicle and testament of the creative ability of a people who demonstrated their capacity for suffering, their endurance, their ingenuity and resourcefulness under the most inhuman conditions. The songs reveal a burning will to live as human beings in dignity and self-respect and the determination and ability to organize and fight unto death for that life—in freedom.

In addition to written collections of many of these songs, many recordings have been made since the War. *Songs of the Vilna Ghetto* consists of twelve songs with subjects ranging from resistance to an orphan's lullaby. Music origins include: the unknown, Russian folk music, youthful ghetto composers, and professionals. Words were written by many ghetto members, including Glik. As expected, many songs were written in honor of and some in memory of the fighting boys. Cantor Abraham Brun, one of the few survivors of the Lodz Ghetto in Poland, recorded some of the songs he sang there on the record *Songs of the Ghetto*. Emotions voiced here range from courage to despair or pain. These are but samples of recordings that have been made to remember, to preserve.

Liturgical Music

Joza Karas emphasizes that "in sharp contrast to the adequately documented secular music—whether art music or folk songs—information about liturgical music of the Holocaust is practically nonexistent." In Warsaw, Cantors Gershon Sirota and Moshe Koussevitsky carried on the great tradition of cantorial singing. Choral singing was led by conductors such as David Ajzensztat. In addition to his secular compositions, Ajzensztat had a number of his cantatas and synagogue compositions in manuscript form which did not survive. Liturgical contributions in the ghettos were primarily in the realm of interpretative art rather than in creative art. Karas asserts that "as long as there was life in the ghettos, the cantors continued their work. They doubtlessly enriched the liturgical services with new musical settings."

POST-HOLOCAUST RESPONSES IN ART AND MUSIC

Post-Holocaust Art

Since the main purpose of this chapter is to examine art and music created *during* the Holocaust, only minimal attention will be paid to post-Holocaust works of art and music. Focusing on post-Holocaust art works on the Holocaust, Blatter points out that these latter works are often less realistic than the earlier ones. This trend is partially due to the current abstract trend in art in general. For example, two post-Holocaust Polish artists who abstracted victims by representing them symbolically are Mordecai Ardon and Bronislaw Linke. Ardon used numbers to symbolize and substitute for the victims in his 1963 painting ''Train of Numbers.'' Linke depicted the ruined buildings of Warsaw as victims and witnesses. Another post-Holocaust work displaying a strong abstract influence is *The Warsaw Ghetto: Drawings by Józef Kaliszan.* A collection of forty drawings of the horrors and the bravery of the Jews of the Warsaw Ghetto created by a young Polish artist after the War, many of the completed drawings resemble modern collages.

Collages are seen again in a dramatic post-Holocaust work by a vicarious survivor in *The Nazi Drawings by Mauricio Lasansky.* This is a series of thirty-three widely exhibited life-sized drawings of the Nazi killers and their victims. After twenty-five years of pondering and planning, Lasansky finally (1961–1966) created these harsh and moving studies in horror. Lasansky's Nazi drawings feature such details as the distorted skulls and teeth of the killers and the victims. Throughout the drawings, he emphasizes the same tattooed concentration camp number. A world-renowned printmaker, Lasansky was born in Argentina and has resided in the United States since 1943.

Other styles used to depict the atrocities of camp life range from the muted, dreamlike technique of George Zielezinski to the almost photo realism of Wladyslaw Siwek. Some of post-Holocaust art reveals the influence of such twentieth century trends as (1) Surrealism and (2) the Viennese School of Fantastic Realism.

Although sculpture has already been dismissed as being generally too difficult to successfully execute and preserve during such an event as the Holocaust, the Holocaust (as wars always do) inspired postwar monuments. The task of adequately depicting the enormity of the Holocaust produced various sculptural solutions. The emphasis on human courage and suffering is exemplified by some of these monuments, designed primarily to memorialize. Here, too, art serves historical-psychological-spiritual purposes. Nathan Rappaport's ''Warsaw Memorial to the Warsaw Ghetto Uprising,'' created five years after the insurrection, portrays the youths heroically. Fritz Cremer's gigantic sulpture at Buchenwald consists of a horizontal line of figures seemingly on the verge of releasing themselves from their base in order to avenge their own deaths.

Post-Holocaust Music

In the years immediately after the Holocaust, the majority of the few surviving musical artists did not wish to dwell on the horrors of the Holocaust.

Therefore, most of the Holocaust musical activities almost fell into oblivion. In addition, many survivors, struggling to forget, did not want to produce more works of Holocaust-related music. Nevertheless, in the years since the War, official (and unofficial) commemorations have fostered the completion of many new compositions and the issuance of numerous recordings. To commemorate the tenth anniversary of the Uprising of the Warsaw Ghetto, the Polish conductor-composer Artur Gelbrun was commissioned to write *Lament for the Victims of the Warsaw Ghetto,* a cantata for baritone, mixed choir, and orchestra. The work was dedicated to the composer's mother, who died in the Warsaw Ghetto Uprising. To help commemorate the twentieth anniversary of the liberation of Bergen-Belsen, The World Federation of the Bergen-Belsen Survivors issued a recording of songs of the concentration camps and the ghettos: *Remember: Songs of the Holocaust.* Also twenty years later, the Slovak composer Peter Kolman composed *Monument for Six Million Jews,* dedicated to the memory of the concentration camp victims. For the Auschwitz commemorative service on April 16, 1967, the Polish composer Krzysztof Penderecki wrote his oratorio *"Dies Irae."*

Numerous post-Holocaust musical works have been inspired by works in other media. For example, many musical works have been inspired by the poems and drawings of the children of Theresienstadt. The most famous is Charles Davidson's *I Never Saw Another Butterfly,* a dramatic-choral work for choir plus piano or organ. *"Night and Hope: A Symphonic Poem"* is based on *Night and Hope,* a book by Czech novelist Arnost Lustig which depicts Lustig's Theresienstadt experiences. This symphonic poem by Czech composer Otmar Mácha won first prize at the Prague Music Festival in 1964.

One of the two best-known post-Holocaust musical works, also based on a work in another medium, is Dmitri Shostakovich's Symphony No. Thirteen ("Babi Yar"). Based on five poems by Yevgeny Yevtushenko, this symphony is a powerful document of protest, sensitively uniting music and poetry. Soviet criticism of this symphony-cantata for male chorus and soloist has been directed most sharply toward the first of the five movements, "Babi Yar," especially the text by the poet Yevtushenko. This dark and and heavy movement is a powerful poetic protest against anti-Semitism, implicating the Russians too.

The other famous post-Holocaust musical work is Arnold Schoenberg's *A Survivor from Warsaw.* Written in 1947, it was Schoenberg's last completed orchestral work. *A Survivor from Warsaw* is a short musical drama depicting an episode in the Warsaw Ghetto Uprising. The narrator-survivor tells of a group of Jews being deported to the death camp from the ghetto. At the last moment, a sudden surge of faith and spirit inspires them to suddenly sing the prayer "Shema Yisroel." This musical work for speaker, men's chorus, and orchestra exemplifies the effective use of expressionism in music. (See discussion of the Theresienstadt artists for expressionism in art.) The use of expressionism is most appropriate here for the Holocaust drama being enacted.

Expressionism in music, as in art, reveals starkness, brutality, distortion, and tension. Music critic Harold C. Schonberg points out that "Expressionistic music is dissonant, atonal with jagged melodic leaps, and deals with an intensified realism rather than idealism."

Among other Holocaust musical compositions written after the War is *Yiskor: In Memoriam,* a work for viola and orchestra, written by Israeli composer Oedoen Partos. A composition written in the style of the 1960s is *A Mitzvah for the Dead,* composed for violin and tape by the American Michael Sahl. Sahl's composition utilizes references to Polish dances, waltzes and sentimental ballads, all twisted and distorted by tape recordings. Though post-Holocaust works are not our major focus, these are a sample of many Holocaust-inspired musical works still being composed and performed in many parts of the world.

CONCLUSION: SIGNIFICANCE OF HOLOCAUST ART AND MUSIC

Holocaust historian Lucy Dawidowicz and art archivist Janet Blatter both stress the historical significance of Holocaust art. Art works are specially valuable as historical documents when juxtaposed with literary records and photographs. In Holocaust music, the historical significance of the folk song as a document of spiritual resistance was underlined earlier in this chapter. From the historical perspective of the artist or musician himself, his works might also stand as his later proof or reminder that he had actually survived such horrors.

The music and art of the Holocaust are also significant for their very important psychological function. Dawidowicz points out:

> By the very act of drawing or painting, by producing art works, the artists had a hand in maintaining morale within their own circle of family and friends and often in the community at large.

In the introduction to his book, the artist Alfred Kantor reflects on the magical power of music in Theresienstadt:

> There were moments that seemed strangely magnified by a feeling of make-believe amidst an otherwise cold reality. I remember how overjoyed we were one day by the music of an accordion that someone had smuggled into the barracks. Everyone huddled together in the poorly lit, freezing room; and for a while we forgot our hurt as we listened to the tunes.

The musician or artist himself needed his artistic expression for his own self-preservation, as exemplified by earlier remarks of the artist Alfred Kantor and by some of the professional opera singers. The style of the artist or musician clearly reflected his mental state and his struggle to keep his sanity. Numerous examples in this chapter have shown that these cultural activities afforded the people a temporary escape to normalcy and provided a sense of human dignity and hope.

In the ghettos and camps, some artists often used their art to help immortalize people who were dying of disease or being transported. When Esther Lurie drew portraits of her fellow prisoners in Kovno and Leibitsch, she succeeded in capturing the human dignity and the pride that was left in them.

Of all the purposes of art, Gerald Green asserts in *The Artists of Terezin* that the noblest function of art is "to assist blundering mankind in its pained search for bits and pieces of truth." The artists of Theresienstadt clearly drew to reveal the truth in order to expose the lies of German propaganda about Theresienstadt. The Nazis considered this artwork a horrible distortion of truth. To them, truth was how the world community saw Theresienstadt. Truth, to the Nazis, was the illusion painted and immortalized by their lies. Nazi weapons were unprepared for the spiritual resistance expressed by the Jewish art and music of the Holocaust.

TEACHING THE MUSIC AND ART OF THE HOLOCAUST

An examination of the art and music of the Holocaust has shown how music and art have been powerful tools of spiritual resistance for the Jews. Art and music have exerted the kind of long-range pervasive power that the Jew's meager physical facilities and weapons could not and did not. Furthermore, Holocaust art and music are invaluable as historical documents and as psychological survival kits. Unfortunately, one is limited in teaching about Holocaust art and music by the availability and accessibility of materials. Many works of art and music are still in archives, often unsorted and just piled up. Much material has been lost; much is still to be discovered. For greater ease in teaching, much of the available material has been included in the bibliography at the end of this chapter.

In addition to its inherent value as art and music of a special period, material discussed in this chapter can be useful in rounding out Holocaust studies in such areas as history, psychology and literature. For example, the materials on the art and music of Theresienstadt certainly add important dimensions to one's perception of what happened in Theresienstadt. In discussing the problem of resistance, the student can learn much by focusing on the spiritual resistance developed through the art and music of the Holocaust. The struggle of the suffering Jew to avoid dehumanization and to preserve his sanity is dramatically illustrated by the effect of Holocaust art and music on both the creator and the observer during the Holocaust. The themes recurring in the art and music of the Holocaust echo the themes emerging from a study of the Holocaust in literature, history, psychology or other disciplines. The instructor can effectively incorporate materials on Holocaust art and music that will stimulate and challenge those students with no background as well as those with considerable background.

BIBLIOGRAPHY

Annotation in this bibliography is generally limited to those cited sources *not* discussed or analyzed in the preceding chapter.

Only sources available in English have been used in this bibliography.

I. Art of The Holocaust

Art in a Concentration Camp: Drawings from Terezin. Catalogue from exhibit at New School Art Center in New York City: February 13–March 16, 1967.

AUSCHWITZ MUSEUM. *Obóz Koncentracyjny Oświecim w Tworczości Artystycznej— Katalog Malarstwo w Oświęcimiu, prac Graficznych Mieczyslawa Koscielniaka.* (Auschwitz: Wydawnictwo Państwowego Muzeum w Oświecimiu, 1962). A multilingual illustrated catalogue of the works of the non-Jewish Auschwitz artist Mieczyslaw Kościelniak.

BANASIEWICZ, CZESLAW Z., ed. *The Warsaw Ghetto: Drawings by Józef Kaliszan* (New York: Thomas Yoseloff, 1968).

BLATTER, JANET. "The Holocaust in Art." Unpublished paper.

DAVIDOWICZ, LUCY. *Spiritual Resistance: Art from Concentration Camps 1940– 1945* (Philadelphia: Jewish Publication Society, 1978). See also "Spiritual Resistance: Art from Concentration Camps 1940-1945," Introduction by Elaine and Melvin L. Merians; Commentary by Lucy S. Dawidowicz, *Present Tense* 5:2 (Winter 1978), pp. 25–32.

Encyclopaedia Judaica. "Art," Subchapter on "Art in the Concentration Camps and Ghettoes," by B. Mordechai Ansbacher.

FREUDENHEIM, TOM L., "Spiritual Resistance: Art from Concentration Camps," *ARTnews* (May 1978), pp. 72–74.

GREEN, GERALD. *The Artists of Terezin* (New York: Hawthorn Books, 1969). (Available in Schocken paperback, 1978). Focuses on the artwork of Otto Ungar, Bedřich Fritta, Leo Haas and Karel Fleischmann.

. . . I never saw another butterfly . . . ; Children's Drawings and Poems from Terezin Concentration Camp 1942–1944 (New York: McGraw-Hill, 1971).

KANTOR, ALFRED. *The Book of Alfred Kantor* (New York: McGraw-Hill, 1971).

LASANSKY, MAURICIO. *The Nazi Drawings* (Philadelphia: Privately published, 1966).

II. Music of The Holocaust

A. SELECTED WORKS

DAVIDSON, CHARLES. *I Never Saw Another Butterfly;* a dramatic-choral work for choir and piano or organ (Philadelphia: Ashbourne Music Publishers).

EISENSTEIN, JUDITH KAPLAN. *Heritage of Jewish Music: The Music of the Jewish People* (New York: UAHC, 1972). Includes the music, English translation and discussion of the Vilna Ghetto folk song "Dance of Death" and Hirsh Glik's "Song of the Partisans."

FÉNELON, FANIA, AND ROUTIER, MARCELLE. *Playing For Time.* Translated by Judith Landry (New York: Atheneum, 1977).

''Israeli Performance of Camp-Written Opera,'' *Martyrdom and Resistance;* Newsletter of the American Federation of Jewish Fighters, Camp Inmates and Nazi Victims, Inc. (May–June 1978) 4:4, p. 2.

KARAS, JOZA. ''The Holocaust in Music.'' In *Philadelphia Conference on Teaching the Holocaust: November 16–18, 1977.* Edited by Josephine Knopp (Philadelphia: 1977), pp. 75–90. Includes discussion of works by Pavel Haas, Franz Eugen Klein and Viktor Ullmann.

KUNA, MILAN. ''Arts in Terezin—Music.'' In *1973—Memorial Terezin.* Edited by Olivia Pechová et al. Translated by Hana Kvičalová.

RUBIN, RUTH. *Voices of a People: The Story of Yiddish Folksong.* 2nd ed. (New York: McGraw-Hill, 1973). Includes English translation and discussion of M. Gebirtig's ''It Is Burning'' and Hirsh Glik's ''Song of the Partisans.''

SCHONBERG, HAROLD C. *The Lives of the Great Composers* (New York: W. W. Norton, 1970).

SCHULMAN, ELIAS, ''The Holocaust in Yiddish Literature.'' Unpublished paper.

B. SELECTED RECORDINGS

Babi Yar: Symphony No. 13 by Dmitri Shostakovich. Angel Sr-40212 and RCA-LSC 3162.

Dies Irae (Auschwitz Oratorio) by Krzysztof Penderecki. Phillips 839701.

I Never Saw Another Butterfly by Srul Irving Glick. CCI-5073. A song cycle for voice and piano, inspired by the poem ''I Never Saw Another Butterfly.''

Lament for the Victims of the Warsaw Ghetto by Arthur Gelbrun. Everest-3273.

''Monument for Six Million Jews'' by Peter Kolman. In *A Memorial to the Victims of War.* Everest-3315.

Oh, the Chimneys by Shulamit Ran. Turn.-34435. A choral and instrumental composition based on Holocaust poetry by Nelly Sachs.

Remember: Songs of the Holocaust. Sung by Sidor Belarsky. World Federation of the Bergen-Belsen Associations BB-65. Includes M. Gebirtig's ''It Is Burning'' and Hirsh Glik's ''Song of the Partisans.''

Songs of the Ghetto. Sung by Cantor Abraham Brun. Folkways-FW 8739.

Songs of the Vilna Ghetto. CBS-63345 and Hed Arzi BAN-14080. Includes Glik's ''Song of the Partisans.''

A Survivor from Warsaw by Arnold Schoenberg. RCA-LSC 7055 and Columbia-M2S-679.

Terezin by Robert Stern. CRI S-264. A collection of songs featuring a soprano voice accompanied by cello and piano.

Yiskor: In Memoriam by Oedoen Partos. Mace 5-10033.

ADDENDUM

KARAS, JOZA, ''The Use of Music as a Means of Education in Terezin,'' *SHOAH: A Review of Holocaust Studies and Commemorations* 1:2 (Fall 1978).

MILTON, SYBIL, "Concentration Camp Art and Artists," *SHOAH* 1:2 (Fall, 1978).

SZONYI, DAVID, "Art from the Holocaust at the Jewish Museum: A Review," *SHOAH* 1:2 (Fall, 1978).

TOLL, NELLY. *Without Surrender: Art of the Holocaust* (Philadelphia: Running Press paperback, 1978).

Jewish and Christian Theology Encounters the Holocaust

Byron L. Sherwin

The occurrence of natural disasters (e.g. earthquakes, floods) and humanly induced catastrophes (e.g. wars, massacres) often has compelled Jewish and Christian theologians to reexamine their theological assumptions. The clash between the claims of faith and the harsh realities of human experience often has precipitated a reformulation of theological suppositions. The existence of evil and suffering in the world, presumably created and sustained by a benevolent and omnipotent God, has caused the problem of *theodicy* to become a perennial and central issue in Jewish and Christian theological reflection.

Theodicy is derived from two Greek words meaning *deity* and *justice*. It refers to the attempt to justify God's goodness and maintain His omnipotence in the face of the manifold evil present in the world. Simply put, the problem of theodicy raises the following dilemma: either God is able to prevent evil and will not, or He is willing to prevent it and cannot. If the former, we can no longer assume He is benevolent. If the latter, we can no longer assume He is omnipotent. How, then, can we account for evil while still affirming God's goodness and his power?

Throughout the centuries, Jewish and Christian theologians and philosophers have sought to resolve this ancient dilemma by denying or modifying one or more of its premises. Some have maintained that evil is not real but is only the privation of the good; that is, "evil" is not an entity in itself but only an indication that the good is absent. Thus, if evil does not really exist, the problem of evil dissolves into irrelevancy.

Others have attempted to resolve the dilemma by denying or modifying the claim that God is omnipotent. If God is not all-powerful, evil is not explained, but God's failure to prevent or to halt evil is explained by His lack of omnipotence. A variation of this position is the assertion that God's omnipotence is compromised not by His nature but by His will. God chooses to limit His power so that mankind may realize its essence through the exercise of human freedom.

Other theologians modify the premise that God is wholly benevolent. They offer a variety of possibilities:

As the source of creation which embraces good and evil, God's nature too must contain both good and evil.

God created both good and evil and is, consequently, responsible for the existence of evil.

God created the good and the potentiality for evil.

A source other than God, such as human sin or the Devil, introduced evil into the world.

Still other theologians argue that evil is a mystery, beyond human comprehension. Evil exists, but we cannot know why. We can only affirm faith and should not question Providence.

The problem of theodicy emerged as being particularly acute in the wake of trauma and tragedy. Previously formulated responses to the problem of theodicy often proved inadequate for the survivors of immense catastrophe and for their immediate descendants. Theologians had to reformulate their assumptions when confronted with existential crisis.

In the history of Jewish theology, for example, traumatic events such as the destruction of the Second Temple in the first century and the expulsion of Spanish Jewry in the sixteenth, engendered a total reevaluation of Jewish religious belief. Based on tragic events such as the Lisbon earthquake of 1755 and World War I, for example, Christian theologians felt it necessary to reconstruct the then current theological assumptions grounded in evolutionary and idealistic thought. Human existence was not on a progressive onward march as had been assumed by many eighteenth and nineteenth century theologians. Therefore, theological assertions had to be reevaluated in the light of contemporary historical experience.

One would expect that in the wake of World War II, Jewish and Christian theologians would have felt obliged to articulate a theodicy for the post-Holocaust era. However, such has not been the case. Theological response to the Holocaust has been sparse.

In the following discussion, we shall review a number of the more significant attempts of theologians to resolve the theological problems engendered by the Holocaust. First, we shall examine the views of those who attempt to integrate the Holocaust into classical theological categories, such as divine retribution.

DIVINE RETRIBUTION

The most common explanation in classical Jewish theology for tragedy and trauma has been the doctrine of divine retribution; i.e., suffering is punishment for sin.

For the most part, Jewish theologians of the Holocaust have broken with past tradition and have affirmed the unique nature of the Holocaust by rejecting the doctrine of divine retribution as being applicable to the Holocaust. Nevertheless, three theologians have persisted in maintaining the relevance of the doctrine of divine retribution with regard to the Holocaust.

An Israeli scholar, Immanuel Hartom, has claimed that the Holocaust was a punishment visited upon Jewry for the sin of assimilation, for Jews having surrendered traditional Judaism under the impact of the European Enlightenment.

Joel Teitelbaum, the Satmerer rebbe, a leading figure in contemporary Hasidic life, maintains that the sins of the Zionists caused the Holocaust.

According to Teitelbaum, reiterating past traditions, Jews must passively await the messianic advent. They should pursue spiritual quietism and must not seek involvement in the political realm. Any attempt to restore and to maintain Jewish political independence in the Land of Israel can only be interpreted as a gesture of defiance against God, as a rejection of the divine plan for history, as an attempt to quicken the hand of history. Since the Zionists attempted to force the Jewish people to surrender its ahistorical, apolitical role and to reestablish Jewish political independence, they are guilty of rejecting God. They are culpable for having committed the most heinous sin; therefore, the most severe punishment—i.e., the Holocaust—was required. For Teitelbaum, that *any* Jews were spared extermination is a sign of divine mercy. Divine justice required complete extermination.

Unlike most theologians of the Holocaust who perceive the State of Israel as a modicum of counter testimony to the Holocaust, Teitelbaum believes the continued existence of the State of Israel to be a dangerous continuation of the sin which engendered the Holocaust. Unlike those who see Israel as a prelude to the final redemption, Teitelbaum sees Israel as a demonic prelude to disaster.

Ignaz Maybaum, a British Reform rabbi, also utilizes a version of the divine retribution argument to answer the question—why did so many die?

Maybaum claims that "the millions who died in Auschwitz died 'because of the sins of others.' The Holocaust is the twentieth century calvary of the Jewish people."

A similar approach to that of Maybaum is asserted by Ulrich Simon in his *A Theology of Auschwitz*. A Christian of Jewish origins whose family was murdered at Auschwitz, Simon attempts to interpret the Holocaust in classical Christian categories. For Simon, "the pattern of Christ's sacrifice" is the "reality behind Auschwitz." Like Maybaum, Simon seems to identify the Holocaust as the Calvary of the Jewish people. The Jews of Europe, Simon claims, went to their death as martyrs for the truth as did Christ. As Christ was resurrected, so were the Jews, claims Simon, when they were restored to their homeland. Now, insists Simon, Jews must never forget the Holocaust as it serves "to remind Israel that its election as God's servant is no mean thing to be bartered away for advantages which accrue from being like the Gentiles."

Like Hartom, Simon seems to imply that the Holocaust was some kind of punishment for the "sin" of assimilation into modern culture. Like Maybaum, he portrays the victims of the Holocaust as sacrifices required to atone for the sins of mankind.

Critique

Hartom, Teitelbaum, Maybaum and Simon attempt to offer a traditional theological rubric to explain the Holocaust. They do so by invoking the doctrine of divine retribution in one form or another. However, in so doing they exacerbate rather than assuage the theological perplexities engendered by the Holocaust.

As Eliezer Berkovits notes, to claim that millions of people were brutally murdered as a punishment for their sins is an "obscene" retreat to the luxury of self-righteousness which no one can afford. To defend God's actions by suggesting that He acted justly in condemning millions of people, including a million innocent children to a terrible death because they sinned, is the height of moral arrogance, the acme of injustice. Similarly, Emil Fackenheim perceives the application of the divine retribution argument to the Holocaust to be an "absurdity and a sacrilege." Furthermore, Fackenheim notes, the millions who perished were not killed because they failed to keep the covenant with God. They died because their great-grandparents had affirmed it by remaining Jews.

Irving Greenberg considers the claim that the victims died as punishment for their sins to be the ultimate betrayal and indignity: "Now that they have been cruelly tortured and killed, boiled into soap, their hair made into pillows and their bones into fertilizer, their unknown graves and the very fact of their death denied to them, the theologian would commit the only indignity left to inflict on them—to insist that it was done because of their sins."

To contend that God willed the death of millions not only presumes to know the divine will, but it confronts the theologian with a monstrous God who does not inspire faith or devotion. Having "explained" the Holocaust to their satisfaction, those who maintain the applicability of the divine retribution argument to the Holocaust, may no longer be concerned with the problem of theodicy, but they should be compelled to confront the problem of God. How can one maintain faith in a bloodthirsty, vindictive God?

The moral implications of affirming the divine retribution argument are also disturbing. To hold the victims liable for their own annihilation seeks not only to free God but also the murderers from responsibility. The perpetrators become agents of God rather than moral criminals. Maybaum, for example, calls Hitler God's "servant," God's agent in the destruction of the Jews. Thus, Jewish and Christian theologians who interpret the Holocaust as the product of human sinfulness—either that of the victims or that of all mankind—only pervert justice while self-righteously invoking the notion of justice.

Simon's position is additionally problematic. Nothing is gained by associating the Holocaust with the passion of Jesus which had no meaning whatever for the majority of the victims. And, for Simon, an apostate Jew, to claim that the Holocaust should be a constant reminder to the Jews not to "become like the Gentiles," is the height of arrogance.

Underlying Simon's and Maybaum's claim that the victims of the Holocaust died for the sins of humanity is the assumption that the Holocaust was an inevitable scene in the divinely authored historical drama. The sacrifice, like the passion of Jesus, must occur so that a modicum of redemption might be achieved. Maybum develops a philosophy of history which deigns to explain why the Holocaust *had to* occur.

According to Maybum, two kinds of pivotal events highlight Jewish history: *Gezerot* (evil decrees) and *Hurban* (destruction). In this arbitrary distinction, *gezerot* are avertable catastrophes which do not signify the termination of one era and the initiation of a new and better era. Examples of such events are the expulsion of Jews from Spain in 1492 and the Chmielnicki massacres in Poland between 1648 and 1658. *Hurban,* on the other hand, refers to unavoidable events which signify a necessary transition between one period and the initiation of a new and better period. Examples of such events are the destructions of the First and Second Temples and the Holocaust.

The Holocaust, Maybaum asserts, was a necessary and inevitable event required to insure human progress. It was needed in order to effect the transition from medievalism to modernity. Amongst the clearest vestiges of medievalism was the life-style of Eastern European Jewry. Thus, to effect this transition from medieval parochialism to modernity, the destruction of Eastern European Jewry was necessary. Now, in the post-Holocaust era, the teachings of "prophetic Judaism" when linked with western democracy, can realize the destiny of the modern era to initiate a period of messianic peace and universal brotherhood. The promise of this attainment in a sense "justifies" and "explains" the enormity of the catastrophe, according to Maybaum.

Though Maybaum attempts to foster future optimism by describing his vision of the future, his position can only invoke extreme pessimism and despair. If God can intercede into history at any time, utilizing such "servants" as Adolph Hitler, what hope is there for mankind? What place has human freedom in determining human fate? Furthermore, is the progress Maybaum claims to be the price of wholesale slaughter even assured? Have we witnessed the ''progress'' in the ''democratic'' west which Maybaum envisaged? Have we not seen since World War II the weakening of western democracies, the moral decay of western civilization; have we not been witness to Viet Nam, Biafra, Watergate, and countless other tragedies and scandals? Does the technocracy, corruption, and strife of recent times represent a real advance over the ''medieval'' world which, in Maybaum's view, had to be destroyed for mankind's advancement? And, even if it were, was not the death of millions too high a price to pay? Rather than interpret the Holocaust as a fulfillment of the view that history is ''necessary progress,'' it would seem more prudent and more correct to agree with Emil Fackenheim's observation that the Holocaust ''gave the final lie to the view that history is necessary progress.'' To attempt to subsume the tragedy of others under an abstract philosophy of history is morally callous. Neither does Fackenheim accept the revised version of the ''history as necessary progress'' argument which contends that there may be occasional lapses into barbarism (e.g., Roland Gittelsohn's position). For Fackenheim, the Holocaust represents, ''not a relapse. . . . but a total blackout.''

Irving Greenberg has suggested that any Holocaust theology must pass the test of being credible in the presence of burning children. Would an innocent Eastern European Jewish child, being led to the gas chamber or to the crematorium, be content to know that Ignaz Maybaum contends that his or her death is helping to end a medieval life-style and bring about modernity? Thus, Maybaum's response to the Holocaust embodies claims which are theologically perplexing and morally offensive.

RICHARD RUBENSTEIN

The dilemma posed by those who affirm the doctrine of divine retribution is: a cruel God or none, a cosmic sadist or a rejection of the God of history. Given such a dilemma, Richard Rubenstein maintains that the only viable theological option *After Auschwitz* is to reject the God of history.

For Rubenstein, a forthright encounter with the death camps must convince us that ''God is dead,'' that human existence is neither planned nor purposeful, that God can no longer serve as the guarantor for human meaning or morality, that the cosmos is indifferent to human affairs, that the human condition is devoid of any transcendental purpose, that history reveals no providence. For Rubenstein, no rationalization, theological or otherwise, can affirm a viable posture for traditional Jewish belief after the Holocaust. Realization that ''God is dead'' means that the Jew must confirm the termination of his covenant with God, that the people of Israel can no longer be conceived as the "chosen people" of God. A new basis for Jewish existence after the Holocaust is required.

For Rubenstein, it is precisely because human existence bears no intrinsic meaning that human beings turn toward one another in the framework of a community to find a new basis for human existence. The religious community gains heightened status, since without God human interdependence in community now becomes a desperate individual need. For the Jew, only participation in his religious community can provide authentic existence. Only within the Jewish community can the Jew best express his aspirations and ideals.

As the God of history can no longer be the basis for Jewish faith, according to Rubenstein, the modern Jew must reaffirm the God of Nature. Rubenstein interprets the establishment of the State of Israel as an expression of this reaffirmation. The Jewish people returned to the soil, to Nature.

For Rubenstein, the State of Israel also represents a response to the two-thousand-year-long condition of Jewish powerlessness. The Holocaust demonstrated the ultimate conclusion of Jewish powerlessness. Jews must now be involved in a "power struggle" for existence. Since the strategy of Jewish survival by powerless appeasement has been proven specious by the Holocaust, the contemporary Jew must forge a new image, from powerlessness to power. For Rubenstein, the modern Israeli is the prototype of this new image. The way of attaining this goal is by reasserting a pagan theology, rooted in Nature. The God of Nature must replace the God of history so that the potent image of the Jew can replace the image of Jewish impotence.

Critique

Rubenstein, in a sense, agrees with those who hold that the doctrine of divine retribution is the only viable theological explanation for the Holocaust. However, while they stop with the assertion that the Holocaust was punishment for sin, Rubenstein goes a step further. Rubenstein maintains that since the only viable theological explanation for the Holocaust is divine retribution and since that explanation is theologically problematic and morally repugnant, one must therefore reject the possibility of dealing with the Holocaust from the assumptions of classical Jewish theology. One must deny the God of history and affirm "Jewish paganism." In effect, Rubenstein constructs an either/or proposition: either a cruel God or none. Since the former is unacceptable, one must opt for the latter.

The problem with Rubenstein's presentation of the options is that it is too limited. There are other options. Rejection of the divine retribution argument does not necessarily entail rejection of the God of history. Indeed, other Holocaust theologians, such as Fackenheim, Greenberg and Eliezer Berkovits, begin with the assumption that a theological response to the Holocaust which rejects the divine retribution argument without denying the God of history may be articulated.

Having denied the basic categories of Jewish theology, Rubenstein is in a problematič position as a theologian of Judaism. To claim that his response to the Holocaust is a *Jewish* theological response is equally questionable. Indeed, one Christian critic of Rubenstein, George Boyd, has claimed that Rubenstein, having found Jewish theological categories to be inapplicable to the Holocaust, has utilized a number of basic Christian symbols and themes in formulating his Holocaust theology.

Eliezer Berkovits finds moral as well as theological difficulties with Rubenstein's position. Rubenstein's world-view, deeply influenced by French existentialists such as Sartre and Camus, denies an objective source of human meaning and human morality. It is, therefore, ultimately pessimistic and morally anarchistic, claims Berkovits. Since only subjective values exist in this view, anything can be morally justified. Hence, Berkovits maintains, Nazism itself could be justified by such an approach.

RE-FUSED FAITH

The majority of Jewish theologians who have confronted the Holocaust reject both the applicability of the divine retribution argument to the Holocaust and the complete denial of the validity of classical Jewish theology after the Holocaust á la Rubenstein. They seek to articulate a response to the Holocaust which utilizes reconstructed categories drawn from classical Jewish theology. Rather than attempting to solve the unsolvable problem of theodicy, they concentrate their efforts upon justifying the possibility of faith after the Holocaust. Rather than seeking solutions, they are engaged in articulating responses.

Irving Greenberg, for example, maintains that "After the Holocaust there should be no final solutions, not even theological ones." This sentiment is shared by Eliezer Berkovits, Emil Fackenheim and Abraham Joshua Heschel. In Heschel's words, "There is no answer to Auschwitz... to try to answer is to commit a supreme blasphemy." Similarly, novelists such as Elie Wiesel, who have explored the theological implications of the Holocaust, have also arrived at this conclusion. For Wiesel, "one cannot conceive of the Holocaust except as a mystery begotten by the dead. . . . Auschwitz defies the novelist's language, the historian's analysis, the vision of the prophet." Elsewhere, Wiesel remarks, "Perhaps some day someone will explain how, on the level of man, Auschwitz was possible; but on the level of God, it will forever remain the most disturbing of mysteries."

The most extensive theological analysis of the problem of evil after the Holocaust has been *Evil and the God of Love* by the Protestant theologian John Hick. In his erudite and thorough study of the problem of theodicy in

Western Christian tradition, Hick reaches a conclusion which approximates those just noted:

"Our 'solution' then to this baffling problem of excessive and undeserved suffering is a frank appeal to the positive power of mystery. Such suffering remains unjust and inexplicable, haphazard and cruelly excessive. The mystery of dysteleological suffering is a real mystery, impenetrable to the rationalizing human mind."

Thus, these Holocaust theologians echo Dostoyevsky's statement in *The Brothers Karamazov* that all the explanations of all the philosophers cannot explain the unjustified death of one innocent child. To explain the deaths of millions of people, including over one million children, certainly transcends the possibilities of human comprehension. Then, why attempt to respond theologically to the Holocaust? Why be concerned with theological works which articulate some response to the cataclysm? Perhaps the answer to these questions was best expressed by Nikos Kazantzakis in *Zorba the Greek*. When tragedy strikes, Zorba asks his employer, "Well, all those damned books you read—what good are they? Why do you read them? If they don't tell you that, what *do* they tell you?"

The employer responds, "They tell me about the perplexity of mankind, who can give no answer to the question you've just put to me, Zorba."

In the ensuing pages, we shall discuss the attempts of two significant Jewish theologians to assuage their perplexity by articulating a theological response to the Holocaust.

ELIEZER BERKOVITS

Berkovits asserts that affirmations of faith may be made after the Holocaust as they were made after other catastrophes in Jewish history. For Berkovits, unlike Elie Wiesel, Emil Fackenheim and Richard Rubenstein, the Holocaust is unique only in magnitude but not in kind; it is unique in horror, but not unique in the kinds of theological questions it raises. Consequently, one can and must deal with the Holocaust by attempting to evaluate and utilize Jewish theological responses to past traumas. For Berkovits, a serious shortcoming of other literary and theological examinations of the Holocaust is that "they deal with the holocaust in isolation, as if there had been nothing else in Jewish experience but this holocaust. The holocaust . . . cannot be considered independently either of that experience or of the teaching that accompanied that experience." For Berkovits, "while the holocaust is unique in the objective magnitude of its inhumanity, it is not unique as a problem of faith resulting from Jewish historical experience. Indeed, one might say that the problem is as old as Judaism itself." Thus for Berkovits, "each generation had its Auschwitz problem.'' Therefore, it behooves the contemporary Jewish theologian to incorporate the responses of past generations to their ''Auschwitz problem'' into his own response to his own ''Auschwitz problem.'' Berkovits proceeds to address the contemporary Jew's ''Auschwitz problem'' by examining the various theological options formulated in past generations.

Having rejected the divine retribution argument, Berkovits is similarly unable to accept the medieval Jewish philosophical view that evil is a privation of the good—that ''evil'' is not a real entity but a state wherein goodness is absent. Like the divine retribution argument, the ''privation argument'' seeks to absolve God from responsibility for evil in the world. For if evil does not actually exist, if it is just a state where nothing is present but something (i.e., the good) is absent, then God cannot be held responsible for its (i.e., evil's) existence.

While this argument may be philosophically defensible, Berkovits finds it unacceptable. It is too facile a solution, paling into irrelevancy in the face of human suffering. It does not adequately explain suffering to the one who suffers. It does not sufficiently justify or defend God's allowance of suffering and injustice; God remains responsible. While intellectually attractive, the ''privation'' argument is existentially insipid.

As Berkovits rejects the ''privation'' argument because it proves to be an unacceptable attempt to circumvent the vital issues of theodicy, he also denies the position of those who assert that God is detached from the world, if He exists at all. This approach is unacceptable because it tries to ''solve'' the problem of theodicy by denying it exists. Here Berkovits attacks the atheistic French existentialists such as Sartre and Camus and the ''God is dead'' theologians, specifically Richard Rubenstein (though never mentioning him by name).

To deny the existence of God or to reject divine providence solves nothing, Berkovits insists. In fact, it only creates additional problems. For if the ''God-hypothesis'' is removed from an attempt to explain human events, then one is left with a view of reality in which everything happens either because of chance or because it has been predetermined.

Having rejected the viability of other options—classical and contemporary—Berkovits attempts to articulate a response of his own. Drawing upon classical Judaica and western philosophy, Berkovits formulates a posture for defending the viability of Jewish faith after the Holocaust.

For Berkovits, as for classical Jewish tradition, Jewish faith is rooted in the reality of the divine-human encounter which takes place in revelation and history. The divine-human encounter, however, embodies a paradox: God must conceal His essence in order to reveal His presence.

Since God is ''wholly other'' and since His essence eludes human comprehension, God must both reveal and conceal Himself in the moment of encounter. While revealing His concern for man and His commandments to man, He must conceal His essence from man. For Berkovits, God "must reveal Himself as the 'hiding God' that man may live in His sight." So as not to overpower man while expressing divine concern for the human condition, God must conceal Himself from men. So as not to totally overwhelm man, depriving him of spiritual independence or even his very survival, God must conceal Himself in the act of revealing Himself. Thus, divine concealment, "the hiding of God," is necessary to the divine-human encounter which forms the basis for religious faith.

Berkovits carefully distinguishes between the "hiding God" and the Biblical phrase "the hiding face of God." While the "hiding God" is basic to the divine-human relationship, the "hiding face of God" represents a breakdown in that relationship and an inexplicable withdrawal of divine concern. It may be that Berkovits' identification of the category of "the hiding face of God" convinced him of the impossibility of a viable theodicy. There are inexplicable moments of Divine withdrawal which the human mind cannot fathom.

Rather than seeking to rest his argument for faith after the Holocaust in the mystery of God's actions, Berkovits proceeds to construct a modern interpretation of the freewill argument as a basis for reaffirming faith after the Holocaust. For just as God must impose self-restraint in revelation, He must limit His activities once moral choice is given to mankind.

According to Berkovits, a perfect God creates an imperfect world in order to provide human beings with the possibility of meaningful existence by exercising their freedom of choice. Unless human beings had free choice, they would be automatons, devoid of freedom, unable to realize any goals, unable to attain meaning by means of freely chosen deeds. The price of human freedom, however, is the interjection of a chaotic, uncertain element into creation.

While human choice may succeed in generating both meaning and morality, it may also fail to do so. Thus, human failure, human meaninglessness, human destructiveness are implicit within human choice. Man's moral potentiality reflects a metaphysical state. Evil is implicit within the order of creation. Human choice can make evil explicit. Thus, Berkovits expresses a modern version of an argument found in the Book of Genesis and refined by medieval Jewish philosophy: evil is implicit within the structure of creation; man's misuse of his freedom translates evil from a potential danger into an actual entity.

In this view, if God is guilty of anything, it is His creation of man as a free moral agent. Though God is all-powerful, He does not intervene in human affairs because to do so, whether to prevent evil or good, would be to deny the viability of human volition. For Berkovits, God must necesarily withdraw from the arena of human history in order to insure human freedom of will. Thus, Berkovits is left with a paradox: divine providence means that God must tolerate the persecutor, the sinner, and He must abandon the victim, the innocent, in order to insure human freedom. God who is omnipotent restrains His power to make human history possible. Berkovits' paradox means: God must be present for human meaning but He must be absent for human freedom.

Berkovits utilizes his free will argument to project God out of the orbit of moral responsibility. True, Berkovits asserts, God is responsible for human freedom and the potential for evil is implicit within that freedom. However, claims Berkovits, God creates and is responsible for only the potentiality and not the reality of evil. Only man, and not God, is responsible for what is done with human freedom. For Berkovits, God is beyond good and evil. Since good and evil are inextricably interrelated, a moral agent cannot be good *or* evil, but must be both good *and* evil. Since God, by definition, is not evil, He can also not be good.

One may take issue with this view of Berkovits. First of all, how can the Source of morality not be moral? How can the Source of morality be amoral? Secondly, why must one assume that God is bereft of any evil element? This assumption, for example, was not universally accepted in Jewish mystical tradition. Finally, while the human freedom argument may explain moral evil, it leaves untouched the question of ''natural evil''—disease, typhoons, etc. While one may find some merit in Berkovits' free-will argument in explaining the Holocaust on the human level, one must also suggest that he has not adequately defended his attempt to remove responsibility from God.

Berkovits finds the source for faith after the Holocaust within history; specifically, Jewish history. For Berkovits, evidence of the ''hiding God'' within history may be found in the persistent survival of the Jewish people for thousands of years in a state of virtual powerlessness. Berkovits maintains that the continuous survival of Israel, which cannot be explained on natural or scientific grounds, is itself the best testimony to God's presence in history. The persistence of the Jewish people in the face of continual adversity is proof that God's presence is not totally eclipsed. Specifically, Berkovits sees the State of Israel as testimony to the Divine presence in history. For Berkovits, the birth of the State of Israel provides a basis for the possibility of ''faith after the Holocaust.'' He perceives the events of the establishment of the State of Israel in 1948 and the Israeli victory in 1967 as contemporary revelation, as positive proof of God's presence in history. If at Auschwitz and at all other previous tragedies in Jewish history the Jewish people have witnessed ''the hiding face of God,'' in Israel they have ''seen a smile on the face of God. It is enough.'' Because the State of Israel expresses the presence of God in history after the Holocaust for Berkovits, it is not surprising to have him claim that the continuous existence of Israel is indispensable both to the Jewish people and to God.

In his most recent reflections concerning the Holocaust and the State of Israel, Berkovits appears to have gone beyond the position stated in *Faith*

After the Holocaust. In an essay entitled "Crisis and Faith" (now included in his volume of the same name), Berkovits seems to reject his earlier view that the Holocaust represents a continuation of Jewish history. Now Berkovits claims that the Holocaust was a break with past history, a "radically new event."

In this latest view Berkovits maintains that the Holocaust differed from past persecutions both in *quality* and in scope in that it represented, for the first time, a threat of total annihilation for the Jewish people. It represented the destruction of the "exile" itself and not only the destruction of a single diasporan community.

For Berkovits, the response to such a radical event had to be equally radical. This response was the rise of the State of Israel, which Berkovits interprets as an expression of providence. Hence, God had to intercede in history in order to insure the survival of the Jewish people. Now that the diaspora is at an end, the State of Israel continues as the basis for Jewish survival. The continued existence of the State and its military victories are, therefore, crucial for Jewish existence.

In response to Berkovits' newly stated position, one may ask whether he would presently accept the validity of some of his former positions which were predicated upon understanding the Holocaust within the framework of Jewish history rather than as a departure from that history. One may challenge Berkovits' assumption that the Jewish people stood in threat of *total* annihilation in 1940–1945, in 1948, 1967, 1973, or today. One may question Berkovits' premise that Judaism needs the State of Israel to survive. One may deny Berkovits' assertion that the diasporan experience is at an end.

While Berkovits provides a metaphysically oriented philosophy of Jewish history, he offers neither an intellectually nor an existentially satisfying theodicy. However, it was never his intended purpose to do so. Berkovits only claimed to attempt to defend the viability of Jewish faith after the Holocaust. Whether he has realized this attempt must be personally determined by the individual reader of his work, for the conclusion of his argument, in the long run, is more inviting on the personal level, than on the abstract, intellectual level.

EMIL FACKENHEIM

For Emil Fackenheim, an inevitable obligation of the contemporary Jewish theologian and of the contemporary Jewish believer is an encounter with the Holocaust. Such an encounter precludes the acceptance of predetermined categories of explanation; e.g., "the 'progressive ideology' which asserts that memory is unnecessary, that Auschwitz was an accidental 'relapse into tribalism'; the 'psychiatric' ideology which holds that memory is masochism even as Auschwitz itself was sadism, thus safely belittling both; the 'liberalist-universalistic' ideology which asserts that memory is actually immoral.'' Thus, for Fackenheim, any attempt to struggle with the anxieties of contemporary Jewish existence in general and with the Holocaust in particular cannot authentically emerge out of fixed categories of classical or contemporary Jewish theology.

Following Buber, Fackenheim insists that existential encounter with God cannot be replaced by "concepts of God." God must be encountered in the crucible of history; He cannot be neatly categorized and defined. Theodicy must be a personal struggle of faith, not an exercise in categorical gymnastics. Like Eliezer Berkovits, Fackenheim directs his analysis not only to medieval and early modern formulations of the "God-idea," but to the contemporary views of "religious naturalism."

For Fackenheim, the naturalists are guilty of "subjectivist reductionism." Like the scientist who reduces God to an hypothesis and the psychologist who reduces God to a projection of feeling, the naturalist reduces God to an idea or a concept, to a projection of his own view of morality. Fackenheim maintains that the "God-idea" of the naturalist, like the "God-hypothesis" of the scientist, has nothing in common with the God encountered in history. Consequently, these expressions of "subjectivist reductionism" are totally irrelevant to Jewish religious faith which is grounded in the historical and contemporary encounter of the Jew and the Jewish people with the "living God." Thus, for Fackenheim, essentialism, abstract philosophy and subjectivist reductionism are not only untenable in general, but are irrelevant to contemporary Jewish thought in its attempt to speak out of concrete historical existence and in its existential need to grapple with the overwhelming reality of the Holocaust.

Fackenheim begins with experiences rather than with ideological constructs. He understands Judaism to be a series of encounters between God and Israel. Thus, he assumes the experience of God's presence; he assumes revelation. The experience of God takes precedence over any attempt to "prove" or "define" God or to formulate a "God-idea" or a "God-hypothesis." What is primary is the encounter; the ideas and concepts are merely human reflection upon the encounter. For Fackenheim, "A religious concern with Jewish living presupposes the assertion that revelation *actually* happened." Thus, Fackenheim posits a supernatural existential approach to Judaism. Fackenheim assumes the presence of God within history. This presence, while providing history with meaning, does not destroy human freedom. To the contrary, it binds mankind to responsibility.

In the course of Jewish history, the assumption that God is indeed present in history was continually challenged by the impact of contemporary events. Jewish history abounds with examples of the refusal to forfeit faith in the wake of trauma and tragedy. Jewish history and Jewish theology continually attempted to confront the apparent contradictions between "old faith" and contemporary experience. Surrendering to abject despair through total rejection of the God who acts in history was never a viable option for classical Jewish thought; nor is it an option for Fackenheim.

Fackenheim rejects any approach relating the deaths of Holocaust victims to the victims' sins or the sins of others (i.e., vicarious suffering). He also contends that the traditional recourse to martyrdom as a source of meaning is irrelevant with regard to the Holocaust. Traditional martyrdom assumed that the potential martyr had at least the theoretical choice of death or conversion. During the Holocaust, however, there was no choice. Without a choice, there can be no martyrdom. The Holocaust murdered martyrdom itself, depriving the victims of choice and of dignity. The Inquisition destroyed the bodies to save souls; it had some meaning and purpose. The Nazis destroyed both bodies and souls; they murdered for no purpose, only for the sake of murder.

Fackenheim finds neither the theology of protest which challenges the justice of an omnipotent God to be viable, nor does he accept the various attempts to confront evil by positing a less than omnipotent God. For Fackenheim, the rabbinic notion of a less than omnipotent God, a God in exile, is irrelevant after the Holocaust. For Fackenheim, to assert God's powerlessness means to claim God's death. Furthermore, Fackenheim rejects the more recent attempt of Buber to respond to the Holocaust with his image of the "eclipse of God." Fackenheim contends that if all *present* access to the God of history is lost, obscured by an eclipse, then the God of history Himself is lost. A divine eclipse which is total in the present cuts off both past and future. Thus, one is left either with the presence of God in history or without it. "The God of Israel cannot be God of either past or future unless He is still God of the present." For Fackenheim, as for Arthur Cohen, Buber's "eclipse of God" is an evasive concept.

Fackenheim recognizes the sobering fact that "Jewish theology still does not know how to respond to Auschwitz." However, he maintains, "Jews themselves . . . have responded all along." This response is in the desire of Jews—religionists and secularists—to remain Jews and to have their children remain Jews after the Holocaust. Nineteenth century Jews condemned their great-grandchildren to death by retaining Jewish identity. Contemporary Jews remain Jews despite the shattering immensity of the Holocaust, in spite of the fact that their decision to remain Jews might be a condemnation of their descendants in some future holocaust. In this existential affirmation, no distinction is made between religionist and secularist. To remain a Jew after the Holocaust is an affirmation which may be made by the secular and by the religious Jew alike. In past generations, the religious Jew bore witness to the presence of God in history by his continued existence. But, "after Auschwitz even the most secularist of Jews bears witness, by the mere affirmation of his Jewishness, against the devil." In the wake of the Holocaust, Fackenheim maintains, former distinctions between the secular and the religious Jew are obsolete. Now, the distinction is between unauthentic Jews who flee from their Jewishness and authentic Jews who affirm it. "The latter group includes religious and secular Jews. They are united by a commanding Voice which speaks from Auschwitz."

Fackenheim claims that the Voice from Auschwitz is a revelatory voice "as was the voice of Sinai." This Voice issues a commandment, now grafted onto the 613 commandments of the Torah. This 614th commandment forbids Jews—secularist and religionist alike—"to hand Hitler posthumous victories," and orders Jews to survive as Jews, lest the Jewish people perish.

In articulating this position, Fackenheim expresses his opposition to any Jewish version of the "God is dead" theology; i.e., to Richard Rubenstein. To deny the presence of God in history, to despair of man and the world, to give up hope, to embrace an atheistic nihilism is to violate the commandment which emerged from Auschwitz. To deny these things is to render a posthumous victory to Hitler; it is to perpetuate Hitler's attempt to destroy Judaism, Jewish faith, Jewish hope.

According to Fackenheim, the midrashic framework, "the greatest theology ever produced within Judaism," is dialectical "because it must hold fast to contradictory affirmations." The post-Holocaust midrash, therefore, can dialectically affirm both a revelation at Sinai and a revelation at Auschwitz at once. For Fackenheim, this commanding Voice of God was heard "by the Jews of Israel in May and June 1967 when they refused to lie down and be slaughtered." This last affirmation, linking the Voice of Auschwitz to the Israeli experience, leads to an examination of Fackenheim's position on the relationship between the Holocaust and the State of Israel.

Like Abraham Heschel, Fackenheim asserts that both the Holocaust and the State of Israel resist rational explanation and that one cannot posit a cause and effect explanation between them. Israel is neither an answer to the problem posed by the Holocaust, nor does it represent a new revelation. However, it is a response to the Holocaust. For Fackenheim, Israel is a collective fulfillment of the commandment given at Auschwitz. The Six Day War was not a revelatory event as others had claimed. It was, however, a response to the commanding Voice of Auschwitz, the Voice which commands Jewish survival. Hence, for Fackenheim, one must live in the dialectic of faith after the Holocaust. One must exist between Sinai and Auschwitz, between hope and despair, never surrendering to one or to the other.

Most critics of Fackenheim's response to the Holocaust have stressed the problems attendant upon his unique contribution to Holocaust theology; i.e., his claim that there was a commanding Voice at Auschwitz. Despite its novelty, this approach is replete with difficulties.

First of all, by admitting the possibility of revelation today, Fackenheim opens a theological Pandora's Box. For centuries a major stream of Jewish theology insisted that revelation ceased with the Bible. To posit new revelations potentially poses a challenge to the authority of former revelations. How can one be assured of the validity of a new revelation? Who else but Fackenheim has heard the commanding Voice from Auschwitz? Was there such a Voice? Did it impose a new commandment? Is there a need for an additional commandment?

It would seem that Fackenheim's innovation poses more problems than it solves. If revelation was possible at Auschwitz, why can we not assume that it was present in 1948, 1967, 1973? How can we determine which contemporary events are revelatory and which are not? Which bestow commandments and which do not? How can we prevent random and arbitrary claims to new revelations and new commandments? Is not the commandment to survive as Jews implicit within the already existing commandments? Is not the commandment to remember the Holocaust and other past tragedies covered by the commandment to remember ''Amalek'' and by the commandments related to the observance of such holidays as *Tisha B'Av*? Is there a need, a justification, a rationale for a new commandment? Furthermore, even if we were to grant that God's Voice was revealed at Auschwitz, would not such a revelation, such a commandment—to survive as Jews—in such a place, portray God as a ''cosmic sadist'' (Rubenstein)? Finally, what are the implications of accepting the commandment to survive as Jews so as not to allow Hitler a posthumous victory?

To base Jewish survival on the need to avoid giving Hitler posthumous victories implies that Jews should remain Jews after the Holocaust because of Hitler, as if there were no other reasons for doing so. If Judaism is to survive, it must be because it is intrinsically worthy of survival and not because Hitler sought to destroy it. To place Hitler's evil design at the center of Jewish faith is totally inappropriate and unnecessary. A Jew is obliged to preserve Judaism because it is worthy of preservation and not because the Nazis wanted to annihilate it. Thus, Fackenheim's ''negative theology'' is superfluous. It fails to adequately recognize the intrinsic validity of Judaism in and of itself.

Fackenheim's commanding Voice requires uncompromising survival, Jewish survival for Jewish survival's sake. This represents a shift from his early position which rejected a survivalist mentality. One may question the morality of this stance. Is unconditional survival for survival's sake morally defensible? Is there no moral value greater than sheer survival? Is unconditional survival defensible within the framework of Jewish morality which claims that there are things worth dying for? What does the absolute demand for Jewish survival mean in light of the perennial search for Jewish meaning? Is not the quest for survival penultimate to but linked with the struggle for meaning (see Viktor Frankl)?

CHRISTIAN THEOLOGIANS AND THE HOLOCAUST

Jewish theologians, such as Fackenheim, Berkovits and Greenberg, have consistently maintained that the Holocaust poses as great, if not greater problems for Christian theology than for Jewish theology. A number of Christian theologians have concurred with this observation. Consequently, a small but vocal group of Christian theologians has maintained that the continued pertinence of Christianity may be related to its response to the implications of the Holocaust. For example, a Protestant theologian, Franklin Littell, has identified the Holocaust as "the major event in recent church history—signalizing as it does the rebellion of the baptised against the Lord of History.... Christianity itself has been 'put to the question'—by the apostasy of millions of the baptised, by being witting or silent accomplices in the murder of most of the European Jews."

Similarly, Fredrich Heer, a Catholic theologian who has written on the relationship of Christian anti-Semitism and the Holocaust, contends that the future of Christianity is inextricably bound up with how it relates to Judaism and to Jews in the post-Holocaust era. In Heer's words, "Christianity cannot continue to exist unless Christians are constantly aware of their responsibility for the continued existence of Jews on this ... earth."

Profoundly shaken, both personally and theologically, by the roles played by Christian theological anti-Semitism and by professing Christians in making the Holocaust possible, some Christian theologians have responded to the Holocaust on personal and theological levels.

Christian theologians who have encountered the Holocaust have largely circumvented the problem of theodicy (John Hick is a notable exception) and have concentrated instead upon the socio-theological problems engendered by the Holocaust. The focal point of Christian Holocaust theology has not been the problem of evil, but the problem of Christian anti-Semitism and what to do about it. Not the relationship between God and man but the relationship between Christianity and Judaism, has largely concerned Christian theologians attempting to respond to the Holocaust.

A number of Christian historians and theologians have attempted to articulate the challenge to Christian faith posed by the Holocaust by describing the history of Christian anti-Semitism and its implicit role in making the Holocaust possible (see bibliography below and Chapter Three above). Others have examined the role of the Church in various countries during World War II vis-à-vis Nazism in general and the Jews in particular. Their findings, together with the findings of non-Christian scholars writing in these areas, have stimulated some theological reassessment of Christian attitudes towards Jews and Judaism.

Generally, speaking, one may identify three positions in post-Holocaust Christian theology regarding Jews and Judaism. The first position maintains that both theological anti-Semitism and its corollary, social anti-Semitism, are endemic to Christian faith. In this view, the Holocaust, rather than posing a challenge to Christian belief, represents an affirmation of classical Christian attitudes towards Jews and Judaism. The fate of the Jews during World War II demonstrates that they are the rejected people of God, doomed to degradation and death for having rejected and murdered Jesus Christ. This position, discussed in part above, reaffirms the applicability of the doctrine of divine retribution to the Holocaust. The weakness of this stance is that it fails to come to grips with the challenge the Holocaust poses to Christian faith by simply failing to recognize that such a challenge exists.

The second position maintains that the premises of Christian theological anti-Judaism are so essential to the structure of Christian faith that to alter them would virtually entail the self-dismantling of Christian theology. However, social anti-Semitism, which reached its apogee during the Holocaust, ought to be repudiated as moral behavior unbefitting civilized humanity, much less a professing Christian. Thus, many church leaders, institutions and organizations, both during and after World War II, have deplored anti-Semitism, but have hesitatingly refused to alter the theological positions which serve as the ideological basis for anti-Semitic attitudes. The problem with this stance is in not realizing the intrinsic relationship between theological and social anti-Semitism. To deplore the effect while refusing to deal with the cause does not insure the assuaging of Christian anti-Semitism.

The third position affirms the close relationship between Christian theological and social anti-Semitism. It therefore maintains that since social anti-Semitism is the praxis of which theological anti-Semitism is the theory, one must deplore social anti-Semitism while attempting to reformulate Christian doctrine so as to eliminate or radically modify the premises from which theological anti-Semitism flows. The problem with this stance is that its theological reformulation of basic Christian doctrines may be interpreted as too radical for Christian self-understanding. In restructuring the Christian theological edifice, these theological architects may in effect be dismantling its very foundations.

Those who advocate the first position basically affirm the same theological assumptions as those who advocate the second position. Those advocating the third position call for a reevaluation of these assumptions, and some have articulated new formulations of basic Christian doctrines based upon that reevaluation. Thus, in order to understand and to appreciate the Christian theological response to the Holocaust, it is important to delineate the basic theological posture maintained by those who advocate the first and second positions. It will then be necessary to further distinguish the first position from the second. Finally, the reformulations offered by the advocates of position three will require discussion. To be sure, not all Christian responses may be exactly subsumed by one or another of these positions. However, the differentiation of these three postures does account for much of post-Holocaust Christian speculation and does provide a rubric for understanding post-Holocaust Christian theology.

Theological Problems and Premises

The first and second positions, mentioned above, embrace a theology which stresses the uniqueness and finality of Christ as the sole mediator of salvation, as the final messiah whose advent represents the fulfillment of Jewish hopes and prophecies. Christ, in this view, is the embodiment of the New Israel which succeeds and replaces the Old Israel. His teaching, as contained in the New Testament, represents the new Torah, the new covenant with the New Israel, the Church. Just as the New Israel succeeds the Old Israel, so does the new Torah succeed the Old Testament.

According to this theological stance, Judaism is an obsolete faith. Jewish existence in itself has no intrinsic value since the Jew is only a potential Christian. Having rejected Christ, the recalcitrant contemporary Jew perpetuates the sins of his ancestors who murdered Christ (deicide) and who consequently were condemned by God to eternal degradation, wandering and punishment. The salvation of the Jew lies in his casting off the stubbornness of his forefathers and his affirmation of Jesus as the Christ. Christians, therefore, must persist in their "mission to the Jews."

This position, expressed here in oversimplified terms, has been identified as a contributing cause of the Holocaust. For those Christian theologians who maintain this position in the wake of the Holocaust, the fact that this stance helped make the Holocaust possible, appears irrelevant. That the missionary imperative embodied by this position calls for "religious genocide," for a theological "Final Solution to the Jewish problem," has not affected those who affirm this approach.

Rosemary Ruether and Franklin Littell have both noted that the "displacement myth," which claims that with the coming of Christ the Old Israel was displaced by the New Israel, is the "cornerstone of Christian anti-semitism which already rings with a genocidal note" (Littell). The displacement myth assigns the Jewish people to obsolescence. The premise that Jews have no right to exist as Jews easily slides into the claim that the Jews have no right to exist at all. As Raul Hilberg so poignantly put it, "The missionaries of Christianity had said in effect: You have no right to live among us as Jews. The secular rulers who followed had proclaimed: You have no right to live among us. The German Nazis at last decreed: you have no right to live."

The displacement myth, as incorporated into Christian theology, raises the following questions formulated by Gregory Baum: "Does the self-understanding of the Christian church leave theological room for Jewish self-understanding? Or does the claim of the church to be the people of God, the true Israel, make it impossible for Christians to acknowledge the special place which Jewish self-understanding demands?'' If the answer to the first question is ''no,'' then Christian anti-Semitism becomes theologically and logically inevitable.

What differentiates the second aforementioned position from the first is its rejection of social anti-Semitism while generally affirming the theological premises just outlined. The tension inherent in this second position is the clash of two forces: a revulsion against social anti-Semitism and a commitment to theological ''truth.'' This tension appears, for example, in the writings of the eminent Catholic theologian, Cardinal Charles Journet. While expressing revulsion and horror in the face of Auschwitz, Journet reiterates the displacement myth. For Journet, Israel's ''no'' to Christ inevitably transforms it into a guilty people. The fate of Israel in history is life under a divine curse. Jewish tragedy is the product of the ''patrimony of infidelity'' which prevents the Jew from affirming Christ.

The eminent Catholic philosopher Jacques Maritain takes a position similar to that of Journet. He expresses moral revulsion towards social anti-Semitism of every shade, from the Dreyfus trial to Nazism. He affirms opposition to anti-Semitism as a Christian moral duty, and he rebukes those who would speak or write a word which could be used as an excuse for engendering hatred. At the same time, Maritain reaffirms the theological claim that the continuous Jewish rejection of Christ is at the root of the Jews' historical troubles. As long as they continue in their defiant path, the Jews will invoke the enmity of their neighbors and will court disaster. Even a Catholic ''liberal'' such as Jean Danielou, who outspokenly denounced the doctrine of Jewish guilt for the Crucifixion and unceasingly opposed social anti-Semitism, nevertheless maintains that the sorry fate of the Jewish people in history is the result of their abiding rejection of Christ.

Amongst Protestant theologians and Church organizations, a similar approach is evident. For example, at the Second Assembly of the World Council of Churches which convened in Evanston, Illinois in 1954, future relations with the Jewish community were a primary subject of discussion. The outcome of these theological deliberations was a condemnation of social anti-Semitism, especially of Nazism. The Assembly even went so far as to express remorse and ''the grievous guilt of the Christian people towards the Jews throughout the history of the church.'' However, when it came to a theological reappraisal of the Church's attitude toward the Jews, the missionary imperative and the successionist doctrine were reaffirmed. The Assembly proclaimed that ''the Church cannot rest until the title of Christ to the Kingdom is recognized by His own People according to the flesh.''

The position of the important Protestant theologian Karl Barth is relevant to this discussion. Like so many European Protestants who actively opposed Hitler and Nazism at great risk, Barth was virtually silent regarding the Nazis' "Final Solution."

Barth was at the forefront of the German Church's opposition to Nazism. He considered Christian Nazis as idolaters and heretics. He perceived Nazism as a profound threat to Christianity. For Barth, there can only be Christ *or* Hitler, not Christ *and* Hitler. He urged his followers to actively oppose Hitler and Nazism. Barth, however, did not speak out against Nazi persecution of the Jews. His only major discussion of Jews and Judaism appears in his theological writings where he reaffirms the myth of supersession and describes the Jew as the reluctant witness to Christian faith. For Barth, the Jew symbolizes man's "unwillingness, incapacity and unworthiness" with respect to God's love. The onus of this role is the malice of those who do not wish to be reminded of their unwillingness, incapacity and unworthiness. This stance assigns Jewry a tragic fate. Barth's position approximates what Hannah Arendt has called "eternal anti-Semitism," a doctrine in which "Jew hatred is a normal and natural reaction to which history only gives more or less opportunity."

Theological Premises, Problems, and Prospects

The third position introduced above condemns social anti-Semitism while also attempting to dismiss the premises which lie at the root of theological anti-Semitism. Certain advocates of this position reject these premises but do not offer a reconstructed theology to replace them. Other advocates of this position offer a radical restructuring of Christian faith which rejects the displacement myth and its correlative claims in a variety of degrees.

The two most eminent Protestant theologians writing in the United States in the post-World War II era were Paul Tillich and Reinhold Niebuhr. Both rejected the displacement myth, denied the acceptibility of the "mission to the Jews," and actively opposed social anti-Semitism in general and Nazism in particular.

Tillich opposed Nazism in his native Germany in the 1930's. He considered it an "honor" to have been the "first non-Jewish professor to be dismissed from a German university in 1933." Tillich not only affirmed the right of Judaism to exist as a continually viable faith, but he also proclaimed that Christianity required the continued existence of an authentic Judaism for its own authenticity and moral rectitude. For Tillich, "Judaism is a permanent ethical corrective of sacramental Christianity. And this is the main significance of Judaism for Protestant theology." Considering his background in German Protestant theology, Tillich is amazingly free of the theological anti-Semitism which has characterized that theological community. Thus, Tillich affirms the integrity of Judaism and its pertinence for Christian self-understanding. His theology, therefore, is inclusionary rather than exclusionary. Theological truth is not a monopoly of the Church.

Reinhold Niebuhr was a persistent opponent of Nazism. He perceived the monstrous sinfulness of man at work in Hitler's treatment of the Jews, and sought to demonstrate its ramifications and combat its consequences in numerous books, essays and speeches. He saw a continuing significance for Christianity in the Holocaust, not only because it manifested the demonic dimensions of sin, but also because it demonstrated the need for Christians to be involved in trying to achieve at least relative justice through involvement in social and political affairs.

While Niebuhr wrote little directly related to the Jewish experience during the Holocaust, he was a persistent opponent of both social and theological anti-Semitism. The first major American theologian to reject the myth of supersession and to call for an end to "the mission to the Jews," Niebuhr always affirmed the theological integrity of Judaism and, like Tillich, considered the continued flourishing of Judaism to be important for the continued authenticity of the Church.

Always a staunch supporter of the State of Israel, Niebuhr regarded "the thrilling emergence of the State of Israel as a kind of penance of the world for the awful atrocities committed against the Jews."

As has been mentioned above, one of the most significant American Protestant voices condemning the displacement myth as being scripturally unjustifiable is Franklin Littell. As early as 1960, when he published *The German Phoenix*, Littell expressed his profound concern with social and theological anti-Semitism. In *The Crucifixion of the Jews* Littell admonishes his fellow Christians for not resolving the "acute identity crisis" which the Holocaust should have caused for them. He contends that not only the Holocaust but also the emergence of the State of Israel represents a strong challenge to Christians and to Christianity. For Littell, the Holocaust demonstrates the murderous implications of the displacement myth, thus dispelling its moral and theological viability. The resurrection of Israel, represented by the State of Israel, offers a living "refutation of the traditional Christian myth about their end [i.e., the Jewish people] in the historic process."

According to Littell, Christian theology has remained oblivious to its two major challenges: confrontation with the implications of the Holocaust and of the State of Israel. Only if Christians confront these two issues do they have the possibility of recovering their true identity. In the meantime, the apostasy of Christians who do not want to admit their guilt and their rebellion against God, epitomized by Christian attitudes towards Jews during and after the Holocaust, characterizes the presently alienated condition of the Christian community. Thus, for Littell, the Church must encounter the theological implications of the Holocaust to insure its own identity, its own meaning, its own integrity. The Holocaust may represent a more vital challenge to Christian faith than to Jewish faith. The Holocaust and the State of Israel offer an essential challenge to Christian self-understanding. In Littell's words, "perhaps the question put to us by the Holocaust and [the State of] Israel is whether we [Christians] are still able to grasp the meaning of Crucifixion and resurrection."

Like Littell, Protestant theologian Roy Eckardt interprets the Holocaust as Christian apostasy without the assumption of guilt and repentence. In Eckardt's words, "the church that collaborated in the Nazi 'final solution' dealt itself mortal blows. From that Jewish crucifixion and Christian self-crucifixion there could and did come a Jewish resurrection—the State of Israel—but not a Christian resurrection. For the church has nowhere now to go." Thus, for Eckardt, as for Littell, the Holocaust seems to represent a more severe challenge to Christian theology than it does to Jewish theology.

Eckardt formulates a Christology which leaves adequate room for both Jewish and Christian self-understanding. For Eckardt, the significance of Jesus is his making salvation available to the Gentiles. The Jewish non-acceptance of Jesus is, therefore, to be understood as an act of faithfulness to God and not as an act of faithlessness towards God.

Eckardt maintains that Jesus partially fulfilled messianic expectations insofar as the pagans were brought into salvation. Judaism and Christianity, therefore, operate in a dialectical tension within a single covenant. Each has a vocation to the world and to one another—to announce the revelation which God has given in their respective histories. The events of Israel's history are no less revelatory and final than those of Christians. Rather than excluding one another, they complement one another. For Eckardt, the covenant between God and the Christian community in no way supersedes or supplants the covenant with Israel. Consequently, any mission to the Jews is untenable. The Christian covenant is not a new and better covenant. Rather, it reveals a new dimension of the covenant with Israel. The original covenant expands to embrace all men. It becomes open to the Gentiles.

Eckardt is quick to point out that while Christians are bound to recognize the validity of the original covenant with Israel, Jews are not bound to acknowledge the truth of the expanded dimension of the covenant, especially its Christological implications. In Eckardt's words, "As a Christian, I can and must affirm unreservedly, that Jewish faith is true *for me*. But a Jew simply cannot take an equivalent position with respect to the Christian faith."

Eckardt's discussion of the covenant and its pertinence for the Christian-Jewish relationship after the Holocaust has been explored by other Christian theologians. While Eckardt opts for a single covenantal theory, they affirm a double covenant, where neither covenant is inclusive of the other.

The Jewish philosopher, Franz Rosenzweig (d. 1929), was an early advocate of the double-covenant or two covenant theory. He appears to have been the first Jewish thinker to maintain that Judaism and Christianity are both authentic manifestations of religious truth.

For Rosenzweig, the Jewish covenant and the Christian covenant are equally valid views of reality. Through his covenant, the Jew is already with God. For the Gentile, however, Christ provides the road to the Father. Thus, for the Jew, Christ is an "unnecessary detour" to the Father.

For the Gentile, Christ is the necessary path to the Father. The task of the Christian covenant, therefore, is not to supersede the Jewish covenant, but to provide the means for the unconverted pagan Gentile to approach God. The imperative of the Christian covenant is the conversion of the pagan Gentiles. This covenant excludes a mission to the Jews, while it proclaims a mission to the Gentiles. Without the Christian covenant, the Gentiles would never know God. However, without the Jewish covenant, which is the fire from which the Christian covenant feeds, its historical source and its spiritual origin, the Christian covenant would dissipate. Hence, for Rosenzweig, the two covenants are mutually exclusive in terms of their respective claims to "truth," albeit a partial "truth." (The final truth is vouchsafed only at the end of history.) However, they are mutually interdependent in terms of their respective missions within history. A similar position appears in the writings of Abraham J. Heschel.

For Heschel, no religion can claim a monopoly on truth. "No religion is an Island." Judaism and Christianity in particular are mutually interdependent. In Heschel's words, "A Christian ought to realize that a world without Israel will be a world without the God of Israel. A Jew, on the other hand, ought to acknowledge the eminent role and part of Christianity in God's design for the redemption of all men."

The two-covenant theory, as articulated by Rosenzweig, has been adopted, modified and articulated by Christian theologians in an attempt to develop a bridge theology between Judaism and Christianity which rejects the supersessionist doctrine. A major characteristic of the Christian version of the double-covenant theory, as formulated by theologians such as Peter Chirico, is the assertion that Christ's advent represents a partial, rather than a complete, fulfillment of messianic prophecies. Thus, a major characteristic of Christian formulations of the double-covenant theory is a rejection of the "finality" attached to the advent of Christ by representatives of the first and second aforementioned positions.

Probably the most radical theological response to the Holocaust in Christian circles has been that of Rosemary Ruether. A vocal opponent of the supersessionist myth and an advocate of a double-covenant theory, Ruether offers an extreme reformulation of Christology. Her restructured theology is partially aimed at eliminating the basis for theological and for social anti-Semitism. Her confrontation with the horror of the Holocaust is a vital motive for her painstaking scholarship and creative theological suggestions.

In *Faith and Fratricide*, Ruether provides an extensive historical survey of the "Theological Roots of Anti-Semitism" in the New Testament, Church Fathers and medieval Christian culture. She also demonstrates how motives and stereotypes found in this literature were adopted by modern religious and secular ideologies, including Nazism.

Ruether contends that Christ's failure to appear in final messianic victory after the resurrection stimulated early Christian writers to provide revisionist understanding of Hebrew messianic prophecies and of the role of the Jewish people in history.

In this revisionist view, Jesus is considered the final Messiah, the ultimate fulfillment of Jewish prophecies, the only way to God. The Jewish rejection of Jesus is foreshadowed in Hebrew prophecy. The Hebrew prophets already realized that the Jews are a faithless people, rebellious against God, unrehabilitable criminals who murdered the prophets and the Christ. Rejected by God, they are "of the devil," punished with eternal degradation. Their continued degraded state is necessary to demonstrate their rejected status and the truth of the supersessionist claim of the Church. Ruether terms Christian theological anti-Semitism, the product of this revisionist view, the "left hand of Christology."

Ruether considers this revisionist position to be the flawed and illegitimate interpretation of promise and fulfillment, positively applied to Jesus as Messiah and final revelation and negatively applied to the Jews as a blind, reprobate, rejected people of God. This revisionist position has had its expression in social anti-Semitism, with its logical, if not inevitable, conclusion in the Holocaust. What must be attempted, therefore, is a radical rethinking and restructuring of Christology. In this restructuring, the myth of supersession must be eliminated and the integrity of Jewish faith must be affirmed.

In Ruether's restructured Christology, the advent of Jesus two thousand years ago represents only a partial fulfillment of earlier prophecies. Final redemption did not occur. History and tragedy remained. Jesus represents not the paradigm of fulfillment, but the symbol of hope, of future fulfillment. "Jesus is our paradigm of hoping . . . Christ stands as the symbol of the fulfillment of that hope. Jesus Christ, then, stands for that unification of man with his destiny which has still not come, but in whose light we continue to hope and struggle." Thus, although the advent of Jesus provides hope, Jesus is not yet the Christ. Only when evil is eradicated and God's reign is established, will Jesus become the Christ. In the meantime, belief in Jesus provides the hope that evil will be conquered. He provides the strength to struggle to conquer evil. For Ruether, just as the Exodus assures the Jews of final vindication in the struggle against evil, so does the resurrection of Jesus assure Christians of final redemption. Neither event—Exodus or Resurrection—invalidates or supplants or supersedes the other. Each event simply speaks to a different group of people.

So far, Ruether's position represents the most radical and the most expansive formulation of the third position. She not only condemns social anti-Semitism, but affirms its link with theological anti-Semitism. From that affirmation she has proceeded to construct a new foundation for Christian theology in the post-Holocaust era which eliminates the premises upon which Christian theological anti-Semitism has been based. Her efforts, no doubt, will continue to be the center of criticism and controversy. However, they have met the challenge posed by the Holocaust to Christian theology. Whether other Christian theologians will follow her lead and whether the Christian theological edifice can survive such extensive remodeling and remain intact, only the future will be able to decide.

TOPICS FOR FURTHER RESEARCH AND FOR CLASS DISCUSSION

The preceding discussion has limited itself to a survey of the responses of a limited number of Jewish and Christian theologians to the Holocaust. Additional theological responses to those noted above might be explored in class. Amongst Jewish thinkers, responses of the following individuals might be discussed: Martin Buber, Mordecai Kaplan, Arthur Cohen, Jacob Agus, etc. In addition, the theological implications of responsa (i.e., Jewish legal decisions) which emerged from the Holocaust period might be analyzed. Amongst Christian theologians, the following individuals' responses might be explored: Jurgen Moltmann, Fredrich Heer, Edward Schillebeeckx, Paul Van Buren, etc. Discussion of these theologians has been omitted here only for reasons of space, not because their contributions are not pertinent.

The theological responses of those who deal with the Holocaust implicitly, but not explicitly, would provide a major contribution to understanding Holocaust theology. The thought of Abraham J. Heschel and of Leo Baeck would be relevant to this task.

While the problem of theodicy has not been central to theological reflections regarding the Holocaust, it should be. The major theological issue raised by the Holocaust is, after all, the problem of evil. Further study of earlier theodicies and their possible applicability or actual irrelevance to the theological implications of the Holocaust should be considered.

Theological responses to historical events become part of the life of a faith-community when they are incorporated into its liturgy. To date, limited attempts have been made in liturgies as a response to the Holocaust. Noteworthy is the *Yom Ha-Shoah* (Day in Memory of the Holocaust) liturgy for the synagogue incorporated in the new Reform prayerbook *Gates of Prayer* and for the church at the end of Littell's *The Crucifixion of the Jews*. The composition of liturgical-theological responses to the Holocaust would anchor awareness of the theological implications of the Holocaust in worship. This would expand the theological impact of the Holocaust into the faith-community rather than having it just be a subject for theological speculation by a limited number of theologians.

To further expand a theological encounter with the Holocaust, Holocaust studies should be integrated into religious school curricula at a variety of levels. How to do this requires discussion, analysis and efforts in curriculum design. In addition, Christian scholars would have to re-think the teaching of New Testament, dogmatics, etc., in view of the theological anti-Semitism contained in such studies. How to deal with the anti-Jewish texts in the New Testament, writings of the Church Fathers, etc., provides a challenge to Christian educators. To be sure, the process of eliminating anti-Jewish notions from Church texts has already begun, but much remains to be done.

Research is still in an incipient stage regarding the role of the Church—Protestant, Catholic, Orthodox—during World War II vis-à-vis the "Final Solution." Studies of the activities of the Vatican have been marred by the inaccessibility of Vatican documents. Study of the Church struggle against Nazism in Germany and elsewhere in Europe is still in its infancy. No doubt, untapped archives and documents will reveal much. The problem of whether anti-Nazi Christians only opposed Hitler or whether they also defended Jews awaits definitive analysis. In the specific case of Dietrich Bonhoeffer, who so profoundly influenced post-World War II Christian theology, this issue is widely discussed. Until the Bonhoeffer archives have been totally and carefully examined, one can reach no definitive position.

While research into the attitudes of European churches to the plight of the Jews in Europe during the Holocaust years is important, so is an investigation of reactions amongst American Jewry and Christianity most pertinent. Research in this area has also just begun. Sociological inquiry into Christian attitudes toward Jews at present as compared to the pre-Holocaust period is also a desideratum. Though such efforts have begun (e.g., the Glock and Stock studies), continuous updates are needed. On the other hand, present Jewish attitudes towards Christians and Christianity and their relationship to the Holocaust also ought to be analyzed by sociologists. For example, a number of prominent Jewish scholars, such as Eliezer Berkovits, have denied the possibility of Jewish-Christian dialogue in the wake of the Holocaust. Furthermore, the emergence of the State of Israel and its effect upon Holocaust theology and Jewish-Christian dialogue bears analysis.

Holocaust theology, in the broadest sense, has not only been written by professional theologians but by novelists, poets, and other literary artists. Indeed, Holocaust literature has made a significant impact upon many theologians' responses to the Holocaust. Especially noteworthy in this regard is novelist Elie Wiesel, whose works have had a profound influence upon Jewish theologians such as Fackenheim and Greenberg and Christian theologians such as Jurgen Moltmann, Roy Eckardt and Robert MacAfee Brown. Attention to the theological implications of the works of literary artists other than Wiesel would prove additionally fruitful; for example: Andre Schwartz-Bart's novel *The Last of the Just*; Arthur Cohen's novel, *In the Days of Simon Stern*; Hayyim Grade's collection of short stories, *Seven Little Lanes*; Zvi Kolitz's short story, ''Yossel Rackover's Appeal to God;'' Soma Morgenstern's novel *The Third Pillar*; the poetry of Uri Zvi Greenberg, Jacob Glatstein, Kadia Molodowsky, Aaron Zeitlin; the drama of H. Leivick, etc. (see also section above on Holocaust literature).

BIBLIOGRAPHY

The following bibliography is divided into sections which roughly correspond to the order of topics dealt with in the preceding discussion. Where it was felt necessary, annotation has been provided. Often titles and subtitles have been sufficient to describe the basic focus of the works listed.

I. Review Essays

ECKARDT, ALICE, "The Holocaust: Christian and Jewish Responses," *Journal of the American Academy of Religion* (1974) 42:453–470. A fine review essay of Jewish and Christian responses to the Holocaust up to 1973.

ECKARDT, ALICE AND ROY, "German Thinkers View the Holocaust," *Christian Century* (March 17, 1976) 93,9 pp. 249–252.

JACOBS, LOUIS, "The Problem of Evil in Our Times," *Judaism* (1968) 17:347–352. Review essay of current theodicies, Jewish and Christian. Discussion of Hick, Simon, and others.

KATZ, STEVEN, ed., *Jewish Philosophers* (New York: Bloch, 1975) (Available in paperback). Sections on Rubenstein, Maybaum, Fackenheim, and Berkovits. Also in *Encyclopedia Judaica Yearbook 1975/76*.

KAUFMAN, WILLIAM E., *Contemporary Jewish Philosophers* (New York: Reconstructionist and Behrman Press, 1976) (Available in paperback). Chapters on Buber, Rubenstein, Fackenheim, A. Cohen.

WILLIS, ROBERT E., "Christian Theology After Auschwitz," *Journal of Ecumenical Studies* 12:4 (Fall 1975), pp. 493–521. Review of Jewish and Christian theologies.

II. The Problem of Theodicy

(Some examples of theodicies, mostly recent)

MACGREGOR, GEDDES. *Introduction to Religious Philosophy* (Boston: Houghton Mifflin, 1959) (Available in paperback). "The Mystery of Evil"—Part Seven.

PIKE, NELSON ed., *God and Evil* (New Jersey: Prentice Hall, 1964).

RICOEUR, PAUL. *The Symbolism of Evil* (Boston: Beacon, 1967; paperback, 1970).

SHERWIN, BYRON L., "Theodicy: Reason and Mystery," *Central Conference of American Rabbis Journal* (June 1971) 18:62–76.

TSANOFF, RADOSLAV. *The Nature of Evil* (New York: Macmillan, 1931).

III. History of Christian Anti-Semitism

(Some important historical studies. Historical data is also found in theological responses noted below.)

FLANNERY, EDWARD H. *The Anguish of the Jews* (New York: Macmillan, 1965) (Available in paperback).

HAY, MALCOLM. *Europe and the Jews* (Boston: Beacon, 1960) (Available in paperback).

PARKES, JAMES. *The Conflict of the Church and Synagogue* (New York: Atheneum, 1974) (Available in paperback).

_____. *The Jew in the Medieval Community* (New York: Hermon, 1976-2nd ed.) (Available in paperback).

TAL, URIEL. *Christians and Jews in Germany: Religion, Politics, and Ideology in the Second Reich, 1870–1914* (Ithaca, New York: Cornell University Press, 1974).

IV. Richard Rubenstein

RUBENSTEIN, RICHARD. *After Auschwitz* (Indianapolis: Bobbs Merrill, 1968; paperback, 1969).

_____. *The Cunning of History* (New York: Harper and Row, 1975).

_____, "God as Cosmic Sadist: In Reply to Emil Fackenheim," *Christian Century* (July 29, 1970) pp. 921–923.

_____, "Job and Auschwitz," *Union Seminary Quarterly Review* 25:4 (Summer 1970) pp. 421–430.

_____. *Morality and Eros* (New York: McGraw Hill, 1971).

_____. *My Brother Paul* (New York: Harper and Row, 1972; paperback, 1975).

_____. *Power Struggle* (New York: Scribners, 1974) (Available in paperback).

_____. *The Religious Imagination* (Indianapolis: Bobbs Merrill, 1968; paperback ed. 1970).

BOYD, GEORGE N. "Richard Rubenstein and Radical Christianity," *Union Seminary Quarterly Review* (Fall 1974) 20:41–51. A Christian critique of Rubenstein. Claims Rubenstein utilizes Christian concepts.

GORDIS, ROBERT, "A Cruel God or None—Is There No Other Choice," *Judaism* (1972) 21:277–285. A Jewish critique of Rubenstein.

V. Eliezer Berkovits

BERKOVITS, ELIEZER. *Crisis and Faith* (New York: Scribe, 1976).

_____. *Faith After the Holocaust* (New York: Ktav, 1973; paperback ed., 1975).

_____. *God, Man and History* (New York: Jonathan and David, 1959, paperback ed., 1968) pp. 75–85.

FOX, MARVIN, "Berkovits' Treatment of the Problem of Evil," *Tradition* 14:3 (1974), pp. 116–125.

VI. Emil Fackenheim

FACKENHEIM, EMIL. *Encounters Between Judaism and Modern Philosophy* (New York: Basic, 1973).

_____. *God's Presence in History* (New York: New York University Press, 1970). (Reprint: New York: Harper paperback, 1973).

_____. *The Human Condition After Auschwitz* (Syracuse, New York: Syracuse University Press, 1971).

_____. *The Jewish Return Into History* (New York: Schocken, 1978).

_____. *Metaphysics and Historicity* (Milwaukee: Marquette University Press, 1961).

_____. *Paths to Jewish Belief* (New York: Behrman House, 1960) pp. 59–75.

_____. *Quest for Past and Future* (Boston: Beacon, 1968; paperback, 1970).

MEYER, MICHAEL, "Judaism After Auschwitz: The Religious Thought of Emil Fackenheim," *Commentary* (June 1972) pp. 55–62.

VII. Other Jewish Responses

AGUS, JACOB. *Dialogue and Tradition* (New York: Abelard Schumann, 1971) pp. 243–275. Towards a "new" theodicy.

BOROWITZ, EUGENE. *How Can a Jew Speak of Faith Today?* (Philadelphia: Westminster, 1969) pp. 15–61.

BUBER, MARTIN. *The Eclipse of God* (New York: Harper and Row, 1952; paperback ed., 1957). On evil and suffering.

_____. *Good and Evil* (New York: Scribners, 1952; paperback ed., 1953). On the problem of evil.

_____. *On Judaism* (New York: Schocken, 1967; paperback, 1972) pp. 177–237. Buber's clearest response to the Holocaust.

_____. *Pointing the Way* (New York: Schocken, 1957; paperback ed., 1974). "Genuine Dialogue and the Possibilities of Dialogue."

CAIN, SEYMOUR, "The Question and Answers After Auschwitz," *Judaism* (Summer 1971) 20:263–279. Review of Holocaust theologies.

CARMEL, L., "The Problem of Evil: The Jewish Synthesis," *Proceedings of the Association of Orthodox Jewish Scientists* 1:92–101.

COHEN, ARTHUR A. *Thinking the Tremendum: Some Theological Implications of the Death Camps* (New York: Leo Baeck Institute, 1974). An important essay. Cohen's novel, *In the Days of Simon Stern,* has much theological import.

ECKSTEIN, JEROME, "The Holocaust and Jewish Theology," *Midstream* (April 1977) pp. 36–45. (Review of Berkovits, Fackenheim, etc.)

GREENBERG, IRVING, "Judaism and Christianity After the Holocaust," *Journal of Ecumenical Studies* 12:4 (Fall 1975) pp. 521–553. An important essay. Develops a dialectical post-Holocaust theology.

GUTTMAN, ALEXANDER, "Humane Insights of the Rabbis Particularly with Respect to the Holocaust," *Hebrew Union College Annual* (1975) 46:433–55. The response to the Holocaust in responsa literature.

HAMMER, ROBERi .ND SILVERMAN, DAVID, "Holocaust," *Conservative Judaism* 31:2 (Fall 1976) pp. 16–42.

JACOBS, LOUIS. *Faith* (New York: Basic, 1968) pp. 113–126. The problem of evil in Jewish theology.

_____. *A Jewish Theology* (New York: Behrman House, 1973) pp. 72–81, 125–136. The problem of evil in Jewish theology.

JONAS, HANS, "Immorality and the Modern Temper," *Harvard Theological Review* (1962) 55:1–20. A philosophical-theological response to the Holocaust.

KAPLAN, MORDECAI M. *Questions Jews Ask* (New York: Reconstructionist Press, 1965) pp. 115–125. Founder of Reconstructionist Judaism on the problem of evil.

LAMM, NORMAN, "The Ideology of the Neturei Karta—According to the Satmerer Version," *Tradition* (Fall 1971) 13:38–54. Good review of Teitelbaum's theology.

LELYVELD, ARTHUR. *Atheism is Dead* (Cleveland: World Publishing Co., 1968).

Critique of the "God is dead" theology and Jewish theological response to the Holocaust.

MAYBAUM, IGNAZ. *The Face of God After Auschwitz* (Holland: Polak and Van Gennup, 1965).

NEUSNER, JACOB, "The Implications of the Holocaust," *The Journal of Religion* 53:3 (July 1973) pp. 293–309. Claims nothing has changed as a result of the Holocaust; "the tradition endures."

ROSENBAUM, IRVING. *The Holocaust and Halakah* (New York: Ktav, 1976). Responsa literature during the Holocaust.

SCHINDLER, PESACH, "The Holocaust and *Kiddush Ha Shem* in Hasidic Thought," *Tradition* (Spring 1973) 13:88–105. Hasidic responses to the Holocaust. Part of author's dissertation.

SCHLESINGER, G. N., "Divine Benevolence," *Proceedings of the Association of Orthodox Jewish Scientists* 1:101–106. Free-will argument and problem of evil.

SHERWIN, BYRON L., "The Impotence of Explanation and the European Holocaust," *Tradition* (Winter 1972) 12:99–107.

SIEGEL, SEYMOUR. "Theological Reflections on the Destruction of European Jewry," *Conservative Judaism* 18:4 (Summer 1964) pp. 2–10.

STECKEL, CHARLES, "God and the Holocaust," *Judaism* (Summer 1971) 20:279–286. Critique and review.

TEITELBAUM, JOEL (Satmerer Rebbe). *Al Ha-Geulah ve-al Ha Temurah* (Hebrew) (Brooklyn: Deutsch, 1967). Divine retribution stance. Unavailable in English.

_____. *Va Yoel Moshe* (Hebrew) (New York: Jerusalem Publishing, n. d.). Divine retribution theory. Unavailable in English.

WYSCHOGROD, MICHAEL, "Faith and the Holocaust" *Judaism* (Summer 1971) pp. 286–295. Good critique of Fackenheim.

_____, "Some Theological Reflections on the Holocaust," *Response* (Spring 1975) 9:65–69. Contains critique of Wiesel.

ZIMMELS, H. J. *The Echo of the Nazi Holocaust in Rabbinic Literature* (Ireland, 1975). Responsa literature and the Holocaust.

VIII. Christian Theology

AAGARD, JOHANNES, "The Church and the Jews in Eschatology," *Lutheran World* (1964) pp. 270–278. Advocates a supersessionist position.

AAGARD, BOLEWSKI, SIRALA, et al, "Christians, Jews and the Mission of the Church," *Lutheran World* 11:3 (July 1964).

BARTH, MARKUS. *Israel and the Church* (Richmond: John Knox Press, 1969). Rejects mission to the Jews; advocates Christian repentence for social anti-Semitism.

BEA, AUGUSTINE CARDINAL. *The Church and the Jewish People* (London: Geoffrey Chapman, 1966). Holds second position discussed above.

BOWLER, MAURICE G., "Rosenzweig on Judaism and Christianity—The Two Covenant Theory," *Judaism* (1973) 22:475–481.

CHIRICO, PETER, "Christian and Jew Today from a Theological Perspective," *Journal of Ecumenical Studies* (1970) 7:37–51. Double-covenant theory.

DANIELOU, JEAN. *Dialogue with Israel* (Baltimore: Helicon Press, 1966). Position two discussed above.

_____. *The Theology of Jewish Christianity* (Chicago: Regnery, 1964).

DAVIES, ALAN T. *Anti-Semitism and the Christian Mind: The Crisis of Conscience After Auschwitz* (New York: Herder, 1969). A pivotal work on Christian post-Holocaust theology.

ECKARDT, ROY, "Theological Approaches to Anti-Semitism," *Jewish Social Studies* (1971) 33:272-284.

_____, "Jurgen Moltmann, The Jewish People and the Holocaust," *Journal of the American Academy of Religion* 44:4 (December 1976) pp. 675-693.

_____, "Is the Holocaust Unique?" *Worldview* 18, 9 (September 1974) pp. 31-35. Discusses God and the Holocaust, etc.

FLANNERY, EDWARD, "Anti-Zionism and the Christian Psyche," *Journal of Ecumenical Studies* 6:2 (1969) pp. 173-185. Among other claims, the author maintains that "there is a strong probability that many Christians harbor a deeply repressed death wish for the Jewish people."

FLEISCHNER, EVA, ed., *Auschwitz: Beginning of a New Era?* (New York: Ktav, 1977). A collection of important essays by Ruether, Greenberg, Pawlikowski, etc.

FLEISCHNER, EVA. *Judaism in German Christian Theology Since 1945* (Metuchen, New Jersey: Scarecrow Press, 1975).

FRIEDLANDER, ALBERT H., "A Final Conversation with Paul Tillich," *Reconstructionist* 31:14 (November 12, 1965) pp. 21-25.

HEER, FREDRICH. *God's First Love* (New York: Weybright and Talley, 1970). An uneven but important Catholic response to the Holocaust.

HELLWIG, MONIKA, "Christian Theology and the Covenant with Israel," *Journal of Ecumenical Studies* (1970) 7:37-51. Single covenant theory.

HICK, JOHN. *Evil and the God of Love* (New York: Harper and Row, 1966) (Available in paperback). An extensive, scholarly, erudite examination of Christian theodicies and their relationship to theodicy after the Holocaust.

HRUBY, KURT, "Peoplehood in Judaism and Christianity," *Theology Digest* (1974) 22:3-12. Advocates supersessionist theology.

JOCZ, JAKOB. *The Jewish People and Jesus Christ* (London: SPCK, 1958).

LITTELL, FRANKLIN, "Christendom, Holocaust and Israel," *Journal of Ecumenical Studies* (1973) 10:483-497.

_____, "Christians and Jews and Ecumenism," *Dial* (1970) 10:249-255.

_____. *The Crucifixion of the Jews* (New York: Harper and Row, 1975), pp. 52-53; also 24-44. A pivotal response by a Protestant scholar to the Holocaust. Condemns supersessionist theory and "Christian apostasy" during and after the Holocaust.

McGARRY, MICHAEL B. *Christology After Auschwitz* (New York: Paulish Press, 1977). An excellent review of theological responses by Christian theologians and Church groups to the Holocaust, including a fine analysis of the Vatican statements on the Jews.

MARITAIN, JACQUES. *Antisemitism* (London: Centenary Press, 1939). Advocates position two discussed above.

MARTIN, BERNARD, "Paul Tillich and Judaism," *Judaism* (Spring 1966) 15:180-188.

MOLTMANN, JURGEN. *The Crucified God* (New York: Harper, 1974). Also note Eckardt's essay on Moltmann.

OPSAHL, PAUL AND TANENBAUM, MARC, eds. *Speaking of God Today: Jews and Lutherans in Conversation* (Philadelphia: Fortress Press, 1974). Especially note the essay by F. Sherman which adopts some of Heschel's ideas for a Christian theological response to the problem of theodicy and Uriel Tal's ''Lutheran Theology and the Third Reich.''

PARKES, JAMES. *The Foundations of Judaism and Christianity* (Chicago: Quadrangle Books, 1960). Advocates the two-covenant theory. Has done extensive work on the history of Jewish-Christian relations.

————. *Judaism and Christianity* (London: Victor Gallancz, 1948).

————. *Prelude to Dialogue: Jewish-Christian Relationships* (New York: Schocken, 1969).

RICE, DAN, ''Reinhold Niebuhr and Judaism,'' *Journal of the American Academy of Religion* 45:1 (March 1977), *Supplement,* pp. 101-146.

RUETHER, ROSEMARY. *Faith and Fratricide: The Theological Roots of Anti-semitism* (New York: Seabury, 1974). A pivotal work, historically and theologically.

————, ''An Invitation to Jewish-Christian Dialogue: In What Sense Can We Say that Jesus was the Christ?,'' *The Ecumenist* (1972) 10:17-24. Beginnings of Ruether's ''radical'' Christology.

RYLAARSDAM, J. COERT, ''Jewish Christian Relationship: The Two Covenants and the Dilemmas of Christology,'' *Journal of Ecumenical Studies* (1972) 9:249-270. Finds roots of double-covenant in Hebrew Bible.

SCHREITER, ROBERT, ''Christology in the Jewish-Christian Encounter; An Essay Review of Edward Schillebeeckx,'' *Journal of the American Academy of Religion* (1976) 44:693-703. Review of an attempt to redo Christology after the Holocaust.

SHERMAN, FRANKLIN, ''Speaking of God After Auschwitz,'' *Worldview* 17:9 (September 1974) pp. 26-30. Essentially a Christian articulation of a Heschelian position on theodicy.

SIMON, ULRICH. *A Theology of Auschwitz* (London: Victor Gollancz, 1967) (Reprinted by John Knox Press, 1979). Attempt to integrate the Holocaust into classical Christian categories.

SMITH, ELWYN, ''The Christian Meaning of the Holocaust,'' *Journal of Ecumenical Studies* (Summer 1969) 6:419-423.

TIEFEL, HANS, ''Holocaust Interpretations and Religious Assumptions,'' *Judaism* 25:2 (Spring 1976), pp. 135-150.

WILLIS, ROBERT, ''Auschwitz and the Nurturing of Conscience,'' *Religion in Life* (Winter 1975) 44:432-447.

IX. The Role of Christian Churches During the Holocaust

BARTH, KARL. *The German Church Conflict* (Richmond: John Knox Press, 1965).

CONWAY, JOHN. *The Nazi Persecution of the Churches 1933-1945* (New York: Basic, 1969).

DAVIES, ALAN T., ''The Aryan Christ: A Motif in Christian Anti-Semitism,'' *Journal of Ecumenical Studies* (1975) 22:569-581.

FALCONI, CARLO. *The Silence of Pius XII* (Boston: Little, Brown, 1965).

FRIEDLANDER, SAUL. *Pius XII and the Third Reich* (New York: Knopf, 1966).

LEWY, GUENTER. *The Catholic Church and Nazi Germany* (New York: Holt, 1974).

LITTELL, FRANKLIN. *The German Phoenix* (New York: Doubleday, 1963). The German Church experience under the Nazis.

LITTELL, FRANKLIN H., AND LOCKE, HUBERT G., eds. *The German Church Struggle and the Holocaust* (Detroit: Wayne State University Press, 1974).

MICKLEM, NATHANIEL. *National Socialism and the Roman Catholic Church, 1933-1938* (London: Oxford University Press, 1939).

SNOEK, JOHAN M. *The Grey Book: A Collection of Protests Against Anti-Semitism and Persecution of Jews Issued by Non-Roman Catholic Churches and Church Leaders During Hitler's Rule* (Assen: van Gorcum, 1969). Note the fine introduction by Uriel Tal.

ZAHN, GORDON. *German Catholics and Hitler's Wars* (New York: Sheed and Ward, 1962).

BETHGE, EBERHARD. *Dietrich Bonhoeffer* (New York: Harper, 1970).

PECK, WILLIAM J., "From Cain to the Death Camps: An Essay on Bonhoeffer and Judaism," *Union Seminary Quarterly Review* 28 (Winter 1973) pp. 158-177.

ZERNER, RUTH, "Dietrich Bonhoeffer and the Jews," *Jewish Social Studies* 37 (Summer 1975) pp. 235-250.

X. Theological Themes in Holocaust Literature

(Examples of some probings into the theological implications of Elie Wiesel)

BERENBAUM, MICHAEL, "Elie Wiesel and Contemporary Jewish Theology," *Conservative Judaism* (Spring 1976) 30:19-40.

SHERWIN, BYRON L., "Elie Wiesel and Jewish Theology," *Judaism* (1969) 18:39-53. Reprinted in *Responses to Elie Wiesel* (N.Y.: Persea, 1979).

———, "Elie Wiesel on Madness," *Central Conference of American Rabbis Journal* 19:3 (1972) pp. 24-33.

———, "Jewish Messianism and Elie Wiesel," *Perspectives in Jewish Learning—Volume Five* (1973) pp. 48-60. Reprinted in *Notre Dame Journal of English* 9:1 (October 1978).

XI. Christian Attitudes After the Holocaust: Educational and Sociological Surveys

GLOCK, CHARLES, AND STARK, RODNEY. *Christian Beliefs and Anti-Semitism* (New York: Harper and Row, 1966) (Available in paperback). Detailed study of anti-Semitism in American Churches.

OLSON, BERNHARD. *Faith and Prejudice* (New Haven: Yale University Press, 1963).

PAWLIKOWSKI, JOHN T. *Catechetics and Prejudice* (New York: Paulist Press, 1973).

STROBER, GERALD. *Portrait of the Elder Brother: Jews and Judaism in Protestant Teaching Materials* (New York: NCCJ/AJC, 1972).

Philosophical Reactions to and Moral Implications of the Holocaust

Byron L. Sherwin

PHILOSOPHY AFTER AUSCHWITZ

"Philosophy cannot be the same after Auschwitz and Hiroshima. Certain assumptions about humanity have been proved to be specious, have been smashed," writes Abraham J. Heschel. Yet, contemporary philosophy and philosophers have failed to encounter the philosophical and moral implications of the Holocaust. Though a severely limited number of historians of philosophy have explored the possible influences of leading philosophers of the pre-Holocaust era (e.g., Kant, Hegel, Fichte) upon the genesis and development of Nazi ideology, the efforts amongst professional philosophers to allow the Holocaust to have an impact upon post-Holocaust philosophies and ideologies have been negligible.* While recent discussions of such moral issues as abortion and euthanasia occasionally invoke the spectre of Nazi eugenic policies and medical experiments upon concentration camp inmates, little in-depth analysis of the moral and philosophical implications of Nazism's inhuman use of human beings has been forthcoming. Thus, to an overwhelming degree, philosophical speculation and moral theory after Auschwitz proceed as if the Holocaust had not occurred. It has, therefore, been largely left to theologians, novelists, jurists, sociologists, and political scientists to explore the philosophical and moral implications of the Holocaust. Indeed, the failure of philosophy to encounter the Holocaust may account for the

*See chapter on "Ideological Antecedents of the Holocaust."

repudiation of the viability of philosophy present in Holocaust literature. Rationality and logic as paths to wisdom and truth are denied by some significant writers responding to the Holocaust. Chaim Grade, for example, writes,

> Reason is like a dog on a leash who follows sedately in his master's footsteps—until he sees a bitch. . . . Any man can rationalize whatever he wants to do . . . . The philosopher himself is cold and gloomy and empty. He is like a man who wants to celebrate a marriage with himself.

Similarly, Elie Wiesel approvingly quotes Ephraim Kishon's remark, "Logic, too, went up in smoke at Auschwitz."

The only major philosopher who has dealt with some of the philosophical and moral implications of the Holocaust has been the German existentialist, Karl Jaspers (b. 1883). In *The Question of German Guilt* (1947), Jaspers applies his medical and philosophical training to the question of the nature and extent of the guilt of a modern nation for the world's greatest crime. The interest in psychopathology which characterizes Jaspers' other works is the focal point of this work.

Karl Jaspers

Born in 1883, Karl Jaspers is generally considered to have been one of contemporary Germany's most significant philosophers. A physician and a psychologist by training, Jaspers was a central architect of modern existentialism. In 1946 (English edition, 1947) this profound and prolific, but often prolix and obscure, thinker published his reflections upon the fate of European Jewry during World War II and its relationship to *The Question of German Guilt (Die Schuldfrage, ein Beitrag zur deutschen Frage)*.

Jaspers was affected personally as well as intellectually by the rise of Nazi Germany and by Nazi persecution of the Jews. Having held the prestigious position of professor of philosophy at Heidelberg University for sixteen years, in 1937 Jaspers was relieved of his duties by the National Socialist regime. He became a refugee from his native Germany and through his Jewish wife, Gertrude, Jaspers shared some of the agony of the Jewish people during the War years. The present discussion will not be concerned with his vast philosophical and psychological writings, but only with a presentation and an analysis of some of the pivotal ideas explored in *The Question of German Guilt*.

Jaspers distinguishes amongst four varieties of guilt: criminal guilt, political guilt, moral guilt and metaphysical guilt (pp. 31–32). "Criminal guilt" is the result of "crimes" having been committed. For Jaspers, "crimes are acts capable of objective proof and violate unequivocal laws." Jurisdiction over crimes "rests with the court, which in formal proceedings can be relied upon to find the facts and apply the law.'' Such crimes should meet with punishment.

''Political guilt'' involves ''the deeds of statesmen and the citizenry of a state.'' Each citizen bears the consequences of the state under whose power the citizen is governed. Jurisdiction over such deeds rests with ''the power and will of the victor, in both domestic and foreign politics.'' Liability for political guilt may result in the destruction of the vanquished state or, at least, in the vanquished making reparation and restitution for its actions.

''Moral guilt'' emerges from the responsibility of each individual for all his deeds, ''including the execution of political and military orders.'' Jurisdiction rests with the individual's conscience. ''The outgrowth of the moral guilt is insight, which involves penance and renewal. It is an inner development then also taking effect in the world of reality.''

''Metaphysical guilt'' derives from the solidarity of all mankind which makes each individual ''co-responsible for every wrong and every injustice in the world, especially for crimes committed in his presence or with his knowledge. If I fail to do whatever I can to prevent them, I too am guilty.'' All human beings share in ''metaphysical guilt.'' ''Jurisdiction rests with God alone.'' Metaphysical guilt should result in ''a transformation of human self-consciousness before God.''

Having characterized these four types of guilt, Jaspers analyzes their specific relevancy or irrelevancy to German guilt in the aftermath of World War II. To be sure, these distinctions are arbitrary. Jaspers himself admits that the sharp distinctions he has drawn cannot be absolutely maintained. Each form of guilt, especially moral and political guilt, is interrelated with each other form of guilt (p. 77). As we shall see below, Jaspers' definitions of each of these varieties of guilt are too restrictive. They serve to absolve the guilty from their guilt, rather than to establish the guilt of the guilty.

For Jaspers, criminal guilt is applicable only to individuals, not to nations. He, therefore, approved of the Nuremberg trials which prosecuted individuals rather than the German people as a whole. In adopting this position, Jaspers denies that there is ''such a thing as a national character extending to every single member of a nation.'' He, thereby, rejects the often made assertion that traits such as militarism and unquestioning obedience to orders are essential characteristics of the German people as a whole. However, in his claim that only certain individuals were guilty of criminal acts during World War II, he in effect exonerates hundreds of individuals from criminal responsibility by redefining their guilt as political, moral or metaphysical, rather than criminal. One might say that he defines too many *crimes* out of existence. Jaspers' position implies that since only those criminally charged are criminally guilty, those who were not *criminally* charged are *criminally* innocent. Furthermore, Jaspers assumes that crimes can be atoned for (p. 117). However, what

atonement can be made for the death camps and for their victims which
Jaspers never directly mentions when discussing German guilt?

While Jaspers maintains that not all Germans were criminally guilty for the
actions of Nazi Germany, he does claim that all Germans are collectively
politically *liable* for those deeds and actions. The determination of the consequences of this liability rests not with the guilty parties but with the
"victors." A problem with this claim is that it posits "liability" but not
necessarily "responsibility." It assigns the definition and execution of "liability" to the will and whim of the "victors." It does not contend that justice
is required, nor does it assume that the "victor" will necessarily execute
justice. One might say that Jaspers' assertion that all Germans share political
guilt for the actions of the Third Reich, palls into irrelevancy in view of his
failure to define the concrete implications of "liability." Furthermore, as
Jaspers assumes crimes can be atoned for, so does he presume that political
liability can be limited by a peace treaty and thus brought to an end (p. 117).
However, one must query as to whether the political liability incurred by
Germany during the War can simply be limited by a peace treaty
supplemented by reparation payments and thus brought to an end.

On the question of moral guilt, as in the question of criminal guilt, Jaspers
insists that only individuals and not a people as a whole may be held culpable.
He, thereby, frees many from moral guilt for deeds committed during the War.

According to Jaspers, jurisdiction for moral guilt rests only with the individual's conscience. "Morally man can condemn only himself [and] not
another"; "no one can morally judge another" (p. 39). By adopting this
stance, Jaspers implies that no one has a right to pass moral judgment upon the
deeds committed during the Holocaust years, that anti-Nazi Germans cannot
morally judge those involved in genocide, that the victims cannot express
moral outrage against their persecutors. For Jaspers, moral guilt rests in the
conscience of the individual. Those who sense their own moral guilt must
seek penance and renewal. Thus, Jaspers makes moral guilt contingent upon
the individual's conscience and upon his will to seek penance and renewal.
The problem with this position is that it defines out of existence the moral
guilt of those whose consciences are unconscious, who fail to have quirks of
conscience for the deeds they committed or allowed to be done, who refuse to
seek penance, who see no need for renewal. Thus, Jaspers assigns "Hitler and
his accomplices" to a state "beyond moral guilt for as long as they do not feel
it." In so doing, Jaspers in effect frees from moral guilt and responsibility, as
they are generally understood (as opposed to his own limiting definition), the
most morally culpable individuals. By making penance a *sine qua non* of
moral guilt he actually frees all those morally culpable for the Holocaust; for
what penance could be done to atone for what was done during the Holocaust?

Though Jaspers contends that one may not judge the moral guilt of another,
he does so himself. For example, Jaspers maintains that blind German

nationalism under the spell of Nazism incurs moral guilt (p. 65). In Jaspers' words:

> What finally turned this conduct into full-fledged moral guilt was the eagerness to obey—that compulsive conduct, feeling itself conscientious and, in fact, forsaking all conscience. (p. 66)

Furthermore, Jaspers maintains that those who remained inactive and passive to the deeds of the Reich, as well as those who actively participated in those deeds, are also morally guilty (p. 69). Here Jaspers twice contradicts his earlier position: (1) He denies his assertion that only the individual may assess his own moral guilt; (2) Whereas Jaspers had previously maintained that moral guilt is evoked by the individual's conscience, he now claims that moral guilt may be engendered by a lack of conscience.

Finally, there is metaphysical guilt. For Jaspers, all those who were alive at the close of the War "are guilty of being alive" (p. 72). Their failure to have expressed "absolute solidarity" with all other human beings—by action or inaction—makes them metaphysically guilty. Jaspers is quick to distinguish the metaphysical guilt engendered by the Holocaust from original sin; i.e., from the inevitable guilt of being human. For Jaspers, "The question of original sin may not become a way to dodge German guilt" (p. 100).

The problem with Jaspers' discussion of metaphysical guilt is that *if all are guilty, then none are guilty*. In this regard, Elie Wiesel has written, "To be sure, Karl Jaspers set himself the task of investigating German guilt, but with the specific intention of thereby demonstrating the universal guilt. As a result, his investigation succeeded in allaying many fears in occupied Germany, in reassuring many uneasy minds. . . . The world, indeed, had more than a few lessons to learn—but not from a German professor" (*Legends of Our Time,* p. 169).

By asserting universal metaphysical guilt, Jaspers, in effect, assuages the specific guilt of the perpetrators of and the apathetic bystanders to the Holocaust. Jaspers himself was aware, but not adequately convinced that "our dissection of the guilt concepts can be turned into a trick, for getting rid of guilt" (p. 74). If he were totally convinced, then it is likely that he never would have written *The Question of German Guilt.*

MORAL IMPLICATIONS OF THE HOLOCAUST

For both victims and perpetrators of the Holocaust, the War years compelled one to live a "condensed life." In the course of a day or a week, an individual was confronted with a plethora of moral problems which in normal circumstances might arise over the course of an entire lifetime, if at all. Individuals were forced to make extreme moral decisions *in extremis*. It is therefore questionable whether usual norms for evaluating the morality of human behavior can be applied to the Holocaust; the unique nature of the Holocaust experience may cause one to examine moral decisions made during the Holocaust with a completely different framework of moral criteria. Moral decisions are conditioned by the existential and human situation of the individual involved in making a specific moral choice. To apply usual moral criteria to moral choices made during the Holocaust would infer an unjustifiable comparison between the conditions surrounding such a choice during the Holocaust and during "normal" times. To evaluate moral decisions, therefore, one must consider the conditions under which they were made.

In the following pages we shall offer two models for considering moral implications of the Holocaust. These models are not meant to be inclusive or representative of all moral choices occasioned by the Holocaust. They merely seek to offer the instructor or student of Holocaust studies an approach for treating the moral implications of the Holocaust.

The first model attempts to raise moral questions occasioned by particular historical situations endemic to the Holocaust. Well suited for role-playing discussion, the first model is situated within the uniqueness of Holocaust experience and the framework of the Holocaust. The second model attempts to raise moral questions related to the Holocaust experience but not necessarily unique to the Holocaust. This model treats the more universal, moral implications of the Holocaust.

Model #1

One method of approaching the moral implications of the Holocaust would be to construct a paradigm situation and to delineate some of the moral decisions which would have to be made by an individual in such a situation. To construct the setting, one should consult historical documents, diaries and literary works. Thus, the first model might be called "the historical setting situation."

Any evaluation of the moral choices made by individuals during the Holocaust must consider the conditions under which those choices were made. Furthermore, in making any such evaluation one must honestly ask oneself: What would I have done? For example, one must confront questions such as:

Would I as a non-Jew take risks to save a Jew? To what degree? Would I risk my life, the lives of my family, the lives of my fellow villagers?

Would I as a businessman in Nazi Germany help increase my profits, satisfy my stockholders, and please the regime by using slave labor? Would I take the economic and personal risks which noncompliance might entail?

Would I as a German Christian defy my church and my government to oppose the regime, to help Jews? At what risk?

Would I as a Jew take risks to save a fellow Jew, a non-Jew? To what degree? Would I collaborate with the enemy to secure certain benefits and privileges? To what degree? Would I become a *Kapo,* a guard?

Would I as a German soldier obey my superiors when commanded to participate in the deportation and extermination of Jews, Gypsies, etc? Would I take the risks which such disobedience might entail? To what degree?

Would I as a citizen of a country occupied by the Nazis join the Resistance or help my Jewish compatriots? To what degree of risk?

Would I as a woman save my life by becoming a prostitute in a German brothel?

Would I as a member of the Resistance kill a Nazi soldier if I knew that retaliation for such an act might entail the deaths of my family or of a group of my countrymen? If captured, would I betray my comrades in order to save my own life?

Would I as a Jewish leader in a ghetto, aware that transports were sending people to the gas chambers of Auschwitz, inform the inhabitants of the ghetto of this fact? Would I sign transport lists of people selected to go to Auschwitz? Would I put my own name and/or the names of members of my family on these lists rather than sign them? If told by the Nazis that my choice was to compose a transport list of 10,000 names or have 25,000 people arbitrarily chosen and transported by the Nazi authorities, what would I do?

If I were a parent told by a Nazi officer—I will kill one of your four children and if you cannot decide which one within a span of 60 seconds, I shall kill all—what would I do?

If I were a ghetto inmate awaiting transport, would I choose suicide rather than transport?

If I were a camp inmate or a survivor and a Nazi appealed to me to save his life, would I do so? If a concentration camp guard on his deathbed asked me to forgive him for his crimes, would I forgive him?

If I were a survivor and the German government offered me reparations for the death of my wife/husband, son/daughter, mother/father, would I accept them?

None of the preceding examples are based upon fiction or speculation. They are all actual decisions which individuals had to make during and after the Holocaust. In teaching or studying about the Holocaust, one should honestly confront such questions as these. In doing so, one must be constantly aware of the life-conditions under which they were made.

In the following example of how Model #1 may be implemented, the moral dilemmas of membership on a ghetto *Judenrat* (Jewish Community Council) will be explored.

To be sure, conditions varied from ghetto to ghetto and the composition of *Judenrate* differed from ghetto to ghetto and from time to time. Thus, the reconstruction of a paradigm situation would necessarily be historically inaccurate. However, in that moral options did not radically differ from ghetto to ghetto, the paradigm situation would still be pedagogically useful. The immediately following pages offer such a paradigm situation, written in a "personal" tone rather than as an "objective" description.

Setting the Scene

Before the War you were a prominent member of your community. Once the Nazis invaded your country, you found yourself and your family hastily stripped of your rights and possessions. As a Jew, you were denied your citizenship, and with it all civil rights. You could no longer vote, no longer bring suit in the courts. Your children were ejected from the public schools. Your license to practice your profession was revoked. Your office was "Aryanized." Your money, deposited in a bank, was confiscated. Your house was raided and searched, and most of your valuables were taken by the local police. You approached various foreign embassies in an attempt to emigrate. You were told that visas were unavailable but could be gotten for a price. With your depleted funds you could "buy out" one member of your family of five people—but which one? Or, would it be necessary to conserve these meager resources for future emergencies which might save the entire family? Besides, the consulate might take your money and then recant on the visa. Can you take the chance?

You must now wear a yellow star. The penality for noncompliance is death for you and sanctions against your family. Your identity card is stamped with a large "J." To be without an identity card means certain imprisonment if caught. What would your family do if you are caught?

You cannot travel to another city as such travel is prohibited. Noncompliance carries stiff penalties. Even if you were allowed travel, it might be impossible to do so. Your automobile has been confiscated. Funds for train travel are unavailable and identity papers are checked on the trains.

You cannot communicate easily with others to elicit their help. Your phone has been confiscated. Mail service is virtually unavailable. Public places are off-limits to you; this includes public phone booths. Your radio has also been confiscated. You can trust no one: everyone is either desperate or an informer. You and your family are systematically and rapidly losing all vestiges of your former life-style. Despite the penalties for smuggling, you purchase food and clothing from smugglers at an exorbitant price. Your financial resources are quickly disappearing.

An order from the Nazi commandant of your city announces the establishment of a Jewish section, a ghetto. An area which previously housed 60,000 people now must house 150,000 people. You must leave your home with only what can be carried and move to the most dilapidated section of the city where the ghetto has been established.

Your new living quarters now house five people per room. From a five room apartment, your family now dwells in a single room of an ancient building. In other rooms are people from your city, from other cities, and even from other countries. Some speak a language you do not understand. Privacy is absent. Plumbing is virtually nonexistent. Winter is coming and fuel for heat is unavailable.

Sexual relations with your wife have all but ceased. You have no privacy or opportunity. In any case, pregnancy is punishable by death. Children are hungry, sick and cranky. Stress and tension mount.

A new order has made the area of the ghetto smaller. Although you do not have to move, crowding in your building increases. Another family of four now shares your room. You are always afraid that one of your neighbors might steal the few possessions you have, especially your food or clothing. You are in a constant state of anxiety and fear. The future is unknown.

Food allocations have been regular but sparse. The public kitchen dispenses food of the worst quality and little quantity. You are living on less than 500 calories a day. Your money is almost gone and smuggled food is becoming increasingly exorbitant. The only way to "earn" money is through joining a labor brigade. You join, knowing the hours are long, the pay is insignificant and your family will be left alone. But, it's the only way, so you enlist, knowing that you will be destroying what little good health you have. Besides, you know that without "volunteer" labor, there will be forced labor.

Typhus, dysentery and starvation are rampant in the ghetto. All cats and dogs in the ghetto have already been eaten. Cases of cannibalism have been reported. Your children are sick and starving. Your wife looks like a skeleton. She has been giving most of her rations to the children.

Winter begins early. The cold is bitter. Fuel is nonexistent. You've already burnt all your "furniture." Disease is more frequent and more serious. There are no drugs, not even vitamins. The food ration has been cut to 300 calories per day. Food distribution is irregular. If conceivable, the food's quality has also become worse. Raids by the Nazis and by the Jewish police have become frequent. Your wife's wedding ring has been confiscated. The money you had hidden is missing. The police beat your wife and your son because the ring was not handed over earlier. Beatings are now common in homes and on the streets. Corpses are everywhere.

You have been in the ghetto four months. It seems like forty years. Transports have begun. No one knows where they are going, but there are rumors of death camps.

You have developed ulcers. Your daughter is dying. Your son can hardly stand; he has rickets. Your wife may have tuberculosis. You are weak from labor. People in your building have been transported only to be replaced by new, strange people. Things are getting worse and worse. Perhaps the War will end soon!

A member of the Jewish police wakes you while it is still dark. You have been called by the head of the Judenrat to his office. You ask: Am I being transported? The policeman does not answer. You tell your wife you must go. Fear flushes across your face.

Since arriving at the ghetto you, like most of the other inhabitants of the ghetto, were cursing the members of the Judenrat. They were collaborating with the Nazis and forsaking their brethren. They and their families were living comparatively well while your family was cramped and starving. They had salaried jobs and were not forced laborers working for a pittance. They used their influence to help their families and their friends. They took bribes. They controlled the cruel ghetto police who confiscated people's jewelry and money, who beat people for no reason, who rounded up people for transports. They ate good food while they provided you with barely edible food from the public kitchens. It was their fault that there were no drugs or vitamins for the sick and for the children. They could not be trusted. They were corrupt and haughty, arbitrarily deciding matters of life and death for thousands. Their housing department is a den of corruption. A band of dishonest, obnoxious career seekers, the members of the Judenrat exploit their brethren for their own aggrandisement. They want to control everything in the ghetto, all facets of life—even the schools and the scheduling of religious services. Their rules and the sanctions for breaking them have been unduly harsh. They helped the Nazis round up fellow Jews who bravely fought the Nazis with guns and molotov cocktails. They make up lists for transports and help find people hiding from the roundups. Now, you are going to confront those you accuse. Will you risk your life and that of your family to speak your mind? What do they want from you?

Two Nazi guards stand outside the office of the Judenrat. You climb the stairs and enter a conference room. A Nazi officer stands in the center of the room with his gun drawn. Eleven members of the Judenrat stand against a wall ashen-faced. The twelfth lies on the floor, bleeding to death from a bullet wound. The officer greets you with the words, "Jewish swine, against the wall." You stand against the wall. Any other gesture and you would be shot. The officer stands behind you, his gun behind your ear. He whispers, "You have been selected . . . " For transport? For what? He waits a moment while the blood rushes from your face. He continues, " . . . for membership on the Judenrat."

Without a choice you have been named to the Judenrat. You are simultaneously distressed and relieved. Chances of survival have been enhanced. There will be better lodgings, more food, no more hard labor. Anxiety, however, increases. The moral decisions you will have to make will become increasingly difficult. You have been awarded a dubious honor.

A week before, like other inhabitants of the ghetto, you were cursing the Judenrat. But now, you are part of it. Now decisions regarding the lives of your fellow ghetto residents are in your hands. Despite the advantages of your new position, you would prefer not to have to make decisions of life and death. But someone has to do it. Now, that someone is you.

It is light outside. Surrounded by Jewish police, you return "home." You and your family are moved to new quarters. As you leave, the people in your building give you gifts, bribes, asking you to remember them should they need favors. Some curse you as a "collaborator."

Your new quarters are better, but not good. You fear for your children. The ghetto resistance fighters and other dissidents within the ghetto are known to capture the children of Judenrat members and hold them for ransom. You are protected but still anxious.

You must report immediately to assume your duties. The head of the Judenrat greets you and reviews the situation. He is not the first head of the Judenrat but the third. The first had committed suicide when he heard about the death camps and realized that the transports he signed were sending people there. He left a letter in which he claimed that suicide was the only viable moral choice. Rather than send others to their death, he had decided to take his own life. The second head of the Judenrat appointed by the Nazis refused to sign the transport lists. However, he felt suicide was equally immoral. A religious Jew, he believed that only God who gave life could take life. The Nazis disagreed. They tortured him to death. The present head of the Judenrat felt that he had to comply. His own death would solve nothing. Only cooperation with the Nazis could insure that at least some would survive. Better sacrifice some than risk all.

The head of the Judenrat paints a dismal picture. The Judenrat members were in constant danger from Jews and Germans. They had to provide food, jobs, clothing and housing to an economically dead society. In addition, they had to mediate amongst the various nationalities, and political, social, and religious groups in the ghetto. They had to administer schools, hospitals, orphanages and libraries, and to arrange cultural events. They had to raise money through taxes and confiscations in order to provide bribes and gifts to the German authorities in exchange for certain favors and benefits for themselves and for their community. They ran courts and jails. They controlled and paid a Jewish police force rather than have a Nazi police force in the ghetto. They prepared numerous reports for the German authorities. They were responsible and accountable both to their fellow Jews and to the Nazis, clearly an impossible situation. The only hope was that the War would end before the ghetto inhabitants were all transported.

Having been briefed by the head of the Judenrat, you are informed that the Nazis have demanded a transport list of 1,000 names for the following day. As a member of the Judenrat, as a formerly prominent citizen of the city, and as an acquaintance of many of its inhabitants, you are to help compose the list. The Nazis have specified the transport of all children under fourteen plus any individuals with tuberculosis or typhus. Your children are under fourteen and your wife has tuberculosis. You can save them by substituting names of others. You can save one member of your family by putting your own name on the list, but this would leave your family without you, destitute, without protection. You could refuse and be shot or tortured to death. You could commit suicide and thereby insure the transport of your family. Before making a final decision, you discuss the possibility of armed resistance with the head of the Judenrat. In doing so, you take a risk. He might report you to the Gestapo. He listens patiently and responds.

The head of the Judenrat informs you that armed resistance was already considered, but rejected. There were few guns and little ammunition in the ghetto. It was almost impossible to get additional arms. The local resistance failed to help. The Allies would make no air drops. Funds to pay the exorbitant prices necessary to secure smuggled arms were not available. Even if there were arms, few people knew how to use them. Besides, people were weak and sick. They had been stripped of their will to fight. What chance would they have against the German army? Furthermore, there would be harsh sanctions for armed resistance. At the last act of resistance, one hundred Jews were rounded up and shot for each German soldier killed. Therefore, the Judenrat had decided to denounce armed resisters to the Nazis. Resistance was too dangerous. The entire ghetto might be destroyed and all its inhabitants killed if resistance succeeded to any significant degree. Thus, resistance was not a viable option.

The head of the Judenrat then took his seat at the head of the table. The other members were seated at the table including you. He began to read out names of your family, relatives, friends, business associates, acquaintances, former neighbors and strangers. One thousand of these must be put on the list for transport. As the freshman member of the Judenrat, you are responsible for composing the first half of the list. What do you do?

Model #2

A second possible model for dealing with the moral implications of the Holocaust would begin by identifying a broad moral problem which emerges from the Holocaust experience and which may be applied to a variety of situations. This problem would then be analyzed in three steps:

1. How the problem emerges from the Holocaust experience.

2. How Anglo-American legal/moral tradition might deal with the problem.

3. How one other legal/moral system, e.g., Jewish law and morals, might treat the problem.

One of the many moral problems emerging from a consideration of the Holocaust experience, and reflected in Holocaust literature but not unique to the Holocaust, is the problem of apathy. While the focal point of discussion regarding the moral implications of the Holocaust is usually the moral behavior of the perpetrators and/or of the victims, the question of the moral behavior of the bystander must also be considered in any attempt to come to grips with the moral implications of the Holocaust. While the morality or immorality of actions must be evaluated, the morality or immorality of lack of action also must be examined. Moral questions specifically pertinent to the Holocaust experience must be discussed with a clear awareness of the conditions under which they had to be decided (Model #1); furthermore, moral questions invoked by the Holocaust, but with implications clearly transcending the Holocaust and possibly related to many other situations, should be examined within any discussion of the moral implications of the Holocaust.

The question of the moral culpability of the bystander to the Holocaust was raised by a variety of individuals in a variety of contexts both during and after World War II. Historians, novelists, diarists, jurists, playwrights, and poets have raised this question. Thus, an interdisciplinary approach to the Holocaust may be usefully employed in discussing moral implications of the Holocaust in general and the problem of apathy in particular. For example, the implications of the apathy of German non-Jews to the fate of the Jews and others persecuted by the Nazis was discussed by Pastor Niemoller, among others. A prominent German clergyman and a hero of the First World War, Niemoller was at first a supporter of Hitler. After having become aware of Nazi persecution and atrocities, he became an active opponent of the regime. Reflecting upon his own initial apathy to Nazi persecution of others, he wrote:

When the gestapo came and took away the Jews, I did not protest because I was not a Jew. When they came to take away the Communists, I did not protest because I was not a Communist. When they came to take me away, no one was left who could protest.

In a similar vein, the apathy of Polish Warsaw to the fate of the inhabitants of the Warsaw Ghetto as it burned was described by a survivor of the ghetto:

As the Warsaw Ghetto was burning down, extinguishing the lives of its inhabitants, on the other side of the wall, citizens of the capital (Warsaw) strolled, played and enjoyed themselves.

The apparent apathy of the Pope, not only towards the fate of the Jews but to the fate of Polish Catholics as well, has been widely discussed by historians, theologians, and playwrights. In August of 1943, for example, the Polish underground published a pamphlet which read:

The world is silent. The world knows what is going on—it cannot help but know, and is silent. And in the Vatican, the deputy of God is silent too.

Similarly, the apparent apathy of the Allies has been explored from the perspectives of a variety of academic and literary disciplines. *While Six Million Died,* Arthur Morse's study of the reactions of the Roosevelt administration to the destruction of European Jewry, is aptly subtitled, "A Chronicle of American Apathy." Governments other than that of the United States were equally apathetic to the fate of European Jewry and to the fate of refugees seeking a new home.* Gordon Thomas' and Max Witts' reportage and the film based upon it, both entitled *Voyage of the Damned,* provide a graphic description of this fact. In a similar vein, a survivor of the Warsaw Ghetto, Itzhak Katzenelson, condemned the apathy of the Allies. He wrote:

Sure enough, the nations did not interfere, nor did they protest, nor shake their heads, nor did they warn the murderers, never a murmur. It was as if the leaders of the nations were afraid that the killings might stop.

In 1943, Szmul Zygiebojm, a Jewish member of the Polish government in exile in England committed suicide. He left a note which read:

By my death, I wish to make final protest against the passivity with which the world is looking on and permitting the extermination of the Jewish people.

World Jewry, too, was largely apathetic to the fate of their co-religionists. Historians, novelists and others have discussed this matter in essays and historical studies. Elie Wiesel, for example, has written (*Legends of Our Times,* p. 165):

And finally, in order to keep inviolate the historical truth, the prosecutor should have removed the last taboo: to reveal the sorry but nonetheless ineluctable fact that the Jews themselves failed to do everything they should have done: they ought to have done more, they could have done better. . . . we know the reasons and justifications [for inaction or inadequate action]: they are not good enough. There can be no justification nor any explanation for passivity when an effort had to be made to save five or ten thousand Jews from murder each day.

To this point, it should be evident that the problem of apathy cuts across interdisciplinary lines and is related to the behavior of Germans, Allies,

*See Chapter Five.

victims, citizens of occupied countries, neutrals, etc. Thus, apathy emerges as one of the central concerns for any discussion of the moral implications of the Holocaust. As Elie Wiesel put it:

> I pinched my face. Was I still alive? Was I awake? I could not believe it. How could it be possible for them to burn people, children, and for the world to keep silent? (*Night*, p. 42)

> This, this was the thing I had wanted to understand ever since the war. Nothing else. How a human being can remain indifferent. The executioners I understood; also the victims, though with more difficulty. But the others, all the others, those who were neither for nor against, those who sprawled in passive patience, those who told themselves, 'The storm will blow over and everything will be normal again,' those who thought themselves above the battle, those who were permanently and merely spectators—all those were closed to me, incomprehensible. (*Town Beyond the Wall*, p. 149)

> I take my head in my hand and I think: it is insanity, that is the explanation, the only conceivable one. When so great a number of men carry their indifference to an extreme, it becomes sickness, it resembles madness. (*Legends of Our Time*, p. 191)

Dealing with Apathy

Those who have been concerned with the moral implications of the Holocaust insist that the possibility of a future Holocaust can only be lessened if mankind comes to grips with the problem of apathy, of indifference. Arthur Morse, for example, has written:

> If genocide is to be prevented in the future, we must understand how it happened in the past—not in terms of the killers and the killed, but of the bystanders.

Therefore, in discussing the moral implications of the Holocaust, it would be useful to investigate how moral/legal traditions have dealt with the problem of apathy. It is particularly relevant for American students to be aware of how Anglo-American law and morality have traditionally related to the problem of apathy. As moral attitudes of society are generally crystalized in the laws of a society, one must investigate a society's laws in order to best understand how it enforces its moral presumptions. Therefore, in examining the reaction to the problem of apathy in Anglo-American tradition, the most fertile field for investigation would be Anglo-American law. Before doing so, however, some reactions of traditions other than the Anglo-American to the problem of apathy will be offered.

THE "GOOD SAMARITAN"

The "Good Samaritan" epitomizes the opposite of the apathetic bystander. The idea of the "Good Samaritan" has its origin in the New Testament (Luke 10:29-37):

> But he wanted to vindicate himself, so he said to Jesus, "And who is my neighbor?" Jesus replied "A man was on his way from Jerusalem down to Jericho when he fell in with robbers, who stripped him, beat him, and went off leaving him half dead. It so happened that a priest was going down by the same road; but when he saw him, he went past on the other side. So too a Levite came to the place, and when he saw him went past on the other side. But a Samaritan who was making the journey came upon him, and when he saw him was moved to pity. He went up and bandaged his wounds, bathing them with oil and wine. Then he lifted him on to his own beast, brought him to an inn, and looked after him there. Next day he produced two silver pieces and gave them to the inn-keeper, and said, 'Look after him; and if you spend any more, I will repay you on my way back.' Which of these three do you think was neighbor to the man who fell into the hands of the robbers?" He answered, "The one who showed him kindness." Jesus said, "Go and do as he did."

In this tale of the Good Samaritan, Jesus adopts a typically rabbinic tactic by answering a question with a story. The question—Who is my neighbor?—may in fact have been a request for Jesus to interpret the meaning of the Scriptural verse: You should love your neighbor as yourself, I am the Lord (Leviticus 19:18). The questioner was asking for a definition of "neighbor."

In his parable, Jesus seems to be interpreting "neighbor" to mean anyone, even a stranger. That is, one is obliged to help one's neighbor and since everyone is one's neighbor, one is obliged to help any imperiled individual.

The parable carefully relates that it was not the members of the victim's community, the priest and the levite, who helped him, but one of the despised Samaritans—a member of the outgroup—who helped him. Thus, the victim's kinsmen, his neighbors, failed to meet their obligations as neighbors. Only the Samaritan who was not technically the victim's neighbor helped him. Jesus' rhetorical question at the end of the parable (v. 36) indicates that the true neighbor is not determined by kindred blood. The neighbor is one who aids the imperiled stranger. The neighbor is one who fulfills the commandment as interpreted by Jesus—any person is my neighbor. Therefore, I am obliged to help anyone in peril. My obligation to love my neighbor means to love all people. Love is not essentially an emotional requirement, but a moral one. I am required to act—to help my neighbor, to help an imperiled victim. Jesus' parable clearly reflects the attitude of Jewish law and tradition, not only of his time but of both earlier and later times as well. Summarizing the attitude of the Hebrew prophets of the Bible who chronologically preceded Jesus vis-à-vis the problem of apathy, Abraham Heschel has written (*The Prophets,* p. 284):

> Indifference to evil is more insidious than evil itself; it is more universal, more contagious, more dangerous. A silent justification, it makes possible an evil erupting as an exception becoming the rule and being in turn accepted.

> The knowledge of evil is something which the first man acquired; it was not something that the prophets had to discover. Their great contribution to humanity was the discovery of the evil of indifference.

In Talmudic literature, contemporaneous with and subsequent to Jesus' life, the problem of apathy is discussed. In one possible interpretation of why Job suffered, one may perceive the rabbinic view of the sin of indifference.

CASE #1—JOB

Job emerges from the book which bears his name as being wholly righteous. No sin of his is uncovered despite the suggestions of his friends that Job is a sinner.

God's anger is kindled against Job's friends. Job prays on their behalf. Only then, when Job becomes the selfless intercessor on behalf of his friends did God restore his fortune:

> "the Lord restored the fortune of Job when he had prayed for his friends" (42:10)

Only when Job verbalizes a deep concern for others is he restored, are his afflictions ended. Could it be then that Job was not completely righteous? That though he was not liable for any sin of commission, he was dreadfully liable for a sin of omission—the failure to express concern for others? Could apathy have been the sin which brought torture and tragedy to Job? The Talmud, in fact, suggests this to have been the case:

> R. Hiyya b. Abba said in the name of R. Simai: There were three in the plan (to exterminate the Jewish people in Egypt) (Exodus 1:22) i.e. Balaam, Job and Jethro . . . Job who silently acquiesced was inflicted with sufferings (*Sota* 11a, *Sanhedrin* 106a).

Apathy in the face of the extermination of a people would warrant afflictions of chastisement and of instruction. Job learned the lesson of his infliction. He interceded and was restored.

CASE #2—Why Destruction?

One of the central problems for rabbinic theology after the destruction of the Second Temple in 70 C.E. was: Why had the Temple been destroyed? What sin had required such severe punishment as the destruction of the Second Temple and the Second Jewish Commonwealth?

When the First Temple was destroyed in 586 B.C.E. the cause was clear. The prophets had warned that the sins of idolatry, etc. would result in the destruction of the Temple. Immediately before the destruction, Jeremiah predicted its imminent occurrence. However, no such prophetic prediction had preceded the destruction of the Second Temple. The generation was judged to be pious, learned and righteous. Why then was the Temple destroyed?

Talmudic literature offers a variety of suggestions. One suggestion was that the Temple in Jerusalem was destroyed because the people were apathetic to evil; that apathy, itself a tragedy, engenders tragedy.

> Rabbi Hanina said, Jerusalem was destroyed only because they did not rebuke each other . . . (i.e.) that generation ''hid their faces in the earth'' (i.e., shut their eyes to evil) and did not protest (*Sabbath,* 119b).

Is the failure to protest evil such a grave sin that it may cause the destruction of the Temple? Is it such a grave sin that it warrants the life of the sinner? Consider this story where the identical expression—''they hid their faces in the earth''—is used:

> An incident happened with a slave of King Jannai who killed a man. Simeon b. Shetach said to the sages: ''Set your eyes boldly upon him and let us judge him.'' So they sent the King word, saying: ''Your slave has killed a man.'' Thereupon he sent him to them to be tried. But they again sent him a message: ''You must come here too, for the Torah says, 'If warning has been given to its owners,' teaching that the owner of the ox must come and stand by his ox.'' The king accordingly came and sat down. Then Simeon b. Shetach said: ''Stand on your feet, King Jannai, and let the witness testify against you; yet it is not before us that you stand, but before Him who spoke and the world came into being, as it is written 'Then both men between whom the controversy is, shall stand . . .' '' ''I shall not act in accordance with what you say, but in accordance with what your colleagues say,'' he answered. Simeon then turned first to the right and then to the left but they all (for fear of the king) HID THEIR FACES IN THE EARTH. Then said Simeon b. Shetach to them: ''Are you wrapped in thoughts? Let the master of thoughts (i.e. God) come and CALL YOU TO ACCOUNT!'' Instantly, Gabriel came and smote them to the ground and they died (*Sanhedrin* 19 a–b)

Similarly, Abner is punished with a dishonorable death for not protesting Saul's evildoings (i.e., the murder of the priests of Nob—Rashi) (I Samuel 22:18, *Sanhedrin* 20a).

Apathy in the face of injustice, failure to protest evildoing, may allow for one's punishment, one's death, or even the destruction of Jerusalem.

According to the Talmud, the destruction of the Second Temple came only through an incident regarding two men: Kamza and Bar Kamza, but also because "the rabbis who were present did not protest." The text interprets the rabbis' apathetic inaction as an assent to the unjust act of the man who made the party and to the humiliation of Bar Kamza. The reaction of this text seems to imply that the story of Kamza and Bar Kamza (according to R. Jonathan) is illustrative of the verse:

> Blessed is the man who fears the Lord always,
> *But he who hardens his heart will fall into evil.*
>
> (Proverbs 28:14; *Gittin* 55b–56a)

The view here is that apathy in the face of evil will lead to a more devastating evil. Apathy serves as a catalyst for evil. It intensifies evil, encourages wrongdoing, and thus is to be considered evil itself.

After the destruction of the First Temple, Zedekiah was named king. He was a righteous man and was held in esteem by Jeremiah. When the Temple was destroyed, it was as if cosmic calamity had struck. One rabbinic view is that God desired to return the cosmos to chaos directly after the destruction of the First Temple but did not do so on account of Zedekiah's righteousness (*Sanhedrin* 103a). Zedekiah, however, was not wholly righteous. Besides the good "he did that which was evil in the sight of the Lord (II Kings 24:19)— (That denotes) that he could have protested against (the evil of others) and did not" (*Sanhedrin* 103a). Thus, for the Talmudic rabbis, apathy is not morally neutral. In being a lack of action, it becomes an action. By being a lack of good, it is considered evil. The rabbis insisted that one is obliged not only to help an imperiled individual but is also forbidden to remain apathetic to the problems of his community. For example, one Talmudic source declares:

> When the community is in trouble let *not* a man say: I will go to my dwelling and will eat and drink and all will be well with me. (*Taanit* 11a)

MEDIEVAL REFLECTIONS

This Talmudic approach to the problem of apathy was continued and was expanded in medieval Jewish legalistic and moralistic literature. Legal discussions of the problem in the Talmud, for example, were interpolated and restated in medieval codes of Jewish law. The following instance is a case in point.

According to the Talmud:

He who sees his fellow being drowned, being mauled by a beast or being attacked by armed bandits, is obliged to save him. As it is written, "Do not stand by your neighbor's blood." (Leviticus 19:16) *Sanhedrin* 74a (*Sifra on Lev*. 19:16). [*circa* 3rd century (?)]

In the twelfth century, Maimonides codified this law:

If one person is able to save another and does not save him, he transgresses the commandment: Neither shall you stand idly by the blood of your neighbor. (Lev. 19:16). Similarly, if one person sees another drowning in the sea, or being attacked by bandits, or being attacked by wild animals, and although able to rescue him either alone or by hiring others, does not rescue him; or if one hears heathen or informers plotting evil against another or laying a trap for him and does not call it to the other's attention and let him know; or if one knows that a heathen or a violent person is going to attack another and although able to appease him on behalf of the other and make him change his mind, he does not do so; or if one acts in any similar way—he transgresses in each case the injunction: Neither shall you stand idly by the blood of your neighbor.

If one sees someone pursuing another in order to kill him, or sees someone pursuing a woman forbidden to him in order to ravish her, and although able to save them does not do so, he thereby disregards the positive commandment: Then you shall cut off her hand (Deut. 25:12) and transgresses two negative commandments: Thine eye shall have no pity, and, Neither shall you stand idly by the blood of your neighbor. Although there is no flogging for these prohibitions, because breach of them involves no action, the offense is most serious, for if one destroys the life of a single Israelite, it is regarded as though he destroyed the whole world, and if one preserves the life of a single Israelite, it is regarded as if he preserved the whole world.

(Laws of Murder and Preservation of Life: *Mishneh Torah*, Chapter One, Paragraphs 14, 15, 16.)

It is significant that Maimonides reiterates his legal position in his philosophical work, *The Guide of the Perplexed* (3:40):

. . . . just as one who is able to save an individual from perishing and refrains from saving him may be said to have killed him.

POST-MEDIEVAL REFLECTIONS

The moral and legal imperative against apathetic behavior towards an imperiled victim continued in late medieval and modern Jewish literature. Two examples, one from the eighteenth century and one from the twentieth century, make this apparent. The first is a Hasidic story and the second is a modern poem.

Rabbi Moses Leib of Sassov (d. 1807) once suggested to his students that every object and every thought was created by God for a purpose. "What about atheism?'' asked a shrewd student. ''That too,'' replied the rabbi. ''When you see someone in peril, at that moment be an atheist. Pretend that there is no God to help him and only you can do so.''

> ''If you sit fenced off in your apathy,'' says God
> ''If you sit entrenched. I don't give a hang,'' says God
> ''If you look at the stars and yawn
> If you see suffering and don't cry out
> If you don't praise and you don't revile
> Then I have created you in vain,'' says God.

(Aaron Zeitlin)

From the preceding discussion, it should be clear that for Jewish and Christian tradition, apathy towards a potential or actual victim of evil is considered sinful. The duty to intercede is absolute. In the following discussion, we shall see how another approach, that of Anglo-American jurisprudence, has traditionally dealt with the problem of apathy and indifference.

THE ''GOOD SAMARITAN'' IN ANGLO-AMERICAN JURISPRUDENCE

At 3:34 A.M., March 13, 1964, Catherine Genovese's screams ''I'm dying, I'm dying,'' reached the ears of her neighbors in Kew Gardens, New York. They opened their windows and put on their lights. The killer vanished. None of the witnesses went to help her. None chased the attacker. None called the police. Minutes passed. The killer returned and inflicted the mortal wound. At 3:50 A.M. the police received a call from a man who, after phoning friends for advice, had finally decided to ask an elderly woman in an adjacent building to make the call because ''I didn't want to get involved.''

The murder of Kitty Genovese in 1964 and similar incidents demonstrate once again the murderous implications of apathy. On the individual level, apathy can facilitate murder; on the national level, apathy can facilitate genocide. We have seen that Jewish and Christian tradition consider it both a moral and legal duty to help an imperiled person. The purpose of the present section is to see how Anglo-American jurisprudence deals with the apathetic bystander.

To be sure, Anglo-American law posits no affirmative legal duty to aid an imperiled party. While Jewish law might have found the apathetic witnesses to the Genovese murder guilty of accessory to murder, Anglo-American law could not hold any of them legally culpable in any way. The position of American law in this regard was aptly summed up by Justice Sweeny, Chief Judge of the U.S. District Court in Massachusetts, in the 1951 case of *Lacey vs. The United States* (98 Federal Supplement 219). In his decision, Sweeney wrote:

It is well settled common law that a mere bystander incurs no liability where he fails to take any action, however negligent or even intentionally, to rescue another in distress.

Numerous cases decided in American courts reaffirm the right of the bystander to remain apathetic toward an imperiled victim. In his authoritative *Law of Torts,* William Prosser offers a number of examples drawn from decisions of judges in actual cases. Prosser writes (p. 340):

> . . . . the law has persistently refused to recognize the moral obligation of common decency and common humanity, to come to the aid of another human being, even though the outcome is to cost him his life. Some of the decisions have been shocking in the extreme. The expert swimmer, with a boat and a rope at hand, who sees another drowning before his eyes, is not required to do anything about it, but may sit on the dock and smoke his cigarette, and watch the man drown. A physician is under no duty to answer the call of one who is dying and might be saved, nor is anyone required to play the part of Florence Nightingale and bind up the wounds of a stranger who is bleeding to death, or to prevent a neighbor's child from hammering on a dangerous explosive, or to remove a stone from the highway where it is a menace to traffic, or a train from a place where it blocks a fire engine on its way to save a house, or even to cry a warning to one who is walking into the jaws of a dangerous machine.

Generally speaking, American courts have categorized the duty to rescue an imperiled party as a moral duty, unenforceable by the courts. Limiting their jurisdiction to legal obligations, the courts have removed private moral duties from the purview of their authority. Thus in dealing with the apathetic bystander, American courts express a basic presumption of much of Anglo-American jurisprudence: morality and law are separate realms; to enforce morality is to impinge upon human liberties and upon civil rights. This attitude, with specific reference to the apathetic bystander, is most clearly evident in the often quoted decision of Judge C. J. Carpenter in the 1897 case of *Buch vs. Armory Manufacturing Co.* (69 NH 257):

> With purely moral obligations the law does not deal. For example, the priest and the levite who passed by on the other side were not, it is supposed, liable at law for the continued suffering of the man who fell among thieves, which they might, and morally ought to have, prevented or relieved. Suppose, A, standing close by a railroad sees a two year old babe on the track, and a car approaching. He can easily rescue the child with entire safety to himself, and the instincts of humanity require him to do so. If he does not, he may, perhaps, justly, be styled a ruthless savage and a moral monster; but he is not liable for the child's injury or indictable under the statutes for its death.

Rather than seeking to impose a legal duty upon the apathetic bystander, American courts have appealed to the moral sensitivities of society, to the "higher law," to the "voice of conscience." A case in point is the New York decision in *Zelenko vs. Gimbels* (287 NYS 134). In this case Justice Lauer held:

> We will assume that the defendant owed her [the plaintiff] no duty at all—that the defendant could have let her die.

Thus, no legal duty could be imposed upon the defendant to help the plaintiff. Consequently, the court left it to the moral sensitivities of other bystanders to rescue the imperiled plaintiff. In the words of the court:

> ... beyond doubt, some bystander, who would be influenced more by charity than by legalistic duty would have summoned an ambulance.

A similar view was taken in the 1903 case of *Union Pacific vs. Cappier* (66 Kansas 649, 72 Pacific 281):

> With the humane side of the question courts are not concerned. It is the omission or negligent discharge of legal duties only which come within the sphere of judicial cognizance. For withholding relief from the suffering, for failure to respond to the calls of worthy charity, or for faltering in the bestowment of brotherly love on the unfortunate, penalties are found not in the laws of men, but in that higher law, the violation of which is condemned by the voice of conscience, whose sentence of punishment for the recreant act is swift and sure. In the law of contracts it is now well understood that a promise founded on a moral obligation will not be enforced in the courts.
> ... The moral law would obligate an attempt to rescue a person in a perilous position—as a drowning child—but the law of the land does not require it, no matter how little personal risk it might involve, provided that the person who declines to act is not responsible for the peril.

Yet, in the Genovese case, as in so many others, bystanders were not "influenced. ... by charity" and the imperiled victim perished.

A significant number of legal precedents assume an act of rescue to be a violation of the right of privacy both of the bystander and of the victim. Consequently, American jurisprudence categorizes the "Good Samaritan" as the "altruistic *intermeddler*" or as the "*officious* intermeddler." Not only is his intercession not required, but it is discouraged and sometimes punishable. For while the bystander is under no legal obligation to help an imperiled party, he becomes liable for negligence once he intercedes to help someone in distress. It is a general principle of American tort law that while the law imposes no duty to rescue, it does hold the "altruistic intermeddler" subject

to liability for negligent acts performed in the course of the act of rescue
(Prosser and Wade, *Torts,* p. 417). Thus, as one authority on Anglo-
American jurisprudence has put it, "The Good Samaritan is a character unes-
teemed by English law." (*Salmon on Torts,* p. 46)

As one scholar has written, reflecting upon the present state of the law
(Rudolph, 44 *Nebraska Law Review* 501):

> Under the present state of the law an individual would be foolish to come to
> the aid of a stranger, for if he made the stranger's position worse, he would
> be liable. Moreover, if he went to the aid of another and were injured, he
> would not be indemnified, nor would he be paid for his time. Only he who
> does nothing is not liable.

Though the thrust of Anglo-American law refuses to impose a legal duty
upon the bystander and may actually punish the "Good Samaritan" for his
altruistic intermeddling, efforts have been made in a limited number of decisions of courts and state legislatures to reverse the *status quo.* It has by now
become well established that one has a legal duty to rescue an individual with
whom one maintains a specific kind of relationship. For example, a husband
is required to rescue his wife (*Territory* [*Montana*] *vs. Manton* 19 Pacific 389
[1899]), but not his mistress (*People vs. Beardsley,* 1908, 113 Northwestern
1128). A parent has a duty to rescue his child (*People vs. Piersen* 176 NY
201). In addition, the law is presently moving towards requiring an employer
to rescue an endangered employee in the course of his employment, a shop-
keeper to aid a business visitor, a host to aid a social guest, etc. (Prosser,
Torts 342). Some states, specifically Massachusetts and Washington, have
enacted Good Samaritan laws in order to free from liability physicians who
render unsolicited aid to individuals in need of medical aid. Such bills have
been under consideration in other states. In Illinois, for instance, Governor
Otto Kerner vetoed a "Good Samaritan bill" in 1964. A number of states
have also enacted "hit and run driver" statutes which result in civil liability
for failure to stop and aid a person injured in an automobile accident, even
without the fault of the driver (Prosser, 343).

Perhaps the earliest attempt to reverse the trend which dissuades the potential Good Samaritan was the opinion of Justice Cordoza in the case of *Wagner
vs. International Railroad* (232 NYS 180). Cordoza wrote:

> Danger invites rescue. The cry of distress is the summons to relief. The law
> does not ignore these reactions of the mind in tracing conduct to its conse-
> quences. It recognizes them as normal. It places their effects within the range
> of the natural and probable. The wrong that imperils life is a wrong to the
> imperiled victim; it is a wrong also to his rescuer.

Cordoza's argument, in effect, says that the event of one in peril, justifies assuming a relationship between the "Good Samaritan" and the victim by their sharing in the event. For example, one hearing a cry of "Help" is no longer a stranger, but a participant in the event of "danger" as well as an invitee to respond with rescue. Thus, Cordoza virtually stands alone in American jurisprudence in his insistence that "danger invites rescue," rather than escape or apathy. The precedent he established was not followed by subsequent decisions.

Legal scholars, repulsed by the treatment of the "Good Samaritan" and the apathetic bystander in many legal decisions, have turned their attention as well toward rectifying the situation. The eminent legal scholar Roscoe Pound, for example, has long been an advocate of limiting individual sovereignty and of translating the duty to rescue from a moral duty into an affirmative legal duty. In this regard, Pound has written (*Introduction to the Philosophy of Law*, p. 101):

> In the case put there is nothing intrinsic in the moral principle which should prevent legal recognition of it and the working out of appropriate legal rules to give it effect. Indeed a movement in this direction is visible in recent American decisions. We must reject the opposition of law and morals when pushed so far as to justify ignoring the moral aspects of such a case as this.

Pound attempts to expand the humanitarian doctrine in order to insure the right of the member of a highly civilized society to a good life (p. 97). This necessitates the "involuntary Good Samaritan" whose right to privacy is not infringed upon, who does not become a slave to another party, but who, because of a given situation, by his role as participant in that situation, whether active or passive, is called upon to serve society by compromising his freedom to aid a stranger. Such a compromise is not a total one. For an individual is never really free of duties to help "others." The state is never free of its responsibility to try to fulfill the expectations of its citizens where their own life and safety is concerned.

Besides Pound, others have argued that while the rugged individualist doctrine which produced the court's reluctance to impose a duty to rescue might have been tenable for rural America, it is anachronistic for urban, megalopolis America.

The direction of American law at present seems to be towards removing liability from the actual "Good Samaritan" and towards encouraging action by the potential "Good Samaritan." Whether the future Kitty Genoveses will ultimately be spared by the results of these developments, only time and the courts will tell. Whether future Holocausts will be prevented because apathetic bystanders decide to become "Good Samaritans," only history will reveal.

FURTHER SUGGESTIONS FOR CLASS DISCUSSION AND RESEARCH

As was noted above, the two models offered herein are not meant to be totally inclusive or wholly representative of all moral implications of the Holocaust. They do, however, offer two possible approaches which may be effectively utilized in teaching about the Holocaust. Neither are the aforementioned specific issues treated by these models—Judenrat and apathy—the only issues which might be utilized by the application of the two models. Each model may be applied to a discussion of a plethora of moral questions emerging out of an encounter with the Holocaust.

Besides historical studies, legal sources and diaries, and novels and films provide a fine basis for discussion of moral implications of the Holocaust. Moral issues raised by Holocaust literature and art may be integrated into the aforementioned models or may form the basis for alternative models.

For example, the notion of justice in works such as Jerzy Kosinski's *Painted Bird* might be discussed and compared with other notions of justice in literature and philosophy. Arnost Lustig's *Prayer for Katerina Horovitzova* might serve as the basis for a discussion of the meaning of courage. Primo Levi's *Auschwitz* might be utilized as the focal point for study and reflection regarding dehumanization during the Holocaust and in its aftermath. In addition, works such as Richard Rubenstein's *Cunning of History,* a nonliterary work, provide excellent material for a discussion of some of the moral problems evoked by the Holocaust and their relevance today. Both provocative and frightening, Rubenstein's work demonstrates that the inhuman use of human beings, epitomized by the Holocaust experience, is a feature of our daily lives and a possibly dominant threat to our future.

The moral and philosophical implications of the Holocaust are virtually limitless. Only a lack of imagination and daring on the part of the instructor or student of Holocaust studies can limit them.

BIBLIOGRAPHY

(English only; annotation is provided when necessary)

1. Karl Jaspers

JASPERS, KARL. *The Question of German Guilt* (New York: Dial, 1947). (available in paperback).

2. Moral Implications

MODEL #1—JUDENRAT (SELECTED)

ARENDT, HANNAH. *Eichmann in Jerusalem* (New York: Viking, 1963). Controversial reflections upon the Eichmann trial, including a condemnation of the *Judenrate*.

BLOOM, SOLOMON, "Dictator of the Lodz Ghetto," *Commentary* (1949) 7:111–112. Discussion of the head of the *Judenrat* of Lodz.

BLOOM, SOLOMON, "Toward the Ghetto Dictator," *Jewish Social Studies* (1950) 12:73–78. The plight of *Judenrate* heads.

DAUBE, DAVID. *Collaboration with Tyranny in Rabbinic Law* (Oxford: Oxford University Press, 1965). A careful analysis of the relationship between the oppressed and the oppressor in ancient (1–3 century) rabbinic law. Important for understanding Holocaust responsa and the history of Jewish behavioral patterns.

DAWIDOWICZ, LUCY. *The War Against the Jews* (New York: Holt, 1975), Chapter Eleven. History of the Holocaust, including extensive discussion of the *Judenrate*.

FRIEDMAN, PHILIP, "Aspects of the Jewish Communal Crisis in the Period of the Nazi Regime in Germany, Austria and Czechoslovakia," in *Essays on Jewish Life and Thought* (New York: Columbia University Press, 1959).

_____. "Two 'Saviors' Who Failed," *Commentary* (1958) 16:479–491. Discussion of two heads of *Judenrate*.

GOLDSTEIN, BERNARD. *The Stars Bear Witness* (New York: Viking, 1949). Life in the ghetto, reflection upon the role of the *Judenrate*.

GRINGANZ, SAMUEL, "The Ghetto as an Experiment of Jewish Social Organization," *Jewish Social Studies* (January 1949), 11:3–20.

HILBERG, RAUL. *The Destruction of the European Jews* (Chicago: Quadrangle, 1961). A standard, but controversial history of the Holocaust, which strongly suggests that Jews collaborated in the process of their own destruction. Extensive discussion of *Judenrate* members and other Jewish leaders during the War.

KATSH, ABRAHAM, ed. *The Warsaw Diary of Chaim A. Kaplan* (New York: Collier, 1965). Warsaw diary including reflections of life in the ghetto and the behavior of the *Judenrat*.

LEVIN, NORA. *The Holocaust* (New York: Schocken, 1968). A standard history of the Holocaust with many references to *Judenräte*.

LUSTIG, ARNOST. *Night and Hope* (Washington: Inscape, 1977) (Avon paperback, 1978). Film: TRANSPORT FROM PARADISE. An attempt to portray some of the moral problems attendant upon life in the Theresienstadt Ghetto by a survivor of that ghetto and of death and labor camps. On the film, see Chapter Eleven; on Lustig's novels, see Chapter Nine.

RINGELBLUM, EMMANUEL. *Notes from the Warsaw Ghetto* (New York: Schocken, 1974). Warsaw Ghetto diary including reflections of life in the ghetto and the behavior of the *Judenrat*.

ROBINSON, JACOB. *And the Crooked Shall Be Made Straight* (New York: Macmillan, 1965), esp. pp. 142–220. A point by point rebuttal of Arendt's *Eichmann in Jerusalem*.

TUSHNET, LEONARD. *The Pavement of Hell* (New York: St. Martin's Press, 1972). An attempt to understand the behavior of *Judenrat* members.

TRUNK, ISAIAH. *Judenrat* (New York: Macmillan, 1972). The classic study of the *Judenrat*: historically, sociologically, economically, etc.

MODEL #2—GOOD SAMARITAN

BOHLEN, FRANCIS, "The Moral Duty to Aid Others as a Basis of Tort Liability," (1908) *Univ. of Pa. Law Review* 56:217–244.

CAHN, EDMOND. *The Moral Decision* (Bloomington: University of Indiana Press, 1966), pp. 183–197. The Good Samaritan in law, literature and moral discourse.

DARLEY, J. M., AND LATUNE, B., "Bystander Intervention in Emergencies: Diffusion of Responsibility," *Journal of Personality and Social Psychology* (1968) 8:377–383. (Also see the authors' later articles in this journal on this subject.) A psychological discussion of aiding distressed parties.

DAWSON, JOHN. "*Negotorium Gestio*: The Altruistic Intermeddler," *Harvard Law Review* (1960–1) 74:817–66, 1073–1130.

DAWSON, JOHN P., AND PALMER, GEORGE E. *Cases on Restitution* (New York: Bobbs Merrill, 2nd ed., 1969) pp. 48–59. Legal discussion of rewards and liabilities for altruistic behavior.

DEVLIN, PATRICK. *The Enforcement of Morals* (London: Oxford, 1965). Discussion regarding the relationship of law and morality in Anglo-American law.

(Editors of) *Columbia Law Review*, "The Failure to Rescue: A Comparative Study," (1964) 52:631. The duty to rescue in a variety of legal systems.

(Editors of) *Columbia Law Review*, "Good Samaritans and Liability for Medical Malpractice," (1964) 52:1301–1322.

FULLER, LON. *The Morality of Law* (New Haven: Yale University Press, 1964). Law and morality in Anglo-American jurisprudence, with some attention paid to the quandry of the Good Samaritan.

GREGORY, CHARLES, "Gratuitous Undertakings and the Duty of Care," *De Paul Law Review* (1951) 1:30. A discussion of the status of the Good Samaritan in Anglo-American law.

GREGORY, CHARLES, "Trespass to Negligence to Absolute Liability," *Virginia Law Review* (1951) 37:359.

HART, H. L. A. *Law, Liberty and Morality* (New York: Vintage, 1963). Discussion of the relationship between law and morals in Anglo-American jurisprudence.

HEUSTON, R. F. V., *Salmond on the Law of Torts* (London: Sweet and Maxwell, 1965). Some discussion of the Good Samaritan in American law.

HOCHHUTH, ROLF. *The Deputy* (New York: Grove, 1964). An indictment in drama of the apathy of the Pope to the plight of the Jews in Nazi Europe. Historical studies, noted in other units, regarding the Vatican policies towards the "Final Solution" ought to be consulted for additional information.

HORN, ALBERT, "Should a Physician be Required to Render Aid in Emergencies," *Alabama Law Review* (1956) 8:332–335.

JASPERS, KARL, AND AUGSTEIN, RUDOLF, "The Criminal State and German Responsibility," *Commentary* (February 1966) 41:33–39.

KOGAN, N., AND WALLACH, M., "Risk Taking as a Function of the Situation, the Person and the Group," *New Directions in Psychology III* (New York: Holt, 1967). Psychologically oriented discussion of bystander reaction to crisis.

LINCK, LEO, "Torts—The Duty to Aid One Not Imperiled by the Defendants Fault," *The Notre Dame Lawyer* (1941) 17:51–64.

MILGRAM, STANLEY, AND HOLLANDER, PAUL, "Murder They Heard," *The Nation* (1964) 198:602–604. Reflection about the Genovese murder.

MINOR, H. D., "Moral Obligations as a Basis of Liability," *Virginia Law Review* (1923) 9:420–431. Discussion of morality and law, with specific reference to the duty to rescue.

MORSE, ARTHUR. *While Six Million Died: A Chronicle of American Apathy* (New York: Random House, 1967). The apathetic and even malevolent attitude of the American Government, especially the State Department, to the Jewish plight in Nazi Europe.

POUND, ROSCOE. *Introduction to the Philosophy of Law* (New Haven: Yale, 1922). Discussion of the relationship of law and morality in American jurisprudence with reference to the duty to rescue.

———. *Law and Morals* (Oxford: Oxford University Press, 1926).

PROSSER, WILLIAM. *Law of Torts* (St. Paul, Minnesota: West, 1971). A standard work on American tort law, with discussion of the status of the Good Samaritan.

PROSSER, WILLIAM, AND WADE, JOHN. *Torts: Cases and Materials* (New York: Foundation Press, 1971). Standard case-book on American tort law, with discussion of the quandry of the Good Samaritan.

RATCLIFFE, JAMES, ed. *The Good Samaritan and the Law* (New York: Anchor, 1966). The best and most complete single volume collection of essays on the duty to rescue in legal, moral, psychological and sociological discourse.

ROSENTHAL, A. M. *Thirty Eight Witnesses* (New York: McGraw Hill, 1966). The story of the Genovese murder. A TV movie, based upon the Genovese case, is also worthy of reference: *Death Scream*—1975, made-for-TV film with Nancy Walker, Kate Jackson and others.

RUDOLPH, WALLACE, "The Duty to Act: A Proposed Rule," *Nebraska Law Review* (1965) 44:499.

THOMAS, GORDON, AND WITTS, MAX. *Voyage of the Damned* (New York: Fawcett Crest, 1974). The true story of refugees from Hitler's Germany, in search of a home in an apathetic world.

VILHAEUR, JACOB, "Negligence—Malpractice Criticism of Existing Good Samaritan Statutes," *Columbia Law Review* (1964) 64:328–349.

3. Miscellaneous

DES PRES, TERRENCE. *The Survivor* (Oxford: Oxford University Press, 1976). A controversial analysis of the quest to stay human in death camps.

MILGRAM, STANLEY. *Obedience to Authority* (New York: Harper and Row, 1974). A classic psychological study of obedience to malevolent authority. The implication of this study, based upon experiments done with American subjects, is that most people, including Americans, would obey malevolent orders. Important, but frightening. Also noteworthy is the TV film based upon these experiments, *The Tenth Level,* starring William Shatner.

ROSENBLOOM, IRVING J. *The Holocaust and Halakhah* (New York: Ktav, 1976) (Available in paperback). Discussion of responses in rabbinic law to the Holocaust. Many moral issues discussed in a legal framework.

RUBENSTEIN, RICHARD. *The Cunning of History* (New York: Harper and Row, 1975) (Available in Harper paperback). A penetrating and frightening discussion of "Mass Death and the American Future." Relates the Holocaust experience to things happening to us today and which may happen in the future.

WIESENTHAL, SIMON, ed. *The Sunflower* (New York: Schocken, 1976). The moral implications of forgiveness or withholding forgiveness from Nazis, discussed by a wide variety of philosophers, writers, theologians, etc.

ZIMMELS, H. J. *The Echo of the Nazi Holocaust in Nazi Literature* (New York: Ktav, 1977). Extensive discussion of responses to the moral implications of the Holocaust in Jewish law. Some reflection upon problems relating to the *Judenräte*.

Addendum

KIRSCHENBAUM, AARON. *The "Good Samaritan" and Jewish Law* (Tel Aviv: Tel Aviv University, 1978).

Resources for the Study of the Holocaust*

Beverly Yusim

SELECTED ARCHIVES WITH LARGE COLLECTIONS OF HOLOCAUST RELATED MATERIALS IN UNITED STATES AND ABROAD

American Jewish Archives
3101 Clifton Avenue
Cincinnati, Ohio 45220

Extensive Collections, such as:

> Stephen S. Wise Collection; Cincinnati Jewish Community Relations Committee Records; Labor Zionist Organization of America Records; William Rosenau Collection, Chaim Weizmann Collection; Harry Arunstein: Activities during and after World War II (political); Kaplan Family: Activities during and after World War II (rel. to Lodz and Warsaw); Collections of their papers and transcripts of speeches and interviews; etc.

American Jewish Committee
165 E. 65th Street
New York, New York 10022
(212) 751-4060

Large collection—their own archives, including:

> Conference for the Relief of German Jewry—Reports and Resolutions

*A basic reference work extensively utilized in compiling the following information is *Guide to Jewish History Under Nazi Impact,* edited by Robinson and Friedman, Ktav, 1973.

American Jewish Congress
15 E. 84th Street
New York, New York 10028
(212) 879-4500

Their own archives, including:

> Hitlerism and the American Jewish Congress; A Confidential Record of
> Activities, March–December, 1933; Recent Activities of AJC and WJC in
> Behalf of Jews Abroad—July–August, 1941; Reports on the Work of the
> AJC; Proceedings of all Emergency Sessions.

American Jewish Historical Society
2 Thornton Road
Waltham, Massachusetts 02154

Collections of Archival Material, including:

> Hebrew Orphan Asylum of New York City; American Jewish Press Asso-
> ciation; Union of Orthodox Jewish Congregations of America; American
> Jewish Conference—Transcriptions; Synagogue Council of America; Coun-
> cil of Jewish Federations and Welfare Funds; Society for the Advance-
> ment of Judaism; Jewish Reconstructionist Foundation; American Asso-
> ciation for Jewish Education; American Jewish Congress; National Refugee
> Service; United Service for New Americans; Hebrew Immigrant Aid So-
> ciety of Boston; Jewish War Veterans of the United States; Personal
> Papers of Individuals covering Holocaust and Post-Holocaust; Gertrude
> Wolf (Secretary to Stephen Wise); Norman Solit (President of Synagogue
> Council of America); Judge Jonah J. Goldstein (Jewish Communal Leader);
> Leon David Cristohl (Canadian Parliament); Nathan Perlman (U.S. Repre-
> sentative); Albert Gordon (Sociologist); Abraham J. Multer (U.S. Repre-
> sentative); Label A. Katz (Jewish Communal Leader); Selman A. Waksman
> (Scientist); Stephen S. Wise (Jewish Communal Leader).

American Jewish Joint Distribution Committee
3 East 54th Street
New York, New York

Archives include:

> Records of JDC meetings; Records of distribution of funds collected for
> Jewish war victims' relief and rehabilitation.

Archives of Kibbutz Arzi-Hashomer Hazair Movement
Merchavia, Israel

Collection includes:

> Vilna Ghetto Collection; Warsaw Ghetto Collection; Lodz Ghetto Collection; Bialystok Ghetto revolt; The Hashomer Hazair Movement in Poland during the Nazi Period.

Archives and Museum of the Jewish Labor Movement
32 President Weizmann St., P.O. Box 303
Tel Aviv, Israel

Archives include:

> Personal narratives of illegal immigrants and refugees; Bergen-Belsen—Post liberation.

Berlin Document Center (BDC)
U.S. Mission
Berlin-Zehlendorf, Germany
APO 742
Postmaster N.Y. (Under Auspices of U.S. Department of State)

Archives include:

> Biographical Records; NSDAP Membership Records; NSDAP Membership Applications; Party Letters; SA Names; SS Service Records and Applications; Personal Backgrounds of SS and their wives and fiancees, Naturalization Records; Nazi-affiliated Organizations; Cultural, Artistic; Gestapo Arrests; NSDAP Awards; Reich Officials; Speer Ministry; Special Collections of varying scope relating to organizations and individuals; Miscellaneous material including: Directives, Circulars, Correspondence and Material of a general nature; Dead storage material of minor historical significance, such as cost of tool production, etc.

Bund Archives for the Jewish Labor Movement
25 E. 78th Street
New York, New York 10021

> Specializes in materials relating to the history of the Jewish Labor Movement in Eastern Europe, the Americas and other countries in many languages.

Related to Holocaust:

> Complete collection of the Bund's dailies, weeklies, monthlies and other publications in Poland, 1918–1948; Complete collection of the Bund's Yiddish and English Press in the U.S. since 1941; Documents and publications during World War II and after of: American Representation of the Bund in Poland, World Coordinating Committee, New York Committee of the Bund; Jewish Socialist Farband; German Nazi Party Leaflets, pamphlets and other materials; Documents and posters protesting anti-Semitism from Jewish and non-Jewish organizations; Literature, photos and posters of the Bund's campaign against anti-Semitism in Russia, Poland, France, the U.S., etc.; Jewish Communists: Newspapers, periodicals, leaflets, documents, from Russia, Poland, U.S., etc.

Canadian Jewish Congress
493 Sherbrooke Str. W.
Montreal, Canada

Archives include:

> Reports and proceedings from ten plenary sessions from 1934–1956; Minutes and reports of all regional committees dealing with United Jewish Relief Agencies and the war effort, refugees, war orphans, overseas relief and Canadian Immigration (1933–1959).

Center for Holocaust Studies
1605 Avenue J
Brooklyn, New York 11230

> (see below, "Oral History" and "Institutions")

Central Zionist Archives
1, Rehov Ibn Gavirol
P.O. Box 92
Jerusalem, Israel

Archives include:

> Central Office of the Zionist Organization Files; Jewish Agency Files; Archives of Principal Institutions of the Jewish Community in Palestine; Records of the Jewish Agency Offices: London, Istanbul, Geneva, Spain, Lisbon.
> Library of Archives: 35,000 volumes—periodicals, leaflets, photographs, tapes, films.

Jabotinsky Institute in Israel
P.O. Box 2171
Tel Aviv, Israel

Material on Jewish heroism during the Nazi period; Records of ghetto songs.

Jewish Historical General Archives in Jerusalem
The Jewish Historical Society of Israel
Yad Vashem Building
Har Hazikaron
P.O. Box 1062
Jerusalem, Israel

Dedicated to the recovery of the archival remains of the destroyed Jewish communities of Europe; Records of approximately 1,000 destroyed Jewish communities of dozens of countries, including over 700,000 frames of microfilm; Archives of institutions and organizations, public and private records, historical documents collected from the diaspora.

Kibbutz Lohamei Ha-geta'ot
Haifa, Israel

Ghetto Fighters House in Memory of Yitzhak Katzenelson.
Educational materials: a library; archival collections; a permanent museum; research on resistance aspects of the Holocaust.
Special archives on Yitzhak Katzenelson.
Publications in Hebrew.

Leo Baeck Institute
129 E. 73rd Street
New York, New York 10021

Archival Material concerning:

German Jewry prior to 1939; Gurs C. C. 1941–1944; Theresienstadt Ghetto; Collections of two German Jews who survived in the underground: Pineas, Adolf Loebel; Complete History of National Socialism; Nazi Authorities and properties, financial matters, legal papers; Rabbi Leo Baeck papers; Joint Restitution Successor Organization: pertaining to content and history of 446 destroyed synagogues; memoirs of 1933–1935; unpublished or privately published.

National Ethnic Archives Branch of the Public Archives of Canada
P.A.C. 395 Wellington
Ottawa, Canada

Archival material concentrating upon Holocaust survivors in Canada.

Sisler Collection
Wayne State University Hillel
Detroit, Michigan

Over 600 documents relating to the German Church under the Nazi regime
on Microfilm.

United Jewish Appeal
1290 Avenue of the Americas
New York, New York 10019

Records of fund-raising in the American Jewish Community and the channeling of those funds to other organizations.

United States National Archives and Records Service
8th and Pennsylvania Avenue
Washington, D.C.
Renamed: World War II Records Division of National Archives
King and Union Streets
Alexandria, Virginia

Contains:

Captured German documents and related records (21,000 linear feet of microfilm, over 15,000,000 pages); War Crimes Trials in Nuremberg; Wartime activities of War Refugee Board; Many guides published of the records microfilmed at Alexandria, Virginia.

Wiener Library and Research Institute
4 Devonshire W I
London, England

Contains:

Nuremberg materials; War Crimes documents not introduced at Nuremberg;
1000 unpublished eyewitness reports on Nazism and persecution of Jews;

Archives of Dutch Refugee Committee. (*Note:* Wiener Library will relocate in Tel Aviv, Israel.)

World Jewish Congress
15 East 84th Street
New York, New York 10028 (Offices in Jerusalem, London, Buenos Aires)

Contains:

Collections of Resolutions; Records of meetings; Records of Rescue activities; correspondence with governments-in-exile (London office); Bermuda Conference on Refugees (Australian section).

Yad Vashem—Martyrs and Heroes Memorial Authority
Har Hazikaron
P.O. Box 84
Jerusalem, Israel

Archival material of:

Historical commissions in Germany, Austria and Italy; Collections of DP Archival material.

Non-Jewish Origins: Slovakian documents; Munich's Municipal Archives; Archives of Gau Wiew of NSDAP; Nazi documents.

Jewish Origins: Union Generale des Israelites de France; World Jewish Congress; Joint Distribution Committees; Joodsche Raad of Uriesland; Joodsche Coordinatie Commissie of Dutch Jews in Switzerland; World Center of Hechaliltz in Geneva; Documentation Section of the Jewish Agency for Palestine; JDC of Budapest and Rumanian, German and Czech Collections; Personal narratives.

Microphotoarchives: Arolsen Archives; Centre de Documentation Juive Contemporaine Yivo; Auswartiges Amt; Lodz Ghetto; Bialystok Jewish Underground; Rijksinstituit voor Oorlogsdocumentatie; Warsaw Ghetto Archives; Hashomer Hazair movement; Wiener Library collection of personal narratives; Records of defunct Jewish rescue institutions, refugees, DP.

Yivo Institute for Jewish Research
1048 5th Avenue
New York, New York 10028

Nazi Records: The Berlin Collection: 40,000 pages; Mauthausen Registers; Institut zur Erforschung der Judenfrage; *Der Sturmer* and other German Agencies.

Jewish Records: Zonabend Collection: Lodz Ghetto; Sukewar-Kaczerginski Collection: Vilna; Wasser Collection: Occupation of Poland; Joodsche Raad voor Amsterdam: Jews in Holland; Theresienstadt; Jews in France during World War II; Kehilat-ha-haredim: Lubavitcher Hassidim during Nazi occupation of France; Shanghai Jewish Community 1920-1948; Hungary, Rumania: Nazi persecution; Sheerit ha-Pleta: Jewish DP activities in Austria, Germany, Italy.

World Art Union (Geneva): Hias-Hicem; Collection of the Board of Deputies and Joint Foreign Committee; United Hujas—Rescue records (Lisbon, France); Joint Boycott Council 1933-1941; German Jewish Childrens Aid; Union for the Protection of the Health of Jews (relates to immigration of children to America); Plans for rescue presented at Evian Conference.

Joseph Tenenbaum Papers (Anti-Nazi Boycott); Rabbi Hirshler (Work of Jewish Chaplaincy in Camp in France during World War II); Union General des Israelites de France: The French Judenrat; Records of the Paris Underground.

Records of Polish Judenrate; Records of Polish Government in Exile.

Rescue by American Jewish Organizations.

Art from Ghettos and Camps.

Eyewitness Accounts—over 2000—Clippings, microfilms, personal narratives, diaries.

Photographic Collection—15,000.

United Service for New Americans; Chamberlain's Collection: Aid to German-Jewish refugees in U.S.A.; Records of defunct Jewish rescue institutions; refugee, DP.

SELECTED LIBRARIES WITH SUBSTANTIAL HOLOCAUST-RELATED HOLDINGS (Mostly in U.S.A.)

American Jewish Committee Library
165 E. 65th Street
New York, New York 10022

Collection includes:

Nazi Collection of Anti-Semitica: 400 books and pamphlets; Nazica: 1000 catalogued books and pamphlets; Nazi periodicals and newspapers: 50 catalogued volumes; Jewish periodicals and newspapers published in Germany: 50 catalogued volumes; Nazi period: 1000 catalogued books and pamphlets; AJC's own publications from this period: books, pamphlets, bulletins.

Anti-Defamation League Library
315 Lexington
New York, New York

Collection includes:

> Anti-Semitica; Holocaust collection (general and small); Film library and archives (1978 project).

Asher Library of Spertus College of Judaica
618 South Michigan Avenue
Chicago, Illinois 60605

Large collection (about 5500 volumes and bound periodicals) of Holocaust and related material, including:

> Transcripts of Eichmann trial; Nuremberg Trial transcripts and documentation; Microfilmed transcripts of oral histories of survivors done at Hebrew University; Institute of Contemporary Jewry's Oral History Division.

Brandeis University
Waltham, Massachusetts

Large collection of Holocaust and related volumes; specialties:

> Resistance throughout Europe; Memorial books (in rare book collection).

Center for Holocaust Studies
1605 Avenue J
Brooklyn, New York 11230

(See also "Institutions")

Harvard University
Widener Library
Cambridge, Massachusetts 02164

> Hebraic Collection of World War II: approx. 175 volumes.
> Specific countries: approx. 200 volumes.

Hebrew Union College
Klau Library
3101 Clifton Avenue
Cincinnati, Ohio 45220

Branch Libraries:40 W. 68th St., New York, N.Y. 10023
                  3077 University Mall, Los Angeles, CA 90007
                  13 King David St., Jerusalem, Israel
                  (collection mainly English)

> Valuable holdings on Contemporary Jewish history.
> World War II: about 750 volumes.
> Concentration Camps: about 150 volumes.

Hoover Institution on War, Revolution and Peace
Stanford University
Stanford, California

Collection includes:

> Valuable collections on Belgium, Germany and Poland; Material from the
> concentration camps of Oranienburg and Dachau; Material from the ghettos
> of Lodz and Theresienstadt; A set of *Der Sturmer*: Vols. 1–13 complete;
> Vols. 14–17 and Vol. 22, scattered issues.
> German documents relating to Jews, such as: Himmler files; Goebbels Di-
> ary; Guide to captured German documents.

The Jewish National University Library
Hebrew University
Jerusalem, Israel

Extensive collection, including:

> Rich collection of Nazica including periodicals; some Jewish collections
> assembled by Jacob Lestschinsky.
> Publications: *Bibliographical Quarterly of the Jewish National and Univer-
> sity Library; Kirjath Sepher.*

Jewish Public Library
5151 Cote St. Catherine Road
Montreal, Quebec H3W 1M6 Canada

Large collection of Holocaust and related volumes:

> Nuremberg transcripts; Eichmann transcripts; Press of DP camps in Ger-

many, Austria, Italy; Vertical file and periodical collection divided by country, concentration camp, ghetto:
200 tapes of survivors.

Jewish Theological Seminary
3080 Broadway
New York, New York 10027

Valuable holdings in the field of contemporary Jewish history.

Leo Baeck Institute
129 E. 73rd Street
New York, New York 10021

Memoir manuscript collection; History of Jews in Germany and Europe by towns; Periodical collection of Germany in the 30's; small collection of Holocaust and related volumes.
Publications: Leo Baeck Yearbook I-XXI, Secker and Warburg, London; Leo Baeck Bulletin, Verlac, Bitaon, Ltd., Tel Aviv, Israel.

Library of Congress
Washington, D.C.

Rich collection of books, pamphlets, periodical articles and archival material dealing with the Nazi period itself and the Holocaust specifically.
Headings: Jews (general and individual countries/localities); Concentration Camps (also individual camps); Atrocities; Underground Movements; Personal Narratives; World War 1939-1945; Refugees; Displaced Persons; Prisoners and Prison; Emigration and Immigration Law.
Special Collections: Nuremberg Military Tribunals, Subsequent trials; Hitler's Private Library; Captured German Records; Films (under control of Alien Property Custodian).

Ludwig Rosenburger Library
Chicago, Illinois

Largest private collection of Anti-Semitica:

Books, pamphlets, manuscripts relating to the political, social, cultural history of the Jews and to the Jewish question.
20,000 works—approximately 900 Nazi-related.

Mendell Gottesman Library
Yeshiva University
500 W. 185th St.
New York, New York 10033

Valuable holdings in the field of contemporary Jewish history.

New York Public Library
Jewish Division
42nd and Fifth Avenue
New York, New York
(collection mainly English)

World War II—1933–1945 (1000 volumes); Anti-Semitica (950 volumes);
Jewish question (500 volumes); Large collection of Nazi publications.

Royal Institute of International Affairs
Chatham House
10 St. James Square
London S.W.I., England

Rich collection of newspaper clippings, books on World War II and
Holocaust-related subjects.

Wiener Library and Research Institute
LTD
4 Devonshire St. WI
London, England

Very large collection of Holocaust and related volumes including:

Persecution, terror, resistance in Nazi Germany; Weimar to Hitler in Ger-
many: 1918–1933; Rise and Fall of the Third Reich; History of Jewish
Emancipation and Anti-Semitism; German Political Trends; History of
German-speaking Jews.
Rich collection of books, pamphlets, reports and press clippings on Central
Europe since 1945.
Pub: *Wiener Library Bulletin* (Tri-yearly).

Yad Vashem
Jerusalem, Israel

> Main repository of Holocaust-related material.

Yivo Institute for Jewish Research
1048 Fifth Avenue
New York, New York 10028

Largest collection of Holocaust-related material in U.S.A.:

> 150,000 volumes on general Jewish History.
> 80,000 volumes of Jewish periodicals.
> 1933–1945—Extensive collection.
> Special collections: Nazi publications (4500 volumes); Memorial volumes;
> Catastrophe literature (3000 volumes).

INSTITUTES AND INSTITUTIONS (EXCLUSIVELY) RELATED TO HOLOCAUST STUDIES*

Brookline Holocaust Center
Brookline, Massachusetts
HEW Title IV Grant

Project Director:Margot Stern Strom
25 Kennard Road
Brookline, Massachusetts 02146

> Facing History and Ourselves.
> Holocaust and Human Behavior: An Example of Curriculum Development
> and Dissemination and In-Service Education.
> Curriculum: Facing History and Ourselves; Holocaust and Human Behavior,
> by Margot Stern Strom and William Parsons.
> Resource Center—Library; Teacher Training; Documentation of Curriculum.
> Change and Implementation.

---

*The development of centers for Holocaust research is rapidly taking place, as is the construction of memorials in many communities. The Zell Holocaust Exhibit at Chicago's Spertus College of Judaica may serve as a model for such memorials, especially if they are educationally oriented. Cities such as Tulsa, Oklahoma; Hartford, Connecticut; Montreal, Canada; etc., are in the process of establishing such centers.

Center for Holocaust Studies
1605 Avenue J
Brooklyn, New York 11230

Dir: Professor Yaffa Eliach

> Collects and preserves documents and oral histories of the Holocaust period
> for purposes of documentation and research.
> Develops educational materials and curricula to teach Holocaust in public
> and religious schools; booklets; audio-visual aids for young students (avail-
> able for rental).
> Publishes a newsletter.

Israel Institute of Historical Documentation
Society for Research on the Activities of Nazi Criminals Against the Jewish
People
8 Herzl Street, P.O. Box 4950
Haifa, Israel

> Publishes mimeographed material on particular trials.

Leo Baeck Institute of Jews from Germany
18 Bezalel St., Jerusalem, Israel
8 Fairfax Mansions, London, England
1239 Broadway, New York, N.Y., U.S.A.

> Research on the history of the Jewish Community in Germany and in
> German-speaking countries—chiefly interested in the rise and decline of the
> emancipation and in the dispersion that took place after Hitler gained power.
> Publications: Yearbook, newsletter.

National Institute on the Holocaust
Temple University
Department of Religious Studies
Philadelphia, Pennsylvania

Dir: Dr. Josephine Knopp

> Holocaust Resource Center; Annual Conference; PhD Program; Newsletter

National Jewish Conference Center
250 West 57th Street, Suite 923
New York, New York

> A newly formed division of the NJCC will coordinate activities among local Holocaust centers in the United States and Canada. In addition, curriculum research, preparation of study material and Holocaust-related liturgies will be implemented. The NJCC also publishes *Shoah,* a newsletter on Holocaust-related activities. In due time it is expected that this newsletter will develop into a scholarly journal.

St. Louis Holocaust Center
Central Agency for Jewish Education
225 S. Meramec
St. Louis, Missouri 63105

Dir: Alex Grobman

> Recently established center (1977). First institution dedicated to the Holocaust supported by a local Jewish Federation.
> Seeks to advise schools and implement Holocaust studies in St. Louis area at religious schools, secular schools, universities. Will establish film and book library. Local programming and conferences.

Simon Wiesenthal Center for Holocaust Studies
9760 W. Pico Blvd.
Los Angeles, California 90033

Dir: Ephraim Zuroff

> A new center for curriculum development and research.

Yad Vashem—Martyrs' and Heroes' Memorial Authority
Har Hazikaron
P.O. Box 84
Jerusalem, Israel

> Purpose: to commemorate the Jewish Catastrophe under Nazism and to conduct research on this period and its background. Also encourages creative writing on this period.

Yivo Institute for Jewish Research
1048 Fifth Avenue
New York, New York 10028

> Research on the social history of the Jews with particular emphasis upon the history of the Jews in Eastern Europe, the Yiddish language, the folklore, the literature.
> Presently doing research on the history of the Holocaust in cooperation with Yad Vashem.

SPECIALIZED PERIODICALS ON HOLOCAUST (English only)

Holocaust Studies Newsletter
National Institute on the Holocaust
P.O. Box 2147
Philadelphia, PA 19103
Dr. Josephine Knopp, Editor

Leo Baeck Yearbook
129 East 73rd Street
New York, New York 10021

Martyrdom and Resistance
American Federation of Jewish Fighters, Camp Inmates and Nazi Victims
315 Lexington Avenue
New York, New York 10016

News of the YIVO
Yiddish Scientific Institute
1048 Fifth Avenue,
New York, New York

Newsletter,
Center for Holocaust Studies
1605 Avenue J
Brooklyn, New York 11230

Shoah
National Jewish Conference Center
250 West 57th St.
New York, New York, 10019
  Jane Gerber, Editor

Quarterly Review, the Official Publication of the American Council of Polish
   Cultural Club
CZAS Publishing Co., Inc.
142 Grand Street
Brooklyn, New York 11211

Wiener Library Bulletin
Wiener Library and Research Institute
LTD
4 Devonshire St. WI
London, England

Yad Vashem Bulletin (1957–1968; new series 1969–)
Yad Vashem
Jerusalem, Israel   (No longer published)

Yad Vashem Studies (annual publication)
Yad Vashem
Jerusalem, Israel
   Livia Rotkirschen, Editor

Yivo Annual of Jewish Social Science
New York: Yiddish Scientific Institute, Yivo, 1946—
(Periodicals contain material referring to Holocaust, but Vol. 8–1953 deals
   exclusively with Holocaust)
Yivo Institute
1048 Fifth Avenue
New York, New York

AUDIO VISUAL RESOURCES (selected)

American Association of Jewish Education
National Council on Jewish Audio Visual Aids
114 5th Avenue
New York, New York 10011

   Catalog available.

Jewish Films in the United States
Stuart Fox Comp.; G. K. Hall & Co.
Boston, Massachusetts 1976; index

Jewish Media Service
15 E. 26 Street
New York, New York 10010

> Social Evil: Complicity and Resistance; East European and Soviet Jewry
> Lists of over 300 Holocaust-related films.

Anti-Defamation League of Bnai Brith
315 Lexington Avenue
New York, New York 10016

> Publications/Audio Visual Bulletin: Material from ADL on Holocaust.

(SIGNIFICANT) ORAL HISTORY COLLECTIONS: Eyewitness Accounts as a special type of mass documentation

American Jewish Committee
165 East 65th St.
New York, New York 10022

> Refugee and immigration experience (in the process of being transcribed and
> published in book form).

Brandeis University
Waltham, Massachusetts

> General histories of survivors across the U.S.

Canadian Jewish Congress
1590 MacGregor Avenue
Montreal, Quebec, Canada

> General histories of survivors who emigrated to Canada.

Center for Holocaust Studies
1605 Avenue J
Brooklyn, New York 11230

> Hasidim—Response to the Holocaust; American soldiers who liberated con-
> centration camps; Children during the event; Greek survivors.

Institute of Contemporary Jewry
Oral History Division
Hebrew University
Jerusalem, Israel

Personal accounts of life in concentration camps, resistance and rescue.

Jewish Public Library
5151 Cote St. Catherine Road
Montreal, Quebec H3W 1M6 Canada

200 tapes of survivors who emigrated to Canada.

Research Foundation for Jewish Immigration
570 7th Avenue
New York, New York 10018

Survivors of the Holocaust from Germany.

Yad Vashem
Jerusalem, Israel

RESOURCES FOR DOING ORAL HISTORIES*

1. *The Art of Asking Questions,* Stanley L. Payne; Princeton N.J.: Princeton University Press, 1951. XIV, 249 p.
2. *A Bibliography of Oral History,* ed. by Donald Shippers and Adelaide Tusler; Oral History Association, North Texas State University, Denton, Texas.
3. *Bibliography on Oral History,* compiled and annotated by Manfred Waserman; Oral History Association, North Texas State University, 1975, Denton, Texas.
4. *Interviewing in Social Research*; Hubert Hiram Hayman, W. J. Coff and others; forward by Samuel A. Stauffer—Chicago: University of Chicago Press, 1954, SIV, 415.

*Note: Oral history projects have been begun in many and varied places, e.g., Oral History Division at University of California at Berkeley; contact Willa Baum, Regional Oral History Office, Bancroft Library. University of California, Berkeley, California 94720.

5. *Oral History for the Local Historical Society,* Willa K. Baum; American Association for State and Local History, Nashville, Tennessee, 1974.
6. *Oral History in the United States*: A Directory, comp. Gary Shumway; ed. and pub. Columbia Office for the Oral History Association, 1971. New York.

SAMPLE QUESTIONNAIRES FOR USE IN OBTAINING ORAL HISTORIES*

Preliminary Questionnaire
Center for Holocaust Studies
in Conjunction with
Yeshiva of Flatbush and Hebrew University

Telephone: ————————————
Interviewer: ————————————
Date: ————————————
Name: ——————————————————————————————
             Last   First   Middle

          ————————————————————————————————
           Maiden Name
Address: ——————————————————————————————
          ————————————————————————————————
Telephone Number: ————————————
Date of Birth: ————————————
Place of Birth: ————————————
             City   Country
Number of Children in Family
(Do *not* include yourself)
Boys: ————————————
Dates of Birth: ————————————
——————————————————
——————————————————
Girls: ————————————
Dates of Birth: ————————————
——————————————————
——————————————————

*From the Center for Holocaust Studies in Brooklyn, New York.

Parents' Occupation:
    Father: ————————————
    Mother: ————————————

What were you doing before the war broke out?

What groups did you belong to (e.g., Bund)?

Were you in the army?

Circumstances of arrest?

Holocaust stations—ghettos, prisons, camps: give dates

Did you have any special function (e.g., Blockalteste, Stubhova)?

Circumstances of liberation

Briefly, what have you done since the liberation?

Name of Interviewer: ————————————————————
Address & Telephone Number: ————————————————

Questionnaire
Liberation of Concentration Camps by
the American Army—1945

Prof. Yaffa Eliach
Brooklyn College &
Center for Holocaust Studies
1605 Avenue J
Brooklyn, New York

                          Date: ————————————————

Name ————————————————————————————
Address ——————————————————————————————
                ————————————————————————————

Telephone Number _____

Date of Birth _____

Place of Birth _____

When did you enter the American Army?

Did you enlist or were you drafted?

What was your military rank in 1945?

What were your duties then?

What was your army serial number then?

What were you doing prior to 1941?

What was your occupation after WW II?

What is your current occupation?

What numbered U.S. Army were you in when you came to the Concentration Camp?

What division were you in?

What regiment or separate battalion were you in?

Please give full names of your leaders:
1) squad
2) platoon
3) company
4) battalion
5) regiment
6) Division commander in 1945.

What concentration camp did your unit liberate?

When? Specify day and month.

What was your exact job (please be specific) at the time you helped with the liberation of the camp?

Did you become especially friendly with individuals liberated by your unit?

If yes, how long did you maintain contact with them?

What were their names?

When did the military government or rear echelon units take over the camp your unit liberated?

Did you visit any displaced persons camps? State when and where.

Are you the recipient of any honors bestowed by the U.S. Army?

Attach picture of yourself in uniform.

Please indicate the names, addresses, and telephone numbers of any other American veterans, currently residing in America, who also liberated concentration camps in 1945.

name	Address	phone

1. When did you land in Europe? Name of your regimental Commander?

2. Describe the direction your Division took; name relevant cities, battles, and extent of warfare.

3. Were there Jewish soldiers to the Battles different from the attitudes of the non-Jews?

4. Were there Jewish soldiers in your unit?

5. Did anyone express the feeling that he was fighting not only for the American cause but also for a Jewish cause; to put an end to Nazi brutality?

6. What concentration camp did you enter? Date? Can you describe the vicinity in relation to near-by cities?

7. Before you entered the camp, what was your knowledge about the German treatment of the inmates? What was the source of this information?

8. What was your initial reaction? Do you recall the reactions of others?

9. What was the impact upon entrance? What did you see?

10. Who were the prisoners? Nationality? Political prisoners? Approximate number of Jews and non-Jews? Total number in camp? Sex? Age?

11. What type of camp was it? Labor? Death? Were there extermination facilities?

12. What was the nature of your contact with survivors? Do you recall conversations, aid that was extended? What was the reaction of survivors to liberators?

13. Did you meet any outstanding inmate personalities in the camp?

14. How much time did you spend in the camp?

15. Did you have any official duties? Describe in detail.

16. Did you see any German personnel? Did you find any German records?

17. Did you have contacts with Germans in vicinity of camp? What was the extent of conversation? What was their attitude to war? Did they have knowledge of the camp?

18. Did you have contact with U.S. Army Chaplains? Specify.

19. Where did your unit go after this incident?

20. Do you have any personal letters or photos of that time?

Resistance

A. *Ghettos*

1. In which ghetto did you join a resistance group? Were you a member of an organized group (state which) or did you join as an individual? Describe the group you belonged to—numbers, personalities, activities, in the ghetto.

2. Describe the steps leading up to armed resistance in your group— discussions, education, etc. At what point (date) did the group decide on armed resistance? Did the decision come before or after the actions?

3. Who were the leading personalities in the resistance? What do you know of their background and later fate? Did any survive? Where are they now?

4. Were there any tensions within your group? Between your group and other groups? What were the reasons? How, if at all, were they resolved? Were ideological considerations (Zionists, Bundists, Communists) important?

5. What was the attitude of the Judenrat to the resistance?

6. What was the attitude of the ghetto population to the resistance?

7. Were there religious people, or rabbis, among the resistance people? If so, can you tell us details?

8. Was there a discussion as to leaving the ghetto or fighting within it? What were the arguments and how were they resolved?

9. Where and how did you get arms?

10. What, if any, were your contacts with the non-Jewish underground outside? Who helped you—who did not? At what points of time did such contacts take place?

11. Were there any emissaries from one ghetto to another that you know about or can tell us anything about?

12. Tell us please the story of the end of the resistance group in the ghetto.

Resistance

B. *Forests*

1. How did you get to the forest?

2. Were you a member of a predominantly non-Jewish group, (at first, or all through)? If so, what was its name, who were the commanders, where did it fight?

3. If you joined a predominantly non-Jewish group, how were you received? Tell us the name of the unit, its size, names of commanders, where it fought.

4. Tell us, in chronological sequence, your experiences, mentioning the details contained in the following questions regarding each of the units in which you fought.

5. Describe the relations between commanders and men in each unit in which you fought.

6. Describe the relations between Jews and non-Jews (both in predominantly Jewish and in predominantly non-Jewish units). Was there animosity? Quote examples as you tell your story. Relations between the surrounding population and Jewish partisans.

7. Describe armed actions, especially those in which you yourself participated.

8. Discuss relations with "family groups" or individual unarmed Jews hiding in the forest. If you yourself belonged to such a group, tell us its history, relating to it all the relevant questions in this questionnaire. Did the fighting units protect the family groups or not? What was the attitude of the non-Jewish commanders and men to the family groups?

9. Did your unit do anything to bring Jews into the forest?

10. Were people (including yourself) received in the unit if they were unarmed to start with?

11. Where did you get arms?

12. Where and how did you obtain food?

13. Was the discipline harsh, strict, mild? Were people punished? What for? How?

14. What was the fate of women partisans? What work did they do? Were they treated with consideration, or exploited sexually?

15. Were there children among the partisans? How were they treated?

16. What were the emotional and/or rational personal motivations of Jewish partisans for fighting?

17. Was there any social activity—bonfires, stories, songs? If so, can you remember and record any?

18. Did you take prisoners? What did you do with them?

19. When and how were you liberated? Relate briefly what happened to you after liberation.

Transnistria

1. Where were you at the time the war broke out?

2. What was the communal organization in your town? Who were the leaders, what parties or ideologies did they adhere to, what youth movements existed, who were the rabbis, what was the influence of orthodoxy, were there Jewish schools?

3. What was the economic situation of Jews in your town? In your family?

4. What were the changes—economic, political, educational, communal— as a result of the Russian occupation after June 1940? How did the changes effect your families and you personally?

5. What were the relations between Jews and non-Jews in your town before and during the Russian occupation?

6. Were there accusations by non-Jews that the Jews had cooperated with the Russians? Was there any truth in these accusations? Were there arrests by Russians?

7. What happened when the Russians re-occupied your district? Did the Russians allow Jews to retreat with them? Please tell us about persecu-

tion, pograms, etc. Who was the responsible authority, what was the attitude of the non-Jewish population, was there any organized Jewish reaction—or an organized one?

8. Describe the steps leading up to the eviction of the Jews of your town?

9. Describe the eviction and the deportation to Transnistria.

10. Describe in detail your own personal experience in Transnistria.

11. Were you in a ghetto? What was the relationship between local and Rumanian Jews? What did you live on? Did the ghetto authorities try to help? Can you describe administrative set-up of the ghetto? Did the ghetto leadership collaborate with the military?

12. What were your relations with the non-Jews. Can you tell us about individual incidents?

13. Did you receive help from the Rumanian Jewish community? In what form?

14. Was there armed resistance of Jews in partisan detachments? Was there underground Zionist or Communist organization of Jews?

15. How and when did you leave Transnistria?

16. Please tell us in a general way what you did between the return from Transnistria.

Labor

1. How old were you when drafted to the labor force? When were you drafted?

2. Did you know you were to serve as a forced laborer in the Hungarian Army?

3. Describe the unit in which you served. How many Jews? Who were the officers in charge? Were there non-Jews among the forced labor soldiers?

4. What were the attitudes of the officers toward the Jews? Relate cases showing positive, negative or indifferent attitudes.

5. When were you sent to Russia? What were you told you would do there? What kind of equipment did you get?

6. Where did you work? Relate in detail your experiences on the front in each of the places you were sent to. Tell us about meeting with the local population, local Jews, German soldiers, Russian prisoners-of-war. What was the attitude of the Hungarian officers? How high was the mortality among the men? Did you see anything of the destruction of the Jewish communities? Can you tell us about it?

7. If you were captured by the Russians, please tell us in detail of the place, the date, the fate of your fellow-workers, and your experiences as a prisoner of the Russians.

8. If you escaped and became a partisan in the Ukraine, please answer our questionnaire on forests and resistance.

9. If you came back to Hungary, please describe your evacuation/flight, the fate of your fellow-workers, the attitudes towards you during the retreat of the Hungarians in charge, and your experiences after your return from Russia. How and when were you released from the labor force?

CONTRIBUTORS

SUSAN G. AMENT is co-editor of this volume and Vice-President of Impact Press, Inc.

M. CHERIF BASSIOUNI is Professor of International Law at De Paul University Law School—Chicago, Illinois. He is the author of ten books and scores of monographs on international law and politics.

YAFFA ELIACH is Associate Professor of Jewish Studies at Brooklyn College of the City University of New York, and, Directress of the Center for Holocaust Studies. In addition to her published poetry, short stories and scholarly essays, she is co-author of *The Last Jew,* a Holocaust-related play.

HELEN FEIN is Associate Professor of Sociology at Queens College of the City University of New York. She has written many scholarly articles and is the author of a book on genocide.

JOSEPHINE Z. KNOPP is Adjunct Professor in the Department of Religion at Temple University in Philadelphia. She also serves as Directress of Research for the National Institute on the Holocaust. Well known for her many articles and essays on literary and theological themes, she also has written a study of contemporary Jewish literature entitled *The Trial of Judaism.*

RUTH G. KUNZER is Associate Professor in the Department of Germanic Languages and Literature at the University of California—Los Angeles.

ARNOST LUSTIG is Associate Professor of Literature and Film at American University in Washington, D.C. A survivor of Theresienstadt, Auschwitz and other Nazi camps, he has written many novels and film scripts dealing with the Holocaust. His novels and films have won many international awards. Lustig's most recent books are *Night and Hope, Darkness Casts No Shadow, Diamonds of the Night* and *Dita Saxova.*

JOSEPH LUSTIG is a Ph.D. candidate in film at New York University and is the son of Arnost Lustig.

JACK N. PORTER teaches at the University of Lowell, in Massachusetts. Besides his many articles and essays, his book on Jewish partisans during the Holocaust will soon be published.

BYRON L. SHERWIN is co-editor of this volume and Professor of Jewish Religious Thought at Chicago's Spertus College of Judaica. He has written extensively on the Holocaust, Jewish mysticism and Jewish philosophy. Besides his other books and articles, Sherwin has written a volume on Holocaust theology, to be published by Impact Press, Inc.

MARIE SYRKIN is Professor Emeritus at Brandeis University. In 1957 she offered the first credit-bearing course in Holocaust studies at an American University. She is the author of many books and articles. For many years she was editor of the *Jewish Frontier, Midstream* and Herzl Press. Her book, *Blessed is the Match: The Story of Jewish Resistance,* has recently been reissued by the Jewish Publication Society.

DAVID WEINBERG is Associate Professor of History at Bowling Green State University in Ohio. The author of many articles and essays, his most recent book is *A Community on Trial,* a study of Jewish life in Vichy, France.

BEVERLY YUSIM teaches Holocaust studies in the Chicago area.